SHE

HENRY RIDER HAGGARD was born in Bradenham in Norfolk in 1856. He was the sixth son of a lawyer and was educated in Ipswich. In 1875, his father procured for him the post of junior secretary to the Governor of Natal, Sir Henry Bulwer. He set sail for South Africa and spent six years there, fascinated by its landscape, wild-life, tribal society and mysterious past. He returned to England in 1880 and was called to the bar at Lincoln's Inn four years later. His first novel, *King Solomon's Mines*, was published soon after he had qualified in 1885 and was so successful that Haggard was able to move back to Norfolk where he could concentrate on his writing. He went on to produce a series of extravagant romances set in far flung corners of the world; Iceland, Constantinople, Mexico and Ancient Egypt, and of course, Africa. Both *She* and *Allan Quatermain* were published in 1887 and by 1890, at the age of thirty-four Haggard had become both an enormously successful writer and a household name. He used his position to further causes, accepting an honorary post and giving countless after dinner speeches. He was great friends with fellow writer Rudyard Kipling, and with the anthropologist and scholar Andrew Lang, to whom *She* is inscribed.

A private man, Haggard was deeply shattered by the death of his son in 1891, and for many months afterwards was rarely to be seen outside his Norfolk home. After an unsuccessful stand for Parliament in 1894 Haggard threw himself into his campaigning and writing again. He wrote extensively about the state of British agriculture, and his *A Farmer's Year* (1898) and *Rural England* (1902) made a substantial contribution to alleviating the plight of farmers and small-holders of the time. Throughout his life Haggard continued to travel widely, visiting exotic places which helped fuel his imagination for new stories. He was knighted in 1912 and died in 1925.

PATRICK BRANTLINGER is Professor of English at Indiana University. He received his MA and PhD degrees from Harvard University (1965, 1968). He served as Editor of *Victorian Studies* from 1980 to 1990, and as Chair of his department from 1990 to 1994. He was a Guggenheim Fellow in 1978, and an NEH Fellow in 1983. The author of seven books, mainly on nineteenth-century British culture, his works include *Rule of Darkness: British Literature and Imperialism 1830–1914* (1988) and *The Reading Lesson: The Threat of Mass Literacy in Nineteenth-Century British Fiction* (1998).

H. Rider Haggard

SHE

A History of Adventure

Edited with an Introduction and Notes by
PATRICK BRANTLINGER

PENGUIN BOOKS

PENGUIN BOOKS

Published by the Penguin Group
Penguin Books Ltd, 27 Wrights Lane, London W8 5TZ, England
Penguin Putnam Inc., 375 Hudson Street, New York, New York 10014, USA
Penguin Books Australia Ltd, Ringwood, Victoria, Australia
Penguin Books Canada Ltd, 10 Alcorn Avenue, Toronto, Ontario, Canada M4V 3B2
Penguin Books India (P) Ltd, 11, Community Centre, Panchsheel Park, New Delhi – 110 017, India
Penguin Books (NZ) Ltd, Cnr Rosedale and Airborne Roads, Albany, Auckland, New Zealand
Penguin Books (South Africa) (Pty) Ltd, 5 Watkins Street, Denver Ext 4, Johannesburg 2094, South Africa

Penguin Books Ltd, Registered Offices: Harmondsworth, Middlesex, England

First published 1886
Published in Penguin Classics 2001
1

Editorial matter copyright © Patrick Brantlinger, 2001
All rights reserved

The moral right of the editor has been asserted

Set in 10/12.5 pt Monotype Imprint
Typeset by Rowland Phototypesetting Ltd, Bury St Edmunds, Suffolk
Printed in Great Britain by Clays Ltd, St Ives plc

Except in the United States of America, this book is sold subject
to the condition that it shall not, by way of trade or otherwise, be lent,
re-sold, hired out, or otherwise circulated without the publisher's
prior consent in any form of binding or cover other than that in
which it is published and without a similar condition including this
condition being imposed on the subsequent purchaser

Contents

Introduction vii
Further Reading xxix
Note on the Text xxxiii

SHE 11

Notes 315

Introduction

I. HAGGARD, SOUTH AFRICA, AND THE BRITISH EMPIRE

Henry Rider Haggard, bestselling author of many works of fiction based on more or less fantastic versions of Africa, was born in 1856, the sixth son of an eccentric, domineering Norfolk farmer and a literary mother. Squire William Meybohm Rider Haggard apparently had too little income to educate all ten of his children equally, so 'Rider' was not given the chance to follow his two oldest brothers to university. Instead, his desultory formal schooling ended with his failing the Armed Services exam and then cramming for the Foreign Service exams that he never took. Haggard's beloved mother Ella, however, was a talented poet and author of, among other works, *Myra, or the Rose of the East: A Tale of the Afghan War* (1857). And rather than as a colonial official, an explorer, a gold or diamond miner, a big-game hunter, or even an ostrich farmer in South Africa, Haggard would make his fame and fortune in Britain as an author, but with his South African experience as the basis for his imaginary adventures.

When, in August 1875, Haggard arrived at Cape Town, South Africa, limitless opportunities for adventure, power and profit seemed to beckon him. Instead of the ne'er-do-well his father had predicted he would become, he had been accepted, aged nineteen, as an unpaid assistant to his father's friend, Sir Henry Bulwer. Bulwer had been appointed lieutenant-governor of the British frontier colony of Natal, established in 1842. Haggard even began to think that he, too, might become a colonial governor (*Days* 1:102).* But he was to discover that, though adventure came easily in Africa, power and profit were more elusive.

Like Joseph Conrad in the Congo in 1890, Haggard found the realities of colonialism in South Africa deeply disillusioning. Little that he witnessed matched the romantic depictions of 'the dark continent' in boys' adventure novels, in the press and even in such bestselling explorers' journals as David Livingstone's *Missionary Travels and Researches in South Africa* (1857) and Henry Morton Stanley's *How I Found Livingstone* (1872). In 1884, just as Haggard was starting his novel-writing career, most of the blanks on the map of central Africa had been filled in and the 'scramble for Africa' was commencing (the Berlin Conference of 1884 is the event usually cited as the start of the imperialist partitioning of Africa by the European powers). But whereas Conrad, in *Heart of Darkness* (1899), would puncture what Henry James called 'the balloon of romance', Haggard, writing a decade earlier, chose to keep it soaring. South African reality might be disappointing, but romance could nurture youthful daydreams and, perhaps, even make them immortal.

Having failed to make his fortune or even to establish a stable career in South Africa (though more through the vexed political and military situation there than through any fault of his own), Haggard returned to Britain and studied to become a lawyer. Soon he also began to emulate his mother and his older brother, Andrew, by writing fiction. After publishing two novels that received little attention from the reading public (*Dawn* and *The Witch's Head*, both in 1884), Haggard struck gold with *King Solomon's Mines* (1885), a novel written for boys in the style of Robert Louis Stevenson's *Treasure Island* (1883). He quickly followed up that stunning success with his second bestseller, *She*, which first appeared as a serial in the *Graphic* in 1886 and

* Works quoted in this Introduction are listed in Further Reading. *Days* refers to Haggard's autobiography, *The Days of My Life*; *Cloak* refers to Lilias Haggard's biography, *The Cloak That I Left*.

then, revised and expanded, in volume format in 1887. Though Haggard wrote many other romances as well as more realistic novels, he is known today primarily as the author of these two adventure stories, both of which depict quests by British heroes into mysterious regions of central Africa. Since their first publication, *King Solomon's Mines* and *She* have never been out of print and have been remade many times over into plays, movies and countless closely related quest romances such as the 1987 film, *Allan Quatermain and the City of Gold*.

Haggard's fantasies about fabulous treasures, lost civilizations, ferocious savages and beautiful, forbidding women 'who must be obeyed' seem to have little to do with the disillusioning realities that he experienced in South Africa. But they have everything to do with the daydreams of the young man who, sure to be a failure at home (so his father told him), had sailed for Cape Town in 1875, only to return six years later, disappointed both with himself and with the ways, as he saw it, that the British government was mismanaging the affairs of the Empire.

For Haggard, the key event during his time in South Africa was the British take-over of the Boer republic of the Transvaal in 1877. Haggard accompanied Sir Theophilus Shepstone, Secretary for Native Affairs in Natal, to the Transvaal on a mission ostensibly to discuss mutual defence against the Zulus. Shepstone's intention, however, was to establish British rule over the Boer republic, an event that took place on 24 May 1877. On that day, which happened to be Queen Victoria's birthday, Haggard helped to raise the Union Jack in Pretoria, capital of the Transvaal. He later wrote to his mother:

> It will be some years before people at home realise how great an act it has been, an act without parallel. I am very proud of having been connected with it. Twenty years hence it will be a great thing to have hoisted the Union Jack over the Transvaal for the first time. (*Days* 1:107)

Even before this 'great act', Haggard had penned his first publications: three journal articles about South Africa. One, 'The Transvaal', which appeared in *Macmillan's Magazine* in May 1877, both predicted and advocated the British annexation of that republic. According to Haggard, the Boers were even less capable of self-government than the Zulus, and, having just lost a small war with the Pedi under their chief, Secococeni, the Boers needed, and would soon demand, British protection from an invasion led by Cetywayo, 'king' of the Zulus. Further, Haggard expresses the jingoistic view that it is Britain's 'mission to conquer and hold in subjection' the lesser peoples of the world, 'not from thirst of conquest but for the sake of law, justice, and order'. This is partly because, Haggard declares, 'we alone of all the nations in the world appear to be able to control coloured races without the exercise of cruelty' (78). (It is at least true that officials in the Colonial Office in London advocated humanitarian policies toward indigenous peoples and also that the Boers continued to practise slavery long after Britain had outlawed it in 1833 throughout its territories.) The other two articles, 'A Zulu War Dance' and 'A Visit to the Chief Secococeni', both published later in 1877 in the *Gentleman's Magazine*, express similar imperialist views.

When Haggard published his first book, *Cetywayo and His White Neighbours* (1882), which includes versions of all three articles, circumstances in the Transvaal and the rest of South Africa had drastically altered. The 1877 essays emphasize, with glowing optimism, the benefits that British rule will bring both to the Transvaal and to the Zulus. In contrast, *Cetywayo*, though it defends the annexation of the Transvaal and continues to hero-worship Shepstone, is an embittered record of defeat and disaster. The treacherous take-over of the fragile republic – which had been founded, after the Boers' trek from the Cape across the Vaal river, to avoid British interference in the first place – only fuelled anger and patriotic fervour among the Boers.

The annexation also prompted the British to try to end the

threat of the Zulus to both Natal and the Transvaal by attacking Cetywayo and his 'impis' or regiments. Though the British troops under Sir Garnet Wolseley ultimately defeated the Zulus, it was a Pyrrhic victory. In a major battle at Isandhlwana in January 1879, the Zulus crushed their adversaries; out of 1,800 troops on the British side (nearly half of whom were 'native' soldiers), only 55 survived (Morris 387). 'Nobody, either at home or in the colonies,' Haggard declares in the first paragraph of *Cetywayo*, 'wishes to see another Zulu war, or anything approaching to it' (1). Although the British, using rifles, machine guns and cavalry, finally defeated Cetywayo's forces at the Zulu center of Ulundi in 1879, both the end of the Zulu threat and the evident military vulnerability of the British emboldened the Transvaal Boers to rebel. In this first Boer War Transvaal 'commandos' soundly defeated the British troops at Majuba Hill in February 1881 – a defeat that also foreshortened Haggard's youthful aspirations for a career in South Africa.

In *Cetywayo*, Haggard tries to counteract the British public reaction to these catastrophes. The second-guessers at home believed that if Shepstone had stayed out of the Transvaal, then just a few months later the Boers and the Zulus would have gone to war. The British would have avoided the humiliations of Isandhlwana and Majuba, and might even have been welcomed by the Transvaal as its destined rulers and protectors against the Zulus. According to Haggard:

> There is no doubt that such a consummation of affairs would have cleared the political atmosphere wonderfully; the Zulus would have got enough fighting to last them some time, and the remainder of the Boers would have entreated our protection and become contented British subjects; there would have been no Isandhlwana and no Majuba Hill. (*Cetywayo* 26)

But, Haggard insists, Shepstone's annexation of the Transvaal was not premature; it was the sensible, humane, right thing to do. It is just unfortunate that neither the Boers nor the Zulus –

nor, for that matter, the British public – saw the wisdom of that 'great act'.

The dismal results of the British take-over of the Transvaal, of the Anglo–Zulu War (even though technically the British won) and of the first Boer War caused Liberal Prime Minister Gladstone to decide not to pursue either British rule over the Transvaal or the federation, under British hegemony, of the whole of South Africa. Like other British colonizers in South Africa, Haggard experienced 'this great betrayal' by the imperial government back in London with a 'bitterness . . . no lapse of time ever can solace or even alleviate' (*Days* 1:194).

The 'retrocession' of the Transvaal was a débâcle for which Haggard never forgave Gladstone or the Liberal party. Although his friend, Andrew Lang, convinced him to delete it, Haggard included an attack on Gladstone in the original manuscript of *She*, and he explicitly condemns the Liberal Prime Minister in several of his other novels: *Dawn*, *The Witch's Head*, *Jess*, *Colonel Quaritch*, *VC*, and *The Way of the Spirit*. Thus, in *Dawn*, the immoral Liberal politician, Lord Minster, calls Gladstone a 'great man' because he knows how to manipulate the spirit of the age, 'the instinct of robbery' (222). The blunt expression of his politics may be one reason why Haggard's first novel did not fare well with the reading public.

The military and political disasters of the Anglo–Zulu and first Boer Wars were compounded for Haggard by the obstacles he encountered in marrying the woman he loved and in establishing an ostrich farm in northern Natal. Shortly before going to South Africa, Haggard had fallen in love with Lilith Jackson, whom he intended to marry and always remembered as 'the girl with the golden hair and violets in her hand' (*Cloak* 32). Squire Haggard, however, made short work of his son's intention; shipping him off to Africa ensured that his son did not marry Lilith. When Haggard returned to Britain in 1880, Lilith had married somebody else. Haggard then met and quickly married, with his father's approval, Louisa Margitson, about whom he could write to his brother William:

> *Je vais me marier* – to such a brick of a girl . . . I love her sincerely, as I think she does me . . . I think we have as good a prospect of happiness as most people. She is good and sensible . . . (*Days* 1:166)

One might suspect that Louisa was 'good and sensible' in inverse proportion to Ayesha, who is *not* good and sensible. Louisa may have been 'a brick' of a wife and mother, but she was also available and, Haggard clearly felt, rather ordinary. Louisa was real; Lilith was romance. The woman of Haggard's dreams would always be Lilith – or Ayesha, or Cleopatra, or Sheba, or Helen of Troy . . . In *She*, the portrayal of Ayesha as an unattainable and yet eternally faithful lover, who is at once blindingly beautiful, dangerous, magical, all-powerful in the world of the Amahagger, and yet far more vulnerable than she realizes, owes something to his idealization of Lilith.

As to ostriches, they soon proved to be tough, intractable creatures. Also, though the 3,000-acre farm which Haggard and his friend Arthur Cochrane purchased in northern Natal might have become profitable, the defeats that the Boers inflicted on the British made life there precarious. Haggard and Louisa, who delivered their first child at the farmstead during the fighting, were close enough to hear gunfire from several skirmishes. Some 500 Boer soldiers bivouacked at the farm next to theirs, and might also have occupied their farm. By the summer of 1881, after the Battle of Majuba Hill and the 'retrocession' of the Transvaal, Haggard reluctantly decided to return to Britain for good.

The disappointments of his South African experience help to explain several aspects of Haggard's beliefs and stories, including *She*. His romances of exploration and discovery bring to the fore the ideological nexus of empire, race, and what Anne McClintock has called 'the porno-tropic tradition' in imperialist discourse. He was always a staunch believer in empire, or at least in the British Empire, and also in the inferiority of the 'dark races' of the world compared to the 'white race', and especially the English 'race'. Like many post-Darwinian intellectuals, though Haggard seems to have viewed humanity as a single species, he believed there were great biological as well as cultural differences among the races, and that the English race was superior to all others. Yet he was able to depict at least one 'dark race', the Zulus, with a good deal of sympathy if not exactly realism. In several of his novels, the Zulus are 'noble savages', at once seemingly superior to Europeans in their natural honesty, dignity and martial valour, and irredeemably primitive, superstitious and bloodthirsty.

During his five years in South Africa, Haggard came to admire the Zulus but to despise the Boers in just about equal measure. The Zulus were noble savages and natural 'gentlemen', but they were also, Haggard at first thought, uncivilizable: 'Savages they are, and savages they will remain, and in the struggle between them and civilisation it is possible that they may be conquered, but I do not believe that they will be converted. The Zulu . . . is incompatible with civilisation' (*Cetywayo* 58). By the time he penned *Nada the Lily* (1892), featuring a Zulu cast of characters, Haggard had decided that that African 'race' might be at least partially civilizable. He clearly felt that the treatment the Zulus received after their defeat by the British in 1879 was unjust (*Cetywayo* 1–48). In 1914, as a result of his penultimate visit to South Africa, he sent an impassioned defence of their rights to the Colonial Office in London, in which he declared:

> . . . if in the place of help, education and good counsel, [the Zulus] receive from the white man, their master, little save his dislike, his disease and his drink; if their lands continue to be taken from them and the morality of their women corrupted; ultimately they will add all his vices to their own.

Haggard added that, 'in the case of the Zulus, civilization has one of its great opportunities, for certainly in them there is a spirit which can be led on to higher things' (*Cloak* 242).

While Haggard developed a respect for the Zulus and their potential, at least, for 'civilisation', that respect did not extend to other, supposedly lesser or inferior African 'races'. In *She*,

Haggard's portrayal of the downtrodden, brutal Amahagger expresses the low regard in which he held most non-Zulu Africans, perhaps including the Boers. Haggard had difficulty overcoming his intense early prejudice against that 'race' of European origin. Though white, the typical Boer farmer, Haggard declared in *Cetywayo*, 'has no romance in him, nor any of the higher feelings and aspirations that are found in almost every other race . . . unlike the Zulu he despises, there is little of the gentleman in his composition . . .' (80). Ignorant in the extreme, according to Haggard, the Boers wanted only complete freedom from all laws and even, despite their fanatical Calvinism, from moral restraint; they wanted especially the freedom to practise slavery and to shoot at will any blacks who opposed them.

In politics, Haggard was always, like his father, a Tory for whom the British Empire represented the highest ideal that anyone could strive to serve. But, after his South African experience, Haggard set the standards of service to that ideal so high that only heroes could meet them. Ordinary mortals – especially ordinary businessmen and ordinary (liberal or radical) politicians – were forever betraying the Empire, as Gladstone, according to Haggard, had done not only in the case of the Transvaal but also by failing to support General Gordon at Khartoum and by advocating Home Rule for Ireland. Self-sacrificing heroes in Haggard's novels, like Robert Ullershaw in *The Way of the Spirit* (1906), are often, as Haggard and a large portion of the British public considered Gordon to be, martyrs to the cause of the Empire. Like Haggard himself, Ullershaw is

> an imperialist, believing in the mission of Britain among the peoples of the earth, and desiring the consolidation of her empire's might because it meant justice, peace, and individual security; because it freed the slave, paralysed the hands of rapine, and caused the corn to grow and the child to laugh. (151)

For his heroic service to the imperial cause, Ullershaw is rewarded by being ignored at home and captured, tortured and maimed for life by Arabs in the Sudan. Ullershaw struggles on, however, without help or acknowledgement from home, turning the Sudanese oasis of Tama into 'an Eden flowing with milk and honey' (292). Haggard compares Ullershaw to other hero-martyrs of empire, and specifically to General Gordon. Such heroes, says imperialist Lord Devene, 'pass away in a blaze of glory and become immortal, like Gordon, or they vanish silently, unnoted, and unremembered, like many another man almost as brave and great as he' (137).

After the disillusionments of the second Boer War of 1899–1902, Haggard seems to have felt very much like a Gordon or an Ullershaw himself, a Tory imperialist left high and dry by others' bad politics and by several bad wars. During the second Boer War, he declined an invitation to go to South Africa to write about it. Instead, he increasingly turned his political attention to the agricultural situation in Britain, writing a number of books about farming and about rural poverty, including *Rural England* (1902). He was also commissioned by the British government to study and write about the social work of the Salvation Army, which led to his book, *Regeneration* (1910). For these works, but more obviously for his fiction, Haggard was knighted in 1912. He travelled widely, including journeys to Egypt and South Africa, and wrote many new works of fiction between World War I and his death in 1925.

2. *SHE*, RACE, AND SEXUALITY

In *The Interpretation of Dreams* (1900), Sigmund Freud analyses a dream of his own in which he performed surgery on his legs. After the operation, he went on a strange journey, taking a cab part of the way to protect his injured extremities and then gingerly crossing some slippery terrain where he saw several strangers, including a girl, 'sitting on the ground like Red Indians or gipsies'. The event that had triggered the dream was a request by one of his patients for something to read. In lieu of yet-unpublished books of his own, Freud had offered her a copy of Haggard's *She*. 'A *strange* book, but full of hidden meaning', Freud recalls telling her, '[depicting] the eternal feminine, the immortality of our emotions . . .' (490). Elements of his dream, Freud explains, had been prompted by his memory of reading 'two imaginative novels' by Haggard, *She* and *Heart of the World*. Both entail 'perilous journeys' in which 'the guide is a woman . . . *She* describes an adventurous road that had scarcely ever been trodden before, leading to an undiscovered region' (491). Freud continues:

> The end of the adventure in *She* is that the guide, instead of finding immortality for herself and the others, perishes in the mysterious subterranean fire. A fear of that kind was unmistakably active in [my] dream-thoughts. (491)

Freud's recollection of Haggard's story, inaccurate in some ways, emphasizes several aspects of its appeal that are quite obvious rather than 'strange' or 'hidden': the 'perilous journey' into 'an undiscovered region' (analogous to Freud's probings of the unconscious), love and jealous rage that last forever, the 'eternal feminine', the prospect of immortality versus the fear of death. Freud does not add that while Ayesha, supposedly the *eternal* feminine, perishes in 'the mysterious subterranean fire', 'the others' – at least, Horace Holly and Leo Vincey – escape and return to civilization, presumably to pursue further adventures. Their escape is not simply from the Amahagger, nor from the murderous 'pillar of fire' that can supposedly also confer immortality but, above all, from Ayesha herself, 'she who must be obeyed'. According to his daughter, Lilias, Haggard recalled that he got that phrase from a rag doll 'of particularly hideous aspect':

> This doll was something of a fetish, and Rider, as a small child, was terrified of her, a fact soon discovered by an unscrupulous nurse who made full use of it to frighten him into obedience. Why or how it came

to be called She-Who-Must-Be-Obeyed he could not remember . . . (*Cloak* 28).

Nor is it clear whether Ayesha owes more to the doll or to the 'unscrupulous nurse' who terrorized Haggard into obedience. The recollection doesn't make *She* psychoanalytically more complex or mysterious, but it does suggest that Haggard was eager to connect his story-telling to romantic and Victorian conceptions of childhood, imagination and buried layers of the psyche. Rather than just a harmless female guide as in Freud's account, moreover, Ayesha is a terrifying and, at least in the domain of the Amahagger, an all-powerful dictator and *femme fatale*. According to Sandra Gilbert and Susan Gubar, *She* is a prominent instance of the misogynistic 'fictive explorations of female authority' by male writers that ushered in literary modernism (7). Ayesha is at once the star attraction of Haggard's fantasy – a key instance of 'the porno-tropic tradition' in the discourse of western imperialism – and its main source of nightmarish terror, involving, as Holly's blatant misogyny suggests, the male fear of domination or engulfment by 'the eternal feminine'.

Some of the terror that Ayesha evokes both in the male characters and in readers derives from her apparently undying passion for Kallikrates, whose embalmed corpse she has worshipped for 2,000 years while waiting for his descendant (or incarnation?), Leo, to arrive. That true love can and should last forever is a pleasant cliché, but Ayesha's millennial passion has crystallized into a murderous fanaticism that makes Miss Havisham's vindictive obsession in Dickens's *Great Expectations* look almost reasonable by comparison. And, as if it weren't enough that the ruined civilization of Kôr is a vast necropolis with a necrophiliac for its queen, Ayesha's tyranny has also made the lives of the inferior 'race' of the Amahagger a living hell. Of course, the Amahagger have their own nightmarish, terroristic attributes, notably their savage customs of 'hot-potting' and cannibalism. In several of his other stories, Haggard presents positive, albeit stereotypic, images of Africans as noble savages. This is especially so of his portrayals of Zulus in *The Witch's Head*, *King Solomon's Mines*, *Allan Quatermain*, *Nada the Lily*, and his Zulu trilogy of *Marie*, *Child of Storm*, and *Finished*. In contrast, the Amahagger have few, if any, redeeming qualities. Perhaps this is because they are not a 'pure' black race like the Zulus, but are instead a mixed, brown-skinned race, the 'bastard brood of the mighty sons of Kôr' and 'the barbarians from the south', as Ayesha speculates (181). In any event, the Amahagger are a dour, treacherous and violent people who apparently both need and deserve Ayesha's tyranny.

The image of the white (or, at least, light-skinned) queen ruling a black or brown-skinned, savage race is a powerfully erotic one. Its twin is the image of the helpless white woman, captured by savages and threatened, at least, with rape. Haggard seems to have thought that he had at least one actual source for the first image in the beliefs of the Zulus; in the introduction to *Finished*, the last novel in his Zulu trilogy, he writes of 'the *white* goddess, or spirit of the Zulus, who is, or was, called Nomkubulwana or Inkosazana-y-Zulu, i.e., the Princess of Heaven' (xi). Though the Amahagger aren't a particularly sexy people, the racist stereotype that identifies both blackness and savagery with animality and unbridled lust is central to Haggard's fantasy. Ayesha both inspires and dominates male, savage desire. But her domination of the abject Amahagger 'race' is less impressive than her sexual conquests of Holly and Leo. Andrew Lang complained to Haggard that Leo is only a brainless hunk, a beautiful specimen of masculinity without an interesting thought in his head. In contrast, the main narrator and therefore interpreter of the entire quest, Holly, represents the mind–body dichotomy in a peculiarly schizophrenic and supposedly comic way. Holly is a Cambridge scholar or don, mentally superior to every other character in the story except Ayesha, and yet his body seems to be a grotesque Darwinian atavism or biological regression to a pre-human stage of evolution. That Holly should be both ape-like in appearance and a thoroughgoing woman-hater, a figure of repressed or, rather, of badly sublimated lust, is no accident: Ayesha's 'unveilings' or stripteases play havoc with his inhibitions.

Ayesha rules as much through sex appeal as through magic, immortality and sheer will-power. Though she dies at the end of Haggard's first story about her, she was and is destined to be immortal, and not just through the popularity of *She*, but also through Haggard's resurrections of her in subsequent romances and through her career in the movies. The idea of reincarnation, prominent in *She*, involves a sort of grave-robbing logic that allowed Haggard to effect a number of rebirths in later works. The resurrections include *Ayesha: The Return of She* (1905), in which Holly and Leo rediscover her in Tibet; *She and Allan* (1921), which also resurrects Allan Quatermain; and *Wisdom's Daughter* (1923), which purports to be the original, true story of Kallikrates, Amenartas and Ayesha. The movies include seven silent films, starting in 1899, and nearly as many more recent ones, the best known of which is Robert Day's 1965 *She*, starring Ursula Andress. Haggard also wrote other romances featuring beautiful, domineering, queenly women. These include *Cleopatra* (1889), *The World's Desire* (1890 – focused on Helen of Troy and co-authored by Andrew Lang), *Montezuma's Daughter* (1893), and *Queen Sheba's Ring* (1910).

Although Haggard wrote several comparatively realistic novels that draw upon his time in South Africa, this is not the case with *She* or most of his other fantasies about light-skinned sex goddesses. *King Solomon's Mines* seems almost as fantastic as *She*, but both the noble savage Umbopa (based on an actual Zulu warrior) and the Kukuanas are portraits of what Haggard knew and thought about the Zulus. The Amahagger, in contrast, are like no African people whom Haggard had ever encountered or read about. He denied that, when he wrote *She*, he knew about the Lovedu, a matriarchal tribe supposedly ruled by a light-skinned queen. And although there are general parallels between Ayesha and various goddesses worshipped by Zulus and other African societies, these parallels extend to mythologies and religions around the world. Morton Cohen, Haggard's biographer, concludes his extensive survey of such parallels and possible sources for Ayesha by declaring that 'She is the archetypal Great Mother' (110), which is tantamount to saying that no one specific source, and nothing specifically African, characterizes her.

So, too, the ruined civilization of Kôr, though it has its analogue in the lost, white civilization in *King Solomon's Mines*, seems, like Ayesha herself, to be a transplanted version of Haggard's fantasizing about ancient Egypt. Like the white sex goddess ruling a dark-skinned people, the fantasy of a lost civilization, built by white or light-skinned people in 'the heart of darkness', appealed to Haggard for a number of reasons, not least because it reinforced the notion that black Africans needed white civilization (which meant, for Haggard, that they needed the British Empire) in order, if not to become civilized themselves, then at least to escape from the worst effects of their own savagery and superstitions.

When the German explorer Karl Mauch publicized the ruins of Great Zimbabwe in the early 1870s, no European commentators believed they could have been constructed by black Africans. Instead, they must have been built by ancient Egyptians, or Phoenicians, or one of the lost tribes of Israel. That they might even be the ruins of King Solomon's Golden Ophir is the version Haggard favours in *King Solomon's Mines*. The persistent myth that they could only have been produced by a supposedly higher, fairer race, capable of civilization, began to be challenged by archaeologists only in 1906 (Davidson 250–5). Well after that date, Haggard was still wondering, 'Who built the vast Zimbabwe – and other temples or fortresses?' (*Days* 1:242). Despite his high regard for the Zulus, Haggard couldn't imagine them, or any other black 'race', constructing elaborate temples and cities of stone. As recently as 1973, in a cinematic version of *She* called *The Virgin Goddess*, South African director Dirk de Villiers shot the film in the ruins of Great Zimbabwe and turned the Amahagger into black Africans. In this remake, writes Norman Etherington, Ayesha's 'immortality depends on the preservation of her virginity . . . De Villiers was able to cash in on the sexual anxieties of white South Africans while reinforcing the hoary and politically convenient belief that a lost white civilization rather than black men raised the walls of the spectacular buildings at Zimbabwe' ('Introduction' xxxix).

If Ayesha is an Arabian sorceress, if the lost civilization of Kôr was the work of a white-skinned race, and if the Amahagger bear no particular resemblance to any actual African society, then *She* would seem to have little or nothing to do with Haggard's experience in, and considerable knowledge of, South Africa. But, along with several of Haggard's other romances, including *King Solomon's Mines* and *Allan Quatermain*, *She* is a wish-fulfilment fantasy that, in some very precise ways, compensates for what Haggard felt he had lost, or failed to discover, during his five years in South Africa.

3. THE ROMANCE OF *SHE*

Like a number of other Victorian and early modern writers who believed in what Haggard's friend, Rudyard Kipling, called 'the white man's burden' to govern the non-white races of the world, Haggard preferred the fictional mode or genre of 'romance' to materialistic realism. That imperialist writers should so often have employed the romance form is due to several factors. The main one is that the realities of imperial domination are, like Robert Ullershaw's maiming, grim and often disillusioning, as Haggard discovered in South Africa. Marlow, the main narrator of Conrad's *Heart of Darkness*, declares: 'The conquest of the earth, which mostly means the taking it away from those who have a different complexion or slightly flatter noses than ourselves, is not a pretty thing when you look into it too much.' In contrast to Marlow, Haggard's heroes, including Ullershaw, are never critical of imperialism in the abstract, and they oppose anyone who betrays imperialist ideals. Even savages are preferable to anti-imperialist liberals and Home-Rulers. No matter how disillusioning reality may be, fidelity to the ideals of empire is ultimately what counts. And, no matter how unrealistic or fantastic Haggard's romances may be, they express those ideals in part through their generic refusal of disappointing reality.

In her perceptive analysis of Haggard and the fiction of empire, Wendy Katz writes: '. . . the romance is fundamentally idealist in character, presenting experience as a confirmation of *a priori* truths' (82). Applied to empire, the romance form occludes the materialist, economic forces of expansion and exploitation that Conrad's Marlow criticizes. It is also fundamentally nostalgic, harking back to an ahistorical, childlike realm of myths and daydreams. Although the romance form could be turned to utopian, radical and anti-imperialist ends, as does William Morris in *News from Nowhere* (1894), it is more typically reactionary – a sort of holding out for an earlier, simpler model of experience untrammelled by the complications of the modern world and of mundane, material reality. And, insofar as romance simplifies the complexities of the real world, tending to reduce them to binary oppositions of light versus darkness, good versus evil, and civilization versus savagery, it is also inherently a regressive, childlike form. The late Victorian and Edwardian proponents and practitioners of imperialist romance – Haggard, Lang, Stevenson, Kipling, Sir Arthur Conan Doyle and the poet and publicist W. E. Henley, along with a host of writers of boys' adventure fiction such as Captain Mayne Reid, G. E. Henty and Dr Gordon Stables – all recognized that their aim, as Lang put it, was to evoke and excite 'the Eternal Boy' (*Days* 2:206) in their readers.

Often, too, the romance entails an interest in spiritualism and the occult. The turn to romance in the 1880s and 1890s was, in part, a reaction both against fictional realism and against scientific materialism. But the romance form tends to express mysteries rather than to assert new truth or orthodoxies. Thus, in *She*, Haggard simultaneously invokes Darwinism and notions of reincarnation and immortality. Haggard's interest in spiritualism and the occult waxed and waned throughout his career (*Days*

1:38–40; 2:234–260). Although he never became a total believer in spiritualism, or any other alternative religion, he found such alternatives intriguing, in part as ways of counteracting what he saw as the false materialism, commercialism, and scientism of his age. The ideas about life after death that Ayesha expresses are at once part of the Gothic romance apparatus of *She* and an eclectic mix that includes elements of Darwinism. Holly's 'gorilla-like' appearance and a woman's cruel comment that he proves 'the monkey-theory' allude to the theory of evolution, while Ayesha's horrible death, shrivelling into the form of a monkey, seems to be evolution running in reverse. It is also an instance of time taking its revenge on a character who has, for 2,000 years, made time stand still. But what exactly is Haggard saying about either 'the monkey-theory' or time, death, and immortality? *She* raises many questions about religion, evolution, and life after death, but provides no clear conclusions. As Norman Etherington puts it, 'From the earliest reviews readers have complained that *She* serves up shallow and confused philosophy. It is difficult to refute the charge' ('Introduction' xxix).

The tradition of the Gothic romance, from Horace Walpole's *Castle of Otranto* (1764) to Bram Stoker's *Dracula* (1897) and beyond, is characterized partly by its stress on the supernatural, and especially on the ghostly and demonic. Many Victorian writers employed Gothic conventions in their fiction and participated in, or at least expressed curiosity about, the rise of the spiritualist movement (starting in the 1860s), in the activities of the Psychical Research Society (founded in 1883), in séances, magic, mysticism and in such alternative religions as Buddhism and Theosophy.* Connected to imperialist adventure fiction, these interests often imply anxieties about the stability of Britain, of the British Empire or, more generally, of western civilization. Repressed, demonic forces from the primitive or barbaric regions

* For a recent consideration of the proliferation of Gothic romances in the late Victorian period including *She*, see Robert Mighall's *A Geography of Victorian Gothic Fiction*.

of the world are often depicted as invading, infecting or subverting Britain, as happens, for example, in *Dracula*. Ayesha threatens a similar Gothic-demonic invasion when, toward the end of the story, she announces her intention to come to Britain with Leo and overthrow Queen Victoria. According to Holly:

> The terrible *She* had evidently made up her mind to go to England, and it made me absolutely shudder to think what would be the result of her arrival there . . . It might be possible to control her for a while, but her proud, ambitious spirit would be certain to break loose and avenge itself for the long centuries of its solitude . . . In the end she would, I had little doubt, assume absolute rule over the British dominions, and probably over the whole earth . . . (256).

So Ayesha ultimately threatens to substitute a dictatorial matriarchy and a demonic imperialism for Haggard's idealistic versions of the benign rule of Queen Victoria and of the British Empire. Perhaps Ayesha's tyranny would not be too different from the universal vampirism and deadly immortality threatened by Count Dracula.

In 'About Fiction' (1887), one of his few commentaries on literature, Haggard antagonized his critics by insisting that romance was the only sort of fiction worth reading – that the dominant fictional realism of his age was bunk – and by strongly implying that his own romances were especially worth reading. 'It is a self-opinionated article', says Peter Berresford Ellis, 'a pretentious, dogmatic attack on the literary world' (122). In it, Haggard declares: '. . . really good romance writing is perhaps the most difficult art practised by the sons of man. It might even be maintained that none but a great man or woman can produce a *really* great work of fiction' (172–3). Despite, or perhaps because of, his instant popularity, the attacks on Haggard began immediately, and included accusations of plagiarism. These accusations arose partly because many earlier myths, romances and adventure stories which Haggard read or might have read are analogues, if not direct sources, for *She*. Also, Haggard was always a slapdash writer who didn't like the hard labour of revision; he boasted that he had written *She* in six weeks and never revised it (which was not true): 'The fact is that it was written at white heat, almost without rest, and that is the best way to compose' (*Days* 1:245). Despite his claims to the contrary, hasty writing did not encourage originality.

Haggard certainly read the works of Sir Henry Bulwer's famous uncle, Edward Bulwer-Lytton, and these included *A Strange Story* (1862), which tells of a search for the elixir of life and of a mysterious, veiled woman named 'Ayesha'. Another Bulwer-Lytton fantasy, *The Coming Race* (1871), narrates the discovery of an underground civilization populated by superhuman beings, the Vril-ya, who possess a mysterious form of energy called 'vril', which seems a lot like electricity and which gives them quasi-magical powers. *The Coming Race* was itself inspired by Jules Verne's *Journey to the Centre of the Earth* (1864), and these and other romances about subterranean worlds and lost civilizations form part of the background of *She* with its caves of Kôr.

Along with such Gothic romances as Mary Shelley's *Frankenstein* and *The Last Man*, and Robert Louis Stevenson's *Dr Jekyll and Mr Hyde*, Haggard's stories also form part of the early history of science fiction (H. G. Wells called his non-realistic fictions, starting with *The Time Machine* in 1895, 'scientific romances'). Haggard may seem peripheral to the development of science fiction, and yet his African quest romances could easily be transposed to other planets and galaxies. In his popular account of science fiction, *Billion Year Spree*, Brian Aldiss notes the frequency with which Ayesha's horrific death in the pillar of fire has been imitated (plagiarized?) by science fiction writers. According to Aldiss: 'From Haggard on, crumbling women, priestesses, or empresses – all symbols of women as Untouchable and Unmakeable – fill the pages of many a scientific "romance"' (139). The misogynistic traits of *She* and more generally of imperialist adventure fiction also characterize much science fiction with its fantasies about alien invaders and the exploration and conquest of outer space. One of Haggard's most successful imitators was American Edgar Rice Burroughs, author both of the Tarzan-of-the-Apes stories and of several interplanetary exploration romances, including *A Princess of Mars* (1917).

Along with the charges of plagiarism, *She* evoked many parodies, both by Haggard's critics and by his friends and admirers. So Haggard's friend and critical champion, Andrew Lang, who offered much valuable advice to Haggard when he read the manuscript version of *She*, first wrote an apparently serious sonnet called 'She' and dedicated to Haggard, and then parodied his own sonnet with 'Twosh', dedicated to 'Hyder Ragged' (Ellis 115). Lang proceeded to co-author, with W. H. Pollock, a work called *He*, and subtitled: 'by the authors of "It", "King Solomon's Wives", "Bess", "Much Darker Days", "Mr Morton's Subtler" and other romances' (Ellis 115). Many other parodies appeared, including George Forrest's 'The Deathless Queen' and George Sims's 'The Lost Author'. But even the wittiest parodies in *Punch* and elsewhere, like the charges of plagiarism, only added to the publicity that *She* and its author were receiving. Whether one considered *She* a major, highly original work of fiction, or an overly imitative trifle by an undereducated young man who should have had better things to do with his time, it was and would remain a bestseller. Even that great supposed betrayer of empire, Gladstone, became an ardent reader of Haggard's romances.

From the publication of *King Solomon's Mines* onwards, Haggard has never lacked fans and admirers. Andrew Lang thought *She* was 'one of the most astonishing romances I ever read. The more impossible it is, the better you do it, till it seems like a story from the literature of another planet' (*Days* 1:247). The realist novelist Walter Besant told Haggard that *She* put him 'at the head – a long way ahead – of all contemporary imaginative writers. If fiction is best cultivated in the field of pure invention then you are certainly the first of modern novelists' (*Days* 1:249). And Edmund Gosse wrote to tell Haggard that he could not remember ever being 'thrilled and terrified by any literature as

I have by [the climax] of *She*. It is simply unsurpassable' (*Days* 1:250). And then there was Freud, giving his patient Haggard's 'strange book' to read and telling her that it is 'full of hidden meaning . . . the eternal feminine, the immortality of our emotions . . .' Haggard has had countless such enthusiastic readers, and will continue to have many more.

Patrick Brantlinger

Further Reading

SELECTED WORKS BY H. RIDER HAGGARD

'About Fiction'. *Contemporary Review*, 51 (February 1887): 172–180.

Allan and the Ice-gods: A Tale of Beginnings. London: Hutchinson, 1927.

Allan Quatermain, Being an Account of His Further Adventures and Discoveries in Company with Sir Henry Curtis, Bart, Commander John Good, R N, and One Umslopogaas. London: Longmans, Green, 1887.

The Ancient Allan. London: Cassell, 1920.

Ayesha: The Return of She. London: Ward, Lock, 1905.

Cetywayo and His White Neighbours; or, Remarks on Recent Events in Zululand, Natal, and the Transvaal. London: Trübner, 1882.

Child of Storm. London: Cassell, 1913.

Cleopatra, Being an Account of the Fall and Vengeance of Harmachis, the Royal Egyptian, as Set Forth by His Own Hand. London: Longmans, Green, 1889.

Dawn. London: Hurst and Blackett, 1884.

The Days of My Life. (2 vols). London: Longmans, Green, 1926.

Finished. London: Ward, Lock, 1917.

King Solomon's Mines. London: Cassell, 1885.

Marie. London: Cassell, 1912.

Nada the Lily. London: Longmans, Green, 1892.

Regeneration, Being an Account of the Social Work of the Salvation Army in Great Britain. London: Longmans, Green, 1910.

*Rural England, Being an Account of Agricultural and Social

Researches Carried Out in the Years 1901 and 1902. (2 vols). London: Longmans, Green, 1902.

She and Allan. London: Hutchinson, 1921.

'The Transvaal'. *Macmillan's Magazine*, 36 (May 1877): 71–79.

The Way of the Spirit. London: Hutchinson, 1906.

Wisdom's Daughter: The Life and Love Story of She-Who-Must-Be-Obeyed. London: Hutchinson, 1923.

The World's Desire (co-authored by Andrew Lang). London: Longmans, Green, 1890.

WORKS ABOUT HAGGARD AND SOUTH AFRICA

Cohen, Morton N. *Rider Haggard: His Life and Works*. New York: Walker, 1960.

Davidson, Basil. *The Lost Cities of Africa* (rev. ed.). Boston/Toronto: Little, Brown, 1970.

Ellis, Peter Berresford. *H. Rider Haggard: A Voice from the Infinite*. London: Routledge and Kegan Paul, 1978.

Etherington, Norman. 'Introduction'. *The Annotated She: A Critical Edition*. Bloomington: Indiana UP, 1991: xv–xliii.

——. *Rider Haggard*. Boston: Twayne, 1984.

Freud, Sigmund. *The Interpretation of Dreams*. James Strachey (Translator). New York: Avon Books, 1965.

Gilbert, Sandra M., and Susan Gubar. *No Man's Land: The Place of the Woman Writer in the Twentieth Century*. Vol. 2: *Sexchanges*. New Haven: Yale UP, 1989.

Haggard, Lilias Rider. *The Cloak That I Left: A Biography of the Author Henry Rider Haggard KBE*. London: Hodder and Stoughton, 1951.

Higgins, D. S. *Rider Haggard: The Great Storyteller*. London: Cassell, 1981.

Katz, Wendy R. *Rider Haggard and the Fiction of Empire: A Critical Study of British Imperial Fiction*. Cambridge: CUP, 1987.

McClintock, Anne. *Imperial Leather: Race, Gender and Sex-*

uality in the Colonial Contest. New York and London: Routledge, 1995.

Mighall, Robert. *A Geography of Victorian Gothic Fiction: Mapping History's Nightmares*. Oxford: OUP, 1999.

Morris, Donald R. *The Washing of the Spears: A History of the Rise of the Zulu Nation under Shaka and Its Fall in the Zulu War of 1879*. New York: Simon and Schuster, 1965.

Pocock, Tom. *Rider Haggard and the Lost Empire*. London: Weidenfeld and Nicolson, 1993.

Scott, J. E. *A Bibliography of the Works of Sir Henry Rider Haggard 1856–1925*. Bishop's Stortford: Elkin Matthews, 1947.

Note on the Text

This volume reproduces the first edition of H. Rider Haggard's *She* to appear in book format, published by Longmans, Green & Company of London in 1887. The 1887 edition was a revised version of the serial that had appeared in the *Graphic* from 2 October 1886 to 8 January 1887. For the first Longmans edition, Haggard revised the opening scenes at Cambridge in Chapters 1–3, added the 'facsimile' illustrations and the elaborate account of 'the sherd of Amenartas' in Chapter 3, changed the cause of Mahomed's death in Chapter 8 from 'hot-potting' to a bullet from Horace Holly's pistol, improved some of the information about geography and the history of ancient civilizations in Chapters 4, 13 and 17, and made various other minor changes. Haggard continued to revise his prose for later editions up to 1896; thus, the 'New Edition' of 1888, the basis for *The Annotated She* edited by Norman Etherington, included some 400 minor stylistic changes. The illustrations of the sherd in the Longmans edition of 1887 were photographs of a vase of antique appearance that Haggard's sister-in-law, Agnes Barber, made for him. As the footnotes indicate, Haggard got help from two classical scholars in composing the Greek and Latin inscriptions on the sherd.

SHE

A HISTORY OF ADVENTURE

BY

H. RIDER HAGGARD

AUTHOR OF

'KING SOLOMON'S MINES' 'DAWN' 'THE WITCH'S HEAD' ETC.

IN EARTH AND SKIE AND SEA
STRANGE THYNGES THER BE

Doggerel couplet from the Sherd of Amenartas

THIRD EDITION

LONDON

LONGMANS, GREEN, AND CO.

1887

All rights reserved

I INSCRIBE THIS HISTORY

TO

ANDREW LANG

IN TOKEN OF PERSONAL REGARD

AND OF

MY SINCERE ADMIRATION FOR HIS LEARNING AND HIS WORKS

Contents

		Page
	Introduction	11
I.	My visitor	17
II.	The Years Roll By	26
III.	The Sherd of Amenartas	33
IV.	The Squall	56
V.	The Head of the Ethiopian	66
VI.	An Early Christian Ceremony	77
VII.	Ustane Sings	89
VIII.	The Feast, and After!	100
IX.	A Little Foot	110
X.	Speculations	118
XI.	The Plain of Kôr	128
XII.	'She'	138
XIII.	Ayesha Unveils	149
XIV.	A Soul in Hell	162
XV.	Ayesha Gives Judgment	171
XVI.	The Tombs of Kôr	180
XVII.	The Balance Turns	191
XVIII.	Go, Woman!	203
XIX.	'Give Me a Black Goat!'	215
XX.	Triumph	224
XXI.	The Dead and Living Meet	236
XXII.	Job Has a Presentiment	245
XXIII.	The Temple of Truth	257
XXIV.	Walking the Plank	266

XXV.	The Spirit of Life	277
XXVI.	What We Saw	290
XXVII.	We Leap	300
XXVIII.	Over the Mountain	308

Plates

Facsimile of the Sherd of Amenartas one-half size.
Facsimile of the Reverse of the Sherd of Amenartas, one-half size.

FACSIMILE OF THE SHERD OF AMENARTAS

ONE 1/2 SIZE

Greatest length of the original	*10 1/2 inches*
Greatest breadth	*7 inches*
Weight	*1lb 5½ oz*

FACSIMILE OF THE REVERSE OF THE SHERD OF AMENARTAS

ONE 1/2 SIZE

Introduction

Introduction

In giving to the world the record of what, looked at as an adventure only, is I suppose one of the most wonderful and mysterious experiences ever undergone by mortal men, I feel it incumbent on me to explain what my exact connection with it is. And so I may as well say at once that I am not the narrator but only the editor of this extraordinary history, and then go on to tell how it found its way into my hands.

Some years ago I, the editor, was stopping with a friend, '*vir doctissimus et amicus meus*,'[1] at a certain University, which for the purposes of this history we will call Cambridge, and was one day much struck with the appearance of two people whom I saw going arm-in-arm down the street. One of these gentlemen was I think, without exception, the handsomest young fellow I have ever seen. He was very tall, very broad, and had a look of power and a grace of bearing that seemed as native to him as it is to a wild stag. In addition his face was almost without flaw – a good face as well as a beautiful one, and when he lifted his hat, which he did just then to a passing lady, I saw that his head was covered with little golden curls growing close to the scalp.

'Good gracious!' I said to my friend, with whom I was walking, 'why, that fellow looks like a statue of Apollo come to life. What a splendid man he is!'

'Yes,' he answered, 'he is the handsomest man in the University, and one of the nicest too. They call him "the Greek god"; but look at the other one, he's Vincey's (that's the god's name) guardian, and supposed to be full of every kind of information.

They call him "Charon." '[2] I looked and found the older man quite as interesting in his way as the glorified specimen of humanity at his side. He appeared to be 40 years of age, and was I think as ugly as his companion was handsome. To begin with, he was shortish, rather bow-legged, very deep chested, and with unusually long arms. He had dark hair and small eyes, and the hair grew right down on his forehead, and his whiskers grew right up to his hair, so that there was uncommonly little of his countenance to be seen. Altogether he reminded me forcibly of a gorilla,[3] and yet there was something very pleasing and genial about the man's eye. I remember saying that I should like to know him.

'All right,' answered my friend, 'nothing easier. I know Vincey; I'll introduce you,' and he did, and for some minutes we stood chatting—about the Zulu people,[4] I think, for I had just returned from the Cape at the time. Presently, however, a stoutish lady, whose name I do not remember, came along the pavement, accompanied by a pretty fair-haired girl, and these two Mr. Vincey, who clearly knew them well, at once joined, walking off in their company. I remember being rather amused because of the change in the expression of the elder man, whose name I discovered was Holly, when he saw the ladies advancing. He suddenly stopped short in his talk, cast a reproachful look at his companion, and, with an abrupt nod to myself, turned and marched off alone across the street. I heard afterwards that he was popularly supposed to be as much afraid of a woman as most people are of a mad dog, which accounted for his precipitate retreat. I cannot say, however, that young Vincey showed much aversion to feminine society on this occasion. Indeed I remember laughing, and remarking to my friend at the time that he was not the sort of man whom it would be desirable to introduce to the lady one was going to marry, since it is exceedingly probable that the acquaintance would end in a transfer of her affections. He was altogether too good-looking, and, what is more, he had none of that consciousness and conceit about him which usually afflicts handsome men, and makes them deservedly disliked by their fellows.

That same evening my visit came to an end, and this was the last I saw or heard of 'Charon' and 'the Greek god' for many a long day. Indeed, I have never seen either of them from that hour to this, and do not think it probable that I shall. But a month ago I received a letter and two packets, one of manuscript, and on opening the first found that it was signed by 'Horace Holly,' a name that at the moment was not familiar to me. It ran as follows:—

'—— College, Cambridge, May 1, 18–

'MY DEAR SIR,—You will be surprised, considering the very slight nature of our acquaintance, to get a letter from me. Indeed, I think I had better begin by reminding you that we once met, now some five years ago, when I and my ward Leo Vincey were introduced to you in the street at Cambridge. To be brief and come to my business. I have recently read with much interest a book of yours describing a Central African adventure.[5] I take it that this book is partly true, and partly an effort of the imagination. However this is, it has given me an idea. It happens, how you will see in the accompanying manuscript (which together with the Scarab, the "Royal Son of the Sun,"[6] and the original sherd, I am sending to you by hand), that my ward, or rather my adopted son Leo Vincey and myself have recently passed through a real African adventure, of a nature so much more marvellous than the one which you describe, that to tell you the truth I am almost ashamed to submit it to you for fear lest you should disbelieve my tale. You will see it stated in this manuscript that I, or rather we, had made up our minds not to make this history public during our joint lives. Nor should we alter our determination were it not for a circumstance which has recently arisen. We are for reasons that, after perusing this manuscript, you may be able to guess, going away again, this time to Central Asia where, if anywhere upon this earth, wisdom is to be found, and we anticipate that our sojourn there will be a long one. Possibly we shall not return. Under these altered conditions it has become a question whether we are justified in withholding from the world an account of a phenomenon which we believe to be of unparalleled interest, merely because our private life is involved, or because we are afraid of ridicule and doubt being cast upon our statements. I hold one view about this matter, and Leo holds another, and finally, after much discussion, we have come to a compromise, namely, to send the history to you, giving you full leave to publish it if you think fit, the only stipulation being that you shall disguise our real names, and as much concerning our personal identity as is consistent with the maintenance of the *bona fides*[7] of the narrative.

'And now what am I to say further? I really do not know beyond once more repeating that everything is described in the accompanying manuscript exactly as it happened. As regards *She* herself I have nothing to add. Day by day we have greater occasion to regret that we did not better avail ourselves of our opportunities to obtain more information from that marvellous woman. Who was she? How did she first come to the Caves of Kôr, and what was her real religion? We never ascertained, and now, alas! we never shall, at least not yet. These and many other questions arise in my mind, but what is the good of asking them now?

'Will you undertake the task? We give you complete freedom, and as a reward you will, we believe, have the credit of presenting to the world the most wonderful history, as distinguished from romance, that its records can show. Read the manuscript (which I have copied out fairly for your benefit), and let me know.

'Believe me, very truly yours,

'L. Horace Holly.

'P.S.—Of course, if any profit results from the sale of the writing should you care to undertake its publication, you can do what you like with it, but if there is a loss I will leave instructions with my lawyers, Messrs. Geoffrey and Jordan, to meet it. We entrust the sherd, the scarab, and the parchments to your keeping till such time as we demand them back again.—L.H.H.'

This letter, as may be imagined, astonished me considerably, but when I came to look at the MS., which the pressure of other work prevented me from doing for a fortnight, I was still more astonished, as I think the reader will be also, and at once made up my mind to press on with the matter. I wrote to this effect to Mr. Holly, but a week afterwards received a letter from that gentleman's lawyers, returning my own, with the information that their client and Mr. Leo Vincey had already left this country for Thibet, and they did not at present know their address.

Well, that is all I have to say. Of the history itself the reader must judge. I give it him, with the exception of a very few alterations, made with the object of concealing the identity of the actors from the general public, exactly as it has come to me. Personally I have made up my mind to refrain from comments. At first I was inclined to believe that this history of a woman on whom, clothed in the majesty of her almost endless years, the shadow of Eternity itself lay like the dark wing of Night, was some gigantic allegory of which I could not catch the meaning. Then I thought that it might be a bold attempt to portray the possible results of practical immortality, informing the substance of a mortal who yet drew her strength from Earth, and in whose human bosom passions yet rose and fell and beat as in the undying world around her the winds and the tides rise and fall and beat unceasingly. But as I went on I abandoned that idea also. To me the story seems to bear the stamp of truth upon its face. Its explanation I must leave to others, and with this slight preface, which circumstances make necessary, I introduce the world to Ayesha and the Caves of Kôr.—THE EDITOR.

P.S.—There is on consideration one circumstance that, after a reperusal of this history, struck me with so much force that I cannot resist calling the attention of the reader to it. He will observe that so far as we are made acquainted with him there appears to be nothing in the character of Leo Vincey which in the opinion of most people would have been likely to attract an intellect so powerful as that of Ayesha. He is not even, at any rate to my view, particularly interesting. Indeed, one might imagine that Mr. Holly would under ordinary circumstances have easily out-stripped him in the favour of *She*. Can it be that extremes meet, and that the very excess and splendour of her mind led her by means of some strange physical reaction to worship at the shrine of matter? Was that ancient Kallikrates nothing but a splendid animal beloved for his hereditary Greek beauty? Or is the true explanation what I believe it to be—namely, that Ayesha, seeing further than we can see, perceived the germ and smouldering spark of greatness which lay hid within her lover's soul, and well knew that under the influence of her gift of life, watered by her wisdom, and shone upon with the sunshine of her presence, it would bloom like a flower and flash out like a star, filling the world with light and fragrance?

Here also I am not able to answer, but must leave the reader to form his own judgment on the facts before him, as detailed by Mr. Holly in the following pages.

I

My Visitor

There are some events of which each circumstance and surrounding detail seems to be graven on the memory in such fashion that we cannot forget it, and so it is with the scene that I am about to describe. It rises as clearly before my mind at this moment as though it had happened yesterday.

It was in this very month something over twenty years ago that I, Ludwig Horace Holly, was sitting one night in my rooms at Cambridge, grinding away at some mathematical work, I forget what. I was to go up for my fellowship within a week, and was expected by my tutor and my college generally to distinguish myself. At last, wearied out, I flung my book down, and, going to the mantelpiece, took down a pipe and filled it. There was a candle burning on the mantelpiece, and a long, narrow glass at the back of it; and as I was in the act of lighting the pipe I caught sight of my own countenance in the glass, and paused to reflect. The lighted match burnt away till it scorched my fingers, forcing me to drop it; but still I stood and stared at myself in the glass, and reflected.

'Well,' I said aloud, at last, 'it is to be hoped that I shall be able to do something with the inside of my head, for I shall certainly never do anything by the help of the outside.'

This remark will doubtless strike anybody who reads it as being slightly obscure, but I was in reality alluding to my physical deficiencies. Most men of twenty-two are endowed at any rate with some share of the comeliness of youth, but to me even this was denied. Short, thick-set, and deep-chested almost to deformity, with long sinewy arms, heavy features, deep-set grey eyes, a low brow half overgrown with a mop of thick black hair, like a deserted clearing on which the forest had once more begun to encroach; such was my appearance nearly a quarter of a century ago, and such, with some modification, is it to this day. Like Cain, I was branded—branded by Nature with the stamp of abnormal ugliness, as I was gifted by Nature with iron and abnormal strength and considerable intellectual powers. So ugly was I that the spruce young men of my College, though they were proud enough of my feats of endurance and physical prowess, did not even care to be seen walking with me. Was it wonderful that I was misanthropic and sullen? Was it wonderful that I brooded and worked alone, and had no friends—at least, only one? I was set apart by Nature to live alone, and draw comfort from her breast, and hers only. Women hated the sight of me. Only a week before I had heard one call me a 'monster' when she thought I was out of hearing, and say that I had converted her to the monkey theory.[1] Once, indeed, a woman pretended to care for me, and I lavished all the pent-up affection of my nature upon her. Then money that was to have come to me went elsewhere, and she discarded me. I pleaded with her as I have never pleaded with any living creature before or since, for I was caught by her sweet face, and loved her; and in the end by way of answer she took me to the glass, and stood side by side with me, and looked into it.

'Now,' she said, 'if I am Beauty, who are you?' That was when I was only twenty.

And so I stood and stared, and felt a sort of grim satisfaction in the sense of my own loneliness; for I had neither father, nor mother, nor brother; and as I did so there came a knock at my door.

I listened before I went to open it, for it was nearly twelve o'clock at night, and I was in no mood to admit any stranger. I had but one friend in the College, or, indeed, in the world—perhaps it was he.

Just then the person outside the door coughed, and I hastened to open it, for I knew the cough.

A tall man of about thirty, with the remains of great personal beauty, came hurrying in, staggering beneath the weight of a massive iron box which he carried by a handle with his right hand. He placed the box upon the table, and then fell into an awful fit of coughing. He coughed and coughed till his face became quite purple, and at last he sank into a chair and began to spit up blood. I poured out some whisky into a tumbler, and gave it to him. He drank it, and seemed better; though his better was very bad indeed.

'Why did you keep me standing there in the cold?' he asked pettishly. 'You know the draughts are death to me.'

'I did not know who it was,' I answered. 'You are a late visitor.'

'Yes; and I verily believe it is my last visit,' he answered, with a ghastly attempt at a smile. 'I am done for, Holly. I am done for. I do not believe that I shall see to-morrow!'

'Nonsense!' I said. 'Let me go for a doctor.'

He waved me back imperiously with his hand. 'It is sober sense; but I want no doctors. I have studied medicine, and I know all about it. No doctors can help me. My last hour has come! For a year past I have only lived by a miracle. Now listen to me as you never listened to anybody before; for you will not have the opportunity of getting me to repeat my words. We have been friends for two years; now tell me how much do you know about me?'

'I know that you are rich, and have had a fancy to come to College long after the age that most men leave it. I know that you have been married, and that your wife died; and that you have been the best, indeed almost the only friend I ever had.'

'Did you know that I have a son?'

'No.'

'I have. He is five years old. He cost me his mother's life, and I have never been able to bear to look upon his face in consequence. Holly, if you will accept the trust, I am going to leave you that boy's sole guardian.'

I sprang almost out of my chair. '*Me!*' I said.

'Yes, you. I have not studied you for two years for nothing.

I have known for some time that I could not last, and since I realised the fact I have been searching for some one to whom I could confide the boy and this,' and he tapped the iron box. 'You are the man, Holly; for, like a rugged tree, you are hard and sound at core. Listen; the boy will be the only representative of one of the most ancient families in the world, that is, so far as families can be traced. You will laugh at me when I say it, but one day it will be proved to you beyond a doubt, that my sixty-fifth or sixty-sixth lineal ancestor was an Egyptian priest of Isis,[2] though he was himself of Grecian extraction, and was called Kallikrates.* His father was one of the Greek mercenaries raised by Hak-Hor,[3] a Mendesian Pharaoh of the twenty-ninth dynasty, and his grandfather, I believe, was that very Kallikrates mentioned by Herodotus.†[4] In or about the year 339 before Christ, just at the time of the final fall of the Pharaohs, this Kallikrates (the priest) broke his vows of celibacy and fled from Egypt with a Princess of Royal blood who had fallen in love with him, and was finally wrecked upon the coast of Africa, somewhere, as I believe, in the neighbourhood of where Delagoa Bay[5] now is, or rather to the north of it, he and his wife being saved, and all the remainder of their company destroyed in one way or another. Here they endured great hardships, but were at last entertained

* The Strong and Beautiful, or, more accurately, the Beautiful in strength.

† The Kallikrates here referred to by my friend was a Spartan, spoken of by Herodotus (Herod. ix. 72) as being remarkable for his beauty. He fell at the glorious battle of Platæa (September 22, BC 479), when the Lacedæmonians and Athenians under Pausanias routed the Persians, putting nearly 300,000 of them to the sword. The following is a translation of the passage, 'For Kallikrates died out of the battle, he came to the army the most beautiful man of the Greeks of that day—not only of the Lacedæmonians themselves, but of the other Greeks also. He when Pausanias was sacrificing was wounded in the side by an arrow; and then they fought, but on being carried off he regretted his death, and said to Arimnestus, a Platæan, that he did not grieve at dying for Greece, but at not having struck a blow, or, although he desired so to do, performed any deed worthy of himself.' This Kallikrates, who appears to have been as brave as he was beautiful, is subsequently mentioned by Herodotus as having been buried among the ἰρένες (young commanders), apart from the other Spartans and the Helots.—L.H.H.

by the mighty Queen of a savage people, a white woman of peculiar loveliness, who, under circumstances which I cannot enter into, but which you will one day learn, if you live, from the contents of the box, finally murdered my ancestor, Kallikrates. His wife, however, escaped, how I know not, to Athens, bearing a child with her, whom she named Tisisthenes, or the Mighty Avenger. Five hundred years or more afterwards the family migrated to Rome under circumstances of which no trace remains, and here, probably with the idea of preserving the idea of vengeance which we find set out in the name of Tisisthenes, they appear to have pretty regularly assumed the cognomen of Vindex, or Avenger. Here, too, they remained for another five centuries or more, till about 770 AD, when Charlemagne invaded Lombardy, where they were then settled, whereon the head of the family seems to have attached himself to the great Emperor, and to have returned with him across the Alps, and finally to have settled in Brittany. Eight generations later his lineal representative crossed to England in the reign of Edward the Confessor, and in the time of William the Conqueror was advanced to great honour and power. From that time till the present day I can trace my descent without a break. Not that the Vinceys—for that was the final corruption of the name after its bearers took root in English soil—have been particularly distinguished—they never came much to the fore. Sometimes they were soldiers, sometimes merchants, but on the whole they have preserved a dead level of respectability, and a still deader level of mediocrity. From the time of Charles II. till the beginning of the present century they were merchants.[6] About 1790 my grandfather made a considerable fortune out of brewing, and retired. In 1821 he died, and my father succeeded him, and dissipated most of the money. Ten years ago he died also, leaving me a net income of about two thousand a year. Then it was that I undertook an expedition in connection with *that*,' and he pointed to the iron chest, 'which ended disastrously enough. On my way back I travelled in the South of Europe, and finally reached Athens. There I met my beloved wife, who might well also have been called the "Beautiful," like my old Greek ancestor. There I married her, and there, a year afterwards, when my boy was born, she died.'

He paused a while, his head sunk upon his hand, and then continued—

'My marriage had diverted me from a project which I cannot enter into now. I have no time, Holly—I have no time! One day, if you accept my trust, you will learn all about it. After my wife's death I turned my mind to it again. But first it was necessary, or, at least, I conceived that it was necessary, that I should attain to a perfect knowledge of Eastern dialects, especially Arabic. It was to facilitate my studies that I came here. Very soon, however, my disease developed itself, and now there is an end of me.' And as though to emphasise his words he burst into another terrible fit of coughing.

I gave him some more whisky, and after resting he went on—

'I have never seen my boy, Leo, since he was a tiny baby. I never could bear to see him, but they tell me that he is a quick and handsome child. In this envelope,' and he produced a letter from his pocket addressed to myself, 'I have jotted down the course I wish followed in the boy's education. It is a somewhat peculiar one. At any rate, I could not entrust it to a stranger. Once more, will you undertake it?'

'I must first know what I am to undertake,' I answered.

'You are to undertake to have the boy, Leo, to live with you till he is twenty-five years of age—not to send him to school, remember. On his twenty-fifth birthday your guardianship will end, and you will then, with the keys that I give you now' (and he placed them on the table), 'open the iron box, and let him see and read the contents, and say whether or no he is willing to undertake the quest. There is no obligation on him to do so. Now, as regards terms. My present income is two thousand two hundred a year. Half of that income I have secured to you by will for life contingently on your undertaking the guardianship—that is, one thousand a year remuneration to yourself, for you will have to give up your life to it, and one hundred a year to pay for the board of the boy. The rest is to accumulate till Leo is twenty-five, so that there may be a sum in hand should he wish to undertake the quest of which I spoke.'

'And suppose I were to die?' I asked.

'Then the boy must become a ward of Chancery[7] and take his chance. Only be careful that the iron chest is passed on to him by your will. Listen, Holly, don't refuse me. Believe me, this is to your advantage. You are not fit to mix with the world—it would only embitter you. In a few weeks you will become a Fellow of your College, and the income that you will derive from that combined with what I have left you will enable you to live a life of learned leisure, alternated with the sport of which you are so fond, such as will exactly suit you.'

He paused and looked at me anxiously, but I still hesitated. The charge seemed so very strange.

'For my sake, Holly. We have been good friends, and I have no time to make other arrangements.'

'Very well,' I said, 'I will do it, provided there is nothing in this paper to make me change my mind,' and I touched the envelope he had put upon the table by the keys.

'Thank you, Holly, thank you. There is nothing at all. Swear to me by God that you will be a father to the boy, and follow my directions to the letter.'

'I swear it,' I answered solemnly.

'Very well, remember that perhaps one day I shall ask for the account of your oath, for though I am dead and forgotten, yet shall I live. There is no such thing as death, Holly, only a change, and, as you may perhaps learn in time to come, I believe that even here that change could under certain circumstances be indefinitely postponed,' and again he broke into one of his dreadful fits of coughing.

'There,' he said, 'I must go, you have the chest, and my will will be found among my papers, under the authority of which the child will be handed over to you. You will be well paid, Holly, and I know that you are honest, but if you betray my trust, by Heaven I will haunt you.'

I said nothing, being, indeed, too bewildered to speak.

He held up the candle, and looked at his own face in the glass. It had been a beautiful face, but disease had wrecked it. 'Food for the worms,' he said. 'Curious to think that in a few hours I shall be stiff and cold—the journey done, the little game played out. Ah me, Holly! life is not worth the trouble of life, except when one is in love—at least, mine has not been; but the boy Leo's may be if he has the courage and the faith. Good-bye, my friend!' and with a sudden access of tenderness he flung his arm about me and kissed me on the forehead, and then turned to go.

'Look here, Vincey,' I said, 'if you are as ill as you think, you had better let me fetch a doctor.'

'No, no,' he said earnestly. 'Promise me that you won't. I am going to die, and, like a poisoned rat, I wish to die alone.'

'I don't believe that you are going to do anything of the sort,' I answered. He smiled, and, with the word 'Remember' on his lips, was gone. As for myself, I sat down and rubbed my eyes, wondering if I had been asleep. As this supposition would not bear investigation I gave it up, and began to think that Vincey must have been drinking. I knew that he was, and had been, very ill, but still it seemed impossible that he could be in such a condition as to be able to know for certain that he would not outlive the night. Had he been so near dissolution surely he would scarcely have been able to walk, and carry a heavy iron box with him. The whole story, on reflection, seemed to me utterly incredible, for I was not then old enough to be aware how many things happen in this world that the common sense of the average man would set down as so improbable as to be absolutely impossible. This is a fact that I have only recently mastered. Was it likely that a man would have a son five years of age whom he had never seen since he was a tiny infant? No. Was it likely that he could foretell his own death so accurately? No. Was it likely that he could trace his pedigree for more than three centuries before Christ, or that he would suddenly confide the absolute guardianship of his child, and leave half his fortune, to a college friend? Most certainly not. Clearly Vincey was either drunk or mad. That being so, what did it mean? and what was in the sealed iron chest?

The whole thing baffled and puzzled me to such an extent that at last I could stand it no longer, and determined to sleep over it. So I jumped up, and having put the keys and the letter that Vincey had left away into my despatch-box, and stowed the iron chest in a large portmanteau, I turned in, and was soon fast asleep.

As it seemed to me, I had only been asleep for a few minutes when I was awakened by somebody calling me. I sat up and rubbed my eyes; it was broad daylight—eight o'clock, in fact.

'Why, what is the matter with you, John?' I asked of the gyp[8] who waited on Vincey and myself. 'You look as though you had seen a ghost!'

'Yes, sir, and so I have,' he answered, 'leastways I've seen a corpse, which is worse. I've been in to call Mr. Vincey, as usual, and there he lies stark and dead!'

II

The Years Roll By

Of course, poor Vincey's sudden death created a great stir in the College; but, as he was known to be very ill, and a satisfactory doctor's certificate was forthcoming, there was no inquest. They were not so particular about inquests in those days as they are now; indeed, they were generally disliked, as causing a scandal. Under all these circumstances, as I was asked no questions, I did not feel called upon to volunteer any information about our interview of the night of Vincey's decease, beyond saying that he had come into my rooms to see me, as he often did. On the day of the funeral a lawyer came down from London and followed my poor friend's remains to the grave, and then went back with his papers and effects, except, of course, the iron chest which had been left in my keeping. For a week after this I heard no more of the matter, and, indeed, my attention was amply occupied in other ways, for I was up for my Fellowship, a fact that had prevented me from attending the funeral or seeing the lawyer. At last, however, the examination was over, and I came back to my rooms and sank into an easy chair with a happy consciousness that I had got through it very fairly.

Soon, however, my thoughts, relieved of the pressure that had crushed them into a single groove during the last few days, turned to the events of the night of poor Vincey's death, and again I asked myself what it all meant, and wondered if I should hear anything more of the matter, and if I did not, what it would be my duty to do with the curious iron chest. I sat there and thought and thought till I began to grow quite disturbed over the whole occurrence: the mysterious midnight visit, the prophecy of death so shortly to be fulfilled, the solemn oath that I had taken, and which Vincey had called on me to answer to in another world than this. Had the man committed suicide? It looked like it. And what was the quest of which he spoke? The circumstances were almost uncanny, so much so that, though I am by no means nervous, or apt to be alarmed at anything that may seem to cross the bounds of the natural, I grew afraid, and began to wish I had had nothing to do with it. How much more do I wish it now, over twenty years afterwards!

As I sat and thought, there was a knock at the door, and a letter, in a big blue envelope, was brought in to me. I saw at a glance that it was a lawyer's letter, and an instinct told me that it was connected with my trust. The letter, which I still have, runs thus:—

'SIR,—Our client, the late M. L. Vincey, Esq., who died on the 9th instant in —— College, Cambridge, has left behind him a Will, of which you will please find copy enclosed, and of which we are the executors. By this Will you will perceive that you take a life-interest in about half of the late Mr. Vincey's property, now invested in Consols,[1] subject to your acceptance of the guardianship of his only son, Leo Vincey, at present an infant, aged five. Had we not ourselves drawn up the document in question in obedience to Mr. Vincey's clear and precise instructions, both personal and written, and had he not then assured us that he had very good reasons for what he was doing, we are bound to tell you that its provisions seem to us of so unusual a nature, that we should have felt bound to call the attention of the Court of Chancery to them, in order that such steps might be taken as seemed desirable to it, either by contesting the capacity of the testator or otherwise, to safeguard the interests of the infant. As it is, knowing that the testator was a gentleman of the highest intelligence and acumen, and that he has absolutely no relations living to whom he could have confided the guardianship of the child, we do not feel justified in taking this course.

'Awaiting such instructions as you please to send us as regards the delivery of the infant and the payment of the proportion of the dividends due to you,

'We remain, Sir, faithfully yours,

'GEOFFREY AND JORDAN.'

I put down the letter, and ran my eye through the Will, which appeared, from its utter unintelligibility, to have been drawn on the strictest legal principles. So far as I could discover, however, it exactly bore out what my friend had told me on the night of his death. So it was true after all. I must take the boy. Suddenly I remembered the letter which he had left with the chest. I fetched it and opened it. It only contained such directions as he had already given to me as to opening the chest on Leo's twenty-fifth birthday, and laid down the outlines of the boy's education, which was to include Greek, the higher Mathematics, and *Arabic*. At the bottom there was a postscript to the effect that if the boy died under the age of twenty-five, which, however, he did not believe would be the case, I was to open the chest, and act on the information I obtained if I saw fit. If I did not see fit, I was to destroy all the contents. On no account was I to pass them on to a stranger.

As this letter added nothing material to my knowledge, and certainly raised no further objection in my mind to undertaking the task I had promised my dead friend to undertake, there was only one course open to me—namely, to write to Messrs. Geoffrey and Jordan, and express my readiness to enter on the trust, stating that I should be willing to commence my guardianship of Leo in ten days' time. This done I proceeded to the authorities of my college, and, having told them as much of the story as I considered desirable, which was not very much, after considerable difficulty succeeded in persuading them to stretch a point, and, in the event of my having obtained a fellowship, which I was pretty certain I had done, allow me to have the child to live with me. Their consent, however, was only granted on the condition that I vacated my rooms in college and took lodgings. This I did, and with some difficulty succeeded in obtaining very good apartments quite close to the college gates. The next thing was to find a nurse. And on this point I came to a determination. I would have no woman to lord it over me about the child, and steal his affections from me. The boy was old enough to do without female assistance, so I set to work to hunt up a suitable male attendant. With some difficulty I succeeded in hiring a most respectable round-faced young man, who had been a helper in a hunting-stable, but who said that he was one of a family of seventeen and well-accustomed to the ways of children, and professed himself quite willing to undertake the charge of Master Leo when he arrived. Then, having taken the iron box to town, and with my own hands deposited it at my banker's, I bought some books upon the health and management of children, and read them, first to myself, and then aloud to Job—that was the young man's name—and waited.

At length the child arrived in the charge of an elderly person, who wept bitterly at parting with him, and a beautiful boy he was. Indeed, I do not think that I ever saw such a perfect child before or since. His eyes were grey, his forehead broad, and his face, even at that early age, clean cut as a cameo, without being pinched or thin. But perhaps his most attractive point was his hair, which was pure gold in colour and tightly curled over his shapely head. He cried a little when his nurse finally tore herself away and left him with us. Never shall I forget the scene. There he stood, with the sunlight from the window playing upon his golden curls, his fist screwed in one eye, whilst he took us in with the other. I was seated in a chair, and stretched out my hand to him to induce him to come to me, while Job, in the corner, was making a sort of clucking noise, which, arguing from his previous experience, or from the analogy of the hen, he judged would have a soothing effect, and inspire confidence in the youthful mind, and running a wooden horse of peculiar hideousness backwards and forwards in a way that was little short of inane. This went on for some minutes, and then all of a sudden the lad stretched out both his little arms and ran to me.

'I like you,' he said: 'you is ugly, but you is good.'

Ten minutes afterwards he was eating large slices of bread and butter, with every sign of satisfaction; Job wanted to put jam on to them, but I sternly reminded him of the excellent works we had read, and forbade it.

In a very little while (for, as I expected, I got my fellowship) the boy became the favourite of the whole College—where, all orders and regulations to the contrary notwithstanding, he was continually in and out—a sort of chartered libertine, in whose favour all rules were relaxed. The offerings made at his shrine were simply without number, and I had a serious difference of opinion with one old resident Fellow, now long dead, who was usually supposed to be the crustiest man in the University, and to abhor the sight of a child. And yet I discovered, when a frequently recurring fit of sickness had forced Job to keep a strict look-out, that this unprincipled old man was in the habit of enticing the boy to his rooms and there feeding him upon unlimited quantities of brandy-balls, and making him promise to say nothing about it. Job told him that he ought to be ashamed of himself, 'at his age, too, when he might have been a grandfather if he had done what was right,' by which Job understood had got married, and thence arose the row.

But I have no space to dwell upon those delightful years, around which memory still fondly hovers. One by one they went by, and as they passed we two grew dearer and yet more dear to each other. Few sons have been loved as I love Leo, and few fathers know the deep and continuous affection that Leo bears to me.

The child grew into the boy, and the boy into the young man, as one by one the remorseless years flew by, and as he grew and increased so did his beauty and the beauty of his mind grow with him. When he was about fifteen they used to call him Beauty about the College, and me they nicknamed the Beast. Beauty and the Beast was what they called us when we went out walking together, as we used to do every day.[2] Once Leo attacked a great strapping butcher's man, twice his size, because he sang it out after us, and thrashed him, too—thrashed him fairly. I walked on and pretended not to see, till the combat got too exciting, when I turned round and cheered him on to victory. It was the chaff of the College at the time, but I could not help it. Then when he was a little older the undergraduates got fresh names for us. They called me Charon and Leo the Greek god! I will pass over my own appellation with the humble remark that I was never handsome, and did not grow more so as I grew older. As for his, there was no doubt about its fitness. Leo at twenty-one might have stood for a statue of the youthful Apollo. I never saw anybody to touch him in looks, or anybody so absolutely unconscious of them. As for his mind, he was brilliant and keen-witted, but not a scholar. He had not the dulness necessary for that result. We followed out his father's instructions as regards his education strictly enough, and on the whole the results, especially so far as the Greek and Arabic went, were satisfactory. I learnt the latter language in order to help to teach it to him, but after five years of it he knew it as well as I did—almost as well as the professor who instructed us both. I always was a great sportsman—it is my one passion—and every autumn we went away somewhere shooting or fishing, sometimes to Scotland, sometimes to Norway, once even to Russia. I am a good shot, but even in this he learnt to excel me.

When Leo was eighteen I moved back into my rooms, and entered him at my own College, and at twenty-one he took his degree—a respectable degree, but not a very high one. Then it was that I, for the first time, told him something of his own story, and of the mystery that loomed ahead. Of course he was very curious about it, and of course I explained to him that his curiosity could not be gratified at present. After that, to pass the time away, I suggested that he should get himself called to the Bar; and this he did, reading at Cambridge, and only going up to London to eat his dinners.[3]

I had only one trouble about him, and that was that every young woman who came across him, or, if not every one, nearly so, would insist on falling in love with him. Hence arose difficulties which I need not enter into here, though they were troublesome enough at the time. On the whole, he behaved fairly well; I cannot say more than that.

And so the time went by till at last he reached his twenty-fifth birthday, at which date this strange and, in some ways, awful history really begins.

III

The Sherd of Amenartas

On the day preceding Leo's twenty-fifth birthday we both proceeded to London, and extracted the mysterious chest from the bank where I had deposited it twenty years before. It was, I remember, brought up by the same clerk who had taken it down. He perfectly remembered having hidden it away. Had he not done so, he said, he should have had difficulty in finding it, it was so covered up with cobwebs.

In the evening we returned with our precious burden to Cambridge, and I think that we might both of us have given away all the sleep we got that night and not have been much the poorer. At daybreak Leo arrived in my room in a dressing-gown, and suggested that we should at once proceed to business. I scouted the idea as showing an unworthy curiosity. The chest had waited twenty years, I said, so it could very well continue to wait until after breakfast. Accordingly at nine—an unusually sharp nine—we breakfasted; and so occupied was I with my own thoughts that I regret to state that I put a piece of bacon into Leo's tea in mistake for a lump of sugar. Job, too, to whom the contagion of excitement had, of course, spread, managed to break the handle off my Sèvres china tea-cup, the identical one I believe that Marat had been drinking from just before he was stabbed in his bath.[1]

At last, however, breakfast was cleared away, and Job, at my request, fetched the chest, and placed it upon the table in a somewhat gingerly fashion, as though he mistrusted it. Then he prepared to leave the room.

'Stop a moment, Job,' I said. 'If Mr. Leo has no objection, I should prefer to have an independent witness to this business, who can be relied upon to hold his tongue unless he is asked to speak.'

'Certainly, Uncle Horace,' answered Leo; for I had brought him up to call me uncle—though he varied the appellation somewhat disrespectfully by calling me 'old fellow,' or even 'my avuncular relative.'

Job touched his head, not having a hat on.

'Lock the door, Job,' I said, 'and bring me my despatch-box.'

He obeyed, and from the box I took the keys that poor Vincey, Leo's father, had given me on the night of his death. There were three of them; the largest a comparatively modern key, the second an exceedingly ancient one, and the third entirely unlike anything of the sort that we had ever seen before, being fashioned apparently from a strip of solid silver, with a bar placed across to serve as a handle, and some nicks cut in the edge of the bar. It was more like a model of some antediluvian railway key than anything else.

'Now are you both ready?' I said, as people do when they are going to fire a mine.[2] There was no answer, so I took the big key, rubbed some salad oil into the wards, and after one or two bad shots, for my hands were shaking, managed to fit it, and shoot the lock. Leo bent over and caught the massive lid in both his hands, and with an effort, for the hinges had rusted, leaned it back. Its removal revealed another case covered with dust. This we extracted from the iron chest without any difficulty, and removed the accumulated filth of years from it with a clothes-brush.

It was, or appeared to be, of ebony, or some such close-grained black wood, and was bound in every direction with flat bands of iron. Its antiquity must have been extreme, for the dense heavy wood was actually in parts commencing to crumble away from age.

'Now for it,' I said, inserting the second key.

Job and Leo bent forward in breathless silence. The key

turned, and I flung back the lid, and uttered an exclamation, as did the others; and no wonder, for inside the ebony case was a magnificent silver casket, about twelve inches square by eight high. It appeared to be of Egyptian workmanship, for the four legs were formed of Sphinxes, and the dome-shaped cover was also surmounted by a Sphinx. The casket was of course much tarnished and dinted with age, but otherwise in fairly sound condition.

I drew it out and set it on the table, and then, in the midst of the most perfect silence, I inserted the strange-looking silver key, and pressed this way and that until at last the lock yielded, and the casket stood open before us. It was filled to the brim with some brown shredded material, more like vegetable fibre than paper, the nature of which I have never been able to discover. This I carefully removed to the depth of some three inches, when I came to a letter enclosed in an ordinary modern-looking envelope, and addressed in the handwriting of my dead friend Vincey.

'To my son Leo, should he live to open this casket.'

I handed the letter to Leo, who glanced at the envelope, and then put it down upon the table, making a motion to me to go on emptying the casket.

The next thing that I found was a parchment carefully rolled up. I unrolled it, and seeing that it was also in Vincey's handwriting, and headed 'Translation of the Uncial Greek[3] Writing on the Potsherd,' put it down by the letter. Then followed another ancient roll of parchment, that had become yellow and crinkled with the passage of years. This I also unrolled. It was likewise a translation of the same Greek original, but into black-letter Latin[4] this time, which at the first glance appeared to me from the style and character to date from somewhere about the beginning of the sixteenth century. Immediately beneath this roll was something hard and heavy, wrapped up in yellow linen, and reposing upon another layer of the fibrous material. Slowly and carefully we unrolled the linen, exposing to view a very large but undoubtedly ancient potsherd of a dirty yellow colour!* This potsherd had in my judgment once been a part of an ordinary amphora[5] of medium size. For the rest, it measured ten and a half inches in length by seven in width, was about a quarter of an inch thick, and densely covered on the convex side that lay towards the bottom of the box with writing in the later uncial Greek character, faded here and there, but for the most part perfectly legible, the inscription having evidently been executed with the greatest care, and by means of a reed pen, such as the ancients often used. I must not forget to mention that in some remote age this wonderful fragment had been broken in two, and rejoined by means of cement and eight long rivets. Also there were numerous inscriptions on the inner side, but these were of the most erratic character, and had clearly been made by different hands and in many different ages, and of them, together with the writings on the parchments, I shall have to speak presently.

'Is there anything more?' asked Leo, in a kind of excited whisper.

I groped about, and produced something hard, done up in a little linen bag. Out of the bag we took first a very beautiful miniature done upon ivory, and, secondly, a small chocolate-coloured composition *scarabæus*, marked thus:[6]

symbols which, we have since ascertained, mean 'Suten se Rā,' which is being translated the 'Royal Son of Rā or the Sun.' The miniature was a picture of Leo's Greek mother—a lovely, dark-eyed creature. On the back of it was written, in poor Vincey's handwriting, 'My beloved wife.'

'That is all,' I said.

* *See* Frontispiece.—EDITOR.

'Very well,' answered Leo, putting down the miniature, at which he had been gazing affectionately; 'and now let us read the letter,' and without further ado he broke the seal, and read aloud as follows:—

My Son Leo,—When you open this, if you ever live to do so, you will have attained to manhood, and I shall have been long enough dead to be absolutely forgotten by nearly all who knew me. Yet in reading it remember that I have been, and for anything you know may still be, and that in it, through this link of pen and paper, I stretch out my hand to you across the gulf of death, and my voice speaks to you from the unutterable silence of the grave. Though I am dead, and no memory of me remains in your mind, yet am I with you in this hour that you read. Since your birth to this day I have scarcely seen your face. Forgive me this. Your life supplanted the life of one whom I loved better than women are often loved, and the bitterness of it endureth yet. Had I lived I should in time have conquered this foolish feeling, but I am not destined to live. My sufferings, physical and mental, are more than I can bear, and when such small arrangements as I have to make for your future well-being are completed it is my intention to put a period to them. May God forgive me if I do wrong. At the best I could not live more than another year.'

'So he killed himself,' I exclaimed. 'I thought so.'

'And now,' Leo went on, without replying, 'enough of myself. What has to be said belongs to you who live, not to me, who am dead, and almost as much forgotten as though I had never been. Holly, my friend (to whom, if he will accept the trust, it is my intention to confide you), will have told you something of the extraordinary antiquity of your race. In the contents of this casket you will find sufficient to prove it. The strange legend that you will find inscribed by your remote ancestress upon the potsherd was communicated to me by my father on his deathbed, and took a strong hold upon my imagination. When I was only nineteen years of age I determined, as, to his misfortune, did one of our ancestors about the time of Elizabeth, to investigate its truth.

Into all that befell me I cannot enter now. But this I saw with my own eyes. On the coast of Africa, in a hitherto unexplored region,[7] some distance to the north of where the Zambesi falls into the sea, there is a headland, at the extremity of which a peak towers up, shaped like the head of a negro, similar to that of which the writing speaks. I landed there, and learnt from a wandering native, who had been cast out by his people because of some crime which he had committed, that far inland are great mountains, shaped like cups, and caves surrounded by measureless swamps. I learnt also that the people there speak a dialect of Arabic, and are ruled over by a *beautiful white woman* who is seldom seen by them, but who is reported to have power over all things living and dead. Two days after I had ascertained this the man died of fever contracted in crossing the swamps, and I was forced by want of provisions and by symptoms of an illness which afterwards prostrated me to take to my dhow[8] again.

'Of the adventures that befell me after this I need not now speak. I was wrecked upon the coast of Madagascar, and rescued some months afterwards by an English ship that brought me to Aden, whence I started for England, intending to prosecute my search as soon as I had made sufficient preparations. On my way I stopped in Greece, and there, for "Omnia vincit amor,"[9] I met your beloved mother, and married her, and there you were born and she died. Then it was that my last illness seized me, and I returned hither to die. But still I hoped against hope, and set myself to work to learn Arabic, with the intention, should I ever get better, of returning to the coast of Africa, and solving the mystery of which the tradition has lived so many centuries in our family. But I have not got better, and, so far as I am concerned, the story is at an end.

'For you, however, my son, it is not at an end, and to you I hand on these the results of my labour, together with the hereditary proofs of its origin. It is my intention to provide that they shall not be put into your hands until you have reached an age when you will be able to judge for yourself whether or no you will choose to investigate what, if it is true, must be the greatest mystery in the world, or to put it by as an idle fable, originating in the first place in a woman's disordered brain.

'I do not believe that it is a fable; I believe that if it can only be re-discovered there is a spot where the vital forces of the world visibly exist. Life exists; why therefore should not the means of preserving it indefinitely exist also? But I have no wish to prejudice your mind about the matter. Read and judge for yourself. If you are inclined to undertake the search, I have so provided that you will not lack for means. If, on the other hand, you are satisfied that the whole thing is a chimera, then, I adjure you, destroy the potsherd and the writings, and let a cause of troubling be removed from our race for ever. Perhaps that will be wisest. The unknown is generally taken to be terrible, not as the proverb would infer, from the inherent superstition of man, but because it so often is terrible. He who would tamper with the vast and secret forces that animate the world may well fall a victim to them. And if the end were attained, if at last you emerged from the trial ever beautiful and ever young, defying time and evil, and lifted above the natural decay of flesh and intellect, who shall say that the awesome change would prove a happy one? Choose, my son, and may the Power who rules all things, and who says "thus far shalt thou go, and thus much shalt thou learn," direct the choice to your own happiness and the happiness of the world, which, in the event of your success, you would one day certainly rule by the pure force of accumulated experience.—Farewell!'

Thus the letter, which was unsigned and undated, abruptly ended.

'What do you make of that, Uncle Holly?' said Leo, with a sort of gasp, as he replaced it on the table. 'We have been looking for a mystery, and we certainly seem to have found one.'

'What do I make of it? Why, that your poor dear father was off his head, of course,' I answered, testily. 'I guessed as much that night, 20 years ago, when he came into my room. You see he evidently hurried his own end, poor man. It is absolute balderdash.'

'That's it, sir!' said Job, solemnly. Job was a most matter-of-fact specimen of a matter-of-fact class.

'Well, let's see what the potsherd has to say, at any rate,' said Leo, taking up the translation in his father's writing, and commencing to read:—

'I, Amenartas, of the Royal House of the Pharaohs of Egypt, wife of Kallikrates (the Beautiful in Strength), *a Priest of Isis*[10] *whom the gods cherish and the demons obey, being about to die, to my little son Tisisthenes* (the Mighty Avenger). *I fled with thy father from Egypt in the days of Nectanebes,* causing him through love to break the vows that he had vowed. We fled southward, across the waters, and we wandered for twice twelve moons on the coast of Libya* (Africa) *that looks towards the rising sun, where by a river is a great rock carven like the head of an Ethiopian. Four days on the water from the mouth of a mighty river were we cast away, and some were drowned and some died of sickness. But us wild men took through wastes and marshes, where the sea fowl hid the sky, bearing us ten days' journey till we came to a hollow mountain, where a great city had been and fallen, and where there are caves of which no man hath seen the end; and they brought us to the Queen of the people who place pots upon the heads of strangers, who is a magician having a knowledge of all things, and life and loveliness that does not die. And she cast eyes of love upon thy father, Kallikrates, and would have slain me, and taken him to husband, but he loved me and feared her, and would not. Then did she take us, and lead us by terrible ways, by means of dark magic, to where the great pit is, in the mouth of which the old philosopher lay dead, and showed to us the rolling Pillar of Life that dies not, whereof the voice is as the voice of thunder; and she did stand in the flames, and come forth unharmed, and yet more beautiful. Then did she swear to make thy father undying even as she is, if he would but slay me, and give himself to her, for me she could not slay because of the magic of my own people that I have, and that prevailed thus far against her. And he held his hand before his eyes to hide her beauty, and would not. Then in her rage did she smite him by her magic, and he died; but she wept over him, and bore him thence with lamentations: and being afraid, me she sent to the mouth of the great river where the ships come, and I was carried far away on the ships where I gave thee birth, and hither to Athens I came at last after many wanderings. Now I say to thee, my son, Tisisthenes, seek out the woman, and learn the secret of Life, and if thou mayest find a way slay her, because of thy father Kallikrates; and if thou*

* Nekht-nebf, or Nectanebo II., the last native Pharaoh of Egypt fled from Ochus to Ethiopia, BC339.—EDITOR.

dost fear or fail, this I say to all of thy seed who come after thee, till at last a brave man be found among them who shall bathe in the fire and sit in the place of the Pharaohs. I speak of those things, that though they be past belief, yet I have known, and I lie not.'

'May the Lord forgive her for that,' groaned Job, who had been listening to this marvellous composition with his mouth open.

As for myself, I said nothing: my first idea being that my poor friend, being demented, had composed the whole thing, though it scarcely seemed likely that such a story could have been invented by anybody. It was too original. To solve my doubts I took up the potsherd and began to read the close uncial Greek writing on it; and very good Greek of the period it is,[11] considering that it came from the pen of an Egyptian born. Here is an exact transcript of it:—

ΑΜΕΝΑΡΤΑΣΤΟΥΒΑΣΙΛΙΚΟΥΓΕΝΟΥΣΤΟΥΑΙΓΥ
ΓΤΙΟΥΗΤΟΥΚΑΛΛΙΚΡΑΤΟΥΣΙΣΙΔΟΣΙΕΡΕΩΣΗΝ
ΟΙΜΕΝΘΕΟΙΤΡΕΦΟΥΣΙΤΑΔΕΔΑΙΜΟΝΙΑΥΓΟΤΑ
ΣΣΕΤΑΙΗΔΗΤΕΛΕΥΤΩΣΑΤΙΣΙΣΘΕΝΕΙΤΩΓΑΙΔΙΕ
ΓΙΣΤΕΛΛΕΙΤΑΔΕΣΥΝΕΦΥΓΟΝΓΑΡΓΟΤΕΕΚΤΗΣ
ΑΙΓΥΓΤΙΑΣΕΓΙΝΕΚΤΑΝΕΒΟΥΜΕΤΑΤΟΥΣΟΥΓΑ
ΤΡΟΣΔΙΑΤΟΝΕΡΩΤΑΤΟΝΕΜΟΝΕΓΙΟΡΚΗΣΑΝΤ
ΟΣΦΥΓΟΝΤΕΣΔΕΓΡΟΣΝΟΤΟΝΔΙΑΓΟΝΤΙΟΙΚΑΙ
ΚΔΜΗΝΑΣΚΑΤΑΤΑΓΑΡΑΘΑΛΗΑΣΣΙΑΤΗΣΛΙΒΥ
ΗΣΤΑΓΡΟΣΗΛΙΟΥΑΝΑΤΟΛΑΣΓΛΑΝΗΘΕΝΤΕΣΕ
ΝΘΑΓΕΡΓΕΤΡΑΤΙΣΜΕΓΑΛΗΓΛΥΓΤΟΝΟΜΟΙΩΜ
ΑΑΙΘΙΟΓΟΣΚΕΦΑΛΗΣΕΙΤΑΗΜΕΡΑΣΔΑΓΟΣΤΟ
ΜΑΤΟΣΓΟΤΑΜΟΥΜΕΓΑΛΟΥΕΚΓΕΣΟΝΤΕΣΟΙΜ
ΕΝΚΑΤΕΓΟΝΤΙΣΘΗΜΕΝΟΙΔΕΝΟΣΩΙΑΓΕΘΑΝΟ
ΜΕΝΤΕΛΟΣΔΕΥΓΑΓΡΙΩΝΑΝΘΡΩΓΩΝΕΦΕΡΟΜ
ΕΘΑΔΙΑΕΛΕΩΝΤΕΚΑΙΤΕΝΑΓΕΩΝΕΝΘΑΓΕΡΓΤ
ΗΝΩΝΓΛΗΘΟΣΑΓΟΚΡΥΓΤΕΙΤΟΝΟΥΡΑΝΟΝΗΜ
ΕΡΑΣΙΕΩΣΗΛΘΟΜΕΝΕΙΣΚΟΙΛΟΝΤΙΟΡΟΣΕΝΘ
ΑΓΟΤΕΜΕΓΑΛΗΜΕΝΓΟΛΙΣΗΝΑΝΤΡΑΔΕΑΓΕΙΡ

ΟΝΑΗΓΑΓΟΝΔΕΩΣΒΑΣΙΛΕΙΑΝΤΗΝΤΩΝΞΕΝΟΥ
ΣΧΥΤΡΑΙΣΣΤΕΦΑΝΟΥΝΤΩΝΗΤΙΣΜΑΓΕΙΑΜΕΝΕ
ΧΡΗΤΟΕΓΙΣΤΗΜΗΔΕΓΑΝΤΩΝΚΑΙΔΗΚΑΙΚΑΛΛ
ΟΣΑΙΡΩΜΗΝΑΓΗΡΩΣΗΝΗΔΕΚΑΛΛΙΚΡΑΤΟΥΣΤ
ΟΥΣΟΥΓΑΤΡΟΣΕΡΑΣΘΕΙΣΑΤΟΜΕΝΓΡΩΤΟΝΣΥ
ΝΟΙΚΕΙΝΕΒΟΥΛΕΤΟΕΜΕΔΕΑΝΕΛΕΙΜΕΓΕΙΤΑ
ΩΣΟΥΚΑΝΕΓΕΙΘΕΝΕΜΕΓΑΡΥΓΕΡΕΦΙΛΕΙΚΑΙΤ
ΗΝΞΕΝΗΝΕΦΟΒΕΙΤΟΑΓΗΓΑΓΕΝΗΜΑΣΥΓΟΜΑ
ΓΕΙΑΣΚΑΘΟΔΟΥΣΣΦΑΛΕΡΑΣΕΝΘΑΤΟΒΑΡΑΘΡ
ΟΝΤΟΜΕΓΑΟΥΚΑΤΑΣΤΟΜΑΕΚΕΙΤΟΟΓΕΡΩΝΟ
ΦΙΛΟΣΟΦΟΣΤΕΘΝΕΩΣΑΦΙΚΟΜΕΝΟΙΣΔΕΔΕΙΞ
ΕΦΩΣΤΟΥΒΙΟΥΕΥΘΥΟΙΟΝΚΙΟΝΑΕΛΙΣΣΟΜΕΝ
ΟΝΦΩΝΗΝΙΕΝΤΑΚΑΘΑΓΕΡΒΡΟΝΤΗΣΕΙΤΑΔΙΑ
ΓΥΡΟΣΒΕΒΗΚΥΙΑΑΒΛΑΒΗΣΚΑΙΕΤΙΚΑΛΛΙΩΝΑ
ΥΤΗΕΑΥΤΗΣΕΞΕΦΑΝΗΕΚΔΕΤΟΥΤΩΝΩΜΟΣΕΚ
ΑΙΤΟΝΣΟΝΓΑΤΕΡΑΑΘΑΝΑΤΟΝΑΓΟΔΕΙΞΕΙΝΕΙ
ΣΥΝΟΙΚΕΙΝΟΙΒΟΥΛΟΙΤΟΕΜΕΔΕΑΝΕΛΕΙΝΟΥΓ
ΑΡΟΥΝΑΥΗΑΝΕΛΕΙΝΙΣΧΥΕΝΥΓΟΤΩΝΗΜΕΔΑΓ
ΩΝΗΝΚΑΙΑΥΤΗΕΧΩΜΑΓΕΙΑΣΟΔΟΥΔΕΝΤΙΜΑΛ
ΛΟΝΗΘΕΛΕΤΩΧΕΙΡΕΤΩΝΟΜΜΑΤΩΝΓΡΟΙΣΧΩ
ΝΙΝΑΔΗΤΟΤΗΣΓΥΝΑΙΚΟΣΚΑΛΛΟΣΜΗΟΡΩΗΕΓ
ΕΙΤΑΟΡΓΙΣΘΕΙΣΑΚΑΤΕΓΟΗΤΕΥΣΕΜΕΝΑΥΤΟΝ
ΑΓΟΛΟΜΕΝΟΝΜΕΝΤΟΙΚΛΑΟΥΣΑΚΑΙΟΔΥΡΟΜ
ΕΝΗΕΚΕΙΘΕΝΑΓΗΝΕΓΚΕΝΕΜΕΔΕΦΟΒΩΙΑΦΗ
ΚΕΝΕΙΣΣΤΟΜΑΤΟΥΜΕΓΑΛΟΥΓΟΤΑΜΟΥΤΟΥΜ
ΝΑΥΣΙΓΟΡΟΥΓΟΡΡΩΔΕΝΑΥΣΙΝΕΦΩΝΓΕΡΓΛΕ
ΟΥΣΑΕΤΕΚΟΝΣΕΑΓΟΓΛΕΥΣΑΣΑΜΟΛΙΣΓΟΤΕΔ
ΕΥΡΟΑΘΗΝΑΖΕΚΑΤΗΓΑΓΟΜΗΝΣΥΔΕΩΤΙΣΙΣΘ
ΕΝΕΣΩΝΕΓΙΣΤΕΛΛΩΜΗΟΛΙΓΩΡΕΙΔΕΙΓΑΡΤΗΝ
ΓΥΝΑΙΚΑΑΝΑΖΗΤΕΙΝΗΝΓΩΣΤΟΤΟΥΒΙΟΥΜΥΣΤ
ΗΡΙΟΝΑΝΕΥΡΗΣΚΑΙΑΝΑΙΡΕΙΝΗΝΓΟΥΓΑΡΑΣΧ
ΗΔΙΑΤΟΝΣΟΝΓΑΤΕΡΑΚΑΛΛΙΚΡΑΤΗΝΕΙΔΕΦΟΒ
ΟΥΜΕΝΟΣΗΔΙΑΑΛΛΟΤΙΑΥΤΟΣΛΕΙΓΕΙΤΟΥΕΡΓ
ΟΥΓΑΣΙΤΟΙΣΥΣΤΕΡΟΝΑΥΤΟΤΟΥΤΟΕΓΙΣΤΕΛΛ
ΩΕΩΣΓΟΤΕΑΓΑΘΟΣΤΙΣΓΕΝΟΜΕΝΟΣΤΩΓΥΡΙΛ
ΟΥΣΑΣΘΑΙΤΟΛΜΗΣΕΙΚΑΙΤΑΑΡΙΣΤΕΙΑΕΧΩΝΒΑ

ΣΙΛΕΥΣΑΙΤΩΝΑΝΘΡΩΓΩΝΑΓΙΣΤΑΜΕΝΔΗΤΑΤ
ΟΙΑΥΤΑΛΕΓΩΟΜΩΣΔΕΑΑΥΤΗΕΓΝΩΚΑΟΥΚΕΨ
ΕΥΣΑΜΗΝ

For general convenience in reading, I have here accurately transcribed this inscription into the cursive character:—

Ἀμενάρτας, τοῦ βασιλικοῦ γένους τοῦ Αἰγυπτίου, ἡ τοῦ Καλλικράτους Ἴσιδος ἱερέως, ἣν οἱ μὲν θεοὶ τρέφουσι τὰ δὲ δαιμόνια ὑποτάσσεται, ἤδη τελευτῶσα Τισισθένει τῷ παιδὶ ἐπιστέλλει τάδε· συνέφυγον γάρ ποτε ἐκ τῆς Αἰγυπτίας ἐπὶ Νεκτανέβου μετὰ τοῦ σοῦ πατρός, διὰ τὸν ἔρωτα τὸν ἐμὸν ἐπιορκήσαντος. φυγόντες δὲ πρὸς νότον διαπόντιοι καὶ κ΄δ΄ μῆνας κατὰ τὰ παραθαλάσσια τῆς Λιβύης τὰ πρὸς ἡλίου ἀνατολὰς πλανηθέντες, ἔνθαπερ πέτρα τις μεγάλη, γλυπτὸν ὁμοίωμα Αἰθίοπος κεφαλῆς, εἶτα ἡμέρας δ΄ ἀπὸ στόματος ποταμοῦ μεγάλου ἐκπεσόντες, οἱ μὲν κατεποντίσθημεν, οἱ δὲ νόσῳ ἀπεθάνομεν· τέλος δὲ ὑπ' ἀγρίων ἀνθρώπων ἐφερόμεθα διὰ ἑλέων τε καὶ τεναγέων ἔνθαπερ πτηνῶν πλῆθος ἀποκρύπτει τὸν οὐρανὸν, ἡμέρας ί, ἕως ἤλθομεν εἰς κοῖλόν τι ὄρος, ἔνθα ποτὲ μεγάλη μὲν πόλις ἦν, ἄντρα δὲ ἀπείρονα· ἤγαγον δὲ ὡς βασίλειαν τὴν τῶν ξένους χύτραις στεφανούντων, ἥτις μαγείᾳ μὲν ἐχρῆτο ἐπιστήμῃ δὲ πάντων καὶ δὴ καὶ κάλλος καὶ ῥώμην ἀγήρως ἦν· ἡ δὲ Καλλικάτους τοῦ σοῦ πατρὸς ἐρασθεῖσα τὸ μὲν πρῶτον συνοικεῖν ἐβούλετο ἐμὲ δὲ ἀνελεῖν· ἔπειτα, ὡς οὐκ ἀνέπειθεν, ἐμὲ γὰρ ὑπερεφίλει καὶ τὴν ξένην ἐφοβεῖτο, ἀπήγαγεν ἡμᾶς ὑπὸ μαγείας καθ' ὁδοὺς σφαλερὰς ἔνθα τὸ βάραθρον τὸ μέγα, οὗ κατὰ στόμα ἔκειτο ὁ γέρων ὁ φιλόσοφος τεθνεώς, ἀφικομένοις δ' ἔδειξε φῶς τοῦ βίου εὐθύ, οἷον κίονα ἑλισσόμενον φώνην ἱέντα καθάπερ βροντῆς, εἶτα διὰ πυρὸς βεβηκυῖα ἀβλαβὴς καὶ ἔτι καλλίων αὐτὴ ἑαυτῆς ἐξεφάνη· ἐκ δὲ τούτων ὤμοσε καὶ τὸν σὸν πατέρα ἀθάνατον ἀποδέίξειν, εἰ συνοικεῖν οἱ βούλοιτο ἐμὲ δε ἀνελεῖν, οὐ γὰρ οὖν αὐτὴ ἀνελεῖν ἴσχυεν ὑπὸ τῶν ἡμεδαπῶν ἣν καὶ αὐτὴ ἔχω μαγείας. ὁ δ' οὐδέν τι μᾶλλον ἤθελε, τὼ χεῖρε τῶν ὀμμάτων προίσχων ἵνα δὴ τὸ τῆς γυναικὸς κάλλος μὴ ὁρῴη· ἔπειτα ὀργισθεῖσα κατεγοήτευσε μὲν αὐτόν, ἀπολόμενον μέντοι κλάουσα καὶ ὀδυρομένη ἐκεῖθεν ἀπήνεγκεν, ἐμὲ δὲ φόβῳ ἀφῆκεν εἰς στόμα τοῦ μεγάλου ποταμοῦ τοῦ ναυσιπόρου, πόρρω δὲ ναυσίν, ἐφ' ὧνπερ πλέουσα ἔτεκόν σε, ἀποπλεύσασα μόλις ποτὲ δεῦρο 'Αθηνάζε κατηγαγόμην. σὺ δέ, ὦ Τισίσθενες, ὧν ἐπιστελλω μὴ ὀλιγώρει· δεῖ γὰρ τῆν γυναῖκα ἀναζητεῖν ἥν πως τὸ τοῦ βίου μυστήριον ἀνεύρῃς, καὶ ἀναιρεῖν, ἥν που παρασχῇ, διὰ τὸν σὸν πατέρα Καλλικράτην. εἰ δὲ φοβούμενος ἢ διὰ ἄλλο τι αὐτὸς λείπει τοῦ ἔργου, πᾶσι τοῖς ὕστερον αὐτὸ τοῦτο ἐπιστέλλω, ἕως ποτὲ ἀγαθός τις γενόμενος τῷ πυρὶ λούσασθαι τολμήσει καὶ τὰ ἀριστεῖα ἔχων βασιλεῦσαι τῶν ἀνθρώπων· ἄπιστα μὲν δὴ τὰ τοιαῦτα λέγω, ὅμως δὲ ἃ αὐ αὐτὴ ἔγνωκα οὐκ ἐφευσάμην.

The English translation was, as I discovered on further investigation, and as the reader may easily see by comparison, both accurate and elegant.

Besides the uncial writing on the convex side of the sherd at the top, painted in dull red, on what had once been the lip of the amphora, was the cartouche[12] already mentioned as being on the *scarabæus*, which we had also found in the casket. The hieroglyphics or symbols, however, were reversed, just as though they had been pressed on wax. Whether this was the cartouche of the original Kallikrates,* or of some Prince or Pharaoh from whom his wife Amenartas was descended, I am not sure, nor can I tell if it was drawn upon the sherd at the same time that the uncial Greek was inscribed, or copied on more recently from the Scarab by some other member of the family. Nor was this all. At the foot of the writing, painted in the same dull red, was the faint outline of a somewhat rude drawing of the head and shoulders of a Sphinx wearing two feathers, symbols of majesty, which, though common enough upon the effigies of sacred bulls and gods, I have never before met with on a Sphinx.

Also on the right-hand side of this surface of the sherd, painted

* The cartouche, if it be a true cartouche, cannot have been that of Kallikrates, as Mr. Holly suggests. Kallikrates was a priest and not entitled to a cartouche, which was the prerogative of Egyptian royalty, though he might have inscribed his name or title upon an *oval*.—EDITOR.

obliquely in red on the space not covered by the uncial, and signed in blue paint, was the following quaint inscription:—

IN EARTH AND SKIE AND SEA
STRANGE THYNGES THER BE.
HOC FECIT
DOROTHEA VINCEY.[13]

Perfectly bewildered, I turned the relic over. It was covered from top to bottom with notes and signatures in Greek, Latin, and English. The first in uncial Greek was by Tisisthenes, the son to whom the writing was addressed. It was, 'I could not go. Tisisthenes to his son, Kallikrates.' Here it is in fac-simile with its cursive equivalent:—

ΟΥΚΑΝΔΥΝΑΙΜΗΝΓΟΡΕΥΕCΘΑΙΤΙCΙCΘΕΝΗCΚ
ΑΛΛΙΚΡΑΤΕΙΤΩΙΓΑΙΔΙ

οὐκ ἂν δυναίμην πορεύεσθαι.
Τισισθένης Καλλικράτει τῷ παιδί.

This Kallikrates (probably, in the Greek fashion, so named after his grandfather) evidently made some attempt to start on the quest, for his entry written in very faint and almost illegible uncial is, 'I ceased from my going, the gods being against me. Kallikrates to his son.' Here it is also:—

ΤΩΝΘΕΩΝΑΝΤΙΣΤΑΝΤΩΝΕΓΑΥΣΑΜΗΝΤΗΣΓΟ
ΡΕΙΑΣΚΑΛΛΙΚΡΑΤΗΣΤΩΙΓΑΙΔΙ

τῶν θεῶν ἀντιστάντων ἐπαυσάμην τῆς πορείας.
Καλλικράτης τῷ παιδί.

Between these two ancient writings, the second of which was inscribed upside down and was so faint and worn that, had it not been for the transcript of it executed by Vincey, I should scarcely have been able to read it, since, owing to its having been written on that portion of the tile which had, in the course of ages, undergone the most handling, it was nearly rubbed out—was the bold, modern-looking signature of one Lionel Vincey, 'Ætate sua 17,'[14] which was written thereon, I think, by Leo's grandfather. To the right of this were the initials 'J. B. V.,' and below came a variety of Greek signatures, in uncial and cursive character, and what appeared to be some carelessly executed repetitions of the sentence τῷ παιδί (to my son), showing that the relic was religiously passed on from generation to generation.

The next legible thing after the Greek signatures was the word 'ROMAE, A.U.C.,' showing that the family had now migrated to Rome. Unfortunately, however, with the exception of its termination (cvi) the date of their settlement there is for ever lost, for just where it had been placed a piece of the potsherd is broken away.

Then followed twelve Latin signatures, jotted about here and there, wherever there was a space upon the tile suitable to their inscription. These signatures, with three exceptions only, ended with the name 'Vindex' or 'the Avenger,' which seems to have been adopted by the family after its migration to Rome as a kind of equivalent to the Grecian 'Tisisthenes,' which also means an avenger. Ultimately, as might be expected, this Latin cognomen of Vindex was transformed first into De Vincey, and then into the plain, modern Vincey. It is very curious to observe how the idea of revenge, inspired by an Egyptian before the time of Christ, is thus, as it were, embalmed in an English family name.

A few of the Roman names inscribed upon the sherd I have actually since found mentioned in history and other records. They were, if I remember right,

MVSSIVS. VINDEX

SEX. VARIVS. MARVLLVS

C. FVFIDIVS. C. F. VINDEX

and

LABERIA POMPEIANA. CONIVX. MACRINI. VINDICIS

the last being, of course, the name of a Roman lady.

The following list, however, comprises all the Latin names upon the sherd:—

C. CAECILIVS VINDEX

M. AIMILIVS VINDEX

SEX. VARIVS. MARVLLVS

Q. SOSIVS PRISCVS SENECIO VINDEX

L. VALERIVS COMINIVS VINDEX

SEX. OTACILIVS. M. F.

L. ATTIVS. VINDEX

MVSSIVS VINDEX

C. FVFIDIVS. C. F. VINDEX

LICINIVS FAVSTVS

LABERIA POMPEIANA CONIVX MACRINI VINDICIS

MANILLA LVCILLA CONIVX MARVLLI VINDICIS[15]

After the Roman names there is evidently a gap of very many centuries. Nobody will ever know now what was the history of the relic during those dark ages, or how it came to have been preserved in the family. My poor friend Vincey had, it will be remembered, told me that his Roman ancestors finally settled in Lombardy, and when Charlemagne invaded it, returned with him across the Alps, and made their home in Brittany, whence they crossed to England in the reign of Edward the Confessor.[16] How he knew this I am not aware, for there is no reference to Lombardy or Charlemagne upon the tile, though, as will presently be seen, there is a reference to Brittany. To continue: the next entries on the sherd, if I may except a long splash either of blood or red colouring matter of some sort, consist of two crosses drawn in red pigment, and probably representing Crusaders' swords, and a rather neat monogram ('D. V.') in scarlet and blue, perhaps executed by that same Dorothea Vincey who wrote, or rather painted, the doggrel couplet. To the left of this, inscribed in faint blue, were the initials A. V., and after them a date, 1800.

Then came what was perhaps as curious an entry as anything upon this extraordinary relic of the past. It is executed in black letter, written over the crosses or Crusaders' swords, and dated fourteen hundred and forty-five. As the best plan will be to allow it to speak for itself, I here give the black-letter fac-simile, together with the original Latin without the contractions, from which it will be seen that the writer was a fair mediæval Latinist.[17] Also we discovered what is still more curious, an English version of the black-letter Latin. This, also written in black-letter, we found inscribed on a second parchment that was in the coffer, apparently somewhat older in date than that on which was inscribed the mediæval Latin translation of the uncial Greek of which I shall speak presently. This I also give in full.

Fac-simile of Black-Letter Inscription on the Sherd of Amenartas.

Iſta reliq̄ia eſt valde miſticū et myrificu op̄s, q̄d maiores mei ex Armorica ſſ Brittania mīore ſecū cōvehebāt et q̄dm ſcs clerīcs ſēper p̄ri meo in manu ferebat q̄d pēitus illud deſtrueret affirmās q̄d eſſet ab ipſo ſathana cōflatū preſtigioſa et dyabolica arte, q̄re p̄ter meus cōfregit illud ī duas p̄tes q̄s q̄dm ego Johs̄ de Vīceto ſalvas ſervavi et adaptavi ſicut ap̄paret die lūe p̄r̄ poſt ſeſt beate Mrie virg anni gr̄e mccccxlv

Expanded Version of the above Black-Letter Inscription

'ISTA reliquia est valde misticum et myrificum opus, quod majores mei ex Armorica, scilicet Britannia Minore, secum convehebant; et quidam sanctus clericus semper patri meo in manu ferebat quod penitus illud destrueret, affirmans quod esset ab ipso Sathana conflatum prestigiosa et dyabolica arte, quare pater meus confregit illud in duas partes, quas quidem ego Johannes de Vinceto salvas servavi et adaptavi sicut apparet die lune proximo post festum beate Marie Virginis anni gratie MCCCCXLV.

Fac-simile of the Old English Black-Letter Translation of the above Latin Inscription from the Sherd of Amenartas found inscribed upon a parchment

Thys rellike ys a ryghte miſtycall worke & a marveylous ye whyche myne aunceteres afore tyme dyd conveighe hider w^{t} y^{m} ffrom Armoryke wh^{e} ys to ſeien Britayne ye leſſe & a certayne holye clerke ſhoulde allweyes beare my ffadir on honde y^{t} he owghte uttirly ffor to ffruſſhe y^{e} ſame affirmynge y^{t} yt was ffourmyd & conſflatyd off ſathanas hym ſelffe by arte magike & dyvellyſſhe wherefore my ffadir dyd take y^{e} ſame & to braſt yt yn tweyne but I, John de Vincey dyd ſave whool ye tweye p̄tes therof & topeecyd y^{m} togydder agayne ſoe as yee ſe on y^{s} deye mondaye next ffolowynge after ye ffeeſte of ſeynte Marye ye bleſſed vyrgyne yn ye yeere of ſalvacioun ffowertene hundreth & ffyve & ffowrti.

Modernised Version of the above Black-Letter Translation

Thys rellike ys a ryghte mistycall worke and a marvaylous, ye whyche myne aunceteres aforetyme dyd conveigh hider with them from Armoryke which ys to seien Britaine ye Lesse and a certayne holye clerke should allweyes beare my fadir on honde that he owghte uttirly for to frusshe ye same, affyrmynge that yt was fourmed and conflatyd of Sathanas hym selfe by arte magike and dyvellysshe wherefore my fadir dyd take ye same and tobrast yt yn tweyne, but I, John de Vincey, dyd save whool ye tweye partes therof and topeecyd them togydder agayne soe as yee se, on this daye mondaye next followynge after ye feeste of Seynte Marye ye Blessed Vyrgyne yn ye yeere of Salvacioun fowertene hundreth and fyve and fowerti.'[18]

The next and, save one, last entry was Elizabethan, and dated 1564, 'A most strange historie, and one that did cost my father his life; for in seekynge for the place upon the east coast of Africa, his pinnance[19] was sunk by a Portuguese galleon off Lorenzo Marquez,[20] and he himself perished.—JOHN VINCEY.'

Then came the last entry, apparently, to judge by the style of writing, made by some representative of the family in the middle of the eighteenth century. It was a misquotation of the well-known lines in Hamlet, and ran thus: 'There are more things in Heaven and earth than are dreamt of in your philosophy, Horatio.'*

And now there remained but one more document to be examined—namely, the ancient black-letter translation into mediæval Latin of the uncial inscription on the sherd. As will be seen, this translation was executed and subscribed in the year 1495, by a certain 'learned man,' Edmundus de Prato (Edmund Pratt) by name, licentiate in Canon Law, of Exeter College, Oxford, who had actually been a pupil of Grocyn,[21] the first scholar who taught Greek in England.† No doubt on the fame of this new learning reaching his ears, the Vincey of the day, perhaps that same John de Vincey who years before had saved the relic from destruction and made the black-letter entry on the sherd in 1445, hurried off to Oxford to see if perchance it might avail to solve the secret of the mysterious inscription. Nor was he disappointed, for the learned Edmundus was equal to the task. Indeed his rendering is so excellent an example of mediæval learning and latinity that, even at the risk of sating the learned reader with too many antiquities, I have made up my mind to give it in fac-simile,

* Another thing that makes me fix the date of this entry at the middle of the eighteenth century is that, curiously enough, I have an acting copy of 'Hamlet,' written about 1740, in which these two lines are misquoted almost exactly in the same way, and I have little doubt but that the Vincey who wrote them on the potsherd heard them so misquoted at that date. Of course, the lines really run:—

> There are more things in heaven and earth, Horatio,
> Than are dreamt of in your philosophy—L. H. H.

† Grocyn, the instructor of Erasmus, studied Greek under Chalcondylas the Byzantine at Florence, and first lectured in the Hall of Exeter College, Oxford, in 1491.—EDITOR

together with an expanded version for the benefit of those who find the contractions troublesome. The translation has several peculiarities on which this is not the place to dwell, but I would in passing call the attention of scholars to the passage 'duxerunt autem nos ad reginam *advenaslasaniscoronantium*,'[22] which strikes me as a delightful rendering of the original, 'ἤγαγον δὲ ὡς βασίλειαν τὴν τῶν ξένους χύτραις στεφανούντων.'

Mediæval Black-Letter Latin Translation of the Uncial Inscription on the Sherd of Amenartas

Amenartas e gen. reg. Egyptii uxor Callicratis ſacerdot̄ Iſidis quā dei fovēt demonia attēdūt filiol' ſuo Tiſiſtheni iā moribūda ita mādat: Effugi quōdā ex Egypto regnāte Nectanebo cū patre tuo, p̄pter mei amorē pejerato. Fugiētes autē v'ſus Notū trans mare et xxiiij mēſes p'r litora Libye v'ſus Oriētē errant̄ ubi eſt petra quedā m̄gna ſculpta inſtar Ethiop̄ capit̄, deinde dies iiij ab oſt̄ flum̄ m̄gni eiecti p'tim ſubmerſi ſumus p'tim morbo mortui ſum̄: in fine autē a fer̄ hōīb̄s portabamur p̄r palud̄ et vada. ubi aviū m'titudo celū obūbrat dies x. donec advenim̄ ad cavū quedā montē, ubi olim m̄gna urbs erat, caverne quoq̄ im̄ēſe: durerūt autē nos ad reginā Advenaſlaſaniſcoronātiū que magic̄ utebat̄r et peritia omniū rer̄ et ſaltē pulcrit̄ et vigore īſēēſcibil' erat. Hec m̄gno patr̄ tui amore p̄culſa p'mū q'dē q'dē ei coñubiñ michi mortē parabat. poſtea v'ro recuſāte Callicrate amore mei et timore regine affecto nos p̄r magicā abduxit p'r vias horribil' ubi eſt puteus ille p̄fūdus, cuius iuxta aditū iacebat ſenior̄ philoſophi cadaver, et advēiētib̄ mōſtravit flam̄ā Vite erectā, īſtar columne volutātis, voces emittētē q̄ſi tonitrus: tūc p̄r ignē īpetu nociuo expers trāſiit et iā ipa ſeſe formoſior viſa eſt.

Quib̄ fact̄ iuravit ſe patrē tuū quoq̄ im̄ortalē oſtēſurā eſſe, ſi me prius occiſa regine cōtuberniū mallet; neq̄ enī ipſa me occidere valuit, p̄pter noſtratū m̄gicā cuius egomet p̄tem habeo. Ille vero nichil huius gen̄ maluit, manib ante ocul paſſis ne mulier̄ formoſitatē adſpiceret: poſtea eū m̄gica p̄cuſſit arte, at mortuū efferebat īde cū fletib̄ et vagitib̄, me p̄r timorē expulit ad oſtiū m̄gni flumiñ veliuoli porro in nave in qua te peperi, vix poſt dies huc Athenas invecta fū. At tu, O Tiſiſtheñ, ne q'd quorū mādo nauci fac: necesse enī est mulierē exquirere si qua Vite mysteriū īpetres et vīdicare, quātū in te est, patrē tuū Callicratī in regine morte. Sin timore seu aliq̄ causa rē relīquis īfectā, hoc ipsū oīb̄ posterī mādo, dū bonus q̄s inveniatur qui ignis lavacrū nō p̄rhorrescet et p̄tentia dign̄ dōīabiī hōīū.

Talia dico incredibilia q̄dē at mīīe ficta de reb̄ michi cognitis.

Hec Grece scripta Latine reddidit vir doctus Edm̄ds de Prato, in Decretis Licenciatus e Coll. Exon: Oxon: doctissimi Grocyni quondam e pupillis, Id. Apr. Aº. Dñi. MCCCCLXXXXVº.

Expanded Version of the above Mediæval Latin Translation

AMENARTAS, e genere regio Egyptii, uxor Callicratis, sacerdotis Isidis, quam dei fovent demonia attendunt, filiolo suo Tisistheni jam moribunda ita mandat: Effugi quondam ex Egypto, regnante Nectanebo, cum patre tuo, propter mei amorem pejerato. Fugientes autem versus Notum trans mare, et viginti quatuor menses per litora Libye versus Orientem errantes, ubi est petra quedam magna sculpta instar Ethiopis capitis, deinde dies quatuor ab ostio fluminis magni ejecti partim submersi sumus partim morbo mortui sumus: in fine autem a feris hominibus portabamur per paludes et vada, ubi avium multitudo celum obumbrat, dies decem, donec advenimus ad cavum quendam montem, ubi olim magna urbs erat, caverne quoque immense; duxerunt autem nos ad reginam Advenaslasaniscoronantium, que magicâ utebatur et peritiâ omnium rerum, et saltem pulcritudine et vigore insenescibilis erat. Hec magno patris tui amore perculsa, primum quidem ei connubium michi mortem parabat; postea vero, recusante Callicrate, amore mei et timore regine affecto nos per magicam abduxit per vias horribiles ubi est puteus ille profundus, cujus juxta aditum jacebat senioris philosophi cadaver, et advenientibus monstravit flammam Vite erectam, instar columne volutantis, voces emittentem quasi tonitrus: tunc per ignem impetu nocivo expers transiit et jam ipsa sese formosior visa est.

Quibus factis juravit se patrem tuum quoque immortalem ostensuram esse, si me prius occisa regine contubernium mallet; neque enim ipsa me occidere valuit, propter nostratum magicam cujus egomet partem habeo. Ille vero nichil hujus generis malebat, manibus ante oculos passis, ne mulieris formositatem adspiceret: postea illum magica percussit arte, at mortuum efferebat inde cum fletibus et vagitibus, at me per timorem expulit ad ostium magni fluminis, velivoli, porro in nave, in qua te peperi, vix post dies huc Athenas invecta sum. At tu, O Tisisthenes, ne quid quorum mando nauci fac: necesse enim est mulierem exquirere si qua Vite mysterium impetres et vindicare, quantum in te est, patrem tuum Callicratem in regine morte. Sin timore seu aliqua causa rem relinquis infectam, hoc ipsum omnibus posteris mando, dum bonus quis inveniatur qui ignis lavacrum non perhorrescet, et potentia dignus dominabitur hominum.

Talia dico incredibilia quidem at minime ficta de rebus michi cognitis.

Hec Grece scripta Latine reddidit vir doctus Edmundus de Prato, in Decretis Licenciatus, e Collegio Exoniensi Oxoniensi doctissimi Grocyni quondam e pupillis, Idibus Aprilis Anno Domini MCCCCLXXXXV°.[23]

'Well,' I said, when at length I had read out and carefully examined these writings and paragraphs, at least those of them that were still easily legible, 'that is the conclusion of the whole matter, Leo, and now you can form your own opinion on it. I have already formed mine.'

'And what is it?' he asked, in his quick way.

'It is this. I believe that potsherd to be perfectly genuine, and that, wonderful as it may seem, it has come down in your family from since the fourth century before Christ. The entries absolutely prove it, and therefore, however improbable it may seem, it must be accepted. But there I stop. That your remote ancestress, the Egyptian princess, or some scribe under her direction, wrote that which we see on the sherd I have no doubt, nor have I the slightest doubt but that her sufferings and the loss of her husband had turned her head, and that she was not right in her mind when she did write it.'

'How do you account for what my father saw and heard there?' asked Leo.

'Coincidence. No doubt there are bluffs on the coast of Africa that look something like a man's head, and plenty of people who speak bastard Arabic. Also, I believe that there are lots of swamps. Another thing is, Leo, and I am sorry to say it, but I do not believe that your poor father was quite right when he wrote that letter. He had met with a great trouble, and also he had allowed this story to prey on his imagination, and he was a very imaginative man. Anyway, I believe that the whole thing is the most unmitigated rubbish. I know that there are curious things and forces in nature which we rarely meet with, and, when we do meet them, cannot understand. But until I see it with my own eyes, which I am not likely to, I never will believe that there is any means of avoiding death, even for a time, or that there is or was a white sorceress living in the heart of an African swamp. It is bosh, my boy, all bosh!—What do you say, Job?'

'I say, sir, that it is a lie, and, if it is true, I hope Mr. Leo won't meddle with no such things, for no good can't come of it.'

'Perhaps you are both right,' said Leo, very quietly. 'I express no opinion. But I say this. I am going to set the matter at rest once and for all, and if you won't come with me I will go by myself.'

I looked at the young man, and saw that he meant what he said. When Leo means what he says he always puts on a curious look about the mouth. It has been a trick of his from a child. Now, as a matter of fact, I had no intention of allowing Leo to go anywhere by himself, for my own sake, if not for his. I was far too much attached to him for that. I am not a man of many ties or affections. Circumstances have been against me in this respect, and men and women shrink from me, or, at least, I fancy they do, which comes to the same thing, thinking, perhaps, that my somewhat forbidding exterior is a key to my character. Rather than endure this, I have, to a great extent, secluded myself from the world, and cut myself off from those opportunities which with most men result in the formation of relations more or less intimate. Therefore Leo was all the world to me—brother, child, and friend—and until he wearied of me, where he went there I should go too. But, of course, it would not do to let him see how great a hold he had over me; so I cast about for some means whereby I might let myself down easy.

'Yes, I shall go, Uncle; and if I don't find the "rolling Pillar of Life," at any rate I shall get some first-class shooting.'

Here was my opportunity, and I took it.

'Shooting?' I said. 'Ah! yes; I never thought of that. It must be a very wild stretch of country, and full of big game. I have always wanted to kill a buffalo before I die. Do you know, my boy, I don't believe in the quest, but I do believe in big game, and really, on the whole, if, after thinking it over, you make up your mind to go, I will take a holiday, and come with you.'

'Ah,' said Leo, 'I thought that you would not lose such a chance. But how about money? We shall want a good lot.'

'You need not trouble about that,' I answered. 'There is all your income that has been accumulating for years, and besides that I have saved two-thirds of what your father left to me, as I consider, in trust for you. There is plenty of cash.'

'Very well, then, we may as well stow these things away and go up to town to see about our guns. By the way, Job, are you coming too? It's time you began to see the world.'

'Well, sir,' answered Job, stolidly, 'I don't hold much with foreign parts, but if both you gentlemen are going you will want somebody to look after you, and I am not the man to stop behind after serving you for twenty years.'

'That's right, Job,' said I. 'You won't find out anything wonderful, but you will get some good shooting. And now look here, both of you. I won't have a word said to a living soul about this nonsense,' and I pointed to the pot-sherd. 'If it got out, and anything happened to me, my next of kin would dispute my will on the ground of insanity, and I should become the laughing stock of Cambridge.'

That day three months we were on the ocean, bound for Zanzibar.[24]

IV

The Squall

How different is the scene that I have now to tell from that which has just been told! Gone are the quiet college rooms, gone the wind-swayed English elms and cawing rooks, and the familiar volumes on the shelves, and in their place there rises a vision of the great calm ocean gleaming in shaded silver lights beneath the beams of the full African moon. A gentle breeze fills the huge sail of our dhow, and draws us through the water that ripples musically against our sides. Most of the men are sleeping forward, for it is near midnight, but a stout swarthy Arab, Mahomed by name, stands at the tiller, lazily steering by the stars. Three miles or more to our starboard is a low dim line. It is the Eastern shore of Central Africa. We are running to the southward, before the North East Monsoon, between the mainland and the reef that for hundreds of miles fringes that perilous coast. The night is quiet, so quiet that a whisper can be heard fore and aft the dhow; so quiet that a faint booming sound rolls across the water to us from the distant land.

The Arab at the tiller holds up his hand, and says one word:—'*Simba* (lion)!'

We all sit up and listen. Then it comes again, a slow, majestic sound, that thrills us to the marrow.

'To-morrow by ten o'clock,' I say, 'we ought, if the Captain is not out in his reckoning, which I think very probable, to make this mysterious rock with a man's head, and begin our shooting.'

'And begin our search for the ruined city and the Fire of Life,' corrected Leo, taking his pipe from his mouth, and laughing a little.

'Nonsense!' I answered. 'You were airing your Arabic with that man at the tiller this afternoon. What did he tell you? He has been trading (slave-trading[1] probably) up and down these latitudes for half of his iniquitous life, and once landed on this very "man" rock. Did he ever hear anything of the ruined city or the caves?'

'No,' answered Leo. 'He says that the country is all swamp behind, and full of snakes, especially pythons, and game, and that no man lives there. But then there is a belt of swamp all along the East African coast, so that does not go for much.'

'Yes,' I said, 'it does—it goes for malaria.[2] You see what sort of an opinion these gentry have of the country. Not one of them will go with us. They think that we are mad, and upon my word I believe that they are right. If ever we see old England again I shall be astonished. However, it does not greatly matter to me at my age, but I am anxious for you, Leo, and for Job. It's a Tom Fool's business, my boy.'

'All right, Uncle Horace. So far as I am concerned, I am willing to take my chance. Look! What is that cloud?' and he pointed to a dark blotch upon the starry sky, some miles astern of us.

'Go and ask the man at the tiller,' I said.

He rose, stretched his arms, and went. Presently he returned.

'He says it is a squall, but it will pass far on one side of us.'

Just then Job came up, looking very stout and English in his shooting-suit of brown flannel, and with a sort of perplexed appearance upon his honest round face that had been very common with him since he got into these strange waters.

'Please, sir,' he said, touching his sun hat, which was stuck on to the back of his head in a somewhat ludicrous fashion, 'as we have got all those guns and things in the whale-boat astern, to say nothing of the provisions in the lockers, I think it would be best if I got down and slept in her. I don't like the looks' (here he dropped his voice to a portentous whisper) 'of these black gentry; they have such a wonderful thievish way about them. Supposing now that some of them were to slip into the boat at night and cut the cable, and make off with her? That would be a pretty go, that would.'

The whale-boat, I may explain, was one specially built for us at Dundee, in Scotland. We had brought it with us, as we knew that this coast was a network of creeks, and that we might require something to navigate them with. She was a beautiful boat, thirty feet in length, with a centre-board for sailing, copper-bottomed to keep the worm out of her, and full of water-tight compartments. The captain of the dhow had told us that when we reached the rock, which he knew, and which appeared to be identical with the one described upon the sherd and by Leo's father, he would probably not be able to run up to it on account of the shallows and breakers. Therefore we had employed three hours that very morning, whilst we were totally becalmed, the wind having dropped at sunrise, in transferring most of our goods and chattels to the whale-boat, and placing the guns, ammunition, and preserved provisions in the water-tight lockers specially prepared for them, so that when we did sight the fabled rock we should have nothing to do but step into the boat, and run her ashore. Another reason that induced us to take this precautionary step was that Arab captains are apt to run past the point that they are making, either from carelessness or owing to a mistake in its identity. Now, as sailors know, it is quite impossible for a dhow which is only rigged to run before the monsoon to beat back against it. Therefore we got our boat ready to row for the rock at any moment.

'Well, Job,' I said, 'perhaps it would be as well. There are lots of blankets there, only be careful to keep out of the moon, or it may turn your head or blind you.'

'Lord, sir! I don't think it would much matter if it did; it is that turned already with the sight of these blackamoors and their filthy, thieving ways. They are only fit for muck, they are; and they smell bad enough for it already.'

Job, it will be perceived, was no admirer of the manners and customs of our dark-skinned brothers.

Accordingly we hauled up the boat by the tow-rope till it was right under the stern of the dhow, and Job bundled into her with all the grace of a falling sack of potatoes. Then we returned and sat down on the deck again, and smoked and talked in little gusts and jerks. The night was so lovely, and our brains were so full of suppressed excitement of one sort and another, that we did not feel inclined to turn in. For nearly an hour we sat thus, and then, I think, we both dozed off. At least I have a faint recollection of Leo sleepily explaining that the head was not a bad place to hit a buffalo, if you could catch him exactly between the horns, or send your bullet down his throat, or some nonsense of the sort.

Then I remember no more; till suddenly—a frightful roar of wind, a shriek of terror from the awakening crew, and a whip-like sting of water in our faces. Some of the men ran to let go the haulyards and lower the sail, but the parrel[3] jammed and the yard would not come down. I sprang to my feet and hung on to a rope. The sky aft was dark as pitch, but the moon still shone brightly ahead of us and lit up the blackness. Beneath its sheen a huge white-topped breaker, 20 feet high or more, was rushing on to us. It was on the break—the moon shone on its crest and tipped its foam with light. On it rushed beneath the inky sky, driven by the awful squall behind it. Suddenly, in the twinkling of an eye, I saw the black shape of the whale-boat cast high into the air on the crest of the breaking wave. Then—a shock of water, a wild rush of boiling foam, and I was clinging for my life to the shroud, ay, swept straight out from it like a flag in a gale.

We were pooped.[4]

The wave passed. It seemed to me that I was under water for minutes—really it was seconds. I looked forward. The blast had torn out the great sail, and high in the air it was fluttering away to leeward like a huge wounded bird. Then for a moment there was comparative calm, and in it I heard Job's voice yelling wildly, 'Come here to the boat.'

Bewildered and half drowned as I was, I had the sense to rush aft. I felt the dhow sinking under me—she was full of water.

Under her counter the whale-boat was tossing furiously, and I saw the Arab Mahomed, who had been steering, leap into her. I gave one desperate pull at the tow-rope to bring the boat alongside. Wildly I sprang also, and Job caught me by one arm and I rolled into the bottom of the boat. Down went the dhow bodily, and as she did so Mahomed drew his curved knife and severed the fibre-rope by which we were fast to her, and in another second we were driving before the storm over the place where the dhow had been.

'Great God!' I shrieked, 'where is Leo? *Leo! Leo!*'

'He's gone, sir, God help him!' roared Job into my ear; and such was the fury of the squall that his voice sounded like a whisper.

I wrung my hands in agony. Leo was drowned, and I was left alive to mourn him.

'Look out;' yelled Job, 'here comes another.'

I turned; a second huge wave was overtaking us. I half hoped that it would drown me. With a curious fascination I watched its awful advent. The moon was nearly hidden now by the wreaths of the rushing storm, but a little light still caught the crest of the devouring breaker. There was something dark on it—a piece of wreckage. It was on us now, and the boat was nearly full of water. But she was built in air-tight compartments—Heaven bless the man who invented them!—and lifted up through it like a swan. Through the foam and turmoil I saw the black thing on the wave hurrying right at me. I put out my right arm to ward it from me, and my hand closed on another arm, the wrist of which my fingers gripped like a vice. I am a very strong man, and had something to hold to, but my arm was nearly torn from its socket by the strain and weight of the floating body. Had the rush lasted another two seconds I must either have let go or gone with it. But it passed, leaving us up to our knees in water.

'Bail out! bail out!' shouted Job, suiting the action to the word.

But I could not bail just then, for as the moon went out and left us in total darkness, one faint, flying ray of light lit upon the face of the man I had gripped, who was now half lying, half floating in the bottom of the boat.

It was Leo. Leo brought back by the wave—back, dead or alive, from the very jaws of Death.

'Bail out! bail out!' yelled Job, 'or we shall founder.'

I seized a large tin bowl with a handle to it, which was fixed under one of the seats, and the three of us bailed away for dear life. The furious tempest drove over and round us, flinging the boat this way and that, the wind and the storm wreaths and the sheets of stinging spray blinded and bewildered us, but through it all we worked like demons with the wild exhilaration of despair, for even despair can exhilarate. One minute! three minutes! six minutes! The boat began to lighten, and no fresh wave swamped us. Five minutes more, and she was fairly clear. Then, suddenly, above the awful shriekings of the hurricane came a duller, deeper roar. Great Heavens! It was the voice of breakers!

At that moment the moon began to shine forth again—this time behind the path of the squall. Out far across the torn bosom of the ocean shot the ragged arrows of her light, and there, half a mile ahead of us, was a white line of foam, then a little space of open-mouthed blackness, and then another line of white. It was the breakers, and their roar grew clearer and yet more clear as we sped down upon them like a swallow. There they were, boiling up in snowy spouts of spray, smiting and gnashing together like the gleaming teeth of hell.

'Take the tiller, Mahomed!' I roared in Arabic. 'We must try and shoot them.' At the same moment I seized an oar, and got it out, motioning to Job to do likewise.

Mahomed clambered aft, and got hold of the tiller, and with some difficulty Job, who had sometimes pulled a tub upon the homely Cam,[5] got out his oar. In another minute the boat's head was straight on to the ever-nearing foam, towards which she plunged and tore with the speed of a racehorse. Just in front of us the first line of breakers seemed a little thinner than to the right or left—there was a gap of rather deeper water. I turned and pointed to it.

'Steer for your life, Mahomed!' I yelled. He was a skilful steersman, and well acquainted with the dangers of this most perilous coast, and I saw him grip the tiller and bend his heavy frame forward, and stare at the foaming terror till his big round eyes looked as though they would start out of his head. The send of the sea was driving the boat's head round to starboard. If we struck the line of breakers fifty yards to starboard of the gap we must sink. It was a great field of twisting, spouting waves. Mahomed planted his foot against the seat before him, and, glancing at him, I saw his brown toes spread out like a hand with the weight he put upon them as he took the strain of the tiller. She came round a bit, but not enough. I roared to Job to back water, whilst I dragged and laboured at my oar. She answered now, and none too soon.

Heavens, we were in them! And then followed a couple of minutes of heart-breaking excitement such as I cannot hope to describe. All I remember is a shrieking sea of foam, out of which the billows rose here, there, and everywhere like avenging ghosts from their ocean grave. Once we were turned right round, but either by chance, or through Mahomed's skilful steering, the boat's head came straight again before a breaker filled us. One more—a monster. We were through it or over it—more through than over—and then, with a wild yell of exultation from the Arab, we shot out into the comparative smooth water of the mouth of sea between the teeth-like lines of gnashing waves.

But we were half full of water again, and not more than half a mile ahead was the second line of breakers. Again we set to and bailed furiously. Fortunately the storm had now quite gone by, and the moon shone brightly, revealing a rocky headland running half a mile or more out into the sea, of which this second line of breakers appeared to be a continuation. At any rate, they boiled around its foot. Probably the ridge that formed the headland ran out into the ocean, only at a lower level, and made the reef also. This headland was terminated by a curious peak that seemed not to be more than a mile away from us. Just as we got the boat pretty clear for the second time, Leo, to my immense relief, opened his eyes and remarked that the clothes had tumbled off the bed, and that he supposed it was time to get up for chapel. I told him to shut his eyes and keep quiet, which he did without in the slightest degree realising the position. As for myself, his reference to chapel made me reflect, with a sort of sick longing, on my comfortable rooms at Cambridge. Why had I been such a fool as to leave them? This is a reflection that has several times recurred to me since, and with ever-increasing force.

But now again we are drifting down on the breakers, though with lessened speed, for the wind had fallen, and only the current or the tide (it afterwards turned out to be the tide) was driving us.

Another minute, and with a sort of howl to Allah from the Arab, a pious ejaculation from myself, and something that was not pious from Job, we were in them. And then the whole scene, down to our final escape, repeated itself, only not quite so violently. Mahomed's skilful steering and the air-tight compartments saved our lives. In five minutes we were through, and drifting—for we were too exhausted to do anything to help ourselves except keep her head straight—with the most startling rapidity round the headland which I have described.

Round we went with the tide, until we got well under the lee of the point, aud then suddenly the speed slackened, we ceased to make way, and finally appeared to be in dead water. The storm had entirely passed, leaving a clean-washed sky behind it; the headland intercepted the heavy sea that had been occasioned by the squall, and the tide, which had been running so fiercely up the river (for we were now in the mouth of a river), was sluggish before it turned, so we floated quietly, and before the moon went down managed to bail out the boat thoroughly and get her a little ship-shape. Leo was sleeping profoundly, and on the whole I thought it wise not to wake him. It was true he was sleeping in wet clothes, but the night was now so warm that I thought (and so did Job) that they were not likely to injure a man of his unusually vigorous constitution. Besides, we had no dry ones at hand.

Presently the moon went down, and left us floating on the waters, now only heaving like some troubled woman's breast, giving us leisure to reflect upon all that we had gone through and all that we had escaped. Job stationed himself at the bow, Mahomed kept his post at the tiller, and I sat on a seat in the middle of the boat close to where Leo was lying.

The moon went slowly down in chastened loveliness, she departed like some sweet bride into her chamber, and long veil-like shadows crept up the sky through which the stars peeped shyly out. Soon, however, they too began to pale before a splendour in the east, and then the quivering footsteps of the dawn came rushing across the new-born blue, and shook the planets from their places. Quieter and yet more quiet grew the sea, quiet as the soft mist that brooded on her bosom, and covered up her troubling, as the illusive wreaths of sleep brood upon a pain-racked mind, causing it to forget its sorrow. From the east to the west sped the angels of the Dawn, from sea to sea, from mountain top to mountain top, scattering light with both their hands. On they sped out of the darkness, perfect, glorious, like spirits of the just breaking from the tomb; on, over the quiet sea, over the low coast line, and the swamps beyond, and the mountains beyond them; over those who slept in peace, and those who woke in sorrow; over the evil and the good; over the living and dead; over the wide world and all that breathes or has breathed thereon.

It was a wonderfully beautiful sight, and yet sad, perhaps from the very excess of its beauty. The arising sun; the setting sun! There we have the symbol and the type of humanity, and all things with which humanity has to do. The symbol and the type, yes, and the earthly beginning, and the end also. And on that morning this came home to me with a peculiar force. The sun that rose to-day for us had set last night for eighteen of our fellow-voyagers!—had set for ever for eighteen whom we knew!

The dhow had gone down with them, they were tossing about now among the rocks and seaweed, so much human drift on the great ocean of death! And we four were saved. But one day a sunrise will come when we shall be among those who are lost, and then others will watch those glorious rays, and grow sad in the midst of beauty, and dream of Death in the full glow of arising Life!

For this is the lot of man.

V

The Head of the Ethiopian

At length the heralds and forerunners of the royal sun had done their work, and, searching out the shadows, had caused them to flee away. Then up he came in glory from his ocean-bed, and flooded the earth with warmth and light. I sat there in the boat listening to the gentle lapping of the water and watched him rise, till presently the slight drift of the boat brought the odd-shaped rock, or peak, at the end of the promontory which we had weathered with so much peril, between me and the majestic sight, and blotted it from my view. I still continued to stare at the rock, however, absently enough, till presently it became edged with the fire of the growing light behind it, and then I started, as well I might, for I perceived that the top of the peak, which was about eighty feet high by one hundred and fifty thick at its base, was shaped like a negro's head and face, whereon was stamped a most fiendish and terrifying expression. There was no doubt about it; there were the thick lips, the fat cheeks, and the squat nose standing out with startling clearness against the flaming background. There, too, was the round skull, washed into shape perhaps by thousands of years of wind and weather, and, to complete the resemblance, there was a scrubby growth of weeds or lichen upon it, which against the sun looked for all the world like the wool on a colossal negro's head. It certainly was very odd; so odd that now I believe that it is not a mere freak of nature but a gigantic monument fashioned, like the well-known Egyptian Sphinx, by a forgotten people out of a pile of rock that lent itself to their design, perhaps as an emblem of warning and defiance to any enemies who approached the harbour. Unfortunately we were never able to ascertain whether or not this was the case, inasmuch as the rock was difficult of access both from the land and the water-side, and we had other things to attend to. Myself, considering the matter by the light of what we afterwards saw, I believe that it was fashioned by man, but whether or not this is so, there it stands, and sullenly stares from age to age out across the changing sea—there it stood two thousand years and more ago, when Amenartas, the Egyptian Princess, and the wife of Leo's remote ancestor Kallikrates, gazed upon its devilish face—and there I have no doubt it will still stand when as many centuries as are numbered between her day and our own are added to the year that bore us to oblivion.

'What do you think of that, Job?' I asked of our retainer, who was sitting on the edge of the boat, trying to get as much sunshine as possible, and generally looking uncommonly wretched, and I pointed to the fiery and demoniacal head.

'Oh Lord, sir,' answered Job, who now perceived the object for the first time, 'I think that the old geneleman[1] must have been sitting for his portrait on them rocks.'

I laughed, and the laugh woke up Leo.

'Hullo,' he said, 'what's the matter with me? I am all stiff—where is the dhow? Give me some brandy, please.'

'You may be thankful that you are not stiffer, my boy,' I answered. 'The dhow is sunk, and everybody on board her is drowned, with the exception of us four, and your own life was only saved by a miracle;' and whilst Job, now that it was light enough, searched about in a locker for the brandy for which Leo asked, I told him the history of our night's adventure.

'Great Heavens!' he said, faintly; 'and to think that we should have been chosen to live through it!'

By this time the brandy was forthcoming, and we all had a good pull at it, and thankful enough we were for it. Also the sun was beginning to get strength, and warm our chilled bones, for we had been wet through for five hours or more.

'Why,' said Leo, with a gasp as he put down the brandy bottle, 'there is the head the writing talks of, the "rock carven like the head of an Ethiopian."'

'Yes,' I said, 'there it is.'

'Well, then,' he answered, 'the whole thing is true.'

'I don't at all see that that follows,' I answered. 'We knew this head was here, your father saw it. Very likely it is not the same head that the writing talks of; or if it is, it proves nothing.'

Leo smiled at me in a superior way. 'You are an unbelieving Jew, Uncle Horace,' he said. 'Those who live will see.'[2]

'Exactly so,' I answered, 'and now perhaps you will observe that we are drifting across a sandbank into the mouth of the river. Get hold of your oar, Job, and we will row in and see if we can find a place to land.'

The river mouth which we were entering did not appear to be a very wide one, though as yet the long banks of steaming mist that clung about its shores had not lifted sufficiently to enable us to see its exact width. There was, as is the case with nearly every East African river, a considerable bar at the mouth, which, no doubt, when the wind was on shore and the tide running out, was absolutely impassable even for a boat drawing only a few inches. But as things were it was manageable enough, and we did not ship a cupful of water. In twenty minutes we were well across it, with but slight assistance from ourselves, and being carried by a strong though somewhat variable breeze, well up the harbour. By this time the mist was being sucked up by the sun, which was getting uncomfortably hot, and we saw that the mouth of the little estuary was here about half a mile across, and that the banks were very marshy, and crowded with crocodiles lying about on the mud like logs. About a mile ahead of us, however, was what appeared to be a strip of firm land, and for this we steered. In another quarter of an hour we were there, and making the boat fast to a beautiful tree with broad shining leaves, and flowers of the magnolia species, only they were rose-coloured and not white,* which hung over the water, we dis-

* There is a known species of magnolia with pink flowers. It is indigenous in Sikkim, and known as *Magnolia Campbellii*.—EDITOR.

embarked. This done we undressed, washed ourselves, and spread our clothes and the contents of the boat in the sun to dry, which they very quickly did. Then, taking shelter from the sun under some trees, we made a hearty breakfast off a 'Paysandu' potted tongue,[3] of which we had brought a good quantity with us from the Army and Navy Stores, congratulating ourselves loudly on our good fortune in having loaded and provisioned the boat on the previous day before the hurricane destroyed the dhow. By the time that we had finished our meal our clothes were quite dry, and we hastened to get into them, feeling not a little refreshed. Indeed, with the exception of weariness and a few bruises, none of us were the worse for the terrifying adventure which had been fatal to all our companions. Leo, it is true, had been half-drowned, but that is no great matter to a vigorous young athlete of five-and-twenty.

After breakfast we started to look about us. We were on a strip of dry land about two hundred yards broad by five hundred long, bordered on one side by the river, and on the other three by endless desolate swamps, that stretched as far as the eye could reach. This strip of land was raised about twenty-five feet above the plain of the surrounding swamps and the river level: indeed it had every appearance of having been made by the hand of man.

'This place has been a wharf,' said Leo, dogmatically.

'Nonsense,' I answered. 'Who would be stupid enough to build a wharf in the middle of these dreadful marshes in a country inhabited by savages, that is if it is inhabited at all?'

'Perhaps it was not always marsh, and perhaps the people were not always savage,' he said drily, looking down the steep bank, for we were standing by the river. 'Look there,' he went on, pointing to a spot where the hurricane of the previous night had torn up one of the magnolia trees, which had grown on the extreme edge of the bank just where it sloped down to the water, by the roots, and lifted a large cake of earth with them. 'Is not that stonework? If not, it is very like it.'

'Nonsense,' I said again, and we clambered down to the spot, and got between the upturned roots and the bank.

'Well?' he said.

But I did not answer this time. I only whistled. For there, laid bare by the removal of the earth, was an undoubted facing of solid stone laid in large blocks and bound together with brown cement, so hard that I could make no impression on it with the file in my shooting knife. Nor was this all; seeing something projecting through the soil at the bottom of the bared patch of walling, I removed the loose earth with my hands, and revealed a huge stone ring, a foot or more in diameter, and about three inches thick. This fairly staggered me.

'Looks rather like a wharf where good-sized vessels have been moored, does it not, Uncle Horace?' said Leo, with an excited grin.

I tried to say 'Nonsense' again, but the word stuck in my throat—the ring spoke for itself. In some past age vessels *had* been moored there, and this stone wall was undoubtedly the remnant of a solidly constructed wharf. Probably the city to which it had belonged lay buried beneath the swamp behind it.

'Begins to look as though there were something in the story after all, Uncle Horace,' said the exultant Leo; and reflecting on the mysterious negro's head and the equally mysterious stone-work, I made no direct reply.

'A country like Africa,' I said, 'is sure to be full of the relics of long dead and forgotten civilisations. Nobody knows the age of the Egyptian civilisation, and very likely it had offshoots. Then there were the Babylonians and the Phœnicians, and the Persians and all manner of people, all more or less civilised, to say nothing of the Jews whom everybody "wants" nowadays.[4] It is possible that they, or any one of them, may have had colonies or trading stations about here. Remember those buried Persian cities that the consul showed us at Kilwa.'*[5]

* Near Kilwa, on the East Coast of Africa, about 400 miles south of Zanzibar, is a cliff which has been recently washed by the waves. On the top of this cliff are Persian tombs known to be at least seven centuries old by the dates still legible upon them. Beneath these tombs is a layer of *débris* representing a city. Farther down the cliff is a second layer representing an older city, and further down still

'Quite so,' said Leo, 'but that is not what you said before.'

'Well, what is to be done now?' I asked, turning the conversation.

As no answer was forthcoming we proceeded to the edge of the swamp, and looked over it. It was apparently boundless, and vast flocks of every sort of waterfowl came flying from its recesses, till it was sometimes difficult to see the sky. Now that the sun was getting high it drew thin sickly looking clouds of poisonous vapour from the surface of the marsh and from the scummy pools of stagnant water.

'Two things are clear to me,' I said, addressing my three companions, who stared at this spectacle in dismay: 'first, that we can't go across there' (I pointed to the swamp), 'and, secondly, that if we stop here we shall certainly die of fever.'

'That's as clear as a haystack, sir,' said Job.

'Very well, then; there are two alternatives before us. One is to 'bout ship, and try and run for some port in the whale-boat, which would be a sufficiently risky proceeding, and the other to sail or row on up the river, and see where we come to.'

'I don't know what you are going to do,' said Leo, setting his mouth,' but I am going up that river.'

Job turned up the whites of his eyes and groaned, and the Arab murmured 'Allah,' and groaned also. As for me, I remarked sweetly that as we seemed to be between the devil and the deep sea, it did not much matter where we went. But in reality I was as anxious to proceed as Leo. The colossal negro's head and the stone wharf had excited my curiosity to an extent of which I was secretly ashamed, and I was prepared to gratify it at any cost. Accordingly, having carefully fitted the mast, restowed the boat, and got out our rifles, we embarked. Fortunately the wind was blowing on shore from the ocean, so we were able to hoist the sail. Indeed, we afterwards found out that as a general rule the

---

a third layer, the remains of yet another city of vast and unknown antiquity. Beneath the bottom city were recently found some specimens of glazed earthenware, such as are occasionally to be met with on that coast to this day. I believe that they are now in the possession of Sir John Kirk.—EDITOR.

wind set on shore from daybreak for some hours, and off shore again at sunset, and the explanation that I offer of this is, that when the earth is cooled by the dew and the night the hot air rises, and the draught rushes in from the sea till the sun has once more heated it through. At least that appeared to be the rule here.

Taking advantage of this favouring wind, we sailed merrily up the river for three or four hours. Once we came across a school of hippopotami, which rose, and bellowed dreadfully at us within ten or a dozen fathoms of the boat, much to Job's alarm, and, I will confess, to my own. These were the first hippopotami that we had ever seen, and, to judge by their insatiable curiosity, I should judge that we were the first white men that they had ever seen. Upon my word, I once or twice thought that they were coming into the boat to gratify it. Leo wanted to fire at them, but I dissuaded him, fearing the consequences. Also we saw hundreds of crocodiles basking on the muddy banks, and thousands upon thousands of waterfowl. Some of these we shot, and among them was a wild goose, which, in addition to the sharp curved spurs on its wings, had a spur about three-quarters of an inch long growing from the skull just between the eyes. We never shot another like it, so I do not know if it was a 'sport' or a distinct species. In the latter case this incident may interest naturalists. Job named it the Unicorn Goose.

About midday the sun grew intensely hot, and the stench drawn up by it from the marshes which the river drains was something too awful, and caused us instantly to swallow precautionary doses of quinine. Shortly afterwards the breeze died away altogether, and as rowing our heavy boat against stream in the heat was out of the question, we were thankful enough to get under the shade of a group of trees—a species of willow—that grew by the edge of the river, and lie there and gasp till at length the approach of sunset put a period to our miseries. Seeing what appeared to be an open space of water straight ahead of us, we determined to row there before settling what to do for the night. Just as we were about to loosen the boat, however, a beautiful water-buck, with great horns curving forward, and a white stripe across the rump, came down to the river to drink, without perceiving us hidden away within fifty yards under the willows. Leo was the first to catch sight of it, and being an ardent sportsman, thirsting for the blood of big game, about which he had been dreaming for months, he instantly stiffened all over, and pointed like a setter dog. Seeing what was the matter, I handed him his express rifle, at the same time taking my own.

'Now then,' I whispered, 'mind you don't miss.'

'Miss!' he whispered back contemptuously; 'I could not miss it if I tried.'

He lifted the rifle, and the roan-coloured buck, having drunk his fill, raised his head and looked out across the river. He was standing right against the sunset sky on a little eminence, or ridge of ground, which ran across the swamp, evidently a favourite path for game, and there was something very beautiful about him. Indeed, I do not think that if I live to a hundred I shall ever forget that desolate and yet most fascinating scene: it is stamped upon my memory. To the right and left were wide stretches of lonely, death-breeding swamp, unbroken and unrelieved so far as the eye could reach, except here and there by ponds of black and peaty water that, mirror-like, flashed up the red rays of the setting sun. Behind us and before stretched the vista of the sluggish river, ending in glimpses of a reed-fringed lagoon, on the surface of which the long lights of the evening played as the faint breeze stirred the shadows. To the west loomed the huge red ball of the sinking sun, now vanishing down the vapoury horizon, and filling the great heaven, high across whose arch the cranes and wild fowl streamed in line, square, and triangle, with flashes of flying gold and the lurid stain of blood. And then ourselves—three modern Englishmen in a modern English boat—seeming to jar upon and looking out of tone with that measureless desolation; and in front of us the noble buck limned out upon a background of ruddy sky.

Bang! Away he goes with a mighty bound. Leo has missed him. *Bang!* right under him again. Now for a shot. I must have one, though he is going like an arrow, and a hundred yards away and more. By Jove! over and over and over! 'Well, I think I've wiped your eye there, Master Leo,' I say, struggling against the ungenerous exultation that in such a supreme moment of one's existence will rise in the best-mannered sportsman's breast.

'Confound you, yes,' growled Leo; and then, with that quick smile that is one of his charms lighting up his handsome face like a ray of light, 'I beg your pardon, old fellow. I congratulate you; it was a lovely shot, and mine were vile.'

We got out of the boat and ran to the buck, which was shot through the spine and stone dead. It took us a quarter of an hour or more to clean it and cut off as much of the best meat as we could carry, and, having packed this away, we had barely light enough to row up into the lagoon-like space, into which, there being a hollow in the swamp, the river here expanded. Just as the light vanished we cast anchor about thirty fathoms from the edge of the lake. We did not dare to go ashore, not knowing if we should find dry ground to camp on, and greatly fearing the poisonous exhalations from the marsh, from which we thought we should be freer on the water. So we lighted a lantern, and made our evening meal off another potted tongue in the best fashion that we could, and then prepared to go to sleep, only, however, to find that sleep was impossible. For, whether they were attracted by the lantern, or by the unaccustomed smell of a white man, for which they had been waiting for the last thousand years or so, I know not; but certainly we were presently attacked by tens of thousands of the most bloodthirsty, pertinacious, and huge mosquitoes that I ever saw or read of. In clouds they came, and pinged and buzzed and bit till we were nearly mad. Tobacco smoke only seemed to stir them into a merrier and more active life, till at length we were driven to covering ourselves with blankets, head and all, and sitting to slowly stew and continually scratch and swear beneath them. And as we sat, suddenly rolling out like thunder through the silence came the deep roar of a lion, and then of a second lion, moving among the reeds within sixty yards of us.

'I say,' said Leo, sticking his head out from under his blanket, 'lucky we ain't on the bank, eh, Avuncular?' (Leo sometimes addressed me in this disrespectful way.) 'Curse it! a mosquito has bitten me on the nose,' and the head vanished again.

Shortly after this the moon came up, and notwithstanding every variety of roar that echoed over the water to us from the lions on the banks, we began, thinking ourselves perfectly secure, to gradually doze off.

I do not quite know what it was that made me poke my head out of the friendly shelter of the blanket, perhaps because I found that the mosquitoes were biting right through it. Anyhow, as I did so I heard Job whisper, in a frightened voice—

'Oh, my stars, look there!'

Instantly we all of us looked, and this was what we saw in the moonlight. Near the shore were two wide and ever-widening circles of concentric rings rippling away across the surface of the water, and in the heart and centre of the circles were two dark moving objects.

'What is it?' asked I.

'It is those damned lions, sir,' answered Job, in a tone which was an odd mixture of a sense of personal injury, habitual respect, and acknowledged fear, 'and they are swimming here to *h*eat us,' he added, nervously picking up an 'h' in his agitation.

I looked again, there was no doubt about it; I could catch the glare of their ferocious eyes. Attracted either by the smell of the newly killed waterbuck meat or of ourselves, the hungry beasts were actually storming our position.

Leo already had his rifle in his hand. I called to him to wait till they were nearer, and meanwhile grabbed my own. Some fifteen feet from us the water shallowed on a bank to the depth of about fifteen inches, and presently the first of them—it was the lioness—got on to it and shook herself and roared. At that moment Leo fired, and the bullet went right down her open mouth and out at the back of her neck, and down she dropped, with a splash, dead. The other lion—a full-grown male—was some two paces behind her. At this second he got his forepaws on to the bank, when a strange thing happened. There was a rush and disturbance of the water, such as one sees in a pond in England when a pike takes a little fish, only a thousand times fiercer and larger, and suddenly the lion gave a most terrific snarling roar and sprang forward on to the bank, dragging something black with him.

'Allah!' shouted Mahomed, 'a crocodile has got him by the leg!' and sure enough he had. We could see the long snout with its gleaming lines of teeth and the reptile body behind it.

And then followed an extraordinary scene indeed. The lion managed to get well on to the bank, the crocodile half standing and half swimming, still nipping his hind leg. He roared till the air quivered with the sound, and then, with a savage, shrieking snarl, turned round and clawed hold of the crocodile's head. The crocodile shifted his grip, having, as we afterwards discovered, had one of his eyes torn out, and slightly turned over, and instantly the lion got him by the throat and held on, and then over and over they rolled upon the bank struggling hideously. It was impossible to follow their movements, but when next we got a clear view the tables had turned, for the crocodile, whose head seemed to be a mass of gore, had got the lion's body in his iron jaws just above the hips, and was squeezing him and shaking him to and fro. For his part the tortured brute, roaring in agony, was clawing and biting madly at his enemy's scaly head, and fixing his great hind claws in the crocodile's, comparatively speaking, soft throat, ripping it open as one would rip a glove.

Then, all of a sudden, the end came. The lion's head fell forward on the crocodile's back, and with an awful groan he died, and the crocodile, after standing for a minute motionless, slowly rolled over on to his side, his jaws still fixed across the carcase of the lion, which we afterwards found he had bitten almost in halves.

This duel to the death was a wonderful and a shocking sight, and one that I suppose few men have seen—and thus it ended.

When it was all over, leaving Mahomed to keep a look out, we managed to spend the rest of the night as quietly as the mosquitoes would allow.

VI

An Early Christian Ceremony

Next morning, at the earliest blush of dawn, we rose, performed such ablutions as circumstances would allow, and generally made ready to start. I am bound to say that when there was sufficient light to enable us to see each other's faces I, for one, burst out into a roar of laughter. Job's fat and comfortable countenance was swollen out to nearly twice its natural size from mosquito bites, and Leo's condition was not much better. Indeed, of the three I had come off much the best, probably owing to the toughness of my dark skin, and to the fact that a good deal of it was covered by hair, for since we started from England I had allowed my naturally luxuriant beard to grow at its own sweet will. But the other two were, comparatively speaking, clean shaved, which of course gave the enemy a larger extent of open country to operate on, though as for Mahomed the mosquitoes, recognising the taste of a true believer, would not touch him at any price. How often, I wonder, during the next week or so did we wish that we were flavoured like an Arab!

By the time that we had done laughing as heartily as our swollen lips would allow, it was daylight, and the morning breeze was coming up from the sea, cutting lanes through the dense marsh mists, and here and there rolling them before it in great balls of fleecy vapour. So we set our sail, and having first taken a look at the two dead lions and the dead alligator, which we were of course unable to skin, being destitute of means of curing the pelts, we started, and, sailing through the lagoon, followed the course of the river on the farther side. At midday, when the breeze dropped, we were fortunate enough to find a convenient piece of dry land on which to camp and light a fire, and here we cooked two wild duck and some of the waterbuck's flesh—not in a very appetising way, it is true, but still, sufficiently. The rest of the buck's flesh we cut into strips and hung in the sun to dry into 'biltong,' as I believe the South African Dutch call flesh thus prepared. On this welcome patch of dry land we stopped till the following dawn, and, as before, spent the night in warfare with the mosquitoes, but without other troubles. The next day or two passed in similar fashion, and without noticeable adventures, except that we shot a specimen of a peculiarly graceful hornless buck, and saw many varieties of water-lilies in full bloom, some of them blue and of exquisite beauty, though few of the flowers were perfect, owing to the prevalence of a white water-maggot with a green head that fed upon them.

It was on the fifth day of our journey, when we had travelled, so far as we could reckon, about one hundred and thirty-five to a hundred and forty miles westwards from the coast, that the first event of any real importance occurred. On that morning the usual wind failed us about eleven o'clock, and after pulling a little way we were forced to halt more or less exhausted at what appeared to be the junction of our stream with another of a uniform width of about fifty feet. Some trees grew near at hand—the only trees in all this country were along the banks of the river, and under these we rested, and then, the land being fairly dry just here, walked a little way along the edge of the river to prospect, and shoot a few waterfowl for food. Before we had gone fifty yards we perceived that all hopes of getting further up the stream in the whale-boat were at an end, for not two hundred yards above where we had stopped were a succession of shallows and mudbanks, with not six inches of water over them. It was a watery *cul-de-sac*.

Turning back, we walked some way along the banks of the other river, and soon came to the conclusion, from various indications, that it was not a river at all, but an ancient canal, like the one which is to be seen above Mombasa, on the Zanzibar coast, connecting the Tana River with the Ozy, in such a way as to enable the shipping coming down the Tana to cross to the Ozy, and reach the sea by it, and thus avoid the very dangerous bar that blocks the mouth of the Tana.[1] The canal before us had evidently been dug out by man at some remote period of the world's history, and the results of his digging still remained in the shape of the raised banks that had no doubt once formed towing-paths. Except here and there, where they had been hollowed out or fallen in, these banks of stiff binding clay were at a uniform distance from each other, and the depth of the water also appeared to be uniform. Current there was little or none, and, as a consequence, the surface of the canal was choked with vegetable growth, intersected by little paths of clear water, made, I suppose, by the constant passage of waterfowl, iguanas, and other vermin. Now, as it was evident that we could not proceed up the river, it became equally evident that we must either try the canal or else return to the sea. We could not stop where we were, to be baked by the sun and eaten up by the mosquitoes, till we died of fever in that dreary marsh.

'Well, I suppose that we must try it,' I said; and the others assented in their various ways—Leo, as though it were the best joke in the world; Job, in respectful disgust; and Mahomed, with an invocation to the Prophet, and a comprehensive curse upon all unbelievers and their ways of thought and travel.

Accordingly, as soon as the sun got low, having little or nothing more to hope for from our friendly wind, we started. For the first hour or so we managed to row the boat, though with great labour; but after that the weeds got too thick to allow of it, and we were obliged to resort to the primitive and most exhausting resource of towing her. For two hours we laboured, Mahomed, Job, and I, who was supposed to be strong enough to pull against the two of them, on the bank, while Leo sat in the bow of the boat, and brushed away the weeds which collected round the cutwater with Mahomed's sword. At dark we halted for some hours to rest and enjoy the mosquitoes, but about midnight we went on again, taking advantage of the comparative cool of the night. At dawn we rested for three hours, and then started once more, and laboured on till about ten o'clock, when a thunder-storm, accompanied by a deluge of rain, overtook us, and we spent the next six hours practically under water.

I do not know that there is any necessity for me to describe the next four days of our voyage in detail, further than to say that they were, on the whole, the most miserable that I ever spent in my life, forming one monotonous record of heavy labour, heat, misery, and mosquitoes. All the way we passed through a region of almost endless swamp, and I can only attribute our escape from fever and death to the constant doses of quinine and purgatives which we took, and the unceasing toil which we were forced to undergo. On the third day of our journey up the canal we had sighted a round hill that loomed dimly through the vapours of the marsh, and on the evening of the fourth night, when we camped, this hill seemed to be within twenty-five or thirty miles of us. We were by now utterly exhausted, and felt as though our blistered hands could not pull the boat a yard farther, and that the best thing that we could do would be to lie down and die in that dreadful wilderness of swamp. It was an awful position, and one in which I trust no other white man will ever be placed; and as I threw myself down in the boat to sleep the sleep of utter exhaustion, I bitterly cursed my folly in ever having been a party to such a mad undertaking, which could, I saw, only end in our death in this ghastly land. I thought, I remember, as I slowly sank into a doze, of what the appearance of the boat and her unhappy crew would be in two or three months' time from that night. There she would lie, with gaping seams and half filled with fœtid water, which, when the mist-laden wind stirred her, would wash backwards and forwards through our mouldering bones, and that would be the end of her, and of those in her who would follow after myths and seek out the secrets of nature.

Already I seemed to hear the water rippling against the desiccated bones and rattling them together, rolling my skull against Mahomed's, and his against mine, till at last Mahomed's stood straight up upon its vertebræ, and glared at me through its empty eyeholes, and cursed me with its grinning jaws, because I, a dog of a Christian, disturbed the last sleep of a true believer. I opened my eyes, and shuddered at the horrid dream, and then shuddered again at something that was not a dream, for two great eyes were gleaming down at me through the misty darkness. I struggled up, and in my terror and confusion shrieked, and shrieked again, so that the others sprang up too, reeling, and drunken with sleep and fear. And then all of a sudden there was a flash of cold steel, and a great spear was held against my throat, and behind it other spears gleamed cruelly.

'Peace,' said a voice, speaking in Arabic, or rather in some dialect into which Arabic entered very largely; 'who are ye who come hither swimming on the water? Speak or ye die,' and the steel pressed sharply against my throat, sending a cold chill through me.

'We are travellers, and have come hither by chance,' I answered in my best Arabic, which appeared to be understood, for the man turned his head, and, addressing a tall form that towered up in the background, said, 'Father, shall we slay?'

'What is the colour of the men?' said a deep voice in answer.

'White is their colour.'

'Slay not,' was the reply. 'Four suns since was the word brought to me from "*She-who-must-be-obeyed*," "White men come; if white men come, slay them not." Let them be brought to the land of "*She-who-must-be-obeyed*." Bring forth the men, and let that which they have with them be brought forth also.'

'Come,' said the man, half leading and half dragging me from the boat, and as he did so I perceived other men doing the same kind office to my companions.

On the bank were gathered a company of some fifty men. In that light all I could make out was that they were armed with huge spears, were very tall, and strongly built, comparatively light in colour, and nude, save for a leopard-skin tied round the middle.

Presently Leo and Job were bundled out and placed beside me.

'What on earth is up?' said Leo, rubbing his eyes.

'Oh, Lord! sir, here's a rum go,' ejaculated Job; and just at that moment a disturbance ensued, and Mahomed came tumbling between us, followed by a shadowy form with an uplifted spear.

'Allah! Allah!' howled Mahomed, feeling that he had little to hope from man, 'protect me! protect me!'

'Father, it is a black one,' said a voice. 'What said "*She-who-must-be-obeyed*" about the black one?'

'She said naught; but slay him not. Come hither, my son.'

The man advanced, and the tall shadowy form bent forward and whispered something.

'Yes, yes,' said the other, and chuckled in a rather blood-curdling tone.

'Are the three white men there?' asked the form.

'Yes, they are there.'

'Then bring up that which is made ready for them, and let the men take all that can be brought from the thing which floats.'

Hardly had he spoken when men came running up, carrying on their shoulders neither more nor less than palanquins—four bearers and two spare men to a palanquin—and in these it was promptly indicated we were expected to stow ourselves.

'Well!' said Leo, 'it is a blessing to find anybody to carry us after having to carry ourselves so long.'

Leo always takes a cheerful view of things.

There being no help for it, after seeing the others into theirs I tumbled into my own litter, and very comfortable I found it. It appeared to be manufactured of cloth woven from grass-fibre, which stretched and yielded to every motion after the body, and, being bound top and bottom to the bearing pole, gave a grateful support to the head and neck.

Scarcely had I settled myself when, accompanying their steps with a monotonous song, the bearers started at a swinging trot. For half an hour or so I lay still, reflecting on the very remarkable experiences that we were going through, and wondering if any of my eminently respectable fossil friends down at Cambridge would believe me if I were to be miraculously set at the familiar dinner-table for the purpose of relating them. I don't want to convey any disrespectful notion or slight when I call those good and learned men fossils, but my experience is that people are apt to fossilise even at a University if they follow the same paths too persistently. I was getting fossilised myself, but of late my stock of ideas has been very much enlarged. Well, I lay and reflected, and wondered what on earth would be the end of it all, till at last I ceased to wonder, and went to sleep.

I suppose I must have slept for seven or eight hours, getting the first real rest that I had had since the night before the loss of the dhow, for when I woke the sun was high in the heavens. We were still journeying on at a pace of about four miles an hour. Peeping out through the mist-like curtains of the litter, which were ingeniously fixed to the bearing pole, I perceived to my infinite relief that we had passed out of the region of eternal swamp, and were now travelling over swelling grassy plains towards a cup-shaped hill. Whether or not it was the same hill that we had seen from the canal I do not know, and have never since been able to discover, for, as we afterwards found out, these people will give little information upon such points. Next I glanced at the men who were bearing me. They were of a magnificent build, few of them being under six feet in height, and yellowish in colour. Generally their appearance had a good deal in common with that of the East African Somali, only their hair was not frizzed up, and hung in thick black locks upon their shoulders. Their features were aquiline, and in many cases exceedingly handsome, the teeth being especially regular and beautiful. But notwithstanding their beauty, it struck me that, on the whole, I had never seen a more evil-looking set of faces. There was an aspect of cold and sullen cruelty stamped upon them that revolted me, and which in some cases was almost uncanny in its intensity.

Another thing which struck me about them was that they never seemed to smile. Sometimes they sang the monotonous song of which I have spoken, but when they were not singing they remained almost perfectly silent, and the light of a laugh never came to brighten their sombre and evil countenances. Of what race could these people be? Their language was a bastard Arabic, and yet they were not Arabs; I was quite sure of that. For one thing they were too dark, or rather yellow. I could not say why, but I know that their appearance filled me with a sick fear of which I felt ashamed. While I was still wondering another litter came up alongside of mine. In it—for the curtains were drawn—sat an old man, clothed in a whitish robe, made apparently from coarse linen, that hung loosely about him, who, I at once jumped to the conclusion, was the shadowy figure who had stood on the bank and been addressed as 'Father.' He was a wonderful-looking old man, with a snowy beard, so long that the ends of it hung over the sides of the litter, and he had a hooked nose, above which flashed out a pair of eyes as keen as a snake's, while his whole countenance was instinct with a look of wise and sardonic humour impossible to describe on paper.

'Art thou awake, stranger?' he said in a deep and low voice.

'Surely, my father,' I answered courteously, feeling certain that I should do well to conciliate this ancient Mammon of Unrighteousness.[2]

He stroked his beautiful white beard, and smiled faintly.

'From whatever country thou camest,' he said, 'and by the way it must be from one where somewhat of our language is known, they teach their children courtesy there, my stranger son. And now wherefore comest thou unto this land, which scarce an alien foot has pressed from the time that man knoweth? Art thou and those with thee weary of life?'

'We came to find new things,' I answered boldly. 'We are tired of the old things; we have come up out of the sea to know that which is unknown. We are of a brave race who fear not death, my very much respected father—that is, if we can get a little fresh information before we die.'

'Humph!' said the old gentleman, 'that may be true; it is rash to contradict, otherwise I should say that thou wast lying, my son. However, I dare say that "*She-who-must-be-obeyed*" will meet thy wishes in the matter.'

'Who is "*She-who-must-be-obeyed*?"' I asked, curiously.

The old man glanced at the bearers, and then answered, with a little smile that somehow sent my blood to my heart—

'Surely, my stranger son, thou wilt learn soon enough, if it be her pleasure to see thee at all in the flesh.'

'In the flesh?' I answered. 'What may my father wish to convey?'

But the old man only laughed a dreadful laugh, and made no reply.

'What is the name of my father's people?' I asked.

'The name of my people is Amahagger' (the People of the Rocks).

'And if a son might ask, what is the name of my father?'

'My name is Billali.'

'And whither go we, my father?'

'That shalt thou see,' and at a sign from him his bearers started forward at a run till they reached the litter in which Job was reposing (with one leg hanging over the side). Apparently, however, he could not make much out of Job, for presently I saw his bearers trot forward to Leo's litter.

And after that, as nothing fresh occurred, I yielded to the pleasant swaying motion of the litter, and went to sleep again. I was dreadfully tired. When I woke I found that we were passing through a rocky defile of a lava formation with precipitous sides, in which grew many beautiful trees and flowering shrubs.

Presently this defile took a turn, and a lovely sight unfolded itself to my eyes. Before us was a vast cup of green from four to six miles in extent, of the shape of a Roman amphitheatre. The sides of this great cup were rocky, and clothed with bush, but the centre was of the richest meadow land, studded with single trees of magnificent growth, and watered by meandering brooks. On this rich plain grazed herds of goats and cattle, but I saw no sheep. At first I could not imagine what this strange spot could be, but presently it flashed upon me that it must represent the crater of some long-extinct volcano, which had afterwards been a lake, and was ultimately drained in some unexplained way. And here I may state that from my subsequent experience of this and a much larger, but otherwise similar spot, which I shall have occasion to describe by-and-by, I have every reason to believe that this conclusion was correct. What puzzled me, however, was that, although there were people moving about herding the goats and cattle, I saw no signs of any human habitation. Where did they all live? I wondered. My curiosity was soon destined to be gratified. Turning to the left the string of litters followed the cliffy sides of the crater for a distance of about half a mile, or perhaps a little less, and then halted. Seeing the old gentleman, my adopted 'father,' Billali, emerge from his litter, I did the same, and so did Leo and Job. The first thing I saw was our wretched Arab companion, Mahomed, lying exhausted on the ground. It appeared that he had not been provided with a litter, but had been forced to run the entire distance, and, as he was already quite worn out when we started, his condition now was one of great prostration.

On looking round we discovered that the place where we had halted was a platform in front of the mouth of a great cave, and piled upon this platform were the entire contents of the whale-boat, even down to the oars and sail. Round the cave stood groups of the men who had escorted us, and other men of a similar stamp. They were all tall and all handsome, though they varied in their degree of darkness of skin, some being as dark as Mahomed, and some as yellow as a Chinese. They were naked, except for the leopard-skin round the waist, and each of them carried a huge spear.

There were also some women among them, who, instead of the leopard-skin, wore a tanned hide of a small red buck, something like that of the oribé,[3] only rather darker in colour. These woman were, as a class, exceedingly good-looking, with large, dark eyes, well-cut features, and a thick bush of curling hair—not crisped like a negro's—ranging from black to chestnut in hue, with all shades of intermediate colour. Some, but very few of them, wore a yellowish linen garment, such as I have described as worn by Billali, but this, as we afterwards discovered, was a mark of rank, rather than an attempt at clothing. For the rest, their appearance was not quite so terrifying as that of the men, and they sometimes, though rarely, smiled. As soon as we had alighted they gathered round us and examined us with curiosity, but without excitement. Leo's tall, athletic form and clear-cut Grecian face, however, evidently excited their attention, and when he politely lifted his hat to them, and showed his curling yellow hair, there was a slight murmur of admiration. Nor did it stop there; for, after regarding him critically from head to foot, the handsomest of the young women—one wearing a robe, and with hair of a shade between brown and chestnut—deliberately advanced to him, and, in a way that would have been winning had it not been so determined, quietly put her arm round his neck, bent forward, and kissed him on the lips.

I gave a gasp, expecting to see Leo instantly speared; and Job ejaculated, 'The hussy—well, I never!' As for Leo, he looked slightly astonished; and then, remarking that we had got into a country where they clearly followed the customs of the early Christians,[4] deliberately returned the embrace.

Again I gasped, thinking that something would happen; but to my surprise, though some of the young women showed traces of vexation, the older ones and the men only smiled slightly. When we came to understand the customs of this extraordinary people the mystery was explained. It then appeared that, in direct opposition to the habits of almost every other savage race in the world, women among the Amahagger are not only upon terms of perfect equality with the men, but are not held to them by any binding ties. Descent is traced only through the line of the mother, and while individuals are as proud of a long and superior female ancestry as we are of our families in Europe, they never pay attention to, or even acknowledge, any man as their father, even when their male parentage is perfectly well known. There is but one titular male parent of each tribe, or, as they call it, 'Household,' and he is its elected and immediate ruler, with the title of 'Father.' For instance, the man Billali was the father of this 'household,' which consisted of about seven thousand individuals all told, and no other man was ever called by that name. When a woman took a fancy to a man she signified her preference by advancing and embracing him publicly, in the same way that this handsome and exceedingly prompt young lady, who was called Ustane, had embraced Leo. If he kissed her back it was a token that he accepted her, and the arrangement continued till one of them wearied of it. I am bound, however, to say that the change of husbands was not nearly so frequent as might have been expected. Nor did quarrels arise out of it, at least among the men, who, when their wives deserted them in favour of a rival, accepted the whole thing much as we accept the income-tax or our marriage laws, as something not to be disputed, and as tending to the good of the community, however disagreeable they may in particular instances prove to the individual.

It is very curious to observe how the customs of mankind on this matter vary in different countries, making morality an affair of latitude, and what is right and proper in one place wrong and improper in another. It must, however, be understood that, as all civilised nations appear to accept it as an axiom that ceremony is the touchstone of morality, there is, even according to our canons, nothing immoral about this Amahagger custom, seeing that the interchange of the embrace answers to our ceremony of marriage, which, as we know, justifies most things.

VII

Ustane Sings

When the kissing operation was finished—by the way, none of the young ladies offered to pet me in this fashion, though I saw one hovering round Job, to that respectable individual's evident alarm—the old man Billali advanced, and graciously waved us into the cave, whither we went, followed by Ustane, who did not seem inclined to take the hints I gave her that we liked privacy.

Before we had gone five paces it struck me that the cave that we were entering was none of Nature's handiwork, but, on the contrary, had been hollowed by the hand of man. So far as we could judge it appeared to be about one hundred feet in length by fifty wide, and very lofty, resembling a cathedral aisle more than anything else. From this main aisle opened passages at a distance of every twelve or fifteen feet, leading, I supposed, to smaller chambers. About fifty feet from the entrance of the cave, just where the light began to get dim, a fire was burning, which threw huge shadows upon the gloomy walls around. Here Billali halted, and asked us to be seated, saying that the people would bring us food, and accordingly we squatted ourselves down upon the rugs of skins which were spread for us, and waited. Presently the food, consisting of goat's flesh boiled, fresh milk in an earthenware pot, and boiled cobs of Indian corn,[1] was brought by young girls. We were almost starving, and I do not think that I ever in my life before ate with such satisfaction. Indeed, before we had finished we literally ate up everything that was set before us.

When we had done, our somewhat saturnine host, Billali, who

had been watching us in perfect silence, rose and addressed us. He said that it was a wonderful thing that had happened. No man had ever known or heard of white strangers arriving in the country of the People of the Rocks. Sometimes, though rarely, black men had come here, and from them they had heard of the existence of men much whiter than themselves, who sailed on the sea in ships, but for the arrival of such there was no precedent. We had, however, been seen dragging the boat up the canal, and he told us frankly that he had at once given orders for our destruction, seeing that it was unlawful for any stranger to enter here, when a message had come from '*She-who-must-be-obeyed*,' saying that our lives were to be spared, and that we were to be brought hither.

'Pardon me, my father,' I interrupted at this point; 'but if, as I understand, "*She-who-must-be-obeyed*" lives yet farther off, how could she have known of our approach?'

Billali turned, and seeing that we were alone—for the young lady, Ustane, had withdrawn when he had begun to speak—said, with a curious little laugh—

'Are there none in your land who can see without eyes and hear without ears? Ask no questions; *She* knew.'

I shrugged my shoulders at this, and he proceeded to say that no further instructions had been received on the subject of our disposal, and this being so he was about to start to interview '*She-who-must-be-obeyed*,' generally spoken of, for the sake of brevity, as 'Hiya' or *She* simply, who he gave us to understand was the Queen of the Amahagger, and learn her wishes.

I asked him how long he proposed to be away, and he said that by travelling hard he might be back on the fifth day, but there were many miles of marsh to cross before he came to where *She* was. He then said that every arrangement would be made for our comfort during his absence, and that, as he personally had taken a fancy to us, he sincerely trusted that the answer he should bring from *She* would be one favourable to the continuation of our existence, but at the same time he did not wish to conceal from us that he thought this doubtful, as every stranger who had ever come into the country during his grandmother's life, his mother's life, and his own life, had been put to death without mercy, and in a way that he would not harrow our feelings by describing; and this had been done by the order of *She* herself, at least he supposed it was by her order. At any rate, she never interfered to save them.

'Why,' I said, 'but how can that be? You are an old man, and the time you talk of must reach back three men's lives. How therefore could *She* have ordered the death of anybody at the beginning of the life of your grandmother, seeing that herself she would not have been born?'

Again he smiled—that same faint, peculiar smile, and with a deep bow departed, without making any answer; nor did we see him again for five days.

When he had gone we discussed the situation, which filled me with alarm. I did not at all like the accounts of this mysterious Queen, '*She-who-must-be-obeyed*,' or more shortly *She*, who apparently ordered the execution of any unfortunate stranger in a fashion so unmerciful. Leo, too, was depressed about it, but proceeded to console himself by triumphantly pointing out that this *She* was undoubtedly the person referred to in the writing on the potsherd and in his father's letter, in proof of which he advanced Billali's allusions to her age and power. I was by this time so overwhelmed with the whole course of events that I had not even got the heart left to dispute a proposition so absurd, so I suggested that we should try and go out and get a bath, of which we all stood sadly in need.

Accordingly, having indicated our wish to a middle-aged individual of an unusually saturnine cast of countenance, even among this saturnine people, who appeared to be deputed to look after us now that the Father of the hamlet had departed, we started in a body—having first lit our pipes. Outside the cave we found quite a crowd of people evidently watching for our appearance, but when they saw us come out smoking they vanished this way and that, calling out that we were great magicians. Indeed, nothing about us created so great a sensation as our tobacco smoke—not even our firearms.* After this we succeeded in reaching a stream that had its source in a strong ground spring, and taking our bath in peace, though some of the women, not excepting Ustane, showed a decided inclination to follow us even there.

By the time that we had finished this most refreshing bath the sun was setting; indeed, when we got back to the big cave it had already set. The cave itself was full of people gathered round fires—for several more had now been lighted—and eating their evening meal by their lurid light, and by that of various lamps which were set about or hung upon the walls. These lamps were of a rude manufacture of baked earthenware, and of all shapes, some of them graceful enough. The larger ones were formed of big red earthenware pots, filled with clarified melted fat, and having a reed wick stuck through a wooden disk which filled the top of the pot, and this sort of lamp required the most constant attention to prevent its going out whenever the wick burnt down, as there were no means of turning it up. The smaller hand lamps, however, which were also made of baked clay, were fitted with wicks manufactured from the pith of a palm-tree, or sometimes from the stem of a very handsome variety of fern. This kind of wick was passed through a round hole at the end of the lamp, to which a sharp piece of hard wood was attached wherewith to pierce and draw it up whenever it showed signs of burning low.

For a while we sat down and watched this grim people eating their evening meal in silence as grim as themselves, till at length, getting tired of contemplating them and the huge moving shadows on the rocky walls, I suggested to our new keeper that we should like to go to bed.

Without a word he rose, and, taking me politely by the hand, advanced with a lamp to one of the small passages that I had noticed opening out of the central cave. This we followed for about five paces, when it suddenly widened out into a small

* We found tobacco growing in this country as it does in every other part of Africa, and, although they are so absolutely ignorant of its other blessed qualities, the Amahagger use it habitually in the form of snuff, and also for medicinal purposes.—L. H. H.

chamber, about eight feet square, and hewn out of the living rock. On one side of this chamber was a stone slab, about three feet from the ground, and running its entire length like a bunk in a cabin, and on this slab he intimated that I was to sleep. There was no window or air-hole to the chamber, and no furniture; and, on looking at it more closely, I came to the disturbing conclusion (in which, as I afterwards discovered, I was quite right) that it had originally served for a sepulchre for the dead rather than a sleeping-place for the living, the slab being designed to receive the corpse of the departed. The thought made me shudder in spite of myself; but, seeing that I must sleep somewhere, I got over the feeling as best I might, and returned to the cavern to get my blanket, which had been brought up from the boat with the other things. There I met Job, who, having been inducted to a similar apartment, had flatly declined to stop in it, saying that the look of the place gave him the horrors, and that he might as well be dead and buried in his grandfather's brick grave at once, and expressed his determination of sleeping with me if I would allow him. This, of course, I was only too glad to do.

The night passed very comfortably on the whole. I say on the whole, for personally I went through a most horrible nightmare of being buried alive, induced, no doubt, by the sepulchral nature of my surroundings. At dawn we were aroused by a loud trumpeting sound, produced, as we afterwards discovered, by a young Amahagger blowing through a hole bored in its side into a hollowed elephant tusk, which was kept for the purpose.

Taking the hint, we got up and went down to the stream to wash, after which the morning meal was served. At breakfast one of the women, no longer quite young, advanced, and publicly kissed Job. I think it was in its way the most delightful thing (putting its impropriety aside for a moment) that I ever saw. Never shall I forget the respectable Job's abject terror and disgust. Job, like myself, is a bit of a mysogynist—I fancy chiefly owing to the fact of his having been one of a family of seventeen – and the feelings expressed upon his countenance when he realised that he was not only being embraced publicly, and without authorisation on his own part, but also in the presence of his masters, were too mixed and painful to admit of accurate description. He sprang to his feet, and pushed the woman, a buxom person of about thirty, from him.

'Well, I never!' he gasped, whereupon probably thinking that he was only coy, she embraced him again.

'Be off with you! Get away, you minx!' he shouted, waving the wooden spoon, with which he was eating his breakfast, up and down before the lady's face. 'Beg your pardon, gentlemen, I am sure I haven't encouraged her. Oh, Lord! she's coming for me again. Hold her, Mr. Holly! please hold her! I can't stand it; I can't, indeed. This has never happened to me before, gentlemen, never. There's nothing against my character,' and here he broke off, and ran as hard as he could go down the cave, and for once I saw the Amahagger laugh. As for the woman, however, she did not laugh. On the contrary, she seemed to bristle with fury, which the mockery of the other women about only served to intensify. She stood there literally snarling and shaking with indignation, and, seeing her, I wished Job's scruples had been at Jericho,[2] forming a shrewd guess that his admirable behaviour had endangered our throats. Nor, as the sequel shows, was I wrong.

The lady having retreated, Job returned in a great state of nervousness, and keeping his weather eye fixed upon every woman who came near him. I took an opportunity to explain to our hosts that Job was a married man, and had had very unhappy experiences in his domestic relations, which accounted for his presence here and his terror at the sight of women, but my remarks were received in grim silence, it being evident that our retainer's behaviour was considered as a slight to the 'household' at large, although the women, after the manner of some of their more civilised sisters, made merry at the rebuff of their companion.

After breakfast we took a walk and inspected the Amahagger herds, and also their cultivated lands. They have two breeds of cattle, one large and angular, with no horns, but yielding beautiful milk; and the other, a red breed, very small and fat, excellent for meat, but of no value for milking purposes. This last breed closely resembles the Norfolk red-pole strain,[3] only it has horns which generally curve forward over the head, sometimes to such an extent that they have to be cut to prevent them from growing into the bones of the skull. The goats are long-haired, and are used for eating only, at least I never saw them milked. As for the Amahagger cultivation, it is primitive in the extreme, being all done by means of a spade made of iron, for these people smelt and work iron.[4] This spade is shaped more like a big spear-head than anything else, and has no shoulder to it on which the foot can be set. As a consequence, the labour of digging is very great. It is, however, all done by the men, the women, contrary to the habits of most savage races, being entirely exempt from manual toil. But then, as I think I have said elsewhere, among the Amahagger the weaker sex has established its rights.

At first we were much puzzled as to the origin and constitution of this extraordinary race, points upon which they were singularly uncommunicative. As the time went on—for the next four days passed without any striking event—we learnt something from Leo's lady friend Ustane, who, by the way, stuck to that young gentleman like his own shadow. As to origin, they had none, at least, so far as she was aware. There were, however, she informed us, mounds of masonry and many pillars near the place where *She* lived, which was called Kôr, and which the wise said had once been houses wherein men lived, and it was suggested that they were descended from these men. No one, however, dared go near these great ruins, because they were haunted: they only looked on them from a distance. Other similar ruins were to be seen, she had heard, in various parts of the country, that is, wherever one of the mountains rose above the level of the swamp. Also the caves in which they lived had been hollowed out of the rocks by men, perhaps the same who built the cities. They themselves had no written laws, only custom, which was, however, quite as binding as law. If any man offended against the custom, he was put to death by order of the Father of the

'Household.' I asked how he was put to death, and she only smiled, and said that I might see one day soon.

They had a Queen, however. *She* was their Queen, but she was very rarely seen, perhaps once in two or three years, when she came forth to pass sentence on some offenders, and when seen was muffled up in a big cloak, so that nobody could look upon her face. Those who waited upon her were deaf and dumb, and therefore could tell no tales, but it was reported that she was lovely as no other woman was lovely, or ever had been. It was rumoured also that she was immortal, and had power over all things, but she, Ustane, could say nothing of all that. What she believed was that the Queen chose a husband from time to time, and as soon as a female child was born this husband, who was never again seen, was put to death. Then the female child grew up and took the place of the Queen when its mother died, and had been buried in the great caves. But of these matters none could speak for certain. Only *She* was obeyed throughout the length and breadth of the land, and to question her command was certain death. She kept a guard, but had no regular army, and to disobey her was to die.

I asked what size the land was, and how many people lived in it. She answered that there were ten 'Households,' like this that she knew of, including the big 'Household,' where the Queen was, that all the 'Households' lived in caves, in places resembling this stretch of raised country, dotted about in a vast extent of swamp, which was only to be threaded by secret paths. Often the 'Households' made war on each other until *She* sent word that it was to stop, and then they instantly ceased. That and the fever which they caught in crossing the swamps prevented their numbers from increasing too much. They had no connection with any other race, indeed none lived near them, or were able to thread the vast swamps. Once an army from the direction of the great river (presumably the Zambesi) had attempted to attack them, but they got lost in the marshes, and at night, seeing the great balls of fire that move about there, tried to come to them, thinking that they marked the enemy's camp, and half of them were drowned. As for the rest, they soon died of fever and starvation, not a blow being struck at them. The marshes, she told us, were absolutely impassable except to those who knew the paths, adding, what I could well believe, that we should never have reached this place where we then were had we not been brought thither.

These and many other things we learnt from Ustane during the four days' pause before our real adventures began, and, as may be imagined, they gave us considerable cause for thought. The whole thing was exceedingly remarkable, almost incredibly so, indeed, and the oddest part of it was that so far it did more or less correspond to the ancient writing on the sherd. And now it appeared that there was a mysterious Queen clothed by rumour with dread and wonderful attributes, and commonly known by the impersonal but, to my mind, rather awesome title of *She*. Altogether, I could not make it out, nor could Leo, though of course he was exceedingly triumphant over me because I had persistently mocked at the whole thing. As for Job, he had long since abandoned any attempt to call his reason his own, and left it to drift upon the sea of circumstance. Mahomed, the Arab, who was, by the way, treated civilly indeed, but with chilling contempt, by the Amahagger, was, I discovered, in a great fright, though I could not quite make out what he was frightened about. He would sit crouched up in a corner of the cave all day long, calling upon Allah and the Prophet to protect him. When I pressed him about it, he said that he was afraid because these people were not men and women at all, but devils, and that this was an enchanted land; and, upon my word, once or twice since then I have been inclined to agree with him. And so the time went on, till the night of the fourth day after Billali had left, when something happened.

We three and Ustane were sitting round a fire in the cave just before bedtime, when suddenly the woman, who had been brooding in silence, rose, and laid her hand upon Leo's golden curls, and addressed him. Even now, when I shut my eyes, I can see her proud, imperial form, clothed alternately in dense shadow and the red flickering of the fire, as she stood, the wild centre of as weird a scene as I ever witnessed, and delivered herself of the burden of her thoughts and forebodings in a kind of rhythmical speech that ran something as follows:—

Thou art my chosen—I have waited for thee from the beginning!
Thou art very beautiful. Who hath hair like unto thee, or skin so white?
Who hath so strong an arm, who is so much a man?
Thine eyes are the sky, and the light in them is the stars.
Thou art perfect and of a happy face, and my heart turned itself towards thee.
Ay, when mine eyes fell on thee I did desire thee,—
Then did I take thee to me—thou, my Beloved,
And hold thee fast, lest harm should come unto thee.
Ay, I did cover thine head with mine hair, lest the sun should strike it;
And altogether was I thine, and thou wast altogether mine.
And so it went for a little space, till Time was in labour with an evil Day;
And then what befell on that day? Alas! my Beloved, I know not!
But I, I saw thee no more—I, I was lost in the blackness.
And she who is stronger did take thee; ay, she who is fairer than Ustane.
Yet didst thou turn and call upon me, and let thine eyes wander in the darkness.
But, nevertheless, she prevailed by Beauty, and led thee down horrible places,
And then, ah! then my Beloved——

Here this extraordinary woman broke off her speech, or chant, which was so much musical gibberish to us, for all that we understood of what she was talking about, and seemed to fix her flashing eyes upon the deep shadow before her. Then in a moment they acquired a vacant, terrified stare, as though they were striving to realise some half-seen horror. She lifted her hand from Leo's head, and pointed into the darkness. We all looked, and could see nothing; but she saw something, or thought she did, and something evidently that affected even her iron nerves, for, without another sound, down she fell senseless between us.

Leo, who was growing really attached to this remarkable young person, was in a great state of alarm and distress, and I, to be perfectly candid, was in a condition not far removed from superstitious fear. The whole scene was an uncanny one.

Presently, however, she recovered, and sat up with an extraordinary convulsive shudder.

'What didst thou mean, Ustane?' asked Leo, who, thanks to years of tuition, spoke Arabic very prettily.

'Nay, my chosen,' she answered with a little forced laugh. 'I did but sing unto thee after the fashion of my people. Surely, I meant nothing. How could I speak of that which is not yet?'

'And what didst thou see, Ustane?' I asked, looking her sharply in the face.

'Nay,' she answered again; 'I saw naught. Ask me not what I saw. Why should I fright ye?' And then, turning to Leo with a look of the most utter tenderness that I ever saw upon the face of a woman, civilised or savage, she took his head between her hands, and kissed him on the forehead as a mother might. 'When I am gone from thee, my chosen; when at night thou stretchest out thine hand and canst not find me, then shouldst thou think at times of me, for of a truth I love thee well, though I be not fit to wash thy feet. And now let us love and take that which is given us, and be happy; for in the grave there is no love and no warmth, nor any touching of the lips. Nothing perchance, or perchance but bitter memories of what might have been. To-night the hours are our own, how know we to whom they shall belong to-morrow?

VIII

The Feast, and After!

On the day following this remarkable scene—a scene calculated to make a deep impression upon anybody who beheld it, more because of what it suggested and seemed to foreshadow than of what it revealed—it was announced to us that a feast would be held that evening in our honour. I did my best to get out of it, saying that we were modest people, and cared little for feasts, but my remarks being received with the silence of displeasure, I thought it wisest to hold my tongue.

Accordingly, just before sundown, I was informed that everything was ready, and, accompanied by Job, went into the cave, where I met Leo, who was, as usual, followed by Ustane. These two had been out walking somewhere, and knew nothing of the projected festivity till that moment. When Ustane heard of it I saw an expression of horror spring up upon her handsome features. Turning, she caught a man who was passing up the cave by the arm, and asked him something in an imperious tone. His answer seemed to reassure her a little, for she looked relieved, though far from satisfied. Next she appeared to attempt some remonstrance with the man, who was a person in authority, but he spoke angrily to her, and shook her off, and then changing his mind, led her by the arm, and sat her down between himself and another man in the circle round the fire, and I perceived that for some reason of her own she thought it best to submit.

The fire in the cave was an unusually big one that night, and in a large circle round it were gathered about thirty-five men and two women, Ustane and the woman to avoid whom Job had played the *rôle* of another Scriptural character.[1] The men were sitting in perfect silence, as was their custom, each with his great spear stuck upright behind him, in a socket cut in the rock for that purpose. Only one or two wore the yellowish linen garment of which I have spoken, the rest had nothing on except the leopard's skin about the middle.

'What's up now, sir?' said Job, doubtfully. 'Bless us and save us, there's that woman again. Now, surely, she can't be after me, seeing that I have given her no encouragement. They give me the creeps, the whole lot of them, and that's a fact. Why, look, they have asked Mahomed to dine, too. There, that lady of mine is talking to him in as nice and civil a way as possible. Well, I'm glad it isn't me, that's all.'

We looked up, and sure enough the woman in question had risen, and was escorting the wretched Mahomed from the corner, where, overcome by some acute prescience of horror, he had been seated, shivering, and calling on Allah. He appeared unwilling enough to come, if for no other reason perhaps because it was an unaccustomed honour, for hitherto his food had been given to him apart. Anyway I could see that he was in a state of great terror, for his tottering legs would scarcely support his stout, bulky form, and I think it was rather owing to the resources of barbarism behind him, in the shape of a huge Amahagger with a proportionately huge spear, than to the seduction of the lady who led him by the hand, that he consented to come at all.

'Well,' I said to the others, 'I don't at all like the look of things, but I suppose that we must face it out. Have you fellows got your revolvers on? because, if so, you had better see that they are loaded.'

'I have, sir,' said Job, tapping his Colt, 'but Mr. Leo has only got his hunting-knife, though that is big enough, surely.'

Feeling that it would not do to wait while the missing weapon was fetched, we advanced boldly, and seated ourselves in a line, with our backs against the side of the cave.

As soon as we were seated, an earthenware jar was passed round containing a fermented fluid, of by no means unpleasant taste, though apt to turn upon the stomach, made of crushed grain—not Indian corn, but a small brown grain that grows upon the stem in clusters, not unlike that which in the southern part of Africa is known by the name of Kafir corn.[2] The vase in which this liquid was handed round was very curious, and as it more or less resembled many hundreds of others in use among the Amahagger I may as well describe it. These vases are of a very ancient manufacture, and of all sizes. None such can have been made in the country for hundreds, or rather thousands, of years. They are found in the rock tombs, of which I shall give a description in their proper place, and my own belief is that, after the fashion of the Egyptians, with whom the former inhabitants of this country may have had some connection, they were used to receive the viscera of the dead. Leo, however, is of opinion that, as in the case of Etruscan amphoræ,[3] they were placed there for the spiritual use of the deceased. They are mostly two-handled, and of all sizes, some being nearly three feet in height, and running from that down to as many inches. In shape they vary, but are all exceedingly beautiful and graceful, being made of a very fine black ware, not lustrous, but slightly rough. On this groundwork were inlaid figures much more graceful and lifelike than any others I have seen on antique vases. Some of these inlaid pictures represented love-scenes with a childlike simplicity and freedom of manner which would not commend itself to the taste of the present day. Others again were pictures of maidens dancing, and yet others of hunting-scenes. For instance, the very vase from which we were then drinking had on one side a most spirited drawing of men, apparently white in colour, attacking a bull-elephant with spears, while on the reverse was a picture, not quite so well done, of a hunter shooting an arrow at a running antelope, I should say from the look of it either an eland or a koodoo.[4]

This is a digression at a critical moment, but it is not too long for the occasion, for the occasion itself was very long. With the exception of the periodical passing of the vase, and the movement necessary to throw fuel on to the fire, nothing happened for the best part of a whole hour. Nobody spoke a word. There we all sat in perfect silence, staring at the glare and glow of the large fire, and at the shadows thrown by the flickering earthenware lamps (which, by the way, were not ancient). On the open space between us and the fire lay a large wooden tray, with four short handles to it, exactly like a butcher's tray, only not hollowed out. By the side of the tray was a great pair of long-handled iron pincers, and on the other side of the fire was a similar pair. Somehow I did not at all like the appearance of this tray and the accompanying pincers. There I sat and stared at them and at the silent circle of the fierce moody faces of the men, and reflected that it was all very awful, and that we were absolutely in the power of this alarming people, who, to me at any rate, were all the more formidable because their true character was still very much of a mystery to us. They might be better than I thought them, or they might be worse. I feared that they were worse, and I was not wrong. It was a curious sort of a feast, I reflected, in appearance, indeed, an entertainment of the Barmecide stamp,[5] for there was absolutely nothing to eat.

At last, just as I was beginning to feel as though I were being mesmerised, a move was made. Without the slightest warning, a man from the other side of the circle called out in a loud voice—

'Where is the flesh that we shall eat?'

Thereon everybody in the circle answered in a deep measured tone, and stretching out the right arm towards the fire as he spoke—

'*The flesh will come.*'

'Is it a goat?' said the same man.

'*It is a goat without horns, and more than a goat, and we shall slay it,*' they answered with one voice, and turning half round they one and all grasped the handles of their spears with the right hand, and then simultaneously let them go.

'Is it an ox?' said the man again.

'*It is an ox without horns, and more than an ox, and we shall slay it,*' was the answer, and again the spears were grasped, and again let go.

Then came a pause, and I noticed, with horror and a rising of the hair, that the woman next to Mahomed began to fondle him, patting his cheeks, and calling him by names of endearment, while her fierce eyes played up and down his trembling form. I do not know why the sight frightened me so, but it did frighten us all dreadfully, especially Leo. The caressing was so snake-like, and so evidently a part of some ghastly formula that had to be gone through.* I saw Mahomed turn white under his brown skin, sickly white with fear.

'Is the meat ready to be cooked?' asked the voice, more rapidly.

'*It is ready; it is ready.*'

'Is the pot hot to cook it?' it continued, in a sort of scream that echoed painfully down the great recesses of the cave.

'*It is hot; it is hot.*'

'Great heavens!' roared Leo, 'remember the writing, "*The people who place pots upon the heads of strangers.*"'

As he said the words, before we could stir, or even take the matter in, two great ruffians jumped up, and, seizing the long pincers, plunged them into the heart of the fire, and the woman who had been caressing Mahomed suddenly produced a fibre noose from under her girdle or moocha, and, slipping it over his shoulders, ran it tight, while the men next him seized him by the legs. The two men with the pincers gave a heave, and, scattering the fire this way and that upon the rocky floor, lifted from it a large earthenware pot, heated to a white heat. In an instant, almost with a single movement, they had reached the spot where Mahomed was struggling. He fought like a fiend, shrieking in the abandonment of his despair, and notwithstanding the noose round him, and the efforts of the men who held his legs, the advancing wretches were for the moment unable to accomplish their purpose, which, horrible and incredible as it seems, was *to put the red-hot pot upon his head.*[6]

* We afterwards learnt that its object was to pretend to the victim that he was the object of love and admiration, and so to soothe his injured feelings, and cause him to expire in a happy and contented frame of mind.—L. H. H.

I sprang to my feet with a yell of horror, and drawing my revolver fired it by a sort of instinct straight at the diabolical woman who had been caressing Mahomed, and was now gripping him in her arms. The bullet struck her in the back and killed her, and to this day I am glad that it did, for, as it afterwards transpired, she had availed herself of the anthropophagous customs[7] of the Amahagger to organise the whole thing in revenge of the slight put upon her by Job. She sank down dead, and as she did so, to my terror and dismay, Mahomed, by a superhuman effort, burst from his tormentors, and, springing high into the air, fell dying upon her corpse. The heavy bullet from my pistol had driven through the bodies of both, at once striking down the murdress, and saving her victim from a death a hundred times more horrible. It was an awful and yet a most merciful accident.

For a moment there was a silence of astonishment. The Amahagger had never heard the report of a firearm before, and its effects dismayed them. But the next a man close to us recovered himself, and seized his spear preparatory to making a lunge with it at Leo, who was the nearest to him.

'Run for it!' I shouted, setting the example by starting up the cave as hard as my legs would carry me. I would have made for the open air if it had been possible, but there were men in the way, and, besides, I had caught sight of the forms of a crowd of people standing out clear against the skyline beyond the entrance to the cave. Up the cave I went, and after me came the others, and after them thundered the whole crowd of cannibals, mad with fury at the death of the woman. With a bound I cleared the prostrate form of Mahomed. As I flew over him I felt the heat from the red hot pot, which was lying close by, strike upon my legs, and by its glow saw his hands—for he was not quite dead—still feebly moving. At the top of the cave was a little platform of rock three feet or so high by about eight deep, on which two large lamps were placed at night. Whether this platform had been left as a seat, or as a raised point afterwards to be cut away when it had served its purpose as a standing-place from which to carry on the excavations, I do not know—at least, I did not then. At any rate, we all three reached it, and, jumping on it, prepared to sell our lives as dearly as we could. For a few seconds the crowd that was pressing on our heels hung back when they saw us face round upon them. Job was on one side of the rock to the left, Leo in the centre, and I to the right. Behind us were the lamps. Leo bent forward, and looked down the long lane of shadows, terminated in the fire and lighted lamps, through which the quiet forms of our would-be murderers flitted to and fro with the faint light glinting on their spears, for even their fury was silent as a bulldog's. The only other thing visible was the red-hot pot still glowing angrily in the gloom. There was a curious light in Leo's eyes, and his handsome face was set like a stone. In his right hand was his heavy hunting-knife. He shifted its thong a little up his wrist, and then put his arm round me and gave me a good hug.

'Good-bye, old fellow,' he said, 'my dear friend—my more than father. We have no chance against those scoundrels; they will finish us in a few minutes, and eat us afterwards, I suppose. Good-bye. I led you into this. I hope you will forgive me. Good-bye, Job.'

'God's will be done,' I said, setting my teeth, as I prepared for the end. At that moment, with an exclamation, Job lifted his revolver and fired, and hit a man—not the man he had aimed at, by the way: anything that Job shot *at* was perfectly safe.

On they came with a rush, and I fired too as fast as I could, and checked them—between us, Job and I, besides the woman, killed or mortally wounded five men with our pistols before they were emptied. But we had no time to reload, and they still came on in a way that was almost splendid in its recklessness, seeing that they did not know but that we could go on firing for ever.

A great fellow bounded up upon the platform, and Leo struck him dead with one blow of his powerful arm, sending the knife right through him. I did the same by another, but Job missed his stroke, and I saw a brawny Amahagger grip him by the middle and whirl him off the rock. The knife not being secured by a thong fell from Job's hand as he did so, and, by a most happy accident for him, lit upon its handle on the rock, just as the body of the Amahagger being undermost, hit upon its point and was transfixed upon it. What happened to Job after that I am sure I do not know, but my own impression is that he lay still upon the corpse of his deceased assailant, 'playing 'possum' as the Americans say. As for myself, I was soon involved in a desperate encounter with two ruffians who, luckily for me, had left their spears behind them; and for the first time in my life the great physical power with which Nature has endowed me stood me in good stead. I had hacked at the head of one man with my hunting-knife, which was almost as big and heavy as a short sword, with such vigour, that the sharp steel had split his skull down to the eyes, and was held so fast by it that as he suddenly fell sideways the knife was twisted right out of my hand.

Then it was that the two others sprang upon me. I saw them coming, and got an arm round the waist of each, and down we all fell upon the floor of the cave together, rolling over and over. They were strong men, but I was mad with rage, and that awful lust for slaughter which will creep into the hearts of the most civilised of us when blows are flying, and life and death tremble on the turn. My arms were round the two swarthy demons, and I hugged them till I heard their ribs crack and crunch up beneath my gripe. They twisted and writhed like snakes, and clawed and battered at me with their fists, but I held on. Lying on my back there, so that their bodies might protect me from spear thrusts from above, I slowly crushed the life out of them, and as I did so, strange as it may seem, I thought of what the amiable Head of my College at Cambridge (who is a member of the Peace Society) and my brother Fellows would say if by clairvoyance they could see me, of all men, playing such a bloody game. Soon my assailants grew faint, and almost ceased to struggle, their breath had failed them, and they were dying, but still I dared not leave them, for they died very slowly. I knew that if I relaxed my grip they would revive. The other ruffians probably thought—for we were all three lying in the shadow of the ledge—

that we were all dead together, at any rate they did not interfere with our little tragedy.

I turned my head, and as I lay gasping in the throes of that awful struggle I could see that Leo was off the rock now, for the lamplight fell full upon him. He was still on his feet, but in the centre of a surging mass of struggling men, who were striving to pull him down as wolves pull down a stag. Up above them towered his beautiful pale face crowned with its bright curls (for Leo is six feet two high), and I saw that he was fighting with a desperate abandonment and energy that was at once splendid and hideous to behold. He drove his knife through one man—they were so close to him and mixed up with him that they could not get at him to kill him with their big spears, and they had no knives or sticks. The man fell, and then somehow the knife was wrenched from his hand, leaving him defenceless, and I thought the end had come. But no; with a desperate effort he broke loose from them, seized the body of the man he had just slain, and lifting it high in the air hurled it right at the mob of his assailants, so that the shock and weight of it swept some five or six of them to the earth. But in a minute they were all up again, except one, whose skull was smashed, and had once more fastened upon him. And then slowly, and with infinite labour and struggling, the wolves bore the lion down. Once even then he recovered himself, and felled an Amahagger with his fist, but it was more than man could do to hold his own for long against so many, and at last he came crashing down upon the rock floor, falling as an oak falls, and bearing with him to the earth all those who clung about him. They gripped him by his arms and legs, and then cleared off his body.

'A spear,' cried a voice—'a spear to cut his throat, and a vessel to catch his blood.'

I shut my eyes, for I saw the man coming with a spear, and myself, I could not stir to Leo's help, for I was growing weak, and the two men on me were not yet dead, and a deadly sickness overcame me.

Then suddenly there was a disturbance, and involuntarily I

opened my eyes again, and looked towards the scene of murder. The girl Ustane had thrown herself on Leo's prostrate form, covering his body with her body, and fastening her arms about his neck. They tried to drag her from him, but she twisted her legs round his, and hung on like a bulldog, or rather like a creeper to a tree, and they could not. Then they tried to stab him in the side without hurting her, but somehow she shielded him, and he was only wounded.

At last they lost patience.

'Drive the spear through the man and the woman together,' said a voice, the same voice that had asked the questions at that ghastly feast, 'so of a verity shall they be wed.'

Then I saw the man with the weapon straighten himself for the effort. I saw the cold steel gleam on high, and once more I shut my eyes.

As I did so I heard the voice of a man thunder out in tones that rang and echoed down the rocky ways—

'*Cease!*'

Then I fainted, and as I did so it flashed through my darkening mind that I was passing down into the last oblivion of death.

IX

A Little Foot

When I opened my eyes again I found myself lying on a skin mat not far from the fire round which we had been gathered for that dreadful feast. Near me lay Leo, still apparently in a swoon, and over him was bending the tall form of the girl Ustane, who was washing a deep spear wound in his side with cold water preparatory to binding it up with linen. Leaning against the wall of the cave behind her was Job, apparently uninjured, but bruised and trembling. On the other side of the fire, tossed about this way and that, as though they had thrown themselves down to sleep in some moment of absolute exhaustion, were the bodies of those whom we had killed in our frightful struggle for life. I counted them: there were twelve beside the woman, and the corpse of poor Mahomed, who had died by my hand, which, the fire-stained pot at its side, was placed at the end of the irregular line. To the left a body of men were engaged in binding the arms of the survivors of the cannibals behind them, and then fastening them two and two. The villains were submitting with a look of sulky indifference upon their faces which accorded ill with the baffled fury that gleamed in their sombre eyes. In front of these men, directing the operations, stood no other than our friend Billali, looking rather tired, but particularly patriarchal with his flowing beard, and as cool and unconcerned as though he were superintending the cutting up of an ox.

Presently he turned, and perceiving that I was sitting up advanced to me, and with the utmost courtesy said that he trusted that I felt better. I answered that at present I scarcely knew how I felt, except that I ached all over.

Then he bent down and examined Leo's wound.

'It is a nasty cut,' he said, 'but the spear has not pierced the entrails. He will recover.'

'Thanks to thy arrival, my father,' I answered. 'In another minute we should all have been beyond the reach of recovery, for those devils of thine would have slain us as they would have slain our servant,' and I pointed towards Mahomed.

The old man ground his teeth, and I saw an extraordinary expression of malignity light up his eyes.

'Fear not, my son,' he answered. 'Vengeance shall be taken on them such as would make the flesh twist upon the bones merely to hear of it. To *She* shall they go, and her vengeance shall be worthy of her greatness. That man,' pointing to Mahomed, 'I tell thee that man would have died a merciful death to the death these hyæna-men shall die. Tell me, I pray of thee, how it came about.'

In a few words I sketched what had happened.

'Ah, so,' he answered. 'Thou seest, my son, here there is a custom that if a stranger comes into this country he may be slain by "the pot", and eaten.'

'It is hospitality turned upside down,' I answered feebly. 'In our country we entertain a stranger, and give him food to eat. Here ye eat him, and are entertained.'

'It is a custom,' he answered, with a shrug. 'Myself I think it an evil one; but then,' he added by an after-thought, 'I do not like the taste of strangers, especially after they have wandered through the swamps and lived on wildfowl. When *She-who-must-be-obeyed* sent orders that ye were to be saved alive she said naught of the black man, therefore, being hyænas, these men lusted after his flesh, and the woman it was, whom thou didst rightly slay, who put it into their evil hearts to hot-pot him. Well, they will have their reward. Better for them would it be if they had never seen the light than that they should stand before

She in her terrible anger. Happy are those of them who died by your hands.

'Ah,' he went on, 'it was a gallant fight that ye fought. Knowest thou, that thou, long-armed old baboon that thou art, hast crushed in the ribs of those two who are laid out there as though they were but as the shell on an egg? And the young one, the lion, it was a beautiful stand that he made—one against so many—three did he slay outright, and that one there'—and he pointed to a body that was still moving a little—'will die anon, for his head is cracked across, and others of those who are bound are hurt. It was a gallant fight, and thou and he have made a friend of me by it, for I love to see a well-fought fray. But tell me, my son, the baboon—and now I think of it thy face, too, is hairy, and altogether like a baboon's—how was it that ye slew those with a hole in them?—Ye made a noise, they say, and slew them—they fell down on their faces at the noise?'

I explained to him as well as I could, but very shortly—I was terribly wearied, and only persuaded to talk at all through fear of offending one so powerful if I refused to do so—what were the properties of gunpowder, and he instantly suggested that I should illustrate what I said by operating on the person of one of the prisoners. One, he said, never would be counted, and it would not only be very interesting to him, but would give me an opportunity of an instalment of revenge. He was greatly astounded when I told him that it was not our custom to avenge ourselves in cold blood, and that we left vengeance to the law and a higher power, of which he knew nothing. I added, however, that when I recovered I would take him out shooting with us, and he should kill an animal for himself, and at this he was as pleased as a child at the promise of a new toy.

Just then Leo opened his eyes beneath the stimulus of some brandy (of which we still had a little) that Job had poured down his throat, and our conversation came to an end.

After this we managed to get Leo, who was in a very poor way indeed, and only half-conscious, safely off to bed, supported by Job and that brave girl Ustane, to whom, had I not been afraid she might resent it, I would certainly have given a kiss for her splendid behaviour in saving my dear boy's life at the risk of her own. But Ustane was not the sort of young person with whom one would care to take liberties unless one were perfectly certain that they would not be misunderstood, so I repressed my inclinations. Then, bruised and battered, but with a sense of safety in my breast to which I had for some days been a stranger, I crept off to my own little sepulchre, not forgetting before I lay down in it to thank Providence from the bottom of my heart that it was not a sepulchre indeed, as were it not for a merciful combination of events that I can only attribute to its protection, it would certainly have been for me that night. Few men have been nearer their end and yet escaped it than we were on that dreadful day.

I am a bad sleeper at the best of times, and my dreams that night when at last I got to rest were not of the pleasantest. The awful vision of poor Mahomed struggling to escape the red-hot pot would haunt them, and then in the background, as it were, a veiled form was always hovering, which, from time to time, seemed to draw the coverings from its body, revealing now the perfect shape of a lovely blooming woman, and now again the white bones of a grinning skeleton, and which, as it veiled and unveiled, uttered the mysterious and apparently meaningless sentence:—

'*That which is alive hath known death, and that which is dead yet can never die, for in the Circle of the Spirit life is naught and death is naught. Yea, all things live for ever, though at times they sleep and are forgotten.*'

The morning came at last, but when it came I found that I was too stiff and sore to rise. About seven Job arrived, limping terribly, and with his face the colour of a rotten apple, and told me that Leo had slept fairly, but was very weak. Two hours afterwards Billali (Job called him 'Billy-goat,' to which, indeed, his white beard gave him some resemblance, or more familiarly 'Billy') came too, bearing a lamp in his hand, his towering form reaching nearly to the roof of the little chamber. I pretended to be asleep, and through the cracks of my eyelids watched his sardonic but handsome old face. He fixed his hawk-like eyes upon me, and stroked his glorious white beard, which, by the way, would have been worth a hundred a year to any London barber as an advertisement.

'Ah!' I heard him mutter (Billali had a habit of muttering to himself), 'he is ugly—ugly as the other is beautiful—a very Baboon, it was a good name. But I like the man. Strange now, at my age, that I should like a man. What says the proverb—"Mistrust all men, and slay him whom thou mistrustest overmuch; and as for women, flee from them, for they are evil, and in the end will destroy thee." It is a good proverb, especially the last part of it: I think it must have come down from the ancients. Nevertheless I like this Baboon, and I wonder where they taught him his tricks, and I trust that *She* will not bewitch him. Poor Baboon! he must be wearied after that fight. I will go lest I should awake him.'

I waited till he had turned and was nearly through the entrance, walking softly on tiptoe, and then I called after him.

'My father,' I said, 'is it thou?'

'Yes, my son, it is I; but let me not disturb thee. I did but come to see how thou didst fare, and to tell thee that those who would have slain thee, my Baboon, are by now well on their road to *She*. *She* said that ye also were to come at once, but I fear ye cannot yet.'

'Nay,' I said, 'not till we have recovered a little; but have me borne out into the daylight, I pray thee, my father. I love not this place.'

'Ah, no,' he answered, 'it hath a sad air. I remember when I was a boy I found the body of a fair woman lying where thou liest now, yes, on that very bench. She was so beautiful that I was wont to creep in hither with a lamp and gaze upon her. Had it not been for her cold hands, almost could I think that she slept and would one day awake, so fair and peaceful was she in her robes of white. White was she, too, and her hair was yellow and lay down her almost to the feet. There are many such still in the tombs at the place where *She* is, for those who set them there had a way I know naught of, whereby to keep their beloved out of the crumbling hand of Decay, even when Death had slain them. Ay, day by day I came hither, and gazed on her till at last, laugh not at me, stranger, for I was but a silly lad, I learned to love that dead form, that shell which once had held a life that no more is. I would creep up to her and kiss her cold face, and wonder how many men had lived and died since she was, and who had loved her and embraced her in the days that long had passed away. And, my Baboon, I think I learned wisdom from that dead one, for of a truth it taught me of the littleness of life, and the length of Death, and how all things that are under the sun go down one path, and are for ever forgotten. And so I mused, and it seemed to me that wisdom flowed into me from the dead, till one day my mother, a watchful woman, but hasty-minded, seeing I was changed, followed me, and saw the beautiful white one, and feared that I was bewitched, as, indeed, I was. So half in dread, and half in anger, she took the lamp, and standing the dead woman up against the wall there, set fire to her hair, and she burnt fiercely, even down to the feet, for those who are thus kept burn excellently well.

'See, my son, there on the roof is yet the smoke of her burning.'

I looked up doubtfully, and there, sure enough, on the roof of the sepulchre, was a peculiarly unctuous and sooty mark, three feet or more across. Doubtless it had in the course of years been rubbed off the sides of the little cave, but on the roof it remained, and there was no mistaking its appearance.

'She burnt,' he went on in a meditative way, 'even to the feet, but the feet I came back and saved, cutting the burnt bone from them, and hid them under the stone bench there, wrapped up in a piece of linen. Surely, I remember it as though it were but yesterday. Perchance they are there if none have found them, even to this hour. Of a truth I have not entered this chamber from that time to this very day. Stay, I will look,' and, kneeling down, he groped about with his long arm in the recess under the stone bench. Presently his face brightened, and with an exclamation he pulled something forth that was caked in dust; which he shook on to the floor. It was covered with the remains of a rotting rag, which he undid, and revealed to my astonished gaze a beautifully shaped and almost white woman's foot, looking as fresh and as firm as though it had but now been placed there.

'Thou seest, my son, the Baboon,' he said, in a sad voice, 'I spake the truth to thee, for here is yet one foot remaining. Take it, my son, and gaze upon it.'

I took this cold fragment of mortality in my hand and looked at it in the light of the lamp with feelings which I cannot describe, so mixed up were they between astonishment, fear, and fascination. It was light, much lighter I should say than it had been in the living state, and the flesh to all appearance was still flesh, though about it there clung a faintly aromatic odour. For the rest it was not shrunk or shrivelled, or even black and unsightly, like the flesh of Egyptian mummies, but plump and fair, and, except where it had been slightly burnt, perfect as on the day of death—a very triumph of embalming.

Poor little foot! I set it down upon the stone bench where it had lain for so many thousand years, and wondered whose was the beauty that it had upborne through the pomp and pageantry of a forgotten civilisation—first as a merry child's, then as a blushing maid's, and lastly as a perfect woman's. Through what halls of Life had its soft step echoed, and in the end, with what courage had it trodden down the dusty ways of Death! To whose side had it stolen in the hush of night when the black slave[1] slept upon the marble floor, and who had listened for its stealing? Shapely little foot! Well might it have been set upon the proud neck of a conqueror bent at last to woman's beauty, and well might the lips of nobles and of kings have been pressed upon its jewelled whiteness.

I wrapped up this relic of the past in the remnants of the old linen rag which had evidently formed a portion of its owner's grave-clothes, for it was partially burnt, and put it away in my Gladstone bag,[2] which I had bought at the Army and Navy Stores—a strange combination, I thought. Then with Billali's help I staggered off to see Leo. I found him dreadfully bruised, worse even than myself, perhaps owing to the excessive whiteness of his skin, and faint and weak with the loss of blood from the flesh wound in his side, but for all that cheerful as a cricket, and asking for some breakfast. Job and Ustane got him on to the bottom, or rather the sacking of a litter, which was removed from its pole for that purpose, and with the aid of old Billali carried him out into the shade at the mouth of the cave, from which, by the way, every trace of the slaughter of the previous night had now been removed, and there we all breakfasted, and indeed spent that day, and most of the two following ones.

On the third morning Job and myself were practically recovered. Leo also was so much better that I yielded to Billali's often expressed entreaty, and agreed to start at once upon our journey to Kôr, which we were told was the name of the place where the mysterious *She* lived, though I still feared for its effects upon Leo, and especially lest the motion should cause his wound, which was scarcely skinned over, to break open again. Indeed, had it not been for Billali's evident anxiety to get off, which led us to suspect that some difficulty or danger might threaten us if we did not comply with it, I would not have consented to go.

X

Speculations

Within an hour of our finally deciding to start five litters were brought up to the door of the cave, each accompanied by four regular bearers and two spare hands, also a band of about fifty armed Amahagger, who were to form the escort and carry the baggage. Three of these litters, of course, were for us, and one for Billali, who, I was immensely relieved to hear, was to be our companion, while the fifth I presumed was for the use of Ustane.

'Does the lady go with us, my father?' I asked of Billali, as he stood superintending things generally.

He shrugged his shoulders as he answered—

'If she wills. In this country the women do what they please. We worship them, and give them their way, because without them the world could not go on; they are the source of life.'

'Ah,' I said, the matter never having struck me quite in that light before.

'We worship them,' he went on, 'up to a certain point, till at last they get unbearable, which,' he added, 'they do about every second generation.'

'And then what do you do?' I asked, with curiosity.

'Then,' he answered, with a faint smile, 'we rise, and kill the old ones as an example to the young ones, and to show them that we are the strongest. My poor wife was killed in that way three years ago. It was very sad, but to tell thee the truth, my son, life has been happier since, for my age protects me from the young ones.'

'In short,' I replied, quoting the saying of a great man whose wisdom has not yet lightened the darkness of the Amahagger, 'thou hast found thy position one of greater freedom and less responsibility.'

This phrase puzzled him a little at first from its vagueness, though I think my translation hit off its sense very well, but at last he saw it, and appreciated it.

'Yes, yes, my Baboon,' he said, 'I see it now, but all the "responsibilities" are killed, at least some of them are, and that is why there are so few old women about just now. Well, they brought it on themselves. As for this girl,' he went on, in a graver tone, 'I know not what to say. She is a brave girl, and she loves the Lion (Leo); thou sawest how she clung to him, and saved his life. Also, she is, according to our custom, wed to him, and has a right to go where he goes, unless,' he added significantly, '*She* would say her no, for her word overrides all rights.'

'And if *She* bade her leave him, and the girl refused? What then?'

'If,' he said, with a shrug, 'the hurricane bids the tree to bend, and it will not; what happens?'

And then, without waiting for an answer, he turned and walked to his litter, and in ten minutes from that time we were all well under weigh.

It took us an hour and more to cross the cup of the volcanic plain, and another half-hour or so to climb the edge on the farther side. Once there, however, the view was a very fine one. Before us was a long steep slope of grassy plain, broken here and there by clumps of trees mostly of the thorn tribe. At the bottom of this gentle slope, some nine or ten miles away, we could make out a dim sea of marsh, over which the foul vapours hung like smoke about a city. It was easy going for the bearers down the slopes, and by midday we had reached the borders of the dismal swamp. Here we halted to eat our midday meal, and then, following a winding and devious path, plunged into the morass. Presently the path, at any rate to our unaccustomed eyes, grew so faint as to be almost indistinguishable from those made by the aquatic beasts and birds, and it is to this day a mystery to me how our bearers found their way across the marshes. Ahead of the cavalcade marched two men with long poles, which they now and again plunged into the ground before them, the reason of this being that the nature of the soil frequently changed from causes with which I am not acquainted, so that places which might be safe enough to cross one month would certainly swallow the wayfarer the next. Never did I see a more dreary and depressing scene. Miles on miles of quagmire, varied only by bright green strips of comparatively solid ground, and by deep and sullen pools fringed with tall rushes, in which the bitterns boomed and the frogs croaked incessantly: miles on miles of it without a break, unless the fever fog can be called a break. The only life in this great morass was that of the aquatic birds, and the animals that fed on them, of both of which there were vast numbers. Geese, cranes, ducks, teal, coot, snipe, and plover swarmed all around us, many being of varieties that were quite new to me, and all so tame that one could almost have knocked them over with a stick. Among these birds I especially noticed a very beautiful variety of painted snipe, almost the size of woodcock, and with a flight more resembling that bird's than an English snipe's. In the pools, too, was a species of small alligator or enormous iguana, I do not know which, that fed, Billali told me, upon the waterfowl, also large quantities of a hideous black water-snake, of which the bite is very dangerous, though not, I gathered, so deadly as a cobra's or a puff adder's. The bull-frogs were also very large, and with voices proportionate to their size; and as for the mosquitoes—the 'musqueteers,' as Job called them—they were, if possible, even worse than they had been on the river, and tormented us greatly. Undoubtedly, however, the worst feature of the swamp was the awful smell of rotting vegetation that hung about it, which was at times positively overpowering, and the malarious exhalations that accompanied it, which we were of course obliged to breathe.

On we went through it all, till at last the sun sank in sullen splendour just as we reached a spot of rising ground about two acres in extent—a little oasis of dry in the midst of the miry wilderness—where Billali announced that we were to camp. The camping, however, turned out to be a very simple process, and consisted, in fact, in sitting down on the ground round a scanty fire made of dry reeds and some wood that had been brought with us. However, we made the best we could of it, and smoked and ate with such appetite as the smell of damp, stifling heat would allow, for it was very hot on this low land, and yet, oddly enough, chilly at times. But, however hot it was, we were glad enough to keep near the fire, because we found that the mosquitoes did not like the smoke. Presently we rolled ourselves up in our blankets and tried to go to sleep, but so far as I was concerned the bull-frogs, and the extraordinary roaring and alarming sound produced by hundreds of snipe hovering high in the air, made sleep an impossibility, to say nothing of our other discomforts. I turned and looked at Leo, who was next me; he was dozing, but his face had a flushed appearance that I did not like, and by the flickering fire-light I saw Ustane, who was lying on the other side of him, raise herself from time to time upon her elbow, and look at him anxiously enough.

However, I could do nothing for him, for we had all already taken a good dose of quinine,[1] which was the only preventive we had; so I lay and watched the stars come out by thousands, till all the immense arch of heaven was sewn with glittering points, and every point a world! Here was a glorious sight by which man might well measure his own insignificance! Soon I gave up thinking about it, for the mind wearies easily when it strives to grapple with the Infinite, and to trace the footsteps of the Almighty as he strides from sphere to sphere, or deduce His purpose from His works. Such things are not for us to know. Knowledge is to the strong, and we are weak. Too much wisdom would perchance blind our imperfect sight, and too much strength would make us drunk, and overweight our feeble reason till it fell, and we were drowned in the depths of our own vanity. For what is the first result of man's increased knowledge interpreted from Nature's book by the persistent effort of his purblind observation? Is it not but too often to make him question the existence of his Maker, or indeed of any intelligent purpose beyond his own? The truth is veiled, because we could no more look upon her glory than we can upon the sun. It would destroy us. Full knowledge is not for man as man is here, for his capacities, which he is apt to think so great, are indeed but small. The vessel is soon filled, and, were one-thousandth part of the unutterable and silent wisdom that directs the rolling of those shining spheres, and the force which makes them roll, pressed into it, it would be shattered into fragments. Perhaps in some other place and time it may be otherwise, who can tell? Here the lot of man born of the flesh is but to endure midst toil and tribulation, to catch at the bubbles blown by Fate, which he calls pleasures, thankful if before they burst they rest a moment in his hand, and when the tragedy is played out, and his hour comes to perish, to pass humbly whither he knows not.

Above me, as I lay, shone the eternal stars, and there at my feet the impish marsh-born balls of fire rolled this way and that, vapour-tossed and earth-desiring, and me-thought that in the two I saw a type and image of what man is, and what perchance man may one day be, if the living Force who ordained him and them should so ordain this also. Oh, that it might be ours to rest year by year upon that high level of the heart to which at times we momentarily attain! Oh, that we could shake loose the prisoned pinions of the soul and soar to that superior point, whence, like to some traveller looking out through space from Darien's giddiest peak,[2] we might gaze with the spiritual eyes of noble thoughts deep into Infinity!

What would it be to cast off this earthy robe, to have done for ever with these earthy thoughts and miserable desires; no longer, like those corpse candles, to be tossed this way and that, by forces beyond our control; or which, if we can theoretically control them, we are at times driven by the exigencies of our nature to obey! Yes, to cast them off, to have done with the foul and thorny places of the world; and, like to those glittering points above me, to rest on high wrapped for ever in the brightness of our better selves, that even now shines in us as fire faintly shines within those lurid balls, and lay down our littleness in that wide glory of our dreams, that invisible but surrounding good, from which all truth and beauty comes!

These and many such thoughts passed through my mind that night. They come to torment us all at times. I say to torment, for, alas! thinking can only serve to measure out the helplessness of thought. What is the use of our feeble crying in the awful silences of space? Can our dim intelligence read the secrets of that star-strewn sky? Does any answer come out of it? Never any at all, nothing but echoes and fantastic visions. And yet we believe that there is an answer, and that upon a time a new Dawn will come blushing down the ways of our enduring night. We believe it, for its reflected beauty even now shines up continually in our hearts from beneath the horizon of the grave, and we call it Hope. Without Hope we should suffer moral death, and by the help of Hope we yet may climb to Heaven, or at the worst, if she also prove but a kindly mockery given to hold us from despair, be gently lowered into the abysses of eternal sleep.

Then I fell to reflecting upon the undertaking on which we were bent, and what a wild one it was, and yet how strangely the story seemed to fit in with what had been written centuries ago upon the sherd. Who was this extraordinary woman, Queen over a people apparently as extraordinary as herself, and reigning amidst the vestiges of a lost civilisation? And what was the meaning of this story of the Fire that gave unending life? Could it be possible that any fluid or essence should exist which might so fortify these fleshy walls that they should from age to age resist the mines and batterings of decay? It was possible, though not probable. The indefinite continuation of life would not, as poor Vincey said, be so marvellous a thing as the production of life and its temporary endurance. And if it were true, what then? The person who found it could no doubt rule the world. He could accumulate all the wealth in the world, and all the power, and all the wisdom that is power. He might give a lifetime to the study of each art or science. Well, if that were so, and this *She* were practically immortal, which I did not for one moment believe, how was it that, with all these things at her feet, she preferred to remain in a cave amongst a society of cannibals? This surely settled the question. The whole story was monstrous, and only worthy of the superstitious days in which it was written. At any rate I was very sure that *I* would not attempt to attain unending life. I had had far too many worries and disappointments and secret bitternesses during my forty odd years of existence to wish that this state of affairs should be continued indefinitely. And yet I suppose that my life has been, comparatively speaking, a happy one.

And then, reflecting that at the present moment there was far more likelihood of our earthly careers being cut exceedingly short than of their being unduly prolonged, I at last managed to get to sleep, a fact for which anybody who reads this narrative, if anybody ever does, may very probably be thankful.

When I woke again it was just dawning, and the guard and bearers were moving about like ghosts through the dense morning mists, getting ready for our start. The fire had died quite down, and I rose and stretched myself, shivering in every limb from the damp cold of the dawn. Then I looked at Leo. He was sitting up, holding his hands to his head, and I saw that his face was flushed and his eye bright, and yet yellow round the pupil.

'Well, Leo,' I said, 'how do you feel?'

'I feel as though I were going to die,' he answered hoarsely. 'My head is splitting, my body is trembling, and I am as sick as a cat.'

I whistled, or if I did not whistle I felt inclined to—Leo had got a sharp attack of fever. I went to Job, and asked him for the quinine, of which fortunately we had still a good supply, only to find that Job himself was not much better. He complained of pains across the back, and dizziness, and was almost incapable of helping himself. Then I did the only thing it was possible to do under the circumstances—gave them both about ten grains of quinine, and took a slightly smaller dose myself as a matter of precaution. After that I found Billali, and explained to him how matters stood, asking at the same time what he thought had best be done. He came with me, and looked at Leo and Job (whom, by the way, he had named the Pig on account of his fatness, round face, and small eyes).

'Ah,' he said, when we were out of earshot, 'the fever! I thought so. The Lion has it badly, but he is young, and he may live. As for the Pig, his attack is not so bad; it is the "little fever" which he has; that always begins with pains across the back, it will spend itself upon his fat.'

'Can they go on, my father?' I asked.

'Nay, my son, they must go on. If they stop here they will certainly die; also, they will be better in the litters than on the ground. By to-night, if all goes well, we shall be across the marsh and in good air. Come, let us lift them into the litters and start, for it is very bad to stand still in this morning fog. We can eat our meal as we go.'

This we accordingly did, and with a heavy heart I once more set out upon our strange journey. For the first three hours all went as well as could be expected, and then an accident happened that nearly lost us the pleasure of the company of our venerable friend Billali, whose litter was leading the cavalcade. We were going through a particularly dangerous stretch of quagmire, in which the bearers sometimes sank up to their knees. Indeed, it was a mystery to me how they contrived to carry the heavy litters at all over such ground as that which we were traversing, though the two spare hands, as well as the four regular ones, had of course to put their shoulders to the pole.

Presently, as we blundered and floundered along, there was a sharp cry, then a storm of exclamations, and, last of all, a most tremendous splash, and the whole caravan halted.

I jumped out of my litter and ran forward. About twenty yards ahead was the edge of one of those sullen peaty pools of which I have spoken, the path we were following running along the top of its bank, that, as it happened, was a steep one. Looking towards this pool, to my horror I saw that Billali's litter was floating on it, and as for Billali himself, he was nowhere to be seen. To make matters clear I may as well explain at once what had happened.

One of Billali's bearers had unfortunately trodden on a basking snake, which had bitten him in the leg, whereon he had, not unnaturally, let go of the pole, and then, finding that he was tumbling down the bank, grasped at the litter to save himself. The result of this was what might have been expected. The litter was pulled over the edge of the bank, the bearers let go, and the whole thing, including Billali and the man who had been bitten, rolled into the slimy pool. When I got to the edge of the water neither of them were to be seen, and, indeed, the unfortunate bearer never was seen again. Either he struck his head against something, or got wedged in the mud, or possibly the snake-bite paralysed him. At any rate, he vanished. But though Billali was not to be seen, his whereabouts was clear enough from the agitation of the floating litter, in the bearing cloth and curtains of which he was entangled.

'He is there! Our father is there!' said one of the men, but he did not stir a finger to help him, nor did any of the others. They simply stood and stared at the water.

'Out of the way, you brutes,' I shouted in English, and throwing off my hat I took a run and sprang well out into the horrid slimy-looking pool. A couple of strokes took me to where Billali was struggling beneath the cloth.

Somehow, I do not quite know how, I managed to push this free of him, and his venerable head all covered with green slime, like that of a yellowish Bacchus[3] with ivy leaves, emerged upon the surface of the water. The rest was easy, for Billali was an eminently practical individual, and had the common sense not to grasp hold of me as drowning people often do, so I got him by the arm, and towed him to the bank, through the mud of which we were with difficulty dragged. Such a filthy spectacle as we presented I have never seen before or since, and it will perhaps give some idea of the almost superhuman dignity of Billali's appearance when I say that, coughing, half-drowned, and covered with mud and green slime as he was, with his beautiful beard coming to a dripping point, like a Chinaman's freshly oiled pigtail, he still looked venerable and imposing.

'Ye dogs,' he said, addressing the bearers, as soon as he had sufficiently recovered to speak, 'ye left me, your father, to drown. Had it not been for this stranger, my son the Baboon, assuredly I should have drowned. Well, I will remember it,' and he fixed them with his gleaming though slightly watery eye, in a way I saw they did not like, though they tried to appear sulkily indifferent.

'As for thee, my son,' the old man went on, turning towards me and grasping my hand, 'rest assured that I am thy friend through good and evil. Thou hast saved my life: perchance a day may come when I shall save thine.'

After that we cleaned ourselves as best we could, fished out the litter, and went on, *minus* the man who had been drowned. I do not know if it was owing to his being an unpopular character, or from native indifference and selfishness of temperament, but I am bound to say that nobody seemed to grieve much over his sudden and final disappearance, unless, perhaps, it was the men who had to do his share of the work.

XI

The Plain of Kôr

About an hour before sundown we at last, to my unbounded gratitude, emerged from the great belt of marsh on to land that swelled upwards in a succession of rolling waves. Just on the hither side of the crest of the first wave we halted for the night. My first act was to examine Leo's condition. It was, if anything, worse than in the morning, and a new and very distressing feature, vomiting, set in, and continued till dawn. Not one wink of sleep did I get that night, for I passed it in assisting Ustane, who was one of the most gentle and indefatigable nurses I ever saw, to wait upon Leo and Job. However, the air here was warm and genial without being too hot, and there were no mosquitoes to speak of. Also we were above the level of the marsh mist, which lay stretched beneath us like the dim smoke-pall over a city, lit up here and there by the wandering globes of fen fire. Thus it will be seen that we were, speaking comparatively, in clover.

By dawn on the following morning Leo was quite light-headed, and fancied that he was divided into halves. I was dreadfully distressed, and began to wonder with a sort of sick fear what the termination of the attack would be. Alas! I had heard but too much of how these attacks generally terminate. As I was doing so Billali came up and said that we must be getting on, more especially as, in his opinion, if Leo did not reach some spot where he could be quiet, and have proper nursing, within the next twelve hours, his life would only be a matter of a day or two. I could not but agree with him, so we got him into the litter, and started on, Ustane walking by Leo's side to keep the flies off him, and see that he did not throw himself out on to the ground.

Within half an hour of sunrise we had reached the top of the rise of which I have spoken, and a most beautiful view broke upon our gaze. Beneath us was a rich stretch of country, verdant with grass and lovely with foliage and flowers. In the background, at a distance, so far as I could judge, of some eighteen miles from where we then stood, a huge and extraordinary mountain rose abruptly from the plain. The base of this great mountain appeared to consist of a grassy slope, but rising from this, I should say, from subsequent observation, at a height of about five hundred feet above the level of the plain, was a most tremendous and absolutely precipitous wall of bare rock, quite twelve or fifteen hundred feet in height. The shape of the mountain, which was undoubtedly of volcanic origin, was round, and of course, as only a segment of its circle was visible, it was difficult to estimate its exact size, which was enormous. I afterwards discovered that it could not cover less than fifty square miles of ground. Anything more grand and imposing than the sight presented by this great natural castle, starting in solitary grandeur from the level of the plain, I never saw, and I suppose I never shall. Its very solitude added to its majesty, and its towering cliffs seemed to kiss the sky. Indeed, generally speaking, they were clothed in clouds that lay in fleecy masses upon their broad and level battlements.

I sat up in my hammock and gazed out across the plain at this thrilling and majestic sight, and I suppose that Billali noticed it, for he brought his litter alongside.

'Behold the House of "*She-who-must-be-obeyed*!"' he said. 'Had ever a queen such a throne before?'

'It is wonderful, my father,' I answered. 'But how do we enter? Those cliffs look hard to climb.'

'Thou shalt see, my Baboon. Look now at the plain below us. What thinkest thou that it is? Thou art a wise man. Come, tell me.'

I looked, and saw what appeared to be the line of roadway running straight towards the base of the mountain, though it was covered with turf. There were high banks on each side of it, broken here and there, but fairly continuous on the whole, the meaning of which I did not understand. It seemed so very odd that anybody should embank a roadway.

'Well, my father,' I answered, 'I suppose that it is a road, otherwise I should have been inclined to say that it was the bed of a river, or rather,' I added, observing the extraordinary directness of the cutting, 'of a canal.'

Billali—who, by the way, was none the worse for his immersion of the day before—nodded his head sagely as he replied—

'Thou art right, my son. It is a channel cut out by those who were before us in this place to carry away water. Of this am I sure: within the rocky circle of the great mountain whither we journey was once a great lake. But those who were before us, by wonderful arts of which I know naught, hewed a path for the water through the solid rock of the mountain, piercing even to the bed of the lake. But first they cut the channel that thou seest across the plain. Then, when at last the water burst out, it rushed down the channel that had been made to receive it, and crossed this plain till it reached the low land behind the rise, and there, perchance, it made the swamp through which we had come. Then when the lake was drained dry, the people whereof I speak built a mighty city, whereof naught but ruins and the name of Kôr yet remaineth, on its bed, and from age to age hewed the caves and passages that thou wilt see.'

'It may be,' I answered; 'but if so, how is it that the lake does not fill up again with the rains and the water of the springs?'

'Nay, my son, the people were a wise people, and they left a drain to keep it clear. Seest thou the river to the right?' and he pointed to a fair-sized stream that wound away across the plain, some four miles from us. 'That is the drain, and it comes out through the mountain wall where this cutting goes in. At first, perhaps, the water ran down this canal, but afterwards the people turned it, and used the cutting for a road.'

'And is there then no other place where one may enter into the great mountain,' I asked, 'except through the drain?'

'There is a place,' he answered, 'where cattle and men on foot may cross with much labour, but it is secret. A year mightest thou search and shouldst never find it. It is only used once a year, when the herds of cattle that have been fatting on the slopes of the mountain, and on this plain, are driven into the space within.'

'And does *She* live there always?' I asked, 'or does she come at times without the mountain?'

'Nay, my son, where she is, there she is.'

By now we were well on to the great plain, and I was examining with delight the varied beauty of its semi-tropical flowers and trees, the latter of which grew singly, or at most in clumps of three or four, much of the timber being of large size, and belonging apparently to a variety of evergreen oak. There were also many palms, some of them more than one hundred feet high, and the largest and most beautiful tree ferns that I ever saw, about which hung clouds of jewelled honeysuckers[1] and great-winged butterflies. Wandering about among the trees or crouching in the long and feathered grass were all varieties of game, from rhinoceroses down. I saw rhinoceros, buffalo (a large herd), eland, quagga,[2] and sable antelope, the most beautiful of all the bucks, not to mention many smaller varieties of game, and three ostriches which scudded away at our approach like white drift before a gale. So plentiful was the game that at last I could stand it no longer. I had a single-barrel sporting Martini[3] with me in the litter, the 'Express' being too cumbersome, and espying a beautiful fat eland rubbing himself under one of the oak-like trees, I jumped out of the litter, and proceeded to creep as near to him as I could. He let me come within eighty yards, and then turned his head, and stared at me, preparatory to running away. I lifted the rifle, and taking him about midway down the shoulder, for he was side on to me, fired. I never made a cleaner shot or a better kill in all my small experience, for the great buck sprang right up into the air and fell dead. The bearers, who had all halted to see the performance, gave a murmur of surprise, an unwonted compliment from these sullen people, who never appear to be surprised at anything, and a party of the guard at once ran off to cut the animal up. As for myself, though I was longing to have a look at him, I sauntered back to my litter as though I had been in the habit of killing eland all my life, feeling that I had gone up several degrees in the estimation of the Amahagger, who looked on the whole thing as a very high-class manifestation of witchcraft. As a matter of fact, however, I had never seen an eland in a wild state before. Billali received me with enthusiasm.

'It is wonderful, my son the Baboon,' he cried; 'wonderful! Thou art a very great man, though so ugly. Had I not seen, surely I would never have believed. And thou sayest that thou wilt teach me to slay in this fashion?'

'Certainly, my father,' I said airily; 'it is nothing.'

But all the same I firmly made up my mind that when 'my father' Billali began to fire I would without fail lie down or take refuge behind a tree.

After this little incident nothing happened of any note till about an hour and a half before sundown, when we arrived beneath the shadow of the towering volcanic mass that I have already described. It is quite impossible for me to describe its grim grandeur as it appeared to me while my patient bearers toiled along the bed of the ancient watercourse towards the spot where the rich brown-clad cliff shot up from precipice to precipice till its crown lost itself in cloud. All I can say is that it almost awed me by the intensity of its lonesome and most solemn greatness. On we went up the bright and sunny slope, till at last the creeping shadows from above swallowed up its brightness, and presently we began to pass through a cutting hewn in the living rock. Deeper and deeper grew this marvellous work, which must, I should say, have employed thousands of men for many years. Indeed how it was ever executed at all without the aid of blasting-powder or dynamite I cannot to this day imagine. It is and must remain one of the mysteries of that wild land. I can only suppose that these cuttings and the vast caves that had been hollowed out of the rocks they pierced were the State undertakings of the people of Kôr, who lived here in the dim lost ages of the world, and, as in the case of the Egyptian monuments, were executed by the forced labour of tens of thousands of captives, carried on through an indefinite number of centuries. But who were the people?

At last we reached the face of the precipice itself, and found ourselves looking into the mouth of a dark tunnel that forcibly reminded me of those undertaken by our nineteenth-century engineers in the construction of railway lines. Out of this tunnel flowed a considerable stream of water. Indeed, though I do not think that I have mentioned it, we had followed this stream, which ultimately developed into the river I have already described as winding away to the right, from the spot where the cutting in the solid rock commenced. Half of this cutting formed a channel for the stream, and half, which was placed on a slightly higher level—eight feet perhaps—was devoted to the purposes of a roadway. At the termination of the cutting, however, the stream turned off across the plain and followed a channel of its own. At the mouth of the cave the cavalcade was halted, and, while the men employed themselves in lighting some earthenware lamps they had brought with them, Billali, descending from his litter, informed me politely but firmly that the orders of *She* were that we were now to be blindfolded, so that we should not learn the secret of the paths through the bowels of the mountains. To this I, of course, assented cheerfully enough, but Job, who was now very much better, notwithstanding the journey, did not like it at all, fancying, I believe, that it was but a preliminary step to being hot-potted. He was, however, a little consoled when I pointed out to him that there were no hot pots at hand, and, so far as I knew, no fire to heat them in. As for poor Leo, after turning restlessly for hours, he had, to my deep thankfulness, at last dropped off into a sleep or stupor, I do not know which, so there was no need to blindfold him. The blindfolding was performed by binding a piece of the yellowish linen whereof those of the Amahagger who condescended to wear anything in particular made their dresses tightly round the eyes. This linen

I afterwards discovered was taken from the tombs, and was not, as I had at first supposed, of native manufacture. The bandage was then knotted at the back of the head, and finally brought down again and the ends bound under the chin to prevent its slipping. Ustane was, by the way, also blindfolded, I do not know why, unless it was from fear that she should impart the secrets of the route to us.

This operation performed we started on once more, and soon, by the echoing sound of the footsteps of the bearers and the increased noise of the water caused by reverberation in a confined space, I knew that we were entering into the bowels of the great mountain. It was an eerie sensation, being borne along into the dead heart of the rock we knew not whither, but I was getting used to eerie sensations by this time, and by now was pretty well prepared for anything. So I lay still, and listened to the tramp, tramp of the bearers and the rushing of the water, and tried to believe that I was enjoying myself. Presently the men set up the melancholy little chant that I had heard on the first night when we were captured in the whale-boat, and the effect produced by their voices was very curious, and quite indescribable on paper. After a while the air began to get exceedingly thick and heavy, so much so, indeed, that I felt as though I were going to choke, till at length the litter took a sharp turn, then another and another, and the sound of the running water ceased. After this the air got fresher again, but the turns were continuous, and to me, blindfolded as I was, most bewildering. I tried to keep a map of them in my mind in case it might ever be necessary for us to try and escape by this route, but, needless to say, failed utterly. Another half-hour or so passed, and then suddenly I became aware that we were once more in the open air. I could see the light through my bandage and feel its freshness on my face. A few more minutes and the caravan halted, and I heard Billali order Ustane to remove her bandage and undo ours. Without waiting for her attentions I got the knot of mine loose, and looked out.

As I anticipated, we had passed right through the precipice, and were now on the farther side, and immediately beneath its beetling face. The first thing I noticed was that the cliff was not nearly so high here, not so high I should say by five hundred feet, which proved that the bed of the lake, or rather of the vast ancient crater in which we stood, was much above the level of the surrounding plain. For the rest, we found ourselves in a huge rock-surrounded cup, not unlike that of the first place where we had sojourned, only ten times the size. Indeed, I could only just make out the frowning line of the opposite cliffs. A great portion of the plain thus enclosed by nature was cultivated, and fenced in with walls of stone placed there to keep the cattle and goats, of which there were large herds about, from breaking into the gardens. Here and there rose great grass mounds, and some miles away towards the centre I thought that I could see the outline of colossal ruins. I had no time to observe anything more at the moment, for we were instantly surrounded by crowds of Amahagger, similar in every particular to those with whom we were already familiar, who, though they spoke little, pressed round us so closely as to obscure the view to a person lying in a hammock. Then all of a sudden a number of armed men arranged in companies, and marshalled by officers who held ivory wands in their hands, came running swiftly towards us, having, so far as I could make out, emerged from the face of the precipice like ants from their burrows. These men as well as their officers were all robed in addition to the usual leopard skin, and, as I gathered, formed the bodyguard of *She* herself.

Their leader advanced to Billali, saluted him by placing his ivory wand transversely across his forehead, and then asked some question which I could not catch, and Billali having answered him the whole regiment turned and marched along the side of the cliff, our cavalcade of litters following in their track. After going thus for about half a mile we halted once more in front of the mouth of a tremendous cave, measuring about sixty feet in height by eighty wide, and here Billali descended finally, and requested Job and myself to do the same. Leo, of course, was far too ill to do anything of the sort. I did so, and we entered the great cave, into which the light of the setting sun penetrated for some distance, while beyond the reach of the light it was faintly illuminated with lamps which seemed to me to stretch away for an almost immeasurable distance, like the gas lights of an empty London street. The first thing that I noticed was that the walls were covered with sculptures in bas-relief, of a sort, pictorially speaking, similar to those that I have described upon the vases;—love-scenes principally, then hunting pictures, pictures of executions, and the torture of criminals by the placing of a presumably red-hot pot upon the *head*, showing whence our hosts had derived this pleasant practice. There were very few battle-pieces, though many of duels, and men running and wrestling, and from this fact I am led to believe that this people was not much subject to attack by exterior foes, either on account of the isolation of their position or because of their great strength. Between the pictures were columns of stone characters of a formation absolutely new to me; at any rate they were neither Greek nor Egyptian, nor Hebrew, nor Assyrian—that I am sure of.[4] They looked more like Chinese writings than any other that I am acquainted with. Near to the entrance of the cave both pictures and writings were worn away, but further in they were in many cases absolutely fresh and perfect as the day on which the sculptor had ceased work upon them.

The regiment of guards did not come further than the entrance to the cave, where they formed up to let us pass through. On entering the place itself we were, however, met by a man robed in white, who bowed humbly, but said nothing, which, as it afterwards appeared that he was a deaf mute, was not very wonderful.

Running at right angles to the great cave, at a distance of some twenty feet from the entrance was a smaller, cave or wide gallery, that was pierced into the rock both to the right and to the left of the main cavern. In front of the gallery to our left stood two guards, from which circumstance I argued that it was the entrance to the apartments of *She* herself. The mouth of the right-hand gallery was unguarded, and along it the mute indicated that we were to proceed. Walking a few yards down this passage, which was lighted with lamps, we came to the entrance to a chamber having a curtain made of some grass material, not unlike a Zanzibar mat in appearance, hung over the doorway. This the mute drew back with another profound obeisance, and led the way into a good-sized apartment, hewn, of course, out of the solid rock, but to my great delight lighted by means of a shaft pierced in the face of the precipice. In this room was a stone bedstead, pots full of water for washing, and beautifully tanned leopard skins to serve as blankets.

Here we left Leo, who was still sleeping heavily, and with him stopped Ustane. I noticed that the mute gave her a very sharp look, as much as to say, 'Who are you, and by whose orders do you come here?' Then he conducted us to another similar room which Job took, and then to two more that were respectively occupied by Billali and myself.

XII

'She'

The first care of Job and myself, after seeing to Leo, was to wash ourselves and put on clean clothing, for what we were wearing had not been changed since the loss of the dhow. Fortunately, as I think that I have said, by far the greater part of our personal baggage had been packed into the whale-boat, and was therefore saved—and brought hither by the bearers—although all the stores laid in by us for barter and presents to the natives were lost. Nearly all our clothing was made of a well-shrunk and very strong grey flannel, and excellent I found it for travelling in these places, because though a Norfolk jacket, shirt, and pair of trousers of it only weighed about four pounds, a great consideration in a tropical country, where every extra ounce tells on the wearer, it was warm, and offered a good resistance to the rays of the sun, and best of all to chills, which are so apt to result from sudden changes of temperature.

Never shall I forget the comfort of the 'wash and brush-up,' and of those clean flannels. The only thing that was wanting to complete my joy was a cake of soap, of which we had none.

Afterwards I discovered that the Amahagger, who do not reckon dirt among their many disagreeable qualities, use a kind of burnt earth for washing purposes, which, though unpleasant to the touch till one gets accustomed to it, forms a very fair substitute for soap.

By the time that I was dressed, and had combed and trimmed my black beard, the previous condition of which was certainly sufficiently unkempt to give weight to Billali's appellation for me, the 'Baboon,' I began to feel most uncommonly hungry. Therefore I was by no means sorry when, without the slightest preparatory sound or warning, the curtain over the entrance to my cave was flung aside, and another mute, a young girl this time, announced to me by signs that I could not misunderstand—that is, by opening her mouth and pointing down it—that there was something ready to eat. Accordingly I followed her into the next chamber, which we had not yet entered, where I found Job, who had also, to his great embarrassment, been conducted thither by a fair mute. Job had never got over the advances the former lady had made towards him, and suspected every girl who came near to him of similar designs.

'These young parties have a way of looking at one, sir,' he would say apologetically, 'which I don't call respectable.'

This chamber was twice the size of the sleeping caves, and I saw at once that it had originally served as a refectory, and also probably as an embalming room for the Priests of the Dead; for I may as well say at once that these hollowed-out caves were nothing more or less than vast catacombs, in which for tens of ages the mortal remains of the great extinct race whose monuments surrounded us had been first preserved, with an art and a completeness that has never since been equalled, and then hidden away for all time. On each side of this particular rock-chamber was a long and solid stone table, about three feet wide by three feet six in height, hewn out of the living rock, of which it had formed part, and was still attached to at the base. These tables were slightly hollowed out or curved inward, to give room for the knees of any one sitting on the stone ledge that had been cut for a bench along the side of the cave at a distance of about two feet from them. Each of them, also, was so arranged that it ended right under a shaft pierced in the rock for the admission of light and air. On examining them carefully, however, I saw that there was a difference between them that had at first escaped my attention, viz. that one of the tables, that to the left as we entered the cave, had evidently been used, not to eat upon, but for the purposes of embalming. That this was beyond all question the case was clear from five shallow depressions in the stone of the table, all shaped like a human form, with a separate place for the head to lie in, and a little bridge to support the neck, each depression being of a different size, so as to fit bodies varying in stature from a full-grown man's to a small child's, and with little holes bored at intervals to carry off fluid. And, indeed, if any further confirmation was required, we had but to look at the wall of the cave above to find it. For there, sculptured all round the apartment, and looking nearly as fresh as the day it was done, was the pictorial representation of the death, embalming, and burial of an old man with a long beard, probably an ancient king or grandee of this country.

The first picture represented his death. He was lying upon a couch which had four short curved posts at the corners coming to a knob at the end, in appearance something like a written note of music, and was evidently in the very act of expiring. Gathered round the couch were women and children weeping, the former with their hair hanging down their back. The next scene represented the embalmment of the body, which lay nude upon a table with depressions in it, similar to the one before us; probably, indeed, it was a picture of the same table. Three men were employed at the work—one superintending, one holding a funnel shaped exactly like a port wine strainer, of which the narrow end was fixed in an incision in the breast, no doubt in the great pectoral artery; while the third, who was depicted as standing straddle-legged over the corpse, held a kind of large jug high in his hand, and poured from it some steaming fluid which fell accurately into the funnel. The most curious part of this sculpture is that both the man with the funnel and the man who poured the fluid are drawn holding their noses, either I suppose because of the stench arising from the body, or more probably to keep out the aromatic fumes of the hot fluid which was being forced into the dead man's veins. Another curious thing which I am unable to explain is that all three men were represented as having a band of linen tied round the face with holes in it for the eyes.

The third sculpture was a picture of the burial of the deceased. There he was, stiff and cold, clothed in a linen robe, and laid out on a stone slab such as I had slept upon at our first sojourning-place. At his head and feet burnt lamps, and by his side were placed several of the beautiful painted vases that I have described, which were perhaps supposed to be full of provisions. The little chamber was crowded with mourners, and with musicians playing on an instrument resembling a lyre, while near the foot of the corpse stood a man with a sheet, with which he was preparing to cover it from view.

These sculptures, looked at merely as works of art, were so remarkable that I make no apology for describing them rather fully. They struck me also as being of surpassing interest as representing, probably with studious accuracy, the last rites of the dead as practised among an utterly lost people, and even then I thought how envious some antiquarian friends of my own at Cambridge would be if ever I got an opportunity of describing these wonderful remains to them. Probably they would say that I was exaggerating, notwithstanding that every page of this history must bear so much internal evidence of its truth that it would obviously have been quite impossible for me to have invented it.

To return. As soon as I had hastily examined these sculptures, which I think I omitted to mention were executed in relief, we sat down to a very excellent meal of boiled goat's-flesh, fresh milk, and cakes made of meal, the whole being served upon clean wooden platters.

When we had eaten we returned to see how poor Leo was getting on, Billali saying that he must now wait upon *She*, and hear her commands. On reaching Leo's room we found the poor boy in a very bad way. He had woke up from his torpor, and was altogether off his head, babbling about some boat-race on the Cam, and was inclined to be violent. Indeed, when we entered the room Ustane was holding him down. I spoke to him, and my voice seemed to soothe him; at any rate he grew much quieter, and was persuaded to swallow a dose of quinine.

I had been sitting with him for an hour, perhaps—at any rate I know that it was getting so dark that I could only just make out his head lying like a gleam of gold upon the pillow we had extemporised out of a bag covered with a blanket—when suddenly Billali arrived with an air of great importance, and informed me that *She* herself had deigned to express a wish to see me—an honour, he added, accorded to but very few. I think that he was a little horrified at my cool way of taking the honour, but the fact was that I did not feel overwhelmed with gratitude at the prospect of seeing some savage, dusky queen, however absolute and mysterious she might be, more especially as my mind was full of dear Leo, for whose life I began to have great fears. However, I rose to follow him, and as I did so I caught sight of something bright lying on the floor, which I picked up. Perhaps the reader will remember that with the potsherd in the casket was a composition scarabæus marked with a round O, a goose, and another curious hieroglyphic, the meaning of which signs is 'Suten se Rā,' or 'Royal Son of the Sun.' This scarab, which is a very small one, Leo had insisted upon having set in a massive gold ring, such as is generally used for signets, and it was this very ring that I now picked up. He had pulled it off in the paroxysm of his fever, at least I suppose so, and flung it down upon the rock-floor. Thinking that if I left it about it might get lost, I slipped it on to my own little finger, and then followed Billali, leaving Job and Ustane with Leo.

We passed down the passage, crossed the great aisle-like cave, and came to the corresponding passage on the other side, at the mouth of which the guards stood like two statues. As we came they bowed their heads in salutation, and then lifting their long spears placed them transversely across their foreheads, as the leaders of the troop that had met us had done with their ivory wands. We stepped between them, and found ourselves in an exactly similar gallery to that which led to our own apartments, only this passage was, comparatively speaking, brilliantly lighted. A few paces down it we were met by four mutes—two men and two women—who bowed low and then arranged themselves, the women in front and the men behind of us, and in this order we continued our procession past several doorways hung with curtains resembling those leading to our own quarters, and which I afterwards found opened out into chambers occupied by the mutes who attended on *She*. A few paces more and we came to another doorway facing us, and not to our left like the others, which seemed to mark the termination of the passage. Here two more white-, or rather yellow-robed guards were standing, and they too bowed, saluted, and let us pass through heavy curtains into a great antechamber, quite forty feet long by as many wide, in which some eight or ten women, most of them young and handsome, with yellowish hair, sat on cushions working with ivory needles at what had the appearance of being embroidery-frames. These women were also deaf and dumb. At the farther end of this great lamp-lit apartment was another doorway closed in with heavy Oriental-looking curtains, quite unlike those that hung before the doors of our own rooms, and here stood two particularly handsome girl mutes, their heads bowed upon their bosoms and their hands crossed in an attitude of the humblest submission. As we advanced they each stretched out an arm and drew back the curtains. Thereupon Billali did a curious thing. Down he went, that venerable-looking old gentleman—for Billali is a gentleman at the bottom—down on to his hands and knees, and in this undignified position, with his long white beard trailing on the ground, he began to creep into the apartment beyond. I followed him, standing on my feet in the usual fashion. Looking over his shoulder he perceived it.

'Down, my son; down, my Baboon; down on to thy hands and knees. We enter the presence of *She*, and, if thou are not humble, of a surety she will blast thee where thou standest.'

I halted, and felt scared. Indeed, my knees began to give way of their own mere motion; but reflection came to my aid. I was an Englishman, and why, I asked myself, should I creep into the presence of some savage woman as though I were a monkey in fact as well as in name? I would not and could not do it, that is, unless I was absolutely sure that my life or comfort depended upon it. If once I began to creep upon my knees I should always have to do so, and it would be a patent acknowledgment of inferiority. So, fortified by an insular prejudice against 'kootooing,'[1] which has, like most of our so-called prejudices, a good deal of common sense to recommend it, I marched in boldly after Billali. I found myself in another apartment, considerably smaller than the anteroom, of which the walls were entirely hung with rich-looking curtains of the same make as those over the door, the work, as I subsequently discovered, of the mutes who sat in the antechamber and wove them in strips, which were afterwards sewn together. Also, here and there about the room, were settees of a beautiful black wood of the ebony tribe, inlaid with ivory, and all over the floor were other tapestries, or rather rugs. At the top end of this apartment was what appeared to be a recess, also draped with curtains, through which shone rays of light. There was nobody in the place except ourselves.

Painfully and slowly old Billali crept up the length of the cave, and with the most dignified stride that I could command I followed after him. But I felt that it was more or less of a failure. To begin with, it is not possible to look dignified when you are following in the wake of an old man writhing along on his stomach like a snake, and then, in order to go sufficiently slowly, either I had to keep my leg some seconds in the air at every step, or else to advance with a full stop between each stride, like Mary Queen of Scots[2] going to execution in a play. Billali was not good at crawling, I suppose his years stood in the way, and our progress up that apartment was a very long affair. I was immediately behind him, and several times I was sorely tempted to help him on with a good kick. It is so absurd to advance into the presence of savage royalty after the fashion of an Irishman driving a pig to market, for that is what we looked like, and the idea nearly made me burst out laughing then and there. I had to work off my dangerous tendency to unseemly merriment by blowing my nose, a proceeding which filled old Billali with horror, for he looked over his shoulder and made a ghastly face at me, and I heard him murmur, 'Oh, my poor Baboon!'

At last we reached the curtains, and here Billali collapsed flat on to his stomach, with his hands stretched out before him as though he were dead, and I, not knowing what to do, began to stare about the place. But presently I clearly felt that somebody was looking at me from behind the curtains. I could not see the person, but I could distinctly feel his or her gaze, and, what is more, it produced a very odd effect upon my nerves. I was frightened, I do not know why. The place was a strange one, it is true, and looked lonely, notwithstanding its rich hangings and the soft glow of the lamps—indeed, these accessories added to, rather than detracted from its loneliness, just as a lighted street at night has always a more solitary appearance than a dark one. It was so silent in the place, and there lay Billali like one dead before the heavy curtains, through which the odour of perfume seemed to float up towards the gloom of the arched roof above. Minute grew into minute, and still there was no sign of life, nor did the curtain move; but I felt the gaze of the unknown being sinking through and through me, and filling me with a nameless terror, till the perspiration stood in beads upon my brow.

At length the curtain began to move. Who could be behind it?—some naked savage queen, a languishing Oriental beauty, or a nineteenth-century young lady, drinking afternoon tea? I had not the slightest idea, and should not have been astonished at seeing any of the three. I was getting beyond astonishment. The curtain agitated itself a little, then suddenly between its folds there appeared a most beautiful white hand (white as snow), and with long tapering fingers, ending in the pinkest nails. The hand grasped the curtain, and drew it aside, and as it did so I heard a voice, I think the softest and yet most silvery voice I ever heard. It reminded me of the murmur of a brook.

'Stranger,' said the voice in Arabic, but much purer and more classical Arabic than the Amahagger talk—'stranger, wherefore art thou so much afraid?'

Now I flattered myself that in spite of my inward terrors I had kept a very fair command of my countenance, and was, therefore, a little astonished at this question. Before I had made up my mind how to answer it, however, the curtain was drawn, and a tall figure stood before us. I say a figure, for not only the body, but also the face was wrapped up in soft white, gauzy material in such a way as at first sight to remind me most forcibly of a corpse in its grave-clothes. And yet I do not know why it should have given me that idea, seeing that the wrappings were so thin that one could distinctly see the gleam of the pink flesh beneath them. I suppose it was owing to the way in which they were arranged, either accidentally, or more probably by design. Anyhow, I felt more frightened than ever at this ghost-like apparition, and my hair began to rise upon my head as the feeling crept over me that I was in the presence of something that was not canny. I could, however, clearly distinguish that the swathed mummy-like form before me was that of a tall and lovely woman, instinct with beauty in every part, and also with a certain snake-like grace which I had never seen anything to equal before. When she moved a hand or foot her entire frame seemed to undulate, and the neck did not bend, it curved.

'Why art thou so frightened, stranger?' asked the sweet voice again—a voice which seemed to draw the heart out of me, like the strains of softest music. 'Is there that about me that should affright a man? Then surely are men changed from what they used to be!' And with a little coquettish movement she turned herself, and held up one arm, so as to show all her loveliness and the rich hair of raven blackness that streamed in soft ripples down her snowy robes, almost to her sandalled feet.

'It is thy beauty that makes me fear, oh Queen,' I answered humbly, scarcely knowing what to say, and I thought that as I did so I heard old Billali, who was still lying prostrate on the floor, mutter, 'Good, my Baboon, good.'

'I see that men still know how to beguile us women with false words. Ah, stranger,' she answered, with a laugh that sounded like distant silver bells, 'thou wast afraid because mine eyes were searching out thine heart, therefore wast thou afraid. But being but a woman, I forgive thee for the lie, for it was courteously said. And now tell me how came ye hither to this land of the dwellers among caves—a land of swamps and evil things and dead old shadows of the dead? What came ye for to see? How is it that ye hold your lives so cheap as to place them in the hollow of the hand of *Hiya*, into the hand of "*She-who-must-be-obeyed*"? Tell me also how come ye to know the tongue I talk. It is an ancient tongue, that sweet child of the old Syriac. Liveth it yet in the world? Thou seest I dwell among the caves and the dead, and naught know I of the affairs of men, nor have I cared to know. I have lived, oh stranger, with my memories, and my memories are in a grave that mine own hands hollowed, for truly hath it been said that the child of man maketh his own path evil;' and her beautiful voice quivered, and broke in a note as soft as any wood-bird's. Suddenly her eye fell upon the sprawling frame of Billali, and she seemed to recollect herself.

'Ah! thou art there, old man. Tell me how it is that things have gone wrong in thine household. Forsooth, it seems that these my guests were set upon. Ay, and one was nigh to being slain by the hot pot to be eaten of those brutes, thy children, and had not the others fought gallantly they too had been slain, and not even I could have called back the life which had been loosed from the body. What means it, old man? What hast thou to say that I should not give thee over to those who execute my vengeance?'

Her voice had risen in her anger, and it rang clear and cold against the rocky walls. Also I thought I could see her eyes flash through the gauze that hid them. I saw poor Billali, whom I had believed to be a very fearless person, positively quiver with terror at her words.

'Oh "Hiya!" oh *She*!' he said, without lifting his white head from the floor. 'Oh *She*, as thou art great be merciful, for I am now as ever thy servant to obey. It was no plan or fault of mine, oh *She*, it was those wicked ones who are called my children. Led on by a woman whom thy guest the Pig had scorned, they would have followed the ancient custom of the land, and eaten the fat black stranger who came hither with these thy guests the Baboon and the Lion who is sick, thinking that no word had come from thee about the Black one. But when the Baboon and the Lion saw what they would do, they slew the woman, and slew also their servant to save him from the horror of the pot. Then those evil ones, ay, those children of the Wicked One who lives in the Pit, they went mad with the lust of blood, and flew at the throats of the Lion and the Baboon and the Pig. But gallantly they fought. Oh *Hiya*! they fought like very men, and slew many, and held their own, and then I came and saved them, and the evildoers have I sent on hither to Kôr to be judged of thy greatness, oh *She*! and here they are.'

'Ay, old man, I know it, and to-morrow will I sit in the great hall and do justice upon them, fear not. And for thee, I forgive thee, though hardly. See that thou dost keep thine household better. Go.'

Billali rose upon his knees with astonishing alacrity, bowed his head thrice, and, his white beard sweeping the ground, crawled down the apartment as he had crawled up it, till he finally vanished through the curtains, leaving me, not a little to my alarm, alone with this terrible but most fascinating person.

XIII

Ayesha Unveils

'There,' said *She*, 'he has gone, the white-bearded old fool! Ah, how little knowledge does a man acquire in his life. He gathereth it up like water, but like water it runneth through his fingers, and yet, if his hands be but wet as though with dew, behold a generation of fools call out, "See, he is a wise man!" Is it not so? But how call they thee? "Baboon," he says,' and she laughed; 'but that is the fashion of these savages who lack imagination, and fly to the beasts they resemble for a name. How do they call thee in thine own country, stranger?'

'They call me Holly, oh Queen,' I answered.

'Holly,' she answered, speaking the word with difficulty, and yet with a most charming accent; 'and what is "Holly"?'

' "Holly" is a prickly tree,' I said.

'So. Well, thou hast a prickly and yet a tree-like look. Strong art thou, and ugly, but, if my wisdom be not at fault, honest at the core, and a staff to lean on. Also one who thinks. But stay, oh Holly, stand not there, enter with me and be seated by me. I would not see thee crawl before me like those slaves. I am aweary of their worship and their terror; sometimes when they vex me I could blast them for very sport, and to see the rest turn white, even to the heart.' And she held the curtain aside with her ivory hand to let me pass in.

I entered, shuddering. This woman was very terrible. Within the curtains was a recess, about twelve feet by ten, and in the recess was a couch and a table whereon stood fruit and sparkling water. By it, at its end, was a vessel like a font cut in carved stone, also full of pure water. The place was softly lit with lamps formed out of the beautiful vessels of which I have spoken, and the air and curtains were laden with a subtle perfume. Perfume too seemed to emanate from the glorious hair and white-clinging vestments of *She* herself. I entered the little room, and there stood uncertain.

'Sit,' said *She*, pointing to the couch. 'As yet thou hast no cause to fear me. If thou hast cause, thou shalt not fear for long, for I shall slay thee. Therefore let thy heart be light.'

I sat down on the end of the couch near to the font-like basin of water, and *She* sank down softly on to the other end.

'Now, Holly,' she said, 'how comest thou to speak Arabic? It is my own dear tongue, for Arabian am I by my birth, even "al Arab al Ariba" (an Arab of the Arabs), and of the race of our father Yárab, the son of Kâhtan, for in that fair and ancient city Ozal was I born, in the province of Yaman the Happy. Yet dost thou not speak it as we used to speak. Thy talk doth lack the music of the sweet tongue of the tribes of Hamyar which I was wont to hear.[1] Some of the words too seemed changed, even as among these Amahagger, who have debased and defiled its purity, so that I must speak with them in what is to me another tongue.'*

'I have studied it,' I answered, 'for many years. Also the language is spoken in Egypt and elsewhere.'

'So it is still spoken, and there is yet an Egypt? And what Pharaoh sits upon the throne? Still one of the spawn of the Persian Ochus, or are the Achæmenians gone, for far is it to the days of Ochus.'[2]

* Yárab the son of Kâhtan, who lived some centuries before the time of Abraham, was the father of the ancient Arabs, and gave its name Araba to the country. In speaking of herself as 'al Arab al Ariba,' *She* no doubt meant to convey that she was of the true Arab blood as distinguished from the naturalised Arabs, the descendants of Ismael, the son of Abraham and Hagar, who were known as 'al Arab al mostáreba.' The dialect of the Koreish was usually called the clear or 'perspicuous' Arabic, but the Hamaritic dialect approached nearer to the purity of the mother Syriac.—L. H. H.

'The Persians have been gone from Egypt for nigh two thousand years, and since then the Ptolemies, the Romans, and many others have flourished and held sway upon the Nile, and fallen when their time was ripe,' I said, aghast. 'What canst thou know of the Persian Artaxerxes?'

She laughed, and made no answer, and again a cold chill went through me. 'And Greece,' she said; 'is there still a Greece? Ah, I loved the Greeks. Beautiful were they as the day, and clever, but fierce at heart and fickle, notwithstanding.'

'Yes,' I said, 'there is a Greece; and, just now, is it once more a people.[3] Yet the Greeks of to-day are not what the Greeks of the old time were, and Greece herself is but a mockery of the Greece that was.'

'So! The Hebrews, are they yet at Jerusalem? And does the Temple that the wise king built stand, and if so, what God do they worship therein? Is their Messiah come, of whom they preached so much and prophesied so loudly, and doth He rule the earth?'

'The Jews are broken and gone, and the fragments of their people strew the world, and Jerusalem is no more. As for the temple that Herod built ——'[4]

'Herod!' she said. 'I know not Herod. But go on.'

'The Romans burnt it, and the Roman eagles flew across its ruins, and now Judæa is a desert.'

'So, so! They were a great people, those Romans, and went straight to their end—ay, they sped to it like Fate, or like their own eagles on their prey!—and left peace behind them.'

'Solitudinem faciunt, pacem appellant,' I suggested.[5]

'Ah, thou canst speak the Latin tongue, too!' she said, in surprise. 'It hath a strange ring in my ears after all these days, and it seems to me that thy accent does not fall as the Romans put it. Who was it wrote that? I know not the saying, but it is a true one of that great people. It seems that I have found a learned man—one whose hands have held the water of the world's knowledge. Knowest thou Greek also?'

'Yes, oh Queen, and something of Hebrew, but not to speak them well. They are all dead languages now.'

She clapped her hands in childish glee. 'Of a truth, ugly tree that thou art, thou growest the fruits of wisdom, oh, Holly,' she said, 'but of those Jews whom I hated, for they called me "heathen" when I would have taught them my philosophy. Did their Messiah come, and doth He rule the world?'

'Their Messiah came,' I answered with reverence; 'but He came poor and lowly, and they would have none of Him. They scourged Him, and crucified Him upon a tree, but yet His words and His works live on, for He was the Son of God, and now of a truth He doth rule half the world, but not with an Empire of the World.'

'Ah, the fierce-hearted wolves,' she said, 'the followers of Sense and of many gods—greedy of gain and faction-torn. I can see their dark faces yet. So they crucified their Messiah? Well can I believe it. That he was a Son of the Living Spirit would be naught to them, if indeed He was so, and of that we will talk afterwards. They would care naught for any God if he came not with pomp and power. They, a chosen people, a vessel of Him they call Jehovah, ay, and a vessel of Baal, and a vessel of Astoreth, and a vessel of the gods of the Egyptians—a high-stomached people, greedy of aught that brought them wealth and power. So they crucified their Messiah because He came in lowly guise—and now are they scattered about the earth. Why, if I remember, so said one of their prophets that it should be.[6] Well, let them go—they broke my heart, those Jews, and made me look with evil eyes across the world, ay, and drove me to this wilderness, this place of a people that was before them. When I would have taught them wisdom in Jerusalem they stoned me, ay, at the Gate of the Temple those white-bearded hypocrites and Rabbis hounded the people on to stone me! See, here is the mark of it to this day!' and with a sudden move she pulled up the gauzy wrapping on her rounded arm, and pointed to a little scar that showed red against its milky beauty.

I shrank back horrified.

'Pardon me, oh Queen,' I said, 'but I am bewildered. Nigh upon two thousand years have rolled across the earth since the

Jewish Messiah hung upon His cross at Golgotha. How then canst thou have taught thy philosophy to the Jews before He was? Thou art a woman, and no spirit. How can a woman live two thousand years? Why dost thou befool me, oh Queen?'

She leaned back on the couch, and once more I felt the hidden eyes playing upon me and searching out my heart.

'Oh man!' she said at last, speaking very slowly and deliberately, 'it seems that there are still things upon the earth of which thou knowest naught. Dost thou still believe that all things die, even as those very Jews believed? I tell thee that naught really dies. There is no such thing as Death, though there be a thing called Change. See,' and she pointed to some sculptures on the rocky wall. 'Three times two thousand years have passed since the last of the great race that hewed those pictures fell before the breath of the pestilence which destroyed them, yet are they not dead. E'en now they live; perchance their spirits are drawn toward us at this very hour,' and she glanced round. 'Of a surety it sometimes seems to me that my eyes can see them.'

'Yes, but to the world they are dead.'

'Ay, for a time; but even to the world are they born again and again. I, yes I, Ayesha*—for that is my name, stranger—I say to thee that I wait now for one I loved to be born again, and here I tarry till he finds me, knowing of a surety that hither he will come, and that here, and here only, shall he greet me. Why, dost thou suppose that I, who am all powerful, I, whose loveliness is more than the loveliness of the Grecian Helen, of whom they used to sing, and whose wisdom is wider, ay, far more wide and deep than the wisdom of Solomon the Wise,—I, who know the secrets of the earth and its riches, and can turn all things to my uses,—I, who have even for a while overcome Change, that ye call Death,—why, I say, oh stranger, dost thou think that I herd here with barbarians lower than the beasts?'

'I know not,' I said humbly.

'Because I wait for him I love. My life has perchance been

* Pronounced Assha.—L. H. H.

evil, I know not—for who can say what is evil and what good?—so I fear to die even if I could die, which I cannot until mine hour comes, to go and seek him where he is; for between us there might rise a wall I could not climb, at least, I dread it. Surely easy would it be also to lose the way in seeking in those great spaces wherein the planets wander on for ever. But the day will come, it may be when five thousand more years have passed, and are lost and melted into the vault of Time, even as the little clouds melt into the gloom of night, or it may be to-morrow, when he, my love, shall be born again, and then, following a law that is stronger than any human plan, he shall find me *here*, where once he knew me, and of a surety his heart will soften towards me though I sinned against him; ay, even though he know me not again, yet will he love me, if only for my beauty's sake.'

For a moment I was dumbfounded, and could not answer. The matter was too overpowering for my intellect to grasp.

'But even so, oh Queen,' I said at last, 'even if we men be born again and again, that is not so with thee, if thou speakest truly.' Here she looked up sharply, and once more I caught the flash of those hidden eyes; 'thou,' I went on hurriedly, 'who hast never died?'

'That is so,' she said; 'and it is so because I have, half by chance and half by learning, solved one of the great secrets of the world. Tell me, stranger: life is—why therefore should not life be lengthened for a while? What are ten or twenty or fifty thousand years in the history of life? Why in ten thousand years scarce will the rain and storms lessen a mountain top by a span in thickness? In two thousand years these caves have not changed, nothing has changed, but the beasts and man, who is as the beasts. There is naught that is wonderful about the matter, couldst thou but understand. Life is wonderful, ay, but that it should be a little lengthened is not wonderful. Nature hath her animating spirit as well as man, who is Nature's child, and he who can find that spirit, and let it breathe upon him, shall live with her life. He shall not live eternally, for Nature is not eternal, and she herself must die, even as the nature of the moon hath died. She herself must die, I say, or rather change and sleep till it be time for her to live again. But when shall she die? Not yet, I ween, and while she lives, so shall he who hath all her secret live with her. All I have it not, yet have I some, more perchance than any who were before me. Now, to thee I doubt not that this thing is a great mystery, therefore I will not overcome thee with it now. Another time will I tell thee more if the mood be on me, though perchance I shall never speak thereof again. Dost thou wonder how I knew that ye were coming to this land, and so saved your heads from the hot pot?'

'Ay, oh Queen,' I answered feebly.

'Then gaze upon that water,' and she pointed to the font-like vessel, and then, bending forward, held her hand over it.

I rose and gazed, and instantly the water darkened. Then it cleared, and I saw as distinctly as I ever saw anything in my life—I saw, I say, our boat upon that horrible canal. There was Leo lying at the bottom asleep in it, with a coat thrown over him to keep off the mosquitoes, in such a fashion as to hide his face, and myself, Job, and Mahomed towing on the bank.

I started back aghast, and cried out that it was magic, for I recognised the whole scene—it was one which had actually occurred.

'Nay, nay; oh, Holly,' she answered, 'it is no magic; that is a fiction of ignorance. There is no such thing as magic, though there is such a thing as a knowledge of the secrets of Nature. That water is my glass; in it I see what passes if I care to summon up the pictures, which is not often. Therein I can show thee what thou wilt of the past, if it be anything to do with this country and with what I have known, or anything that thou, the gazer, hast known. Think of a face if thou wilt, and it shall be reflected from thy mind upon the water. I know not all the secret yet—I can read nothing in the future. But it is an old secret; I did not find it. In Arabia and in Egypt the sorcerers knew it centuries ago. So one day I chanced to bethink me of that old canal—some twenty centuries ago I sailed upon it, and I was minded to look thereon again. And so I looked, and there I saw the boat and three men walking, and one, whose face I could not see, but a youth of a noble form, sleeping in the boat, and so I sent and saved ye. And now farewell. But stay, tell me of this youth—the Lion, as the old man calls him. I would look upon him, but he is sick, thou sayest—sick with the fever, and also wounded in the fray.'

'He is very sick,' I answered sadly; 'canst thou do nothing for him, oh Queen! who knowest so much?'

'Of a surety I can. I can cure him; but why speakest thou so sadly? Doth thou love the youth? Is he perchance thy son?'

'He is my adopted son, oh Queen! Shall he be brought in before thee?'

'Nay. How long hath the fever taken him?'

'This is the third day.'

'Good; then let him lie another day. Then will he perchance throw it off by his own strength, and that is better than that I should cure him, for my medicine is of a sort to shake the life in its very citadel. If, however, by to-morrow night, at that hour when the fever first took him, he doth not begin to mend, then will I come to him and cure him. Stay, who nurses him?'

'Our white servant, him whom Billali names the Pig; also,' and here I spoke with some little hesitation, 'a woman named Ustane, a very handsome woman of this country, who came and embraced him when first she saw him, and hath stayed by him ever since, as I understand is the fashion of thy people, oh Queen.'

'My people! speak not to me of my people,' she answered, hastily; 'these slaves are no people of mine, they are but dogs to do my bidding till the day of my deliverance comes; and, as for their customs, naught have I to do with them. Also, call me not Queen—I am sick of flattery and titles—call me Ayesha, the name hath a sweet sound in mine ears, it is an echo from the past. As for this Ustane, I know not. I wonder if it be she against whom I was warned, and whom I in turn did warn? Hath she—stay, I will see;' and, bending forward, she passed her hand over the font of water and gazed intently into it. 'See,' she said quietly, 'is that the woman?'

I looked into the water, and there, mirrored upon its placid surface, was the silhouette of Ustane's stately face. She was bending forward, with a look of infinite tenderness upon her features, watching something beneath her, and with her chestnut locks falling on to her right shoulder.

'It is she,' I said, in a low voice, for once more I felt much disturbed at this most uncommon sight. 'She watches Leo asleep.'

'Leo!' said Ayesha, in an absent voice; 'why, that is "lion" in the Latin tongue. The old man hath named happily for once. It is very strange,' she went on speaking to herself, 'very. So like—but it is not possible!' With an impatient gesture she passed her hand over the water once more. It darkened, and the image vanished silently and mysteriously as it had risen, and once more the lamplight, and the lamplight only, shone on the placid surface of that limpid, living mirror.

'Hast thou aught to ask me before thou goest, oh Holly?' she said, after a few moments' reflection. 'It is but a rude life that thou must live here, for these people are savages, and know not the ways of cultivated man. Not that I am troubled thereby, for, behold my food,' and she pointed to the fruit upon the little table. 'Naught but fruit doth ever pass my lips—fruit and cakes of flour, and a little water. I have bidden my girls to wait upon thee. They are mutes thou knowest, deaf are they and dumb, and therefore the safest of servants, save to those who can read their faces and their signs. I bred them so—it hath taken many centuries and much trouble; but at last I have triumphed. Once I succeeded before, but the race was too ugly, so I let it die away; but now, as thou seest, they are otherwise. Once, too, I reared a race of giants, but after a while Nature would no more of it, and it died away. Hast thou aught to ask of me?'

'Ay, one thing, oh Ayesha,' I said boldly; but feeling by no means as bold as I trust I looked. 'I would gaze upon thy face.'

She laughed out in her bell-like notes. 'Bethink thee, Holly,' she answered; 'bethink thee. It seems that thou knowest the old myths of the gods of Greece. Was there not one Actæon who perished miserably because he looked on too much beauty?[7] If I show thee my face, perchance thou wouldst perish miserably also; perchance thou wouldst eat out thy heart in impotent desire; for know I am not for thee—I am for no man, save one, who hath been, but is not yet.'

'As thou wilt, Ayesha,' I said. 'I fear not thy beauty. I have put my heart away from such vanity as woman's loveliness, that passes like a flower.'

'Nay, thou errest,' she said; 'that does *not* pass. My beauty endures even as I endure; still if thou wilt, oh rash man, have thy will; but blame not me if passion mount thy reason, as the Egyptian breakers used to mount a colt, and guide it whither thou wilt not. Never may the man to whom my beauty hath been unveiled put it from his mind, and therefore even with these savages do I go veiled, lest they vex me, and I should slay them. Say, wilt thou see?'

'I will,' I answered, my curiosity overpowering me.

She lifted her white and rounded arms—never had I seen such arms before—and slowly, very slowly, withdrew some fastening beneath her hair. Then all of a sudden the long, corpse-like wrappings fell from her to the ground, and my eyes travelled up her form, now only robed in a garb of clinging white that did but serve to show its perfect and imperial shape, instinct with a life that was more than life, and with a certain serpent-like grace that was more than human. On her little feet were sandals, fastened with studs of gold. Then came ankles more perfect than ever sculptor dreamed of. About the waist her white kirtle was fastened by a double-headed snake of solid gold, above which her gracious form swelled up in lines as pure as they were lovely, till the kirtle ended on the snowy argent of her breast, whereon her arms were folded. I gazed above them at her face, and—I do not exaggerate—shrank back blinded and amazed. I have heard of the beauty of celestial beings, now I saw it; only this beauty, with all its awful loveliness and purity, was *evil*—at least, at the time, it struck me as evil. How am I to describe it? I cannot—simply, I cannot! The man does not live whose pen could convey a sense of what I saw. I might talk of the great changing eyes of deepest, softest black, of the tinted face, of the broad and noble brow, on which the hair grew low, and delicate, straight features. But, beautiful, surpassingly beautiful as they all were, her loveliness did not lie in them. It lay rather, if it can be said to have had any fixed abiding place, in a visible majesty, in an imperial grace, in a godlike stamp of softened power, which shone upon that radiant countenance like a living halo. Never before had I guessed what beauty made sublime could be—and yet, the sublimity was a dark one—the glory was not all of heaven—though none the less was it glorious. Though the face before me was that of a young woman of certainly not more than thirty years, in perfect health, and the first flush of ripened beauty, yet it had stamped upon it a look of unutterable experience, and of deep acquaintance with grief and passion. Not even the lovely smile that crept about the dimples of her mouth could hide this shadow of sin and sorrow. It shone even in the light of the glorious eyes, it was present in the air of majesty, and it seemed to say: 'Behold me, lovely as no woman was or is, undying and half-divine; memory haunts me from age to age, and passion leads me by the hand—evil have I done, and with sorrow have I made acquaintance from age to age, and from age to age evil I shall do, and sorrow shall I know till my redemption comes.'

Drawn by some magnetic force which I could not resist, I let my eyes rest upon her shining orbs, and felt a current pass from them to me that bewildered and half-blinded me.

She laughed—ah, how musically! and nodded her little head at me with an air of sublimated coquetry that would have done credit to a Venus Victrix.[8]

'Rash man!' she said; 'like Actæon, thou hast had thy will; be careful lest, like Actæon, thou too dost perish miserably, torn to pieces by the ban-hounds[9] of thine own passions. I too, oh Holly, am a virgin goddess, not to be moved of any man, save one, and it is not thou. Say, hast thou seen enough!'

'I have looked on beauty, and I am blinded,' I said hoarsely, lifting my hand to cover up my eyes.

'So! what did I tell thee? Beauty is like the lightning; it is lovely, but it destroys—especially trees, oh Holly!' And again she nodded and laughed.

Suddenly she paused, and through my fingers I saw an awful change come over her countenance. Her great eyes suddenly fixed themselves into an expression in which horror seemed to struggle with some tremendous hope arising through the depths of her dark soul. The lovely face grew rigid, and the gracious, willowy form seemed to erect itself.

'Man,' she half whispered, half hissed, throwing back her head like a snake about to strike—'man, where didst thou get that scarab on thy hand? Speak, or by the Spirit of Life I will blast thee where thou standest!' and she took one light step towards me, and from her eyes there shone such an awful light—to me it seemed almost like a flame—that I fell, then and there, on the ground before her, babbling confusedly in my terror.

'Peace,' she said, with a sudden change of manner, and speaking in her former soft voice, 'I did affright thee! Forgive me! But at times, oh Holly, the almost infinite mind grows impatient of the slowness of the very finite, and I am tempted to use my power out of pure vexation—very nearly wast thou dead, but I remembered ——. But the scarab—about the scarabæus!'

'I picked it up,' I gurgled feebly, as I got on to my feet again, and it is a solemn fact that my mind was so disturbed that at the moment I could remember nothing else about the ring except that I had picked it up in Leo's cave.

'It is very strange,' she said, with a sudden access of womanlike trembling and agitation which seemed out of place in this awful woman—'but once I knew a scarab like that. It—hung round the neck—of one I loved,' and she gave a little sob, and I saw that after all she was only a woman, although she might be a very old one.

'There,' she went on, 'it must be one like it, and yet never did I see one like it, for thereto hung a history, and he who wrote it prized it much.* But the scarab that I knew was not set thus in the bezel of a ring. Go now, Holly, go, and, if thou canst, try to forget that thou hast looked upon Ayesha's beauty,' and, turning from me, she flung herself on her couch, and buried her face in the cushions.

As for me, I stumbled from her presence, and I do not remember how I reached my own cave.

* I am informed by a renowned and most learned Egyptologist, to whom I have submitted this very interesting and beautifully finished scarab, 'Suten se Rā,' that he has never seen one resembling it. Although it bears a title frequently given to Egyptian royalty, he is of opinion that it is not necessarily the cartouche of a Pharaoh, on which either the throne or personal name of the monarch is generally inscribed. What the history of this particular scarab may have been we can now, unfortunately, never know, but I have little doubt but that it played some part in the tragic story of the Princess Amenartas and her lover Kallikrates, the forsworn priest of Isis.—EDITOR.

XIV

A Soul in Hell

It was nearly ten o'clock at night when I cast myself down upon my bed, and began to gather my scattered wits, and reflect upon what I had seen and heard. But the more I reflected the less I could make of it. Was I mad, or drunk, or dreaming, or was I merely the victim of a gigantic and most elaborate hoax? How was it possible that I, a rational man, not unacquainted with the leading scientific facts of our history, and hitherto an absolute and utter disbeliever in all the hocus-pocus that in Europe goes by the name of the supernatural, could believe that I had within the last few minutes been engaged in conversation with a woman two thousand and odd years old? The thing was contrary to the experience of human nature, and absolutely and utterly impossible. It must be a hoax, and yet, if it were a hoax, what was I to make of it? What, too, was to be said of the figures on the water, of the woman's extraordinary acquaintance with the remote past, and her ignorance, or apparent ignorance, of any subsequent history? What, too, of her wonderful and awful loveliness? This, at any rate, was a patent fact, and beyond the experience of the world. No merely mortal woman could shine with such a supernatural radiance. About that she had, at any rate, been in the right—it was not safe for any man to look upon such beauty. I was a hardened vessel in such matters, having, with the exception of one painful experience of my green and tender youth, put the softer sex (I sometimes think that this is a misnomer) almost entirely out of my thoughts. But now, to my intense horror, I *knew* that I could never put away the vision of those glorious eyes; and, alas! the very *diablerie* of the woman, whilst it horrified and repelled, attracted in even a greater degree. A person with the experience of two thousand years at her back, with the command of such tremendous powers and the knowledge of a mystery that could hold off death, was certainly worth falling in love with, if ever woman was. But, alas! it was not a question of whether or no she was worth it, for so far as I could judge, not being versed in such matters, I, a fellow of my college, noted for what my acquaintances are pleased to call my misogyny, and a respectable man now well on in middle life, had fallen absolutely and hopelessly in love with this white sorceress. Nonsense; it must be nonsense! She had warned me fairly, and I had refused to take the warning. Curses on the fatal curiosity that is ever prompting man to draw the veil from woman, and curses on the natural impulse that begets it! It is the cause of half—ay, and more than half, of our misfortunes. Why cannot man be content to live alone and be happy, and let the women live alone and be happy too? But perhaps they would not be happy, and I am not sure that we should either. Here was a nice state of affairs. I, at my age, to fall a victim to this modern Circe![1] But then she was not modern, at least she said not. She was almost as ancient as the original Circe.

I tore my hair, and jumped up from my couch, feeling that if I did not do something I should go off my head. What did she mean about the scarabæus too? It was Leo's scarabæus, and had come out of the old coffer that Vincey had left in my rooms nearly one-and-twenty years before. Could it be, after all, that the whole story was true, and the writing on the sherd was *not* a forgery, or the invention of some crack-brained, long-forgotten individual? And if so, could it be that *Leo* was the man that *She* was waiting for—the dead man who was to be born again! Impossible again! The whole thing was gibberish! Who ever heard of a man being born again?

But if it were possible that a woman could exist for two thousand years, this might be possible also—anything might be possible. I myself might, for aught I knew, be a reincarnation of some other forgotten self, or perhaps the last of a long line of ancestral selves. Well, *vive la guerre*![2] why not? Only, unfortunately, I had no recollection of these previous conditions. The idea was so absurd to me that I burst out laughing, and, addressing the sculptured picture of a grim-looking warrior on the cave wall, called out to him aloud, 'Who knows, old fellow?—perhaps I was your contemporary. By Jove! perhaps I was you and you are I,' and then I laughed again at my own folly, and the sound of my laughter rang dismally along the vaulted roof, as though the ghost of the warrior had uttered the ghost of a laugh.

Next I bethought me that I had not been to see how Leo was, so, taking up one of the lamps which was burning at my bedside, I slipped off my shoes and crept down the passage to the entrance of his sleeping cave. The draught of the night air was lifting his curtain to and fro gently, as though spirit hands were drawing and redrawing it. I slid into the vault-like apartment, and looked round. There was a light by which I could see that Leo was lying on the couch, tossing restlessly in his fever, but asleep. At his side, half-lying on the floor, half-leaning against the stone couch, was Ustane. She held his hand in one of hers, but she too was dozing, and the two made a pretty, or rather a pathetic, picture. Poor Leo! his cheek was burning red, there were dark shadows beneath his eyes, and his breath came heavily. He was very, very ill; and again the horrible fear seized me that he might die, and I be left alone in the world. And yet if he lived he would perhaps be my rival with Ayesha; even if he were not the man, what chance should I, middle-aged and hideous, have against his bright youth and beauty? Well, thank Heaven! my sense of right was not dead. *She* had not killed that yet; and, as I stood there, I prayed to the Almighty in my heart that my boy, my more than son, might live—ay, even if he proved to be the man.

Then I went back as softly as I had come, but still I could not sleep; the sight and thought of dear Leo lying there so ill had but added fuel to the fire of my unrest. My wearied body and overstrained mind awakened all my imagination into preternatural activity. Ideas, visions, almost inspirations, floated before it with startling vividness. Most of them were grotesque enough, some were ghastly, some recalled thoughts and sensations that had for years been buried in the *débris* of my past life. But, behind and above them all, hovered the shape of that awful woman, and through them gleamed the memory of her entrancing loveliness. Up and down the cave I strode—up and down.

Suddenly I observed, what I had not noticed before, that there was a narrow aperture in the rocky wall. I took up the lamp and examined it; the aperture led to a passage. Now, I was still sufficiently sensible to remember that it is not pleasant, in such a situation as ours was, to have passages running into one's bed-chamber from no one knows where. If there are passages, people can come up them; they can come up when one is asleep. Partly to see where it went to, and partly from a restless desire to be doing something, I followed the passage. It led to a stone stair, which I descended; the stair ended in another passage, or rather tunnel, also hewn out of the bed-rock, and running, so far as I could judge, exactly beneath the gallery that led to the entrance of our rooms, and across the great central cave. I went on down it: it was as silent as the grave, but still, drawn by some sensation or attraction that I cannot describe, I followed on, my stockinged feet falling without noise on the smooth and rocky floor. When I had traversed some fifty yards of space, I came to another passage running at right angles, and here an awful thing happened to me: the sharp draught caught my lamp and extinguished it, leaving me in utter darkness in the bowels of that mysterious place. I took a couple of strides forward so as to clear the bisecting tunnel, being terribly afraid lest I should turn up it in the dark if once I got confused as to the direction, and then paused to think. What was I to do? I had no match; it seemed awful to attempt that long journey back through the utter gloom, and yet I could not stand there all night, and, if I did, probably it would not help me much, for in the bowels of the rock it would be as dark at midday as at midnight. I looked back over my shoulder—not a sight or a sound. I peered forward down the darkness: surely, far away, I saw something like the faint glow of fire. Perhaps it was a cave where I could get a light—at any rate, it was worth investigating. Slowly and painfully I crept along the tunnel, keeping my hand against its wall, and feeling at every step with my foot before I put it down, fearing lest I should fall into some pit. Thirty paces—there was a light, a broad light that came and went, shining through curtains! Fifty paces—it was close at hand! Sixty—oh, great heaven!

I was at the curtains, and they did not hang close, so I could see clearly into the little cavern beyond them. It had all the appearance of being a tomb, and was lit up by a fire that burnt in its centre with a whitish flame and without smoke. Indeed, there, to the left, was a stone shelf with a little ledge to it three inches or so high, and on the shelf lay what I took to be a corpse; at any rate, it looked like one, with something white thrown over it. To the right was a similar shelf, on which lay some broidered coverings. Over the fire bent the figure of a woman; she was sideways to me and facing the corpse, wrapped in a dark mantle that hid her like a nun's cloak. She seemed to be staring at the flickering flame. Suddenly, as I was trying to make up my mind what to do, with a convulsive movement that somehow gave an impression of despairing energy, the woman rose to her feet and cast the dark cloak from her.

It was *She* herself!

She was clothed, as I had seen her when she unveiled, in the kirtle of clinging white, cut low upon her bosom, and bound in at the waist with the barbaric double-headed snake, and, as before, her rippling black hair fell in heavy masses down her back. But her face was what caught my eye, and held me as in a vice, not this time by the force of its beauty, but by the power of fascinated terror. The beauty was still there, indeed, but the agony, the blind passion, and the awful vindictiveness displayed upon those quivering features, and in the tortured look of the upturned eyes, were such as surpass my powers of description.

For a moment she stood still, her hands raised high above her head, and as she did so the white robe slipped from her down to her golden girdle, baring the blinding loveliness of her form.

She stood there, her fingers clenched, and the awful look of malevolence gathered and deepened on her face.

Suddenly, I thought of what would happen if she discovered me, and the reflection made me turn sick and faint. But even if I had known that I must die if I stopped, I do not believe that I could have moved, for I was absolutely fascinated. But still I knew my danger. Supposing she should hear me, or see me through the curtain, supposing I even sneezed, or that her magic told her that she was being watched—swift indeed would be my doom.

Down came the clenched hands to her sides, then up again above her head, and, as I am a living and honourable man, the white flame of the fire leapt up after them, almost to the roof, throwing a fierce and ghastly glare upon *She* herself, upon the white figure beneath the covering, and every scroll and detail of the rockwork.

Down came the ivory arms again, and as they did so she spoke, or rather hissed, in Arabic, in a note that curdled my blood, and for a second stopped my heart.

'Curse her, may she be everlastingly accursed.'

The arms fell and the flame sank. Up they went again, and the broad tongue of fire shot up after them; then again they fell.

'Curse her memory—accursed be the memory of the Egyptian.'

Up again, and again down.

'Curse her, the fair daughter of the Nile, because of her beauty.

'Curse her, because her magic hath prevailed against me.

'Curse her, because she kept my beloved from me.'

And again the flame dwindled and shrank.

She put her hands before her eyes, and, abandoning the hissing tone, cried aloud:—

'What is the use of cursing?—she prevailed, and she is gone.'

Then she recommenced with an even more frightful energy:—

'Curse her where she is. Let my curses reach her where she is and disturb her rest.

'Curse her through the starry spaces. Let her shadow be accursed.

'Let my power find her even there.

'Let her hear me even there. Let her hide herself in the blackness.

'Let her go down into the pit of despair, because I shall one day find her.'

Again the flame fell, and again she covered her eyes with her hands.

'It is no use—no use,' she wailed; 'who can reach those who sleep? Not even I can reach them.'

Then once more she began her unholy rites.

'Curse her when she shall be born again. Let her be born accursed.

'Let her be utterly accursed from the hour of her birth until sleep finds her.

'Yea, then, let her be accursed: for then shall I overtake her with my vengeance, and utterly destroy her.'

And so on. The flame rose and fell, reflecting itself in her agonised eyes; the hissing sound of her terrible maledictions, and no words of mine, especially on paper, can convey how terrible they were, ran round the walls and died away in little echoes, and the fierce light and deep gloom alternated themselves on the white and dreadful form stretched upon that bier of stone.

But at length she seemed to wear herself out, and ceased. She sat herself down upon the rocky floor, and shook the dense cloud of her beautiful hair over her face and breast, and began to sob terribly in the torture of a heartrending despair.

'Two thousand years,' she moaned—'two thousand years have I waited and endured; but though century doth still creep on to century, and time give place to time, the sting of memory hath not lessened, the light of hope doth not shine more bright. Oh! to have lived two thousand years, with my passion eating at my heart, and with my sin ever before me. Oh, that for me life cannot bring forgetfulness! Oh, for the weary years that have been and are yet to come, and evermore to come, endless and without end!

'My love! my love! my love! Why did that stranger bring thee back to me after this sort? For five hundred years I have not suffered thus. Oh, if I sinned against thee, have I not wiped away the sin? When wilt thou come back to me who have all, and yet without thee have naught? What is there that I can do? What? What? What? And perchance she—perchance that Egyptian doth abide with thee where thou art, and mock my memory. Oh, why could I not die with thee, I who slew thee? Alas, that I cannot die! Alas! Alas!' and she flung herself prone upon the ground, and sobbed and wept till I thought her heart must burst.

Suddenly she ceased, raised herself to her feet, re-arranged her robe, and, tossing back her long locks impatiently, swept across to where the figure lay upon the stone.

'Oh Kallikrates,' she cried, and I trembled at the name, 'I must look upon thy face again, though it be agony. It is a generation since I looked upon thee whom I slew—slew with mine own hand,' and with trembling fingers she seized the corner of the sheet-like wrapping that covered the form upon the stone bier, and then paused. When she spoke again, it was in a kind of awed whisper, as though her idea were terrible even to herself.

'Shall I raise thee,' she said, apparently addressing the corpse, 'so that thou standest there before me, as of old? I *can* do it,' and she held out her hands over the sheeted dead, while her whole frame became rigid and terrible to see, and her eyes grew fixed and dull. I shrank in horror behind the curtain, my hair stood up upon my head, and whether it was my imagination or a fact I am unable to say, but I thought that the quiet form beneath the covering began to quiver, and the winding sheet to lift as though it lay on the breast of one who slept. Suddenly she withdrew her hands, and the motion of the corpse seemed to me to cease.

'What is the use?' she said gloomily. 'Of what use is it to recall the semblance of life when I cannot recall the spirit? Even if thou stoodest before me thou wouldst not know me, and couldst but do what I bid thee. The life in thee would be *my* life, and not *thy* life, Kallikrates.'

For a moment she stood there brooding, and then cast herself down on her knees beside the form, and began to press her lips against the sheet, and weep. There was something so horrible about the sight of this awe-inspiring woman letting loose her passion on the dead—so much more horrible even than anything that had gone before, that I could no longer bear to look at it, and, turning, began to creep, shaking as I was in every limb, slowly along the pitch-dark passage, feeling in my trembling heart that I had a vision of a Soul in Hell.

On I stumbled, I scarcely know how. Twice I fell, once I turned up the bisecting passage, but fortunately found out my mistake in time. For twenty minutes or more I crept along, till at last it occurred to me that I must have passed the little stair by which I descended. So, utterly exhausted, and nearly frightened to death, I sank down at length there on the stone flooring, and sank into oblivion.

When I came to I noticed a faint ray of light in the passage just behind me. I crept to it, and found it was the little stair down which the weak dawn was stealing. Passing up it I gained my chamber in safety, and, flinging myself on the couch, was soon lost in slumber or rather stupor.

XV

Ayesha Gives Judgment

The next thing that I remember was opening my eyes and perceiving the form of Job, who had now practically recovered from his attack of fever. He was standing in the ray of light that pierced into the cave from the outer air, shaking out my clothes as a makeshift for brushing them, which he could not do because there was no brush, and then folding them up neatly and laying them on the foot of the stone couch. This done, he got my travelling dressing-case out of the Gladstone bag, and opened it ready for my use. First, he stood it on the foot of the couch also, then, being afraid, I suppose, that I should kick it off, he placed it on a leopard skin on the floor, and stood back a step or two to observe the effect. It was not satisfactory, so he shut up the bag, turned it on end, and, having rested it against the foot of the couch, placed the dressing-case on it. Next, he looked at the pots full of water, which constituted our washing apparatus. 'Ah!' I heard him murmur, 'no hot water in this beastly place. I suppose these poor creatures only use it to boil each other in,' and he sighed deeply.

'What is the matter, Job?' I said.

'Beg pardon, sir,' he said, touching his hair. 'I thought you were asleep, sir; and I am sure you look as though you want it. One might think from the look of you that you had been having a night of it.'

I only groaned by way of answer. I had, indeed, been having a night of it, such as I hope never to have again.

'How is Mr. Leo, Job?'

'Much the same, sir. If he don't soon mend, he'll end, sir; and that's all about it; though I must say that that there savage, Ustane, do do her best for him, almost like a baptised Christian. She is always hanging round and looking after him, and if I ventures to interfere, it's awful to see her; her hair seems to stand on end, and she curses and swears away in her heathen talk—at least I fancy she must be cursing from the look of her.'

'And what do you do then?'

'I make her a perlite bow, and I say, "Young woman, your position is one that I don't quite understand, and can't recognise. Let me tell you that I has a duty to perform to my master as is incapacitated by illness, and that I am going to perform it until I am incapacitated too," but she don't take no heed, not she—only curses and swears away worse than ever. Last night she put her hand under that sort of nightshirt she wears and whips out a knife with a kind of a curl in the blade, so I whips out my revolver, and we walks round and round each other till at last she bursts out laughing. It isn't nice treatment for a Christian man to have to put up with from a savage, however handsome she may be, but it is what people must expect as is *fools* enough' (Job laid great emphasis on the 'fools') 'to come to such a place to look for things no man is meant to find. It's a judgment on us, sir—that's my opinion; and I, for one, is of opinion, that the judgment isn't half done yet, and when it is done, we shall be done too, and just stop in these beastly caves with the ghosts and the corpseses for once and all. And now, sir, I must be seeing about Mr. Leo's broth, if that wild cat will let me; and, perhaps, you would like to get up, sir, because it's past nine o'clock.'

Job's remarks were not of an exactly cheering order to a man who had passed such a night as I had; and, what is more, they had the weight of truth. Taking one thing with another, it appeared to me to be an utter impossibility that we should escape from the place where we were. Supposing that Leo recovered, and supposing that *She* would let us go, which was exceedingly doubtful, and that she did not 'blast' us in some moment of vexation, and that we were not hot-potted by the Amahagger, it would be quite impossible for us to find our way across the network of marshes which, stretching for scores and scores of miles, formed a stronger and more impassable fortification round the various Amahagger households than any that could be built or designed by man. No, there was but one thing to do—face it out; and, speaking for my own part, I was so intensely interested in the whole weird story that, so far as I was concerned, notwithstanding the shattered state of my nerves, I asked nothing better, even if my life paid forfeit to my curiosity. What man for whom physiology has charms could forbear to study such a character as that of this Ayesha when the opportunity of doing so presented itself? The very terror of the pursuit added to its fascination, and besides, as I was forced to own to myself even now in the sober light of day, she herself had attractions that I could not forget. Not even the dreadful sight which I had witnessed during the night could drive that folly from my mind; and alas! that I should have to admit it, it has not been driven thence to this hour.

After I had dressed myself I passed into the eating, or rather embalming chamber, and had some food, which was as before brought to me by the girl mutes. When I had finished I went and saw poor Leo, who was quite off his head, and did not even know me. I asked Ustane how she thought he was; but she only shook her head and began to cry a little. Evidently her hopes were small; and I then and there made up my mind that, if it were in any way possible, I would get *She* to come and see him. Surely she would cure him if she chose—at any rate she said she could. While I was in the room, Billali entered, and also shook his head.

'He will die at night,' he said.

'God forbid, my father,' I answered, and turned away with a heavy heart.

'*She-who-must-be-obeyed* commands thy presence, my Baboon,' said the old man as soon as we got to the curtain; 'but, oh my dear son, be more careful. Yesterday I made sure in my heart that *She* would blast thee when thou didst not crawl upon thy stomach before her. She is sitting in the great hall even now to do justice upon those who would have smitten thee and the Lion. Come on, my son; come swiftly.'

I turned, and followed him down the passage, and when we reached the great central cave saw that many Amahagger, some robed, and some merely clad in the sweet simplicity of a leopard skin, were hurrying up it. We mingled with the throng, and walked up the enormous and, indeed, almost interminable cave. All the way its walls were elaborately sculptured, and every twenty paces or so passages opened out of it at right angles, leading, Billali told me, to tombs, hollowed in the rock by 'the people who were before.' Nobody visited those tombs now, he said; and I must say that my heart rejoiced when I thought of the opportunities of antiquarian research which opened out before me.

At last we came to the head of the cave, where there was a rock daïs almost exactly similar to the one on which we had been so furiously attacked, a fact that proved to me that these daïs must have been used as altars, probably for the celebration of religious ceremonies, and more especially of rites connected with the interment of the dead. On either side of this daïs were passages leading, Billali informed me, to other caves full of dead bodies. 'Indeed,' he added, 'the whole mountain is full of dead, and nearly all of them are perfect.'

In front of the daïs were gathered a great number of people of both sexes, who stood staring about in their peculiar gloomy fashion, which would have reduced Mark Tapley[1] himself to misery in about five minutes. On the daïs was a rude chair of black wood inlaid with ivory, having a seat made of grass fibre, and a footstool formed of a wooden slab attached to the framework of the chair.

Suddenly there was a cry of 'Hiya! Hiya!' ('*She! She!*'), and thereupon the entire crowd of spectators instantly precipitated itself upon the ground, and lay still as though it were individually and collectively stricken dead, leaving me standing there like some solitary survivor of a massacre. As it did so a long string of guards began to defile from a passage to the left, and ranged themselves on either side of the daïs. Then followed about a score of male mutes, then as many women mutes bearing lamps, and then a tall white figure, swathed from head to foot, in whom I recognised *She* herself. She mounted the daïs and sat down upon the chair, and spoke to me in *Greek*, I suppose because she did not wish those present to understand what she said.

'Come hither, oh Holly,' she said, 'and sit thou at my feet, and see me do justice on those who would have slain thee. Forgive me if my Greek doth halt like a lame man; it is so long since I have heard the sound of it that my tongue is stiff, and will not bend rightly to the words.'

I bowed, and, mounting the daïs, sat down at her feet.

'How didst thou sleep, my Holly?' she asked.

'I slept not well, oh Ayesha!' I answered with perfect truth, and with an inward fear that perhaps she knew how I had passed the heart of the night.

'So,' she said, with a little laugh, 'I, too, have not slept well. Last night I had dreams, and methinks that thou didst call them to me, oh Holly.'

'Of what didst thou dream, Ayesha?' I asked indifferently.

'I dreamed,' she answered quickly, 'of one I hate and one I love,' and then, as though to turn the conversation, she addressed the captain of her guard in Arabic: 'Let the men be brought before me.'

The captain bowed low, for the guard and her attendants did not prostrate themselves but had remained standing, and departed with his underlings down a passage to the right.

Then came a silence. *She* leant her swathed head upon her hand and appeared to be lost in thought, while the multitude before her continued to grovel upon their stomachs, only screwing their heads round a little so as to get a view of us with one eye. It seemed that their Queen so rarely appeared in public that they were willing to undergo this inconvenience, and even graver risks, to have the opportunity of looking on her, or rather on her garments, for no living man there except myself had ever seen her face. At last we caught sight of the waving of lights, and heard the tramp of men coming along the passage, and in filed the guard, and with them the survivors of our would-be murderers to the number of twenty or more, on whose countenances the natural expression of sullenness struggled with the terror that evidently filled their savage hearts. They were ranged in front of the daïs, and would have cast themselves down on the floor of the cave like the spectators, but *She* stopped them.

'Nay,' she said in her softest voice, 'stand; I pray you stand. Perchance the time will soon be when ye shall grow weary of being stretched out,' and she laughed melodiously.

I saw a cringe of terror run along the rank of the poor doomed wretches, and, wicked villains as they were, I felt sorry for them. Some minutes, perhaps two or three, passed before anything fresh occurred, during which *She* appeared from the movement of her head—for, of course, we could not see her eyes—to be slowly and carefully examining each delinquent. At last she spoke, addressing herself to me in a quiet and deliberate tone.

'Dost thou, oh my guest, who art known in thine own country by the name of the Prickly Tree, recognise these men?'

'Ay, oh Queen, nearly all of them,' I said, and I saw them glower at me as I said it.

'Then tell to me, and this great company, the tale whereof I have heard.'

Thus adjured, I, in as few words as I could, related the history of the cannibal feast, and of the attempted torture of our poor servant. The narrative was received in perfect silence, both by the accused and by the audience, and also by *She* herself. When I had done, Ayesha called upon Billali by name, and, lifting his head from the ground, but without rising, the old man confirmed my story. No further evidence was taken.

'Ye have heard,' said *She* at length, in a cold, clear voice, very different from her usual tones—indeed, it was one of the most remarkable things about this extraordinary creature that her voice had the power of suiting itself in a wonderful manner to the mood of the moment. 'What have ye to say, ye rebellious children, why vengeance should not be done upon you?'

For some time there was no answer, but at last one of the men, a fine, broad-chested fellow, well on in middle life, with deep-graven features and an eye like a hawk's, spoke, and said that the orders that they had received were not to harm the white men; nothing was said of their black servant, so, egged on thereto by a woman who was now dead, they proceeded to try to hot-pot him after the ancient and honourable custom of their country, with a view of eating him in due course. As for their attack upon ourselves, it was made in an access of sudden fury, and they deeply regretted it. He ended by humbly praying that mercy might be extended to them; or, at least, that they might be banished into the swamps, to live or die as it might chance; but I saw it written on his face that he had but little hope of mercy.

Then came a pause, and the most intense silence reigned over the whole scene, which, illuminated as it was by the flicker of the lamps striking out broad patterns of light and shadow upon the rocky walls, was as strange as any I ever saw, even in that unholy land. Upon the ground before the daïs were stretched scores of the corpselike forms of the spectators, till at last the long lines of them were lost in the gloomy background. Before this outstretched audience were the knots of evil-doers, trying to cover up their natural terrors with a brave appearance of unconcern. On the right and left stood the silent guards, robed in white and armed with great spears and daggers, and men and women mutes watching with hard curious eyes. Then, seated in her barbaric chair above them all, with myself at her feet, was the veiled white woman, whose loveliness and awesome power seemed to visibly shine about her like a halo, or rather like the glow from some unseen light. Never have I seen her veiled shape look more terrible than it did in that space, while she gathered herself up for vengeance.

At last it came.

'Dogs and serpents,' *She* began in a low voice that gradually gathered power as she went on, till the place rang with it. 'Eaters of human flesh, two things have ye done. First, ye have attacked these strangers, being white men, and would have slain their servant, and for that alone death is your reward. But that is not all. Ye have dared to disobey me. Did I not send my word unto you by Billali, my servant, and the father of your household? Did I not bid you to hospitably entertain these strangers, whom now ye have striven to slay, and whom, had not they been brave and strong beyond the strength of men, ye would cruelly have murdered? Hath it not been taught to you from childhood that the law of *She* is an ever fixed law, and that he who breaketh it by so much as one jot or tittle shall perish?[2] And is not my lightest word a law? Have not your fathers taught you this, I say, whilst as yet ye were but children? Do ye not know that as well might ye bid these great caves to fall upon you, or the sun to cease its journeying, as to hope to turn me from my courses, or make my word light or heavy, according to your minds? Well do ye know it, ye Wicked Ones. But ye are all evil—evil to the core—the wickedness bubbles up in you like a fountain in the spring-time. Were it not for me, generations since had ye ceased to be, for of your own evil way had ye destroyed each other. And now, because ye have done this thing, because ye have striven to put these men, my guests, to death, and yet more because ye have dared to disobey my word, this is the doom that I doom you to. That ye be taken to the cave of torture,* and given over to the tormentors, and that on the going down of tomorrow's sun those of you who yet remain alive be slain, even as ye would have slain the servant of this my guest.'

* 'The cave of torture.' I afterwards saw this dreadful place, also a legacy from the prehistoric people who lived in Kôr. The only objects in the cave itself were slabs of rock arranged in various positions to facilitate the operations of the torturers. Many of these slabs, which were of a porous stone, were stained quite dark with the blood of ancient victims that had soaked into them. Also in the centre of the room was a place for a furnace, with a cavity wherein to heat the historic pot. But the most dreadful thing about the cave was that over each slab was a sculptured illustration of the appropriate torture being applied. These sculptures were so awful that I will not harrow the reader by attempting a description of them.—L. H. H.

She ceased, and a faint murmur of horror ran round the cave. As for the victims, as soon as they realised the full hideousness of their doom, their stoicism forsook them, and they flung themselves down upon the ground, and wept and implored for mercy in a way that was dreadful to behold. I, too, turned to Ayesha, and begged her to spare them, or at least to mete out their fate in some less awful way. But she was hard as adamant about it.

'My Holly,' she said, again speaking in Greek, which, to tell the truth, although I have always been considered a better scholar of that language than most men, I found it rather difficult to follow, chiefly because of the change in the fall of the accent. Ayesha, of course, talked with the accent of her contemporaries, whereas we have only tradition and the modern accent to guide us as to the exact pronunciation—'My Holly, it cannot be. Were I to show mercy to those wolves, your lives would not be safe among this people for a day. Thou knowest them not. They are tigers to lap blood, and even now they hunger for your lives. How thinkest thou that I rule this people? I have but a regiment of guards to do my bidding, therefore it is not by force. It is by terror. My empire is of the imagination. Once in a generation mayhap I do as I have done but now, and slay a score by torture. Believe not that I would be cruel, or take vengeance on anything so low. What can it profit me to be avenged on such as these? Those who live long, my Holly, have no passions, save where they have interests. Though I may seem to slay in wrath, or because my mood is crossed, it is not so. Thou hast seen how in the heavens the little clouds blow this way and that without a cause, yet behind them is the great wind sweeping on its path whither it listeth. So is it with me, oh Holly. My moods and changes are the little clouds, and fitfully these seem to turn; but behind them ever blows the great wind of my purpose. Nay, the men must die; and die as I have said.' Then, suddenly turning to the captain of the guard—

'As my word is, so be it!'

XVI

The Tombs of Kôr

After the prisoners had been removed Ayesha waved her hand, and the spectators turned round, and began to crawl off down the cave like a scattered flock of sheep. When they were a fair distance from the daïs, however, they rose and walked away, leaving the Queen and myself alone, with the exception of the mutes and the few remaining guards, most of whom had departed with the doomed men. Thinking this a good opportunity, I asked *She* to come and see Leo, telling her of his serious condition; but she would not, saying that he certainly would not die before the night, as people never died of that sort of fever except at nightfall or dawn. Also she said that it would be better to let the sickness spend its course as much as possible before she cured it. Accordingly, I was rising to leave, when she bade me follow her, as she would talk with me, and show me the wonders of the caves.

I was too much involved in the web of her fatal fascinations to say her no, even if I had wished, which I did not. She rose from her chair, and, making some signs to the mutes, descended from the daïs. Thereon four of the girls took lamps, and ranged themselves two in front and two behind us, but the others went away, as also did the guards.

'Now,' she said, 'wouldst thou see some of the wonders of this place, oh Holly? Look upon this great cave. Sawest thou ever the like? Yet was it, and many more like it, hollowed by the hands of the dead race that once lived here in the city on the plain. A great and a wonderful people must they have been, those men of

Kôr, but, like the Egyptians, they thought more of the dead than of the living. How many men, thinkest thou, working for how many years, did it need to the hollowing out this cave and all the galleries thereof?'

'Tens of thousands,' I answered.

'So, oh Holly. This people was an old people before the Egyptians were. A little can I read of their inscriptions, having found the key thereto—and, see thou here, this was one of the last of the caves that they hollowed,' and, turning to the rock behind her, she motioned the mutes to hold up the lamps. Carven over the daïs was the figure of an old man seated in a chair, with an ivory rod in his hand. It struck me at once that his features were exceedingly like those of the man who was represented as being embalmed in the chamber where we took our meals. Beneath the chair, which, by the way was shaped exactly like the one in which Ayesha had sat to give judgment, was a short inscription in the extraordinary characters of which I have already spoken, but which I do not remember sufficient of to illustrate. It looked more like Chinese writing than any other that I am acquainted with. This inscription Ayesha proceeded, with some difficulty and hesitation, to read aloud and translate. It ran as follows:—

'*In the year four thousand two hundred and fifty-nine from the founding of the City of imperial Kôr was this cave (or burial place) completed by Tisno, King of Kôr, the people thereof and their slaves having laboured thereat for three generations, to be a tomb for their citizens of rank who shall come after. May the blessing of the heaven above the heaven rest upon their work, and make the sleep of Tisno, the mighty monarch, the likeness of whose features is graven above, a sound and happy sleep till the day of awakening,* and also the sleep of his servants, and of those of his race who, rising up after him, shall yet lay their heads as low.*'

* This phrase is remarkable, as seeming to indicate a belief in a future state.—EDITOR.

'Thou seest, oh Holly,' she said, 'this people founded the city, of which the ruins yet cumber the plain yonder, four thousand years before this cave was finished. Yet, when first mine eyes beheld it two thousand years ago, was it even as it is now. Judge, therefore, how old must that city have been! And now, follow thou me, and I will show thee after what fashion this great people fell when the time was come for it to fall,' and she led the way down to the centre of the cave, stopping at a spot where a round rock had been let into a kind of large manhole in the flooring, accurately filling it just as the iron plates fill the spaces in the London pavements down which the coals are thrown. 'Thou seest,' she said. 'Tell me, what is it?'

'Nay, I know not,' I answered; whereon she crossed to the left-hand side of the cave (looking towards the entrance) and signed to the mutes to hold up the lamps. On the wall was something painted with a red pigment in similar characters to those hewn beneath the sculpture of Tisno, King of Kôr. This inscription she proceeded to translate to me, the pigment still being quite fresh enough to show the form of the letters. It ran as follows:—

'I, Junis, a priest of the Great Temple of Kôr, write this upon the rock of the burying-place in the year four thousand eight hundred and three from the founding of Kôr. Kôr is fallen! No more shall the mighty feast in her halls, no more shall she rule the world, and her navies go out to commerce with the world. Kôr is fallen! and her mighty works and all the cities of Kôr, and all the harbours that she built and the canals that she made, are for the wolf and the owl and the wild swan, and the barbarian who comes after. Twenty and five moons ago did a cloud settle upon Kôr, and the hundred cities of Kôr, and out of the cloud came a pestilence that slew her people, old and young, one with another, and spared not. One with another they turned black and died—the young and the old, the rich and the poor, the man and the woman, the prince and the slave. The pestilence slew and slew, and ceased not by day or by night, and those who escaped from the pestilence were slain of the famine. No longer could the bodies of the children of Kôr be preserved according to the ancient rites, because of the

number of the dead, therefore were they hurled into the great pit beneath the cave through the hole in the floor of the cave. Then at last, a remnant of this the great people, the light of the whole world, went down to the coast and took ship and sailed northwards; and now am I, the Priest Junis, who write this, the last man left alive[1] *of this great city of men, but whether there be any yet left in the other cities I know not. This do I write in misery of heart before I die, because Kôr the Imperial is no more, and because there are none to worship in her temple, and all her palaces are empty, and her princes and her captains and her traders and her fair women have passed off the face of the earth.*'

I gave a sigh of astonishment—the utter desolation depicted in this rude scrawl was so overpowering. It was terrible to think of this solitary survivor of a mighty people recording its fate before he too went down into darkness. What must the old man have felt as, in ghastly terrifying solitude, by the light of one lamp feebly illumining a little space of gloom, he in a few brief lines daubed the history of his nation's death upon the cavern wall? What a subject for the moralist, or the painter, or indeed for any one who can think!

'Doth it not occur to thee, oh Holly,' said Ayesha, laying her hand upon my shoulder, 'that those men who sailed North may have been the fathers of the first Egyptians?'

'Nay, I know not,' I said; 'it seems that the world is very old.'

'Old? Yes, it is old indeed. Time after time have nations, ay, and rich and strong nations, learned in the arts, been and passed away and been forgotten, so that no memory of them remains. This is but one of several; for Time eats up the works of man, unless, indeed, he digs in caves like the people of Kôr, and then mayhap the sea swallows them, or the earthquake shakes them in. Who knows what hath been on the earth, or what shall be? There is no new thing under the sun, as the wise Hebrew[2] wrote long ago. Yet were not these people utterly destroyed, as I think. Some few remained in the other cities, for their cities were many. But the barbarians from the south, or perchance my people, the Arabs, came down upon them, and took their women to wife, and the race of the Amahagger that is now is a bastard brood of the mighty sons of Kôr, and behold it dwelleth in the tombs with its fathers' bones.* But I know not: who can know? My arts cannot pierce so far into the blackness of Time's night. A great people were they. They conquered till none were left to conquer, and then they dwelt at ease within their rocky mountain walls, with their man servants and their maid servants, their minstrels, their sculptors, and their concubines, and traded and quarrelled, and ate and hunted and slept and made merry till their time came. But come, I will show thee the great pit beneath the cave whereof the writing speaks. Never shall thine eyes witness such another sight.'

Accordingly I followed her to a side passage opening out of the main cave, then down a great number of steps, and along an underground shaft which cannot have been less than sixty feet beneath the surface of the rock, and was ventilated by curious borings that ran upward, I do not know where. Suddenly the passage ended, and she halted and bade the mutes hold up the lamps, and, as she had prophesied, I saw a scene such as I was not likely to see again. We were standing in an enormous pit, or rather on the edge of it, for it went down deeper—I do not know how much—than the level on which we stood, and was edged in with a low wall of rock. So far as I could judge, this pit was about the size of the space beneath the dome of St. Paul's in London, and when the lamps were held up I saw that it was nothing but one vast charnel-house, being literally full of thousands of human skeletons, which lay piled up in an enormous gleaming pyramid, formed by the slipping down of the bodies at the apex as fresh ones were dropped in from above. Anything more appalling than this jumbled mass of the remains of a departed race I cannot imagine, and what made it even more dreadful was that in this dry air a considerable number of the bodies had simply become

* The name of the race Ama-hagger would seem to indicate a curious mingling of races such as might easily have occurred in the neighbourhood of the Zambesi. The prefix 'Ama' is common to the Zulu and kindred races, and signifies 'people,' while 'hagger' is an Arabic word meaning a stone.—EDITOR.[3]

desiccated with the skin still on them, and now, fixed in every conceivable position, stared at us out of the mountain of white bones, grotesquely horrible caricatures of humanity. In my astonishment I uttered an ejaculation, and the echoes of my voice ringing in the vaulted space disturbed a skull that had been accurately balanced for many thousands of years near the apex of the pile. Down it came with a run, bounding along merrily towards us, and of course bringing an avalanche of other bones after it, till at last the whole pit rattled with their movement, even as though the skeletons were getting up to greet us.

'Come,' I said, 'I have seen enough. These are the bodies of those who died of the great sickness, is it not so?' I added, as we turned away.

'Yes. The people of Kôr ever embalmed their dead, as did the Egyptians, but their art was greater than the art of the Egyptians, for whereas the Egyptians disembowelled and drew the brain, the people of Kôr injected fluid into the veins, and thus reached every part. But stay, thou shalt see,' and she halted at haphazard at one of the little doorways opening out of the passage along which we were walking, and motioned to the mutes to light us in. We entered into a small chamber similar to the one in which I had slept at our first stopping-place, only instead of one there were two stone benches or beds in it. On the benches lay figures covered with yellow linen,* on which a fine and impalpable dust had gathered in the course of ages but nothing like to the extent that one would have anticipated, for in these deep-hewn caves there is no material to turn to dust. About the bodies on the stone shelves and floor of the tomb were many painted vases, but I saw very few ornaments or weapons in any of the vaults.

'Uplift the cloths, oh Holly,' said Ayesha, but when I put out my hand to do so I drew it back again. It seemed like sacrilege, and to speak the truth I was awed by the dread solemnity of the

* All the linen that the Amahagger wore was taken from the tombs, which accounted for its yellow hue. If it was well washed, however, and properly rebleached, it acquired its former snowy whiteness, and was the softest and best linen I ever saw.—L. H. H.

place, and of the presences before us. Then, with a little laugh at my fears, she drew them herself, only to discover other and yet finer cloths lying over the forms upon the stone bench. These also she withdrew, and then for the first time for thousands upon thousands of years did living eyes look upon the face of that chilly dead. It was a woman; she might have been thirty-five years of age, or perhaps a little less, and had certainly been beautiful. Even now her calm clear-cut features, marked out with delicate eyebrows and long eyelashes which threw little lines of the shadow of the lamplight upon the ivory face, were wonderfully beautiful. There, robed in white, down which her blue-black hair was streaming, she slept her last long sleep, and on her arm, its face pressed against her breast, there lay a little babe. So sweet was the sight, although so awful, that—I confess it without shame—I could scarcely withhold my tears. It took me back across the dim gulf of the ages to some happy home in dead Imperial Kôr, where this winsome lady girt about with beauty had lived and died, and dying taken her last-born with her to the tomb. There they were before us, mother and babe, the white memories of a forgotten human history speaking more eloquently to the heart than could any written record of their lives. Reverently I replaced the grave-cloths, and, with a sigh that flowers so fair should, in the purpose of the Everlasting, have only bloomed to be gathered to the grave, I turned to the body on the opposite shelf, and gently unveiled it. It was that of a man in advanced life, with a long grizzled beard, and also robed in white, probably the husband of the lady, who, after surviving her many years, came at last to sleep once more for good and all beside her.

We left the place and entered others. It would be too long to describe the many things I saw in them. Each one had its occupants, for the five hundred and odd years that had elapsed between the completion of the cave and the destruction of the race had evidently sufficed to fill these catacombs, numberless as they were, and all appeared to have been undisturbed since the day when they were placed there. I could fill a book with the description of them, but to do so would only be to repeat what I have said, with variations.

Nearly all the bodies, so masterly was the art with which they had been treated, were as perfect as on the day of death thousands of years before. Nothing came to injure them in the deep silence of the living rock: they were beyond the reach of heat and cold and damp, and the aromatic drugs with which they had been saturated were evidently practically everlasting in their effect. Here and there, however, we saw an exception, and in these cases, although the flesh looked sound enough externally, if one touched it it fell in, and revealed the fact that the figure was but a pile of dust. This arose, Ayesha told me, from these particular bodies having, either owing to haste in the burial or other causes, been soaked in the preservative,* instead of its being injected into the substance of the flesh.

About the last tomb we visited I must, however, say one word, for its contents spoke even more eloquently to the human sympathies than those of the first. It had but two occupants, and they lay together on a single shelf. I withdrew the grave-cloths, and there, clasped heart to heart, were a young man and a blooming girl. Her head rested on his arm, and his lips were pressed against her brow. I opened the man's linen robe, and there over his heart was a dagger-wound, and beneath the girl's fair breast was a like cruel stab, through which her life had ebbed

* Ayesha afterwards showed me the tree from the leaves of which this ancient preservative was manufactured. It is a low bush-like tree, that to this day grows in wonderful plenty upon the sides of the mountains, or rather upon the slopes leading up to the rocky walls. The leaves are long and narrow, a vivid green in colour, but turning a bright red in the autumn, and not unlike those of a laurel in general appearance. They have little smell when green, but if boiled the aromatic odour from them is so strong that one can hardly bear it. The best mixture, however, was made from the roots, and among the people of Kôr there was a law, which Ayesha showed me alluded to on some of the inscriptions, to the effect that under heavy penalties no one under a certain rank was to be embalmed with the drugs prepared from the roots. The object and effect of this was, of course, to preserve the trees from extermination. The sale of the leaves and roots was a Government monopoly, and from it the Kings of Kôr derived a large proportion of their private revenue.—L. H. H.

away. On the rock above was an inscription in three words. Ayesha translated it. It was '*Wedded in Death.*'

What was the life-history of these two, who, of a truth, were beautiful in their lives, and in their death were not divided?

I closed my eyelids, and imagination taking up the thread of thought shot its swift shuttle back across the ages, weaving a picture on their blackness so real and vivid in its detail that I could almost for a moment think that I had triumphed o'er the Past, and that my spirit's eyes had pierced the mystery of Time.

I seemed to see this fair girl form—the yellow hair streaming down her, glittering against her garments snowy white, and the bosom that was whiter than the robes, even dimming with its lustre her ornaments of burnished gold. I seemed to see the great cave filled with warriors, bearded and clad in mail, and, on the lighted daïs where Ayesha had given judgment, a man standing, robed, and surrounded by the symbols of his priestly office. And up the cave there came one clad in purple, and before him and behind him came minstrels and fair maidens, chanting a wedding song. White stood the maid against the altar, fairer than the fairest there—purer than a lily, and more cold than the dew that glistens in its heart. But as the man drew near she shuddered. Then out of the press and throng there sprang a dark-haired youth, and put his arm about this long-forgotten maid, and kissed her pale face in which the blood shot up like lights of the red dawn across the silent sky. And next there was turmoil and uproar, and a flashing of swords, and they tore the youth from her arms, and stabbed him, but with a cry she snatched the dagger from his belt, and drove it into her snowy breast, home to the heart, and down she fell, and then, with cries and wailing, and every sound of lamentation, the pageant rolled away from the arena of my vision, and once more the past shut to its book.

Let him who reads forgive the intrusion of a dream into a history of fact. But it came so home to me—I saw it all so clear in a moment, as it were; and, besides, who shall say what proportion of fact, past, present, or to come, may lie in the imagination? What is imagination? Perhaps it is the shadow of the intangible truth, perhaps it is the soul's thought.

In an instant the whole thing had passed through my brain, and *She* was addressing me.

'Behold the lot of man,' said the veiled Ayesha, as she drew the winding sheets back over the dead lovers, speaking in a solemn, thrilling voice, which accorded well with the dream that I had dreamed: 'to the tomb, and to the forgetfulness that hides the tomb, must we all come at last! Ay, even I who live so long. Even for me, oh Holly, thousands upon thousands of years hence; thousands of years after thou hast gone through the gate and been lost in the mists, a day will dawn whereon I shall die, and be even as thou art and these are. And then what will it avail that I have lived a little longer, holding off death by the knowledge I have wrung from Nature, since at last I too must die? What is a span of ten thousand years, or ten times ten thousand years, in the history of time? It is as naught—it is as the mists that roll up in the sunlight; it fleeth away like an hour of sleep or a breath of the Eternal Spirit. Behold the lot of man! Certainly it shall overtake us, and we shall sleep. Certainly, too, we shall awake, and live again and again shall sleep, and so on and on, through periods, spaces, and times, from æon unto æon, till the world is dead, and the worlds beyond the world are dead, and naught liveth save the Spirit that is Life. But for us twain and for these dead ones shall the end of ends be Life, or shall it be Death? As yet Death is but Life's Night, but out of the night is the Morrow born again, and doth again beget the Night. Only when Day and Night, and Life and Death, are ended and swallowed up in that from which they came, what shall be our fate, oh Holly? Who can see so far? Not even I!'

And then, with a sudden change of tone and manner—

'Hast thou seen enough, my stranger guest, or shall I show thee more of the wonders of these tombs that are my palace halls? If thou wilt, I can lead thee to where Tisno, the mightiest and most valorous King of Kôr, in whose day these caves were ended, lies in a pomp that seems to mock at nothingness, and bid the empty shadows of the past do homage to his sculptured vanity!'

'I have seen enough, oh Queen,' I answered. 'My heart is overwhelmed by the power of the present Death. Mortality is weak, and easily broken down by a sense of the companionship that waits upon its end. Take me hence, oh Ayesha!'

XVII

The Balance Turns

In a few minutes, following the lamps of the mutes, which, held out from the body as a bearer holds water in a vessel, had the appearance of floating down the darkness by themselves, we came to a stair which led us to *She's* ante-room, the same that Billali had crept up upon all fours on the previous day. Here I would have bid the Queen adieu, but she would not.

'Nay,' she said, 'enter with me, oh Holly, for of a truth thy conversation pleaseth me. Think, oh Holly: for two thousand years have I had none to converse with save slaves and my own thoughts, and though of all this thinking hath much wisdom come, and many secrets been made plain, yet am I weary of my thoughts, and have come to loathe mine own society, for surely the food that memory gives to eat is bitter to the taste, and it is only with the teeth of hope that we can bear to bite it. Now though thy thoughts are green and tender, as becometh one so young, yet are they those of a thinking brain, and in truth thou dost bring back to my mind certain of those old philosophers with whom in days bygone I have disputed at Athens, and at Becca in Arabia, for thou hast the same crabbed air and dusty look, as though thou hadst passed thy days in reading ill-writ Greek, and been stained dark with the grime of manuscripts. So draw the curtain, and sit here by my side, and we will eat fruit, and talk of pleasant things. See, I will again unveil to thee. Thou hast brought it on thyself, oh Holly; fairly have I warned thee—and thou shalt call me beautiful as even those old philosophers were wont to do. Fie upon them, forgetting their philosophy!'

And without more ado she stood up and shook the white wrappings from her, and came forth shining and splendid like some glittering snake when she has cast her slough; ay, and fixed her wonderful eyes upon me—more deadly than any Basilisk's[1]—and pierced me through and through with their beauty, and sent her light laugh ringing through the air like chimes of silver bells.

A new mood was on her, and the very colour of her mind seemed to change beneath it. It was no longer torture-torn and hateful, as I had seen it when she was cursing her dead rival by the leaping flames, no longer icily terrible as in the judgment-hall, no longer rich, and sombre, and splendid, like a Tyrian cloth,[2] as in the dwellings of the dead. No, her mood now was that of Aphrodité[3] triumphing. Life—radiant, ecstatic, wonderful—seemed to flow from her and around her. Softly she laughed and sighed, and swift her glances flew. She shook her heavy tresses, and their perfume filled the place; she struck her little sandalled foot upon the floor, and hummed a snatch of some old Greek epithalamium.[4] All the majesty was gone, or did but lurk and faintly flicker through her laughing eyes, like lightning seen through sunlight. She had cast off the terror of the leaping flame, the cold power of judgment that was even now being done, and the wise sadness of the tombs—cast them off and put them behind her, like the white shroud she wore, and now stood out the incarnation of lovely tempting womanhood, made more perfect—and in a way more spiritual—than ever woman was before.

'There, my Holly, sit there where thou canst see me. It is by thine own wish, remember—again I say, blame me not if thou dost spend the rest of thy little span with such a sick pain at the heart that thou wouldst fain have died before ever thy curious eyes were set upon me. There, sit so, and tell me, for in truth I am inclined for praises—tell me, am I not beautiful? Nay, speak not so hastily; consider well the point; take me feature by feature, forgetting not my form, and my hands and feet, and my hair, and the whiteness of my skin, and then tell me truly hast thou ever known a woman who in aught, ay, in one little portion of her beauty, in the curve of an eyelash even, or the modelling of a shell-like ear, is justified to hold a light before my loveliness? Now, my waist! Perchance thou thinkest it too large, but of a truth it is not so; it is this golden snake that is too large, and doth not bind it as it should. It is a wise snake, and knoweth that it is ill to tie in the waist. But see, give me thy hands—so—now press them round me, there, with but a little force, thy fingers touch, oh Holly.'

I could bear it no longer. I am but a man, and she was more than a woman. Heaven knows what she was—I do not! But then and there I fell upon my knees before her, and told her in a sad mixture of languages—for such moments confuse the thoughts—that I worshipped her as never woman was worshipped, and that I would give my immortal soul to marry her, which at that time I certainly would have done, and so, indeed, would any other man, or all the race of men rolled into one. For a moment she looked a little surprised, and then she began to laugh, and clap her hands in glee.

'Oh, so soon, oh Holly!' she said. 'I wondered how many minutes it would need to bring thee to thy knees. I have not seen a man kneel before me for so many days, and, believe me, to a woman's heart the sight is sweet, ay, wisdom and length of days take not from that dear pleasure which is our sex's only right.

'What wouldst thou?—what wouldst thou? Thou dost not know what thou doest. Have I not told thee that I am not for thee? I love but one, and thou art not the man. Ah Holly, for all thy wisdom—and in a way thou art wise—thou art but a fool running after folly. Thou wouldst look into mine eyes—thou wouldst kiss me! Well, if it pleaseth thee, *look*,' and she bent herself towards me, and fixed her dark and thrilling orbs upon my own; 'ay, and *kiss* too, if thou wilt, for, thanks be given to the scheme of things, kisses leave no marks, except upon the heart. But if thou dost kiss, I tell thee of a surety wilt thou eat out thy breast with love of me, and die!' and she bent yet further towards me till her soft hair brushed my brow, and her fragrant breath played upon my face, and made me faint and weak. Then of a sudden, even as I stretched out my arms to clasp, she straightened herself, and a quick change passed over her. Reaching out her hand, she held it over my head, and it seemed to me that something flowed from it that chilled me back to common sense, and a knowledge of propriety and the domestic virtues.

'Enough of this wanton play,' she said with a touch of sternness. 'Listen, Holly. Thou art a good and honest man, and I fain would spare thee; but, oh! it is so hard for a woman to be merciful. I have said I am not for thee, therefore let thy thoughts pass by me like an idle wind, and the dust of thy imagination sink again into the depths—well, of despair, if thou wilt. Thou dost not know me, Holly. Hadst thou seen me but ten hours past when my passion seized me, thou hadst shrunk from me in fear and trembling. I am a woman of many moods, and, like the water in that vessel, I reflect many things; but they pass, my Holly; they pass, and are forgotten. Only the water is the water still, and I still am I, and that which maketh the water maketh it, and that which maketh me maketh me, nor can my quality be altered. Therefore, pay no heed to what I seem, seeing that thou canst not know what I am. If thou troublest me again I will veil myself, and thou shalt behold my face no more.'

I rose, and sank on the cushioned couch beside her, yet quivering with emotion, though for a moment my mad passion had left me, as the leaves of a tree quiver still, although the gust be gone that stirred them. I did not dare to tell her that I *had* seen her in that deep and hellish mood, muttering incantations to the fire in the tomb.

'So,' she went on, 'now eat some fruit; believe me, it is the only true food for man. Oh, tell me of the philosophy of that Hebrew Messiah, who came after me, and whom thou sayest doth now rule Rome, and Greece, and Egypt, and the barbarians beyond. It must have been a strange philosophy that He taught, for in my day the peoples would have naught of our philosophies. Revel and lust and drink, blood and cold steel, and the shock of men gathered in the battle—these were the canons of their creeds.'

I had recovered myself a little by now, and, feeling bitterly ashamed of the weakness into which I had been betrayed, I did my best to expound to her the doctrines of Christianity, to which, however, with the single exception of our conception of Heaven and Hell, I found that she paid but faint attention, her interest being all directed towards the Man who taught them. Also I told her that among her own people, the Arabs, another prophet, one Mohammed, had arisen and preached a new faith to which many millions of mankind now adhered.

'Ah!' she said; 'I see—two new religions! I have known so many, and doubtless there have been many more since I knew aught beyond these caves of Kôr. Mankind asks ever of the skies to vision out what lies behind them. It is terror for the end, and but a subtler form of selfishness—this it is that breeds religions. Mark, my Holly, each religion claims the future for its followers; or, at the least, the good thereof. The evil is for those benighted ones who will have none of it; seeing the light the true believers worship, as the fishes see the stars, but dimly. The religions come and the religions pass, and the civilisations come and pass, and naught endures but the world and human nature. Ah! if man would but see that hope is from within and not from without—that he himself must work out his own salvation! He is there, and within him is the breath of life and a knowledge of good and evil as good and evil is to him. Thereon let him build and stand erect, and not cast himself before the image of some unknown God, modelled like his poor self, but with a bigger brain to think the evil thing; and a longer arm to do it.'

I thought to myself, which shows how old such reasoning is, being, indeed, one of the recurring quantities of theological discussion, that her argument sounded very like some that I have heard in the nineteenth century, and in other places than the caves of Kôr, and with which, by the way, I totally disagree, but I did not care to try and discuss the question with her. To begin with, my mind was too weary with all the emotions through which I had passed, and, in the second place, I knew that I should get the worst of it. It is weary work enough to argue with an ordinary materialist, who hurls statistics and whole strata of geological facts at your head, whilst you can only buffet him with deductions and instincts and the snowflakes of faith, that are, alas! so apt to melt in the hot embers of our troubles. How little chance, then, should I have against one whose brain was supernaturally sharpened, and who had two thousand years of experience, besides all manner of knowledge of the secrets of Nature at her command! Feeling that she would be more likely to convert me than I should to convert her, I thought it best to leave the matter alone, and so sat silent. Many a time since then have I bitterly regretted that I did so, for thereby I lost the only opportunity I can remember having had of ascertaining what Ayesha *really* believed, and what her 'philosophy' was.

'Well, my Holly,' she continued, 'and so those people of mine have also found a prophet, a false prophet thou sayest, for he is not thine own, and, indeed, I doubt it not. Yet in my day was it otherwise, for then we Arabs had many gods. Allât there was, and Saba, the Host of Heaven, Al Uzza, and Manah the stony one, for whom the blood of victims flowed, and Wadd and Sawâ, and Yaghûth the Lion of the dwellers in Yaman, and Yäûk the Horse of Morad, and Nasr the Eagle of Hamyar; ay, and many more.[5] Oh, the folly of it all, the shame and the pitiful folly! Yet when I rose in wisdom and spoke thereof, surely they would have slain me in the name of their outraged gods. Well, so hath it ever been;—but, my Holly, art thou weary of me already, that thou dost sit so silent? Or dost thou fear lest I should teach thee my philosophy?—for know I have a philosophy. What would a teacher be without her own philosophy? and if thou dost vex me overmuch beware! for I will have thee learn it, and thou shalt be my disciple, and we twain will found a faith that shall swallow up all others. Faithless man! And but half an hour since thou wast upon thy knees—the posture does not suit thee, Holly—swearing that thou didst love me. What shall we do?—Nay, I have it. I will come and see this youth, the Lion, as the old man Billali calls him, who came with thee, and who is so sick. The fever must have run its course by now, and if he is about to die

I will recover him. Fear not, my Holly, I shall use no magic. Have I not told thee that there is no such thing as magic, though there is such a thing as understanding and applying the forces which are in Nature? Go now, and presently when I have made the drug ready I will follow thee.'*

Accordingly I went, only to find Job and Ustane in a great state of grief, declaring that Leo was in the throes of death, and that they had been searching for me everywhere. I rushed to the couch, and glanced at him: clearly he was dying. He was senseless, and breathing heavily, but his lips were quivering, and every now and again a little shudder ran down his frame. I knew enough of doctoring to see that in another hour he would be beyond the reach of earthly help—perhaps in another five minutes. How I cursed my selfishness and the folly that had kept me lingering by Ayesha's side while my dear boy lay dying! Alas and alas! how easily the best of us are lighted down to evil by the gleam of a woman's eyes! What a wicked wretch was I! Actually, for the last half-hour I had scarcely thought of Leo, and this, be it remembered, of the man who for twenty years had been my dearest companion, and the chief interest of my existence. And now, perhaps, it was too late!

I wrung my hands, and glanced round. Ustane was sitting by the couch, and in her eyes burnt the dull light of despair. Job was blubbering—I am sorry I cannot name his distress by any more delicate word—audibly in the corner. Seeing my eye fixed upon him he went outside to give way to his grief in the passage. Obviously the only hope lay in Ayesha. She, and she alone—unless, indeed, she was an impostor, which I could not believe—could save him. I would go and implore her to come. As I started to do so, however, Job came flying into the room, his hair literally standing on end with terror.

* Ayesha was a great chemist, indeed chemistry appears to have been her only amusement and occupation. She had one of the caves fitted up as a laboratory, and, although her appliances were necessarily rude, the results that she attained were, as will become clear in the course of this narrative, sufficiently surprising.—L. H. H.

'Oh, God help us, sir!' he ejaculated in a frightened whisper, 'here's a corpse a-coming sliding down the passage!'

For a moment I was puzzled, but presently, of course, it struck me that he must have seen Ayesha, wrapped in her grave-like garment, and been deceived by the extraordinary undulating smoothness of her walk into a belief that she was a white ghost gliding towards him. Indeed, at that very moment the question was settled, for Ayesha herself was in the apartment, or rather cave. Job turned, and saw her sheeted form, and then, with a convulsive howl of 'Here it comes!' sprang into a corner, and jammed his face against the wall, and Ustane, guessing whose the dread presence must be, prostrated herself upon her face.

'Thou comest in a good time, Ayesha,' I said, 'for my boy lies at the point of death.'

'So,' she said softly; 'provided he be not dead, it is no matter, for I can bring him back to life, my Holly. Is that man there thy servant, and is that the method wherewith thy servants greet strangers in thy country?'

'He is frightened of thy garb—it hath a death-like air,' I answered.

She laughed.

'And the girl? Ah, I see now. It is her of whom thou didst speak to me. Well, bid them both to leave us, and we will see to this sick Lion of thine. I love not that underlings should perceive my wisdom.'

Thereon I told Ustane in Arabic and Job in English both to leave the room; an order which the latter obeyed readily enough, and was glad to obey, for he could not in any way subdue his fear. But it was otherwise with Ustane.

'What does *She* want?' she whispered, divided between her fear of the terrible Queen and her anxiety to remain near Leo. 'It is surely the right of a wife to be near her husband when he dieth. Nay, I will not go, my lord, the Baboon.'

'Why doth not that woman leave us, my Holly?' asked Ayesha, from the other end of the cave, where she was engaged in carelessly examining some of the sculptures on the wall.

'She is not willing to leave Leo,' I answered, not knowing what to say. Ayesha wheeled round, and, pointing to the girl Ustane, said one word, and one only, but it was quite enough, for the tone in which it was said meant volumes.

'Go!'

And then Ustane crept past her on her hands and knees, and went.

'Thou seest, my Holly,' said Ayesha, with a little laugh, 'it was needful that I should give these people a lesson in obedience. That girl went nigh to disobeying me, but then she did not learn this morn how I treat the disobedient. Well, she has gone; and now let me see the youth,' and she glided towards the couch on which Leo lay, with his face in the shadow and turned toward the wall.

'He hath a noble shape,' she said, as she bent over him to look upon his face.

Next second her tall and willowy form was staggering back across the room, as though she had been shot or stabbed, staggering back till at last she struck the cavern wall, and then there burst from her lips the most awful and unearthly scream that I ever heard in all my life.

'What is it, Ayesha?' I cried. 'Is he dead?'

She turned, and sprang towards me like a tigress.

'Thou dog!' she said, in her terrible whisper, which sounded like the hiss of a snake, 'why didst thou hide this from me?' And she stretched out her arm, and I thought that she was about to slay me.

'What?' I ejaculated, in the most lively terror; 'what?'

'Ah!' she said, 'perchance thou didst not know. Learn, my Holly, learn: there lies—there lies my lost Kallikrates. Kallikrates, who has come back to me at last, as I knew he would, as I knew he would;' and she began to sob and to laugh, and generally to conduct herself like any other lady who is a little upset, murmuring 'Kallikrates, Kallikrates!'

'Nonsense,' thought I to myself, but I did not like to say it; and, indeed, at that moment I was thinking of Leo's life, having forgotten everything else in that terrible anxiety. What I feared now was that he should die while she was 'carrying on.'

'Unless thou art able to help him, Ayesha,' I put in, by way of a reminder, 'thy Kallikrates will soon be far beyond thy calling. Surely he dieth even now.'

'True,' she said, with a start. 'Oh, why did I not come before! I am unnerved—my hand trembles, even mine—and yet it is very easy. Here, thou Holly, take this phial,' and she produced a tiny jar of pottery from the folds of her garment, 'and pour the liquid in it down his throat. It will cure him if he be not dead. Swift, now! Swift! The man dies!'

I glanced towards him; it was true enough, Leo was in his death-struggle. I saw his poor face turning ashen, and heard the breath begin to rattle in his throat. The phial was stoppered with a little piece of wood. I drew it with my teeth, and a drop of the fluid within flew out upon my tongue. It had a sweet flavour, and for a second made my head swim, and a mist gather before my eyes, but happily the effect passed away as swiftly as it had arisen,

When I reached Leo's side he was plainly expiring—his golden head was slowly turning from side to side, and his mouth was slightly open. I called to Ayesha to hold his head, and this she managed to do, though the woman was quivering from head to foot, like an aspen-leaf or a startled horse. Then, forcing the jaw a little more open, I poured the contents of the phial into his mouth. Instantly a little vapour arose from it, as happens when one disturbs nitric acid, and this sight did not increase my hopes, already faint enough, of the efficacy of the treatment.

One thing, however, was certain, the death-throes ceased—at first I thought because he had got beyond them, and crossed the awful river. His face turned to a livid pallor, and his heart-beats, which had been feeble enough before, seemed to die away altogether—only the eyelid still twitched a little. In my doubt I looked up at Ayesha, whose head-wrapping had slipped back in her excitement when she went reeling across the room. She was still holding Leo's head, and, with a face as pale as his own, watching his countenance with such an expression of agonised anxiety as I have never seen before. Clearly she did not know if he would live or die. Five minutes slowly passed, and I saw that she was abandoning hope; her lovely oval face seemed to fall in and grow visibly thinner beneath the pressure of a mental agony whose pencil drew black lines about the hollows of her eyes. The coral faded even from her lips, till they were as white as Leo's face, and quivered pitifully. It was shocking to see her: even in my own grief I felt for hers.

'Is it too late?' I gasped.

She hid her face in her hands, and made no answer, and I too turned away. But as I did so I heard a deep-drawn breath, and looking down perceived a line of colour creeping up Leo's face, then another and another, and then, wonder of wonders, the man we had thought dead turned over on his side.

'Thou seest,' I said in a whisper.

'I see,' she answered hoarsely. 'He is saved. I thought we were too late—another moment—one little moment more—and he had been gone!' and she burst into an awful flood of tears, sobbing as though her heart would break, and yet looking lovelier than ever as she did it. At last she ceased.

'Forgive me, my Holly—forgive me for my weakness,' she said. 'Thou seest after all I am a very woman. Think—now think of it! This morning didst thou speak of the place of torment appointed by this new religion of thine. Hell or Hades thou didst call it—a place where the vital essence lives and retains an individual memory, and where all the errors and faults of judgment, and unsatisfied passions and the unsubstantial terrors of the mind wherewith it hath at any time had to do, come to mock and haunt and gibe and wring the heart for ever and for ever with the vision of its own hopelessness. Thus, even thus, have I lived for full two thousand years—for some six and sixty generations, as ye reckon time—in a Hell, as thou callest it—tormented by the memory of a crime, tortured day and night with an unfulfilled desire—without companionship, without comfort, without death, and led on only down my dreary road by the marsh lights of Hope, which though they flickered here and there, and now glowed strong, and now were not, yet, as my skill told me, would one day lead unto my deliverer.

'And then—think of it still, oh Holly, for never shalt thou hear such another tale, or see such another scene, nay, not even if I give thee ten thousand years of life—and thou shalt have it in payment if thou wilt—think: at last my deliverer came—he for whom I had watched and waited through the generations—at the appointed time he came to seek me, as I knew that he must come, for my wisdom could not err, though I knew not when or how. Yet see how ignorant I was! See how small my knowledge, and how faint my strength! For hours he lay here sick unto death, and I felt it not—I who had waited for him for two thousand years—I knew it not. And then at last I see him, and behold, my chance is gone but by a hair's breadth even before I have it, for he is in the very jaws of death; whence no power of mine can draw him. And if he die, surely must the Hell be lived through once more—once more must I face the weary centuries, and wait, and wait till the time in its fulness shall bring my beloved back to me. And then thou gavest him the medicine, and that five minutes dragged along before I knew if he would live or die, and I tell thee that all the sixty generations that are gone were not so long as that five minutes. But they passed at length, and still he showed no sign, and I knew that if the drug works not then, so far as I have had knowledge, it works not at all. Then thought I that he was once more dead, and all the tortures of all the years gathered themselves into a single venomed spear, and pierced me through and through, because once again I had lost Kallikrates! And then, when all was done, behold! he sighed, behold! he lived, and I knew that he would live, for none die on whom the drug takes hold. Think of it now, my Holly—think of the wonder of it! He will sleep for twelve hours, and then the fever will have left him!'

She stopped, and laid her hand upon the golden head, and then bent down and kissed the brow with a chastened abandonment of tenderness that would have been beautiful to behold had not the sight cut me to the heart—for I was jealous!

XVIII

Go, Woman!

Then followed a silence of a minute or so, during which *She* appeared, if one might judge from the almost angelic rapture of her face—for she looked angelic sometimes—to be plunged in a happy ecstasy. Suddenly, however, a new thought struck her, and her expression became the very reverse of angelic.

'Almost had I forgotten,' she said, 'that woman, Ustane. What is she to Kallikrates—his servant, or ——' and she paused, and her voice trembled.

I shrugged my shoulders. 'I understand that she is wed to him according to the custom of the Amahagger,' I answered; 'but I know not.'

Her face grew dark as a thunder-cloud. Old as she was, Ayesha had not outlived jealousy.

'Then there is an end,' she said; 'she must die, even now!'

'For what crime?' I asked, horrified. 'She is guilty of naught that thou art not guilty of thyself, oh Ayesha. She loves the man, and he has been pleased to accept her love: where, then, is her sin?'

'Truly, oh Holly, thou art foolish,' she answered, almost petulantly. 'Where is her sin? Her sin is that she stands between me and my desire. Well, I know that I can take him from her—for dwells there a man upon this earth, oh Holly, who could resist me if I put out my strength? Men are faithful for so long only as temptations pass them by. If the temptation be but strong enough, then will the man yield, for every man, like every rope, hath his breaking strain, and passion is to men what gold and power are to women—the weight upon their weakness. Believe me, ill will it go with mortal women in that heaven of which thou speakest, if only the spirits be more fair, for their lords will never turn to look upon them, and their heaven will become their hell. For man can be bought with woman's beauty, if it be but beautiful enough; and woman's beauty can be ever bought with gold, if only there be gold enough. So was it in my day, and so it will be to the end of time. The world is a great mart, my Holly, where all things are for sale to him who bids the highest in the currency of our desires.'

These remarks, which were as cynical as might have been expected from a woman of Ayesha's age and experience, jarred upon me, and I answered, testily, that in our heaven there was no marriage or giving in marriage.[1]

'Else would it not be heaven, dost thou mean?' she put in. 'Fie upon thee, Holly, to think so ill of us poor women! Is it, then, marriage that marks the line between thy heaven and thy hell? But enough of this. This is no time for disputing and the challenge of our wits. Why dost thou always dispute? Art thou also a philosopher of these latter days? As for this woman, she must die; for though I can take her lover from her, yet, while she lived, might he think tenderly of her, and that I cannot away with.[2] No other woman shall dwell in my Lord's thoughts; my empire shall be all my own. She hath had her day, let her be content; for better is an hour with love than a century of loneliness—now the night shall swallow her.'

'Nay, nay,' I cried, 'it would be a wicked crime; and from a crime naught comes but what is evil. For thine own sake do not this deed.'

'Is it, then, a crime, oh foolish man, to put away that which stands between us and our ends? Then is our life one long crime, my Holly; for day by day we destroy that we may live, since in this world none save the strongest can endure. Those who are weak must perish; the earth is to the strong, and the fruits thereof. For every tree that grows a score shall wither, that the strong ones may take their share. We run to place and power over the dead bodies of those who fail and fall; ay, we win the food we eat from out the mouths of starving babes. It is the scheme of things. Thou sayest, too, that a crime breeds evil, but therein thou dost lack experience; for out of crimes come many good things, and out of good grows much evil. The cruel rage of the tyrant may prove a blessing to thousands who come after him, and the sweet-heartedness of a holy man may make a nation slaves. Man doeth this and doeth that from the good or evil of his heart; but he knoweth not to what end his moral sense doth prompt him; for when he striketh he is blind to where the blow shall fall, nor can he count the airy threads that weave the web of circumstance. Good and evil, love and hate, night and day, sweet and bitter, man and woman, heaven above and the earth beneath—all these things are necessary, one to the other, and who knows the end of each? I tell thee that there is a hand of Fate that twines them up to bear the burden of its purpose, and all things are gathered in that great rope to which all things are needful. Therefore doth it not become us to say this thing is evil and this good, or the dark is hateful and the light lovely; for to other eyes than ours the evil may be the good and the darkness more beautiful than the day, or all alike be fair. Hearest thou, my Holly?'

I felt it was hopeless to argue against casuistry of this nature, which, if it were carried to its logical conclusion, would absolutely destroy all morality, as we understand it. But her talk gave me a fresh thrill of fear; for what may not be possible to a being who, unconstrained by human law, is also absolutely unshackled by a moral sense of right and wrong, which, however partial and conventional it may be, is yet based, as our conscience tells us, upon the great wall of individual responsibility that marks off mankind from the beasts?

But I was deeply anxious to save Ustane, whom I liked and respected, from the dire fate that overshadowed her at the hands of her mighty rival. So I made one more appeal.

'Ayesha,' I said, 'thou art too subtle for me; but thou thyself hast told me that each man should be a law unto himself, and follow the teaching of his heart. Hath thy heart no mercy towards her whose place thou wouldst take? Bethink thee, as thou sayest—though to me the thing is incredible—him whom thou desirest has returned to thee after many ages, and but now thou hast, as thou sayest also, wrung him from the jaws of death. Wilt thou celebrate his coming by the murder of one who loved him, and whom perchance he loved—one, at the least, who saved his life for thee when the spears of thy slaves would have made an end thereof? Thou sayest also that in past days thou didst grievously wrong this man, that with thine own hand thou didst slay him because of the Egyptian Amenartas whom he loved.'

'How knowest thou that, oh stranger? How knowest thou that name? I spoke it not to thee,' she broke in with a cry, catching at my arm.

'Perchance I dreamed it,' I answered; 'strange dreams do hover about these caves of Kôr. It seems that the dream was, indeed, a shadow of the truth. What came to thee of thy mad crime?—two thousand years of waiting, was it not? And now wouldst thou repeat the history? Say what thou wilt, I tell thee that evil will come of it; for to him who doeth, at the least, good breeds good and evil evil, even though in after days out of evil cometh good. Offences must needs come; but woe to him by whom the offence cometh. So said that Messiah[3] of whom I spoke to thee, and it was truly said. If thou slayest this innocent woman, I say unto thee that thou shalt be accursed, and pluck no fruit from thine ancient tree of love. Also, what thinkest thou? How will this man take thee red-handed from the slaughter of her who loved and tended him?'

'As to that,' she answered, 'I have already answered thee. Had I slain thee as well as her, yet should he love me, Holly, because he could not save himself therefrom any more than thou couldst save thyself from dying, if by chance I slew thee, oh Holly. And yet maybe there is truth in what thou dost say; for in some way it presseth on my mind. If it may be, I will spare this woman; for have I not told thee that I am not cruel for the sake of cruelty? I love not to see suffering, or to cause it. Let her come before me—quick now, before my mood changes,' and she hastily covered her face with its gauzy wrapping.

Well pleased to have succeeded even to this extent, I passed out into the passage and called to Ustane, whose white garment I caught sight of some yards away, huddled up against one of the earthenware lamps that were placed at intervals along the tunnel. She rose, and ran towards me.

'Is my lord dead? Oh, say not he is dead,' she cried, lifting her noble-looking face, all stained as it was with tears, up to me with an air of infinite beseeching that went straight to my heart.

'Nay, he lives,' I answered. '*She* hath saved him. Enter.'

She sighed deeply, entered, and fell upon her hands and knees, after the custom of the Amahagger people, in the presence of the dread *She*.

'Stand,' said Ayesha in her coldest voice, 'and come hither.'

Ustane obeyed, standing before her with bowed head.

Then came a pause, which Ayesha broke.

'Who is this man?' she said, pointing to the sleeping form of Leo.

'The man is my husband,' she answered in a low voice.

'Who gave him to thee for a husband?'

'I took him according to the custom of our country, oh *She*.'

'Thou hast done evil, woman, in taking this man, who is a stranger. He is not a man of thine own race, and the custom fails. Listen: perchance thou didst this thing through ignorance, therefore, woman, do I spare thee, otherwise hadst thou died. Listen again. Go from hence back to thine own place, and never dare to speak to or set thine eyes upon this man again. He is not for thee. Listen a third time. If thou breakest this my law, that moment thou diest. Go.'

But Ustane did not move.

'Go, woman!'

Then she looked up, and I saw that her face was torn with passion.

'Nay, oh *She*, I will not go,' she answered in a choked voice: 'the man is my husband, and I love him—I love him, and I will not leave him. What right hast thou to command me to leave my husband?'

I saw a little quiver pass down Ayesha's frame, and shuddered myself, fearing the worst.

'Be pitiful,' I said in Latin; 'it is but Nature working.'

'I am pitiful,' she answered coldly in the same language; 'had I not been pitiful she had been dead even now.' Then addressing Ustane: 'Woman, I say to thee, go before I destroy thee where thou art!'

'I will not go! He is mine—mine!' she cried in anguish. 'I took him, and I saved his life! Destroy me, then, if thou hast the power! I will not give thee my husband—never—never!'

Ayesha made a movement so swift that I could scarcely follow it, but it seemed to me that she lightly struck the poor girl upon the head with her hand. I looked at Ustane, and then staggered back in horror, for there upon her hair, right across her bronze-like tresses, were three finger-marks *white as snow*. As for the girl herself, she had put her hands to her head, and was looking dazed.

'Great heavens!' I said, perfectly aghast at this dreadful manifestation of inhuman power; but *She* did but laugh a little.

'Thou thinkest, poor ignorant fool,' she said to the bewildered woman, 'that I have not power to slay. Stay, there lies a mirror,' and she pointed to Leo's round shaving-glass that had been arranged by Job with other things upon his portmanteau; 'give it to this woman, my Holly, and let her see that which lies across her hair, and whether or no I have power to slay.'

I picked up the glass, and held it before Ustane's eyes. She gazed, then felt at her hair, then gazed again, and then sank upon the ground with a sort of sob.

'Now, wilt thou go, or must I strike a second time?' asked Ayesha, in mockery. 'Look, I have set my seal upon thee so that I may know thee till thy hair is all as white as it. If I see thy face here again, be sure, too, that thy bones shall soon be whiter than my mark upon thy hair.'

Utterly awed and broken down, the poor creature rose, and,

marked with that awful mark, crept from the room sobbing bitterly.

'Look not so frighted, my Holly,' said Ayesha, when she had gone. 'I tell thee I deal not in magic—there is no such thing. 'Tis only a force that thou dost not understand. I marked her to strike terror to her heart, else must I have slain her. And now I will bid my servants bear my Lord Kallikrates to a chamber near mine own, that I may watch over him, and be ready to greet him when he wakes; and thither, too, shalt thou come, my Holly, and the white man, thy servant. But one thing remember at thy peril. Naught shalt thou say to Kallikrates as to how this woman went, and as little as may be of me. Now, I have warned thee!' and she slid away to give her orders, leaving me more absolutely confounded than ever. Indeed, so bewildered was I, and racked and torn with such a succession of various emotions, that I began to think that I must be going mad. However, perhaps fortunately, I had but little time to reflect, for presently the mutes arrived to carry the sleeping Leo and our possessions across the central cave, so for a while all was bustle. Our new rooms were situated immediately behind what we used to call Ayesha's boudoir—the curtained space where I had first seen her. Where she herself slept I did not then know, but it was somewhere quite close.

That night I passed in Leo's room, but he slept through it like the dead, never once stirring. I also slept fairly well, as, indeed, I needed to do, but my sleep was full of dreams of all the horrors and wonders I had undergone. Chiefly, however, I was haunted by that frightful piece of *diablerie* by which Ayesha left her finger marks upon her rival's hair. There was something so terrible about the swift, snake-like movement, and the instantaneous blanching of that threefold line, that, if the results to Ustane had been much more tremendous, I doubt if they would have impressed me so deeply. To this day I often dream of that awful scene, and see the weeping woman, bereaved, and marked like Cain, cast a last look at her lover, and creep from the presence of her dread Queen.

Another dream that troubled me originated in the huge

pyramid of bones. I dreamed that they all stood up and marched past me in thousands and tens of thousands—in squadrons, companies, and armies—with the sunlight shining through their hollow ribs. On they rushed across the plain to Kôr, their imperial home; I saw the drawbridges fall before them, and heard their bones clank through the brazen gates. On they went, up the splendid streets, on past fountains, palaces, and temples such as the eye of man never saw. But there was no man to greet them in the market-place, and no woman's face appeared at the windows—only a bodiless voice went before them, calling: '*Fallen is Imperial Kôr!—fallen!—fallen! fallen!*'[4] On, right through the city, marched those gleaming phalanxes, and the rattle of their bony tread echoed through the silent air as they pressed grimly on. They passed through the city and climbed the wall, and marched along the great roadway that was made upon the wall, till at length they once more reached the drawbridge. Then, as the sun was sinking, they returned again towards their sepulchre, and luridly his light shone in the sockets of their empty eyes, throwing gigantic shadows of their bones, that stretched away, and crept and crept like huge spider's legs as their armies wound across the plain. Then they came to the cave, and once more one by one flung themselves in unending files through the hole into the pit of bones, and I awoke, shuddering, to see *She*, who had evidently been standing between my couch and Leo's, glide like a shadow from the room.

After this I slept again, soundly this time, till morning, when I awoke much refreshed, and got up. At last the hour drew near at which, according to Ayesha, Leo was to awake, and with it came *She* herself, as usual, veiled.

'Thou shalt see, oh Holly,' she said; 'presently shall he awake in his right mind, the fever having left him.'

Hardly were the words out of her mouth, when Leo turned round and stretched out his arms, yawned, opened his eyes, and, perceiving a female form bending over him, threw his arms round her and kissed her, mistaking her, perhaps, for Ustane. At any rate, he said, in Arabic, 'Hullo, Ustane, why have you tied your head up like that? Have you got the toothache?' and then, in English, 'I say, I'm awfully hungry. Why, Job, you old son of a gun, where the deuce have we got to now—eh?'

'I am sure I wish I knew, Mr. Leo,' said Job, edging suspiciously past Ayesha, whom he still regarded with the utmost disgust and horror, being by no means sure that she was not an animated corpse; 'but you mustn't talk, Mr. Leo, you've been very ill, and given us a great deal of hanxiety, and, if this lady,' looking at Ayesha, 'would be so kind as to move, I'll bring you your soup.'

This turned Leo's attention to the 'lady,' who was standing by in perfect silence. 'Hullo!' he said; 'that is not Ustane—where is Ustane?'

Then, for the first time, Ayesha spoke to him, and her first words were a lie. 'She has gone from hence upon a visit,' she said; 'and, behold, in her place am I here as thine handmaiden.'

Ayesha's silver notes seemed to puzzle Leo's half-awakened intellect, as also did her corpse-like wrappings. However, he said nothing at the time, but drank off his soup greedily enough, and then turned over and slept again till the evening. When he woke for the second time he saw me, and began to question me as to what had happened, but I had to put him off as best I could till the morrow, when he awoke almost miraculously better. Then I told him something of his illness and of my doings, but as Ayesha was present I could not tell him much except that she was the Queen of the country, and well disposed towards us, and that it was her pleasure to go veiled; for, though of course I spoke in English, I was afraid that she might understand what we were saying from the expression of our faces, and besides, I remembered her warning.

On the following day Leo got up almost entirely recovered. The flesh wound in his side was healed, and his constitution, naturally a vigorous one, had shaken off the exhaustion consequent on his terrible fever with a rapidity that I can only attribute to the effects of the wonderful drug which Ayesha had given to him, and also to the fact that his illness had been too short to reduce him very much. With his returning health came back full recollection of all his adventures up to the time when he had lost consciousness in the marsh, and of course of Ustane also, to whom I had discovered he had grown considerably attached. Indeed, he overwhelmed me with questions about the poor girl, which I did not dare to answer, for after Leo's first wakening *She* had sent for me, and again warned me solemnly that I was to reveal nothing of the story to him, delicately hinting that if I did it would be the worse for me. She also, for the second time, cautioned me not to tell Leo anything more than I was obliged about herself, saying that she would reveal herself to him in her own time.

Indeed, her whole manner changed. After all that I had seen I had expected that she would take the earliest opportunity of claiming the man she believed to be her old-world lover, but this, for some reason of her own, which was at the time quite inscrutable to me, she did not do. All that she did was to attend to his wants quietly, and with a humility which was in striking contrast with her former imperious bearing, addressing him always in a tone of something very like respect, and keeping him with her as much as possible. Of course his curiosity was as much excited about this mysterious woman as my own had been, and he was particularly anxious to see her face, which I had, without entering into particulars, told him was as lovely as her form and voice. This in itself was enough to raise the expectations of any young man to a dangerous pitch, and had it not been that he had not as yet completely shaken off the effects of illness, and was much troubled in his mind about Ustane, of whose affection and brave devotion he spoke in touching terms, I have no doubt that he would have entered into her plans, and fallen in love with her by anticipation. As it was, however, he was simply wildly curious, and also, like myself, considerably awed, for though no hint had been given to him by Ayesha of her extraordinary age, he not unnaturally came to identify her with the woman spoken of on the potsherd. At last, quite driven into a corner by his continual questions, which he showered on me while he was dressing on this third morning, I referred him to Ayesha, saying, with perfect truth, that I did not know where Ustane was. Accordingly, after Leo had eaten a hearty breakfast, we adjourned into *She's* presence, for her mutes had orders to admit us at all hours.

She was, as usual, seated in what, for want of a better term, we called her boudoir, and on the curtains being drawn she rose from her couch and, stretching out both hands, came forward to greet us, or rather Leo; for I, as may be imagined, was now quite left in the cold. It was a pretty sight to see her veiled form gliding towards the sturdy young Englishman, dressed in his grey flannel suit; for though he is half a Greek in blood, Leo is, with the exception of his hair, one of the most English-looking men I ever saw. He has nothing of the supple form or slippery manner of the modern Greek about him, though I presume that he got his remarkable personal beauty from his foreign mother, whose portrait he resembles not a little. He is very tall and big-chested, and yet not awkward, as so many big men are, and his head is set upon him in such a fashion as to give him a proud and vigorous air, which was well translated in his Amahagger name of the 'Lion.'

'Greeting to thee, my young stranger lord,' she said in her softest voice. 'Right glad am I to see thee upon thy feet. Believe me, had I not saved thee at the last, never wouldst thou have stood upon those feet again. But the danger is done, and it shall be my care'—and she flung a world of meaning into the words—'that it doth return no more.'

Leo bowed to her, and then, in his best Arabic, thanked her for all her kindness and courtesy in caring for one unknown to her.

'Nay,' she answered softly, 'ill could the world spare such a man. Beauty is too rare upon it. Give me no thanks, who am made happy by thy coming.'

'Humph! old fellow,' said Leo aside to me in English, 'the lady is very civil. We seem to have tumbled into clover. I hope that you have made the most of your opportunities. By Jove! what a pair of arms she has got!'

I nudged him in the ribs to make him keep quiet, for I caught sight of a gleam from Ayesha's veiled eyes, which were regarding me curiously.

'I trust,' went on Ayesha, 'that my servants have attended well upon thee; if there can be comfort in this poor place, be sure it waits on thee. Is there aught that I can do for thee more?'

'Yes, oh *She*,' answered Leo hastily. 'I would fain know whither the young lady who was looking after me has gone to.'

'Ah,' said Ayesha: 'the girl—yes, I saw her. Nay, I know not; she said that she would go, I know not whither. Perchance she will return, perchance not. It is wearisome waiting on the sick, and these savage women are fickle.'

Leo looked both sulky and distressed at this intelligence.

'It's very odd,' he said to me in English; and then addressing *She*, 'I cannot understand,' he said; 'the young lady and I—well—in short, we had a regard for each other.'

Ayesha laughed a little very musically, and then turned the subject.

XIX

'Give Me a Black Goat!'

The conversation after this was of such a desultory order that I do not quite recollect it. For some reason, perhaps from a desire to keep her identity and character in reserve, Ayesha did not talk freely, as she usually did. Presently, however, she informed Leo that she had arranged a dance that night for our amusement. I was astonished to hear this, as I fancied that the Amahagger were much too gloomy a folk to indulge in any such frivolity; but, as will presently more clearly appear, it turned out that an Amahagger dance has little in common with such fantastic festivities in other countries, savage or civilised. Then, as we were about to withdraw, she suggested that Leo might like to see some of the wonders of the caves, and as he gladly assented thither we departed, accompanied by Job and Billali. To describe our visit would only be to repeat a great deal of what I have already said. The tombs we entered were indeed different, for the whole rock was a honeycomb of sepulchres,* but the contents were nearly always similar. Afterwards we visited the pyramid of bones that had haunted my dreams on the previous night, and from thence went down a long passage to one of the great vaults occupied by the bodies of the poorer citizens of Imperial Kôr. These bodies were not nearly so well preserved as were those of the wealthier classes. Many of them had no linen covering on them, also they

* For a long while it puzzled me to know what could have been done with the enormous quantities of rock that must have been dug out of these vast caves; but I afterwards discovered that it was for the most part built into the walls and palaces of Kôr, and also used to line the reservoirs and sewers.—L. H. H.

were buried from five hundred to one thousand in a single large vault, the corpses in some instances being thickly piled one upon another, like a heap of slain.

Leo was of course intensely interested in this stupendous and unequalled sight, which was, indeed, enough to awake all the imagination a man had in him into the most active life. But to poor Job it did not prove attractive. His nerves—already seriously shaken by what he had undergone since we had arrived in this terrible country—were, as may be imagined, still further disturbed by the spectacle of these masses of departed humanity, whereof the forms still remained perfect before his eyes, though their voices were for ever lost in the eternal silence of the tomb. Nor was he comforted when old Billali, by way of soothing his evident agitation, informed him that he should not be frightened of these dead things, as he would soon be like them himself.

'There's a nice thing to say of a man, sir,' he ejaculated, when I translated this little remark; 'but there, what can one expect of an old man-eating savage? Not but what I dare say he's right,' and Job sighed.

When we had finished inspecting the caves, we returned and had our meal, for it was now past four in the afternoon, and we all—especially Leo—needed some food and rest. At six o'clock we, together with Job, waited on Ayesha, who set to work to terrify our poor servant still further by showing him pictures on the pool of water in the font-like vessel. She learnt from me that he was one of seventeen children, and then bid him think of all his brothers and sisters, or as many of them as he could, gathered together in his father's cottage. Then she told him to look in the water, and there, reflected from its stilly surface, was that dead scene of many years gone by, as it was recalled to our retainer's brain. Some of the faces were clear enough, but some were mere blurs and splotches, or with one feature grossly exaggerated; the fact being that, in these instances, Job had been unable to recall the exact appearances of the individuals, or remembered them only by a peculiarity of his tribe, and the water could only reflect what he saw with his mind's eye. For it must be remembered that *She's* power in this matter was strictly limited; she could apparently, except in very rare instances, only photograph upon the water what was actually in the mind of some one present, and then only by his will. But if she was personally acquainted with a locality, she could, as in the case of ourselves and the whale-boat, throw its reflection upon the water, and also it seems the reflection of anything extraneous that was passing there at the time. This power, however, did not extend to the minds of others. For instance, she could show me the interior of my college chapel, as I remembered it, but not as it was at the moment of reflection; for, where other people were concerned, her art was strictly limited to the facts or memories present to *their* consciousness at the moment. So much was this so, that when we tried, for her amusement, to show her pictures of noted buildings, such as St. Paul's or the Houses of Parliament, the result was most imperfect; for, of course, though we had a good general idea of their appearance, we could not recall all the architectural details, and therefore the minutiæ necessary to a perfect reflection were wanting. But Job could not be got to understand this, and so far from accepting a natural explanation of the matter, which was after all, though strange enough in all conscience, nothing more than an instance of glorified and perfected telepathy, he set the whole thing down as a manifestation of the blackest magic. I shall never forget the howl of terror which he uttered when he saw the more or less perfect portraits of his long-scattered brethren staring at him from the quiet water, or the merry peal of laughter with which Ayesha greeted his consternation. As for Leo, he did not altogether like it either, but ran his fingers through his yellow curls, and remarked that it gave him the creeps.

After about an hour of this amusement, in the latter part of which Job did *not* participate, the mutes by signs indicated that Billali was waiting for an audience. Accordingly he was told to 'crawl up,' which he did as awkwardly as usual, and announced that the dance was ready to begin if *She* and the white strangers would be pleased to attend. Shortly afterwards we all rose, and

Ayesha having thrown a dark cloak (the same, by the way, that she had worn when I saw her cursing by the fire) over her white wrappings, we started. The dance was to be held in the open air, on the smooth rocky plateau in front of the great cave, and thither we made our way. About fifteen paces from the mouth of the cave we found three chairs placed, and here we sat and waited, for as yet no dancers were to be seen. The night was almost, but not quite, dark, the moon not having risen as yet, which made us wonder how we should be able to see the dancing.

'Thou wilt presently understand,' said Ayesha, with a little laugh, when Leo asked her; and we certainly did. Scarcely were the words out of her mouth when from every point we saw dark forms rushing up, each bearing with him what we at first took to be an enormous flaming torch. Whatever they were they were burning furiously, for the flames stood out a yard or more behind each bearer. On they came, fifty or more of them, carrying their flaming burdens and looking like so many devils from hell. Leo was the first to discover what these burdens were.

'Great heaven!' he said, 'they are corpses on fire!'

I stared and stared again—he was perfectly right—the torches that were to light our entertainment were human mummies from the caves!

On rushed the bearers of the flaming corpses, and, meeting at a spot about twenty paces in front of us, built their ghastly burdens crossways into a huge bonfire. Heavens! how they roared and flared! No tar barrel could have burnt as those mummies did. Nor was this all. Suddenly I saw one great fellow seize a flaming human arm that had fallen from its parent frame, and rush off into the darkness. Presently he stopped, and a tall streak of fire shot up into the air, illumining the gloom, and also the lamp from which it sprang. That lamp was the mummy of a woman tied to a stout stake let into the rock, and he had fired her hair. On he went a few paces and touched a second, then a third, and a fourth, till at last we were surrounded on all three sides by a great ring of bodies flaring furiously, the material with which they were preserved having rendered them so inflammable that the flames would literally spout out of the ears and mouth in tongues of fire a foot or more in length.

Nero illuminated his gardens with live Christians soaked in tar, and we were now treated to a similar spectacle, probably for the first time since his day, only happily our lamps were not living ones.[1]

But although this element of horror was fortunately wanting, to describe the awful and hideous grandeur of the spectacle thus presented to us is, I feel, so absolutely beyond my poor powers, that I scarcely dare attempt it. To begin with, it appealed to the moral as well as the physical susceptibilities. There was something very terrible, and yet very fascinating, about the employment of the remote dead to illumine the orgies of the living; in itself the thing was a satire, both on the living and the dead. Cæsar's dust—or is it Alexander's?—may stop a bung-hole, but the functions of these dead Cæsars of the past was to light up a savage fetish dance. To such base uses may we come,[2] of so little account may we be in the minds of the eager multitudes that we shall breed, many of whom, so far from revering our memory, will live to curse us for begetting them into such a world of woe.

Then there was the physical side of the spectacle, and a weird and splendid one it was. Those old citizens of Kôr burnt as, to judge from their sculptures and inscriptions, they had lived, very fast, and with the utmost liberality. What is more, there were plenty of them. As soon as ever a mummy had burnt down to the ankles, which it did in about twenty minutes, the feet were kicked away, and another one put in its place. The bonfire was kept going on the same generous scale, and its flames shot up, with a hiss and a crackle, twenty or thirty feet into the air, throwing great flashes of light far out into the gloom, through which the dark forms of the Amahagger flitted to and fro like devils replenishing the infernal fires. We all stood and stared aghast—shocked, and yet fascinated at so strange a spectacle, and half-expecting to see the spirits those flaming forms had once enclosed come creeping from the shadows to work vengeance on their desecrators.

'I promised thee a strange sight, my Holly,' laughed Ayesha, whose nerves alone did not seem to be affected; 'and, behold, I have not failed thee. Also, it hath its lesson. Trust not to the future, for who knows what the future may bring! Therefore, live for the day, and endeavour not to escape the dust which seems to be man's end. What thinkest thou those long-forgotten nobles and ladies would have felt had they known that they should one day flare to light the dance or boil the pot of savages? But see, here come the dancers; a merry crew—are they not? The stage is lit—now for the play.'

As she spoke, we perceived two lines of figures, one male and the other female, to the number of about a hundred, each advancing round the human bonfire, arrayed only in the usual leopard and buck skins. They formed up, in perfect silence, in two lines, facing each other between us and the fire, and then the dance—a sort of infernal and fiendish cancan—began. To describe it is quite impossible, but, though there was a good deal of tossing of legs and double shuffling, it seemed to our untutored minds to be more of a play than a dance, and, as usual with this dreadful people, whose minds seem to have taken their colour from the caves in which they live, and whose jokes and amusements are drawn from the inexhaustible stores of preserved mortality with which they share their homes, the subject appeared to be a most ghastly one. I know that it represented an attempted murder first of all, and then the burial alive of the victim and his struggling from the grave; each act of the abominable drama, which was carried on in perfect silence, being rounded off and finished with a furious and most revolting dance round the supposed victim, who writhed upon the ground in the red light of the bonfire.

Presently, however, this pleasing piece was interrupted. Suddenly there was a slight commotion, and a large powerful woman, whom I had noted as one of the most vigorous of the dancers, came, made mad and drunken with unholy excitement, bounding and staggering towards us, shrieking out as she came:—

'I want a black goat, I must have a black goat, bring me a

black goat!' and down she fell upon the rocky floor foaming and writhing, and shrieking for a black goat, about as hideous a spectacle as can well be conceived.

Instantly most of the dancers came up and got round her, though some still continued their capers in the background.

'She has got a Devil,' called out one of them. 'Run and get a black goat. There, Devil, keep quiet! keep quiet! You shall have the goat presently. They have gone to fetch it, Devil.'

'I want a black goat, I must have a black goat!' shrieked the foaming rolling creature again.

'All right, Devil, the goat will be here presently; keep quiet, there's a good Devil!'

And so on till the goat taken from a neighbouring kraal[3] did at last arrive, being dragged bleating on to the scene by its horns.

'Is it a black one, is it a black one?' shrieked the possessed.

'Yes, yes, Devil, as black as night;' then aside, 'keep it behind thee, don't let the Devil see that it has got a white spot on its rump and another on its belly. In one minute, Devil. There, cut his throat quick. Where is the saucer?'

'The goat! the goat! the goat! Give me the blood of my black goat! I must have it, don't you see I must have it? Oh! oh! oh! give me the blood of the goat.'

At this moment a terrified *bah!* announced that the poor goat had been sacrificed, and the next minute a woman ran up with a saucer full of the blood. This the possessed creature, who was then raving and foaming her wildest, seized and *drank*, and was instantly recovered, and without a trace of hysteria, or fits, or being possessed, or whatever dreadful thing it was she was suffering from. She stretched her arms, smiled faintly, and walked quietly back to the dancers, who presently withdrew in a double line as they had come, leaving the space between us and the bonfire deserted.

I thought that the entertainment was now over, and, feeling rather queer, was about to ask *She* if we could rise, when suddenly what at first I took to be a baboon came hopping round the fire, and was instantly met upon the other side by a lion, or rather a human being dressed in a lion's skin. Then came a goat, then a man wrapped in an ox's hide, with the horns wobbling about in a ludicrous way. After him followed a blesbok, then an impala, then a koodoo,[4] then more goats, and many other animals, including a girl sewn up in the shining scaly hide of a boa constrictor, several yards of which trailed along the ground behind her. When all the beasts had collected they began to dance about in a lumbering, unnatural fashion, and to imitate the sounds produced by the respective animals they represented, till the whole air was alive with roars and bleating and the hissing of snakes. This went on for a long time, till, getting tired of the pantomime, I asked Ayesha if there would be any objection to Leo and myself walking round to inspect the human torches, and, as she had nothing to say against it, we started, striking round to the left. After looking at one or two of the flaming bodies, we were about to return, thoroughly disgusted with the grotesque weirdness of the spectacle, when our attention was attracted by one of the dancers, a particularly active leopard, that had separated itself from its fellow-beasts, and was whisking about in our immediate neighbourhood, but gradually drawing into a spot where the shadow was darkest, equidistant between two of the flaming mummies. Drawn by curiosity, we followed it, when suddenly it darted past us into the shadows beyond, and as it did so erected itself and whispered, 'Come,' in a voice that we both recognised as that of Ustane. Without waiting to consult me Leo turned and followed her into the outer darkness, and I, feeling sick enough at heart, went after them. The leopard crawled on for about fifty paces—a sufficient distance to be quite beyond the light of the fire and torches—and then Leo came up with it, or, rather, with Ustane.

'Oh, my lord,' I heard her whisper, 'so I have found thee! Listen. I am in peril of my life from "*She-who-must-be-obeyed*." Surely the Baboon has told thee how she drove me from thee? I love thee, my lord, and thou art mine according to the custom of the country. I saved thy life! My Lion, wilt thou cast me off now?'

'Of course not,' ejaculated Leo; 'I have been wondering whither thou hadst gone. Let us go and explain matters to the Queen.'

'Nay, nay, she would slay us. Thou knowest not her power—the Baboon there, he knoweth, for he saw. Nay, there is but one way: if thou wilt cleave to me, thou must flee with me across the marshes even now, and then perchance we may escape.'

'For Heaven's sake, Leo,' I began, but she broke in—

'Nay, listen not to him. Swift—be swift—death is in the air we breathe. Even now, mayhap, *She* heareth us,' and without more ado she proceeded to back her arguments by throwing herself into his arms. As she did so the leopard's head slipped from her hair, and I saw the three white finger-marks upon it, gleaming faintly in the starlight. Once more realising the desperate nature of the position, I was about to interpose, for I knew that Leo was not too strong-minded where women were concerned, when—oh! horror!—I heard a little silvery laugh behind me. I turned round, and there was *She* herself, and with her Billali and two male mutes. I gasped and nearly sank to the ground, for I knew that such a situation must result in some dreadful tragedy, of which it seemed exceedingly probable to me that I should be the first victim. As for Ustane, she untwined her arms and covered her eyes with her hands, while Leo, not knowing the full terror of the position, merely coloured up, and looked as foolish as a man caught in such a trap would naturally do.

XX

Triumph

Then followed a moment of the most painful silence that I ever endured. It was broken by Ayesha, who addressed herself to Leo.

'Nay, now my lord and guest,' she said in her softest tones, which yet had the ring of steel about them, 'look not so bashful. Surely the sight was a pretty one—the leopard and the lion!'

'Oh, hang it all!' said Leo in English.

'And thou, Ustane,' she went on, 'surely I should have passed thee by had not the light fallen on the white across thy hair,' and she pointed to the bright edge of the rising moon which was now appearing above the horizon. 'Well! well! the dance is done—see, the tapers have burnt down, and all things end in silence and in ashes. So thou thoughtest it a fit time for love, Ustane, my servant—and I, dreaming not that I could be disobeyed, thought thee already far away.'

'Play not with me,' moaned the wretched woman; 'slay me, and let there be an end.'

'Nay, why? It is not well to go so swift from the hot lips of love down to the cold mouth of the grave,' and she made a motion to the mutes, who instantly stepped up and caught the girl by either arm. With an oath Leo sprang upon the nearest, and hurled him to the ground, and then stood over him with his face set, and his fist ready.

Again Ayesha laughed. 'It was well thrown, my guest; thou hast a strong arm for one who so late was sick. But now out of thy courtesy I pray thee let that man live and do my bidding. He shall not harm the girl; the night air grows chill, and I would welcome her in mine own place. Surely she whom thou dost favour shall be favoured of me also.'

I took Leo by the arm, and pulled him from the prostrate mute, and he, half bewildered, obeyed the pressure. Then we all set out for the cave across the plateau, where a pile of white human ashes was all that remained of the fire that had lit the dancing, for the dancers had vanished.

In due course we gained Ayesha's boudoir—all too soon it seemed to me, having a sad presage of what was to come lying heavy on my heart.

Ayesha seated herself upon her cushions, and, having dismissed Job and Billali, by signs bade the mutes tend the lamps and retire, all save one girl, who was her favourite personal attendant. We three remained standing, the unfortunate Ustane a little to the left of the rest of us.

'Now, oh Holly,' Ayesha began, 'how came it that thou who didst hear my words bidding this evil-doer'—and she pointed to Ustane—'to go from hence—thou at whose prayer I did weakly spare her life—how came it, I say, that thou wast a sharer in what I saw to-night? Answer, and for thine own sake, I say, speak all the truth, for I am not minded to hear lies upon this matter!'

'It was by accident, oh Queen,' I answered. 'I knew naught of it.'

'I do believe thee, oh Holly,' she answered coldly, 'and well it is for thee that I do—then does the whole guilt rest upon her.'

'I do not find any guilt therein,' broke in Leo. 'She is not another man's wife, and it appears that she has married me according to the custom of this awful place, so who is the worse? Any way, madam,' he went on, 'whatever she has done I have done too, so if she is to be punished let me be punished also; and I tell thee,' he went on, working himself up into a fury, 'that if thou biddest one of those deaf and dumb villains to touch her again I will tear him to pieces!' And he looked as though he meant it.

Ayesha listened in icy silence, and made no remark. When he had finished, however, she addressed Ustane.

'Hast thou aught to say, woman? Thou silly straw, thou feather, who didst think to float towards thy passion's petty ends, even against the great wind of my will! Tell me, for I fain would understand. Why didst thou this thing?'

And then I think I saw the most tremendous exhibition of moral courage and intrepidity that it is possible to conceive. For the poor doomed girl, knowing what she had to expect at the hands of her terrible Queen, knowing, too, from bitter experience how great was her adversary's power, yet gathered herself together, and out of the very depths of her despair drew materials to defy her.

'I did it, oh *She*,' she answered, drawing herself up to the full of her stately height, and throwing back the panther skin from her head, 'because my love is stronger than the grave. I did it because my life without this man whom my heart chose would be but a living death. Therefore did I risk my life, and now, that I know that it is forfeit to thine anger, yet am I glad that I did risk it, and pay it away in the risking, ay, because he embraced me once, and told me that he loved me yet.'

Here Ayesha half rose from her couch, and then sank down again.

'I have no magic,' went on Ustane, her rich voice ringing strong and full, 'and I am not a Queen, nor do I live for ever, but a woman's heart is heavy to sink through waters, however deep, oh Queen! and a woman's eyes are quick to see, even through thy veil, oh Queen!

'Listen: I know it, thou dost love this man thyself, and therefore wouldst thou destroy me who stand across thy path. Ay, I die—I die, and go into the darkness, nor know I whither I go. But this I know. There is a light shining in my breast, and by that light, as by a lamp, I see the truth, and the future that I shall not share unroll itself before me like a scroll. When first I knew my lord,' and she pointed to Leo, 'I knew also that death would be the bridal gift he gave me—it rushed upon me of a sudden, but I turned not back, being ready to pay the price, and, behold, death is here! And now, even as I knew that, so do I, standing on the steps of doom, know that thou shalt not reap the profits of thy crime. Mine he is, and, though thy beauty shine like a sun among the stars, mine shall he remain for thee. Never here in this life shall he look thee in the eyes and call thee spouse. Thou too, art doomed, I see'—and her voice rang like the cry of an inspired prophetess; 'ah, I see ——'

Then came an answering cry of mingled rage and terror. I turned my head. Ayesha had risen, and was standing with her outstretched hand pointing at Ustane, who had suddenly stopped speaking. I gazed at the poor woman, and as I gazed there came upon her face that same woful, fixed expression of terror that I had seen once before when she had broken out into her wild chant. Her eyes grew large, her nostrils dilated, and her lips blanched.

Ayesha said nothing, she made no sound, she only drew herself up, stretched out her arm, and, her tall veiled frame quivering like an aspen leaf, appeared to look fixedly at her victim. Even as she did so Ustane put her hands to her head, uttered one piercing scream, turned round twice, and then fell backwards with a thud—prone upon the floor. Both Leo and myself rushed to her—she was stone dead—blasted into death by some mysterious electric agency or overwhelming will-force whereof the dread *She* had command.

For a moment Leo did not quite realise what had happened. But when he did, his face was awful to see. With a savage oath he rose from beside the corpse, and, turning, literally sprang at Ayesha. But she was watching, and, seeing him come, stretched out her hand again, and he went staggering back towards me, and would have fallen, had I not caught him. Afterwards he told me that he felt as though he had suddenly received a violent blow in the chest, and, what is more, utterly cowed, as if all the manhood had been taken out of him.

Then Ayesha spoke. 'Forgive me, my guest,' she said softly, addressing him, 'if I have shocked thee with my justice.'

'Forgive thee, thou fiend,' roared poor Leo, wringing his hands in his rage and grief. 'Forgive thee, thou murdress! By Heaven I will kill thee if I can!'

'Nay, nay,' she answered, in the same soft voice, 'thou dost not understand—the time has come for thee to learn. *Thou* art my love, my Kallikrates, my Beautiful, my Strong! For two thousand years, Kallikrates, have I waited for *thee*, and now at length thou hast come back to me; and as for this woman,' pointing to the corpse, 'she stood between me and thee, and therefore have I removed her, Kallikrates.'

'It is an accursed lie!' said Leo. 'My name is not Kallikrates! I am Leo Vincey; my ancestor was Kallikrates—at least, I believe he was.'

'Ah, thou sayest it—thine ancestor was Kallikrates, and thou, even thou, art Kallikrates reborn, come back—and mine own dear lord!'

'I am not Kallikrates, and as for being thy lord, or having aught to do with thee, I had sooner be the lord of a fiend from hell, for she would be better than thou.'

'Sayest thou so—sayest thou so, Kallikrates? Nay, but thou hast not seen me for so long a time that no memory remains. Yet am I very fair, Kallikrates!'

'I hate thee, murdress, and I have no wish to see thee. What is it to me how fair thou art? I hate thee, I say.'

'Yet within a very little space shalt thou creep to my knee, and swear that thou dost love me,' answered Ayesha, with a sweet, mocking laugh. 'Come, there is no time like the present time, here before this dead girl who loved thee, let us put it to the proof.

'Look now on me, Kallikrates!' and with a sudden motion she shook her gauzy covering from her, and stood forth in her low kirtle and her snaky zone,[1] in her glorious radiant beauty and her imperial grace, rising from her wrappings, as it were, like Venus from the wave, or Galatea from her marble,[2] or a beatified spirit from the tomb. She stood forth, and fixed her deep and glowing eyes upon Leo's eyes, and I saw his clenched fists unclasp, and his set and quivering features relax beneath her gaze. I saw his wonder and astonishment grow into admiration, and then into fascination, and the more he struggled the more I saw the power of her dread beauty fasten on him and take possession of his senses, drugging them, and drawing the heart out of him. Did I not know the process? Had not I, who was twice his age, gone through it myself? Was I not going through it afresh even then, although her sweet and passionate gaze was not for me? Yes, alas, I was! Alas, that I should have to confess that at that very moment I was rent by mad and furious jealousy. I could have flown at him, shame upon me! The woman had confounded and almost destroyed my moral sense, as she was bound to confound all who looked upon her superhuman loveliness. But—I do not quite know how—I got the better of myself, and once more turned to see the climax of the tragedy.

'Oh, great Heaven!' gasped Leo, 'art thou a woman?'

'A woman in truth—in very truth—and thine own spouse, Kallikrates!' she answered, stretching out her rounded ivory arms towards him, and smiling, ah, so sweetly!

He looked and looked, and slowly I perceived that he was drawing nearer to her. Suddenly his eye fell upon the corpse of poor Ustane, and he shuddered and stopped.

'How can I?' he said hoarsely. 'Thou art a murdress; she loved me.'

Observe, he was already forgetting that he had loved her.

'It is naught,' she murmured, and her voice sounded sweet as the night-wind passing through the trees. 'It is naught at all. If I have sinned, let my beauty answer for my sin. If I have sinned, it is for love of thee: let my sin, therefore, be put away and forgotten;' and once more she stretched out her arms and whispered '*Come*,' and then in another few seconds it was over. I saw him struggle—I saw him even turn to fly; but her eyes drew him more strongly than iron bonds, and the magic of her beauty and concentrated will and passion entered into him and overpowered him—ay, even there, in the presence of the body of the woman who had loved him well enough to die for him. It sounds horrible and wicked enough, but he cannot be blamed too much, and be sure his sin will find him out. The temptress who drew him into evil was more than human, and her beauty was greater than the loveliness of the daughters of men.

I looked up again, and now her perfect form lay in his arms, and her lips were pressed against his own; and thus, with the corpse of his dead love for an altar, did Leo Vincey plight his troth to her red-handed murdress—plight it for ever and a day. For those who sell themselves into a like dominion, paying down the price of their own honour, and throwing their soul into the balance to sink the scale to the level of their lusts, can hope for no deliverance here or hereafter. As they have sown, so shall they reap and reap, even when the poppy flowers of passion have withered in their hands, and their harvest is but bitter tares, garnered in satiety.

Suddenly, with a snake-like motion, she seemed to slip from his embrace, and then again broke out into her low laugh of triumphant mockery.

'Did I not tell thee that within a little space thou wouldst creep to my knee, oh Kallikrates? And surely the space has not been a great one!'

Leo groaned in shame and misery; for though he was overcome and stricken down, he was not so lost as to be unaware of the depth of the degradation to which he had sunk. On the contrary, his better nature rose up in arms against his fallen self, as I saw clearly enough later on.

Ayesha laughed again, and then quickly veiled herself, and made a sign to the girl mute, who had been watching the whole scene with curious startled eyes. The girl left, and presently returned, followed by two male mutes, to whom the Queen made another sign. Thereon they all three seized the body of poor Ustane by the arms, and dragged it heavily down the cavern and away through the curtains at the end. Leo watched it for a little while, and then covered his eyes with his hand, and it too, to my excited fancy, seemed to watch us as it went.

'There passes the dead past,' said Ayesha, solemnly, as the

curtains shook and fell back into their places, when the ghastly procession had vanished behind them. And then, with one of those extraordinary transitions of which I have already spoken, she again threw off her veil, and broke out, after the ancient and poetic fashion of the dwellers in Arabia,* into a pæan of triumph or epithalamium, which, wild and beautiful as it was, is exceedingly difficult to render into English, and ought by rights to be sung to the music of a cantata, rather than written and read. It was divided into two parts—one descriptive or definitive, and the other personal; and, as nearly as I can remember, ran as follows:—

Love is like a flower in the desert.

It is like the aloe of Arabia that blooms but once and dies; it blooms in the salt emptiness of Life, and the brightness of its beauty is set upon the waste as a star is set upon a storm.

It hath the sun above that is the spirit, and above it blows the air of its divinity.

At the echoing of a step, Love blooms, I say; I say Love blooms, and bends her beauty down to him who passeth by.

He plucketh it, yea, he plucketh the red cup that is full of honey, and beareth it away; away across the desert, away till the flower be withered, away till the desert be done.

There is only one perfect flower in the wilderness of Life.

That flower is Love!

There is only one fixed star in the mists of our wandering.

That star is Love!

* Among the ancient Arabians the power of poetic declamation, either in verse or prose, was held in the highest honour and esteem, and he who excelled in it was known as 'Khâteb,' or Orator. Every year a general assembly was held at which the rival poets repeated their compositions, when those poems which were judged to be the best were, so soon as the knowledge of the art of writing became general, inscribed on silk in letters of gold, and publicly exhibited, being known as 'Al Modhahabât,' or golden verses. In the poem given above by Mr. Holly, Ayesha evidently followed the traditional poetic manner of her people, which was to embody their thoughts in a series of somewhat disconnected sentences, each remarkable for its beauty and the grace of its expression.—EDITOR.

There is only one hope in our despairing night.
That hope is Love!
All else is false. All else is shadow moving upon water. All else is wind and vanity.
Who shall say what is the weight or the measure of Love?
It is born of the flesh, it dwelleth in the spirit. From each doth it draw its comfort.
For beauty it is as a star.
Many are its shapes, but all are beautiful, and none know where the star rose, or the horizon where it shall set.

Then, turning to Leo, and laying her hand upon his shoulder, she went on in a fuller and more triumphant tone, speaking in balanced sentences that gradually grew and swelled from idealised prose into pure and majestic verse:—

Long have I loved thee, oh, my love; yet has my love not lessened.
Long have I waited for thee, and behold my reward is at hand—is here!
Far away I saw thee once, and thou wast taken from me.
Then in a grave sowed I the seed of patience, and shone upon it with the sun of hope, and watered it with tears of repentance, and breathed on it with the breath of my knowledge. And now, lo! it hath sprung up, and borne fruit. Lo! out of the grave hath it sprung. Yea, from among the dry bones and ashes of the dead.
I have waited and my reward is with me.
I have overcome Death, and Death brought back to me him that was dead.
Therefore do I rejoice, for fair is the future.
Green are the paths that we shall tread across the everlasting meadows.
The hour is at hand. Night hath fled away into the valleys.
The dawn kisseth the mountain tops.
Soft shall we lie, my love, and easy shall we go.
Crowned shall we be with the diadem of Kings.
Worshipping and wonder struck all peoples of the world,

Blinded shall fall before our beauty and our might.
From time unto times shall our greatness thunder on,
Rolling like a chariot through the dust of endless days.
Laughing shall we speed in our victory and pomp,
Laughing like the Daylight as he leaps along the hills.
Onward, still triumphant to a triumph ever new!
Onward, in our power to a power unattained!
Onward, never weary, clad with splendour for a robe!
Till accomplished be our fate, and the night is rushing down.

She paused in her strange and most thrilling allegorical chant, of which I am, unfortunately, only able to give the burden, and that feebly enough, and then said—

'Perchance thou dost not believe my word, Kallikrates—perchance thou thinkest that I do delude thee, and that I have not lived these many years, and that thou hast not been born again to me. Nay, look not so—put away that pale cast of doubt, for oh be sure herein can error find no foothold! Sooner shall the suns forget their course and the swallow miss her nest, than my soul shall swear a lie and be led astray from thee, Kallikrates. Blind me, take away mine eyes, and let the darkness utterly fence me in, and still mine ears would catch the tone of thine unforgotten voice, striking more loud against the portals of my sense than can the call of brazen-throated clarions:—stop up mine hearing also, and let a thousand touch me on the brow, and I would name thee out of all:—yea, rob me of every sense, and see me stand deaf and blind, and dumb, and with nerves that cannot weigh the value of a touch, yet would my spirit leap within me like a quickening child and cry unto my heart, behold Kallikrates! behold thou watcher, the watches of thy night are ended! behold thou who seekest in the night season, thy morning Star ariseth.'

She paused awhile and then continued, 'But stay, if thy heart is yet hardened against the mighty truth and thou dost require a further pledge of that which thou dost find too deep to understand, even now shall it be given to thee, and to thee also, oh my

Holly. Bear each one of you a lamp, and follow after me whither I shall lead you.'

Without stopping to think—indeed, speaking for myself, I had almost abandoned the function in circumstances under which to think seemed to be absolutely useless, since thought fell hourly helpless against a black wall of wonder—we took the lamps and followed her. Going to the end of her 'boudoir,' she raised a curtain and revealed a little stair of the sort that was so common in these dim caves of Kôr. As we hurried down the stair I observed that the steps were worn in the centre to such an extent that some of them had been reduced from seven and a half inches, at which I guessed their original height, to about three and a half. Now, all the other steps that I had seen in the caves had been practically unworn, as was to be expected, seeing that the only traffic which ever passed upon them was that of those who bore a fresh burden to the tomb. Therefore this fact struck my notice with that curious force with which little things do strike us when our minds are absolutely overwhelmed by a sudden rush of powerful sensations; beaten flat, as it were, like a sea beneath the first burst of a hurricane, so that every little object on the surface starts into an unnatural prominence.

At the bottom of the staircase I stood and stared at the worn steps, and Ayesha, turning, saw me.

'Wonderest thou whose are the feet that have worn away the rock, my Holly?' she asked. 'They are mine—even mine own light feet! I can remember when these stairs were fresh and level, but for two thousand years and more have I gone down hither day by day, and see, my sandals have worn out the solid rock!'

I made no answer, but I do not think that anything that I had heard or seen brought home to my limited understanding so clear a sense of this being's overwhelming antiquity as that hard rock hollowed out by her soft white feet. How many millions of times must she have passed up and down that stair to bring about such a result?

The stair led to a tunnel, and a few paces down the tunnel was one of the usual curtain-hung doorways, a glance at which told me that it was the same where I had been a witness of that terrible scene by the leaping flame. I recognised the pattern of the curtain, and the sight of it brought the whole event vividly before my eyes, and made me tremble even at its memory. Ayesha entered the tomb (for it was a tomb), and we followed her—I, for one, rejoicing that the mystery of the place was about to be cleared up, and yet afraid to face its solution.

XXI

The Dead and Living Meet

'See now the place where I have slept for these two thousand years,' said Ayesha, taking the lamp from Leo's hand and holding it above her head. Its rays fell upon a little hollow in the floor, where I had seen the leaping flame, but the fire was out now. They fell upon the white form stretched there beneath its wrappings upon its bed of stone, upon the fretted carving of the tomb, and upon another shelf of stone opposite the one on which the body lay, and separated from it by the breadth of the cave.

'Here,' went on Ayesha, laying her hand upon the rock—'here have I slept night by night for all these generations, with but a cloak to cover me. It did not become me that I should lie soft when my spouse yonder,' and she pointed to the rigid form, 'lay stiff in death. Here night by night have I slept in his cold company—till, thou seest, this thick slab, like the stairs down which we passed, has worn thin with the tossing of my form—so faithful have I been to thee even in thy space of sleep, Kallikrates. And now, mine own, thou shalt see a wonderful thing—living, thou shalt behold thyself dead—for well have I tended thee during all these years, Kallikrates. Art thou prepared?'

We made no answer, but gazed at each other with frightened eyes, the whole scene was so dreadful and so solemn. Ayesha advanced, and laid her hand upon the corner of the shroud, and once more spoke.

'Be not affrighted,' she said; 'though the thing seem wonderful to thee—all we who live have thus lived before; nor is the very shape that holds us a stranger to the sun! Only we know it not, because memory writes no record, and earth hath gathered in the earth she lent us, for none have saved our glory from the grave. But I, by my arts and by the arts of those dead men of Kôr which I have learned, have held thee back, oh Kallikrates, from the dust, that the waxen stamp of beauty on thy face should ever rest before mine eye. 'Twas a mask that memory might fill, serving to fashion out thy presence from the past, and give it strength to wander in the habitations of my thought, clad in a mummery of life that stayed my appetite with visions of dead days.

'Behold now, let the Dead and Living meet! Across the gulf of Time they still are one. Time hath no power against Identity, though sleep the merciful hath blotted out the tablets of our mind, and with oblivion sealed the sorrows that else would hound us from life to life, stuffing the brain with gathered griefs till it burst in the madness of uttermost despair. Still are they one, for the wrappings of our sleep shall roll away as thunder clouds before the wind; the frozen voices of the past shall melt in music like mountain snows beneath the sun; and the weeping and the laughter of the lost hours shall be heard once more most sweetly echoing up the cliffs of immeasurable time.

'Ay, the sleep shall roll away, and the voices shall be heard, when down the completed chain, whereof our each existence is a link, the lightning of the Spirit hath passed to work out the purpose of our being; quickening and fusing those separated days of life, and shaping them to a staff whereon we may safely lean as we wend to our appointed fate.

'Therefore, have no fear, Kallikrates, when thou—living, and but lately born—shalt look upon thine own departed self, who breathed and died so long ago. I do but turn one page in thy Book of Being, and show thee what is writ thereon.

'*Behold!*'

With a sudden motion she drew the shroud from the cold form, and let the lamplight play upon it. I looked, and then shrank back terrified; since, say what she might in explanation, the sight was an uncanny one—for her explanations were beyond the grasp of our finite minds, and when they were stripped from the mists of vague esoteric philosophy, and brought into conflict with the cold and horrifying fact, did not do much to break its force. For there, stretched upon the stone bier before us, robed in white and perfectly preserved, was what appeared to be the body of Leo Vincey. I stared from Leo, standing *there* alive, to Leo lying *there* dead, and could see no difference; except, perhaps, that the body on the bier looked older. Feature for feature they were the same, even down to the crop of little golden curls, which was Leo's most uncommon beauty. It even seemed to me, as I looked, that the expression on the dead man's face resembled that which I had sometimes seen upon Leo's when he was plunged into profound sleep. I can only sum up the closeness of the resemblance by saying that I never saw twins so exactly similar as that dead and living pair.

I turned to see what effect was produced upon Leo by this sight of his dead self, and found it to be one of partial stupefaction. He stood for two or three minutes staring and said nothing, and when at last he spoke it was only to ejaculate—

'Cover it up and take me away.'

'Nay, wait, Kallikrates,' said Ayesha, who, standing with the lamp raised above her head, flooding with its light her own rich beauty and the cold wonder of the death-clothed form upon the bier, resembled an inspired Sibyl[1] rather than a woman, as she rolled out her majestic sentences with a grandeur and a freedom of utterance which I am, alas! quite unable to reproduce.

'Wait; I would show thee something, that no tittle of my crime may be hidden from thee. Do thou, oh Holly, open the garment on the breast of the dead Kallikrates, for perchance my lord may fear to touch himself.'

I obeyed with trembling hands. It seemed a desecration, and an unhallowed thing to touch that sleeping image of the live man by my side. Presently his broad chest was bare, and there upon it, right over the heart, was a wound, evidently inflicted with a spear.

'Thou seest, Kallikrates,' she said. 'Know then that it was *I* who slew thee: in the Place of Life *I* gave thee death. I slew thee because of the Egyptian Amenartas, whom thou didst love, for by her wiles she held thy heart, and her I could not smite as but now I smote the woman, for she was too strong for me. In my haste and bitter anger I slew thee, and now for all these days have I lamented thee, and waited for thy coming. And thou hast come, and none can stand between thee and me, and of a truth now for death I will give thee life—not life eternal, for that none can give, but life and youth that shall endure for thousands upon thousands of years, and with it pomp, and power, and wealth, and all things that are good and beautiful, such as have been to no man before thee, nor shall be to any man who comes after. And now one thing more, and thou shalt rest and make ready for the day of thy new birth. Thou seest this body, which was thine own. For all these centuries it hath been my cold comfort and my companion, but now I need it no more, for I have thy living presence, and it can but serve to stir up memories of that which I would fain forget. Let it therefore go back to the dust from which I held it.

'Behold! I have prepared against this happy hour!' and going to the other shelf, or stone ledge, which, she said, had served her for a bed, she took from it a large vitrified[2] double-handed vase, the mouth of which was tied up with a bladder. This she loosed, and then, having bent down and gently kissed the white forehead of the dead man, she undid the vase, and sprinkled its contents carefully over the form, taking, I observed, the greatest precautions against any drop of them touching us or herself, and then poured out what remained of the liquid upon the chest and head. Instantly a dense vapour arose, and the cave was filled with choking fumes that prevented us from seeing anything while the deadly acid (for I presume it was some tremendous preparation of that sort) did its work. From the spot where the body lay came a fierce fizzing and cracking sound, which ceased, however, before the fumes had cleared away. At last they were all gone, except a little cloud that still hung over the corpse. In a couple of minutes more this too had vanished, and, wonderful as it may seem, it is a fact that on the stone bench that had supported the mortal remains of the ancient Kallikrates for so many centuries there was now nothing to be seen but a few handfuls of smoking white powder. The acid had utterly destroyed the body, and even in places eaten into the stone. Ayesha stooped down, and, taking a handful of this powder in her grasp, threw it into the air, saying at the same time, in a voice of calm solemnity—

'Dust to dust!—the past to the past!—the dead to the dead!—Kallikrates is dead, and is born again!'

The ashes floated noiselessly to the rocky floor, and we stood in awed silence and watched them fall, too overcome for words.

'Now leave me,' she said, 'and sleep if ye may. I must watch and think, for to-morrow night we go hence, and the time is long since I trod the path that we must follow.'

Accordingly we bowed, and left her.

As we passed to our own apartment I peeped into Job's sleeping place, to see how he fared, for he had gone away just before our interview with the murdered Ustane, quite prostrated by the terrors of the Amahagger festivity. He was sleeping soundly, good honest fellow that he was, and I rejoiced to think that his nerves, which, like those of most uneducated people, were far from strong, had been spared the closing scenes of this dreadful day. Then we entered our own chamber, and here at last poor Leo, who, ever since he had looked upon that frozen image of his living self, had been in a state not far removed from stupefaction, burst out into a torrent of grief. Now that he was no longer in the presence of the dread *She*, his sense of the awfulness of all that had happened, and more especially of the wicked murder of Ustane, who was bound to him by ties so close, broke upon him like a storm, and lashed him into an agony of remorse and terror which was painful to witness. He cursed himself—he cursed the hour when we had first seen the writing on the sherd, which was being so mysteriously verified, and bitterly he cursed his own weakness. Ayesha he dared not curse—who dared speak evil of such a woman, whose consciousness for aught we knew was watching us at the very moment?

'What am I to do, old fellow?' he groaned, resting his head against my shoulder in the extremity of his grief. 'I let her be killed—not that I could help that, but within five minutes I was kissing her murdress over her body. I am a degraded brute, but I cannot resist that' (and here his voice sank)—'that awful sorceress. I know I shall do it again to-morrow; I know that I am in her power for always; if I never saw her again I should never think of anybody else during all my life; I must follow her as a needle follows a magnet; I would not go away now if I could; I could not leave her, my legs would not carry me, but my mind is still clear enough, and in my mind I hate her—at least, I think so. It is all so horrible; and that—that body! What can I make of it? It was *me*! I am sold into bondage, old fellow, and she will take my soul as the price of herself!'

Then, for the first time, I told him that I was in a but very little better position; and I am bound to say that, notwithstanding his own infatuation, he had the decency to sympathise with me. Perhaps he did not think it worth while being jealous, realising that he had no cause so far as the lady was concerned. I went on to suggest that we should try to run away, but we soon rejected the project as futile, and, to be perfectly honest, I do not believe that either of us would really have left Ayesha even if some superior power had suddenly offered to convey us from these gloomy caves and set us down in Cambridge. We could no more have left her than a moth can leave the light that destroys it. We were like confirmed opium-eaters: in our moments of reason we well knew the deadly nature of our pursuit, but we certainly were not prepared to abandon its terrible delights.

No man who once had seen *She* unveiled, and heard the music of her voice, and drunk in the bitter wisdom of her words, would willingly give up the sight for a whole sea of placid joys. How much more, then, was this likely to be so when, as in Leo's case, to put myself out of the question, this extraordinary creature declared her utter and absolute devotion, and gave what appeared to be proofs of its having lasted for some two thousand years?

No doubt she was a wicked person, and no doubt she had

murdered Ustane when she stood in her path, but then she was very faithful, and by a law of nature man is apt to think but lightly of a woman's crimes, especially if that woman be beautiful, and the crime be committed for the love of him.

And then for the rest, when had such a chance ever come to a man before as that which now lay in Leo's hand? True, in uniting himself to this dread woman, he would place his life under the influence of a mysterious creature of evil tendencies,* but then that would be likely enough to happen to him in any ordinary marriage. On the other hand, however, no ordinary marriage could bring him such awful beauty—for awful is the only word that can describe it—such divine devotion, such wisdom, and command over the secrets of nature, and the place and power

* After some months of consideration of this statement I am bound to confess that I am not quite satisfied of its truth. It is perfectly true that Ayesha committed a murder, but I shrewdly suspect that, were we endowed with the same absolute power, and if we had the same tremendous interest at stake, we should be very apt to do likewise under parallel circumstances. Also, it must be remembered that she looked on it as an execution for disobedience under a system which made the slightest disobedience punishable by death. Putting aside this question of the murder, her evil-doing resolves itself into the expression of views and the acknowledgment of motives which are contrary to our preaching if not to our practice. Now at first sight this might be fairly taken as a proof of an evil nature, but when we come to consider the great antiquity of the individual it becomes doubtful if it was anything more than the natural cynicism which arises from age and bitter experience, and the possession of extraordinary powers of observation. It is a well-known fact that very often, putting the period of boyhood out of the question, the older we grow the more cynical and hardened we get, indeed many of us are only saved by timely death from utter moral petrifaction if not moral corruption. No one will deny that a young man is on the average better than an old one, for he is without that experience of the order of things that in certain thoughtful dispositions can hardly fail to produce cynicism, and that disregard of acknowledged methods and established custom which we call evil. Now the oldest man upon the earth was but a babe compared to Ayesha, and the wisest man upon the earth was not one-third as wise. And the fruit of her wisdom was this, that there was but one thing worth living for, and that was Love in its highest sense, and to gain that good thing she was not prepared to stop at trifles. This is really the sum of her evil doings, and it must be remembered on the other hand that whatever may be thought of them she had some virtues developed to a degree very uncommon in either sex—constancy, for instance.—L. H. H.

that they must win, or lastly the royal crown of unending youth, if indeed she could give that. No, on the whole, it is not wonderful that though Leo was plunged in bitter shame and grief, such as any gentleman would have felt under the circumstances, he was not ready to entertain the idea of running away from his extraordinary fortune.

My own opinion is that he would have been mad if he had done so. But then I confess that my statement on the matter must be accepted with qualifications. I am in love with Ayesha myself to this day, and I would rather have been the object of her affection for one short week than that of any other woman in the world for a whole lifetime. And let me add that if anybody who doubts this statement, and thinks me foolish for making it, could have seen Ayesha draw her veil and flash out in beauty on his gaze, his view would exactly coincide with my own. Of course, I am speaking of any *man*. We never had the advantage of a lady's opinion of Ayesha, but I think it quite possible that she would have regarded the Queen with dislike, would have expressed her disapproval in some more or less pointed manner, and ultimately have got herself blasted.

For two hours or more Leo and I sat with shaken nerves and frightened eyes, and talked over the miraculous events through which we were passing. It seemed like a dream or a fairy tale, instead of the solemn, sober fact. Who would have believed that the writing on the potsherd was not only true, but that we should live to verify its truth, and that we two seekers should find her who was sought, patiently awaiting our coming in the tombs of Kôr? Who would have thought that in the person of Leo this mysterious woman should, as she believed, discover the being whom she awaited from century to century, and whose former earthly habitation she had till this very night preserved? But so it was. In the face of all we had seen it was difficult for us as ordinary reasoning men any longer to doubt its truth, and therefore at last, with humble hearts and a deep sense of the impotence of human knowledge, and the insolence of its assumption that denies that which it has no experience of to be possible, we laid ourselves down to sleep, leaving our fates in the hands of that watching Providence which had thus chosen to allow us to draw the veil of human ignorance, and reveal to us for good or evil some glimpse of the possibilities of life.

XXII

Job Has a Presentiment

It was nine o'clock on the following morning when Job, who still looked scared and frightened, came in to call me, and at the same time breathe his gratitude at finding us alive in our beds, which it appeared was more than he had expected. When I told him of the awful end of poor Ustane he was even more grateful at our survival, and much shocked, though Ustane had been no favourite of his, or he of hers, for the matter of that. She called him 'pig' in bastard Arabic, and he called her 'hussy' in good English, but these amenities were forgotten in the face of the catastrophe that had overwhelmed her at the hands of her Queen.

'I don't want to say anything as mayn't be agreeable, sir,' said Job, when he had finished exclaiming at my tale, 'but it's my opinion that that there *She* is the old gentleman himself, or perhaps his wife, if he has one, which I suppose he has, for he couldn't be so wicked all by himself. The Witch of Endor[1] was a fool to her, sir; bless you, she would make no more of raising every gentleman in the Bible out of these here beastly tombs than I should of growing cress on an old flannel.[2] It's a country of devils, this is, sir, and she's the master one of the lot; and if ever we get out of it it will be more than I expect to do. I don't see no way out of it. That witch isn't likely to let a fine young man like Mr. Leo go.'

'Come,' I said, 'at any rate she saved his life.'

'Yes, and she'll take his soul to pay for it. She'll make him a witch, like herself. I say it's wicked to have anything to do with those sort of people. Last night, sir, I lay awake and read in my little Bible that my poor old mother gave me about what is going to happen to sorceresses and them sort till my hair stood on end. Lord, how the old lady would stare if she saw where her Job had got to!'

'Yes, it's a queer country, and a queer people too, Job,' I answered, with a sigh, for, though I am not superstitious like Job, I admit to a natural shrinking (which will not bear investigation) from the things that are above Nature.

'You are right, sir,' he answered, 'and if you won't think me very foolish, I should like to say something to you now that Mr. Leo is out of the way'—(Leo had got up early and gone for a stroll)—'and that is that I know it is the last country as ever I shall see in this world. I had a dream last night, and I dreamed that I saw my old father with a kind of night-shirt on him, something like these folks wear when they want to be in particular full-dress, and a bit of that feathery grass in his hand, which he may have gathered on the way, for I saw lots of it yesterday about three hundred yards from the mouth of this beastly cave.

'"Job," he said to me, solemn like, and yet with a kind of satisfaction shining through him, more like a Methody[3] parson when he has sold a neighbour a marked horse for a sound one and cleared twenty pounds by the job than anything I can think on—"Job, time's up, Job; but I never did expect to have to come and hunt you out in this 'ere place, Job. Such ado as I have had to nose you up; it wasn't friendly to give your poor old father such a run, let alone that a wonderful lot of bad characters hail from this place Kôr."'

'Regular cautions,' I suggested.

'Yes, sir—of course, sir, that's just what he said they was—"cautions, downright scorchers"—sir, and I'm sure I don't doubt it, seeing what I know of them and their hot-potting ways,' went on Job, sadly. 'Anyway, he was sure that time was up, and went away saying that we should see more than we cared for of each other soon, and I suppose he was a-thinking of the fact that father and I never could hit it off together for longer nor three days, and I dare say that things will be similar when we meet again.'

'Surely,' I said, 'you don't think that you are going to die because you dreamed you saw your old father; if one dies because one dreams of one's father, what happens to a man who dreams of his mother-in-law?'

'Ah, sir, you're laughing at me,' said Job; 'but, you see, you didn't know my old father. If it had been anybody else—my Aunt Mary, for instance, who never made much of a job—I should not have thought so much of it; but my father was that idle, which he shouldn't have been with seventeen children, that he would never have put himself out to come here just to see the place. No, sir; I know that he meant business. Well, sir, I can't help it; I suppose every man must go some time or other, though it is a hard thing to die in a place like this, where Christian burial isn't to be had for its weight in gold. I've tried to be a good man, sir, and do my duty honest, and if it wasn't for the supercilus kind of way in which father carried on last night—a sort of sniffing at me as it were, as though he hadn't no opinion of my references and testimonials—I should feel easy enough in my mind. Any way, sir, I've been a good servant to you and Mr. Leo, bless him! Why, it seems but the other day that I used to lead him about the streets with a penny whip; and if ever you get out of this place—which, as father didn't allude to you, perhaps you may—I hope you will think kindly of my whitened bones, and never have anything more to do with Greek writing on flower-pots, sir, if I may make so bold as to say so.'

'Come, come, Job,' I said seriously, 'this is all nonsense, you know. You mustn't be silly enough to go getting such ideas into your head. We've lived through some queer things, and I hope that we may go on doing so.'

'No, sir,' answered Job, in a tone of conviction that jarred on me unpleasantly, 'it isn't nonsense. I'm a doomed man, and I feel it, and a wonderful uncomfortable feeling it is, sir, for one can't help wondering how it's going to come about. If you are eating your dinner you think of poison and it goes against your stomach, and if you are walking along these dark rabbit-burrows you think of knives, and Lord, don't you just shiver about the back! I ain't particular, sir, provided it's sharp, like that poor girl, who, now that she's gone, I am sorry to have spoke hard on, though I don't approve of her morals in getting married, which I consider too quick to be decent. Still, sir,' and poor Job turned a shade paler as he said it, 'I do hope it won't be that hot-pot game.'

'Nonsense,' I broke in angrily, 'nonsense!'

'Very well, sir,' said Job, 'it isn't my place to differ from you, sir, but if you happen to be going anywhere, sir, I should be obliged if you could manage to take me with you, seeing that I shall be glad to have a friendly face to look at when the time comes, just to help one through, as it were. And now, sir, I'll be getting the breakfast,' and he went, leaving me in a very uncomfortable state of mind. I was deeply attached to old Job, who was one of the best and honestest men I have ever had to do with in any class of life, and really more of a friend than a servant, and the mere idea of anything happening to him brought a lump into my throat. Beneath all his ludicrous talk I could see that he himself was quite convinced that something was going to happen, and though in most cases these convictions turn out to be utter moonshine—and this particular one especially was to be amply accounted for by the gloomy and unaccustomed surroundings in which its victim was placed—still it did more or less carry a chill to my heart, as any dread that is obviously a genuine object of belief is apt to do, however absurd the belief may be. Presently the breakfast arrived, and with it Leo, who had been taking a walk outside the cave—to clear his mind, he said—and very glad I was to see both, for they gave me a respite from my gloomy thoughts. After breakfast we went for another walk, and watched some of the Amahagger sowing a plot of ground with the grain from which they make their beer. This they did in scriptural fashion—a man with a bag made of goat's-hide fastened round his waist walking up and down the plot and scattering the seed as he went. It was a positive relief to see one of these dreadful people do anything so homely and pleasant as sow a field, perhaps because it seemed to link them, as it were, with the rest of humanity.

As we were returning Billali met us, and informed us that it was *She's* pleasure that we should wait upon her, and accordingly we entered her presence, not without trepidation, for Ayesha was certainly an exception to the rule. Familiarity with her might and did breed passion and wonder and horror, but it certainly did *not* breed contempt.

We were as usual shown in by the mutes, and after these had retired Ayesha unveiled, and once more bade Leo embrace her, which, notwithstanding his heart-searchings of the previous night, he did with more alacrity and fervour than in strictness courtesy required.

She laid her white hand on his head, and looked him fondly in the eyes. 'Dost thou wonder, my Kallikrates,' she said, 'when thou shalt call me all thine own, and when we shall of a truth be for one another and to one another? I will tell thee. First, must thou be even as I am, not immortal indeed, for that I am not, but so cased and hardened against the attacks of Time that his arrows shall glance from the armour of thy vigorous life as the sunbeams glance from water. As yet I may not mate with thee, for thou and I are different, and the very brightness of my being would burn thee up, and perchance destroy thee. Thou couldst not even endure to look upon me for too long a time lest thine eyes should ache, and thy senses swim, and therefore (with a little coquettish nod) shall I presently veil myself again.' (This by the way she did not do.) 'No: listen, thou shalt not be tried beyond endurance, for this very evening, an hour before the sun goes down, shall we start hence, and by tomorrow's dark, if all goes well, and the road is not lost to me, which I pray it may not be, shall we stand in the place of Life, and thou shalt bathe in the fire, and come forth glorified, as no man ever was before thee, and then, Kallikrates, shalt thou call me wife, and I will call thee husband.'

Leo muttered something in answer to this astonishing statement, I do not know what, and she laughed a little at his confusion, and went on.

'And thou, too, oh Holly; on thee also will I confer this boon, and then of a truth shalt thou be an evergreen tree, and this will

I do—well, because thou hast pleased me, Holly, for thou art not altogether a fool, like most of the sons of men, and because, though thou hast a school of philosophy as full of nonsense as those of the old days, yet hast thou not forgotten how to turn a pretty phrase about a lady's eyes.'

'Hulloa, old fellow!' whispered Leo, with a return of his old cheerfulness, 'have you been paying compliments? I should never have thought it of you!'

'I thank thee, oh Ayesha,' I replied, with as much dignity as I could command, 'but if there be such a place as thou dost describe, and if in this strange place there may be found a fiery virtue that can hold off Death when he comes to pluck us by the hand, yet would I none of it. For me, oh Ayesha, the world has not proved so soft a nest that I would lie in it for ever. A stony-hearted mother is our earth, and stones are the bread she gives her children for their daily food.[4] Stones to eat and bitter water for their thirst, and stripes for tender nurture. Who would endure this for many lives? Who would so load up his back with memories of lost hours and loves, and of his neighbour's sorrows that he cannot lessen, and wisdom that brings not consolation? Hard is it to die, because our delicate flesh doth shrink back from the worm it will not feel, and from that unknown which the winding-sheet doth curtain from our view. But harder still, to my fancy, would it be to live on, green in the leaf and fair, but dead and rotten at the core, and feel that other secret worm of recollection gnawing ever at the heart.'

'Bethink thee, Holly,' she said; 'yet doth long life and strength and beauty beyond measure mean power and all things that are dear to man.'

'And what, oh Queen,' I answered, 'are those things that are dear to man? Are they not bubbles? Is not ambition but an endless ladder by which no height is ever climbed till the last unreachable rung is mounted? For height leads on to height, and there is no resting-place upon them, and rung doth grow upon rung, and there is no limit to the number. Doth not wealth satiate and become nauseous, and no longer serve to satisfy or pleasure, or to buy an hour's ease of mind? And is there any end to wisdom that we may hope to reach it? Rather, the more we learn shall we not thereby be able only to better compass out our ignorance? Did we live ten thousand years could we hope to solve the secrets of the suns, and of the space beyond the suns, and of the Hand that hung them in the heavens? Would not our wisdom be but as a gnawing hunger calling our consciousness day by day to a knowledge of the empty craving of our souls? Would it not be but as a light in one of these great caverns, that though bright it burn, and brighter yet, doth but the more serve to show the depths of the gloom around it? And what good thing is there beyond that we may gain by length of days?'

'Nay, my Holly, there is love—love which makes all things beautiful, and doth breathe divinity into the very dust we tread. With love shall life roll gloriously on from year to year, like the voice of some great music that hath power to hold the hearer's heart poised on eagle's wings above the sordid shame and folly of the earth.'

'It may be so,' I answered; 'but if the loved one prove a broken reed to pierce us, or if the love be loved in vain—what then? Shall a man grave his sorrows upon a stone when he hath but need to write them on the water? Nay, oh *She*, I will live my day and grow old with my generation, and die my appointed death, and be forgotten. For I do hope for an immortality to which the little span that perchance thou canst confer will be but as a finger's length laid against the measure of the great world; and, mark this! the immortality to which I look, and which my faith doth promise to me, shall be free from the bonds that here must tie my spirit down. For, while the flesh endures, sorrow and evil and the scorpion whips of sin[5] must endure also; but when the flesh hath fallen from us, then shall the spirit shine forth clad in the brightness of eternal good, and for its common air shall breathe so rare an ether of most noble thoughts, that the highest aspiration of our manhood, or the purest incense of a maiden's prayer, would prove too earthly gross to float therein.'

'Thou lookest high,' answered Ayesha, with a little laugh, 'and speakest clearly as a trumpet and with no uncertain sound. And yet methinks that but now didst thou talk of "that Unknown" from which the winding-sheet doth curtain us. But perchance, thou seest with the eye of Faith, gazing on this brightness that is to be, through the painted-glass of thy imagination. Strange are the pictures of the future that mankind can thus draw with this brush of faith and this many-coloured pigment of imagination! Strange, too, that no one of them doth agree with another! I could tell thee—but there, what is the use? why rob a fool of his bauble? Let it pass, and I pray, oh Holly, that when thou dost feel old age creeping slowly toward thyself, and the confusion of senility making havoc in thy brain, thou mayest not bitterly regret that thou didst cast away the imperial boon I would have given to thee. But so it hath ever been; man can never be content with that which his hand can pluck. If a lamp be in his reach to light him through the darkness, he must needs cast it down because it is no star. Happiness danceth ever a pace before him, like the marsh-fires in the swamps, and he must catch the fire, and he must hold the star! Beauty is naught to him, because there are lips more honey-sweet; and wealth is naught, because others can weigh him down with heavier shekels; and fame is naught, because there have been greater men than he. Thyself thou saidst it, and I turn thy words against thee. Well, thou dreamest that thou shalt pluck the star. I believe it not, and I think thee a fool, my Holly, to throw away the lamp.'

I made no answer, for I could not—especially before Leo—tell her that since I had seen her face I knew that it would always be before my eyes, and that I had no wish to prolong an existence which must always be haunted and tortured by her memory, and by the last bitterness of unsatisfied love. But so it was, and so, alas, is it to this hour!

'And now,' went on *She*, changing her tone and the subject together, 'tell me, my Kallikrates, for as yet I know it not, how came ye to seek me here? Yesternight thou didst say that Kallikrates—him whom thou sawest—was thine ancestor. How was it? Tell me—thou dost not speak overmuch!'

Thus adjured, Leo told her the wonderful story of the casket and of the potsherd that, written on by his ancestress, the Egyptian Amenartas, had been the means of guiding us to her. Ayesha listened intently, and, when he had finished, spoke to me.

'Did I not tell thee one day, when we did talk of good and evil, oh Holly—it was when my beloved lay so ill—that out of good came evil, and out of evil good—that they who sowed knew not what the crop should be, nor he who struck where the blow should fall? See, now: this Egyptian Amenartas, this royal child of the Nile who hated me, and whom even now I hate, for in a way she did prevail against me—see, now, she herself hath been the very means to bring her lover to mine arms! For her sake I slew him, and now, behold, through her he hath come back to me! She would have done me evil, and sowed her seeds that I might reap tares, and behold she hath given me more than all the world can give, and there is a strange square for thee to fit into thy circle of good and evil, oh Holly!

'And so,' she went on after a pause—'and so she bade her son destroy me if he might, because I slew his father. And thou, my Kallikrates, art the father, and in a sense thou art likewise the son; and wouldst thou avenge thy wrong, and the wrong of that far-off mother of thine upon me, oh Kallikrates? See,' and she slid to her knees, and drew the white corsage still farther down her ivory bosom—'see, here beats my heart, and there by thy side is a knife, heavy, and long, and sharp, the very knife to slay an erring woman with. Take it now, and be avenged. Strike, and strike home!—so shalt thou be satisfied, Kallikrates, and go through life a happy man, because thou hast paid back the wrong, and obeyed the mandate of the past.'

He looked at her, and then stretched out his hand and lifted her to her feet.

'Rise, Ayesha,' he said sadly; 'well thou knowest that I cannot strike thee, no, not even for the sake of her whom thou slewest but last night. I am in thy power, and a very slave to thee. How can I kill thee?—sooner should I slay myself.'

'Almost dost thou begin to love me, Kallikrates,' she answered, smiling. 'And now tell me of thy country—'tis a great people, is it not? with an empire like that of Rome! Surely thou wouldst return thither, and it is well, for I mean not that thou shouldst dwell in these caves of Kôr. Nay, when once thou art even as I am, we will go hence—fear not but that I shall find a path—and then shall we cross to this England of thine, and live as it becometh us to live. Two thousand years have I waited for the day when I should see the last of these hateful caves and this gloomy-visaged folk, and now it is at hand, and my heart bounds up to meet it like a child's towards its holiday. For thou shalt rule this England——

'But we have a queen[6] already,' broke in Leo, hastily.

'It is naught, it is naught,' said Ayesha; 'she can be overthrown.'

At this we both broke out into an exclamation of dismay, and explained that we should as soon think of overthrowing ourselves.

'But here is a strange thing,' said Ayesha, in astonishment; 'a queen whom her people love! Surely the world must have changed since I dwelt in Kôr.'

Again we explained that it was the character of monarchs that had changed, and that the one under whom we lived was venerated and beloved by all right-thinking people in her vast realms. Also, we told her that real power in our country rested in the hands of the people, and that we were in fact ruled by the votes of the lower and least educated classes of the community.[7]

'Ah,' she said, 'a democracy—then surely there is a tyrant, for I have long since seen that democracies, having no clear will of their own, in the end set up a tyrant, and worship him.'

'Yes,' I said, 'we have our tyrants.'

'Well,' she answered resignedly, 'we can at any rate destroy these tyrants, and Kallikrates shall rule the land.'

I instantly informed Ayesha that in England 'blasting' was not an amusement that could be indulged in with impunity, and that any such attempt would meet with the consideration of the law and probably end upon a scaffold.

'The law,' she laughed with scorn—'the law! Canst thou not understand, oh Holly, that I am above the law, and so shall my Kallikrates be also? All human law will be to us as the north wind to a mountain. Does the wind bend the mountain, or the mountain the wind?

'And now leave me, I pray thee, and thou too, my own Kallikrates, for I would get me ready against our journey, and so must ye both, and your servant also. But bring no great quantity of things with thee, for I trust that we shall be but three days gone. Then shall we return hither, and I will make a plan whereby we can bid farewell for ever to these sepulchres of Kôr. Yes, surely thou mayst kiss my hand!'

So we went, I, for one, meditating deeply on the awful nature of the problem that now opened out before us. The terrible *She* had evidently made up her mind to go to England, and it made me absolutely shudder to think what would be the result of her arrival there. What her powers were I knew, and I could not doubt but that she would exercise them to the full. It might be possible to control her for a while, but her proud, ambitious spirit would be certain to break loose and avenge itself for the long centuries of its solitude. She would, if necessary, and if the power of her beauty did not unaided prove equal to the occasion, blast her way to any end she set before her, and as she could not die, and for aught I knew could not even be killed,* what was there to stop her? In the end she would, I had little doubt, assume absolute rule over the British dominions, and probably over the whole earth, and, though I was sure that she would speedily make ours the most glorious and prosperous empire that the world has ever seen, it would be at the cost of a terrible sacrifice of life.

* I regret to say that I was never able to ascertain if *She* was invulnerable against the accidents of life. Presumably this was so, else some misadventure would have been sure to put an end to her in the course of so many centuries. True, she offered to let Leo slay her, but very probably this was only an experiment to try his temper and mental attitude towards her. Ayesha never gave way to impulse without some valid object.—L. H. H.

The whole thing sounded like a dream or some extraordinary invention of a speculative brain, and yet it was a fact—a wonderful fact—of which the whole world would soon be called on to take notice. What was the meaning of it all? After much thinking I could only conclude that this wonderful creature, whose passion had kept her for so many centuries chained as it were, and comparatively harmless, was now about to be used by Providence as a means to change the order of the world, and possibly, by the building up of a power that could no more be rebelled against or questioned than the decrees of Fate, to change it materially for the better.

XXIII

The Temple of Truth

Our preparations did not take us very long. We put a change of clothing apiece and some spare boots into my Gladstone bag, also we took our revolvers and an express rifle each, together with a good supply of ammunition, a precaution to which, under Providence, we subsequently owed our lives over and over again. The rest of our gear, together with our heavy rifles, we left behind us.

A few minutes before the appointed time we once more attended in Ayesha's boudoir, and found her also ready, her dark cloak thrown over her winding-sheet like wrappings.

'Are ye prepared for the great venture?' she said.

'We are,' I answered, 'though for my part, Ayesha, I have no faith in it.'

'Ah, my Holly,' she said, 'thou art of a truth like those old Jews—of whom the memory vexes me so sorely—unbelieving, and hard to accept that which they have not known. But thou shalt see; for unless my mirror yonder lies,' and she pointed to the font of crystal water, 'the path is yet open as it was of old time. And now let us start upon the new life which shall end—who knoweth where?'

'Ah,' I echoed, 'who knoweth where?' and we passed down into the great central cave, and out into the light of day. At the mouth of the cave we found a single litter with six bearers, all of them mutes, waiting, and with them I was relieved to see our old friend Billali, for whom I had conceived a sort of affection. It appeared that, for reasons not necessary to explain at length,

Ayesha had thought it best that, with the exception of herself, we should proceed on foot, and this we were nothing loth to do, after our long confinement in these caves, which, however suitable they might be for sarcophagi—a singularly inappropriate word, by the way, for these particular tombs, which certainly did not consume the bodies given to their keeping—were depressing habitations for breathing mortals like ourselves.[1] Either by accident or by the orders of *She*, the space in front of the cave where we had beheld that awful dance was perfectly clear of spectators. Not a soul was to be seen, and consequently I do not believe that our departure was known to anybody, except perhaps the mutes who waited on *She*, and they were, of course, in the habit of keeping what they saw to themselves.

In a few minutes' time we were stepping out sharply across the great cultivated plain or lake bed, framed like a vast emerald in its setting of frowning cliff, and had another opportunity of wondering at the extraordinary nature of the site chosen by these old people of Kôr for their capital, and at the marvellous amount of labour, ingenuity, and engineering skill that must have been brought into requisition by the founders of the city to drain so huge a sheet of water, and to keep it clear of subsequent accumulations. It is, indeed, so far as my experience goes, an unequalled instance of what man can do in the face of nature, for in my opinion such achievements as the Suez Canal or even the Mont Cenis Tunnel[2] do not approach this ancient undertaking in magnitude and grandeur of conception.

When we had been walking for about half an hour, enjoying ourselves exceedingly in the delightful cool which about this time of the day always appeared to descend upon the great plain of Kôr, and which in some degree atoned for the want of any land or sea breeze—for all wind was kept off by the rocky mountain wall—we began to get a clear view of what Billali had informed us were the ruins of the great city. And even from that distance we could see how wonderful those ruins were, a fact which with every step we took became more evident. The city was not very large if compared to Babylon or Thebes, or other cities of remote antiquity; perhaps its outer wall contained some twelve square miles of ground, or a little more. Nor had the walls, so far as we could judge when we reached them, been very high, probably not more than forty feet, which was about their present height where they had not through the sinking of the ground, or some such cause, fallen into ruin. The reason of this, no doubt, was that the people of Kôr, being protected from any outside attack by far more tremendous ramparts than any that the hand of man could rear, only required them for show and to guard against civil discord. But on the other hand they were as broad as they were high, built entirely of dressed stone, hewn, no doubt, from the vast caves, and surrounded by a great moat about sixty feet in width, some reaches of which were still filled with water. About ten minutes before the sun finally sank we reached this moat, and passed down and through it, clambering across what evidently were the piled-up fragments of a great bridge in order to do so, and then with some little difficulty up the slope of the wall to its summit. I wish that it lay within the power of my pen to give some idea of the grandeur of the sight that then met our view. There, all bathed in the red glow of the sinking sun, were miles upon miles of ruins—columns, temples, shrines, and the palaces of kings, varied with patches of green bush. Of course, the roofs of these buildings had long since fallen into decay and vanished, but owing to the extreme massiveness of the style of building, and to the hardness and durability of the rock employed, most of the party walls and great columns still remained standing.*

Straight before us stretched away what had evidently been the

* In connection with the extraordinary state of preservation of these ruins after so vast a lapse of time—at least six thousand years—it must be remembered that Kôr was not burnt or destroyed by an enemy or an earthquake, but deserted, owing to the action of a terrible plague. Consequently the houses were left unharmed; also the climate of the plain is remarkably fine and dry, and there is very little rain or wind; as a result of which these relics have only to contend against the unaided action of time, that works but slowly upon such massive blocks of masonry.—L. H. H.

main thoroughfare of the city, for it was very wide, wider than the Thames Embankment,[3] and regular. Being, as we afterwards discovered, paved, or rather built, throughout of blocks of dressed stone, such as were employed in the walls, it was but little overgrown even now with grass and shrubs that could get no depth of soil to live in. What had been the parks and gardens, on the contrary, were now dense jungle. Indeed, it was easy even from a distance to trace the course of the various roads by the burnt-up appearance of the scanty grass that grew upon them. On either side of this great thoroughfare were vast blocks of ruins, each block, generally speaking, being separated from its neighbour by a space of what had once, I suppose, been garden-ground, but was now dense and tangled bush. They were all built of the same coloured stone, and most of them had pillars, which was as much as we could make out in the fading light as we passed swiftly up the main road, that I believe I am right in saying no living foot had pressed for thousands of years.*

Presently we came to an enormous pile, which we rightly took to be a temple covering at least four acres of ground, and apparently arranged in a series of courts, each one enclosing another of smaller size, on a principle of a Chinese nest of boxes, which were separated one from the other by rows of huge columns. And, whilst I think of it, I may as well state a remarkable thing about the shape of these columns, which resembled none that I have ever seen or heard of, being fashioned with a kind of waist in the centre, and swelling out above and below. At first we thought that this shape was meant to roughly symbolise or suggest the female form, as was a common habit

* Billali told me that the Amahagger believe that the site of the city is haunted, and could not be persuaded to enter it upon any consideration. Indeed, I could see that he himself did not at all like doing so, and was only consoled by the reflection that he was under the direct protection of *She*. It struck Leo and myself as very curious that a people which has no objection to living amongst the dead, with whom their familiarity has perhaps bred contempt, and even using their bodies for purposes of fuel, should be terrified at approaching the habitations that these very departed had occupied when alive. After all, however, it is only a savage inconsistency.—L. H. H.

amongst the ancient religious architects of many creeds. On the following day, however, as we went up the slopes of the mountain, we discovered a large quantity of the most stately looking palms, of which the trunks grew exactly in this shape, and I have now no doubt but that the first designer of those columns drew his inspiration from the graceful bends of those very palms, or rather of their ancestors, which then, some eight or ten thousand years ago, as now, beautified the slopes of the mountain that had once formed the shores of the volcanic lake.

At the *façade* of this huge temple, which, I should imagine, is almost as large as that of El-Karnac, at Thebes,[4] some of the largest columns, which I measured, being between eighteen to twenty feet in diameter at the base, by about seventy feet in height, our little procession was halted, and Ayesha descended from her litter.

'There used to be a spot here, Kallikrates,' she said to Leo, who had run up to help her down, 'where one might sleep. Two thousand years ago did thou and I and that Egyptian asp rest therein, but since then have I not set foot here, nor any man, and perchance it has fallen,' and, followed by the rest of us, she passed up a vast flight of broken and ruined steps into the outer court, and looked round into the gloom. Presently she seemed to recollect, and, walking a few paces along the wall to the left, halted.

'It is here,' she said, and at the same time beckoned to the two mutes, who were loaded with provisions and our little belongings, to advance. One of them came forward, and, producing a lamp, lit it from his brazier (for the Amahagger when on a journey nearly always carried with them a little lighted brazier, from which to provide fire). The tinder of this brazier was made of broken fragments of mummy carefully damped, and, if the admixture of moisture was properly managed, this unholy compound would smoulder away for hours.* As soon as the lamp

* After all we are not much in advance of the Amahagger in these matters. 'Mummy,' that is pounded ancient Egyptian, is, I believe, a pigment much used by artists, and especially by those of them who direct their talents to the reproduction of the works of the old masters.—EDITOR.

was lit we entered the place before which Ayesha had halted. It turned out to be a chamber hollowed in the thickness of the wall, and, from the fact of there still being a massive stone table in it, I should think that it had probably served as a living-room, perhaps for one of the door-keepers of the great temple.

Here we stopped, and after cleaning the place out and making it as comfortable as circumstances and the darkness would permit, we ate some cold meat, at least Leo, Job, and I did, for Ayesha, as I think I have said elsewhere, never touched anything except cakes of flour, fruit, and water. While we were still eating, the moon, which was at her full, rose above the mountain-wall, and began to flood the place with silver.

'Wot ye why I have brought you here to-night, my Holly?' said Ayesha, leaning her head upon her hand and watching the great orb as she rose, like some heavenly queen, above the solemn pillars of the temple. 'I brought you—nay, it is strange, but knowest thou, Kallikrates, that thou liest at this moment upon the very spot where thy dead body lay when I bore thee back to those caves of Kôr so many years ago? It all returns to my mind now. I can see it, and horrible is it to my sight!' and she shuddered.

Here Leo jumped up and hastily changed his seat. However the reminiscence might affect Ayesha, it clearly had few charms for him.

'I brought you,' went on Ayesha presently, 'that ye might look upon the most wonderful sight that ever the eye of man beheld—the full moon shining over ruined Kôr. When ye have done your eating—I would that I could teach thee to eat naught but fruit, Kallikrates, but that will come after thou hast laved in the fire. Once I, too, ate flesh like a brute beast. When ye have done we will go out, and I will show you this great temple and the God whom men once worshipped therein.'

Of course we got up at once, and started. And here again my pen fails me. To give a string of measurements and details of the various courts of the temple would only be wearisome, supposing that I had them, and yet I know not how I am to describe what we saw, magnificent as it was even in its ruin, almost beyond the power of realisation. Court upon dim court, row upon row of mighty pillars—some of them (especially at the gateways) sculptured from pedestal to capital—space upon space of empty chambers that spoke more eloquently to the imagination than any crowded streets. And over all, the dead silence of the dead, the sense of utter loneliness, and the brooding spirit of the Past! How beautiful it was, and yet how drear! We did not dare to speak aloud. Ayesha herself was awed in the presence of an antiquity compared to which even her length of days was but a little thing; we only whispered, and our whispers seemed to run from column to column, till they were lost in the quiet air. Bright fell the moonlight on pillar and court and shattered wall, hiding all their rents and imperfections in its silver garment, and clothing their hoar majesty with the peculiar glory of the night. It was a wonderful sight to see the full moon looking down on the ruined fane of Kôr. It was a wonderful thing to think for how many thousands of years the dead orb above and the dead city below had gazed thus upon each other, and in the utter solitude of space poured forth each to each the tale of their lost life and long-departed glory. The white light fell, and minute by minute the quiet shadows crept across the grass-grown courts like the spirits of old priests haunting the habitations of their worship—the white light fell, and the long shadows grew till the beauty and grandeur of the scene and the untamed majesty of its present Death seemed to sink into our very souls, and speak more loudly than the shouts of armies concerning the pomp and splendour that the grave had swallowed, and even memory had forgotten.

'Come,' said Ayesha, after we had gazed and gazed, I know not for how long, 'and I will show you the stony flower of Loveliness and Wonder's very crown, if yet it stands to mock time with its beauty and fill the heart of man with longing for that which is behind the veil,' and, without waiting for an answer, she led us through two more pillared courts into the inner shrine of the old fane.

And there, in the centre of the inmost court, that might have been some fifty yards square, or a little more, we stood face to face with what is perhaps the grandest allegorical work of Art that the genius of her children has ever given to the world. For in the exact centre of the court, placed upon a thick square slab of rock, was a huge round ball of dark stone, some forty feet in diameter, and standing on the ball was a colossal winged figure of a beauty so entrancing and divine that when I first gazed upon it, illuminated and shadowed as it was by the soft light of the moon, my breath stood still, and for an instant my heart ceased its beating.

The statue was hewn from marble so pure and white that even now, after all those ages, it shone as the moonbeams danced upon it, and its height was, I should say, a trifle under twenty feet. It was the winged figure of a woman of such marvellous loveliness and delicacy of form that the size seemed rather to add to than to detract from its so human and yet more spiritual beauty. She was bending forward and poising herself upon her half-spread wings as though to preserve her balance as she leant. Her arms were outstretched like those of some woman about to embrace one she dearly loved, while her whole attitude gave an impression of the tenderest beseeching. Her perfect and most gracious form was naked, save—and here came the extraordinary thing—the face, which was thinly veiled, so that we could only trace the marking of her features. A gauzy veil was thrown round and about the head, and of its two ends one fell down across her left breast, which was outlined beneath it, and one, now broken, streamed away upon the air behind her.

'Who is she?' I asked, as soon as I could take my eyes off the statue.

'Canst thou not guess, oh Holly?' answered Ayesha. 'Where then is thy imagination? It is Truth standing on the World, and calling to its children to unveil her face. See what is writ upon the pedestal. Without doubt it is taken from the book of the Scriptures of these men of Kôr,' and she led the way to the foot of the statue, where an inscription of the usual Chinese-looking hieroglyphics was so deeply graven as to be still quite legible, at least to Ayesha. According to her translation it ran thus:—

'Is there no man that will draw my veil and look upon my face, for it is very fair? Unto him who draws my veil shall I be, and peace will I give him, and sweet children of knowledge and good works.'

And a voice cried, 'Though all those who seek after thee desire thee, behold! Virgin art thou, and Virgin shalt thou go till Time be done. No man is there born of woman who may draw thy veil and live, nor shall be. By Death only can thy veil be drawn, oh Truth!'

And Truth stretched out her arms and wept, because those who sought her might not find her, nor look upon her face to face.

'Thou seest,' said Ayesha, when she had finished translating, 'Truth was the Goddess of the people of old Kôr, and to her they built their shrines, and her they sought; knowing that they should never find, still sought they.'

'And so,' I added sadly, 'do men seek to this very hour, but they find not; and, as this scripture saith, nor shall they; for in Death only is Truth found.'

Then with one more look at this veiled and spiritualised loveliness—which was so perfect and so pure that one might almost fancy that the light of a living spirit shone through the marble prison to lead man on to high and ethereal thoughts—this poet's dream of beauty frozen into stone, which I never shall forget while I live, though I find myself so helpless when I attempt to describe it, we turned and went back through the vast moonlit courts to the spot whence we had started. I never saw the statue again, which I the more regret, because on the great ball of stone representing the World whereon the figure stood, lines were drawn, that probably, had there been light enough, we should have discovered to be a map of the Universe as it was known to the people of Kôr. It is at any rate suggestive of some scientific knowledge that these long-dead worshippers of Truth had recognised the fact that the globe is round.

XXIV

Walking the Plank

Next day the mutes woke us before the dawn; and by the time that we had got the sleep out of our eyes, and gone through a perfunctory wash at a spring which still welled up into the remains of a marble basin in the centre of the North quadrangle of the vast outer court, we found *She* standing by the litter ready to start, while old Billali and the two bearer mutes were busy collecting the baggage. As usual, Ayesha was veiled like the marble Truth (by the way, I wonder if she originally got the idea of covering up her beauty from that statue?). I noticed, however, that she seemed very depressed, and had none of that proud and buoyant bearing which would have betrayed her among a thousand women of the same stature, even if they had been veiled like herself. She looked up as we came—for her head was bowed—and greeted us. Leo asked her how she had slept.

'Ill, my Kallikrates,' she answered, 'ill. This night have strange and hideous dreams come creeping through my brain, and I know not what they may portend. Almost do I feel as though some evil overshadowed me; and yet how can evil touch me? I wonder,' she went on with a sudden outbreak of womanly tenderness, 'I wonder if, should aught happen to me, so that I slept awhile and left thee waking, wouldst thou think gently of me? I wonder, my Kallikrates, if thou wouldst tarry till I came again, as for so many centuries I have tarried for thy coming?'

Then, without waiting for an answer, she went on: 'Come, let us be setting forth, for we have far to go, and before another day is born in yonder blue should we stand in the place of Life.'

In another five minutes we were once more on our way through the vast ruined city, which loomed at us on either side in the grey dawning in a way that was at once grand and oppressive. Just as the first ray of the rising sun shot like a golden arrow athwart this storied desolation we gained the further gateway of the outer wall, and having given one more glance at the hoar and pillared majesty through which we had passed, and (with the exception of Job, for whom ruins had no charms) breathed a sigh of regret that we had not had more time to explore it, passed through the great moat, and on to the plain beyond.

As the sun rose so did Ayesha's spirits, till by breakfast-time they had regained their normal level, and she laughingly set down her previous depression to the associations of the spot where she had slept.

'These barbarians declare that Kôr is haunted,' she said, 'and of a truth I do believe their saying, for never did I know so ill a night save once. I remember it now. It was on that very spot when thou didst lie dead at my feet, Kallikrates. Never will I visit it again; it is a place of evil omen.'

After a very brief halt for breakfast we pressed on with such good will that by two o'clock in the afternoon we were at the foot of the vast wall of rock that formed the lip of the volcano, and which at this point towered up precipitously above us for fifteen hundred or two thousand feet. Here we halted, certainly not to my astonishment, for I did not see how it was possible that we should go any farther.

'Now,' said Ayesha, as she descended from her litter, 'doth our labour but commence, for here do we part with these men, and henceforward must we bear ourselves;' and then, addressing Billali, 'do thou and these slaves remain here, and abide our coming. By to-morrow at the midday shall we be with thee—if not, wait.'

Billali bowed humbly, and said that her august bidding should be obeyed if they stopped there till they grew old.

'And this man, oh Holly,' said *She*, pointing to Job; 'best is it that he should tarry also, for if his heart be not high and his courage great, perchance some evil might overtake him. Also, the secrets of the place whither we go are not fit for common eyes.'

I translated this to Job, who instantly and earnestly entreated me, almost with tears in his eyes, not to leave him behind. He said he was sure that he could see nothing worse than he had already seen, and that he was terrified to death at the idea of being left alone with those 'dumb folk,' who, he thought, would probably take the opportunity to hot-pot him.

I translated what he said to Ayesha, who shrugged her shoulders, and answered, 'Well, let him come, it is naught to me; on his own head be it, and he will serve to bear the lamp and this,' and she pointed to a narrow plank, some sixteen feet in length, which had been bound above the long bearing-pole of her hammock, as I had thought to make curtains spread out better, but, as it now appeared, for some unknown purpose connected with our extraordinary undertaking.

Accordingly, the plank, which, though tough, was very light, was given to Job to carry, and also one of the lamps. I slung the other on to my back, together with a spare jar of oil, while Leo loaded himself with the provisions and some water in a kid's skin. When this was done *She* bade Billali and the six bearer mutes to retreat behind a grove of flowering magnolias about a hundred yards away, and remain there under pain of death till we had vanished. They bowed humbly, and went, and, as he departed, old Billali gave me a friendly shake of the hand, and whispered that he had rather that it was I than he who was going on this wonderful expedition with '*She-who-must-be-obeyed*,' and upon my word I felt inclined to agree with him. In another minute they were gone, and then, having briefly asked us if we were ready, Ayesha turned, and gazed up the towering cliff.

'Goodness me, Leo,' I said, 'surely we are not going to climb that precipice!'

Leo shrugged his shoulders, being in a condition of half fascinated, half expectant mystification, and as he did so, Ayesha with a sudden move began to climb the cliff, and of course we had to follow her. It was perfectly marvellous to see the ease and grace with which she sprang from rock to rock, and swung herself along the ledges. The ascent was not, however, so difficult as it seemed, although there were one or two nasty places where it did not do to look behind you, the fact being that the rock still sloped here, and was not absolutely precipitous as it was higher up. In this way we, with no great labour, mounted to the height of some fifty feet above our last standing place, the only really troublesome thing to manage being Job's board, and in doing so drew some fifty or sixty paces to the left of our starting point, for we went up like a crab, sideways. Presently we reached a ledge, narrow enough at first, but which widened as we followed it, and moreover sloped inwards like the petal of a flower, so that as we followed it we gradually got into a kind of rut or fold of rock that grew deeper and deeper, till at last it resembled a Devonshire lane in stone, and hid us perfectly from the gaze of anybody on the slope below, if there had been anybody to gaze. This lane (which appeared to be a natural formation) continued for some fifty or sixty paces, and then suddenly ended in a cave, also natural, running at right angles to it. I am sure that it was a natural cave, and not hollowed by the hand of man, because of its irregular and contorted shape and course, which gave it the appearance of having been blown bodily in the mountain by some frightful eruption of gas following the line of the least resistance. All the caves hollowed by the ancients of Kôr, on the contrary, were cut out with the most perfect regularity and symmetry. At the mouth of this cave Ayesha halted, and bade us light the two lamps, which I did, giving one to her and keeping the other myself. Then, taking the lead, she advanced down the cavern, picking her way with great care, as indeed it was necessary to do, for the floor was most irregular—strewn with boulders like the bed of a stream, and in some places pitted with deep holes, in which it would have been easy to break one's leg.

This cavern we pursued for twenty minutes or more, it being, so far as I could form a judgment—owing to its numerous twists and turns no easy task—about a quarter of a mile long.

At last, however, we halted at its farther end, and whilst I was still trying to pierce the gloom a great gust of air came tearing down it, and extinguished both the lamps.

Ayesha called to us, and we crept up to her, for she was a little in front, and were rewarded with a view that was positively appalling in its gloom and grandeur. Before us was a mighty chasm in the black rock, jagged and torn and splintered through it in a far past age by some awful convulsion of Nature, as though it had been cleft by stroke upon stroke of the lightning. This chasm, which was bounded by a precipice on the hither, and presumably, though we could not see it, on the farther side also, may have measured any width across, but from its darkness I do not think that it can have been very broad. It was impossible to make out much of its outline, or how far it ran, for the simple reason that the point where we were standing was so far from the upper surface of the cliff, at least fifteen hundred or two thousand feet, that only a very dim light struggled down to us from above. The mouth of the cavern that we had been following gave on to a most curious and tremendous spur of rock, which jutted out in mid air into the gulf before us, for a distance of some fifty yards, coming to a sharp point at its termination, and resembling nothing that I can think of so much as the spur upon the leg of a cock in shape. This huge spur was attached only to the parent precipice at its base, which was, of course, enormous, just as the cock's spur is attached to its leg. Otherwise it was utterly unsupported.

'Here must we pass,' said Ayesha. 'Be careful lest giddiness overcome you, or the wind sweep you into the gulf beneath, for of a truth it hath no bottom;' and, without giving us any further time to get scared, she started walking along the spur, leaving us to follow her as best we might. I was next to her, then came Job, painfully dragging his plank, while Leo brought up the rear. It was a wonderful sight to see this intrepid woman gliding fearlessly along that dreadful place. For my part, when I had gone but a very few yards, what between the pressure of the air and the awful sense of the consequences that a slip would entail, I found it necessary to go down on my hands and knees and crawl, and so did the other two.

But Ayesha never condescended to this. On she went, leaning her body against the gusts of wind, and never seeming to lose her head or her balance.

In a few minutes we had crossed some twenty paces of this awful bridge, which got narrower at every step, and then all of a sudden a great gust came tearing along the gorge. I saw Ayesha lean herself against it, but the strong draught got under her dark cloak, and tore it from her, and away it went down the wind flapping like a wounded bird. It was dreadful to see it go, till it was lost in the blackness. I clung to the saddle of rock, and looked round, while the great spur vibrated with a humming sound beneath us, like a living thing. The sight was a truly awesome one. There we were poised in the gloom between earth and heaven. Beneath us were hundreds upon hundreds of feet of emptiness that gradually grew darker, till at last it was absolutely black, and at what depth it ended is more than I can guess. Above were space upon space of giddy air, and far, far away a line of blue sky. And down this vast gulf upon which we were pinnacled the great draught dashed and roared, driving clouds and misty wreaths of vapour before it, till we were nearly blinded, and utterly confused.

The whole position was so tremendous and so absolutely unearthly, that I believe it actually lulled our sense of terror, but to this hour I often see it in my dreams, and wake up covered with cold perspiration at its mere phantasy.

'On! on!' cried the white form before us, for now the cloak had gone *She* was robed in white, and looked more like a spirit riding down the gale than a woman; 'On, or ye will fall and be dashed to pieces. Keep your eyes fixed upon the ground, and closely hug the rock.'

We obeyed her, and crept painfully along the quivering path, against which the wind shrieked and wailed as it shook it, causing it to murmur like a vast tuning-fork. On we went, I do not know for how long, only gazing round now and again, when it was absolutely necessary, until at last we saw that we were on the very tip of the spur, a slab of rock, little larger than an ordinary table, and that throbbed and jumped like any over-engined steamer. There we lay on our stomachs, clinging to the ground, and looked about us, while Ayesha stood leaning out against the wind, down which her long hair streamed, and, absolutely heedless of the hideous depth that yawned beneath, pointed before her. Then we saw why the narrow plank, which Job and I had painfully dragged along between us, had been provided. Before us was an empty space, on the other side of which was something, as yet we could not see what, for here—either owing to the shadow of the opposite cliff, or from some other cause—the gloom was that of night.

'We must wait awhile,' called Ayesha; 'soon there will be light.'

At the moment I could not imagine what she meant. How could more light than there was ever come to this dreadful spot? Whilst I was still debating in my mind, suddenly, like a great sword of flame, a beam from the setting sun pierced the Stygian gloom,[1] and smote upon the point of rock whereon we lay, illumining Ayesha's lovely form with an unearthly splendour. I only wish that I could describe the wild and marvellous beauty of that sword of fire, laid across the darkness and rushing mist-wreaths of the gulf. How it got there I do not to this moment know, but I presume that there was some cleft or hole in the opposing cliff, through which it pierced when the setting orb was in a direct line therewith. All I can say is, that the effect was the most wonderful that I ever saw. Right through the heart of the darkness that flaming sword was stabbed, and where it lay there was the most surpassingly vivid light, so vivid that even at a distance one could see the grain of the rock, while, outside of it—yes, within a few inches of its keen edge—was naught but clustering shadows.

And now, by this ray of light, for which *She* had been waiting, and timed our arrival to meet, knowing that at this season for thousands of years it had always struck thus at sunset, we saw what was before us. Within eleven or twelve feet of the very tip of the tongue-like rock whereon we stood there arose, presumably from the far bottom of the gulf, a sugarloaf-shaped cone, of which the summit was exactly opposite to us. But had there been a summit only it would not have helped us much, for the nearest point of its circumference was some forty feet from where we were. On the lip of this summit, however, which was circular and hollow, rested a tremendous flat stone, something like a glacier stone—perhaps it was one, for all I know to the contrary—and the end of this stone approached to within twelve feet or so of us. This huge boulder was nothing more or less than a gigantic rocking-stone, accurately balanced upon the edge of the cone or miniature crater, like a half-crown on the rim of a wine-glass; for, in the fierce light that played upon it and us, we could see it oscillating in the gusts of wind.

'Quick!' said Ayesha; 'the plank—we must cross while the light endures; presently it will be gone.'

'Oh, Lord, sir!' groaned Job, 'surely she don't mean us to walk across that there place on that there thing,' as in obedience to my direction he pushed the long board towards me.

'That's it, Job,' I halloaed in ghastly merriment, though the idea of walking the plank was no pleasanter to me than to him.

I pushed the board on to Ayesha, who deftly ran it across the gulf so that one end of it rested on the rocking-stone, the other remaining on the extremity of the trembling spur. Then placing her foot upon it to prevent it from being blown away, she turned to me.

'Since last I was here, oh Holly,' she called, 'the support of the moving stone hath lessened somewhat, so that I am not sure if it will bear our weight and fall or no. Therefore will I cross the first, because no harm will come unto me,' and, without further ado, she trod lightly but firmly across the frail bridge, and in another second was standing safe upon the heaving stone.

'It is safe,' she called. 'See, hold thou the plank! I will stand on the farther side of the stone so that it may not overbalance with your greater weights. Now come, oh Holly, for presently the light will fail us.'

I struggled to my knees, and if ever I felt sick in my life I felt sick then, and I am not ashamed to say that I hesitated and hung back.

'Surely thou art not afraid,' called this strange creature in a lull of the gale, from where she stood, poised like a bird on the highest point of the rocking-stone. 'Make then way for Kallikrates.'

This settled me; it is better to fall down a precipice and die than be laughed at by such a woman; so I clenched my teeth, and in another instant I was on that horrible, narrow, bending plank, with bottomless space beneath and around me. I have always hated a great height, but never before did I realise the full horrors of which such a position is capable. Oh, the sickening sensation of that yielding board resting on the two moving supports. I grew dizzy, and thought that I must fall; my spine *crept*; it seemed to me that I was falling, and my delight at finding myself sprawling upon that stone, which rose and fell beneath me like a boat in a swell, cannot be expressed in words. All I know is that briefly, but earnestly enough, I thanked Providence for preserving me so far.

Then came Leo's turn, and, though he looked rather queer, he came across like a rope-dancer. Ayesha stretched out her hand to clasp his own, and I heard her say,

'Bravely done, my love—bravely done! The old Greek spirit lives in thee yet!'

And now only poor Job remained on the farther side of the gulf. He crept up to the plank, and yelled out, 'I can't do it, sir. I shall fall into that beastly place.'

'You must,' I remember saying with inappropriate facetiousness—'you must, Job, it's as easy as catching flies.' I suppose that I said it to satisfy my conscience, because although the expression conveys a wonderful idea of facility, as a matter of fact I know no more difficult operation in the whole world than catching flies—that is, in warm weather, unless, indeed, it is catching mosquitoes.

'I can't, sir—I can't, indeed.'

'Let the man come, or let him stop and perish there. See, the light is dying! In a moment it will be gone!' said Ayesha.

I looked. She was right. The sun was passing below the level of the hole or cleft in the precipice through which the ray reached us.

'If you stop there, Job, you will die alone,' I called; 'the light is going.'

'Come, be a man, Job,' roared Leo; 'it's quite easy.'

Thus adjured, the miserable Job, with a most awful yell, precipitated himself face downwards on the plank—he did not dare, small blame to him, to try to walk it, and commenced to draw himself across in little jerks, his poor legs hanging down on either side into the nothingness beneath.

His violent jerks at the frail board made the great stone, which was only balanced on a few inches of rock, oscillate in a most sickening manner, and, to make matters worse, when he was half-way across the flying ray of lurid light suddenly went out, just as though a lamp had been extinguished in a curtained room, leaving the whole howling wilderness of air black with darkness.

'Come on, Job, for God's sake!' I shouted in an agony of fear, while the stone, gathering motion with every swing, rocked so violently that it was difficult to hang on to it. It was a truly awful position.

'Lord have mercy on me!' cried poor Job from the darkness. 'Oh, the plank's slipping!' and I heard a violent struggle, and thought that he was gone.

But at that moment his outstretched hand, clasping in agony at the air, met my own, and I hauled—ah, how I did haul, putting out all the strength that it has pleased Providence to give me in such abundance—and to my joy in another minute Job was gasping on the rock beside me. But the plank! I felt it slip, and heard it knock against a projecting knob of rock, and it was gone.

'Great heavens!' I exclaimed. 'How are we going to get back?'

'I don't know,' answered Leo, out of the gloom. '"Sufficient to the day is the evil thereof."[2] I am thankful enough to be here.'

But Ayesha merely called to me to take her hand and creep after her.

XXV

The Spirit of Life

I did as I was bid, and in fear and trembling felt myself guided over the edge of the stone. I sprawled my legs out, but could touch nothing.

'I am going to fall!' I gasped.

'Nay, let thyself go, and trust to me,' answered Ayesha.

Now, if the position is considered, it will be easily understood that this was a greater demand upon my confidence than was justified by my knowledge of Ayesha's character. For all I knew she might be in the very act of consigning me to a horrible doom. But in life we sometimes have to lay our faith upon strange altars, and so it was now.

'Let thyself go!' she cried, and, having no choice, I did.

I felt myself slide a pace or two down the sloping surface of the rock, and then pass into the air, and the thought flashed through my brain that I was lost. But no! In another instant my feet struck against a rocky floor, and I felt that I was standing on something solid, and out of reach of the wind, which I could hear singing away overhead. As I stood there thanking Heaven for these small mercies, there was a slip and a scuffle, and down came Leo alongside of me.

'Hulloa, old fellow!' he called out, 'are you there? This is getting interesting, is it not?'

Just then, with a terrific yell, Job arrived right on the top of us, knocking us both down. By the time that we had struggled to our feet again Ayesha was standing among us, and bidding us light the lamps, which fortunately remained uninjured, as also did the spare jar of oil.

I got out my box of Bryant and May's wax matches, and they struck as merrily, there, in that awful place, as they could have done in a London drawing-room.

In a couple of minutes both the lamps were alight; and a curious scene they revealed. We were huddled together in a rocky chamber, some ten feet square, and scared enough we looked; that is, except Ayesha, who was standing calmly with her arms folded, and waiting for the lamps to burn up. The chamber appeared to be partly natural, and partly hollowed out of the top of the cone. The roof of the natural part was formed of the swinging stone, and that of the back part of the chamber, which sloped downwards, was hewn from the live rock. For the rest, the place was warm and dry—a perfect haven of rest compared to the giddy pinnacle above, and the quivering spur that shot out to meet it in mid-air.

'So!' said *She*, 'safely have we come, though once I feared that the rocking stone would fall with you, and precipitate you into the bottomless deeps beneath, for I do believe that the cleft goeth down to the very womb of the world. The rock whereon the stone resteth hath crumbled beneath the swinging weight. And now that he,' nodding towards Job, who was sitting on the floor, feebly wiping his forehead with a red cotton pocket-handkerchief, 'whom they rightly call the "Pig," for as a pig is he stupid, hath let fall the plank, it will not be easy to return across the gulf, and to that end must I make a plan. But now rest a while, and look upon this place. What think ye that it is?'

'We know not,' I answered.

'Wouldst thou believe, oh Holly, that once a man did choose this airy nest for a daily habitation, and did here endure for many years; leaving it only but one day in every twelve to seek food and water and oil that the people brought, more than he could carry, and laid as an offering in the mouth of the tunnel through which we passed hither?'

We looked up wonderingly, and she continued—

'Yet so it was. There was a man—Noot, he named himself—who, though he lived in the latter days, had of the wisdom of the sons of Kôr. A hermit was he, and a philosopher, and skilled in the secrets of Nature, and he it was who discovered the Fire that I shall show you, which is Nature's blood and life, and also that he who bathed therein, and breathed thereof, should live while Nature lives. But like unto thee, oh Holly, this man, Noot, would not turn his knowledge to account. "Ill," he said, "was it for man to live, for man was born to die." Therefore did he tell his secret to none, and therefore did he come and live here, where the seeker after Life must pass, and was revered of the Amahagger of the day as holy, and a hermit. And when first I came to this country—knowest thou how I came, Kallikrates? Another time will I tell thee, it is a strange tale—I heard of this philosopher, and waited for him when he came to fetch his food, and returned with him hither, though greatly did I fear to tread the gulf. Then did I beguile him with my beauty and my wit, and flatter him with my tongue, so that he led me down and showed me the Fire, and told me the secrets of the Fire, but he would not suffer me to step therein, and, fearing lest he should slay me, I refrained, knowing that the man was very old, and soon would die. And I returned, having learned from him all that he knew of the wonderful Spirit of the World, and that was much, for the man was wise and very ancient, and by purity and abstinence, and the contemplations of his innocent mind, had worn thin the veil between that which we see and the great invisible truths, the whisper of whose wings at times we hear as they sweep through the gross air of the world. Then—it was but a very few days after, I met thee, my Kallikrates, who hadst wandered hither with the beautiful Egyptian Amenartas, and I learned to love for the first and last time, once and for ever, so that it entered into my mind to come hither with thee, and receive the gift of Life for thee and me. Therefore came we, with that Egyptian who would not be left behind, and, behold, we found the old man Noot lying but newly dead. *There* he lay, and his white beard covered him like a garment,' and she pointed to a spot near where

I was sitting; 'but surely he hath long since crumbled into dust, and the wind hath borne his ashes hence.'

Here I put out my hand and felt in the dust, and presently my fingers touched something. It was a human tooth, very yellow, but sound. I held it up and showed it to Ayesha, who laughed.

'Yes,' she said, 'it is his without a doubt. Behold what remaineth of Noot and the wisdom of Noot—one little tooth! And yet that man had all life at his command, and for his conscience' sake would have none of it. Well, he lay there newly dead, and we descended whither I shall lead you, and then, gathering up all my courage, and courting death that I might perchance win so glorious a crown of life, I stepped into the flames, and behold! life such as ye can never know until ye feel it also, flowed into me, and I came forth undying, and lovely beyond imagining. Then did I stretch out mine arms to thee, Kallikrates, and bid thee take thine immortal bride, and behold, as I spoke, thou, blinded by my beauty, didst turn from me, and throw thine arms about the neck of Amenartas. And then a great fury filled me, and made me mad, and I seized the javelin that thou didst bear, and stabbed thee, so that there, at my very feet, in the place of Life, thou didst groan and go down into death. I knew not then that I had strength to slay with mine eyes and by the power of my will, therefore in my madness slew I with the javelin.*

'And when thou wast dead, ah! I wept, because I was undying and thou wast dead. I wept there in the place of Life so that had

* It will be observed that Ayesha's account of the death of Kallikrates differs materially from that written on the potsherd by Amenartas. The writing on the sherd says, 'Then in her rage did she smite him *by her magic*, and he died.' We never ascertained which was the correct version, but it will be remembered that the body of Kallikrates had a spear-wound in the breast, which seems conclusive, unless, indeed, it was inflicted after death. Another thing that we never ascertained was *how* the two women—*She* and the Egyptian Amenartas—managed to bear the corpse of the man they both loved across the dread gulf and along the shaking spur. What a spectacle the two distracted creatures must have presented in their grief and loveliness as they toiled along that awful place with the dead man between them! Probably however the passage was easier then.—L. H. H.

I been mortal any more my heart had surely broken. And she, the swart Egyptian—she cursed me by her gods. By Osiris did she curse me and by Isis, by Nephthys and by Hekt, by Sekhet, the lion-headed, and by Set, calling down evil on me, evil and everlasting desolation.[1] Ah! I can see her dark face now lowering o'er me like a storm, but she could not hurt me, and I—I know not if I could hurt her. I did not try; it was naught to me then; so together we bore thee hence. And afterwards I sent her—the Egyptian—away through the swamps, and it seems that she lived to bear a son and to write the tale that should lead thee, her husband, back to me, her rival and thy murdress.

'Such is the tale, my love, and now is the hour at hand that shall set a crown upon it. Like all things on the earth, it is compounded of evil and of good—more of evil than of good, perchance; and writ in letters of blood. It is the truth; naught have I hidden from thee, Kallikrates. And now one thing before the final moment of thy trial. We go down into the presence of Death, for Life and Death are very near together, and—who knoweth?—that might happen which should separate us for another space of waiting. I am but a woman, and no prophetess, and I cannot read the future. But this I know—for I learnt it from the lips of the wise man Noot—that my life is but prolonged and made more bright. It cannot live for aye. Therefore, before we go, tell me, oh Kallikrates, that of a truth thou dost forgive me, and dost love me from thy heart. See, Kallikrates: much evil have I done—perchance it was evil but two nights gone to strike that girl who loved thee cold in death—but she disobeyed me and angered me, prophesying misfortune to me, and I smote. Be careful when power comes to thee also, lest thou too shouldst smite in thine anger or thy jealousy, for unconquerable strength is a sore weapon in the hands of erring man. Yea, I have sinned—out of the bitterness born of a great love have I sinned—but yet do I know the good from the evil, nor is my heart altogether hardened. Thy love, oh Kallikrates, shall be the gate of my redemption, even as aforetime my passion was the path down which I ran to evil. For deep love unsatisfied is the hell of noble hearts and a portion for the accursed, but love that is mirrored back more perfect from the soul of our desired doth fashion wings to lift us above ourselves, and make us what we might be. Therefore, Kallikrates, take me by the hand, and lift my veil with no more fear than though I were some peasant girl, and not the wisest and most beauteous woman in this wide world, and look me in the eyes, and tell me that thou dost forgive me with all thine heart, and that with all thine heart thou dost worship me.'

She paused, and the strange tenderness in her voice seemed to hover round us like a memory. I know that the sound of it moved me more even than her words, it was so very human—so very womanly. Leo, too, was strangely touched. Hitherto he had been fascinated against his better judgment, something as a bird is fascinated by a snake, but now I think that all this passed away, and he realised that he really loved this strange and glorious creature, as, alas! I loved her also. At any rate, I saw his eyes fill with tears, and he stepped swiftly to her and undid the gauzy veil, and then took her by the hand, and, gazing into her deep eyes, said aloud—

'Ayesha, I love thee with all my heart, and so far as forgiveness is possible I forgive thee the death of Ustane. For the rest, it is between thee and thy Maker; I know naught of it. I only know that I love thee as I never loved before, and that I will cleave to thee to the end.'

'Now,' answered Ayesha, with proud humility—'now when my lord doth speak thus royally and give with so free a hand, it cannot become me to lag behind in words, and be beggared of my generosity. Behold!' and she took his hand and placed it upon her shapely head, and then bent herself slowly down till one knee for an instant touched the ground—'Behold! in token of submission do I bow me to my lord! Behold!' and she kissed him on the lips, 'in token of my wifely love do I kiss my lord. Behold!' and she laid her hand upon his heart, 'by the sin I sinned, by my lonely centuries of waiting wherewith it was wiped out, by the great love wherewith I love, and by the Spirit—the Eternal

Thing that doth beget all life, from whom it ebbs, to whom it doth return again—I swear:—

'I swear, even in this first most holy hour of completed Womanhood, that I will abandon Evil and cherish Good. I swear that I will be ever guided by thy voice in the straightest path of Duty. I swear that I will eschew Ambition, and through all my length of endless days set Wisdom over me as a guiding star to lead me unto Truth and a knowledge of the Right. I swear also that I will honour and will cherish thee, Kallikrates, who hast been swept by the wave of time back into my arms, ay, till the very end, come it soon or late. I swear—nay, I will swear no more, for what are words? Yet shalt thou learn that Ayesha hath no false tongue.

'So I have sworn, and thou, my Holly, art witness to my oath. Here, too, are we wed, my husband, with the gloom for bridal canopy—wed till the end of all things; here do we write our marriage vows upon the rushing winds which shall bear them up to heaven, and round and continually round this rolling world.

'And for a bridal gift I crown thee with my beauty's starry crown, and enduring life, and wisdom without measure, and wealth that none can count. Behold! the great ones of the earth shall creep about thy feet, and their fair women shall cover up their eyes because of the shining glory of thy countenance, and their wise ones shall be abased before thee. Thou shalt read the hearts of men as an open writing, and hither and thither shalt thou lead them as thy pleasure listeth. Like that old Sphinx of Egypt shalt thou sit aloft from age to age, and ever shall they cry to thee to solve the riddle of thy greatness that doth not pass away, and ever shalt thou mock them with thy silence!

'Behold! once more I kiss thee, and by that kiss I give to thee dominion over sea and earth, over the peasant in his hovel, over the monarch in his palace halls, and cities crowned with towers, and those who breathe therein. Where'er the sun shakes out his spears, and the lonesome waters mirror up the moon, where'er storms roll, and Heaven's painted bows arch in the sky—from the pure North clad in snows, across the middle spaces of the world, to where the amorous South, lying like a bride upon her blue couch of seas, breathes in sighs made sweet with the odour of myrtles—there shall thy power pass and thy dominion find a home. Nor sickness, nor icy-fingered fear, nor sorrow, and pale waste of form and mind hovering ever o'er humanity, shall so much as shadow thee with the shadow of their wings. As a God shalt thou be, holding good and evil in the hollow of thy hand, and I, even I, I humble myself before thee. Such is the power of Love, and such is the bridal gift I give unto thee, Kallikrates, beloved of Rā, my Lord and Lord of All.

'And now it is done, and come storm, come shine, come good, come evil, come life, come death, it never, never can be undone. For, of a truth, that which is, is, and, being done, is done for aye, and cannot be altered. I have said —— Let us hence, that all things may be accomplished in their order;' and, taking one of the lamps, she advanced towards the end of the chamber that was roofed in by the swaying stone, where she halted.

We followed her, and perceived that in the wall of the cone there was a stair, or, to be more accurate, that some projecting knobs of rock had been so shaped as to form a good imitation of a stair. Down this Ayesha began to climb, springing from step to step, like a chamois,[2] and after her we followed with less grace. When we had descended some fifteen or sixteen steps we found that they ended in a tremendous rocky slope, running first outwards and then inwards—like the slope of an inverted cone, or tunnel. The slope was very steep, and often precipitous, but it was nowhere impassable, and by the light of the lamps we went down it with no great difficulty, though it was gloomy work enough travelling on thus, no one of us knew whither, into the dead heart of a volcano. As we went, however, I took the precaution of noting our route as well as I could; and this was not difficult, owing to the extraordinary and most fantastic shape of the rocks that were strewn about, many of which in that dim light looked more like the grim faces carven upon mediæval gargoyles than ordinary boulders.

For a long period we travelled on thus, half an hour I should say, till, after we had descended for many hundreds of feet, I perceived that we were reaching the point of the inverted cone. In another minute we were there, and found that at the very apex of the funnel was a passage, so low and narrow that we had to stoop as we crept along it in indian file. After some fifty yards of this creeping, the passage suddenly widened into a cave, so huge that we could see neither the roof nor the sides. We only knew that it was a cave by the echo of our tread and the perfect quiet of the heavy air. On we went for many minutes in absolute awed silence, like lost souls in the depths of Hades, Ayesha's white and ghost-like form flitting in front of us, till once more the cavern ended in a passage which opened into a second cavern much smaller than the first. Indeed, we could clearly make out the arch and stony banks of this second cave, and, from their rent and jagged appearance, discovered that, like the first long passage down which we had passed through the cliff before we reached the quivering spur, it had to all appearance been torn in the bowels of the rock by the terrific force of some explosive gas. At length this cave ended in a third passage, through which gleamed a faint glow of light.

I heard Ayesha give a sigh of relief as this light dawned upon us.

'It is well,' she said; 'prepare to enter the very womb of the Earth, wherein she doth conceive the Life that ye see brought forth in man and beast—ay, and in every tree and flower.'

Swiftly she sped along, and after her we stumbled as best we might, our hearts filled like a cup with mingled dread and curiosity. What were we about to see? We passed down the tunnel; stronger and stronger the light beamed, reaching us in great flashes like the rays from a lighthouse, as one by one they are thrown wide upon the darkness of the waters. Nor was this all, for with the flashes came a soul-shaking sound like that of thunder and of crashing trees. Now we were through it, and—oh, heavens!

We stood in a third cavern, some fifty feet in length by perhaps as great a height, and thirty wide. It was carpeted with fine white sand, and its walls had been worn smooth by the action of I know not what. The cavern was not dark like the others, it was filled with a soft glow of rose-coloured light, more beautiful to look on than anything that can be conceived. But at first we saw no flashes, and heard no more of the thunderous sound. Presently, however, as we stood in amaze, gazing at the wonderful sight, and wondering whence the rosy radiance flowed, a dread and beautiful thing happened. Across the far end of the cavern, with a grinding and crashing noise—a noise so dreadful and awe-inspiring that we all trembled, and Job actually sank to his knees—there flamed out an awful cloud or pillar of fire, like a rainbow many-coloured, and like the lightning bright. For a space, perhaps forty seconds, it flamed and roared thus, turning slowly round and round, and then by degrees the terrible noise ceased, and with the fire it passed away—I know not where—leaving behind it the same rosy glow that we had first seen.

'Draw near, draw near!' cried Ayesha, with a voice of thrilling exultation. 'Behold the very Fountain and Heart of Life as it beats in the bosom of the great world. Behold the substance from which all things draw their energy, the bright Spirit of the Globe, without which it cannot live, but must grow cold and dead as the dead moon. Draw near, and wash you in the living flames, and take their virtue into your poor frames in all its virgin strength—not as it now feebly glows within your bosoms, filtered thereto through all the fine strainers of a thousand intermediate lives, but as it is here in the very fount and seat of earthly Being.'

We followed her through the rosy glow up to the head of the cave, till at last we stood before the spot where the great pulse beat and the great flame passed. And as we went we became sensible of a wild and splendid exhilaration, of a glorious sense of such a fierce intensity of Life that the most buoyant moments of our strength seemed flat and tame and feeble beside it. It was the mere effluvium of the flame, the subtle ether that it cast off as it passed, working on us, and making us feel strong as giants and swift as eagles.

We reached the head of the cave, and gazed at each other in the glorious glow, and laughed aloud—even Job laughed, and he had not laughed for a week—in the lightness of our hearts and the divine intoxication of our brains. I know that I felt as though all the varied genius of which the human intellect is capable had descended upon me. I could have spoken in blank verse of Shakespearean beauty, all sorts of great ideas flashed through my mind; it was as though the bonds of my flesh had been loosened, and left the spirit free to soar to the empyrean of its native power. The sensations that poured in upon me are indescribable. I seemed to live more keenly, to reach to a higher joy, and sip the goblet of a subtler thought than ever it had been my lot to do before. I was another and most glorified self, and all the avenues of the Possible were for a space laid open to the footsteps of the Real.

Then, suddenly, whilst I rejoiced in this splendid vigour of a new-found self, from far, far away there came a dreadful muttering noise, that grew and grew to a crash and a roar, which combined in itself all that is terrible and yet splendid in the possibilities of sound. Nearer it came, and nearer yet, till it was close upon us, rolling down like all the thunder-wheels of heaven behind the horses of the lightning. On it came, and with it came the glorious blinding cloud of many-coloured light, and stood before us for a space, turning, as it seemed to us, slowly round and round, and then, accompanied by its attendant pomp of sound, passed away I know not whither.

So astonishing was the wondrous sight that one and all of us, save *She*, who stood up and stretched her hands towards the fire, sank down before it, and hid our faces in the sand.

When it was gone, Ayesha spoke.

'Now, Kallikrates,' she said, 'the mighty moment is at hand. When the great flame comes again thou must stand in it. First throw aside thy garments, for it will burn them, though thee it will not hurt. Thou must stand in the flame while thy senses will endure, and when it embraces thee suck the fire down into thy very heart, and let it leap and play around thy every part, so that thou lose no moiety of its virtue. Hearest thou me, Kallikrates?'

'I hear thee, Ayesha,' answered Leo, 'but, of a truth—I am no coward—but I doubt me of that raging flame. How know I that it will not utterly destroy me, so that I lose myself and lose thee also? Nevertheless will I do it,' he added.

Ayesha thought for a minute, and then said—

'It is not wonderful that thou shouldst doubt. Tell me, Kallikrates: if thou seest me stand in the flame and come forth unharmed, wilt thou enter also?'

'Yes,' he answered, 'I will enter even if it slay me. I have said that I will enter now.'

'And that will I also,' I cried.

'What, my Holly!' she laughed aloud; 'methought that thou wouldst naught of length of days. Why, how is this?'

'Nay, I know not,' I answered, 'but there is that in my heart that calleth to me to taste of the flame, and live.'

'It is well,' she said. 'Thou art not altogether lost in folly. See now, I will for the second time bathe me in this living bath. Fain would I add to my beauty and my length of days if that be possible. If it be not possible, at the least it cannot harm me.

'Also,' she continued, after a momentary pause, 'is there another and a deeper cause why I would once again dip me in the flame. When first I tasted of its virtue full was my heart of passion and of hatred of that Egyptian Amenartas, and therefore, despite my strivings to be rid thereof, have passion and hatred been stamped upon my soul from that sad hour to this. But now it is otherwise. Now is my mood a happy mood, and filled am I with the purest part of thought, and so would I ever be. Therefore, Kallikrates, will I once more wash and make me pure and clean, and yet more fit for thee. Therefore also, when thou dost in turn stand in the fire, empty all thy heart of evil, and let sweet contentment hold the balance of thy mind. Shake loose thy spirit's wings, and take thy stand upon the utter verge of holy contemplation; ay, dream upon thy mother's kiss, and turn thee towards the vision of the highest good that hath ever swept on silver wings across the silence of thy dreams. For from the germ of what thou art in that dread moment shall grow the fruit of what thou shalt be for all unreckoned time.

'Now prepare thee, prepare! even as though thy last hour were at hand, and thou wast about to cross to the land of shadows, and not through the gates of glory into the realms of Life made beautiful. Prepare, I say!'

XXVI

What We Saw

Then came a few moments' pause, during which Ayesha seemed to be gathering up her strength for the fiery trial, while we clung to each other, and waited in utter silence.

At last, from far far away, came the first murmur of sound, that grew and grew till it began to crash and bellow in the distance. As she heard it, Ayesha swiftly threw off her gauzy wrapping, loosened the golden snake from her kirtle, and then, shaking her lovely hair about her like a garment, beneath its cover slipped the kirtle off and replaced the snaky belt around her and outside the masses of falling hair. There she stood before us as Eve might have stood before Adam, clad in nothing but her abundant locks, held round her by the golden band; and no words of mine can tell how sweet she looked—and yet how divine. Nearer and nearer came the thunder wheels of fire, and as they came she pushed one ivory arm through the dark masses of her hair and flung it round Leo's neck.

'Oh, my love, my love!' she murmured, 'wilt thou ever know how I have loved thee?' and she kissed him on the forehead, and then went and stood in the pathway of the flame of Life.

There was, I remember, to my mind something very touching about her words and that embrace upon the forehead. It was like a mother's kiss, and seemed to convey a benediction with it.

On came the crashing, rolling noise, and the sound thereof was as the sound of a forest being swept flat by a mighty wind, and then tossed up by it like so much grass, and thundered down a mountain-side. Nearer and nearer it came; now flashes of light, forerunners of the revolving pillar of flame, were passing like arrows through the rosy air; and now the edge of the pillar itself appeared. Ayesha turned towards it, and stretched out her arms to greet it. On it came very slowly, and lapped her round with flame. I saw the fire run up her form. I saw her lift it with both hands as though it were water, and pour it over her head. I even saw her open her mouth and draw it down into her lungs, and a dread and wonderful sight it was.

Then she paused, and stretched out her arms, and stood there quite still, with a heavenly smile upon her face, as though she were the very Spirit of the Flame.

The mysterious fire played up and down her dark and rolling locks, twining and twisting itself through and around them like threads of golden lace; it gleamed upon her ivory breast and shoulder, from which the hair had slipped aside; it slid along her pillared throat and delicate features, and seemed to find a home in the glorious eyes that shone and shone, more brightly even than the spiritual essence.

Oh, how beautiful she looked there in the flame! No angel out of heaven could have worn a greater loveliness. Even now my heart faints before the recollection of it, as she stood and smiled at our awed faces, and I would give half my remaining time upon this earth to see her once like that again.

But suddenly—more suddenly than I can describe—a kind of change came over her face, a change which I could not define or explain on paper, but none the less a change. The smile vanished, and in its place there came a dry, hard look; the rounded face seemed to grow pinched, as though some great anxiety were leaving its impress upon it. The glorious eyes, too, lost their light, and, as I thought, the form its perfect shape and erectness.

I rubbed my eyes, thinking that I was the victim of some hallucination, or that the refraction from the intense light produced an optical delusion; and, as I did so, the flaming pillar slowly twisted and thundered off whithersoever it passes to in the bowels of the great earth, leaving Ayesha standing where it had been.

As soon as it was gone, she stepped forward to Leo's side—it seemed to me that there was no spring in her step—and stretched out her hand to lay it on his shoulder. I gazed at her arm. Where was its wonderful roundness and beauty? It was getting thin and angular. And her face—by Heaven!—*her face was growing old before my eyes!* I suppose that Leo saw it also; certainly he recoiled a step or two.

'What is it, my Kallikrates?' she said, and her voice—what was the matter with those deep and thrilling notes? They were quite high and cracked.

'Why, what is it—what is it?' she said confusedly. 'I feel dazed. Surely the quality of the fire hath not altered. Can the principle of Life alter? Tell me, Kallikrates, is there aught wrong with my eyes? I see not clear,' and she put her hand to her head and touched her hair—and oh, *horror of horrors!*—it all fell upon the floor.

'Oh, *look!—look!—look!*' shrieked Job, in a shrill falsetto of terror, his eyes nearly dropping out of his head, and foam upon his lips. '*Look!—look!—look!* she's shrivelling up! she's turning into a monkey!' and down he fell upon the ground, foaming and gnashing in a fit.

True enough—I faint even as I write it in the living presence of that terrible recollection—she *was* shrivelling up; the golden snake that had encircled her gracious form slipped over her hips and to the ground; smaller and smaller she grew; her skin changed colour, and in place of the perfect whiteness of its lustre it turned dirty brown and yellow, like an old piece of withered parchment. She felt at her head: the delicate hand was nothing but a claw now, a human talon like that of a badly-preserved Egyptian mummy, and then she seemed to realise what kind of change was passing over her, and she shrieked—ah, she shrieked!—she rolled upon the floor and shrieked!

Smaller she grew, and smaller yet, till she was no larger than a baboon. Now the skin was puckered into a million wrinkles, and on the shapeless face was the stamp of unutterable age. I never saw anything like it; nobody ever saw anything like the frightful age that was graven on that fearful countenance, no bigger now than that of a two-months' child, though the skull remained the same size, or nearly so, and let all men pray to God they never may, if they wish to keep their reason.

At last she lay still, or only feebly moving. She, who but two minutes before had gazed upon us the loveliest, noblest, most splendid woman the world has ever seen, she lay still before us, near the masses of her own dark hair, no larger than a big monkey, and hideous—ah, too hideous for words. And yet, think of this—at that very moment I thought of it—it was the *same* woman!

She was dying: we saw it, and thanked God—for while she lived she could feel, and what must she have felt? She raised herself upon her bony hands, and blindly gazed around her, swaying her head slowly from side to side as a tortoise does. She could not see, for her whitish eyes were covered with a horny film. Oh, the horrible pathos of the sight! But she could still speak.

'Kallikrates,' she said in husky, trembling notes. 'Forget me not, Kallikrates. Have pity on my shame; I shall come again, and shall once more be beautiful, I swear it—it is true! *Oh—h—h—*' and she fell upon her face, and was still.

On the very spot where more than twenty centuries before she had slain Kallikrates the priest, she herself fell down and died.

Overcome with the extremity of horror, we too fell on the sandy floor of that dread place, and swooned away.

I know not how long we remained thus. Many hours, I suppose. When at last I opened my eyes, the other two were still outstretched upon the floor. The rosy light yet beamed like a celestial dawn, and the thunder-wheels of the Spirit of Life yet rolled upon their accustomed track, for as I awoke the great pillar was passing away. There, too, lay the hideous little monkey frame, covered with crinkled yellow parchment, that once had been the glorious *She*. Alas! it was no hideous dream—it was an awful and unparalleled fact!

What had happened to bring this shocking change about? Had the nature of the life-giving Fire changed? Did it, perhaps, from time to time send forth an essence of Death instead of an essence of Life? Or was it that the frame once charged with its marvellous virtue could bear no more, so that were the process repeated—it mattered not at what lapse of time—the two impregnations neutralised each other, and left the body on which they acted as it was before it ever came into contact with the very essence of life? This, and this alone, would account for the sudden and terrible ageing of Ayesha, as the whole length of her two thousand years took effect upon her. I have not the slightest doubt myself but that the frame now lying before me was just what the frame of a woman would be if by any extraordinary means life could be preserved in her till she at length died at the age of two-and-twenty centuries.

But who can tell what had happened? There was the fact. Often since that awful hour I have reflected that it requires no great stretch of imagination to see the finger of Providence in the matter. Ayesha locked up in her living tomb waiting from age to age for the coming of her lover worked but a small change in the order of the World. But Ayesha strong and happy in her love, clothed in immortal youth and godlike beauty, and the wisdom of the centuries, would have revolutionised society, and even perchance have changed the destiny of Mankind. Thus she opposed herself against the eternal Law, and, strong though she was, by it was swept back to nothingness—swept back with shame and hideous mockery!

For some minutes I lay faintly turning these terrors over in my mind, while my physical strength came back to me, which it quickly did in that buoyant atmosphere. Then I bethought me of the others, and staggered to my feet, to see if I could arouse them. But first I took up Ayesha's kirtle and the gauzy scarf with which she had been wont to hide her dazzling loveliness from the eyes of men, and, averting my head so that I might not look upon it, covered up that dreadful relic of the glorious dead, that shocking epitome of human beauty and human life. I did this hurriedly, fearing lest Leo should recover, and see it again.

Then, stepping over the perfumed masses of dark hair that lay upon the sand, I stooped down by Job, who was lying upon his face, and turned him over. As I did so his arm fell back in a way that I did not like, and which sent a chill through me, and I glanced sharply at him. One look was enough. Our old and faithful servant was dead. His nerves, already shattered by all he had seen and undergone, had utterly broken down beneath this last dire sight, and he had died of terror, or in a fit brought on by terror. One had only to look at his face to see it.

It was another blow; but perhaps it may help people to understand how overwhelmingly awful was the experience through which we had passed—we did not feel it much at the time. It seemed quite natural that the poor old fellow should be dead. When Leo came to himself, which he did with a groan and trembling of the limbs about ten minutes afterwards, and I told him that Job was dead, he merely said, 'Oh!' And, mind you, this was from no heartlessness, for he and Job were much attached to each other; and he often talks of him now with the deepest regret and affection. It was only that his nerves would bear no more. A harp can give out but a certain quantity of sound, however heavily it is smitten.

Well, I set myself to recovering Leo, who, to my infinite relief, I found was not dead, but only fainting, and in the end I succeeded, as I have said, and he sat up; and then I saw another dreadful thing. When we entered that awful place his curling hair had been of the ruddiest gold, now it was turning grey, and by the time we gained the outer air it was snow white. Besides, he looked twenty years older.

'What is to be done, old fellow?' he said in a hollow, dead sort of voice, when his mind had cleared a little, and a recollection of what had happened forced itself upon it.

'Try and get out, I suppose,' I answered; 'that is, unless you would like to go in there,' and I pointed to the column of fire that was once more rolling by.

'I would go in if I were sure that it would kill me,' he said with a little laugh. 'It was my cursed hesitation that did this. If I had not been doubtful she might never have tried to show me the road. But I am not sure. The fire might have the opposite effect upon me. It might make me immortal; and, old fellow, I have not the patience to wait a couple of thousand years for her to come back again as she did for me. I had rather die when my hour comes—and I should fancy that it isn't far off either—and go my ways to look for her. Do you go in if you like.'

But I merely shook my head, my excitement was as dead as ditch-water, and my distaste for the prolongation of my mortal span had come back upon me more strongly than ever. Besides, we neither of us knew what the effects of the fire might be. The result upon *She* had not been of an encouraging nature, and of the exact causes that produced that result we were, of course, ignorant.

'Well, my boy,' I said, 'we cannot stop here till we go the way of those two,' and I pointed to the little heap under the white garment and to the stiffening corpse of poor Job. 'If we are going we had better go. But, by the way, I expect that the lamps have burnt out,' and I took one up and looked at it, and sure enough it had.

'There is some more oil in the vase,' said Leo indifferently—'if it is not broken, at least.'

I examined the vessel in question—it was intact. With a trembling hand I filled the lamps—luckily there was still some of the linen wick unburnt. Then I lit them with one of our wax matches. While I did so we heard the pillar of fire approaching once more as it went on its never-ending journey, if, indeed, it was the same pillar that passed and repassed in a circle.

'Let's see it come once more,' said Leo; 'we shall never look upon its like again in this world.'

It seemed a bit of idle curiosity, but somehow I shared it, and so we waited till, turning slowly round upon its own axis, it had flamed and thundered by; and I remember wondering for how many thousands of years this same phenomenon had been taking place in the bowels of the earth, and for how many more thousands it would continue to take place. I wondered also if any mortal eyes would ever again mark its passage, or any mortal ears be thrilled and fascinated by the swelling volume of its majestic sound. I do not think that they will. I believe that we are the last human beings who will ever see that unearthly sight. Presently it had gone, and we too turned to go.

But before we did so we each took Job's cold hand in ours and shook it. It was a rather ghastly ceremony, but it was the only means in our power of showing our respect to the faithful dead and of celebrating his obsequies. The heap beneath the white garment we did not uncover. We had no wish to look upon that terrible sight again. But we went to the pile of rippling hair that had fallen from her in the agony of that hideous change which was worse than a thousand natural deaths, and each of us drew from it a shining lock, and these locks we still have, the sole memento that is left to us of Ayesha as we knew her in the fulness of her grace and glory. Leo pressed the perfumed hair to his lips.

'She called to me not to forget her,' he said hoarsely; 'and swore that we should meet again. By Heaven! I never will forget her. Here I swear that, if we live to get out of this, I will not for all my days have anything to say to another living woman, and that wherever I go I will wait for her as faithfully as she waited for me.'

'Yes,' I thought to myself, 'if she comes back as beautiful as we knew her. But supposing she came back like that!'*

Well, and then we went. We went, and left those two in the presence of the very well and spring of Life, but gathered to the cold company of Death. How lonely they looked as they lay there, and how ill assorted! That little heap had been for two thousand years the wisest, loveliest, proudest creature—I can hardly call her woman—in the whole universe. She had been

* What a terrifying reflection it is, by the way, that nearly all our deep love for women who are not our kindred depends—at any rate, in the first instance—upon their personal appearance. If we lost them, and found them again dreadful to look on, though otherwise they were the very same, should we still love them?—L. H. H.

wicked, too, in her way; but, alas! such is the frailty of the human heart, her wickedness had not detracted from her charm. Indeed, I am by no means certain that it did not add to it. It was after all of a grand order, there was nothing mean or small about Ayesha.

And poor Job, too! His presentiment had come true, and there was an end of him. Well, he has a strange burial-place—no Norfolk hind[1] ever had a stranger, or ever will; and it is something to lie in the same sepulchre with the poor remains of the imperial *She*.

We looked our last upon them and the indescribable rosy glow in which they lay, and then with hearts far too heavy for words we left them, and crept thence broken-down men—so broken down that we even renounced the chance of practically immortal life, because all that made life valuable had gone from us, and we knew even then that to prolong our days indefinitely would only be to prolong our sufferings. For we felt—yes, both of us—that having once looked Ayesha in the eyes, we could not forget her for ever and ever while memory and identity remained. We both loved her now and for always, she was stamped and carven on our hearts, and no other woman or interest could ever raze that splendid die. And I—there lies the sting—I had and have no right to think thus of her. As she told me, I was naught to her, and never shall be through the unfathomed depth of Time, unless, indeed, conditions alter, and a day comes at last when two men may love one woman, and all three be happy in the fact. It is the only hope of my broken-heartedness, and a rather faint one. Beyond it I have nothing. I have paid down this heavy price, all that I am worth here and hereafter, and that is my sole reward. With Leo it is different, and often and often I bitterly envy him his happy lot, for if *She* was right, and her wisdom and knowledge did not fail her at the last, which, arguing from the precedent of her own case, I think most unlikely, he has some future to look forward to. But I have none, and yet—mark the folly and the weakness of the human heart, and let him who is wise learn wisdom from it—yet I would not have it otherwise. I mean that I am content to give what I have given and must always give, and take in payment those crumbs that fall from my mistress's table, the memory of a few kind words, the hope one day in the far undreamed future of a sweet smile or two of recognition, a little gentle friendship, and a little show of thanks for my devotion to her—and Leo.

If that does not constitute true love, I do not know what does, and all I have to say is that it is a very bad state of mind for a man on the wrong side of middle age to fall into.

XXVII

We Leap

We passed through the caves without trouble, but when we came to the slope of the inverted cone two difficulties stared us in the face. The first of these was the laborious nature of the ascent, and the next the extreme difficulty of finding our way. Indeed, had it not been for the mental notes that I had fortunately taken of the shape of various rocks, etc., I am sure that we never should have managed it at all, but have wandered about in the dreadful womb of the volcano—for I suppose it must once have been something of the sort—until we died of exhaustion and despair. As it was we went wrong several times, and once nearly fell into a huge crack or crevasse. It was terrible work creeping about in the dense gloom and awful stillness from boulder to boulder, and examining it by the feeble light of the lamps to see if I could recognise its shape. We rarely spoke, our hearts were too heavy for speech, we simply stumbled about, falling sometimes and cutting ourselves, in a rather dogged sort of way. The fact was that our spirits were utterly crushed, and we did not greatly care what happened to us. Only we felt bound to try and save our lives whilst we could, and indeed a natural instinct prompted us to it. So for some three or four hours, I should think—I cannot tell exactly how long, for we had no watch left that would go—we blundered on. During the last two hours we were completely lost, and I began to fear that we had got into the funnel of some subsidiary cone, when at last I suddenly recognised a very large rock which we had passed in descending but a little way from the top. It is a marvel that I should have recognised it, and, indeed, we had already passed it going at right angles to the proper path, when something about it struck me, and I turned back and examined it in an idle sort of way, and, as it happened, this proved our salvation.

After this we gained the rocky natural stair without much further trouble, and in due course found ourselves back in the little chamber where the benighted Noot had lived and died.

But now a fresh terror stared us in the face. It will be remembered that owing to Job's fear and awkwardness, the plank upon which we had crossed from the huge spur to the rocking-stone had been whirled off into the tremendous gulf below.

How were we to cross without the plank?

There was only one answer—we must try and *jump* it, or else stop there till we starved. The distance in itself was not so very great, between eleven and twelve feet I should think, and I have seen Leo jump over twenty when he was a young fellow at college; but then, think of the conditions. Two weary, worn-out men, one of them on the wrong side of forty, a rocking-stone to take off from, a trembling point of rock some few feet across to land upon, and a bottomless gulf to be cleared in a raging gale! It was bad enough, God knows, but when I pointed out these things to Leo, he put the whole matter in a nutshell by replying that, merciless as the choice was, we must choose between the certainty of a lingering death in the chamber and the risk of a swift one in the air. Of course, there was no arguing against this, but one thing was clear, we could not attempt that leap in the dark; the only thing to do was to wait for the ray of light which pierced through the gulf at sunset. How near to or how far from sunset we might be, neither of us had the faintest notion; all we did know was, that when at last the light came it would not endure more than a couple of minutes at the outside, so that we must be prepared to meet it. Accordingly, we made up our minds to creep on to the top of the rocking-stone and lie there in readiness. We were the more easily reconciled to this course by the fact that our lamps were once more nearly exhausted—

indeed, one had gone out bodily, and the other was jumping up and down as the flame of a lamp does when the oil is done. So, by the aid of its dying light, we hastened to crawl out of the little chamber and clamber up the side of the great stone.

As we did so the light went out.

The difference in our position was a sufficiently remarkable one. Below, in the little chamber, we had only heard the roaring of the gale overhead—here, lying on our faces on the swinging stone, we were exposed to its full force and fury, as the great draught drew first from this direction and then from that, howling against the mighty precipice and through the rocky cliffs like ten thousand despairing souls. We lay there hour after hour in terror and misery of mind so deep that I will not attempt to describe it, and listened to the wild storm-voices of that Tartarus,[1] as, set to the deep undertone of the spur opposite against which the wind hummed like some awful harp, they called to each other from precipice to precipice. No nightmare dreamed by man, no wild invention of the romancer, can ever equal the living horror of that place, and the weird crying of those voices of the night, as we clung like shipwrecked mariners to a raft, and tossed on the black, unfathomed wilderness of air. Fortunately the temperature was not a low one; indeed, the wind was warm, or we should have perished. So we clung and listened, and while we were stretched out upon the rock a thing happened which was so curious and suggestive in itself, though doubtless a mere coincidence, that, if anything, it added to, rather than deducted from, the burden on our nerves.

It will be remembered that when Ayesha was standing on the spur, before we crossed to the stone, the wind tore her cloak from her, and whirled it away into the darkness of the gulf, we could not see whither. Well—I hardly like to tell the story; it is so strange. As we lay there upon the rocking-stone, this very cloak came floating out of the black space, like a memory from the dead, and fell on Leo—so that it covered him nearly from head to foot. We could not at first make out what it was, but soon discovered by its feel, and then poor Leo, for the first time, gave way, and I heard him sobbing there upon the stone. No doubt the cloak had been caught upon some pinnacle of the cliff, and was thence blown hither by a chance gust; but still, it was a most curious and touching incident.

Shortly after this, suddenly, without the slightest previous warning, the great red knife of light came stabbing the darkness through and through—struck the swaying stone on which we were, and rested its sharp point upon the spur opposite.

'Now for it,' said Leo, 'now or never.'

We rose and stretched ourselves, and looked at the cloud-wreaths stained the colour of blood by that red ray as they tore through the sickening depths beneath, and then at the empty space between the swaying stone and the quivering rock, and, in our hearts, despaired, and prepared for death. Surely we could not clear it—desperate though we were.

'Who is to go first?' said I.

'Do you, old fellow,' answered Leo. 'I will sit upon the other side of the stone to steady it. You must take as much run as you can, and jump high; and God have mercy on us, say I.'

I acquiesced with a nod, and then I did a thing I had never done since Leo was a little boy. I turned and put my arm round him, and kissed him on the forehead. It sounds rather French, but as a fact I was taking my last farewell of a man whom I could not have loved more if he had been my own son twice over.

'Good-bye, my boy,' I said, 'I hope that we shall meet again, wherever it is that we go to.'

The fact was I did not expect to live another two minutes.

Next I retreated to the far side of the rock, and waited till one of the chopping gusts of wind got behind me, and then, commending my soul to God, I ran the length of the huge stone, some three or four and thirty feet, and sprang wildly out into the dizzy air. Oh! the sickening terrors that I felt as I launched myself at that little point of rock, and the horrible sense of despair that shot through my brain as I realised that I had *jumped short*! But so it was, my feet never touched the point, they went down into space, only my hands and body came in contact with it. I gripped at it with a yell, but one hand slipped, and I swung right round, holding by the other, so that I faced the stone from which I had sprung. Wildly I stretched up with my left hand, and this time managed to grasp a knob of rock, and there I hung in the fierce red light, with thousands of feet of empty air beneath me. My hands were holding to either side of the under part of the spur, so that its point was touching my head. Therefore, even if I could have found the strength, I could not pull myself up. The most that I could do would be to hang for about a minute, and then drop down, down into the bottomless pit. If any man can imagine a more hideous position, let him speak! All I know is that the torture of that half-minute nearly turned my brain.

I heard Leo give a cry, and then suddenly saw him in mid-air springing up and out like a chamois. It was a splendid leap that he took under the influence of his terror and despair, clearing the horrible gulf as though it were nothing, and, landing well on to the rocky point, he threw himself upon his face, to prevent his pitching off into the depths. I felt the spur above me shake beneath the shock of his impact, and as it did so I saw the huge rocking-stone, that had been violently depressed by him as he sprang, fly back when relieved of his weight till, for the first time during all these centuries, it got beyond its balance, and fell with a most awful crash right into the rocky chamber which had once served the philosopher Noot for a hermitage, as I have no doubt, for ever hermetically sealing the passage that leads to the Place of Life with some hundreds of tons of rock.

All this happened in a second, and curiously enough, notwithstanding my terrible position, I noted it involuntarily, as it were. I even remember thinking that no human being would go down that dread path again.

Next instant I felt Leo seize me by the right wrist with both hands. By lying flat on the point of rock he could just reach me.

'You must let go and swing yourself clear,' he said in a calm and collected voice, 'and then I will try and pull you up, or we will both go together. Are you ready?'

By way of answer I let go, first with my left hand and then

with the right, and swayed out as a consequence clear of the overshadowing rock, my weight hanging upon Leo's arms. It was a dreadful moment. He was a very powerful man, I knew, but would his strength be equal to lifting me up till I could get a hold on the top of the spur, when owing to his position he had so little purchase?

For a few seconds I swung to and fro, while he gathered himself for the effort, and then I heard his sinews cracking above me, and felt myself lifted up as though I were a little child, till I got my left arm round the rock, and my chest was resting on it. The rest was easy; in two or three more seconds I was up, and we were lying panting side by side, trembling like leaves, and with the cold perspiration of terror pouring from our skins.

And then, as before, the light went out like a lamp.

For some half-hour we lay thus without speaking a word, and then at length began to creep along the great spur as best we might in the dense gloom. As we drew towards the face of the cliff, however, from which the spur sprang out like a spike from a wall, the light increased, though only a very little, for it was night overhead. After that the gusts of wind decreased, and we got along rather better, and at last reached the mouth of the first cave or tunnel. But now a fresh trouble stared us in the face: our oil was gone, and the lamps were, no doubt, crushed to powder beneath the fallen rocking-stone. We were even without a drop of water to stay our thirst, for we had drunk the last in the chamber of Noot. How were we to see to make our way through this last boulder-strewn tunnel?

Clearly all that we could do was to trust to our sense of feeling, and attempt the passage in the dark, so in we crept, fearing that if we delayed to do so our exhaustion would overcome us, and we should probably lie down and die where we were.

Oh, the horrors of that last tunnel! The place was strewn with rocks, and we fell over them, and knocked ourselves up against them till we were bleeding from a score of wounds. Our only guide was the side of the cavern, which we kept touching, and so bewildered did we grow in the darkness that we were several times seized with the terrifying thought that we had turned, and were travelling the wrong way. On we went, feebly, and still more feebly, for hour after hour, stopping every few minutes to rest, for our strength was spent. Once we fell asleep, and, I think, must have slept for some hours, for, when we woke, our limbs were quite stiff, and the blood from our blows and scratches had caked, and was hard and dry upon our skin. Then we dragged ourselves on again, till at last, when despair was entering into our hearts, we once more saw the light of day, and found ourselves outside the tunnel in the rocky fold on the outer surface of the cliff that, it will be remembered, led into it.

It was early morning—that we could tell by the feel of the sweet air and the look of the blessed sky, which we had never hoped to see again. It was, so near as we knew, an hour after sunset when we entered the tunnel, so it followed that it had taken us the entire night to crawl through that dreadful place.

'One more effort, Leo,' I gasped, 'and we shall reach the slope where Billali is, if he hasn't gone. Come, don't give way,' for he had cast himself upon his face. He got up, and, leaning on each other, we got down that fifty feet or so of cliff—somehow, I have not the least notion how. I only remember that we found ourselves lying in a heap at the bottom, and then once more began to drag ourselves along on our hands and knees towards the grove where *She* had told Billali to wait her re-arrival, for we could not walk another foot. We had not gone fifty yards in this fashion when suddenly one of the mutes emerged from some trees on our left, through which, I presume, he had been taking a morning stroll, and came running up to see what sort of strange animals we were. He stared, and stared, and then held up his hands in horror, and nearly fell to the ground. Next, he started off as hard as he could for the grove some two hundred yards away. No wonder that he was horrified at our appearance, for we must have been a shocking sight. To begin, Leo, with his golden curls turned a snowy white, his clothes nearly rent from his body, his worn face and his hands a mass of bruises, cuts, and blood-encrusted filth, was a sufficiently alarming spectacle, as he painfully dragged himself along the ground, and I have no doubt that I was little better to look on. I know that two days afterwards when I looked at my face in some water I scarcely recognised myself. I have never been famous for beauty, but there was something beside ugliness stamped upon my features that I have never got rid of until this day, something resembling that wild look with which a startled person wakes from deep sleep more than anything else that I can think of. And really it is not to be wondered at. What I do wonder at is that we escaped at all with our reason.

Presently, to my intense relief, I saw old Billali hurrying towards us, and even then I could scarcely help smiling at the expression of consternation on his dignified countenance.

'Oh, my Baboon! my Baboon!' he cried, 'my dear son, is it indeed thee and the Lion? Why, his mane that was ripe as corn is white like the snow. Whence come ye? and where is the Pig, and where too *She-who-must-be-obeyed*?'

'Dead, both dead,' I answered; 'but ask no questions; help us, and give us food and water, or we too shall die before thine eyes. Seest thou not that our tongues are black for want of water? How can we talk then?'

'Dead!' he gasped. 'Impossible. *She* who never dies—dead, how can it be?' and then, perceiving, I think, that his face was being watched by the mutes who had come running up, he checked himself, and motioned to them to carry us to the camp, which they did.

Fortunately when we arrived some broth was boiling on the fire, and with this Billali fed us, for we were too weak to feed ourselves, thereby I firmly believe saving us from death by exhaustion. Then he bade the mutes wash the blood and grime from us with wet cloths, and after that we were laid down upon piles of aromatic grass, and instantly fell into the dead sleep of absolute exhaustion of mind and body.

XXVIII

Over the Mountain

The next thing I recollect is a feeling of the most dreadful stiffness, and a sort of vague idea passing through my half-awakened brain that I was a carpet that had just been beaten. I opened my eyes, and the first thing they fell on was the venerable countenance of our old friend Billali, who was seated by the side of the improvised bed upon which I was sleeping, and thoughtfully stroking his long beard. The sight of him at once brought back to my mind a recollection of all that we had recently passed through, which was accentuated by the vision of poor Leo lying opposite to me, his face knocked almost to a jelly, and his beautiful crowd of curls turned from yellow to white,* and I shut my eyes again and groaned.

'Thou has slept long, my Baboon,' said old Billali.

'How long, my father?' I asked.

'A round of the sun and a round of the moon, a day and a night hast thou slept, and the Lion also. See, he sleepeth yet.'

'Blessed is sleep,' I answered, 'for it swallows up recollection.'

'Tell me,' he said, 'what hath befallen ye, and what is this strange story of the death of Her who dieth not. Bethink thee, my son: if this be true, then is thy danger and the danger of the Lion very great—nay, almost is the pot red wherewith ye shall be potted, and the stomachs of those who shall eat ye are already

* Curiously enough, Leo's hair has lately been to some extent regaining its colour—that is to say, it is now a yellowish grey, and I am not without hopes that it will in time come quite right.—L. H. H.

hungry for the feast. Knowest thou not that these Amahagger, my children, these dwellers in the caves, hate ye? They hate ye as strangers, they hate ye more because of their brethren whom *She* put to the torment for your sake. Assuredly, if once they learn that there is naught to fear from Hiya, from the terrible One-who-must-be-obeyed, they will slay ye by the pot. But let me hear thy tale, my poor Baboon.'

Thus adjured, I set to work and told him—not everything, indeed, for I did not think it desirable to do so, but sufficient for my purpose, which was to make him understand that *She* was really no more, having fallen into some fire, and, as I put it—for the real thing would have been incomprehensible to him—been burnt up. I also told him some of the horrors we had undergone in effecting our escape, and these produced a great impression on him. But I clearly saw that he did not believe in the report of Ayesha's death. He believed indeed that we thought that she was dead, but his explanation was that it had suited her to disappear for a while. Once, he said, in his father's time, she had done so for twelve years, and there was a tradition in the country that many centuries back no one had seen her for a whole generation, when she suddenly reappeared, and destroyed a woman who had assumed the position of Queen. I said nothing to this, but only shook my head sadly. Alas! I knew too well that Ayesha would appear no more, or at any rate that Billali would never see her again.

'And now,' concluded Billali, 'what wouldst thou do, my Baboon?'

'Nay,' I said, 'I know not, my father. Can we not escape from this country?'

He shook his head.

'It is very difficult. By Kôr ye cannot pass, for ye would be seen, and as soon as those fierce ones found that ye were alone, well,' and he smiled significantly, and made a movement as though he were placing a hat on his head. 'But there is a way over the cliff whereof I once spake to thee, where they drive the cattle out to pasture. Then beyond the pastures are three days' journey through the marshes, and after that I know not, but I have heard that seven days' journey from thence is a mighty river, which floweth to the black water. If ye could come thither, perchance ye might escape, but how can ye come thither?'

'Billali,' I said, 'once, thou knowest, I did save thy life. Now pay back the debt, my father, and save me mine and my friend's, the Lion's. It shall be a pleasant thing for thee to think of when thine hour comes, and something to set in the scale against the evil-doing of thy days, if perchance thou hast done any evil. Also, if thou be right, and if *She* doth but hide herself, surely when she comes again she shall reward thee.'

'My son the Baboon,' answered the old man, 'think not that I have an ungrateful heart. Well do I remember how thou didst rescue me when those dogs stood by to see me drown. Measure for measure will I give thee, and if thou canst be saved, surely I will save thee. Listen: by dawn to-morrow be prepared, for litters shall be here to bear ye away across the mountains, and through the marshes beyond. This will I do, saying that it is the word of *She* that it be done, and he who obeyeth not the word of *She* food is he for the hyænas. Then when ye have crossed the marshes, ye must strike with your own hands, so that perchance, if good fortune go with you, ye may live to come to that black water whereof ye told me. And now, see, the Lion wakes, and ye must eat the food I have made ready for you.'

Leo's condition when once he was fairly aroused proved not to be so bad as might have been expected from his appearance, and we both of us managed to eat a hearty meal, which indeed we needed sadly enough. After this we limped down to the spring and bathed, and then came back and slept again till evening, when we once more ate enough for five. Billali was away all that day, no doubt making arrangements about litters and bearers, for we were awakened in the middle of the night by the arrival of a considerable number of men in the little camp.

At dawn the old man himself appeared, and told us that he had by using *She's* dreaded name, though with some difficulty, succeeded in getting the necessary men and two guides to conduct us across the swamps, and that he urged us to start at once, at the same time announcing his intention of accompanying us so as to protect us against treachery. I was much touched by this act of kindness on the part of that wily old barbarian towards two utterly defenceless strangers. A three—or in his case, for he would have to return, six—days' journey through those deadly swamps was no light undertaking for a man of his age, but he consented to do it cheerfully in order to promote our safety. It shows that even among those dreadful Amahagger—who are certainly with their gloom and their devilish and ferocious rites by far the most terrible savages that I ever heard of—there are people with kindly hearts. Of course self-interest may have had something to do with it. He may have thought that *She* would suddenly reappear and demand an account of us at his hands, but still, allowing for all deductions, it was a great deal more than we could expect under the circumstances, and I can only say that I shall for as long as I live cherish a most affectionate remembrance of my nominal parent, old Billali.

Accordingly, after swallowing some food, we started in the litters, feeling, so far as our bodies went, wonderfully like our old selves after our long rest and sleep. I must leave the condition of our minds to the imagination.

Then came a terrible pull up the cliff. Sometimes the ascent was natural, more often it was a zig-zag roadway cut, no doubt, in the first instance by the old inhabitants of Kôr. The Amahagger say they drive their spare cattle over it once a year to pasture outside; all I know is that those cattle must be uncommonly active on their feet. Of course the litters were useless here, so we had to walk.

By midday, however, we reached the great flat top of that mighty wall of rock, and grand enough the view was from it, with the plain of Kôr, in the centre of which we could clearly make out the pillared ruins of the Temple of Truth to the one side, and the boundless and melancholy marsh on the other. This wall of rock, which had no doubt once formed the lip of the crater, was about a mile and a half thick, and still covered with clinker. Nothing grew there, and the only thing to relieve our eyes were occasional pools of rain-water (for rain had lately fallen) wherever there was a little hollow. Over the flat crest of this mighty rampart we went, and then came the descent, which, if not so difficult a matter as the getting up, was still sufficiently break-neck, and took us till sunset. That night, however, we camped in safety upon the mighty slopes that rolled away to the marsh beneath.

On the following morning, about eleven o'clock, began our dreary journey across those awful seas of swamps which I have already described.

For three whole days, through stench and mire, and the all-prevailing flavour of fever, did our bearers struggle along, till at length we came to open rolling ground quite uncultivated, and mostly treeless, but covered with game of all sorts, which lies beyond that most desolate, and without guides utterly impracticable, district. And here on the following morning we bade farewell, not without some regret, to old Billali, who stroked his white beard and solemnly blessed us.

'Farewell, my son the Baboon,' he said, 'and farewell to thee too, oh Lion. I can do no more to help you. But if ever ye come to your country, be advised, and venture no more into lands that ye know not, lest ye come back no more, but leave your white bones to mark the limit of your journeyings. Farewell once more; often shall I think of you, nor wilt thou forget me, my Baboon, for though thy face is ugly thy heart is true.' And then he turned and went, and with him went the tall and sullen-looking bearers, and that was the last that we saw of the Amahagger. We watched them winding away with the empty litters like a procession bearing dead men from a battle, till the mists from the marsh gathered round them and hid them, and then, left utterly desolate in the vast wilderness, we turned and gazed around us and at each other.

Three weeks or so before four men had entered the marshes of Kôr, and now two of us were dead, and the other two had gone through adventures and experiences so strange and terrible that death himself hath not a more fearful countenance. Three weeks—and only three weeks! Truly time should be measured by events, and not by the lapse of hours. It seemed like thirty years since we saw the last of our whale-boat.

'We must strike out for the Zambesi, Leo,' I said, 'but God knows if we shall ever get there.'

Leo nodded. He had become very silent of late, and we started with nothing but the clothes we stood in, a compass, our revolvers and express rifles, and about two hundred rounds of ammunition, and so ended the history of our visit to the ancient ruins of mighty and imperial Kôr.

As for the adventures that subsequently befell us, strange and varied as they were, I have, after deliberation, determined not to record them here. In these pages I have only tried to give a short and clear account of an occurrence which I believe to be unprecedented, and this I have done, not with a view to immediate publication, but merely to put on paper while they are yet fresh in our memories the details of our journey and its result, which will, I believe, prove interesting to the world if ever we determine to make them public. This, as at present advised, we do not intend should be done during our joint lives.

For the rest, it is of no public interest, resembling as it does the experience of more than one Central African traveller. Suffice it to say, that we did, after incredible hardships and privations, reach the Zambesi, which proved to be about a hundred and seventy miles south of where Billali left us. There we were for six months imprisoned by a savage tribe, who believed us to be supernatural beings, chiefly on account of Leo's youthful face and snow-white hair. From these people we ultimately escaped, and, crossing the Zambesi, wandered off southwards, where, when on the point of starvation, we were sufficiently fortunate to fall in with a half-caste Portuguese elephant-hunter who had followed a troop of elephants farther inland than he had ever been before. This man treated us most hospitably, and ultimately through his assistance we, after innumerable sufferings and adventures, reached Delagoa Bay, more than eighteen months from the time when we emerged from the marshes of Kôr, and the very next day managed to catch one of the steamboats that run round the Cape to England. Our journey home was a prosperous one, and we set our foot on the quay at Southampton exactly two years from the date of our departure upon our wild and seemingly ridiculous quest, and I now write these last words with Leo leaning over my shoulder in my old room in my college, the very same into which some two-and-twenty years ago my poor friend Vincey came stumbling on the memorable night of his death, bearing the iron chest with him.

And that is the end of this history so far as it concerns science and the outside world. What its end will be as regards Leo and myself is more than I can guess at. But we feel that is not reached yet. A story that began more than two thousand years ago may stretch a long way into the dim and distant future.

Is Leo really a reincarnation of the ancient Kallikrates of whom the inscription tells? Or was Ayesha deceived by some strange hereditary resemblance? The reader must form his own opinion on this as on many other matters. I have mine, which is that she made no such mistake.

Often I sit alone at night, staring with the eyes of the mind into the blackness of unborn time, and wondering in what shape and form the great drama will be finally developed, and where the scene of its next act will be laid. And when that *final* development ultimately occurs, as I have no doubt it must and will occur, in obedience to a fate that never swerves and a purpose that cannot be altered, what will be the part played therein by that beautiful Egyptian Amenartas, the Princess of the royal race of the Pharaohs, for the love of whom the Priest Kallikrates broke his vows to Isis, and, pursued by the inexorable vengeance of the outraged Goddess, fled down the coast of Libya to meet his doom at Kôr?

FINIS.

Notes

INTRODUCTION

1. Latin phrase, meaning 'a most learned man and my friend'.
2. Holly is 'Charon' to Leo's 'Apollo'. In Greek mythology, the sun-god Apollo was dazzlingly beautiful; Charon was the boatman who ferried the souls of the deceased over the River Styx to Hades, realm of the dead.
3. Gorillas had been first brought to European notice by French explorer Paul du Chaillu in the 1860s.
4. See my Introduction for information about the Zulus and Haggard's knowledge of them.
5. Haggard is alluding to *King Solomon's Mines*.
6. Scarabs were precious stones carved in the image of *scarabaeus sacer*, a type of beetle held sacred by the ancient Egyptians; the Egyptian god of the sun was Ra.
7. Latin for good faith, or in this case for the truthfulness of the manuscript.

CHAPTER I

1. The theory of evolution; Darwin's *Origin of Species* had appeared in 1859.
2. The ancient Egyptian goddess of fertility; wife of Osiris.
3. The third Pharoah of the 29th dynasty, which had originated in the ancient Egyptian city of Mendes.
4. The Greek historian, called 'the Father of History'; his account of Ancient Greece begins with its mythic origins and comes down to the Persian Wars (431–404 BC) that Holly mentions in his second footnote. In that footnote, the Lacedaemonians are the Spartans; the Helots are Greeks enslaved by the Spartans.

5. The site of a Portuguese settlement on the coast of Mozambique; later called Lourenço Marques. The modern African port is named Maputo.
6. Vincey makes several references to European history in his letter. CHARLEMAGNE, or Charles the Great, King of the Franks, became ruler of the Holy Roman Empire in 800 AD; EDWARD THE CONFESSOR was King of England from 1042–1066, when he was deposed by the invading Normans under WILLIAM THE CONQUEROR. CHARLES II was King of England from 1660–1685.
7. Part of the High Court system in England and Wales, dealing with issues of property and inheritance. Dickens satirized the slowness and redtape involved in Chancery suits in his novel, *Bleak House* (1854).
8. A college servant at Cambridge.

CHAPTER II

1. Government bonds or annuities.
2. Fairy tale about the love affair between a beautiful maiden and a highly sensitive, intelligent 'beast'. The allusion feminizes Leo while reinforcing the image of Holly as ape-like. Whether consciously on Haggard's part or not, it also lends an undertone of latent homosexuality to their relationship.
3. Leo studies law at the university, but travels to London to dine at the Inns of Court with other law students; this was a requirement for membership of the Inns of Court.

CHAPTER III

1. Jean Paul Marat was a French revolutionary who was assassinated by Charlotte Corday while he was bathing; Holly apparently owns the tea cup, made in Sèvres, France, from which Marat had been drinking at the time of his death.
2. To set off an explosion.
3. Ancient Greek writing composed of large, rounded, separate letters.
4. Black-letter Latin: Gothic script on which early 'black letter' typefaces were based.
5. A jar with two handles.
6. Scarab; *see* Introduction to the narrative n6.

7. By the time Haggard wrote *She*, most of central Africa, including the territory 'to the north of where the Zambesi falls into the sea', had been explored by Europeans. *See*, for instance, David and Charles Livingstone, *Narrative of an Expedition to the Zambezi and Its Tributaries* (1865). The famous meeting of Henry Morton Stanley and David Livingstone in 1871 took place at Lake Tanganyika, 500 miles north of the Zambezi River.
8. An Arabian or African boat with a single, triangular sail.
9. A Latin phrase, from Virgil's *Eclogues* (x:69), meaning 'love conquers all'.
10. *See* Chapter 1 n2.
11. Haggard made sure the Greek was 'very good'; he got his former headmaster, Dr Hubert Holden of Ipswich Grammar School, to write the inscription.
12. In Egyptian hieroglyphics, an oval or oblong around the name or symbol of a deity or a ruler.
13. 'This was made by Dorothy Vincey.' In other words, she supposedly wrote the Latin translation that appears on the sherd. The spelling of the words in the English couplet is meant to suggest that she did so in the 1500s.
14. Latin phrase, indicating that Lionel Vincey signed the sherd when he was 17 years old.
15. In the list of Roman names on the sherd, *Vindex* is supposedly the Latin version of 'Vincey'; *conivx* (coniux) means married to or wife of.
16. *See* Chapter 1 n6.
17. In *Days of My Life* (1:251), Haggard says that the author of the medieval Latin and 'old English' inscriptions was his 'friend Dr. [John] Raven who was a very great authority on monkish Latin and medieval English'.
18. 'This relic is a right mystical work and a marvellous, the which my ancestors of long ago did convey here with them from Armoric which is to say Britain the Less [Brittany] and a certain holy clerk was always telling my father that he should destroy the same [potsherd], affirming that it was formed and conflated by Satan himself by magic and devilish art whereby my father did take the same and broke it in two, but I, John Vincey, did save the two parts thereof and pieced them together again as you see, on this day monday next following after the feast of St. Mary the Blessed Virgin in the year of Salvation fourteen hundred and forty five.'
19. A pinnace, small boat.

20. *See* Chapter I n5.
21. The Editor's footnote explains who Grocyn was; Edmund Pratt is fictional.
22. Latin: 'they brought us to the Queen of the people who place pots upon the heads of strangers . . .'
23. Latin: 'This Greek writing was rendered into Latin by the learned Edmund Pratt, licensed in canon law, from Exeter College at Oxford and an ex-student of the most learned Grocyn, on the Ides of April in the year of the Lord 1495.' This is a translation of the same text in 'uncial Greek' that Leo's father has translated; *see* pp. 40–41.
24. An island and city off the coast of modern Tanzania; in the decades before Haggard wrote *She*, Zanzibar was the starting place for a number of the attempts by European explorers to discover the sources of the Nile in central Africa.

CHAPTER IV

1. The abolitionist movement in Britain had led to the outlawing of the slave trade in 1807 and of slavery in all British territories in 1833. But the slave trade and slavery continued in many parts of the world (the USA, for instance, until the end of the Civil War) including much of Africa. Helping to end slavery, and the slave trade, within Africa was one of the motivations frequently expressed, at least, for its exploration and imperialization by Europeans.
2. Diseases, and especially malaria, helped to keep Europeans out of central Africa and prevented major colonies of 'white settlement' from being established there. From the late 1850s, the use of quinine as a prophylactic against malaria made it somewhat safer for Europeans to travel in central Africa.
3. A rope attaching a yard-arm to a mast on the dhow.
4. Swamped; the wave has crashed over the stern or poop of the dhow.
5. Rowed a boat upon the Cam River in Cambridge.

CHAPTER V

1. 'The old geneleman' is the devil.
2. Acts 14:2.
3. A brand of canned meat.

4. An allusion to speculations about the lost tribes of Israel, who were sometimes thought to have founded lost civilizations like that at Kilwa (*see* note 5 below) or like Kôr. Holly's rather contemptuous tone expresses Haggard's anti-semitism.
5. Kilwa, on the coast of modern Tanzania, is indeed the site of the ruins of at least one 'long dead and forgotten' civilization. Modern scholars no longer think that that civilization was Persian, however. For European interpretations of these and other 'lost' civilizations – the ruins of Great Zimbabwe among them – see my introduction, pp. xxi–xxii. For more information about this favourite theme of Haggard, 'lost' cities and civilizations in Africa, *see* Basil Davidson, *The Lost Cities of Africa*. In the Editor's note, Sir John Kirk, who had helped Livingstone explore the Zambezi, was British Consul at Zanzibar for many years.

CHAPTER VI

1. Mombasa is a port city in modern Kenya; the Tana River is also in Kenya, well north of Zanzibar Island but on the 'Zanzibar coast' – that is, the east coast of central Africa. The Ozy isn't named on modern maps, but was apparently a part of the Tana delta. There is no evidence today of a canal in that location.
2. Luke 16:9.
3. The oribi is a variety of South Africa antelope.
4. Romans 16:16; 1 Peter 5:14.

CHAPTER VII

1. Later, Holly says that it is 'not Indian corn', but something like the 'Kafir corn' grown in South Africa (*see* p. 102).
2. That is, Holly wishes that Job hadn't had any 'scruples'.
3. Reddish type of cattle that Haggard was familiar with from Norfolk in England; see his *Rural England* (1902).
4. Though the farming of the Amahagger is 'primitive in the extreme', they have apparently progressed out of the 'stone age' into the 'iron age'. Whether they passed through a 'bronze age' is unclear. Nineteenth-century archaeology hierarchized both past and present social formations largely in terms of their tool-making and metal-working capacities.

Mankind in general, it was thought, developed from the pre-historic stone ages ('palaeolithic' and 'neolithic') through the barbaric 'bronze age' to a pre-civilized and civilized 'iron age'. The African builders of Great Zimbabwe and other major ruins throughout south-central Africa knew how to forge iron and other metals, including copper, gold, and silver.

CHAPTER VIII

1. Besides the biblical Job after whom he is named, Haggard's Job, in rejecting the Amahagger woman, is like Joseph, who in Genesis 39:7–12 rejects Potiphar's wife.
2. *See* Chapter VII n 1.
3. *See* Chapter III n 4; ancient Etruscan civilization pre-dated Roman civilization in Italy.
4. Types of African antelopes.
5. In *The Arabian Nights*, Prince Barmecide serves an imaginary feast to a poor man.
6. In the first, serial version of *She* in the *Graphic*, Mahomed is indeed 'hot-potted' to death. When that episode was criticized for being too gruesome, Haggard changed it so that Mahomed is inadvertently but less painfully shot by Holly.
7. Cannibalism.

CHAPTER IX

1. Though the Amahagger are 'savages' and 'cannibals', Holly assumes that the slaves of the rulers of Kôr must have been 'black' Africans. The phrase is symptomatic of Haggard's own racial assumptions.
2. A type of travelling bag named after the Prime Minister, William Ewart Gladstone.

CHAPTER X

1. See Chapter IV n 2.
2. 'Darien' is an obsolete name for Panama. Balboa is supposed to have first sighted the Pacific Ocean from a peak in Darien. In his sonnet, 'On

First Looking into Chapman's Homer', Keats mistakenly has Cortés discovering the Pacific, gazing at it from 'upon a peak in Darien'.
3. The Roman god of wine and good times.

CHAPTER XI

1. Small South African birds.
2. A type of zebra that was extinct by the early 1880s.
3. A brand of rifle.
4. Another indication that the founders of the lost civilization of Kôr cannot have been sub-Saharan Africans. *See* my Introduction on the ruins of Great Zimbabwe, pp. xxi–xxii.

CHAPTER XII

1. 'Kowtowing': bowing, kneeling, or crawling before a person of high status or power.
2. Mary Queen of Scots was imprisoned and ultimately beheaded in 1587 on the orders of Queen Elizabeth I. Haggard may be alluding to Schiller's play *Mary Stuart*.

CHAPTER XIII

1. Ayesha's account of her 'Arabian' origin includes the origin of the Arab 'race' in Yemen, south-western Arabia ('Yaman the Happy'). This account stems partly from Genesis 21:9–21. 'Ayesha' was the name of one of Mohammed's favourite wives. Both Haggard's and Ayesha's insistence on her linguistic and racial purity, in contrast to the Amahagger, 'who have debased and defiled' both the language and, apparently, 'the true Arab blood' (*see* Holly's footnote) underscore the racist elements of the novel.
2. The Achaemenian dynasty ruled Persia under Cyrus I and eventually conquered Egypt.
3. Greece gained its independence from the Ottoman Empire in 1829.
4. Holly mistakes Herod's New Testament temple for the one Ayesha refers to, built by 'the wise king', Solomon (1 Kings 6).
5. Latin, meaning they create a desert and call it peace.

6. Several Old Testament prophets predicted the coming of the Messiah and the destruction and diaspora of the Jewish people.
7. In Greek mythology, the hunter who angers the goddess Artemis when he sees her bathing; she transforms him into a stag and he is then killed by his dogs.
8. Conquering Venus; name of a statue sculpted by Antonio Canova, eighteenth-century Italian sculptor.
9. Hounds which carry out a ban or curse; in this case, Actaeon's hunting dogs.

CHAPTER XIV

1. A sorceress in Homer's *Odyssey*, book 10; she turns Odysseus' men into swine.
2. A French phrase, meaning the war or the struggle lives on; Holly means something like, 'so it goes'.

CHAPTER XV

1. Unflappably good-humoured character in Charles Dickens's novel, *Martin Chuzzlewit*.
2. Matthew 5:18.

CHAPTER XVI

1. Junis's lament for Kôr and about being 'the last man' or the sole survivor of his 'race' was a familiar sort of fantasy in the nineteenth century, from Mary Shelley's *The Last Man* (1826), in which the entire human species perishes from the plague (much as Kôr has perished from 'pestilence'), down to H. G. Wells's *The War of the Worlds* (1896), in which the 'last man' narrator also witnesses the near-extinction of humanity. The theme was important, too, to early anthropologists, humanitarians, and biologists (including Darwin), as they worried about the causes of the extinction or near-extinction of at least some if not all primitive or pre-civilized races. From the late eighteenth century forward, archaeological discoveries of numerous 'lost civilizations' like Kôr reinforced the theme and fascinated Haggard. Junis's lament also echoes the traditional *ubi sunt* ('where have they gone?') theme in literary elegies, back to the Bible and beyond (compare Revelation 18).

2. Ecclesiastes 1:9.

3. The Editor's footnote suggests that the Amahagger 'race' may have been the product of miscegenation between the white or light-skinned people of Kôr and black-skinned Africans. For Haggard, racial hybridization of any sort entailed degeneration, a falling off or decline from the 'pure' blood of the two earlier races. If so, an aspect of their degeneration is the idea that the Amahagger have lost whatever elements of civilization their Kôr ancestors may have imparted to them. Instead of progressing, they have regressed into savagery. While 'hagger' means stone in Arabic, Haggard seems also to be playing upon his own name.

CHAPTER XVII

1. A fabled dragon-like monster; its breath and glance were lethal.
2. Beautiful fabric from the Phoenician city of Tyre.
3. In Greek mythology, the goddess of love.
4. A song or poem celebrating a wedding.
5. Ayesha reels off the names of some of the many gods worshipped by Arabic peoples before the prophet Mohammed instituted the monotheistic belief in Allah, the basis of modern Islam.

CHAPTER XVIII

1. Mark 12:25.
2. That I cannot abide. In later editions, Haggard revised this odd phrasing to 'that I cannot suffer'.
3. Matthew 18:7.
4. Compare Revelation 18:2.

CHAPTER XIX

1. Infamous for his cruelty and depravity, Nero was one of several Roman emperors who persecuted the early Christians. He ruled from 54–68 AD.
2. Holly is echoing *Hamlet* V.i.197–208.

3. A South African term for a pen or corral for animals.
4. Types of African antelopes.

CHAPTER XX

1. Skirt and belt.
2. In Greek mythology, Pygmalion sculpts a statue of a beautiful maiden, Galatea, and falls in love with it; Aphrodité brings it to life for him. Venus, the Roman equivalent of Aphrodité, goddess of beauty and love, was born from the sea.

CHAPTER XXI

1. In Greek and Roman mythology, a female prophet or soothsayer.
2. Hardened into glass.

CHAPTER XXII

1. 1 Samuel 28: 7–20.
2. Watercress. Job here imagines growing it on a piece of cloth.
3. Methodist.
4. Matthew 7:9.
5. 1 Kings 12:11.
6. Queen Victoria, whose diamond jubilee in 1887 coincided with the publication of the Longmans first edition of *She*.
7. Holly here expresses Haggard's disapproval of democracy, and particularly of the expansion of the franchise to many working-class voters that had just occurred in 1884, when Parliament passed the Third Reform Bill.

CHAPTER XXIII

1. A sarcophagus is a limestone coffin or burial vault; the word derives from Greek roots meaning flesh-eating, because it was thought that limestone consumed the flesh of the dead.

2. The Suez Canal was completed in 1869; the Mont Cenis Tunnel between Italy and France was completed in 1871.
3. Constructed between 1868–1874 to protect London from flooding by the River Thames, the Embankment runs from Westminster to the City of London.
4. Ancient Egyptian ruins near Luxor on the Nile.

CHAPTER XXIV

1. As dark as Hades. 'Stygian' refers to the River Styx. *See* Introduction n2.
2. Matthew 6:34.

CHAPTER XXV

1. In ancient Egyptian mythology, Osiris, consort of Isis (whose priest Kallikrates had been), was lord of the underworld and the dead. Nephthys was Osiris's sister and Set was his twin. Hekt was a goddess associated with birth, and Sekhet was the goddess of war.
2. A goat-like antelope found in the mountains of Europe and the Caucasus.

CHAPTER XXVI

1. Peasant or farm labourer.

CHAPTER XXVII

1. In Greek mythology, the abyss below Hades into which Zeus hurled the rebellious Titans; it then became a place of punishment for wrongdoers.

[illegible]

[illegible]

[illegible]

[illegible]

[illegible]

• Competitions with prizes and

[illegible]

PENGUIN CLASSICS

www.penguinclassics.com

- *Details about every Penguin Classic*
- *Advanced information about forthcoming titles*
- *Hundreds of author biographies*
- *FREE resources including critical essays on the books and their historical background, reader's and teacher's guides.*
- *Links to other web resources for the Classics*
- *Discussion area*
- *Online review copy ordering for academics*
- *Competitions with prizes, and challenging Classics trivia quizzes*

PENGUIN CLASSICS ONLINE

READ MORE IN PENGUIN

In every corner of the world, on every subject under the sun, Penguin represents quality and variety – the very best in publishing today.

For complete information about books available from Penguin – including Puffins, Penguin Classics and Arkana – and how to order them, write to us at the appropriate address below. Please note that for copyright reasons the selection of books varies from country to country.

In the United Kingdom: Please write to *Dept. EP, Penguin Books Ltd, Bath Road, Harmondsworth, West Drayton, Middlesex UB7 ODA*

In the United States: Please write to *Consumer Sales, Penguin Putnam Inc., P.O. Box 12289 Dept. B, Newark, New Jersey 07101-5289.* VISA and MasterCard holders call 1-800-788-6262 to order Penguin titles

In Canada: Please write to *Penguin Books Canada Ltd, 10 Alcorn Avenue, Suite 300, Toronto, Ontario M4V 3B2*

In Australia: Please write to *Penguin Books Australia Ltd, P.O. Box 257, Ringwood, Victoria 3134*

In New Zealand: Please write to *Penguin Books (NZ) Ltd, Private Bag 102902, North Shore Mail Centre, Auckland 10*

In India: Please write to *Penguin Books India Pvt Ltd, 11 Community Centre, Panchsheel Park, New Delhi 110017*

In the Netherlands: Please write to *Penguin Books Netherlands bv, Postbus 3507, NL-1001 AH Amsterdam*

In Germany: Please write to *Penguin Books Deutschland GmbH, Metzlerstrasse 26, 60594 Frankfurt am Main*

In Spain: Please write to *Penguin Books S. A., Bravo Murillo 19, 1º B, 28015 Madrid*

In Italy: Please write to *Penguin Italia s.r.l., Via Benedetto Croce 2, 20094 Corsico, Milano*

In France: Please write to *Penguin France, Le Carré Wilson, 62 rue Benjamin Baillaud, 31500 Toulouse*

In Japan: Please write to *Penguin Books Japan Ltd, Kaneko Building, 2-3-25 Koraku, Bunkyo-Ku, Tokyo 112*

In South Africa: Please write to *Penguin Books South Africa (Pty) Ltd, Private Bag X14, Parkview, 2122 Johannesburg*

READ MORE IN PENGUIN

A CHOICE OF CLASSICS

Matthew Arnold	**Selected Prose**
Jane Austen	**Emma**
	Lady Susan/The Watsons/Sanditon
	Mansfield Park
	Northanger Abbey
	Persuasion
	Pride and Prejudice
	Sense and Sensibility
William Barnes	**Selected Poems**
Mary Braddon	**Lady Audley's Secret**
Anne Brontë	**Agnes Grey**
	The Tenant of Wildfell Hall
Charlotte Brontë	**Jane Eyre**
	Juvenilia: 1829–35
	The Professor
	Shirley
	Villette
Emily Brontë	**Complete Poems**
	Wuthering Heights
Samuel Butler	**Erewhon**
	The Way of All Flesh
Lord Byron	**Don Juan**
	Selected Poems
Lewis Carroll	**Alice's Adventures in Wonderland**
	The Hunting of the Snark
Thomas Carlyle	**Selected Writings**
Arthur Hugh Clough	**Selected Poems**
Wilkie Collins	**Armadale**
	The Law and the Lady
	The Moonstone
	No Name
	The Woman in White
Charles Darwin	**The Origin of Species**
	Voyage of the Beagle
Benjamin Disraeli	**Coningsby**
	Sybil

READ MORE IN PENGUIN

A CHOICE OF CLASSICS

Charles Dickens	**American Notes for General Circulation**
	Barnaby Rudge
	Bleak House
	The Christmas Books (in two volumes)
	David Copperfield
	Dombey and Son
	Great Expectations
	Hard Times
	Little Dorrit
	Martin Chuzzlewit
	The Mystery of Edwin Drood
	Nicholas Nickleby
	The Old Curiosity Shop
	Oliver Twist
	Our Mutual Friend
	The Pickwick Papers
	Pictures from Italy
	Selected Journalism 1850–1870
	Selected Short Fiction
	Sketches by Boz
	A Tale of Two Cities
George Eliot	**Adam Bede**
	Daniel Deronda
	Felix Holt
	Middlemarch
	The Mill on the Floss
	Romola
	Scenes of Clerical Life
	Silas Marner
Fanny Fern	**Ruth Hall**
Elizabeth Gaskell	**Cranford/Cousin Phillis**
	The Life of Charlotte Brontë
	Mary Barton
	North and South
	Ruth
	Sylvia's Lovers
	Wives and Daughters

READ MORE IN PENGUIN

A CHOICE OF CLASSICS

Edward Gibbon	**The Decline and Fall of the Roman Empire** (in three volumes)
	Memoirs of My Life
George Gissing	**New Grub Street**
	The Odd Women
William Godwin	**Caleb Williams**
	Concerning Political Justice
Thomas Hardy	**Desperate Remedies**
	The Distracted Preacher and Other Tales
	Far from the Madding Crowd
	Jude the Obscure
	The Hand of Ethelberta
	A Laodicean
	The Mayor of Casterbridge
	A Pair of Blue Eyes
	The Return of the Native
	Selected Poems
	Tess of the d'Urbervilles
	The Trumpet-Major
	Two on a Tower
	Under the Greenwood Tree
	The Well-Beloved
	The Woodlanders
George Lyell	**Principles of Geology**
Lord Macaulay	**The History of England**
Henry Mayhew	**London Labour and the London Poor**
George Meredith	**The Egoist**
	The Ordeal of Richard Feverel
John Stuart Mill	**The Autobiography**
	On Liberty
	Principles of Political Economy
William Morris	**News from Nowhere and Other Writings**
John Henry Newman	**Apologia Pro Vita Sua**
Margaret Oliphant	**Miss Marjoribanks**
Robert Owen	**A New View of Society and Other Writings**
Walter Pater	**Marius the Epicurean**
John Ruskin	**Unto This Last and Other Writings**

READ MORE IN PENGUIN

A CHOICE OF CLASSICS

Walter Scott	**The Antiquary**
	Heart of Mid-Lothian
	Ivanhoe
	Kenilworth
	The Tale of Old Mortality
	Rob Roy
	Waverley
Robert Louis Stevenson	**Kidnapped**
	Dr Jekyll and Mr Hyde and Other Stories
	In the South Seas
	The Master of Ballantrae
	Selected Poems
	Weir of Hermiston
William Makepeace Thackeray	**The History of Henry Esmond**
	The History of Pendennis
	The Newcomes
	Vanity Fair
Anthony Trollope	**Barchester Towers**
	Can You Forgive Her?
	Doctor Thorne
	The Eustace Diamonds
	Framley Parsonage
	He Knew He Was Right
	The Last Chronicle of Barset
	Phineas Finn
	The Prime Minister
	The Small House at Allington
	The Warden
	The Way We Live Now
Oscar Wilde	**Complete Short Fiction**
Mary Wollstonecraft	**A Vindication of the Rights of Woman**
	Mary and Maria (includes Mary Shelley's **Matilda**)
Dorothy and William Wordsworth	**Home at Grasmere**

HENRY VAUGHAN

The Border Lines Series

Series Editor: John Powell Ward

Bruce Chatwin	Nicholas Murray
The Dymock Poets	Sean Street
Edward Elgar: Sacred Music	John Allison
Eric Gill & David Jones at Capel-y-Ffin	Jonathan Miles
A.E. Housman	Keith Jebb
Francis Kilvert	David Lockwood
Wilfred Owen	Merryn Williams
Edith Pargeter: Ellis Peters	Margaret Lewis
Dennis Potter	Peter Stead
Philip Wilson Steer	Ysanne Holt
Henry Vaughan	Stevie Davies
Mary Webb	Gladys Mary Coles
Samuel Sebastian Wesley	Donald Hunt
Raymond Williams	Tony Pinkney

HENRY VAUGHAN

Stevie Davies

for Alan Rudrum
with thanks
for all you have
shown me —
Stevie Davies
23 April 95
Brecon

Border Lines Series Editor
John Powell Ward

seren

seren is the book imprint of
Poetry Wales Press Ltd
Wyndham Street, Bridgend,
Mid Glamorgan, CF31 1EF
Wales

Text © Stevie Davies, 1995
Editorial & Afterword © John Powell Ward, 1995

ACIP record for this book is available at the
British Library Cataloguing in Publication Data Office

ISBN 1-85411-142-6
1-85411-143-4 paperback

All rights reserved. No part of this publication may be reproduced, stored in a retrieval system, or transmitted at any time or by any means electronic, mechanical, photocopying, recording or otherwise, without the prior permission of the publisher

The publisher acknowledges the financial support of the Arts Council of Wales

Cover illustration: detail from *Olor Iscanus*

Printed in Palatino by WBC Book Manufacturers Ltd

Contents

7 Preface and Acknowledgements

9 Introduction: Meditation in Llansantffraed Churchyard

28 1. The Crucible of Twinship

56 2. 'Handsome Dubious Eggs Called Possibilities'

78 3. 'Putting On The New Man': William Vaughan and George Herbert

105 4. Meditation, Reading and Night-Thoughts

128 5. 'Who Taught The Spider His Mathematicks?'

152 6. Christ Coming In Triumph To Brecon

171 7. 'Such Low & Forgotten Things, As My Brother And My Selfe'

195 Conclusion: 'Into The World Of Light'

199 Bibliography

203 Index

209 Series Afterword

To Frank, my life's companion

Preface and Acknowledgements

No portrait exists of Henry Vaughan, the details of whose life are tantalisingly sparse and cryptic. He lived and wrote during one of the most turbulent epochs of history, the English Civil Wars and the Interregnum — a maelstrom which, throwing him back on his inner resources and his Welsh origins, generated the stressful beauty of his poetry. I wanted to imagine him and his twin brother, Thomas, as real and breathing persons in a landscape both geographical and historical. The vestiges of his life are just sufficient to make this possible, in a delicate skeining of certainty with intuition. Through the poetry a landscape of the mind is revealed — dappled, mountainous and riven. Through the documents that survive, inklings and intuitions of a person can be discerned — an odd-man-out, a bonded but bereft twin, a loser who turned failure into glory, most himself in silence, at night and out-of-doors in the green world. Most clearly I felt he remained in the landscape of his home in the Usk Valley, the Beacons and the Black Mountains. My book is attentive to the countryside, testing my sightings against documentary historical evidence and seeing by the light of the poetry. I have quoted whole poems wherever space permits, so that the reader can experience the full and immediate joy of the finest of Vaughan's sacred poems. I came to see my work as a journey, undertaken literally in viewing the places Vaughan inhabited, or imaginatively in that hazarding time-travel to which all biography is committed. I have built something of my own search into my account. It seemed right for Henry Vaughan, who himself scanned backwards toward long-evacuated origins for traces of an earlier self, and found — as I did — an empty nest, the echo of wings and a requiem of birdsong.

Anyone who writes about Henry Vaughan is burdened with debt to five people who have created a structure of documentation and scholarship without which we would be in no position to comprehend the poet's life. These are Louise Guiney, Gwenllian Morgan,

L.C. Martin, F.E. Hutchinson and Alan Rudrum. Louise Guiney and Gwenllian Morgan collaborated in the late nineteenth and early twentieth centuries to bring to light all extant evidence from the historical record: a labour of love which rescued Vaughan from the sediment of time which had formed above his memory. Together they restored his grave. However, they did not live to publish or arrange their material: this was handed to F.E. Hutchinson who used it as the basis for his critical biography of 1947, *Henry Vaughan: A Life and Interpretation*. Though this book is rather dull reading, it is an essential part of the salvage work which has been completed by the formidable textual and interpretative work of Alan Rudrum in his editions of *The Complete Poems* and (with Jennifer Drake-Brockman) of *The Works of Thomas Vaughan*, by Henry's alchemist twin brother, essential reading equally for its occultism and for clues to the Vaughan psychology. Henry's prose works are still only accessible in L.C. Martin's compendious Clarendon Press edition of 1914 (reprinted in 1957). The present author acknowledges her debt to the work of these five scholarly lovers of Vaughan.

I have received invaluable help in my researches from David Moore, M.A., A.M.A., Curator of Brecknock Museum. I thank Rev Dr J. Daryll Evans, Chaplain of Christ College, Brecon, for a wonderful correspondence on the churchyard yews of the area. Dr William Linnard, the Welsh forest-historian, was generous with his knowledge and helpful in applying it to the Silurist. I also thank Mrs Margaret Roderick, owner of Newton Farm, Scethrog, (probable site of Vaughan's first home), for her kind communications.

Frank Regan read Vaughan's poems alongside me and our shared thoughts constantly replenished me: I thank him for this and for endless practical help and support. I acknowledge here the caring and counsel of Barbara Everett, which have been invaluable. The strength of Ann Mackay's friendship sustained me throughout. Margaret Argyle's sensitive art gave clues to visual understanding. I thank Joy Anderson, Beth Brownhill, Daphne Cooper, Lyndall Gordon, Andrew Howdle, Bryan Loughrey, Ruth Smith, Leon Stoger, Barbara Wilson, Joyce Workman and my mother, Monica, for all the courage they have given for the road. In publishing this book, I also remember my father, Harry, in his deep love of the hills and poetry of Wales, his native country.

Stevie Davies, Roehampton Institute July 1994

Introduction: Meditation in Llansantffraed Churchyard

Henry Vaughan is buried at the eastern top of the steeply sloping churchyard of St Bride's, Llansantffraed, near Brecon, beneath a two-centuries-old yew tree. The tomb is private, sequestered and far from illustrious. The branches of the over-arching yew cast a rocking network of shadows which reinforce the perpetual obscurity of this special and cryptic man. For on the face of it he has left so little that is tangible behind him, beyond his poetry. Most of his life was spent within a mile of his tomb. The house at Newton in which he and his twin brother Thomas were born and in which he lived out the greater part of his life is now gone; so too is the cottage in Scethrog where he moved in 1689 — all save the lintel, carved with his initials, which has been brought to the tomb and placed at its foot. Even the church is not the same. In 1884 the old church with the beehive tower was replaced by a new one, the thirteenth century font and and certain monuments being retained. The great yew at the front overlooking the road is eight or nine hundred years old: Vaughan would have passed it on his way into and out of church. His tombstone is authentic, its characters recut by the loving ministrations of Louise Guiney and Gwenllian Morgan who in the late nineteenth and early twentieth centuries collaborated to retrieve all of Vaughan that had not perished.

From the poet's resting-place, one looks down over the valley of the Usk across the green plain and the river to the Brecon Beacons. Unlike the mortal fabric of a house or church, this diviner architecture takes longer to degrade or corrupt. This too is Vaughan's personal space, where, looking into the boundless light and the reach of nature into horizon beyond horizon, it is possible to feel that one shares space with his mind; that where he once was, we are now. Vaughan, the 'Swan of Usk', identified himself with the river and promised to immortalise it:

> When I am laid to *rest* hard by thy *streams,*
> And my *sun sets,* where first it *sprang* in beams,
> I'll leave behind me such a *large, kind light,*
> As shall *redeem* thee from oblivious *night* ...
> ('To the River Isca', 27-30)

But this boast was made in Vaughan's early, classicising phase, written around 1647, when Vaughan was in his mid-twenties. A Welsh Horace, he retired to his native version of the Tusculan farm, garbing his native land in an assumed Latinity. Vaughan soon learned that it did not lie with him to 'redeem' but to be redeemed; nor to confer a '*large, kind light*' upon landscape but to receive it as a gift and token of Grace. The modern eye-witness from the graveyard is aware of the same lightscape, whether veiled through films of cloud; breaking through with powerful, searching rays; troubled and turbulent; or an expanse of turquoise like his description in 'Regeneration':

> The unthrift Sun shot vital gold
> A thousand pieces,
> And heaven its azure did unfold
> Chequered with snowy fleeces...
> (41-4)

Even on dull days, he witnessed and recorded a shining. The dulness was in oneself: light lived on the thither side of our cloudy vision.

Standing in Llansantffraed, the visitor can imagine sharing Vaughan's eyebeam and hearing with his ears. Such visions and sights are confused, however, by the ruthless iconoclasm of modernity. A fast stretch of the A40 passes directly alongside and beneath the churchyard and the sporadic bellowing of traffic often drowns out the birdsong which affected him (especially in the dawn chorus) like a gospelling. The Usk, biographers used to remark, can be heard in its purling throughout the entire valley: but no longer. Traffic has drowned out this music, and the silence which must have invested the area with a quality of listening stillness is destroyed. Only in the pauses between vehicles do we receive the eloquence of brimming light and silence in which the messages of running water and birdsong can be registered in their fulness. To listen thus is also to be aware that the Vaughan who sleeps in Llansantffraed was a poet not of a pastoral but of a georgic working world. Brecon was and remains a predominantly agricultural area: a sparsely populated farming community where the land is there to be worked rather than admired. The smell of manure is in the air. Across the hedge from the poet's grave, horses whinny and dogs bark. Sheep roam and bleat in the churchyard itself, cropping the grass between the graves, and beside the poet's slab with its Latin inscription a scatter of sheep-droppings indicates the irreverence of creaturely life for human pretensions. Vaughan, with his eye for mortifying irony and his uniquely high valuation of animals, might well have appreciated that and read in it a green message from the Creator to the created.

The impression of the churchyard is vehemently lively, as if to invert the familiar Biblical paradox and insist that in the midst of death we are in life. Moles have burrowed in the neighbourhood of the poet's head, and the ground is dotted with their hillocks. Rooks caw in the trees. The grass is thick and lush, full of celandines, nettles, ivy, and weeds of great beauty. To Vaughan, all plants and trees were sacred: a fresh-air and outdoor person, he read the divine in the humblest root; as a doctor, he knew the curative efficacy of all plants and herbs, scorning none as weeds. Yet his grave has been maintained clear of the vegetation which buries the semi-legible tombs of two of Llansantffraed's later ministers, whose august raised slabs are bedded in a rich quilting of ivy, celandine, grass and nettles. For its period and area, Vaughan's is an opulent tomb, the stone being of an unusual size and thickness, approximately seven by three feet, and probably fetched from the quarry of Bwlch-yr-Arllwys in the adjoining parish of Cwmdu (*H*, p.40). As soon as we begin to read the inscription, some of his life's central paradoxes and conflicts come into play, pulling the eye in and out of focus. For it is a gentry-grave. But it is the prostration-place of a man who exclaims (in Latin) that he is the lowest of worms. The Latin identifies Vaughan as an Oxford-educated member of the social élite; the magnitude of the stone amplifies this; the coat of arms carved into the tombstone between the name and date and the pious exclamations proclaims his high breeding as a member of the Tretower Vaughan dynasty. But the coat of arms is simple and elementary, almost childish: a chevron between three boys' heads, each of whom has a snake wreathed round his neck. As a member of a high-standing family of the county, Vaughan had the right to be buried inside the church. Yet he seems to have chosen to occupy the common earth. Probably he chose his own form of words too:

HENRICUS
VAUGHAN — SILURIS
M.D. OBIIT. AP.23. ANNO
SAL.1695.AETAT. SUAE. 73

QUOD IN SEPUCHRUM
VOLUIT
SERVUS INUTILIS:
PECCATOR MAXIMUS
HIC IACEO
+
GLORIA MISERERE

The Latinised form of his name proclaims Vaughan a member of the European cultural élite. It is immediately followed by the title he had adopted as a poet: 'the Silurist'. This defines him as a provincial: a Welshman native to the south-east region of Wales in which Tacitus recorded the existence of a tribe called the Silures, stern resisters of the Roman conquest. The self-styled 'Silurist' upheld the outsiders against the insiders, the back-of-beyond against the centre, 'Taffy' against the scoffing English overlords. He turned his back upon the corrupt '*cities* of the plain' inhabited by the children of Lot ('Retirement', *[II] 15)*. But this complex Welshman can also boast of being 'M.D.': another enigma. 'My profession,' he wrote to John Aubrey in 1673, 'allso is physic, wch I have practised now for many years with good successe (I thank god!) & a repute big enough for a person of greater parts than my selfe' (*HV*, p.688). But no one has been able to discover where or when he acquired his degree. All known university records are innocent of his name. Perhaps indeed he displays what he never officially earned? Such a thought shocks the sensibilities of those who cannot imagine the Vaughan of the poetry as disreputably trading on a fabricated qualification. But an 'M.D.' is only a piece of paper: perhaps the practitioner, serving God through cure of bodies on the basis of experience and much prayer, and practising an alternative ('Hermetic') form of medicine, felt he could honourably claim a degree no academy had awarded. 'Doctor' Vaughan was a homeopath whose holistic view of health, in relation to the Creator, nature and astral influence, prefigures alternative developments in modern medicine. Standing in the churchyard at Llansantffraed and viewing the letters after his name, we are exactly placed to appreciate Vaughan's sense of the inter-relatedness of spirit and matter: the wind was the breath of God, water, plants, minerals and sunlight his cordial agencies. Vaughan's doctoring was the poet's active ministry. Nature was one great pharmacopeia, if one had only skill to read the directions the Creator had written in hieroglyphic handwriting.

If there is a consciousness of professional honour in Vaughan's 'M.D.', the coat of arms signals awareness of family nobility. Here his final testimonial records noble descent from a Vaughan lineage which traced its heritage back to Agincourt, linking the family with the powerful Herbert dynasty through the daughter of the warrior Dafydd ap Llewellen. In the fifteenth century Gwladys ap Llewellen first married Roger Vaughan of Bredwardine; then Sir William Herbert, lord of Raglan. Through labyrinths of intricate intermarriage which over centuries connected the nobility and gentry families of Wales in intricate meshes of kinship, Vaughan was related to the Earls of Pembroke, the Vaughans of Tretower and the Somersets of Raglan who were the grandest magnates in Wales. The coat of arms proclaims that the remains in this tomb are those of Someone in the world; not a nameless nobody or an anybody like the modern visitor, bred in a world of democratic assumption. We represent the 'populus' for whom, as an ardent royalist in a period of Civil War and regicide, he expressed contempt. Yet so did Milton, the republican and Vaughan's natural enemy, when he poured gall upon the degenerate people of England as 'a credulous and hapless herd, begott'n to servility' (*Eikonoklastes, CPW*, III, p.601). And here again there is a complexity in Vaughan, who wonders eloquently about the implications of the word 'descent'. If 'descent' means 'coming down' we are all so far down, viewed from the heights of Heaven, as to be indistinguishable not only from one another but from the earth which is our communal source and destination. The ascendency of the Divinity's 'close house/ Above the morning-star' ('Retirement' [I], 2-3) looks down from Baroque vistas of infinite space at God's other house where, interred in church and churchyard, '*Name*, and *honour*' are equalised in the pedigree of dust:

A faithful school where thou may'st see
In heraldry
Of stones, and speechless earth
Thy true descent
Where dead men preach, who can turn feasts, and mirth
To funerals, and *Lent*.
(38, 45-50).

Vaughan was fond of the 'Vanity' theme and liked to show his reader a death's-head; though this was seldom in the spirit of Donne's blood-curdling sermons of feasting maggots, putrefying flesh and slimy dissolutions. The spirit of Vaughan's meditations is kindly, friendly. The heraldry of 'stones, and speechless earth' fails to appal. Vaughan loved stones. He valued and respected them. In his extraordinary poem beginning 'And do they so?' he exclaims with awe spiced with a kind of child-like incredulity at the thought that mere stones are not dead matter, but, on the model of magnetic stones, living force-fields of energy which yearn back up to the Creator.

Revelation is also revaluation for the poet. All things fall into a new alignment at the recognition that nothing in the universe is dead. Such displacement is revolutionary, saturnalian. Stones become superior to man in the fidelity of their homing sympathy toward the Creator:

And do they so? have they a sense
Of ought but influence?
Can they their heads lift, and expect,
And groan too? why the elect
Can do no more: my volumes said
They were all dull, and dead,
They judged them senseless, and their state
Wholly inanimate.
Go, go; seal up thy looks,
And burn thy books.
(1-10)

Nothing in the universe of Vaughan's poetry is insentient. Spirit flows boundlessly through all creation, pouring back the Divine love to its source. For this reason, while the mortal 'descent' of man into earth is on the one hand a mortification and calamity, and the 'descent' from Adam's loins carries the corruption of sin from generation to generation, yet to acknowledge affinity with the earth is to be restored to hope. If nature is vital, to lie amongst stones is to be among friends. And the underlying 'dead men' who in 'Retirement [I]' 'preach' in a graveyard testify in their silent sermons to having fallen to a safe place and a refuge. Hence we may locate a coat of arms beyond and around the coat of arms carved on to the seven-foot slab which covers Vaughan's bones. It contradicts the carver's pattern and marks genealogy as a rooted tree made of real timber, confirming man's family link with mossed stones and mountain masses.

Stones are strewn throughout Vaughan's poetry. Far less dead than man's stone-cold heart, they lie in the streams of his verse with extraordinary solidity and weight, resisting the commonsense impulse to make light of them as objects of no account:

> So hills and valleys into singing break,
> And though poor stones have neither speech nor tongue,
> While active winds and streams both run and speak,
> Yet stones are deep in admiration.
>
> ('The Bird', 13-16)

He seems to handle them with his eyes, and must have eyed them with his hands, turning them over and taking their weight, pondering these ponderous objects in all their otherness. He overhears the intense silences they keep. In them he meditates the resistance of the objects we take for granted to our low account of creation. He compares his own variable and insubstantial heart with their downright substantiality; his insecurity with their solidity; his untruth to himself and God to their fixed fidelity. What is a stone? It is always and forever a stone: a tautology which a man (gadding, giddy, feckless and distractible) might in all conscience do well to envy. 'Deep in admiration', the stone is so immersed in the subconscious equivalent of prayer that its very being is prayer. In another poem, entitled 'The Stone', the sand, dust and 'stones/ Which some think dead' (38-9) commit espionage on human sin, and will bear witness against man on the Judgement Day. The literality with which Vaughan reads nature against Scripture is breathtaking. It is absurd. It is painfully and tenderly moving. Standing in the churchyard and pondering these things, I found that I had unconsciously snapped off the dry, skeletal head of a dead stalk of cow-parsley. Would this broken fragment have been holy in his book, I asked, in the light of the gravestone and the poetry? I was forced to confess that if I could not imagine a living blessedness in each humble dandelion or clover leaf, the yellow lichens on the wall, the fork of the yew-root and its scroll-like rust-red bark, the very sheep and their droppings — and stones — I should have failed in my attempt to share, however imperfectly and transiently, Vaughan's line of vision. It seemed a hard trust for one bred up in the post-Newtonian age of mechanistic science and modern technology, in which the vital virtue has been systematically drained from a Godforsaken nature. Modern 'Green' science perhaps comes to our rescue, the vision of the biosphere viewed less as a system in physics than as a living organism, which respires, circulates and nourishes itself through a complex network in which all the parts are meaningful. Vaughan too believed that man was the polluter of this ecological system and that, to be healthy, he must depose himself from his dominant and exploitative position.

The Vaughan interred here advertised himself as 'SERVUS INUTILIS/PECCATOR MAXIMUS', a useless servant and the chief of sinners. No doubt this craftily pious disclaimer of piety was as sincere as it was conventional, following St Paul in his claim to rank as the chief of sinners (I Timothy, 1:15). Donne made the same black boast, spectacularly, wearing his guilt like a flamboyant badge of office. Vaughan's prostration is in a lower key, tired with trying, longing to go home, resigning himself body and soul to the Creator. But as an Arminian follower of Laudian High Church Christianity, with its stress on freewill, he was little troubled by Calvinist terrors of predestination to hell-fire. God's remoteness hurt him, and poem after poem records the baffled straining of his eyes towards a light intuited as shining just over the hill, a music just out of earshot. Homesickness panics or saddens him; and a sense of perpetual exile from the arms of love. Nature at once signalled the immanence of the Divine everywhere around him, flashing its light to him in reflections of his lost parent, and intimated the absence of that parent, for that reflected light was really only a form of shadow. Its assurance of nearness also emphasised the fact of separation; a chronic spiritual eyestrain was the penalty of his obsessive attempt to see through the visible world into the invisible, closing the gap between subject and object. With extreme simplicity of diction and genuine conviction, he records the experience of lying at night waiting for Someone to come:

> So for this night I linger here,
> And full of tossings to and fro,
> Expect still when thou wilt appear
> That I may get me up, and go.
>
> I long, and groan, and grieve for thee,
> For thee my words, my tears do gush,
> *O that I were but where I see!*
> Is all the note within my bush.
>
> As birds robbed of their native wood,
> Although their diet may be fine,
> Yet neither sing, nor like their food,
> But with the thought of home do pine,
>
> So do I mourn ....
>
> ('The Pilgrimage', 9-21)

Sustained on the face of it more than adequately by the diet nature can afford, he tosses restlessly in his mortal bed, in insomniac and brittle-nerved eagerness to continue his westward journey. The text for the poem is from Hebrews (11:13): 'And they confessed that they were strangers, and pilgrims on the earth.' The Bunyanesque homeliness of his Scriptural interpretation discloses the extent of the homelessness experienced by the pilgrim lodged in a world of refugees and emigrants. '*O that I were but where I see!*' The music of 'were' and 'where' which chimes so closely that the two words might in his dialect have been pronounced almost identically, also emphasises the impotent conflict intrinsic to such an attitude of otherworldliness. The conditional form of the verb 'to be' ('were') is an index of failed aspiration; the speaker will always be confined 'here' like a bird in a cage as long as he is alive. These are his terms and conditions. The object of vision is always and only elsewhere, the 'where' that is tantalisingly beyond occupation. One can know and see it, but not 'be' there. The seer and the seen are by their very nature sundered; asunder. For Vaughan the hunger for home was at once a desire for origins and for death; but such a lively form of death as must give us pause. For the nature-image of the pining caged birds hungry for their proper food in their 'native woods' implicitly contradicts the out-of-nature movement of the poem. Our mental eye travels into the foliage of the oak and birchwoods of Vaughan's area. If Heaven is a woodland habitat for the winged soul, it must resemble a nature-beyond-nature, echoing with the fluting of Seraphim, the rustling of human trees, the divine scamper of squirrels, all under an eternal dewfall of Grace. Vaughan makes us feel that, in Emily Brontë's phrase, 'none would ask a Heaven/ More like this Earth than thine' ('Shall Earth no more inspire thee', 23-4).

Ivy nets the dark trunk of the yew in skeins of green; from the tree's base it runs out over the dappled earth around the tomb in tendrils. Daryll Evans, who kindly measured the Llansantffraed yews for this book, estimates this tree as not more than two hundred years old, planted perhaps to commemorate the poet and mark his grave (private correspondence, June 1994). As the yew, symbol of eternal life, drinks being from the burial ground, so the ivy's thirst is fed by the yew's sap, in an ecology which would not have been lost on the poet of *Silex Scintillans* who saw no gaps in God's circulating, recycling creation:

> *Plants* in the *root* with earth do most comply,
> Their *leaves* with water, and humidity,
> The *flowers* to air draw near, and subtlety,
> And *seeds* a kindred fire have with the sky ...
> ('The Tempest', 33-6)

It is a profoundly peaceful scene, though it thrives on competition and milks survival from decomposition. How far is this impression of peace an illusion? A jagged crack completely bisects the tombstone, breaking through the word VOLUIT and branching upwards through SEPULCHRUM. An attempt has been made to heal this breach with cement, but some of the filler has flaked away under the attrition of wind and rain, leaving a dark irregular trench like a deletion through the characters. The poet lived and wrote through the turbulent period of the Civil War and Commonwealth, in the throes of personal disorientation.

Tides of wind buffet the exposed ridge, and the church must have seemed in Vaughan's time a haven and refuge in more than one sense, from the rains and storms that lash the hills in winter. It was his home — the dining-room of his home — where he ate Christ Sunday by Sunday. The meal of the Eucharist is figured in his poetry as a delicious cannibalism, ingested with a literality which brings his account of the Communion close to those of Crashaw and the Catholic devotional poets. He was a blood-relative of recusants, notably the Somersets of Worcester and Raglan Castle. Though his theology was broadly High Anglican, his sensibility was a curious mingling of Reformation with Counter-Reformation. In 'Dressing', he protests against the Puritans who reduce this eating of the Saviour to the status of 'kitchen food':

> Some sit to thee, and eat
> Thy body as their common meat,
> O let me not do so!
> Poor dust should lie still low,
> Then kneel my soul, and body; Kneel, and bow;
> If *Saints*, and *Angels* fall down, much more thou.
> (37-42)

Non-conformists still sit down together to share the symbolic bread and wine, remembering in this fraternal and egalitarian breaking of bread the love-feasts of the primitive church as well as the humanity of God. Vaughan came to St Bridget's to kneel in obeisance, appalled by such beastly eating (33). His mysticism leaned to ritual and he found in his 'Son-days' 'Heaven once a week' (2), 'the combs, and hive,/ And home of rest' (19-20). His liturgical frame of mind expressed a passion for order. As a Royalist, like most of the South Wales gentry, he venerated his king as a father and the viceroy of God on earth; as a lay churchman, and brother and friend of ordained ministers, he adored God as Father-King. When we are standing at the entrance to Llansantffraed Church we are in the footsteps of the Vaughan who worshipped his King through the Book of Common Prayer prescribed by the earthly Stuart king and observed the calendar of the church year with enthusiasm. The church-year circled in accord with the seasons of nature. He can sound like a minister, parsonical, sermonical; and impersonates his beloved mentor George Herbert (a minister-poet and a cousin) like an ecclesiastical ventriloquist.

Of course the surviving church is not the one Vaughan attended to receive on his tongue the sacred meal. His church was rebuilt in 1690, and he will have attended the new church described by the Brecon antiquarian, Theophilus Jones, who took as dim a view of this rickety edifice as he did of the Silurist himself, whose poetry had sunk into obscurity in the century after his death:

> The steeple or tower or whatever it may be called, containing one bell only, has rather a grotesque appearance, and resembles a beehive, or the bottom of a pot turned upwards; the church ... has two low ailes, the wall dividing them bulges considerably: to support it some poles have been placed across, which at the same time that they are unseemly to the sight, have pushed the outward wall out of its perpendicularity, and will in process of time undoubtedly occasion its fall ...
>
> (*J*, p 432)

The monument to the man who pulled down the church and replaced it with the present one in 1884 celebrates J.P.W. Gwynne Holford of Buckland, who died in 1916. The ten-foot high sarcophagus is topped with stone scrollings and embellished with marble inscriptions and a neoclassical portrait of Buckland sporting tremendous sideburns. It is imposing; and it is meant to impose on all who pass by on the road and all who visit the church. Beyond it is the immense panorama of the wooded slopes of the Beacons, across the Usk which curves in near at this point. Holford has closed the door of Vaughan's church against us in perpetuity. And yet, if we cannot get in (because there is nothing left to get into) this in a sense parallels Vaughan's experience in the 1650's: the door of his brother's church was also shut against him. Those Sundays which were 'lamps that light/ Man through his heap of dark days' ('Son-days', 6-7) could not be spent here. Under the 'Act for better Propagation and Preaching the Gospel in Wales' of 1650, Thomas Vaughan was evicted as Rector of the church and not replaced; so were their close friends, Thomas Powell of Cantref, Thomas Lewes of Llanfigan and Matthew Herbert of Llangattock. This exodus happened throughout the area.

Ironically this eviction gave to Henry Vaughan an experience and voice that sometimes seem more Puritan than those of the Puritans. Vaughan's personal testimony to being set adrift as a solitary pilgrim in the wilderness bears uncanny comparison with Bunyan; it shares common spiritual ground with Milton and inhabits a world adjacent to that of George Fox and the Quakers, his inveterate antagonists. The Royalist and High Church poet would no doubt have winced away from the comparison; but the analogy is irresistible. For marginalisation and eventual exclusion from church-services barred Vaughan out from the sanctities of ritual, symbolism and liturgical forms. These to him were the true expression of the essence of the Reformation. Archbishop Laud had spelt this out in his defence of his policy as 'the reducing of it [the church] into order, the upholding of the external worship of God in it, and the settling of it to the rules of its first reformation' (*L & O*, p.45). But what becomes of piety when this 'external worship of God' is not available? Where then is the temple? The believer must fall back on the Holy Scriptures and his own prayerful mind. The temple for Vaughan had to be the house not built with hands, the invisible church of faith constructed in the inner space of the individual believer. This church has the advantage of being transportable and invisible; and therefore inviolable. It could not be raided by Roundhead soldiers smashing stained glass windows, organs, carved pew-ends, altar-rails snd statuary. The temple of the Holy Spirit is not embellished with any of this finery. Neither does it admit a priest. Its choir is the singing spirit; its anthems the poetry which inspire the reclusive worshipper.

Vaughan in the late 1640s and 1650s (the period of his finest poetry) is an exile in a strange land, like Bunyan's Christian fleeing the City of Destruction. Reading his poetry, it is often this sense of the aloneness and foreignness of the pilgrim that haunts and touches us. Vaughan felt himself to be an Israelite in captivity to the Egyptian tyranny: an exact mirror-reversal of the Puritan view of themselves under the Stuarts as the Children of God attempting their journey out of captivity to the powers of this world by the leading of the inner light and under direction from Providence. If some of Vaughan's meditative poetry reminds us of the Catholic Ignatian tradition of contemplation, other poems — like 'The Pilgrimage', 'Praise', 'Peace', 'Anguish' and 'The Law, and the Gospel' — have the plain-spoken spontaneity and heart-shaken emotion of Bunyan's hymns. The simple diction of the wayfarer in 'The Pilgrimage' begs comparison with *The Pilgrim's Progress*. The New Testament assurance of parts of 'The Law, and the Gospel' sounds a note very like the gathered churches on their persecuted journey to the New Jerusalem:

> But now since we to *Sion* came,
> And through thy blood thy glory see,
> With filial confidence we touch even thee;
> And where the other mount all clad in flame,
> And threatening clouds would not so much

As 'bide the touch,
We climb up this, and have too all the way
Thy hand our stay,
Nay, thou tak'st ours, and (which full comfort brings)
Thy Dove too bears us on her sacred wings.
(11-20)

For Vaughan the New Testament is a book with miraculous properties: a Hand reaches from its pages to guide the reader up the steep slopes of a landscape which seems to unscroll from Scripture like a map; finally a Dove, the Holy Spirit, flies out of the Testament and carries the pilgrims on her wings. The Reformation had taken as its source the personal reading of the vernacular Bible. Vaughan as its son did not stand empty-handed at the closed door of the church: he held the Book as a personal message in his right hand. He pondered and studied its meanings in the passionate privacy of his heart, like a letter from a far-away loved-one. His poems are often accompanied by Biblical texts; and those texts may express themselves in a vision of a landscape — Mount Horeb where God first spoke to Moses and Sinai where the Laws were given, the Mount of Olives, Mount Sion. Vaughan played these visionary mountains over the view of Pen y Bryn, Waun Rydd or Pen y Cader, and the ground of Brecknockshire acted as a mnemonic for the Holy Land. The rainbow recalled the Covenant with Noah, the Usk's reddish flood-waters the Red Sea, the Lake of Llangorse the pools of the Testaments. Looking out from Llansantffraed, we need to adjust our vision to take in this dimension of the Scriptural landscape, the Welsh hills beaconing a memorial to the 'everlasting hills' ('Man's Fall, and Recovery', 1). In a secular age, this dimension is perhaps the most difficult of all to summon: his poem 'Holy Scriptures', makes clear how essential the Bible was to Vaughan's life. It gave him birth and kept him alive by feeding him: 'Welcome, dear book, soul's joy, and food! ... life's charter' (1, 3). Its scenes imposed their might and meaning on the visual scene and at the same time took solidity from the mundane landscape.

On the slopes of the ridge running behind the church, Allt-yr-esgair, sheep are pastured, and the air is often riven with bleatings. The wool-trade was the area's major industry; and the keeping of sheep a staple of life. The inventory of Vaughan's father's Newton estate, which passed to Henry in 1658, includes '1 small flax wheele' for turning yarn into thread, as well as 'fower sheep & 1 ram & 2 lambs' (*H*, p.17). Dependence upon sheep-breeding for both food and clothing was a factor in Welsh families' ancient rural way of life which reproduces the basis of the culture and religion of the Israelites. The Bible is a pastoral work from cover to cover. Its flocks were the tribe's livelihood and wealth: sheep had to be tended, watered, mated, slaughtered, bartered, cooked, their fleeces spun and woven. Rachel was a shepherdess, David the Psalmist a shepherd, Christ the Lamb of God and the Good Shepherd whose injunction to Peter was 'Feed my sheep' (John 21:16). A minister of the church was to his parishioner as shepherd was to sheep. For the Puritans the bishops were 'bitesheep' (*Cook* in *Scott* [1811], p.226) and rapacious wolves in sheep's clothing whose vocation was the fleecing of their flocks through tithes and the corruption of their souls through the spreading of diseased doctrine. 'The hungry sheep look up, and are not fed,' wrote Milton in *Lycidas* in 1637:

> But swoln with wind, and the rank mist they draw,
> Rot inwardly, and foul contagion spread;
> Besides what the grim wolf with privy paw
> Daily devours apace, and nothing said...
> (125-9)

A decade or so later, Vaughan was lamenting in 'The British Church' the 'Slain flock, and pillaged fleeces' of the new dispensation (17). The livestock in the meadows were looted and slaughtered by billeted or invading soldiers; meanwhile the spiritual 'flock', deprived of pastors, was hacked to the bone with iron or left to starve for want of sustenance. The land in the 1640s and 1650s was red with carnage.

A convoy of four army lorries appears on the road travelling from the military base at Crickhowell towards Brecon and thunders past the gate of the church. The road here is relatively straight and traffic can pick up speed. These convoys are frequent rather than occasional sights, for the whole region is (as it has always been) heavily militarised. Roman fortresses like Y Gaer are amongst the attractions in this sight-seers' paradise; and Vaughan's very title 'the Silurist' commemorates a violent uprising. In some areas the Ministry of Defence's military ranges have turned the earth into a barren moonscape. Brecon itself is a military centre, with a regimental tradition and a military museum full of trophies from the Empire. The Cathedral celebrates on the stained glass window behind the altar scenes from the Zulu War, in which so many Africans were slaughtered. The Cathedral was once the Benedictine Brecon Priory, seized at the Dissolution of the Monasteries, and its buildings transferred to the Price family, descending to the Royalist Colonel Herbert Price in the mid-seventeenth century.

We cannot 'see' this landscape as it was in the crucial decades of Vaughan's life unless we recognise it as militarised. Although no major Civil War battles took place in Wales, apart from the battle at Montgomery Castle in 1644, the presence of soldiers and the threat of hostility marked the area. Wales, which was nearly monolithically Royalist early in the War, stood for the king for complex reasons and without signal enthusiasm, allegiance wavering as the War progressed. Royalism for the gentry-class meant order, and a hoped-for bastion against the Irish Catholic armies whose invasion was always feared. They distrusted Parliamentary rule as a threat to privilege and property; but a split within the gentry existed between 'ultra-Royalists' allied with Catholics like Vaughan's distant kinsman, the Earl of Worcester, defender of Raglan Castle, and moderates who flinched away from the taint of Catholicism. The ordinary people, often non-English-speaking, did what ordinary people do in times of strife — what their masters told them. However, the Welsh were pliable in their allegiance and the common people became harder to bully into risking their lives for a cause of dubious relevance to their own already impoverished lives. By 1645, the brutal scorched-earth policy of the Royalist Charles Gerard in South Wales, driving off cattle and burning corn, combined with exhaustion and deep popular resentment against martial law, free quarter and taxation, caused mass desertion of the Royalist cause by the civilian population. Widespread bloodshed was hence avoided. The voluntary 'peaceable Army' of Glamorganshire formed to resist the King's exactions. The Breconshire gentry were noted as being 'inclined to be neutral and to join with the stronger party' (*Gaunt* [1991], p.56), and on 23 November 1645, Parliamentary forces were welcomed into Brecon.

Henry Vaughan was a romantic ultra-Royalist who witnessed the turncoat loyalism of his countrymen with shame and scorn, viewing it as an apostasy from God's earthly representative. In 'The King Disguised', he lamented the flight from Oxford of the 'Royal Saint' (8), concealing his majesty from the besetting wolves in homespun garb of wool. And in 'To His Retired Friend, an Invitation to Brecknock', he scorns the 'foul, polluted walls / ... sacked by *Brennus*, and the savage *Gauls*' (13-14), an allusion to the expedient actions of the inhabitants in pulling down Brecon's walls in 1645, in the (successful) effort to avoid garrisoning and siege. Vaughan's attitude in the earlier poetry seems oblique, equivocating. The introductory Latin poem to *Olor Iscanus* claims that 'I took no part in this great overthrow' and 'I have never desecrated what is holy with hideous violence, neither was my mind or my hand stained' (*Ad Posteros*, 20-1; 25-6). This is ambivalent for it could either mean that he remained neutral or that he did not shed innocent (that is, Royalist) blood; or that he fought but did not kill anyone. Some poems testify to his having borne arms, like his brother, in the King's cause; and although he cannot have enlisted at the outbreak of war, being employed by Sir Marmaduke Lloyd, Chief Justice of the Brecon circuit, it is likely that he served under Colonel Price in his campaigns, his name occurring with his brother's on a list of Royalist officers drawn up after the Restoration: 'Price, Sir Herbert (company of) ... Brecon. Vaughan, Hen., L. to Capt. Barth. Price ... Brecon. Prees, Will, Lieut. to Cap. Tho. Vaughan' (*H*, p.65). Price served at Hereford and Chester. However, after the first Civil War, Vaughan was certainly at home, dating the dedication to *Olor Iscanus* from Newton on 17 December 1647.

Henry Vaughan was at this point in his mid-twenties. He was a relative nobody; his cause a failure. A writer of mediocre and dully derivative verse, who had fraternised in the circles of the minor Cavalier literati in London but made no name for himself, he had no degree, no obvious calling, a feckless and litigious father and (by the standards of his class) a meagre patrimony to which to look forward. With the death of his younger brother William in 1648, Vaughan's spirit seems to have sunk into entire desolation. It was at this point that the poetry of George Herbert came to him like manna in the desert, a personal voice and vocation which took over his entire personality. I will speak more fully of this 'conversion experience' later; here is it enough to mention it as a turning-point into that brief blossoming-season which, in the two volumes of *Silex Scintillans* (1650 and 1655), distilled a condition of the mind which was able to translate the experience of defeat, bereavement and dereliction into a language for eternity. Kermode thought this change was not to do primarily with religious but with literary epiphany. 'Something happened, something to do with poetry, and not with prayer; a trumpet sounded and the bones lived' (*Kermode* [1950], p.225). But poetry and prayer were one: the resurrection was Vaughan's song in the 1640's and 1650's. And as it had been born of paradox, it died in paradox.

For Vaughan's music could not survive the experience of the Restoration. He lived to see the military dictatorship swept away, which had invested the hills with menace and filled the road from Abergavenny to Brecon with enemy troopers. King Charles II landed at Dover, whose sands were black with throngs of revellers, and people all along the route to London climbed trees and hung from windows to welcome their Moses, led 'through a *rough Red sea*' to the Promised Land, 'Banish'd David', as the Royalist poets Cowley and Dryden chorused ('Ode Upon His Majesties Restoration and Return', st.8; 'Astraea Redux', 79, 276). The church was re-established and Vaughan's friends vindicated. The ousted Thomas Powell was reinstated at Cantref, awarded the degree of Doctor of Divinity at Oxford and appointed canon of St David's, although he died at the end of 1660. Thomas Lewes was presented to his former rectory of Llanfigan, just over the Usk from Llansantffraed, where Powell's son Hugh became rector in 1668. The old order had been reasserted; but Vaughan's period of poetic ministry was over. He lived for a further thirty-five years after the Restoration, dying in 1695 at the age of about seventy-four. But the stream had all but dried. It is curious to think of John Milton in the 1660's, blind, ostracised, ageing, *persona non grata* in his own country, composing *Paradise Lost* in exile:

> More safe I sing with mortal voice, unchanged
> To hoarse or mute, though fallen on evil days,
> On evil days though fallen, and evil tongues;
> In darkness, and with dangers compassed round,
> And solitude; yet not alone, while thou
> Visit'st my slumbers nightly, or when morn
> Purples the east ....
>
> (VII. 24-30)

Milton's 'evil days' were Vaughan's days of jubilation. The 'evil tongues' which intensified Milton's estrangement in the chamber of his darkness were those of Vaughan's victorious allies. Yet to Milton were vouchsafed the visits of the sacred Muse which illumined the core of his darkness with inner light: 'So much the rather thou celestial Light/ Shine inward' (III. 51-2). The Angels hymn a God 'Dark with excessive bright' (380). Vaughan too had known the solace of mantling himself in inner quiet while the world rang with tumult; he too had apprehended a brilliance in the dark Creator: 'There is in God (some say)/ A deep, but dazzling darkness' ('The Night', 49-50). He had been open in that night to 'His still, soft call/ His knocking time' (34-5) and had shared in the two-way communion between earth and Heaven ('Ascension-Day'). *Silex Scintillans* was Vaughan's *Paradise Lost*.

Some time after 1655, the vein of poetry shrivelled. The Sacred Muse failed in her offices. *Thalia Rediviva,* published in 1678, consists of poems mostly written before the Restoration, many even before 1650. He abandoned authorship for medicine; and his long life petered out in waves of family acrimony. Hutchinson suggests that the poor reception of Vaughan's poetry discouraged him (*H*, p.212) and that he was too busy ministering to the sick to write further poetry. But such deep inwardness as these religious poems maintain seems neither to crave nor to depend upon applause. Allowing for the conscious and sophisticated art which shaped the poems, there is a spontaneous quality which implies a need to write. One cannot know. Perhaps a mere seven years can condense a whole seventy-years' testament; and deliver a soul as completely as it can be born into the light of day.

One:
The Crucible of Twinship

Polixenes: We were as twinn'd lambs that did frisk i' th' sun,
And bleat the one at th'other: what we chang'd
Was innocence for innocence; we knew not
The doctrine of ill-doing, nor dream'd
That any did. Had we pursu'd that life,
And our weak spirits ne'er been higher rear'd
With stronger blood, we should have answer'd heaven
Boldly 'not guilty', the imposition clear'd
Hereditary ours.
Hermione: By this we gather
You have tripp'd since.
(*The Winter's Tale*, I. ii. 67-76)

The pilgrim to the sites of Henry Vaughan's life must back-track along paths that lead to houses which no longer exist or to houses with which he was connected but laterally, not centrally. We move back into history along cooled trails that seem to get colder the nearer we approach to an abdicated source. History assures us 'Vaughan was here' but adds 'Nothing here remembers him'; and our search leads to tokens of absence rather than signs of presence. This mode of backward-looking pilgrimage, balked of tangible discovery, is appropriate to the nature of Vaughan's own quest and the experience of his poetry. He is essentially backward-looking, recidivist, running against Time in the attempt to recapitulate what the individual, society and mankind have lost. Nostalgia is the compulsive force which drives his poems; it is the strongest passion he knows, and the source of his most moving effects. He homes to origins. But origins elude him. His homing instinct therefore has nowhere to go; he is the poet of the dispossessed, whose birthright was loss of inheritance. This is true in the literal as well as the figurative sense. For, although as the firstborn son of Thomas Vaughan, he was his father's heir, that father was a second son who failed to inherit the ancient house of the dynasty. It is important to register, when we visit Vaughan's father's childhood home at Tretower Court, that this imposing mansion was the home Henry Vaughan *did not* inherit. He missed it through a quirk of genealogy whereby what his father was born to think of as his home could not descend to him except through the death of his elder brother.

The house stands several miles south-east of Llansantffraed, on the foothills of Pen Cerrig-calch and near the Rhiangoll River, tributary to the Usk. The court's vast rooms are intensely cold. They remind us of the barbarous conditions which even great and wealthy families of mediaeval and Tudor times had to endure. Immense fires must have roared in the grates of these rooms, with their sombre magnificence and feet-thick walls. The ruthless and powerful Roger Vaughan began the major reconstruction of the Court in around 1450. Built around a central quadrangle, its north range belongs to the fourteenth century, the west range to the fifteenth and the gate-house and wall-walks to the later fifteenth. Diamond lead-paned windows filter in a little light to spaces which for the modern visitor are all the more arresting for their shocking emptiness. There is scarcely a stick of furniture in the building, and in places the inner walls have been exposed to their bare fabric, woven branches and cement: what remains to be viewed by us is pure structure, nude of embellishment. The childhood of Henry Vaughan's father — any childhood — is impossible to reinstate imaginatively in this fortress-like interior, which must once have teemed with retinues of servants. Love must have been made here; babies born; business done; great guests received, but the imagination falters in the high spaces of such a vault. Outside, a trellised mediaeval herb garden has been planted, and a stone fountain dribbles weakly. Here there is human scale; the air carries a tang of herbs. Lush pasturage runs to the foot of deciduous and coniferous woodlands and the spectacular shoulders of the Black Mountains. Everything is watery, a deliquescence in which small streams whose banks are netted with tree-roots descend to the Rhiangoll which in its turn flows into the Usk. Once out in the open air, however, one's gaze is riveted by the remains of the thirteenth century round tower and keep. Thrusting up into the air and perforated with those cyclops eyeholes through which bowmen shot, this defensive stronghold dates from the Norman conquerors of Wales. In these large horizons the tower has a curious double aspect: at once tumescent and defiant, it makes an aggressive assertion which, at close quarters, it seems impotent to confirm. The warriors within that cramped cylinder must have resembled a huddle of soft flesh in a big stone pot.

This estate, with its roots in centuries of militarism and accumulated wealth, is the inheritance that escaped Henry Vaughan. Thomas Vaughan's elder brother, Charles, who died in 1636, bequeathed Tretower to his grandson, Edward. Presumably Henry must have visited the Court in his uncle's and nephew's time, so he knew what he had lost. But the estate for all its baronial-seeming magnificence was encumbered by debt. Charles Vaughan is recorded as being in 1626 a debtor. Money-troubles and wranglings over property run through the Vaughan family, ending in the elderly poet's own legal battles with a son and daughter of his first marriage. Inheritance is the grand theme in such disputes. Property of course travelled primarily down the male line according to the laws of patriarchy and primogeniture. Hence the bond between father and son as the basis of the social order also begot division between brother and brother, whether in the form of feud or in the holding of longterm silent grudges. From Tretower Court to Thomas Vaughan's house at Newton was a step down from the nearly noble to the frankly gentlemanly. In 1611 Thomas Vaughan had married Denise, the sole heir of David Morgan of Llansantffraed, inheritor of an estate of roughly 35 acres, including woodland, meadow and pasture. For years, Thomas and his wife were suing for her property rights; and even at the end of their struggle had only sufficient land and money to cover the needs of their family (although needs must be measured by expectations). Although he was at various times Justice of the Peace, contributor to the local 'trained bands' (equivalent to civil defence forces) and under-sheriff, Thomas Vaughan seems to have been a man of little substance — possibly in more than one sense of the word. He was later forced to part with land in order to service debts. In 1649 he was charged with abuse of charitable funds. John Aubrey did not trust his cousin an inch: he considered him 'a coxcombe and no honester then he should be — he cosened me of 50s. once' (*A*, p.303).

Not a stone remains in its original place of the house at Newton in which Henry Vaughan was born and grew up; to which he returned from Oxford and London to watch his younger brother die, to write *Olor Iscanus* and *Silex Scintillans*, to inherit in 1658, and to occupy until the rancorous disputes between himself and his son Thomas led him to abandon it in 1689, when he was in his late sixties. Its present owner, Margaret Roderick, notes the conspicuously large and ancient timbers in some of the rooms of the present Newton Farm, which may have been adopted from Vaughan's house (private correspondence, June 1994). The farm is situated between Scethrog and Llansantffraed, on a gently inclining plane under the wooded hillside of Allt-yr-esgair. From that spot, the view is not precisely one of grandeur, but over the Usk plain, of bosomy rising ground, patchworked with fields many shades of green, sparsely populated and with a rhythm of dense timbering; the ancient custom of strengthening the hedges by plaiting dead branches into them forming impenetrable wind-breaks and sheep-barriers. Moody alternations of light and shadow chase over the Beacons, turning the tender green of Talybont Forest to the sombrest black, and back again. The chiaroscuro play of light and shadow of which Henry Vaughan was conscious within himself was imaged in the volatile lights and shades of the landscapes. He lamented the rootlessness of mankind ('Man', 16), and saw himself as an aberration lurching from pathological shadow to nervous light: 'What though some clouds defiance bid/ Thy Sun must shine in every part' ('Begging [II]', 15-16). Perhaps because of his volatile insecurity, the poet was a home-bird, settling close to source, without apparent wanderlust. The need for bearings was paramount, and bearings were provided by the house and countryside at Newton.

Some ghostly picture of that house can be built up from the inventory made at his father's death, when Henry Vaughan was thirty-seven. On the ground-floor, the house centred on a carpeted and wainscotted hall, with benches, table and chairs, panelled with (probably) oak, a timber in which the area is rich. This would have been the family's main living room. The three other rooms comprised a large kitchen and a buttery, and also a room designated a 'study' and containing '1 little bed'. This would surely have been Henry Vaughan's room, and would be distinguished by the valuers as a 'study' rather than a withdrawing room because it was full of books and papers. Upstairs were four rooms including a 'little chamber' over the porch: this implies a large porch, so that the house may have had a facade more impressive than the interior. There was a 'great chamber' over the kitchen and two further rooms, together with a garret. The furniture and effects were far from sumptuous, including a standing bed and two feather beds, coffer, 'nine pewter dishes of all sorts ... 7 pewter spoons ... 3 pewter flagons', basic kitchen ware (some derided as 'old'), and churning tub, bill-hooks, wood-knife, milking-pails. The valuers rate the whole property as worth 'Five Pounds of current English money' (*H*, pp.16-17). The poet's inheritance then was neither extensive nor particularly commodious. It belonged to a member of that class so numerous in Wales, a gentry which had never risen far above subsistence, or, conversely, had frayed and unravelled from more finespun origins. Compared with the dynastic house at Tretower, the house was not much more than a working farmstead, and generally shabby and out-at-elbow. The Vaughans did not drink out of silver but from common pewter. All his life Vaughan thought of austerity as sacred, proud of the homespun 'coarse fleece/ I shelter in' ('Content', 2-3), disdaining show and conspicuous consumption. His countryman's garments were always referred back to the Giver and the giver: the God who clothes the bird to withstand nights of storm ('The Bird') is also manifested in the sheep that parts with its fleece to clothe its fellow-creatures. This sense of debt to the creatures which, nominally inferior on the chain of creation, at once outshine and serve him must have come from his outdoor life as a child in the country.

Throughout his writing life, childhood was vital to him. The vitalistic universe of his adult thought witnesses to his retention of delighted childhood impulses and intuitions: stones that commune with stars, green that vibrates in leaves, the golden eye of the cock that raises the sun, the conversational murmur of waters, all recall the magical perceptions of childhood. Thomas's 'magic' art of Hermetism recapitulates the childhood fantasy of omnipotence. Alchemical apparatus was an extension of the serious play of youth. Henry's life from his earliest beginnings — from nine months before his birth — was binary and double. He wrote to Aubrey, 'My brother and I were borne att Newton in the parish of St Brigets in the yeare 1621' (Letter of 1673, *HV*, p.687). Aubrey began his entry in *Brief Lives*, 'There were two Vaughans (Twinnes) both very ingeniose, and writers' (*A*, p.303). Henry's psyche was forged in the crucible of twinship. This fact is at the centre of my reading of Vaughan's life and work: it suggests why identity was experienced as such a problem in later life and why childhood appeared in retrospect so idyllic. He seems eternally looking for himself. Some part of himself had gone missing and he tracked it across-country, back through time to infancy. That phase of 'my first, happy age' was also a landscape:

Fair, shining *mountains* of my pilgrimage,
  And flowery *vales*, whose flowers were stars:
The *days* and *nights* of my first, happy age;
  An age without distaste and wars;
When I by thoughts ascend your *sunny heads*,
  And mind those sacred, *midnight* lights:
By which I walked, when curtained rooms and beds
  Confined, or sealed up others' sights:
    O then how bright
    And quick a light
  Doth brush my heart and scatter night;
    Chasing that shade
    Which my sins made,
  While I so *spring*, as if I could not *fade*!
('Looking Back', 1-14)

Henry speaks of himself in the first person singular; but his origins were in the first person plural. The home-world of the Beacons, the Usk and the Black Mountains had been shared in common with his other self, Thomas. Rudrum explains Henry's idealisation of childhood by claiming that 'Psychologists tell us' (he does not specify which) that such idealisation is generally caused by actual childhoods 'filled with pain and loss, the memory of which has been suppressed' (*Rudrum* [1981], pp.91-2). This seems to me the antithesis of the truth. In ignoring the pathology of twin-psychology, it is an inference based on norms which do not hold for twin-pairings. I hypothesise that Henry's childhood was, as he maintains, relaxedly happy, with a more than normal measure of that sense of wholeness and intimate communion for which the poems of his mature life yearn. Development undid him. The growth of consciousness involved a forfeit of wholeness.

Henry's longing for a return to the 'oceanic' feeling generally associated with assimilation to the mother may have extended to the early years of mirroring by his brother. Identical twinship can delay full individuation, creating a merciful space of easy play and mutual identification: a seedbed for nostalgia. If Henry Vaughan was later visited by intimations of pre-existence and of a ghostly 'Presence', this took the form of a Platonistic Christianity but possessed a literal quality: he had shared space in his mother's body with a companion conception, inseparably linked before birth expelled them, to nurse presumably at the same breasts and share a common childhood. Adult life severed the pair and made Thomas, for long spaces, invisible to Henry. Such early closeness can also involve desperate covert hostility, the need to sheer away from the constraint of the twin-knot. I think this rather shows in Thomas than in Henry, who in later life recalled the bonding rather than the bondage of a childhood which was imagined as an Edenic estate of now forfeit blessedness: 'my Angel-infancy' ('The Retreat', 2). These two angels, then, came into the world together. Thomas Powell, the vicar of Cantref and Henry's closest friend, who ought to have known, said the twins were identical. He phrased his dedicatory poem to *Olor Iscanus*, 'Upon the Most Ingenious Pair of Twins, Eugenius Philalethes, and the Author of these Poems', ('Eugenius Philalethes' being Thomas' *nom de plume*) in these terms:

> What *Planet* ruled your *birth*? what *witty star?*
> That you so like in *souls* as *bodies* are!
> So like in *both*, that you seem *born* to free
> The *starry art* from *vulgar* calumny.
> My *doubts* are solved, from hence my *faith* begins,
> Not only your *faces*, but your *wits* are *twins*.
> When this bright *Gemini* shall from earth ascend,
> They will *new light* to dull-eyed mankind lend,
> Teach the *star-gazers*, and delight their *eyes*,
> Being fixed a *constellation* in the skies.
> (1-10)

Powell's geministical effusion is the only piece of direct evidence we possess as to whether the twins looked alike. Twins were a test-case in Renaissance astrology just as much as in modern psychology (*Shumaker* [1972], pp.39-40). Although Powell's poem is only a squib, performing the seventeenth century equivalent of sales-hype to the book, it seems conclusive. Stellifying the astral miracle of the twins in the cosmos of fame (character was supposed to be generated by celestial influences at the moment of birth), he celebrates them as identical in mind as in body. Had the twins not strikingly resembled one another — for instance, had Henry been dark and Thomas fair — such an assertion would have left the author open to ridicule. I shall treat Henry and Thomas as if they were identical twins, but without making any statement which could not hold for a close fraternal pair. Powell's poem cannot be taken as definitive proof of the Vaughan twins' genetic identity, since contemporaries did not possess the science to make the distinction between monozygotic and dizygotic twins and tended to assume that twins must necessarily be identical; and of course it would be more poetic to fancy that they were. But Powell's poem demonstrates that the two were alike to a conspicuous degree; and what we know about their characters and careers bears out his perception of them as identicals. Identical twins, representing the division of a single fertilised ovum, are genetic replications of one another in every detail, and always of the same sex. Differences (height, weight, character) only emerge as responses to environment or conditioning, whereas fraternal twins are only as alike as any other siblings. Because they are born and brought up simultaneously, fraternal twins may closely resemble one another in habits and behaviour, miming some of the behaviour of identicals (private codes and languages, collusive solidarity). The twin knows little of the aloneness of the singleton; the halving of parental attention tends to be compensated by sibling-closeness. In identicals, doubleness of aspect is often accompanied by a wordless mutual understanding which can seem telepathic to outsiders. They tend to follow parallel paths in life (see *Abeleen* [1974]).

Many of these expectations were fulfilled in the Vaughan twins. Their individual and joint interest in the secret and arcane is fundamental to their work. Their temperaments reflect one another, with significant differences. Each was manifestly insecure and volatile, prodigiously intelligent, complex, eccentric, quick to anger, impetuous and ardent. Thomas expresses his insecurity by belligerence: sure that everybody takes him for a madman, he throws the reader a wild left-hook in advance of prophesied criticism. He is profoundly and demonstratively emotional. Henry is more inward, complex and riven, liable to outbursts of unmediated emotion, self-scrutinising, more respectable in demeanour, with a desire to be seen to be pious which his brother lacks. His cousin, John Aubrey, said in an irritated moment that Henry was 'ingeniose but prowd and humorous' (*A*, p.303): that is, intelligent but arrogant and moody. This moody arrogance is rarely manifest in the published work but his poetry acknowledges 'storm' as part of his temperament ('The Mutiny', 6-10, 'Misery', 83). In 'The Storm', he confesses a tempestuous inner world:

> boiling streams that rave
> With the same curling force, and hiss,
> As doth the mountained wave.
> (6–8)

The tendency appeared in later life in the vitriolic row with his daughter. Vaughan is also tender and reclusive, inclined to solitude and unsociability. Thomas set off for the world; Henry made for home. I think of Thomas as the centrifugal twin; Henry the centripetal twin. The one flies out; the other turns in. They have always been read together, Thomas's copious Hermetic treatises being used as a gloss on the occult ideas and terminology of Henry's poetry. However, though twins are always thought of as coming into the world together, this is not in practice possible. They arrive separately, one after the other, competitors for available space and sustenance. In the case of Henry and Thomas, they came out into different worlds. Having beaten Thomas in the race for precedence, Henry emerged as the elder brother in a system which rewarded elder brothers with the rewards of primogeniture. When Thomas appeared, minutes, hours or a day later, he found himself in the world of younger brothers, condemned to find their own way in the world.

It was unusual in those days of high infant mortality for both twins to survive, so they must have seemed to the neighbourhood, and hence to themselves, as something of a prodigy. Their sense of specialness is discernible throughout their lifetimes, though an unstable sense of identity troubled each in a different way. The bond which secured them in a private world of shared and secret understandings included rivalry as well as complicity, and a drama of envy and self-assertion on Thomas' part and dependence on Henry's seems to have been played out in their development. The problem of constructing a separate self would exercise Henry in the 1640s and '50s against the background of national history in which identity had come into doubt for all members of his class and political affiliation. Thomas was to get away and stay away from Henry. After 1642, they were seldom together, Henry living at home and Thomas at Oxford, then London, dying near Oxford in 1666. But in infancy, their fraternal link would have been paramount, and I think of them as enjoying a buoyant and outdoor childhood together. I imagine they would both have been vocal children, and to judge from the rampant garrulity of his prose-works Thomas must have been the noisiest child known in the Beacons. Wildly effervescing or spoiling for a fight, he shouts (with his hand costively shielding his notebook so that no one can see) that he has found a secret, the best secret in the world. For 'can it bee expected then, that I should prostitute this *Mysterie* to all hands whatsoever, that I should *proclame* it, and *crie* it, as they cry *Oysters*? ... I have been instructed in all the *Secret Circumstances* thereof, which few upon Earth understand'. Thus in *Magia Adamica* Thomas was simultaneously to hug and brag the alchemical Truths which he had received from a sequence of select persons including Adam and Noah (*TV*, p.216). I know what I know, he announces — and you don't. In *The Man-Mouse*, his confutation of Henry More the Cambridge Platonist, he hammers his opponent with puerile abuse as 'a scurvie, slabbie, snotty-snowted thing' (*TW*, p.237). Granted that polemic tended to be carried on in gutter terms during this period, there is something in Thomas so flagrantly naive that it bears eloquent witness to its infantile origins; and he let fly with a wildness that suggests the belligerent agitation of the vulnerable. Emotion, always close to the surface however abstruse the subject, could break out endearingly into song; digression never came amiss; his marvellous earnestness was innocent of humour and left him ever-open to ridicule — which he hated. Everywhere in Thomas Vaughan, we see vestiges of the child he must have been.

Thomas stated that '*English* is a *Language* the *Author* was *not born to*' (*Anthroposophia Theomagica, TV*, p.94). Elsewhere, Henry implies that English was the language of his infancy ('To my Learned Friend, Mr. T. Powell', 1-2). In fact they were almost certainly brought up bilingual, in a Welsh-speaking area where, though English was the master-language, Welsh was still the mother-tongue. Possibly their father (product of the Tretower dynasty) spoke English, and their mother Welsh. This duality complicated and enriched Henry's linguistic inheritance. Hearing the double music of twin tongues around him from cradle days, his mind would have been formed by both languages, relating by alternation, conflict and mingling. When he came to write English sacred poetry, the rhythms, intricate sound-patterns and diction of Welsh language and literature informed it.

The inspirational quality of his poetic voice may have owed something to the Bardic *hwyl* of the Welsh poets, whose work was still passed down from generation to generation on the mountains in a living oral tradition. In a late letter to Aubrey, discussing the 'Awen' or poetic fury of the Welsh poets, he says he has spoken to practising Welsh poets, and:

> as many of them as I have conversed with are (as I may say) gifted or inspired with it. I was told by a very sober & knowing person (now dead) that in his time, there was a young lad father & motherless, & soe very poor that he was forced to beg; but att last was taken up by a rich man, that kept a great stock of sheep upon the mountains not far from the place where I now dwell. who cloathed him & sent him into the mountains to keep his sheep. There in Summer time following the sheep & looking to their lambs, he fell into a deep sleep; In wch he dreamt, that he saw a beautifull young man with a garland of green leafs upon his head, & an hawk upon his fist: with a quiver full of Arrows att his back, coming towards him (whistling several measures or tunes all the way) and att last lett the hawk fly att him, wch (he dreamt) gott into his mouth & inward parts, & suddenly awaked in a great fear & consternation: butt possessed with such a vein, or gift of poetrie, that he left the sheep & went about the Countrey, making songs upon all occasions, and came to be the most famous Bard in all the Countrey in his time.
>
> (*HV*, Letter of 1694, p.696)

This passage transmits a great deal of information about the area in which the Vaughan twins grew up. It is concerned with the perceived link between nature, magic and poetry, the leaf-garlanded young man being a descendant of the 'green man' of ancient fertility myth. His hawk's attack on the dreamer's mouth effects a rape-like penetration whose violence expresses the uncanny generation of 'inspired' poetry in the subconscious mind, whilst reinforcing the ancient link between dream-vision and poetry. The narrative issues from a culture in which poets are highly prized, in a green world saturated in myth. Vaughan attests to the story's veracity by authenticating his source as 'a very sober & knowing person' and grounds it in local reality by saying that the young man kept sheep 'not far from the place where I now dwell' (the Scethrog cottage). An element of folk-tale transcendence is felt in the motif of the orphan-made-good, in his double leap from beggar to shepherd to poet. Aubrey as an antiquarian was interested in the story, which he conflated in the margin of the letter with a parallel tale of a dreamer whose mouth and entrails were invaded by a crow 'whereby he had the gift of Prophesie' (quoted *HV*, p.764n). The story belongs to that wealth of Welsh myth, history, prophecy and poetry which was the local inheritance of Henry and Thomas Vaughan: magical stories of Merlin (whose prophecies gained new currency in England in the Interregnum period [*KT*, pp.374-432]) which seem to have formed part of their education when they were sent as pupils to Matthew Herbert at the age of about eleven. Henry allegorised Herbert as Amphion in 'Daphnis: An Elegiac Eclogue', a pastoral elegy for Thomas:

> Here, when the careless world did sleep, have I
> In dark records and numbers nobly high
> The visions of our black, but brightest bard
> From old *Amphion*'s mouth full often heard;
> With all those plagues poor shepherds since have known,
> And riddles more, which future times must own.
> (59-64)

'Our' means 'Welsh'. The black bard is Merlin, a composite figure to whom were assigned both the nationalist predictions of the bard Myrddin and the prophecies included by Geoffrey of Monmouth in his *History of the Kings of Britain* ('Merlin Ambrosius'). Evidently Herbert had specialised not only in reciting the obscure and secret ('dark') stories, visionary poems and riddles attributed to the Bard but in interpreting them historically. The twins were made aware of their specialness as part of a colonised subculture, with its own myths and magic; a nationalism which would stand in creative conflict with their bid to join the English intellectual élite. Vaughan identified with his native land as 'The Silurist', '*Olor Iscanus*', but he would clothe his Welshness with cosmopolitan Latin for the consumption of the English. For Thomas, the magical and occult Welsh heritage must have been germane to his unfolding obsession with secret knowledge. Their cultural background made it natural for the twins to see their mother-world as a place of wonders and magical affinities and encouraged them to divine the hidden secrets and hieroglyphs of the Book of Nature. It was a world which reverberated with symbol. Vaughan's poetry was to evolve a language to record the failures of that quest for secret knowledge. Thomas pressed on, ever-hopeful. Henry looked back with rue to the lost magical world of childhood.

The Vaughan twins' background was devoutly Christian and Anglican, and like many contemporaries they learned to read by spelling out the simpler passages of the Bible. The nature-magic of the area however would have given an added dimension which opened their minds in later life to Christian Hermetism and the alchemical art which offered the heady promise of a solution to the enigma of the world by a combination of extraordinary spirituality and 'scientific' grasp of the laws of nature. In *Euphrates* (1655) Thomas made it clear that it was in childhood that his intellectual curiosity was first kindled, not by books or teachers but by his response to the natural world around his home. Talking of the interaction of fire and water, he digressed:

> This *Speculation* (I know not how) surpris'd my first youth, long before I saw the University, and certainly *Nature*, whose pupill I was, had even then awaken'd many *Notions* in me, which I met with afterwards, in the *Platonick Philosophie*. I will not forbear to write, how I had then fansied a certain practice on water, out of which, even in those childish dayes, I expected wonders .... This *Consideration* of my self, when I was a Child, hath made me since examine Children, namely, what thoughts they had of these *Elements*, we see about us, and I found thus much by them, that *Nature* in her simplicity, is much more wise, than some men are with their acquired parts, and *Sophistrie* .... A Child I suppose, *in puris Naturalibus*, Before education alters, and ferments him, is a Subject hath not been much consider'd, for men respect him not, till he is companie for them, and then indeed they spoile him.
>
> (*TV*, p.521)

The child is a born experimentalist, with nature as his laboratory. Vaughan says he has interrogated both '*Children* and *Fools* too': for fools, read adults. He has concluded that the 'naturall disposition of Children, before it is *Corrupted* with *Customes* and *Manners*' is the source of human wisdom. This attitude to childhood, shared in common with Henry Vaughan, is a development of Neo-Platonism, with its theory of cognition as recognition, bringing from the pre-birth transcendent world vestiges of immortal knowledge. Insight and intuition precede knowledge: the Thomas-child learns from nature, that is, the light of nature within himself in response to the natural world outside. He denounces indoctrination as 'fermentation', an irreversible process. Vaughan must be referring to children under the age of ten, if not younger. He prefigures Wordsworth in valuing the innocent knowledge of children, their ability to ask fresh questions, free of the tyranny of consensus. His argument is autobiographical, from the storehouse of his own memory of being a boy in Newton, dreaming up for himself original experiments with fire and water. If we find Thomas all his life childlike in his eager responses, that quality is one he would have cherished and not despised. His childhood was the time when he was most himself. Both Thomas and Henry took literally the Gospel attitude to children: 'Suffer the little children to come unto me ...', 'Verily I say unto you, Whosoever shall not receive the kingdom of God as a little child, he shall not enter therein' (Mark 10:14-15). Going forward to God meant back-tracking to Grace at source.

In front of the house at Newton stood an ancient oak tree, with widely-spreading boughs. Thomas Vaughan's subconscious mind recalled it vividly in his bereavement of 1658 as an aspect of his first home. His wife Rebecca and his father Thomas died in that year; his younger brother William had died in 1648. His mourning mind summoned in a dream the lost persons of his father and brother, restoring them to him as he lay beneath the 'shelter' of its branches:

> I went to bed: and dreamed, That I lay full of sores in my feet, and cloathed in certaine Rags, under the shelter of the great Oake, which growes before the Court yard of my fathers house and it rain'd round about mee. My feet that were sore with Boyles, and corrupt matter, troubled mee extremely, soe that being not able to stand up, I was layd all along. I dreamed that my father, & my Brother W. who were both dead came unto mee, and my father sucked the Corruption out of my feete, soe that I was presently well, and stood up with great Joy, and looking on my feete, they appeared very white and cleane, and the sores were quite Gone!
>
> Blessed bee my good God!
>
> Amen!
>
> (*Aqua Vitae: Non Vitis*, *TV*, p.591)

The notebook in which Thomas interspersed alchemical recipes with personal jottings of dreams relating to the loss of his wife is a painfully moving account of his inner life which shows how deeply in touch he was with his own subconscious mind, and how grateful to his dreams as communications from his dead wife and the living God she had joined. He often cried himself to sleep. He recalls petty injuries done to her which now he will never be able to redress. He prays and is answered. The dreams are rich with symbol. The tree outside his home stood for continuity; growth; genealogy; the Tree of Life. In Thomas' dream, he suffers from some Job-like affliction which prostrates him beneath his father's oak. The phrasing, with its unmistakably Biblical ring, brings to mind those passages of Scripture in which plagues and sores are visited upon the corrupt: Isaiah's 'From the sole of the foot ... even to the head ... putrefying sores' (1:6); the judgment in Revelation whereby sores fell on the men with the mark of the Beast (16:2). He suffers grave guilt in relation to the dead. But his father comes with practical and even Christ-like healing, cleansing his feet and restoring him to himself. The oak beneath which the dreamer suffers and is comforted is felt as a protective presence; a symbol of continuity and belonging. Thomas's twin does not feature in the dream. But Henry Vaughan, aged thirty-seven, was at that moment living in their father's house and might have been looking out of the window at that same oak-tree. For the elder brother it was not a dream-tree but the substance of his inheritance.

Two kinds of oak flourish in the Brecon area, the sessile and the pedunculate, each of which can reach about one hundred feet high: taller than the house. The pedunculate, with its characteristic massiveness of girth and the broad spread of its boughs, can live up to eight hundred years or more. Henry Vaughan's love of trees is felt throughout his poetry, especially in the context of the chopping-down of an ancient and beautiful tree. In 'Daphnis', he describes an oak which seems to have grown near Matthew Herbert's rectory at Llangattock and may have resembled the oak-tree at Newton: 'a goodly shelter', from whose top 'with thick diffused boughs/ In distant rounds grew' (49-51). The oak, allegorised as Truth, is felled but with the next spring regenerates as 'the checked sap waked from sleep' (74). This is an accurate description of the ability of oaks to 'coppice' after felling. William Linnard, the forest-historian, has pointed out to me that the 'curs'd' owner of the 'Daphnis' oak seems to have cut off the branches before he felled the tree — a common way of saving the trunks of great oaks from shattering by providing a cushioning of branchwood (personal correspondence, 25 June 1994). The mortality of a fallen tree haunts Henry Vaughan in one of his most tender meditations, the requiem 'The Timber', the extinction of an eternal-seeming habitat for generations of winged lives. Venerable trees were associated with his father's and his second father's home and their sacrifice seemed to threaten the very roots of being. This canopy of leaves, sheltering them as children, must have seemed to both Henry and Thomas a guarantee of security: but, like all earthly sanctuaries, this living refuge was not rootfast. Henry too was deracinated, partly by the commotion of the times and partly because of conflicting needs in himself, and attempted to reroot himself in childhood stability. But childhood is known only by contrast: it is what and where *we are not now*, discernible by hindsight. He coveted its innocent unconsciousness, but the means by which he sought to recuperate it was consciousness, the condition of its destruction. Vaughan's 'Childhood' poems wistfully contemplate the impossibility of the backward journey they address: their greatness lies not in their nostalgia but in their anatomy of failure. Magnetism and natural sympathies structured Henry's imagined cosmos, implying that the principle of twinship pertained throughout the universe, but too often he felt excluded from the system, the left-over half of a twin-pairing cloven from its soul-mate. Vaughan acted out the familiar Renaissance Platonist predicament figured in the bisected beings fantasised in Plato's *Symposium* in which 'each half yearned for the half from which it had been severed', seeking 'the love which restores us to our ancient state' (191a-d). This story had been elaborated by Marsilio Ficino in his influential *Commentary on Plato's 'Symposium'* (1484), as an allegory of the fall.

In Thomas's personal notebook, *Aqua Vitae*, there is only one reference to Henry. The dreamer finds himself:

> in some obscure, large house, where there was a tumultuous rayling people, amongst whom I knew not any, but my Brother H. my deare wife was there with mee, but having conceived som discontent at their disorder, I quitted the place, and went out leaving my dear wife behind mee.
>
> (*TV*, p.593)

Henry seems to be identified with the disorderly household which so offends the dreamer that he stalks off. But no sooner has Thomas exited than he is wrenched with the memory of past unkindnesses to Rebecca and cannot imagine why he has left her. Turning to recall her, he finds instead an old drinking-companion, with whom he continues on his way. Eventually, through the healing chemistry of the dream-work (see p.67 below) he recovers his lost wife. But Henry is in this process left far behind, in that house of chaos and animosity symbolising the realm of death in which his wife has been detained. Thomas's unconscious mind interprets his loss of Rebecca as an abandonment by himself through his own disorderly actions (unkindnesses, drinking-bouts); remorse toward her coexists with hostility to his twin, whom he identifies with the 'tumultuous rayling' elements which have cost him his partner. The feeling toward Henry is negative; his brother is a minor figure in the background. Thomas returned to Llansantffraed at the end of the Civil War long enough to be ejected as minister and make his home in London. For him there was no going back. Henry had circled back to the place of his birth, but in a real way there was no going back for him either.

Two poems in *Silex Scintillans*, 'The Retreat' and 'Child-hood' distil the essence of Vaughan's feeling for his earliest years. The first figures Time as distance: maturation is long-distance travelling from a place of origin which becomes invisible and irretrievable. The poem begins with the word 'Happy' but the happiness it consecrates is signified as bygone through the very act of being written down: the beatitude of the speaker's childhood was pre-literate. The poem ends with the word 'return', tracing a circular journey which can only be accomplished if the way is prepared by the rhyme-word 'urn'. Walking against the crowd, the retreat is to a grave. The pre-conscious pleasure of unformed identity can only be reconstituted as final erasure of self:

> Happy those early days! when I
> Shined in my Angel-infancy.
> Before I understood this place
> Appointed for my second race,
> Or taught my soul to fancy aught
> But a white, celestial thought,
> When yet I had not walked above
> A mile, or two, from my first love.
> And looking back (at that short space,)
> Could see a glimpse of his bright face;
> When on some *gilded cloud*, or *flower*

My gazing soul would dwell an hour,
And in those weaker glories spy
Some shadows of eternity;
Before I taught my tongue to wound
My conscience with a sinful sound,
Or had the black art to dispense
A several sin to every sense,
But felt through all this fleshly dress
Bright *shoots* of everlastingness.
  O how I long to travel back
And tread again that ancient track!
That I might once more reach that plain,
Where first I left my glorious train,
From whence the enlightened spirit sees
That shady city of palm trees;
But (ah!) my soul with too much stay
Is drunk, and staggers in the way.
Some men a forward motion love,
But I with backward steps would move,
And when this dust falls to the urn
In that state I came return.

Of the two dominant and opposing versions of childhood which have preoccupied western thought — that children are little devils or little angels — the Vaughan-child is invariably the latter, immune to the effects of original sin until reason develops. He has no impulses to hooliganism, stamping on flowers, sibling-rivalry. He is all eyes; and very quiet. The Vaughan-child is a meditative being, an outdoor boy in a landscape, who pauses to muse on clouds and flowers; and interprets what he sees through the very substance of his body. Vision for him is communion with an invisible but present beloved. Immortal spirit buds in the child with intuitions of his Creator, which can be felt as scintillations through the whole of his being. These 'Bright *shoots* of everlastingness' tell him whose child he is and that the 'fleshly dress' through which he feels the flashes and quickenings of perception are not the whole of him, but apparel only. All that he sees in nature brings him news of his origins: the cloud margined with gold light, the beautiful face of a flower, mirror another Face — that of 'my first love' whom he has so recently left. The thoughts of the Vaughan-child are characteristically and naturally 'white' (one of the poet's favourite epithets, echoing the Welsh word *gwyn* with its connotations of blessedness and happiness) as against the 'black' manipulations of the corrupted will later in life. For the Vaughan-child is still very near to Eden; if this is his 'second race', this is because, like the Wordsworthian child, he comes 'trailing clouds of glory .../From God, who is our home' ('Ode: Intimations of Immortality from Recollections of Early Childhood', 64-5). He existed before his own birth, and his language as well as his eyesight are close to source, knowing nothing of duplicity. Not only does he stand in the light; he is light: 'I/ Shined'. The placement of 'I' at the culmination of the line as the rhyme-word (though, as here, much rhyme in Vaughan is half-rhyme) allows it a stress which yearns toward the eloquently stressed and chiming 'Shined' which initiates the second line.

How old is the Vaughan-child? Very young, I am sure. 'Infancy' comes from the Latin *infans*, meaning 'languageless'. The Vaughan-child exists on the threshold at which preconscious life meets consciousness, a period prehistoric for most of us, when first memories take root in vivid pictures and surprisingly waylay us in later life as they spring out of otherwise unqualified darkness. It was Vaughan's genius to find images for this earliest season of human perception. The 'Bright *shoots* of everlastingness' which have thrilled through generations of readers suggest at once 'shoots' of light (on the model of 'shooting stars') and the green shoots of the young season which prick through tree-bark in springtime. This is one of many occasions when the sheer beauty of the writing brings to the reader of Vaughan a pang or shiver of response at once sensuous and mental which cannot be translated into the language of critical appraisal. This transmitted tremor is in keeping with the burden of the poem's meaning: it seeks to recreate in us the awe it recalls as the state of Grace.

When we come to the second verse-paragraph, we might ask again, 'How old is the Vaughan-child?', and receive a different answer, for there is a dramatic shift of scale and space. The Vaughan-child now is as remote as the childhood of the race. He dwells in antiquity, just outside the outskirts of the Promised Land. The poet longs to see 'that plain/ Where first I left my glorious train': if we thought we were looking out over the plain of the River Usk from Newton, it will be perplexing to discover that 'palm trees' grow on the Beacons. We relocate ourselves in the final stage of Moses' exodus across the wilderness from Egypt to Jericho. The Baroque shift of perspective creates an effect of double exposure which fazes the inner eye with vistas of time antedating the poet's life-journey by thousands of years and recapitulated within his mere thirty years, as each of us repeats the immemorial journey along an identical 'ancient track'. Mankind lost Eden; was taken into captivity; was rescued and led back to his home in the greatest of all 'retreats'. Moses as a type of Christ points the way to the only person capable of redeeming Vaughan's childhood from oblivion. But the allusion also reinforces the inevitable failure of the poet's pilgrimage, in this life; ironically, Moses's great age excluded him from participation in victory. The Vaughan-child too, though saved, is mortal. Reaching the plain of Moab, Moses clambered up on Mount Nebo to overlook 'the plain of the valley of Jericho, the city of palm trees' (Deuteronomy, 34:3). From this vantage-point, God showed Moses the inheritance of Israel but excluded him from personal participation:

> And the LORD said unto him, This is the land which I sware unto Abraham, unto Isaac, and unto Jacob, saying, I will give it unto thy seed: I have caused thee to see it with thine eyes, but thou shalt not go over thither.
>
> So Moses the servant of the LORD died there in Moab, according to the word of the LORD.
>
> (Deuteronomy, 34:4-5)

Moses was 120 years old when he saw what he could not possess; the Vaughan-child is less than ten. The track that links the two timeless figures is 'ancient', and can be mapped only by language for all other vestiges are entirely lost. The voice of the poet modulates movingly between the child-like (never 'childish') and the ruefully experienced. One cannot go back; and yet back is the only direct way home. As he moves into the final passage, there is a shift in manner into the gentlest of echoes of that verbal 'linking' music of internal rhyme, assonance and alliteration which recalls the Welsh tradition of *cynghanedd* with its dense patterns of sound-reminiscence. 'Travel ... tread ... train' trace the obscure homing path to the place of origin; the rhyme 'back' and 'track' supports the quest. Since the quest is homeward to source, it is fitting that the mother-tongue and its maternal culture should be invoked by the poet who belongs to two worlds, two languages, twin brothers.

To raise the idea of the 'maternal' antecedents of Vaughan's life is to stumble into a perplexing area. When I think of my 'first love', I think of my mother. The mother, who for most of us is the matrix of life as she is its biological source, is erased in Vaughan's poetry and her characteristics displaced on to the father, whether human or divine. Having walked 'A mile, or two, from my first love', the Vaughan-child turns in his tracks and can witness at close quarters a glimpse of *his* bright face' (8-10; emphases added). The mothering lap, arms, breast, nourishment, and especially the exclusive mutual gaze shared by mother and infant, which confirms the baby's identity and value, are transferred to the male Author of Creation. Of course this aberration is germane to the patriarchal religion of Father, Son and Holy Spirit, male disciples and apostles, and, until 1994, an all-male priesthood. The fathers that begat us are the subjects of copious Old Testament genealogies; and indeed in the seventeenth century the father was regarded as the sole biological progenitor, the female providing only a convenient receptacle for that homunculus, his seed. Our fore-mothers have corporately receded into the oblivion of the uncommemorated, their names and deeds eclipsed; only surnames ('sires' names') are cut in marble and handed down in dynastic titles. At marriage, a woman legally ceased to exist, being 'feme covert', 'covered' beneath her husband's tutelage, an eternal minor who could not normally hold property in her own name because she *was* property (*Fraser* [1984]). I spell this out because it represents part of the assumption that structured Vaughan's and his generation's world and minds.

Apart from a concern for 'Mother Church' and a yen for the Virgin Mary whose cult was anathema to Protestantism ('The Knot', *Silex II*), Henry Vaughan's poetry gives the impression that he had been created out of a rib of his father, by pure parthenogenesis. His love-poems are negligible as art and unconvincing in emotion. The poet of *Silex Scintillans* was married to Catherine Wise and had four children, Thomas, Lucy, Frances and Catherine; his wife died while he was writing the second part and the elegy 'Fair and young light!' may be dedicated to her. Otherwise there is little trace of his marriage. Brought up in a predominantly male family, with his twin and younger brother close to his heart, he may also have had a sister whose name has not survived (*H*, p.14). Brothers, father, adoptive father Matthew Herbert, male friends like Thomas Powell, father-king Charles I and God the Father, Son and Spirit are the ground of his affections. We know little about his mother, Denise, except her parentage and inheritance. As sole heiress to the Newton estate, which she inherited as a five-year-old in 1598, she represented a good marriage for a younger son of Tretower. She had been married before at the age of fifteen to Thomas Jenkin of Llandefalle, who died within two years. Henry's father married her when she was eighteen. Hutchinson thinks that she may have been Welsh-speaking. He also feels that she may be the person congratulated as 'a chaste and faithful mother' toward the end of '*Ad Posteros*' (23-4), but if so, what is she doing at the end of an autobiographical poem, when her proper place is at the beginning, between 'Father Usk' and Matthew Herbert? And why is she performing the grammatically secondary function of a simile for Vaughan's own endurance of the Civil War? Others have thought that this mother represents 'Mother Church', which is more likely. In any case, the chastity of one's mother is scarcely proof of more than one's own legitimacy. If Denise Vaughan and the anonymous sister are erased from Henry Vaughan's history, this is in keeping with an age which denied the personal significance of women. Milton, who has left us a Latin encomium to his father, *Ad Patrem*, omitted to marry it to any commemoration of his mother, except perhaps obliquely and back-handedly 'our mother Eve' in *Paradise Lost*. Nor indeed would anyone have expected him to do so, intelligence and greatness being understood to travel exclusively down the male line.

However, Vaughan is a distinctly peculiar case of this endemic condition. He shows every sign of being a 'mother's boy' but this feminine affiliation was detached from its original object and bonded to the male image which it profoundly qualified, and to the mother-world of nature. Perhaps this is related to his twinship, which can reproduce the experience of maternal bonding. As an initiate in Hermetic mysteries, he had access to a concept of a bisexual God and a bisexual nature. But images of feminine gender for God are present in the Scriptures too, where God is featured as a woman in labour (Isaiah 42:14); a nursing mother (49:15, Numbers 11:12–13); midwife (Isaiah 66:9; Psalm 22: 9–10); carer for a household (Psalm 123:2); female beloved. The Indwelling Presence (*Shekhinah*) is feminine and Wisdom is a female figure (*Mollenkott* [1983]). It is important to gather these female images of God because the texts from which they derive (Isaiah, the Psalms, especially the Song of Songs) were inspirational to Vaughan. His preference for his 'first love' in his mother, mother-country and mother-tongue are transferred into a God of boundlessly maternal tenderness, to whom the poet responds with an answering love. Henry Vaughan's mother, a cypher in his history and possibly of little account in his consciousness, inheres as an indwelling presence in the unspoken depths of his psyche. Maternal qualities have been especially associated with the Second Person of the Trinity, Christ, in traditions of Christian mysticism; and so it is with Vaughan, whose poems to Jesus Christ are passionately endeared. The works of Jacob Boehme, the German Protestant visionary (1575-1624), all of which were translated into English during this period, are sometimes compared with Vaughan. What Boehme makes explicit Vaughan veils in implication. Boehme urges the believer to 'become as a child who knows nothing and groans only for the mother who bore it. So too a Christian's will must enter completely into its mother, as into the Spirit of Christ'.'This Word is our eternal mother in whose body we are begotten and nourished' (*The Way to Christ*, pp.140, 112)

The desire to be a child again is scarcely a virile attitude, and went unacknowledged beneath moustached stiff upper lips in Vaughan's day as in ours. Much ink has been wasted on a fruitless critical struggle as to whether Vaughan's backward-looking stance was immature and self-indulgent. T.S. Eliot, wearing his pin-striped city suit, exclaimed clean-shavenly against 'the luxury of reminiscence of childhood', advocated wholesome repression, and damned Vaughan as 'vague, adolescent, fitful and retrogressive' (*Eliot* [1927], pp.260-1, 263). Others hoisted the poet out of the dilemma by explaining that the child was symbolic or hermetic, and hence not a puerile fantasy. But there is no reason to apologise for Vaughan's regressiveness. He *was* regressive. He candidly acknowledged this, asserting his spiritual right to prefer the childlike to the manly. 'Child-hood' states this allegiance and defends it against the social imperative to grow up and be a man. Obsession with relinquishing childhood is an aspect of patriarchy which hardens the male by denying his emotional affinities with the female: he may not cry, is not encouraged to be demonstrative. Vaughan of course does not put his perception in quite this way. But it is because he is seeing along an adjacent eyeline that his insight seems at once so radical and so sympathetic. The fact that Vaughan needs to defend his position in 'Child-hood' implies that he underwent inner conflict on the basis of the manifest abnormality of the vision he espoused. He too may have felt the pang that comes when respectable people advise us that we are 'vague, adolescent, fitful and retrogressive'. Self-confessedly aberrant, he accused the mob of 'the normal' of being suicidal; in flight from life and reality.

The poem begins unforgettably with a plain statement of failure. But in the failure there is something of glory:

> I cannot reach it; and my striving eye
> Dazzles at it, as at eternity.
> Were now that chronicle alive,
> Those white designs that children drive,
> And the thoughts of each harmless hour,
> With their content too in my power,
> Quickly would I make my path even,
> And by mere playing go to Heaven.
>
> (1-8)

'Child-hood' opens, as it ends, with an account of eyestrain; and with a path which varies on the one mapped out in St Matthew's Gospel:

> Enter ye in at the strait gate: for wide is the gate, and broad is the way, that leadeth to destruction, and many there be which go in thereat:
>
> Because strait is the gate, and narrow is the way, which leadeth unto life, and few there be that find it.
>
> (7:13-14)

The eye is a pathfinder in Vaughan's poetry. But both physical and inner eye are maladaptive. The 'striving eye' is also the 'striving I' whose selfconsciousness excludes him from the spontaneity of childhood. We can no more get back to the unselfconsciousness of childhood than we can view eternity, for our optical instrument is incriminated by the Fall. For children, Heaven is literally child's-play. The road is wide open and they see through to the transcendent world beyond the world because their lens is not defective or sullied, their 'designs' being 'white' (blessed, happy and innocent). That guilelessness is also guiltlessness. If Vaughan could re-enter and re-enact that early state of Grace he would not need to undertake the weary labour of seeking the 'strait' gate, the 'narrow' way, for blessedness would be within easy and 'even' reach of Paradise. But it is not so. The poem never pretends that the childhood state is capable of re-enactment. It desires but never fantasises. 'I cannot reach it' dominates the entire poem with its message of inbuilt maladjustment.

The end of the poem rewrites the riddle in terms of searching irony. Nightbound, the adult looks back to the vestiges of morning light:

> How do I study now, and scan
> Thee, more than ere I studied man,
> And only see through a long night
> Thy edges, and thy bordering light!
> O for thy centre and mid-day!
> For sure that is the *narrow way*.
> (39-44)

Vaughan's 'study' of childhood seems to have a telescopic remoteness. Light-years removed from the one-way time-traveller, it is glimpsed as if across cosmic darkness, like the very edges of a remote sunset. The object of meditation is beyond full focus; the stargazer cannot encompass the whole in his spiritual eye. Only the outskirts are lucid to him, the threshold-state of 'edges' and 'bordering light' which remind him of what he cannot (by his very nature) see and comprehend. 'Centre' implies a closed circle; but 'mid-day' is paradoxical. For childhood is our dawn and has set by mid-day. Theologically, however, the child's state of Grace is meridian, and through the needle's eye of that 'centre' the poet envisages a '*narrow way*' home to God. What remains in our minds is perhaps less the theological paradox of the conclusive conceit than the visual paradox Vaughan attains in giving the reader a spectacular eyeline on *what cannot be seen*. The vision is as moving as that of Milton's Satan as he lands on the rim of the universe:

> But now at last the sacred influence
> Of light appears, and from the walls of heaven
> Shoots far into the bosom of dim Night
> A glimmering dawn ....
> (*Paradise Lost*, II. 1034-7)

For Vaughan as for Milton, light was a 'sacred influence' and 'glimmering dawn' a sign of grace written on the page of night. But in the towering perspectives of *Paradise Lost*, we could not imagine a baby or child; Vaughan's vision measures its light by the manger's glow.

It has been insisted that Vaughan's 'retreat' towards childhood has 'nothing to do with a literal nostalgia for boyhood nor is comparable to what we mean by psychological regression' (*Durr* [1962], p.40).

The Vaughan-child is scooped out of the world of the 'real' and put safely behind bars as 'symbol'. This view is a symptom of the very disease Vaughan was trying to cure. 'Verily I say unto you, Whosoever shall not receive the kingdom of God as a little child, he shall not enter therein' (Mark 10:15): Vaughan takes Christ at his word. It is as hard for literary critics as for learned theologians to squeeze through the eye of that needle, if their trade is in polysyllables and their minds are swollen with ratiocination. Vaughan's style has in common with Bunyan a conscious naïveté which embarrasses the scholar, who responds by ignoring it. Vaughan's children are not mere symbols, emblems or types, fond though he was of the figurative. Even when he is represented as light, the Vaughan-child is still a human child and not an abstract. Vaughan's poetry has a blessed literality which posits that value is to be found in each creature as being, simply, itself; just that. The self is a statement. Hopkins in 'As kingfishers catch fire' celebrated a similar perception: 'Each mortal thing/ .../ Selves — goes itself; *myself* it speaks and sings,/ Crying *What I do is me: for that I came*' (5, 7-8). What the Vaughan-child is doing is childing: nothing more is required of it. God designed it to play childish games and to think childish thoughts. Acting in consonance with its own nature, it is also spontaneously and enviably obedient to the divine law.

Vaughan was an ascetic who needed quiet and privacy for his meditations and must therefore have sought detachment from his fellow men. Communing with the Other World, he is generally considered to have had the mistiest attachment to the things and persons of this world. But while he was composing *Silex Scintillans*, Vaughan fathered four babies. In the eight-roomed house at Newton he must have been surrounded by them: they played in his own play-space when a child, ran round the oak-tree of his own childhood, and learned to read and write in the same rooms, sitting on the chairs and at the table where he had traced the words on the pages of the same Book. His son took his father's and brother's name, Thomas. Of course, as a male, Henry Vaughan was exempt from the more menial aspects of child-care, coping with tantrums, ear-aches or the seventeenth century equivalent of nappy-changing; and we cannot know what kind of father he was, whether distant and unapproachable or tender and close. Relations with his first family broke down in later life. But the poetry implies that he observed and pondered in living children those aspects of childhood which brought back his infancy. Granted that he must have had the luxury of conversing with his offspring in their more grave and thoughtful moments (a paternal privilege essential to the preservation of a belief in the 'little angel' theory), this bookish man seems to have prized their simplicity in a world where sagacity generally meant erudition; and listened thoughtfully to the questions they asked which adults, blinkered by 'the obvious', never think of asking. Like Thomas, who was childless, he may have solicited their opinion and shared his own love of green and creaturely life. He viewed the adult man as a calcified organism, an echo of the creating Word which had skewed into a digression. In childhood he witnessed the seed of wisdom. The child was no more conscious of this than a stone is aware of its magnetism or a leaf its sap; and by the time he was in a position to know, the growth of the cognitive faculty destroyed the child's innocence.

The child is distinguished by Vaughan from the adult through its mode of cognition. His comparison of children with angels was not a literary version of that pramside simpering which mistakes a child for a doll, but a literal and indeed rather severe reading of the Scriptural warning, 'Take heed that ye despise not one of these little ones; for I say unto you, that in heaven their angels do always behold the face of my Father which is in heaven' (Matthew, 18:10). Vaughan ached to share this face-to-face beholding. Both child and angel are light-suffused because their mode of knowing is intuitive and immediate, not encumbered by heavy chains of reasoning. Hence Vaughan's claim in 'Child-hood' to 'study' the young carries self-humouring irony: studiousness is an outsiderly activity. The more one falls back on a programme of study, the less one knows spontaneously, and the more distanced seems the beloved face. Vaughan felt the compulsion to defend this attitude against the ideology that equates ethics with maturity; and the heatedness of the debate which takes up the central section of 'Child-hood' implies an excoriated inner conflict produced by awareness of his anomalousness. He explains and excuses himself by a barrage of rhetorical questions and a ballast of proverbs:

Why should men love
A wolf, more than a lamb or dove?
Or choose hell-fire and brimstone streams
Before bright stars and God's own beams?

....

Since all that age doth teach, is ill,
Why should I not love child-hood still?
Why if I see a rock or shelf,
Shall I from thence cast down my self,
Or by complying with the world,
From the same precipice be hurled?
Those observations are but foul
Which make me wise to lose my soul.

And yet the *practice* worldlings call
Business and weighty action all,
Checking the poor child for his play,
But gravely cast themselves away.
(9-12; 19-30)

Defensive argumentativeness turns the octosyllabic couplets into instruments of gnomic persuasion and bereaves them of their wistful quality of emotion. The terms of Vaughan's defence are untypically violent, implying that he has been inwardly stung by the imputation of childishness. Adult preoccupation is treated as destructive, a form of voluntary or involuntary suicide. This is seriously meant. The attitude of those who break Christ's command to 'Take heed that ye despise not one of these little ones' is stigmatised as suicidal because it forfeits the prospect of eternal life through discountenancing the play of God's privileged younger children. He sees in their relationships a love that is neither complicated by sexuality nor compromised by self-interest. Pompous adults, filthy with sin, stand over them and scold: for Vaughan, their scorn and reproach are a kind of blasphemy.

* * *

Thus Vaughan looked back toward his own childhood out of eyes that had read books, seen the world, and viewed at close quarters the atrocity of war. He cast his eyes back with all the more yearning for knowing that this state, glimmerings of whose vestiges he could sometimes indistinctly catch, was as out of bounds as Eden to Adam. At the age of sixteen, he and his twin brother had graduated both from their childhood and from their schooling at Matthew Herbert's rectory, and gone out into the adult world of Oxford. When Henry Vaughan returned, he remained alone.

Two: 'Handsome Dubious Eggs Called Possibilities'

Vaughan's world was bookbound, its landscapes mountains of text through which fluent rivers of poetry streamed. His mind was compounded of many people's writings; the act of reading brought the ancient world to life and made Moses, Plato and Virgil his contemporaries. Oxford was all young men and old minds. These venerable minds either belonged to the teachers or had been shelved between covers and might come to life — their prime of life — in your hands as you opened their testaments. Vaughan would have agreed passionately with Milton's account of the immortality of the author in the book:

> For Books are not absolutely dead things, but doe contain a potencie of life in them to be as active as that soule was whose progeny they are; nay they do preserve as in a violl the purest efficacie and extraction of that living intellect that bred them.
>
> (*Areopagitica*, *CPW*, Vol. II, p.492)

Vaughan's poem, 'On Sir Thomas Bodley's Library; the Author Being Then in Oxford', which probably belongs to his undergraduate days, is a witty exercise in celebration of the library as agent of regeneration. If the skulls of the ancient Hebrew scholars are now empty, the contents of the skulls have been decanted and preserved: 'whoever looks/ In here, shall find their *brains* in all their books' (7-8). A dash through classical antiquity reveals the incorrigible life that siphons shed blood into inkwells, so that Julius Caesar's pen survives his sword and Seneca outlasts his enforced suicide at the hands of the Emperor Nero:

> Afflictions turn our *blood* to *ink*, and we
> Commence when *writing*, our *eternity* ....
> But what care I to whom thy *Letters* be?
> I change the *name*, and thou dost write to me;
> And in this age, as sad almost as thine,
> Thy stately *Consolations* are mine.
> (21-2; 25-8)

This undergraduate frisking along the bookshelves pulling out a tome here, an *Opera Omnia* there, gives notice of personal involvement in the game of literature, a game played to win against no lesser an opponent than mortality itself. He accounts himself a member of the fraternity of writers ('we/ Commence when *writing*'), and with pleasant irreverence thumbs his nose at scholarship by refusing to care whose correspondent Seneca's actually was. 'I change the *name*, and thou dost write to me,' he informs the Stoic, appropriating Donne's scintillating witticisms in 'A Valediction: of my name, in the window', in which Donne's name 'superscribe[s]' his rival's (57). But this appropriation can also express something valid and important about the writer-reader relationship: Seneca's *Consolations* are indeed for all time. They are written to me as well as to Marcia and Lucilius; literature is always an intimate but open letter in which a private message is confided to oneself. Vaughan states an equation between Nero's and the present day: never were *Consolations* so needed.

In willing his fortune to the endowment of a library, Bodley is thanked for making 'us all thine *heirs*' (45). The Celt from the provinces presented himself as the inheritor of the culture of a British élite. Indeed, he seems to have taken this inheritance somewhat literally, for he made off with a book from the library of Jesus College. John Aubrey gossiped to his correspondent Anthony à Wood in 1681 that Vaughan had borrowed a copy of Rhesus's Welsh Grammar and neglected to return it (*H*, p.36); and Vaughan alluded to this very work when passing information to Aubrey about the Welsh druids and Bards whose genres 'are all sett down exactly In the learned John David Rhees, or Rhesus his welch, or British grammer' (*HV*, p.696). Perhaps when Vaughan was writing this to his cousin in 1694, the penultimate year of his life, he had the same pilfered copy open on the table before him that he had pocketed from Jesus College nearly half a century earlier. It is quirkily characteristic of Henry Vaughan that he should filch not a Quintilian or a Cicero but a classic work which led home to his roots in the Welsh language; and that he should take this rather rare loot home from Oxford to Llansantffraed, there to ponder it in its country of birth. Just as a plain John David Rhees (a name two-a-penny throughout Wales) elevated itself and its Welsh heritage to the dignity of a humanistic Latinity as 'Rhesus', so Henricus Vaughan maintained a compound identity as *Olor Iscanus* or 'The Silurist' which sought to marry the high cultural traditions of Oxford and the éclat of an 'Oxford-man' with the songs of the earth of the ancient Welsh traditions. Rhesus's textbook called itself a 'welch, or British grammer', a reminder that the Welsh, antedating the Anglo-Saxons, claimed priority as the original Britons; more occult, more authentic, more venerable than their mighty but callow brothers.

However, when the Vaughan twins went up to Jesus College, they migrated into a home-from-home. The place was full of Welshmen. In 1638, out of the 99 men on the books of the 'national college', 59 came from Wales and the border-counties, a sprinkling from England and the Channel Isles, and 31 from origins not known. Persons with the surname 'Vaughan' were also thick on the ground at Jesus as at Brecon, for it is a common name in South Wales. Although Thomas Vaughan's name is recorded in the Buttery Books for four years, Henry's is not, neither did he matriculate, implying that he was never intended to take a degree but (as eldest son) just to soak up a little erudition and saunter around in the general atmosphere of manliness, knowledge and rank, and then, like Oliver Cromwell, proceed to study law in London. Thomas, as younger brother, was intended for holy orders and continued there, Henry told Aubrey, 'for ten or 12 years' but:

> I stayed not att Oxford to take any degree, butt was sent to London, beinge then designed by my father for the study of the Law, which the sudden eruption of our late civil warres wholie frustrated.
>
> (Letter of 1673, *HV*, p.687)

Henry Vaughan does not mention the active part his brother took in the wars as disrupting his academic career; Thomas's career is presented as intact. He sees his own, by contrast, as truncated; his aspirations thwarted by the Civil War. Of course by going to London he was entering the Parliamentary lion's den. When the battle lines were drawn up in 1642, London declared for Parliament and the king moved his court to Oxford. The division of the kingdom at once disqualified the elder twin from his profession by positioning him in the enemy camp, while the younger twin was in the Royalist camp in Oxford. It is indeed possible, arguing from the poem 'The King Disguised', presumably written soon after April 1646 when Charles I escaped dressed as a servant, that Henry was actually in Oxford at that time: 'A King and no King! Is he gone from *us*...?' (emphases added). But this does not alter the picture of an abortive outset to a life begun according to a conventional gentry-model, which was forced to build itself afresh out of its own inner resources. The iron fist smashed straight through his elegant aspirations.

If we pause to imagine the 19-year-old Henry Vaughan in the capital city in 1640, we can observe a typical test case in the explosive effect of history on individual vocation and direction. Vaughan as a sacred poet is one of the great might-*not*-have-beens of poetry. The development of his career mirrors the indeterminate and embryonic messages given out by young people before the course of their lives has been established. George Eliot put it finely:

> Even Caesar's fortune at one time was but a grand presentiment. We know what a masquerade all development is, and what effective shapes may be disguised in helpless embryos. — In fact, the world is full of hopeful analogies and handsome dubious eggs called possibilities.
>
> (*Middlemarch*, Bk. I, Ch.10)

The glimpses Vaughan allows us of his London period are, with the advantage of hindsight, a graphic illumination of this theme. The chick that would eventually hatch from Vaughan's 'handsome dubious egg' gave small sign of being a home-bird, a bard of God, a reclusive lover of nature. On the contrary, he represented himself as one of the boys, hanging on to the coat-tails of the would-be-great, cutting a literary dash in well-trimmed but undistinguished couplets. Fawning complimentary verse exhibits jarringly the young poet's desire to be carried in the train of glitzy semi-celebrities. The general style is an emulation of that virile verbal swagger adopted by Donne in the Satires, punchy, artily colloquial and worldly. Vaughan was evidently (to judge by his eulogies of Fletcher and Cartwright) a theatre-lover; and he represents himself as a man-about-town frequenter of pubs and observer of often sordid street-life. Yet the London of the early 1640's was in a state of swelling tumult, often bordering on anarchy. In the May Day riots of 1640, mobs of seamen, dock-hands and youths seethed in the streets, emptying a gaol and battering the doors of the hated Archbishop Laud's palace, baying for his blood. Vast crowds welcomed the Puritan 'martyrs', Burton, Bastwicke and Prynne, into London in a triumphal entry said to presage the entry of King Jesus. Strafford and Laud were both impeached and imprisoned, and Strafford was beheaded in May 1641, to scenes of frenzied rapture. Pamphleteers and newspapers kept up a daily cannonade of polemic; crowds bombarded Westminster Hall with the cry of 'No Bishop!'; the King in person invaded the House of Commons to arrest the Six Members, abortively; in 1642, Charles raised his standard at York, and the Civil War exploded (*Wedgwood* [1955], pp.327–90). Meanwhile, to judge by his poetic effusions, the young Henry Vaughan toured the taverns and observed the gallants in their finery; bit the end of his pen, lubricated his Muse with wine and wondered what to write.

'A Rhapsody', which proposes three classically encoded toasts to the Royalists, spends most of its time in the womb-like interior of the pub-world, soaking up atmosphere and alcohol and exhibiting wit in a mildly bacchanalian *jeu d'esprit*. It is easily the most lively and adventurous of the early poems, for the curious reason that its perspective is a frivolous version of that major theme of Vaughan's mature works, the experience of an alternative world. Here however the alternative world is not the transcendent vision of the celestial canopy of God's glory beyond the range of the visible, but a vulgar version of the Baroque: the painted ceiling and walls of a tavern-room in which the youthful Vaughan and his fellow-roisterers sit. A laborious note explains that the party is to be imagined 'at the Globe Tavern, in a Chamber painted over head with a Cloudy Sky and some few Dispersed Stars', the walls showing a landscape with sheep and shepherds:

> Darkness, & stars i' the mid day! they invite
> Our active fancies to believe it night:
> For taverns need no sun, but for a sign,
> Where rich tobacco, and quick tapers shine;
> And royal, witty sack, the poets' soul,

With brighter suns than he doth gild the bowl;
As though the pot, and poet did agree,
Sack should to both illuminator be.
That artificial cloud with its curled brow,
Tells us 'tis late; and that blue space below
Is fired with many stars; mark, how they break
In silent glances o'er the hills, and speak
The evening to the plains; where shot from far,
They meet in dumb salutes, as one great star.
   The room (me thinks) grows darker; & the air
Contracts a sadder colour, and less fair:
Or is't the drawer's skill, hath he no arts
To blind us so, we can't know pints from quarts?
(1–18)

If the exclamatory opening cheats us momentarily into mystical or cosmological expectations, the tongue-in-cheek couplets soon advertise the self-conscious roguery of this cheat, and declare *trompe l'oeil* to be the poem's subject. Yet there is a kindling in the verse, attributable now as later to Vaughan's taking fire at the notion of a reversed reality in which dark counterfeits light, midnight midday; and illumination derives from inner ecstasy, here provided by the ministry of the bottle rather than the Redeemer. *Trompe l'oeil* is recognised as a cheap trick and the painter invited to 'Choke' by the no-doubt hiccupping inebriate who is the persona of the poem (31). Later a choicely satiric word-picture of the outdoor world of London is painted:

   Should we go now a wandering, we should meet
With catchpoles, whores, & carts in every street:
Now when each narrow lane, each nook & cave,
Sign-posts, & shop-doors, pimp for every knave,
When riotous sinful plush, and tell-tale spurs
Walk Fleet street, & the Strand, when the soft stirs
Of bawdy, ruffled silks, turn night to day;
And the loud whip, and coach scolds all the way;
When lust of all sorts, and each itchy blood
From the Tower-wharf to Cymbeline, and Lud,
Hunts for a mate, and the tired footman reels
'Twixt chair-men, torches, & the hackney-wheels ....
(35–46)

Vaughan crams his verse with the traffic which chokes the seedy underworld of a London authenticated by street-signs and area-directions in the manner of Jacobean city-comedy. The covert lust that drives the 'itchy bloods' of this night-scene is betrayed by the luxurious coverings which clank ('tell-tale spurs') and rustle ('bawdy, ruffled silks') while thieves, prostitutes, debt-collectors and rakes stalk their prey and ply their trades amidst a crush of sedans, carts and carriages, in the sickly noon of artificial light. After this fantasy-excursion, poet and cronies return to the serious business of drinking themselves round the clock into a state of 'divine' intoxication.

Evidently Henry Vaughan was doing his best to qualify as an elegantly wild young man in a circle of such young men; but he was remarkably unsuited to the role. An insurmountable sartorial obstacle presented itself, in the form of his constitutional dislike of fine clothes. This resistance, which may have had its origins in his impecunious state, is a consistently touching aspect of his character. In 'To Lysimachus, the Author Being With Him in London', he ridicules with some vivacity the men of fashion strutting their stuff in the public eye and name-dropping in the public ear:

> how the trimmed *gallants* went
> Cringing, & passed each step some compliment?
> What strange, fantastic *diagrams* they drew
> With legs and arms; the like we never knew
> In *Euclid, Archimed;* nor all of those
> *Whose learned lines are neither verse nor prose?*
> What store of *lace* was there? how did the *gold*
> Run in rich *traces* ...?
>
> (3-10)

This puritanical distaste for the sumptuous, linked with an exuberant sense of the ridiculous, compares with the Miltonic disdain for rich array, expressed so unforgettably in relation to the episcopacy in *Of Reformation in England,* published in 1641, when Milton was thirty-two and Vaughan twenty, and both were in London marvelling over the strange geometry of human vanity:

> they would request us to indure still the rustling of their Silken Cassocks, and that we would burst our *midriffes,* rather than laugh to see them under Sayl in all their Lawn and Sarcenet, their shrouds and tackle, with a *geometricall rhomboides* upon their heads ...
>
> (*CPW,* Vol. I, p.611)

For Vaughan rank and pedigree derive from the Heavenly family, and the soul of his friend or brother which is 'kin/ To some bright *star*, or to a *cherubin*' (27-8) need not descend to the trashy glitter of outward adornment. Vaughan as a Royalist belonged to the party of curled and scented men who were walking wardrobes; yet he could never ape them. If he hadn't the cash, neither had he a mind for it. Nevertheless he respected church adornment and never criticised the rhomboidal style of headgear affected by the prelacy. Vaughan's inwardness is at all stages of his writing life austere, and his picture of the 'gallants' is only different in degree from the Puritan revulsion against the Cavalier life-style, ridiculed as lecherous and effete in a squib of 1646:

> PICTURE OF AN ENGLISH ANTICK
> with a list of his ridiculous Habits and apish Gestures ....
> 1 His hat in fashion like a close-stoolepan.
> 2 Set on the top of his noddle like a coxcombe.
> 3 Banded with a calves tail, and a bunch of ribband.....
> 5 Long haire, with ribands tied in it....
> 11 A long wasted dubblet unbuttoned half way.
> 12 Little skirts....
> 15 His breeches unhooked, ready to drop off....
> 17 His codpeece open tied at the top with a great bunch of riband....
> 22 Boot hose tops, tied about the middle of the Calfe, as long as a paire of shirt sleeves, double at the ends like a ruffe band....
> 24 A great pair of spurres, gingling like a Morrice dancer ....
> (*L & O*, pp.63–4)

The Cavalier garb was sexily virile, a quality Henry Vaughan may have secretly coveted but never remotely acquired. He lived uneasily on a difficult threshold where opposites overlap.

The Cavalier poet was primarily a love-poet, in style combining the grace of Ben Jonson with an urbane intellectual wit deriving from Donne and the Metaphysicals. Vaughan tried to be a love-poet too. He therefore selected a pseudonym (Amoret, or 'Little Love', via Lovelace and Waller out of Spenser) for one beloved, and added a second (Etesia) for good measure. He then set about courting, cajoling, instructing, praising and blaming her in lyrics of devastating competence. When we come to 'To Amoret Gone From Him', or 'To Etesia Going Beyond Sea', it is hard to resist the suspicion that the two young women have emigrated out of sheer boredom. His amorous poems have rather a bovine air, as of a lover ruminant and assiduous rather than ardent. The sparkling little somethings tossed off by the Cavaliers with such an appearance of casual élan are not available to Vaughan, whose love is conventional and entirely lacking in eroticism. What shine they do have is reflected from other poets, especially from Donne. Hence Donne's 'Valediction: forbidding mourning':

> Dull sublunary lovers love
> (Whose soule is sense) cannot admit
> Absence, because it doth remove
> Those things which elemented it.
>
> But we by a love so much refin'd,
> That our selves know not what it is,
> Inter-assured of the mind,
> Care lesse, eyes, lips, and hands to misse....
> (13–20)

is served up with syrup by Vaughan in 'To Amoret, of the Difference 'Twixt Him, and Other Lovers, and what True Love is', as:

> Just so base, sublunary lovers' hearts
> Fed on profane desires,
> May for an eye,
> Or face comply:
> But those removed, they will as soon depart,
> And show their art,
> And painted fires.
>
> Whilst I by powerful love, so much refined,
> That my absent soul the same is,
> Careless to miss,
> A glance, or kiss,
> Can with those elements of lust and sense,
> Freely dispense,
> And court the mind.
> (15–28)

It is curious to the point of absurdity that so brazen a plagiarism, which is little more than a rearrangement of the original key-words (*sublunary, absent, care lesse ... to miss, refined, element, sense, mind*) should advertise itself as a discourse on the incomparability of the sagacious poet's kind of love. And yet this perversity goes to the centre of something very deep in Vaughan: his need to twin to another identity in order to be himself. But he and Donne were not very compatible, and he turns the elder poet's hot blood to milk and water. The tense complexity of Donne's tender and passionate Platonism is quite lost in Vaughan's adaptation. His predilection for the idea of correspondences and innate sympathies brings him nearer to the sources of his own inspiration in 'To Amoret, Walking in a Starry Evening' in which he is persuaded ''Twixt thee, and me,/ Of some predestined sympathy' (17–18); and in 'A Song to Amoret', he arrives at his most convincing expression of emotion for a woman in a memorable resolution:

Fortune and beauty thou mightst find
   And greater men then I:
But my true resolved mind,
   They never shall come nigh.

For I not for an hour did love,
   Or for a day desire,
But with my soul had from above,
   This endless holy fire.
(17–24)

Vaughan lines are not really close in feeling to their supposed source in Habington's 'To Castara, enquiring why I loved her'. Their sense of the sacramental, tuned to the quatrains of a serene lyricism, looks back to Spenser's *Amoretti* and across to the philosophy of love expressed in his distant relative Lord Herbert of Cherbury's 'pure heavenly fires' which 'hold in an eternal bond' in 'An Ode upon a Question moved, Whether Love should continue for ever?' (66, 72). Yet Vaughan's amorous verses, even at their best, are just too pat, lacking in sustained force and written as if the speaker were fastidiously determined not to acknowledge, even to himself, that he possesses a body. Vaughan's poetry to a woman is costive with that intimate tenderness which he later lavishes upon his Creator. In reading *Poems, 1646*, we have the impression that Henry Vaughan would rather have liked to be a rip-roaring rake but that the requisite salaciousness and violence were not in his temperament, so that like Bottom canvassing the role of the lion he might have promised, 'I will roar you as gently as any sucking dove; I will roar you and 'twere any nightingale' (*MND*, I. ii. 77-8).

The roaring dove, recalled to Brecon, seems to have worked, possibly from 1642 to 1645, as 'Clarke sometime to Judge Sir Marmaduke Lloyd' (*A*, p.303) and to have wooed his first wife, Catherine Wise, in the grounds of Brecon Priory, where she is thought to have been staying (*H*, p.53). Catherine Vaughan is yet another female character written in invisible ink, who has faded into nonentity, apart from her antecedents. She came of a Warwickshire family, and was a grand-daughter of Sir Charles Egerton. Henry Vaughan tells us precious little about his feelings for her in his poems. This stands in contrast to his twin brother Thomas's jotted dream-record of his love for his wife Rebecca, written during his bereavement in 1658–9, which reveals to us the passionately tender attachment of a highly emotional man, wrestling with his grief in private on the page. Beside the testament in Thomas's *Aqua Vitae*, Henry's love-poems sound like the 'cawing of an amorous rook'. Of course I am comparing unlikes, in formal poems and private memoranda; and the apparent difference may simply be one of the caprices of history, which arbitrarily shreds one set of documents while it preserves another. Or it may point to a significant disaffinity between the two brothers: one cannot know. Thomas Vaughan cleaved to Rebecca with immoderate affection. She was not only his life's companion but his laboratory associate in alchemical experiment. In the first of his entries, he alludes to 'a great glass full of eye-water, made att the pinner of Wakefield, by my deare wife, and my sister vaughan, who are both now with god' (*TV*, p.587). Thomas's 'sister vaughan' can only be Catherine, Henry's wife. In another entry, Rebecca appears in a dream to predict the death of Thomas and Henry's father, which comes to pass (p.589). He often cries himself to sleep, and marvellously dreams her alive:

> I went that night to bed after earnest prayers, and teares, and towards the Day-Breake, or just upon it, I had this following dreame. I thought, that I was againe newly maried to my deare Wife, and brought her along with mee to shew her to some of my friends .... I thought, wee were both left alone, and calling her to mee, I tooke her into my Armes, and shee presently embraced mee, and kissed mee: nor had I in all this vision any Sinnfull desyre, but such a Love to her, as I had to her very soule in my prayers, to which this Dreame was an Answer.
>
> (pp.592–3)

With something of the affecting spirit of Milton's 'Methought I saw my late espoused saint', the dreaming widower remarries his wife, delivered like Alcestis into his arms. In a later, more complex narrative from which I have already quoted (see p.44 above), the dreamer having incomprehensibly abandoned Rebecca, conjures a myth of reunion:

> I had in my hand a very long cane, and at last wee came to a Churchyard, and it was the Brightest day-light, that ever I beheld: when wee were about the middle of the Churchyard, I struck upon the ground with my Cane at the full length, and it gave a most shrill reverberating Eccho. I turned back to looke upon my wife, and shee appeared to mee in greene silks downe to the ground, and much taller, and slenderer then shee was in her life time, but in her face there was so much glorie, and beautie, that noe Angell in Heaven can have more.
>
> (pp.593–4)

The cane breaks, leaving in Thomas's hand the shorter half, which is not a powerful rod but 'a brittle, weake reed'; he is afraid he will die before her. The dream carries vestiges of the Orpheus and Eurydice myth in the husband's 'turn[ing] back' to look upon his wife; but the revelation of the higher than life-size radiant figure, flowing with green silk, recalls the alchemical symbolism in which Thomas's perception was drenched, specifically the divine messenger, Thalia, of *Lumen de Lumine*: 'Attir'd she was in *thin loose silke*, but so *green*, that I never saw the *like*, for the *Colour* was not *Earthly*' (*TV*, p.305). The psyche is engaged in a symbolic chemistry that labours to assimilate and transcend loss. The cane, like 'the rod of his mouth' with which Isaiah prophesies God will 'smite the earth' (Isaiah 11:4) perhaps symbolises the power and authority of the Hermetic magus who can retrieve the dead from the grave; but it turns to an impotent 'staff of reed' such as Ezekiel attributed to Egypt which, when the Israelites leaned upon it 'thou brakest, and madest all their loins to be at a stand' (Ezekiel 29: 7). The troubled dreamer is composed by his wife, who gives him a knife to trim the ragged end of his portion of the rod; and he awakens fortified.

We do not know if Henry Vaughan had the capacity to love a woman with this depth. At Brecon in the early 1640s, Henry sought both professional occupation and a wife. At Brecon Priory, he seems to have found both, for here lived Colonel Herbert Price, the governor of Brecon Castle and MP for the town, the military leader who headed the Vaughans' regiment at Chester. The Price family had acquired the Priory buildings at the Dissolution of the Monasteries and Henry Vaughan celebrates in his poem 'Upon the Priory Grove, His Usual Retirement' the beauty of the grounds in which he courted an unidentified beloved whom it is probably right to recognise as Catherine Wise, since the emblematic vegetation is specifically matrimonial: the wifely woodbine that clasps the husband oak (13–14). Henry Vaughan must have been a welcome guest to the house if he was free to wander the grounds, lie out on the lawns, and court the house-guest:

> Hail sacred shades! cool, leafy house!
> Chaste treasurer of all my vows,
> And wealth! on whose soft bosom laid
> My love's fair steps I first betrayed.
>
> (1-4)

Here the youth we view reclining on the amplitude of the lawns is not slumped sun-bathing but posed in the well-known elegant posture of 'the amorist'. Henry classicises the ecclesiastical Grove by dedicating it to Diana. Though 'cool, leafy house' is attractive, the verse is in general infelicitous, with its incongruous suggestions of the Grove as a bank for chaste vows, its mixed metaphor (do houses or treasurers have 'soft bosoms'?) and the peculiar verb 'betrayed', whose meaning has been debated by scholars with a view to begetting sense in it, but which seems to me likely to have been determined by exigencies of rhyme, leaving the swain with the inappropriate appearance of lying in wait like a snake in the grass. The poet goes on to bless the grove, invoking conventional images of Philomela, 'The amorous Sun' and the moon; and wishes it translated to Elysium when its 'green curls' have gone grey with age. There the poet and the beloved will relive their 'growth, and birth' in eternal freshness beyond time. Tangled metaphor (leaves don't, like human hair, grow grey) and strange word-order ('growth' before 'birth') do not seem accounted for by any esoteric meanings.

The Grove is not there now in its pristine state; it lives, if at all, on the imitation Elysium of the page. The Priory woodlands have been hacked back and built over, and only an avenue of tall rookeried trees standing aslant outside the Priory Church (now the Cathedral) remembers the green world once rooted there. But the Priory Church and Colonel Price's Priory buildings which abut on to the cathedral are the authentic remnant of the power of mediaeval Catholic institutions and their secularisation under the Henrician reforms. The Priory buildings are imposing but, though built on a grand scale to house Benedictine monks, they give the impression of many-eyed small dwellings crowded in together, with a pleasant irregularity of architectural shapes and slopes. In Vaughan's day these buildings represented the centre of the Brecon power-structure in the hands of one of the most prominent local dynasties. Price was MP for Brecon in 1642 and acting governor of Hereford until its surrender to Parliament in April, 1643. Escaping from captivity, he raised troops for the King in Brecon in April 1644 and the following summer entertained King Charles at the Priory. It is conceivable that Vaughan saw or even met the King on this occasion, a possibility which highlights the pitch of his anguish at Charles's execution four years later. Price was with the king on 23 September 1645, the eve of the Battle of Rowton Heath in which Vaughan also seems to have taken part. During the 1650s his estates were sequestrated and he shared in the general Royalist ruin. The afflicted and aspiring had flocked to him, currying favour. Rowland Watkyns, the ousted parson of Llanfrynach, who directed a flattering effusion to everyone he could think of who might offer a hand-out, dedicated to Price his collection of poems chiefly encomiastic, *Flamma Sine Fumo* (1662). Two are addressed to the Colonel's wife: 'To the most incomparable, wise, and vertuous Lady, the Lady *Goditha Prise,* Lady to the Honourable Colonel, Sir *Herbert Prise* Knight':

> As I do live, I wonder how you can
> Forget your sex, and be so much a man!
> In wit and judgment; nay, you are divine
> Transcending far our nature masculine.
> As you are fair, so you disdain the rude
> And sluttish nature of the multitude.
>
> (1-6)

Watkyns, who is entirely without embarrassment, goes on to protest that Goditha's manly bosom houses the Promethean fire, and praises her loftiness by mentioning the resemblance of his own poem to a mole-hill. Vaughan cannot have failed to bump into

Watkyns, whose parish incorporated part of the Aubrey estates (*J*, pp.464-7) and who also practised as a doctor, publishing some very killing cures.

The interior of the Priory Church, with its high, dim spaces in which arched windows cut a white dazzle of sculptured light, still implies its Catholic origins. Money fed in through the ancient tithe barns, now being restored, and the whole is encompassed by military-seeming fortifications. Massive perimeter walls remind us of the hostility between monastic communities and the locality in the mediaeval period. The place, which seems to the visitor such a sanctuary of peace, was in Vaughan's day a zone of conflict, in which the authority of the Royalist Price and his fellow Brecknockshire gentry was under violent stress. The Roundheads smashed their way through 'graven imagery' which commemorated and demanded respect for the sanctities of Royalist caste. Standing in the nave of the cathedral, where now the soles of visitors' feet and murmurs of admiration echo, it is a struggle to conceive the noise as Roundhead troops ransacked the effigies of ancient Brecon families. One aid to imagination survives in the form of a single wooden figure from the sixteenth century ornate wooden monument of the Games family. By some fluke this wooden wife survived while the rest of her tribe perished; severed from her pedigree, she lies with her head on its pillow intact, enclosed in its cap on the tall stem of a high-ruffed collar. Her arms have been cloven just below the shoulder, presumably by Parliamentary axes; but her carved hands still join in prayer upon her breast. This unnamed wife is a small, vulnerable-looking figure of a homely vernacular art, whose simplicity makes it hard for us to comprehend the ferocity of the Puritan attack. This is because she descends to us as the image of a single person, detached from her function in an ecclesiastical and political system abhorrent to the Puritan. This was the system into which Henry Vaughan was born and for which he took up arms to fight; its rout in the 1640s brought the trauma of deracination. The sanctities and certainties of his world shattered.

Military service must have been an initiation which coated his eye with blood. He reacted later with a horror of carnage and a stance that approximates to pacifism; but nearer the time with that defensive, urbane machismo which could turn a heroic couplet in the face of horror. In 'Upon a Cloak Lent Him by Mr. J. Ridsley', a witty, manly piece in which he recounts the ignominious adventures of a rough cloak, he represents himself as a soldier who has been present at the siege of Chester:

> Hadst thou been with me on that day, when we
> Left craggy *Beeston*, and the fatal *Dee*,
> When beaten with fresh storms, and late mishap
> It shared the office of a *cloak*, and *cap*,
> To see how 'bout my clouded head it stood
> Like a thick *turband*, or some lawyer's *hood*,
> While the stiff, hollow pleats on every side
> Like *conduit-pipes* rained from the *bearded hide*,
> I know thou would'st in spite of that day's fate
> Let loose thy mirth at my new shape and state ....
> (19-28)

Vaughan presents himself as a fantasy-figure, turning humiliation to advantage; his grotesque levity seems to deflect awareness of the reality of defeat. Beeston Castle, nine miles south-east of Chester, surrendered to Parliament in November 1645; the 'late mishap' from which Vaughan's comrades had emerged would be the Battle of Rowton Heath in which Vaughan records the loss of a friend in the 'Elegy On the Death of Mr. R.W.' and makes it plain that he was personally present. These battles marked the rout of the Cavaliers. Charles I was watching in person from Chester as his cavalry under Langdale moved out towards Rowton Heath to drive the besiegers from their works but was himself forced back into Chester amidst appalling carnage. The King exclaimed, 'O Lord, O Lord, what have I done that should cause my people to deal thus with me?' (*Wedgwood* [1958]). He withdrew from Chester and left it to hold out until starvation broke its will. After Rowton Heath, the remnant retreated to Beeston Castle, upon whose surrender in November 1645 the defeated Royalists were allowed to march across the Dee into Denbigh. By this time, Brecon had welcomed the Parliamentary troops and the cause in South Wales was lost: there is no further evidence that Thomas and Henry Vaughan took an active part in the war after these engagements.

Both Henry Vaughan's first and third volumes of poetry, *Poems with the Tenth Satire of Juvenal Englished* (1646) and *Olor Iscanus* (1651, but prefaced in 1647) have seemed to readers to cast a disagreeably detached and even callously indifferent eye upon the national crisis. There was a limit to what a Royalist could say in print if he wished to remain out of prison: comment must be veiled or coded. Equally, silence, dissimulation and evasion are themselves statements, perhaps the most eloquent of all in a period in which the poet could find neither personal vocation nor public recognition. In the verse letter 'To His Retired Friend, an Invitation to Brecknock', he adopts a worldly tone of surprising levity, but beneath the surface froth appears a groundswell of turbulence as he deals with the change of masters in Brecon: 'in the *Shire-/-Hall furs* of an old *Saxon Fox* appear,/ With brotherly ruffs and beards' (21-3). The town walls are mortifyingly down, and Vaughan's erstwhile employer, Sir Marmaduke Lloyd, has been replaced by an Englishman (Eltonhead), together with a throng of Puritan shovel-hats whom Vaughan derides as relics of the Elizabethan age. The 'new fine *Worships*' (19), in tandem with the old catarrhal Worships, have displaced the twenty-five year old Henry Vaughan from the only profession for which he was in any way fitted — the law. He twiddles his thumbs in the raucous streets thronged with 'banged mortars, blue aprons, and boys,/ Pigs, dogs, and drums' (16-17), and, looking round for occupation, all he can think of is the securing of a drinking-partner:

> let us
> 'Midst noise and war, of peace, and mirth discuss.
> This portion thou wert born for: why should we
> Vex at the time's ridiculous misery?
> An age that thus hath fooled it self, and will
> (Spite of thy teeth and mine) persist so still.
> (75-80)

Had such an invitation been issued to me, I should have politely declined visiting Brecon. The poem's advertisement of the squalor and noise of a swilling, pig-ignorant, turncoat population is hardly a commendation; and the happily married correspondent would have been well-advised to stay at home. Vaughan, beached in his native land, has no idea what to do with himself; he writes as a displaced person, shorn of purpose and sick of his fellow-men, finding temporary release for his energies in self-dramatisation. Offence has been taken at his shrug of dismissal of 'the time's ridiculous misery' (78); justly, I think, for 'misery' is never 'ridiculous', though it may be the product of absurd behaviour and circumstances. This thoughtless scoff comes of a compensatory phrase-making facility, closely related to the burden of impotence conveyed in the succeeding couplet. It must be confessed that both Henry and Thomas Vaughan possessed a singular capacity for the tactless or uncouth remark; Thomas more so than Henry. In his famous *Anthroposophia Theomagica* (1650) he head-charges the reader in the most wildly neurotic manner and does not seem to know how to address us as though we were rational beings. If we do not accept his 'Exposition of the world and the parts therof' (all accomplished in the space of 637 lines), he advises us to go and boil our heads, as servile lickers-up of the 'Vomits of *Aristotle* and other *illiterate Ethnickes*' (*TV*, pp.66, 67). Again and again, he comes flailing at us, naïve, insecure, excitable and quarrel-picking: 'You see now, if you be not *Durissimae Cervicis Homines*, how men fell ...' (p.81), slamming us with Latin tags in a southpaw manner. He ends the work with 'An Advertisement to the Reader' in which he advises us not to 'slight my *Indeavours* because of *my yeers*, which are but *few*' (p. 95) (he was in his late twenties at the time of writing), having explained the possible infelicities of his expression by the following apology:

> I would not have Thee look here for the *Paint*, and *Trim* of *Rhetorick*, and the rather because *English* is a *Language* the *Author* was *not born to*. Besides, this *Piece* was compos'd in *Haste*, and in my *Dayes* of *Mourning*, on the *sad Occurence* of a *Brother's Death*.
>
> (p. 94)

Thomas seems to know that there is something crassly, and even churlishly, wrong with his literary table-manners, but he possesses neither the humour nor the *savoir faire* to correct his mistakes of tone. I have laughed my way through this most solemn of treatises, often aloud. He relates his fallings-short to his provincialism and to unhappy circumstances of composition, a special pleading which, however, only begs the question of why the importunate author did not slow down his hectic progress or delay composition until his mind was more steady.

Though Henry Vaughan was more adept in calculating his reader's response, his poetic taste could fluctuate not only between poems but between lines. The earlier poetry displays an absence of direction and a want of stable identity. This lack manifests itself in both *Poems, 1646*, and *Olor Iscanus* in his mask of a small-time versifier, impersonating Donne but chiefly wearing the costume of the 'sons of Ben', Cartwright, Cleveland, Davenant, Randolph, Habington, Carew. He plagiarises and flatters; fills out his slender inspiration by translating chunks of Boethius, Casimir, Ovid and Juvenal. As a love-poet he addresses an entirely forgettable Amoret; as a war-poet he swashbuckles in borrowed armour, clanking his heroic couplets and flying facile conceits like pennants. The 'Swan of Usk' seldom mentions his native country in *Olor Iscanus* and, when he does, it resembles an outpost of Ancient Rome, as in the pastoral poem, 'To the River Isca'. The Usk is set aside from the contentious world into an area of glossy pastoral: art, not nature (1-24). For only an art-river could offer sanctuary from the chaos of the Civil Wars. Pastoral, as practised by Virgil, Petrarch, Sidney, Habington, is a confluent river of tradition and continuity as against the displacement which was Vaughan's and his fellow Royalists' experience of modernity. The poem is a smooth and urbane example of its type but like many of the compositions of *Olor Iscanus* severely ruffled by the distress from which he has turned to write it. It takes the form of a blessing and exorcism but in stating what he wishes to exorcise, the poet automatically invokes it: 'Mild, dewy *nights*, and sun-shine *days*,/ The *turtle's voice, joy* without *fear*' (48-9). The voice of the turtle was not being heard in the land whose inhabitants lived in daily fear. Vaughan praises a backwater and hopes to keep it so. The river becomes a symbol of all he is trying to save from ruin (church and state) but, because all this cannot be saved, the river flows into ever deeper areas of churning uncertainty:

And what ever *Fate*
Impose elsewhere, whether the graver state,
Or some toy else, may those *loud, anxious cares*
For *dead* and *dying* things (the common wares
And *shows* of time) ne'er break thy *peace*, nor make
Thy *reposed arms* to a new war *awake*!
But *freedom, safety, joy and bliss*
United in one loving *kiss*
Surround thee quite, and *style* thy borders
The land redeemed from all disorders!
(77-86)

Classicism is infiltrated by the more sombre chords of Biblical allusion ('the voice of the turtle', the 'kiss' of 'union'); the tone of Arcadian levity ('state,/ Or some toy else') is undermined by the memory of war; the poem's final word is *'disorders'*. The persona of 'To the River Isca' is adrift. Vaughan's search for a profession in law had led to nothing. Professional status would have manufactured a 'self' for the young man: this seems to have been the case when he turned to medicine later in life. The problem of constructing a viable 'self' in an age of controversy, civil turmoil and scepticism was shared in common with many contemporaries. 'Our selves', confessed Donne, are 'What we know not'. Montaigne had pointed out and Donne agreed, that the self is a process, changing and in flow like a river ('On Experience', p.348; 'The second Anniversarie', 393). The miasma of ontological uncertainty in a period of scepticism affected many thinking people; and in the period of the Civil Wars and the Commonwealth it was compounded for traditionalists by the disintegration of every norm they had grown up to assume and trust. The King was divinely appointed: he could not be deposed. But he had been killed. The Church was the house of holiness: it had been despoiled and its priests evicted. Inheritance was patrilinear: families were cloven, estates confiscated. Murder and schism were the new norm. The shock was equivalent to an earthquake.

Vaughan's insecurity about personal identity registers the stress and confusion of the times in a personality already in want of bearings. The motif of a lost other self (a remnant, as I read him, of the twin-bond) threads the poetry. He longed for the affirmation of a double or *alter ego* and used for that search the language of union and affinity offered by Hermetism. He espoused the idea of 'magnetism' and 'sympathy' which Thomas had researched in the works of Paracelsus, Cornelius Agrippa, Fludd and the Occultists. A dearly loved friend like Thomas Powell, for all the age-difference, became a second self. In 'To His Learned Friend and Loyal Fellow-Prisoner, Thomas Powell of Cantref, Doctor of Divinity' (written before 1660), Vaughan began, 'If severed friends by *sympathy* can join' ...', *'sympathy'* being understood as the responsive vital energy which exerts a mutual magnetism in beings of like nature. With playful tenderness he learnedly expounds the doctrine of magnetism (7-20) and goes on to imagine that:

> if I were dead,
> Thy love, as now in life, would in that bed
> Of earth and darkness warm me, and dispense,
> Effectual informing influence.

Since then 'tis clear, that friendship is nought else
But a joint, kind propension: and excels
In none, but such whose equal easy hearts
Comply and meet both in their *whole* and *parts*:
And when they cannot meet, do not forget
To mingle souls, but secretly reflect
And some third place their centre make, where they
Silently mix, and make an unseen stay ....
(25-36)

Here, the esoteric pseudo-scientific doctrine of 'magnetic coition' is used as a metaphor for Vaughan's passionate need to meet his friend; to be empathically with him and in him; to share being in the deepest way, so that the fused being seems part of the natural order of things. Passionate neediness is only just masked by the metaphysical dazzle in the display of erudite wit. The poem, which speaks of joint magnetism, is itself a magnet, bidding the friend *come* and come *now*. The desire to 'mingle souls', 'secretly reflect', 'silently mix' is a displacement of the erotic to the bondings of male friendship, conventionally idealised by Renaissance Platonist culture, but in Vaughan this is felt with a peculiar poignancy. An unusual number of his secular poems are invitations to friends to come and see him. 'Let us meet then,' he writes in 'To my Worthy Friend, Master T. Lewes', snowed up in Llanfigan across the frozen Usk (7). 'Come then!' he begs his 'Retired Friend, an Invitation to Brecknock' (73).

Or he laments that dead friends will never come again, reliving the occasion of separation. In the 'Elegy on the Death of R.W.', Vaughan imagines himself on the battlefield at Rowton Heath in 1645, losing sight of 'R.W.':'O that day/ When like the *fathers* in the *fire* and *cloud*/ I missed thy face!' (50-2). Rudrum feels that the likening of 'R.W.'s' face to God's when he enclosed himself in cloud and fire 'seems an oddly flippant allusion' (p.485n). To compare the chaotic cannon- and musket-smoke and flame of the battlefield with the 'cloud' which covered Sinai and the 'devouring fire on the top of the mount' which in Exodus concealed God from the eyes of the Children of Israel (24: 15-17) is disturbing. The rough, jaunty narrative manner of the couplets, assumed from the Satires and Elegies of Donne, reinforces this effect. Yet the superficially frivolous hyperbole goes to the heart of Vaughan's preoccupation with maintaining eye-contact. In losing sight of the twinned friend, perceived as life-guaranteeing, he has lost a human equivalent of the Blessed

Vision. 'I missed thy face' later in the poem becomes 'But here I lost him' (61): in the maelstrom of fighters, the crowd intervenes, and second person 'thee' is distanced and blocked off into third person 'him'. The fall of 'R.W.', in a conceit which confounds logic but not psychology, is compared with the fall of twin trees:

> When unexpected from the angry *North*
> A fatal sullen whirl-wind sallies forth,
> And with a full-mouthed blast rends from the ground
> The *shady twins*, which rushing scatter round
> Their sighing leaves, whilst overborn with strength,
> Their trembling heads bow to a prostrate length;
> So forced fell he ....
> (13-19)

Vaughan is evidently alluding to the 'twin oaks' of Virgil's *Aeneid* (IX. 679-82), conflated with Virgil's unforgettable description of the violent felling of the ash-tree (II. 626-31). For confusion's sake he also plants 'A well-built *elm*, or stately *cedar*' (10), which he then treats as 'twins', though they are grammatical alternatives. The unconscious and unrevised slip turns the singular 'R.W.' into a plural 'twins'. If one falls, both fall. Henry records the threat to his own identity incurred by self-projection. To lose sight of the other (whether man or God) was Vaughan's nightmare: that fear was to be realised in the political and personal catastrophes of the final years of the 1640s. He disintegrated and was renewed.

Three:
'Putting on the New Man': William Vaughan and George Herbert

Vaughan was struck to the heart by the death of his brother William in 1648 at the age of about twenty; and by the execution of his King in 1649. He presents us with an image of that heart on the title-page of *Silex Scintillans: Sacred Poems and Private Ejaculations*, in the form of an engraved emblem. ('*Silex Scintillans*' means 'Flashing Flint'). A jagged, flinty heart suspended in mid-air is being stabbed by iron tools representative of a thunderbolt wielded by a muscular arm which issues from a stormy cloud on the top right-hand corner of the picture. From the heart two tears or blood-drops fall and a fire is struck from the flint at the top. Thus the blows of Providence at once melt the sinful heart into tearful humility, tending downwards, and strike from it ardent fire, tending upwards. Scholars have discerned three faces on the heart, and a man within, looking out through its walls; but, despite much perplexed staring, my eyesight has so far been unable to detect these secret subtleties. A Latin poem, 'The Author's Emblem (Of Himself)' interprets the picture as symbolic of the process of Vaughan's conversion, through the assault of an angrily loving God:

> You draw nearer and break that mass which is my rocky heart, and that which was formerly stone is now made flesh. See how it is torn, its fragments at last setting your heavens alight, and tears from the flint staining my cheeks.
>
> (9-2)

He compares this act of benign violence with the miracle whereby Moses struck the rock in the desert to quench the thirst of the Children of Israel (13-14); and interprets the 'wreck of my worldly resources' in terms of the familiar Christian paradox of dying to be born again (15-16). Penitential affliction has been his route to unmerited grace; and the testaments of time past are no more than spiritually embarrassing betrayals of his hardness of heart. The poet who in 'To His Retired Friend, an Invitation to Brecknock' had located 'the *chimic*, quick fire' with a cup of sack (65) and cracked profane jokes about 'redemption' (43, 44) must now number himself with 'the obtuse/ Rout' (86-7) he had formerly despised.

To our eyes the emblematic mode so deep-rooted in the culture of the seventeenth century and elaborated in the Emblem Books of Quarles, Wither and copious others may seem quaint or naïve. To Vaughan it was another language which could figure forth both intimate personal feelings and their relevance to the human journey along the difficult roads of Scripture. Some poems in *Silex Scintillans* are entirely in emblem-language, such as the riddling 'Regeneration', where the mountaineering narrator discovers a pair of scales on a pinnacle (20) and emblematic stones of various colours and sizes in a fountain (49-56). We wonder where on earth we are. It seems certain we are not in Breconshire. Gradually the intimation dawns that this is the inner space occupied by the man in the heart: Vaughan leads us into his heartland, a terrain both cryptic and alien. By the time we have read a dozen poems of *Silex Scintillans*, we have become intimate with the man in the heart, sharing the privacy of his meditations, longings, pangs, passions and fluctuations of mood. He is cast down and he is exalted. He follows the meditation exercises of the devotional tradition inaugurated by Ignatius Loyola, and moves on the mystic's path to ecstasy — but he never reaches such ecstasy. There is a peculiar integrity about Vaughan's refusal to claim a consummation he never experienced, only longed for. Scatterings of light flare along the way. He catches the swirling hem of light in his mind's eye, and it scintillates on the page for us to share:

What emanations,
Quick vibrations
And bright stirs are there?
....
O what bright quickness,

Active brightness,
And celestial flows ...
('Midnight', 11-13, 27-29)

But this light is always entertained at a remote distance. The 'bright stirs' are star-light in motion, in perpetual kinesis across the abyss of darkness; the 'Active brightness' of the second stanza is the action of the 'firy-liquid light' of which Heaven is made (18), and the streaming, alight spirits of the ardent dead are themselves kindlings of that flaming liquidity. This poem is one of a series of elegies (mostly for his brother), specially marked with a pilcrow in the text of *Silex Scintillans*. How uncavalier Vaughan's vision has become. The star-gazer marvels at God's vibrant light; a cavalier in 1648 admired the shotsilk vibrations of his mistress' dress:

When as in silks my *Julia* goes,
Then, then (me thinks) how sweetly flowes
That liquefaction of her clothes.

Next, when I cast mine eyes and see
That brave Vibration each way free;
O how that glittering taketh me!
(Robert Herrick, 'Upon Julia's Clothes')

At no stage in his career would Vaughan have been capable of this magnificent and subtle eroticism, with its feeling for rich clothes (Julia would have been expensive) and the tender awareness of the contours and motions of the body they at once conceal and reveal, deliquescent in its sexuality. Vaughan has transported his passion to the firmament where it blazes in untouchable splendour of disembodiment.

The death of William altered the course of Henry Vaughan's life. We can date it, bizarrely, from an item of that endless litigation associated with their father, in which Thomas Vaughan (the elder) was arrested for non-payment of a bill for a shroud ordered from a Brecon mercer on 14 July 1648. The shroud which thus passed into the realm of funerary farce was William's. The manner of his death is not known but has been surmised, to my mind unconvincingly, from Thomas Vaughan (the younger)'s retort to the Cambridge Platonist Henry More's attack on the absurdity of *Anthroposophia Theomagica*. In *The Man-Mouse Taken in a Trap, and tortur'd to death for gnawing the Margins of Eugenius Philalethes* (1650), a wild have-at-you which mingles racist insult with ridiculous rant, Thomas comes to the portion of More's *Observations* in which the philosopher unkindly suggests that the brother whose death Vaughan mentioned as having botched the composition of *Anthroposophia* was 'Some young man certainly that killed himselfe by unmercifull studying of *Aristotle.* And Philalethes writ this booke to revenge his Death' (*H*, p.96). Thomas ripostes thus:

> Here *Mr. Mastix,* you tell me, and adde withall *it is certain, I had a Brother who kill'd himself by studying of Aristotel.* Who told thee so, thou *Negro,* thou *Mouse,* thou *Moore*? He did *not kill himself,* and his *death* came not by studying of *Aristotel,* but by *a far more glorious imployment.* (*TV*, p.281)

This suggests to Hutchinson that William may have died of wounds or a disease sustained in the Civil War. But Thomas, punch-drunk with gutter-discourse, does not pause to elaborate. He goes on to ever choicer ravings in which he accuses More of being, for instance, an underwater crocodile 'afraid to be *taken* by the *snout*' (p.281), 'a *Spanniel* over *hot pottage*' (p.282), 'Thou illiterate, insipid, irrational *scribler!*' (285), enquiring, 'Here *Sirrah Mastix,* must I lug thee by the Nose, and it were not amiss if thy Noddle were squees'd in a Press ....' (289). In the midst of this farrago, it seems reckless to attach too much historical significance to a vague assertion thrown forth on the gallop. After all, it must inevitably seem more heroic to have your brother die in a noble cause than of a mere boil or nose-bleed.

However William died, the experience of severance from him was decisive for Henry. It broke him down and readied him to be remade in a second birth. Always for the mature Vaughan tears were nothing to be ashamed of. They were not stigmatised as 'womanish', 'effeminate' — or, if they were so, he accepted a feminine role in relation to his Christ, whose bride he was. In his manual of devotion, *The Mount of Olives: or, Solitary Devotions* (1652), he prescribed them as a sovereign remedy against that spiritual bane, hardness of heart:

> for as the *Dew* which falls by night is most fructifying, and tempers the heat of the *Sun,* so the tears we shed in the night, make the soul fruitful, quench all Concupiscence, and supple the hardnesse we got in the day.
>
> (*HV*, p.143)

This verb 'supple' is important in conveying the tender, melted state of contrition which alone opens the soul to God. Images of liquid represent the possibility or state of Grace throughout his poetry, especially dew, the atoning blood, tears, molten light, the river and waterfall, the sea at once amniotic source and final dissolution. The source is Biblical and conventional, the emphasis unique. 'My dew, my dew!' he calls uninhibitedly in 'The Seed Growing Secretly' (5), as if *Dieu* or *Duw* (the Welsh for 'God') were shed as dew. He even carries a bottle to catch the healing balm, like 'the *weeping lad*' Ishmael in 'Begging [II]' and feels himself to be parching for 'one living drop': 'O fill his bottle! thy child weeps!' ('The Seed Growing Secretly', 16). Grown men, we know, do not speak like this. The Silurist's unembarrassed dismissal of dry-eyed manliness is Vaughan's response to Christ's injunction to become as a little child. If it sometimes verges upon the appearance of infantilism, that is because of a certain literality and an absence of face-saving humour in his temperament. He risks our amusement by equipping his persona with the equivalent of a baby-bottle. The 'suppleness' Vaughan desired for the heart required a thorough softening and 'suppling' of the person through humiliation, without which it was not possible to be 'fruitful'.

What then had Henry lost with his brother William? The poems marked out as elegies, occurring mostly in the 1650 volume of *Silex Scintillans*, deserve our close attention, not only because he did mark them out as special but because of their importance in suggesting ways of viewing his psychology. What William seems to have meant to him (after the event) was life itself and Henry's hold on hope. We naturally expect to lose a mother or father, but a younger brother might be expected always to be there in the world of 'givens', the sustaining mesh of affinities and kinships. Our language has verbs 'to mother', 'to be mothered' and 'to father', 'to be fathered'; it has not been thought necessary to coin a corresponding verb 'to brother' or 'to be brothered', for a sibling is seen as a secondary relation. But for Henry Vaughan it was a primary and securing bond: in Thomas's absence, perhaps he had projected his identity on to William. After William's death he found himself unbrothered. Vaughan has been dismissed as 'not really equipped to describe grief at the death of another person ... for Vaughan to lose this life is, in fact, a gain .... On the whole, Vaughan's poems of grief lack the tension between loss and faith which makes Jonson's epitaphs outstanding'. Parfitt calls the elegies 'glib', predictable, neither individualising nor commemorating the dead person but using his brother's death to demonstrate the vanity of material life and the desirability of escape to union with God. Vaughan's supposed devaluation of life seems a health-risk to some critics, an unwholesome attack on the assumption that life is a good. Parfitt however confesses, 'He can, nevertheless, write quite effectively about loss' (*Parfitt* [1992], pp.117-18). This condescension is absurd. For Vaughan writes unsurpassedly about loss; it is the symphonic theme in his works.

A boy has died, and his brother misses him. Evidently, though (or, as Vaughan might characteristically think, *because*) young, he died full of Christian faith and was ready to die:

O let me (like him,) know my end!
   And be as glad to find it ....
Then make my soul white as his own,
   My faith as pure, and steady ....
(57-8, 61-2)

This is part of the prayer at the end of 'Thou that know'st for whom I mourn': it tells us that William made what is called 'a good death'. Henry has vehemently argued down his wish that his young brother should have been left by God to live into his prime, by reminding himself severely of the affliction that characterises life, the frailty of the human form by comparison with the merest feather, shell, stick, rod (22-3). Affliction is embraced as a 'mother/ Whose painful throes yield many sons, / Each fairer than the other' (46-8). His pangs therefore are birth-pangs; his prayers are wrenched from this labour of loss. He accepts God's bargain; but his final prayer carries the urgent burden of a sublimated anxiety. All is well with his brother now (he knows that, as every Christian must). But what if their separation is indeed forever and *he should never see him again*? He may die full of sin and never cross the threshold over which his brother is safely waiting. Therefore he begs God for the 'whiteness' of an answerable piety, and makes a deep obeisance. This poem has understandably been thought oddly egocentric:

But 'twas my sin that forced thy hand
   To cull this *prim-rose* out,
That by thy early choice forewarned
   My soul might look about.
(9-12)

Survivor's guilt appears here in inverted form. The elder has survived the younger. Why? He finds an acceptable answer that deflects the guilt. God's Providence acts on the innocent to redeem the guilty. The primrose is made immortal so that the hole left by its absence should release the survivor from earthly affections.

A boy has died but, more profoundly, a light has died, a spark or beam of the Divine. The mourner is left in the dark. It is the literality of this belief which transmits the pain: William was literally a light, and has literally been extinguished, at least so far as the poet can see. 'Silence, and stealth of days' counts the hours since the day the light went out: 'Twelve hundred hours', a longer period than fifty days or seven weeks because it is a measure of that dragging, pointless time that hangs interminably on the bereaved. They are going nowhere, looking back, but to a past which steadily recedes:

Silence, and stealth of days! 'tis now
        Since thou art gone,
Twelve hundred hours, and not a brow
        But clouds hang on.
As he that in some cave's thick damp
        Locked from the light,
Fixeth a solitary lamp,
        To brave the night
And walking from his sun, when past
        That glimmering ray
Cuts through the heavy mists in haste
        Back to his day,
So o'er fled minutes I retreat
        Unto that hour
Which showed thee last, but did defeat
        Thy light, and power,
I search, and rack my soul to see
        Those beams again,
But nothing but the snuff to me
        Appeareth plain;
That dark, and dead sleeps in its known,
        And common urn,
But those fled to their Maker's throne,
        There shine and burn;
O could I track them! but souls must
        Track one another,
And now the spirit, not the dust
        Must be thy brother.

Yet I have one *pearl* by whose light
All things I see,
And in the heart of earth, and night
Find Heaven, and thee.

The allegory of the cave in the extended simile remembers Plato's cave of the senses. Claustrophobic darkness encompasses the wanderer like a prison ('in some cave's thick damp/ Locked'). The prisoner has a single and therefore absolutely precious light, his only representation of the sunlight itself, the lamp which he lodges at a fixed point in order to reconnoitre further. Losing contact with this light, he panics and and flees back. The lamp is out. Vaughan in the cave of time repeats this obsessive return-journey of the bereaved imagination's need to recapitulate the 1,200 hours to 'that hour' when the light was last seen — a date in July 1648. Each time the journey becomes longer: tomorrow, on perhaps 2 September, it will be 1,224 hours long, and each time it will lead not to William but to the fresh absence of William. The beloved brother is re-encountered as a corpse ('the snuff' [19]), the black wick of a burnt-out candle-end. William's death replaces William in his memory. Vaughan's anatomy of grief yields moving insights into the psyche in mourning, trapped in a cave of nightmare in which it is doomed to re-enact the trauma of loss; and the person himself becomes literally unimaginable, so vivid are his disease and dying. Anyone who has suffered bereavement will recognise this phenomenon of memory-distortion. When the poet turns, at line 23, from earth to Heaven, he still finds no immediate solace. The lamp is out here; it shines there. This should theoretically bring comfort. Fugitives from earth 'fled to their Maker's throne,/ There shine, and burn' (24). But such light is neither intimate nor near at hand. Its incandescence shares the terrible majesty and mystery of God. But where does this leave the mourner? Grounded at infinite distance from the dazzle of these translated beings, he is still searching out a brother whose footsteps he retrospectively 'tracks', reaching with each pilgrimage the point where his brother forever *is not*. The elegy is anything but 'glib', stringing itself on the tension of alternating long and short lines between desire which contradicts knowledge. The final reversal discloses a hitherto unguessed light-source, a 'pearl' whose sudden appearance might strike a secular reader as an odd find in this dark cave. But the Christian reader would have recognised that 'pearl of great price' for which the merchant 'sold all that he had, and bought it', the 'kingdom of heaven' in Matthew's Gospel (13:45-6). I imagine Vaughan lays his hand on the Bible and its covenant of faith; and, with that blessedness of touching home which solaces even unreachable grief, the mind recalls that there is still someone or something to turn to; and desolation abates. This sudden stabilising does not pretend to miraculous healing or transcendence. The poet is still benighted on earth, but in that dark incarnation his mind is freed from the cycle of abortive withdrawals and recoils to see, here and now, in this darkness, 'Heaven, and thee' (32).

The most 'Metaphysical' of Vaughan's elegies for his brother is the powerful 'Sure, there's a tie of bodies!', which draws upon Hermetic 'science', to establish the concept of a universe in which a sympathetic 'influence' flowing through affined natures links them in intuitive communication by tapping them in to the medium of the universal world-soul. Such natures are telepathically aware of one another: light beams out to light. A modern analogy might be secret transmission over air-waves, but the analogy breaks down because of its mechanical suggestions. The attunement of 'bodies' to one another in Vaughan is organic and natural. Thomas Vaughan claims in *Anthroposophia* that the soul free of the body could 'infuse, and communicate her thoughts to the absent, be the distance never so great' (*TV*, p.82) and goes on to refer to 'her *Magnet*, wherewith she can attract all things as well *Spirituall*, as *Naturall*' (p.83). But the optimist, and indeed triumphalist, tenor of Thomas' science of sympathies, founded in his hopes for the 'empirical' science of alchemy, takes on a sombre and tragic tenor in Henry's meditation. For 'the tie of bodies' is grounded in the senses. When the body dies, so does that energy which once flowed out from the dead person to the survivor. The survivor loses grip on the beloved; his 'tie' is broken, his memories degrade. This poem, whose cryptic conciseness bears comparison with the bitter ellipses of Emily Dickinson, again should be quoted in full:

1
Sure, there's a tie of bodies! and as they
        Dissolve (with it,) to clay,
Love languisheth, and memory doth rust
        O'er-cast with that cold dust;
For things thus *centred*, without *beams*, or *action*
        Nor give, nor take *contaction*,

And man is such a marigold, these fled,
That shuts, and hangs the head.

2
Absents within the line conspire, and *sense*
Things distant doth unite,
Herbs sleep unto the *east*, and some fowls thence
Watch the returns of light;
But hearts are not so kind: false, short delights
Tell us the world is brave,
And wrap us in imaginary flights
Wide of a faithful grave;
Thus *Lazarus* was carried out of town;
For 'tis our foe's chief art
By distance all good objects first to drown,
And then besiege the heart.
But I will be my own *death's-head*; and though
The flatterer say, *I live*,
Because incertainties we cannot know
Be sure, not to believe.

If memory is biodegradable, what is our love worth? The tone, forensic and expository, is also wry and rueful. Vaughan confronts with impressive candour both the mortality of human relationships and the psychology of bereavement and recovery. The opening exclamation mocks us with the appearance of celebration. 'Sure, there's a tie of bodies!' has a memorable physicality. That 'tie' of bonding seems as firm and permanent as an unseen two-way cord between two people. It bears comparison with the sacramental bond of nature Kent describes in *King Lear* as 'the holy cords ... / Which are too intrince t'unloose' (II. ii. 71-2), or to the state of love which 'Interinanimates two soules' in Donne's 'The Extasie' (42). But ties can decay or snap, being no more durable than the bodies they attach. The image which emerges is something like the circulation-system of a Siamese twin-pairing cloven by the death of one partner. The succinct exposition of 'scientific' (Hermetic) observations in the first stanza lays down the foundation of laws of nature as the bedrock of solid fact within which human nature is constrained to live. The buried body neither emits nor responds to any ray of vital warmth and is impervious to our signals. Because love has to be sustained on both sides, it becomes harder to preserve its faith *incommunicado*. We are prone to lose the sense of who the other person was and what he meant to us ('Love languisheth, and memory doth rust').

At the end of the first stanza, Vaughan plants a marigold, the one vestige of colour in the elegy. The colour is sun-yellow. Giordano Bruno, the occultist and Pantheist, had gathered in nature's gold along the line of correspondences which link the creation with God: 'Think thus, of the Sun in the Crocus, in the narcissus, in the heliotrope, in the rooster, in the Lion ... one ascends to Divinity through Nature' (*Bruno* [1584], p.240). Vaughan too saw in the surrounding pattern of similitudes not an arbitrary palette of colours but a reciprocal sequence of reflections of the Divine Ray. So the sunflower is not merely an image of the sun; the sun is an indwelling presence in the sunflower. The sunflower aspires to the heavens which are its origin and in turn incline downwards to the sunflower. This would be true of the most trivial celandine, primrose, vetch. But Vaughan's marigold which stands as an emblem of man in the first stanza belies the completeness of the scheme. Dependent on the flow of external energy for its sustenance, it 'shuts, and hangs the head'.

In the second stanza, Vaughan deepens the idea of reciprocity between earthly creatures and Heavenly light: 'Herbs sleep unto the *east*, and some fowls thence / Watch the return of light'. These plants and birds do not passively await the sunrise but actively incline towards it, assenting to the law of their natures, rooted in primal love in accordance with the secret law of regeneration. Like calls to like and kin to kin. In a later poem, 'Cock-Crowing', Vaughan celebrates that 'sunny seed' planted by the 'Father of lights' in the tawny cock's golden eye, whose 'candle' 'Was tinned and lighted at the sun' (11-12). The creature's magnetic eye, a working beam of ardent light, actually influences the sun to rise. Quaint to us, in the light of Apollo moon missions and the Hubble space-probe, these ideas were magical to generations of vitalists privileged to know nothing of black holes and the impersonal matter of the stars. The sun was alive as God was alive, as I am alive, and the cock crowed every dawn for the resurrection of the whole. Then I could have sung with Vaughan (since I too held the 'sunny seed' of golden original light within me):

> ... brush me with thy light, that I
> May shine unto a perfect day,
> And warm me at thy glorious Eye!
> ('Cock-Crowing', 44-6)

That 'glorious Eye', the sun (warm with the Son), corresponds to the human eye, which also, according to contemporary optics, saw by means of eye-beams which it gave forth to brush the object of its vision.

Yet perhaps, after all, Vaughan and his generation did apprehend an equivalent to black holes. If God was not doubted, his distance was experienced. If Nature was interinanimate, mankind was astray. The elegist was in a cave, a shadow, a trough from which life-warmth had withdrawn. The marigold-man of 'Sure, there's a tie of bodies!' is situated outside or on the periphery of the natural order of circulating lights, for 'hearts are not so kind', that is, 'kinned', and at the death of a partner stand estranged from the circulating beams of sympathy which unite the universe. Parfitt's condemnation of Vaughan's elegies for lacking tension, doubt and conflict is ridiculously wide of the mark in this instance; and Rudrum's distinction between the complexity of the Hermetic thought and the basic simplicity of the idea is, though not ridiculous, a surface reading (*Rudrum* [1981], p. 46). For the poem is deep in the psychic conflict of a double-bind which sooner or later afflicts all who mourn, and, the deeper the mourning, the sharper the conflict. In order to recover from the death of a loved-one, we must leave her or him behind; health depends on allowing Lazarus to be 'carried out of town' (17), that is, out of sight and of mind, so that repression, distraction and re-adaptation to 'normal life' can take place. We become interested in life and pursuits again and indulge in 'imaginary flights/ Wide of a faithful grave' (15-16). But this self-therapy is a kind of apostasy, and the mind protests against its own infidelity, remorsefully determining not to recover but to affirm solidarity with the dead by denying community with the living. Hence Vaughan ends with the mirthless humour and edgy reasoning of his vow: 'I will be my own *death's-head*':

> and though
> The flatterer say, *I live,*
> Because incertainties we cannot know
> Be sure, not to believe.
> (21-4)

Scepticism, forbidding assent even to the obvious, throws all into the realm of uncertainty. Seizing a paradox equal to any of Donne's,

Vaughan enlists with his dead brother by refusing to acknowledge that he has survived him.

If bereavement is a pilgrimage, then it forms an intrinsic part of the longer journey in which the Christian understands himself to be engaged. When memory ceased playing tricks and the vagrant heart could unload its burden of grief so that it no longer staggered from the path of the Gospel promises, Vaughan could see clearly that the life of a mourned person had not simply vanished as if it had never been. It had made a difference. And its testament remained as a constant guide, beaconing to light the way. Beyond mutability and corruption, the soul of brother, wife or friend was fixed everlastingly in the firmament of the mind. To despair is to imply that the person's life was of no account. In 'Joy of my life', he commemorates what his partner (probably his brother, though possibly his wife) means to his own pilgrimage:

1
Joy of my life! while left me here,
        And still my love!
How in thy absence thou dost steer
        Me from above!
        A life well led
        This truth commends,
        With quick, or dead
        It never ends.

2
Stars are of mighty use: the night
        Is dark, and long;
The road foul, and where one goes right,
        Six may go wrong.
        One twinkling ray
        Shot o'er some cloud,
        May clear much way
        And guide a crowd.

3
God's saints are shining lights: who stays
        Here long must pass
O'er dark hills, swift streams, and steep ways
        As smooth as glass;
        But these all night
        Like candles, shed

Their beams, and light
Us into bed.

4
They are (indeed,) our pillar-fires
Seen as we go,
They are that City's shining spires
We travel to;
A swordlike gleam
Kept man for sin
First *out;* this beam
Will guide him *in.*

This is properly speaking not an elegy but a thanksgiving. Yet its beautiful form (each stanza like a 'T' cross, or that pillar of fire that led the vulnerable Israelites across their wilderness) has been fashioned from the strivings of mourning. We must mourn a hundred days or a thousand, to arrive at this certitude. Drawing on the courage of the tender exaltation with which he sets out ('Joy of my life .../ And still my love'), Vaughan is able to tread with assurance the narrow way of the five short lines which make a kind of causeway for the verse to navigate so as to complete the stanza safely. He walks forward with his eyes steadily raised. They are fixed on the life of his partner: all that it has been and meant. That life is now experienced in relation to the commonwealth of stars which represents the achievements of the exemplary. Navigating by the light of this example, and not looking down to panic, the way across the black difficulty of life becomes obvious and plain. The writing, in its simplicity and deftness, scarcely resorting to a word of more than one syllable, deviates neither to right nor left. The poem is perfect in its cadencing of such few words, like a person running with inspired confidence lightly over a very few stepping-stones, making the perils of the crossing appear child's-play. It is so simple. But for the sophisticated, genuine simplicity is the hardest thing of all, if it is to avoid simple-mindedness and platitude. Vaughan's emphases are moving in the fulness of their trust as he confides himself to the guidance of the absent person by putting himself — and us — into object status at line-beginnings: 'thou dost steer/ *Me* from above', they 'light/ *Us* into bed' (emphases added). The leading is tender; the led is full of trust.

Vaughan generalises his one sure star into the constellations of a world-view: 'Stars are of mighty use', 'God's saints are shining lights'. The odds are six to one on that we will err without support. But the witness of all who have lived faithful lives is an abiding fellowship which binds the community of those who have gone before with those still travelling. The whole church is in transit to the same destination. And that destination is ourselves. The grandeur of the final stanza derives in part from its direction to the reading mind to understand the New Jerusalem not as a place but as persons: 'They are that City's shining spires / We travel to' (27-8). Simile and metaphor that search out likeness spell difference; but this is neither simile nor metaphor. It is meant literally. If the soul is a spark or candle of light, then the constellated souls of the saints, in union with the 'Father of lights', are where we are going. As 'pillar-fires', they confirm the presence and safe-keeping of the Divine Presence:

> And the LORD went before them by day in a pillar of a cloud, to lead them the way, and by night in a pillar of fire, to give them light; to go by day and night.
>
> He took not away the pillar of the cloud by day, nor the pillar of fire by night, from before the people.
>
> (Exodus 13:21-2)

The whole span of the Bible is condensed into Vaughan's final stanza, for the pillar-fire from the second Book of Scripture guides the spirit to the promises in the last chapters of the last Book, Revelation:

> And I heard a great voice out of heaven saying, Behold, the tabernacle of God is with men, and he will dwell with them, and they shall be his people, and God himself shall be with them, and be their God.
>
> And God shall wipe away all tears from their eyes; and there shall be no more death, neither sorrow, nor crying, neither shall there be any more pain: for the former things are passed away.
>
> (Revelation 21: 3-4)

Each promise assures humankind of 'God-with-us'. The 'swordlike gleam' of Vaughan's final stanza represents the terror of eviction converted into the sign of final welcome: the exit-sign in Genesis (the flaming sword which barred Adam and Eve from Paradise) becomes an entrance-sign (the shining spires of the just spirits). The God who has travelled with the church waits at the end of the journey to welcome us. If the 'swordlike gleam' also suggests, less consolingly, the Sword of Judgment which will smite the wicked, it is not Vaughan's project to emphasise this. The prospect of Hell for his enemies never appealed to his temperament in the way it did to Milton. He pursues his longing with an entire concentration of spirit. Here the direction is not retrospective and nostalgic but prospective and (covertly and circuitously) nostalgic. The bed of the grave takes us home to eternity, and a gathering in to the persons lost in the past and now restored. The poem is itself a kind of optical signal. Shape was as important to Vaughan as it was to his mentor, George Herbert, though less static and ritualistic, more flowing or flickering. Herbert's 'Easter Wings' had featured two pairs of wings; his 'The Altar' is table-shaped, representing those 'fleshly tables of the heart' on which the 'Spirit of the living God' writes his testament (2 Corinthians 3:3). Each stanza of 'Joy of my life' creates the eye-puzzling effect of 'a swordlike gleam', flickering out at the 'hilt' (1-3) and beaming down in the 'blade' (4-8). The poems ebb and flow on the page; no form is constant or conclusive. Variable rhythms and line-lengths regularly fluctuate. Each poem has its own shape, but shape in Vaughan is fluent as the 'liquid, loose retinue' of 'The Water-fall' (5), which pools in long lines and channels through the 'steep' gulleys of short lines, to pool again, and fall again, so that to see the shape on the page is to image the moving form of water.

Everywhere in *Silex Scintillans* the debt to Herbert is felt; or rather, no debt but a gift received. To understand how Vaughan managed to convert his personal losses to spiritual and poetic gain, it is essential to reflect upon this relationship. Vaughan must have read or re-read George Herbert's *The Temple* in his most needy hours, perhaps while William was dying or in the shadow of his death. It is necessary that we align the two figures: William Vaughan and George Herbert. The man he lost was dead and the man he met was — physically — also dead. But this meeting was the sort which leaves an imprint for life. He was empty and Herbert filled him; exhausted and Herbert refreshed him and relieved his spiritual poverty. Herbert put words in Vaughan's mouth, in a literal sense. He studied and mirrored Herbert; became for a span a latter-day twin of his relative. Herbert taught him not just a poetic manner, the power of virtuoso verse-forms, piety and a confessional art, but a new language of the heart and a means of communicating with his own innermost self. Some people love by marvelling at the specialness of the other person; others by trying to become the object of their love. Vaughan was of this second kind. It was and had to be, of course, a textual love. Presumably, Vaughan had never heard the voice of his cousin in the flesh: he had died at Bemerton where he was parish priest in 1633, when Vaughan was about twelve years old. The younger poet, whose identity had always been an *ad hoc* improvisation of other people's singing-voices (none of which had been quite right for him) found a convincing self-identification in Herbert because his voice spoke to and of something deep in his own psyche. This imprinting belonged both to the work and the life.

In the 1654 Preface to *Silex Scintillans*, Vaughan claimed to be a 'convert' of 'the blessed man, Mr. *George Herbert*' and of his 'holy *life* and *verse*' (p.142). He especially praises Herbert for the integrity of his spiritual quest, which, placing 'perfection' before 'wit', achieved the authenticity of a genuine sacred poetry. It was the transparent sincerity of Herbert's speaking-voice which reached in to him; the root in 'A life well led' such as he felt his brother's had been. No doubt George Herbert was numbered amongst the company of saints whose light beckons, accompanies and will ultimately welcome the pilgrim home in 'that City's shining spires / We travel to'. If the New Jerusalem *was* William Vaughan, it was also George Herbert. He respected in him a spiritual wholeness he coveted for himself; the sense of a person intimately in touch with his God. The longing for nearness and communication which made Vaughan so insecure was recognisable also in Herbert; but Herbert, through personal dialogue, was able to show that such need could be answered by the voice in the heart, if only one could listen attentively enough. He allowed Vaughan to overhear his conflicts and debates with God, his queries, praises, meditations, demands, prayers. And God was heard to answer — not, perhaps, providing the answers the persona wants to hear, but nourishing with tenderness and wisdom, as father to child:

> But as I rav'd, and grew more fierce and wilde
> At every word,
> Me thoughts I heard one calling, *Child*:
> And I reply'd, *My Lord*.
> ('The Collar', 32-5)

When the poet Crashaw read Herbert's volume *The Temple,* he said, 'Divinest love lyes in this booke' ('*On Mr.* George Herbert's *book intituled the Temple of Sacred Poems'*, 2). Vaughan, holding his relative's book in his hands in the mourning house at Newton and turning the pages, found the same. In *The Mount of Olives,* wearing a home-made parsonical hat of his own, he quotes the whole of Herbert's exquisite 'Life' as an exhortation to regard this life as worthless. In fact, the poem does not argue this; the flowers which signal human transience are ephemera valued for their beauty and healing properties:

> Farewell deare flowers, sweetly your time ye spent,
> Fit, while ye liv'd, for smell or ornament,
> And after death for cures.
>
> I follow strait without complaint or grief,
> Since if my sent be good, I care not, if
> It be as short as yours.
> (13-18)

Reconciliation to death is not the same as devaluing of life; and the gentle restraint of Herbert's poem has a melancholy sweetness in its lesson to which Vaughan must have responded. The poems have lodged in him so deeply that, with that eagerness so understandable in ourselves and so annoying in other people, he longs to *say them out loud* to anyone who will listen. In *The Mount of Olives,* he assigns Herbert to the 'many blessed Patterns of a holy life in the *Brittish Church,* though now trodden under foot, and branded with the title of *Antichristian'*. He calls Herbert 'a most glorious true *Saint* and a *Seer'* (*HV,* p.186), and recommends three of the more ecclesiastical poems in *The Temple,* 'Church-musick', 'Church-rents, and schisms' and 'The Church militant' — not the finest of Herbert's poems and not necessarily those which had moved him most deeply. The reasons Vaughan gives for his devotion to Herbert are, though real, not necessarily primary, for they belong to his project to become and to appear as a ministering model of piety. The appeal of Herbert was visceral.

Today, leafing through Herbert's poems, we find their voice just as fresh and individual as if the ink were newly dried. We too receive the sense of a warmly human personality, with the artful artlessness that generates the illusion of privacy overheard. His tone varies between the wry and rueful, tender and grave, excited and exalted, indignant or ironic and self-effacing, dryly witty or playful. He ponders, marvels, jokes with God, and has the kind of charm (it is a debased word, but I can think of none more exact) which is profound; it draws us compellingly to him. His sense of humour is irresistible. Whereas the thunder of Donne tintinnabulates, the quiet of Herbert resounds. Like the Bible, Herbert's verse is full of parable, often quaint, sometimes sublime; like the Psalmist, he is a musician, a practising lutenist, who tunes his prayers of love, grievance or longing with a rare lyric gift. As a writing priest, he ministers to the reader. *The Temple* has a three-part liturgical and eucharistic structure, leading from 'The Church-porch' and 'Superliminare' (the lintel) of the vestibule toward 'The churches mysticall repast' of the communion ('Superliminare', 4). Vaughan took communion in Herbert's Temple. He tasted prevenient Grace there. For Herbert's God is uniquely charitable, offering Vaughan assurance and reassurance.

But he did not administer a tranquilliser. Rather his example showed Vaughan that it is possible both to own up to and to live with a restless, sensitive and volatile temperament. Herbert confessed to having been through 'such spiritual Conflicts, as none can think, but only those that have endur'd them' (*Walton* [1670], p.287). Many of his poems are cast in the form of spiritual autobiography; if they are wise after the event, they do not pretend that the poet was anything but unwise, deluded or despairful during the event. They record a psychological conflict which is only in process of being composed and encompassed in the act of writing the poem. In the autobiographical 'Affliction [1]', the persona tracks the process of his disillusion with the glorious life he had initially proposed for himself in God's service. God has thwarted and taunted him with reversals of fortune. From exaltation to sickness and bereavement, he was suddenly pitched by God into the flattering luxury of the world of academia (at Cambridge he had proudly risen to the position of University Orator), only to be plunged for reasons known only to God, into further mortification, followed by illness (47-54). The speaker's story has never been his own. God, whose plans he could never second-guess, has harried him from one insecurity to another. The persona reaches the dead end of autobiography in a problematic present:

Now I am here, what thou wilt do with me
None of my books will show:
I reade, and sigh, and wish I were a tree;
For sure then I should grow
To fruit or shade ...
(55-9)

In Herbert, this desire to become a tree is a humorous and disarming fantasy bred by frustration. He repeats it in 'Employment [II]': 'Oh that I were an Orenge-tree,/ That busie plant!' (21-2). But the Vaughans had only a limited ration of sense of humour. When Henry Vaughan read George Herbert, he converted such desires into the wellnigh humourless stuff of his own personality — to marvellous effect:

I would I were a stone, or tree,
Or flower by pedigree,
Or some poor high-way herb, or spring
To flow, or bird to sing!
Then should I (tied to one sure state,)
All day expect my date;
But I am sadly loose, and stray
A giddy blast each way;
O let me not thus range!
Thou canst not change!
('And do they so?', 11-20)

Vaughan could genuinely wish to be a tree, loving trees with the passionate sensibility of a person who could imagine all creaturely life as instinct with the sap of Grace. Vaughan subjects Herbert to photosynthesis.

In 'The Temper', Herbert presents a telescopic vision of God's cosmic dualities confronted by that wincing atom, man. Lamenting his own violent mood-swings in reaction to the stress of Divine paradox, he longs for the expansion and durability of tempered steel, without the pain of the heat that conditions it. Highly-strung, he desires an attunement not germane to his temperament:

Although there were some fourtie heav'ns, or more,
Sometimes I peere above them all;
Sometimes I hardly reach a score,
Sometimes to hell I fall.

O rack me not to such a vast extent;
Those distances belong to thee:
The world's too little for thy tent,
A grave too big for me.

Wilt thou meet arms with man, that thou dost stretch
A crumme of dust from heav'n to hell?
Will great God measure with a wretch?
Shall he thy stature spell?

O let me, when thy roof my soul hath hid,
O let me roost and nestle there:
Then of a sinner thou art rid,
And I of hope and fear.
(5-20)

The Baroque dynamic of hyperextension challenging that mite, man, is presented with a simplicity of address at once majestic and child-like. A 'crumme of dust' falls back from this Jacob-like wrestle with the Almighty into a huddle of terror. The roof of God's house is a needful enclosure for his fright and vertigo, presaging his safe grave. He does not mount up on eagle's wings; he roosts like a hen in a hen-house. Racked on the torture of Divine paradox, Herbert encounters a God who seems even more variable than himself, executing lightning-changes between mercy and anger, 'And ev'ry day a new Creatour art' ('The Temper[II]', 8). These experiences of near-breakdown or disintegration are resolved in the very form of the poem, shrinking into short lines, expanding into pentameter, affirming integrity through submission to shocks which the poetry absorbs and controls.

Herbert could sustain these changes and challenges by timing them as seasonal, cyclical. In 'The Flower' he opens with an exclamation of release like an exhalation of long-pent breath: 'How fresh, O Lord, how sweet and clean/ Are thy returns! ev'n as the flowers in spring' (1-2). Organic imagery comprehended the underworld of recurrent depression as a growing-place for seeds of the spirit, belonging to a biology of the heart whose risings and fallings, blights and blossomings could be read as seasonal alternations in a 'natural' pattern:

And now in age I bud again
After so many deaths I live and write;

I once more smell the dew and rain,
And relish versing: O my onely light,
It cannot be
That I am he
On whom thy tempests fell all night.
(36-42)

Such images of regeneration went straight to the heart of Vaughan's malaise and did their quickening work. He stepped from Herbert's garden into open country. In that countryside of the soul where thoughts break through like the growing-tips of green inspiration, Vaughan was entirely at home. As a countryman, he could 'smell the dew and rain' on a daily basis simply by going out of his front-door at one of his favourite times, the early morning, to 'hear / The world read to him!' ('The Tempest', 17-18). 'I smell a dew like *myrrh*', he writes in 'Unprofitableness' (10). Greenness and dewfall, baptismally refreshing, brought their sensuous authenticity from the outdoor to the indoor countryside of the heart, whose climate and perspectives he had learnt from the pages of Herbert.

At first a reader is taken by surprise by the sheer magnitude of Vaughan's borrowing. Herbert had given *The Temple* the subtitle *Sacred Poems and Private Ejaculations*. Vaughan reproduced this in his subtitle, giving a clear signal to read *Silex Scintillans* as an echo of the earlier voice. No attempt is made to cover up the debt; on the contrary, it is advertised on the frontispiece as essential to the meaning of Vaughan's volume. He also presents poems with identical titles, notably the 'Affliction' lyrics, and attempts liturgical poetry in the mode of Herbert. He must have known Herbert's work by heart until it mingled with the circulation-system of his own verbal stock, so that he might have said as Emily Brontë's Catherine said of her dreams that they 'have stayed with me ever after, and changed my ideas; they've gone through and through me, like wine through water, and altered the colour of my mind' (*Wuthering Heights*, Ch. 9). If the colour of Vaughan's mind was altered by this assimilation, he transformed the language of Herbert in solution with his own mental processes. The twinship he felt with Herbert is ratified in 'The Match', Vaughan's answer to an invitation which Herbert had held out in 'Obedience' for a like-minded partner to enter as third party into contractual agreement between themselves and God. These twin poems, playing on extended legal imagery of the conveyancing of an estate, lead to the heart of Vaughan's sense of partnership with the older poet. When he read the last two stanzas of 'Obedience', in which Herbert extends the bond of his writing to include anyone who cares to place his signature to the deed (that is, to the text of the poem), Vaughan must have felt with a tingling sensation of being geministically anticipated that he had received a private call to himself, which he eagerly answered with his own parallel deed of covenant.

For Herbert, a sacred poem is a binding pledge for which the writer must stand answerable. 'Obedience' presents its text as a 'legal' bond. New Testament tradition sees Christ (the 'new Adam') as paying the legal forfeit incurred by Adam under the Old Law. The Christian soul must answer this forfeit by abdication of his own will and property in himself. Herbert inserts a clause at the end of his poem to the effect that the document is open-ended: he is looking for a partner in his enterprise, so that another may be a sharer in the (spiritual) profits:

He that will passe his land,
As I have mine, may set his hand
And heart unto this deed, when he hath read;
And make the purchase spread
To both our goods, if he to it will stand.

How happie were my part,
If some kinde man would thrust his heart
Into these lines: till in heav'ns court of rolls
They were by winged souls
Entred for both, farre above their desert!
(36-45)

To this Vaughan replies in 'The Match':

Dear friend! whose holy, ever-living lines
Have done much good
To many, and have checked my blood,
My fierce, wild blood that still heaves, and inclines,
But is still tamed
By those bright fires which thee inflamed;
Here I join hands, and thrust my stubborn heart
Into thy *deed*,

There from no *duties* to be freed,
And if hereafter *youth*, or *folly* thwart
And claim their share,
Here I renounce the poisonous ware.
(1-12)

Herbert's poem is a structure of orderly reasoning, developing his legalistic imagery in a chain of five-line stanzas, each sealed and self-contained. Vaughan however seems to charge into Herbert's 'lines', pumping adrenalin. His poem is divided into two stanzas of unequal length, in which regular variation of line-lengths in relation to complex rhyme-scheme produces rather an effect of 'fierce, wild blood' than of careful argument. He never undertakes the mimicry of legal discourse that gives Herbert's poem its bite, transmuting worldly jargon to heavenly use. The opening expression of endearment and gratitude to the 'Dear friend' who proposed the bargain gives way to vehement epithets ('fierce, wild') and violent or rash verbs ('heaves', 'thrust my stubborn heart'), giving an impression of that hectic inflammation of youth which he means to quell with Herbert's help. The effect of the whole is perhaps talismanic, being a culling of texts not only from 'Obedience' but also from other Herbert poems, the Bible and the Book of Common Prayer. Vaughan expresses more painfully than Herbert the experience of 'inward strife' (18). His language is headlong, dashing into rhapsodic excess: 'O let me still ...!', 'O do as much..!', 'O hear, and heal ...!', 'Lord, strike dead/ All lusts in me ...!' Having clasped the hand of the 'dear friend', Vaughan still finds himself running amok, and has to chase himself to the end of the poem, calling out against his own intransigence, distractibility, lust-afflicted and dust-blinded (24, 33, 34-5). While Herbert is typically understating and recuperative, intellectually organised, Vaughan tends to the intuitive and expressionist. His heart is often on his sleeve as it is on the frontispiece for all to see, bleeding copiously.

Edmund Blunden perhaps unfairly characterised Herbert's work as 'God according to vestry arrangements', as opposed to Vaughan's articulation of 'solar, personal, firmamental, flower-whispering, rainbow-browed, ubiquitous, magnetic Love' (*Blunden* [1927], p.48). Because he is excited, Vaughan is often, despite his unevenness, more exciting, having access to and courage to express extreme emotion. Blunden brings out the fresh-air quality of Vaughan; the occasional vicarishness of Herbert. Whereas the centre of Herbert's world is ceremonial, the round of the church-year, Vaughan as a layman is inevitably an outsider, except insofar as in Protestantism every man *is* his own priest. Some of Herbert's more churchy poems do seem to have been written wearing his surplice, musty from the vestry; Vaughan tried to mime him in poems such as the sermonical 'Rules and Lessons', the liturgical 'The Passion', the eucharistic 'The Holy Communion'. But Herbert could not have written as he did had he survived into the 1640s and '50s. He would have been sequestered, evicted and perhaps imprisoned. The earthly church as he knew, praised and counselled it had been outlawed and its sacred architecture, from which he took his bearings, smashed. Vaughan was left alone with his Bible, the Book of Nature and the moodily chiaroscuro resources of his inner spirit. *Silex Scintillans* presents a black bitterness of satire unknown to Herbert. The order the priest-poet had valued and depended upon for stability had been overturned and replaced by disorder: a disorder he had foreseen in 'The Church Militant'. Insiders were now outsiders. Ancient customs and pieties were stamped underfoot. Herbert's God had been officially abolished. Vaughan and his generation had entered the problematic of the modern period.

Like another better self, Herbert taught Vaughan to look in to the spirit for his consolations, and to seek them in the midst of affliction. This is why I have linked the loss of William Vaughan so intimately with Vaughan's meeting with Herbert. The revelatory character of suffering is after all the centre of the Christian Gospel. Dying to rise, being humbled to aspire, losing to find were the paradox displayed by Jesus's arms splayed on the Cross. The pure joy of that first discovery, through Scripture, through Herbert and through William, came like an inspiration; a being breathed upon by the Spirit. The breadth and depth of Vaughan's verbal debt to Herbert is the testament of Pentecost:

> When first I saw true beauty, and thy joys
> Active as light, and calm without all noise
> Shined on my soul, I felt through all my powers
> Such a rich air of sweets, as evening showers
> Fanned by a gentle gale convey and breathe
> On some parched bank, crowned with a flowery wreath;
> Odours, and myrrh, and balm in one rich flood
> O'er-ran my heart, and spirited my blood,

My thoughts did swim in comforts, and mine eye
Confessed, *The world did only paint and lie.*
And where before I did no safe course steer
But wandered under tempests all the year,
Went bleak and bare in body as in mind,
And was blown through by every storm and wind,
I am so warmed now by this glance on me,
That, midst all storms I feel a ray of thee;
So have I known some beauteous *paisage* rise
In sudden flowers and arbours to my eyes,
And in the depth and dead of winter bring
To my cold thoughts a lively sense of spring.
    Thus fed by thee, who dost all beings nourish,
My withered leaves again look green and flourish,
I shine and shelter underneath thy wing
Where sick with love I strive thy name to sing,
Thy glorious name! which grant I may so do
That these may be thy *Praise*, and my *Joy* too.
('Mount of Olives [II]')

This is Vaughan's account of his conversion-experience and what that experience has meant to his ensuing life, as a person and as a writer. By 'conversion-experience' I do not mean assent to any particular set of theological principles but that sudden once-for-all change in the quality of consciousness which makes the believer feel reborn, confirmed in God's love and his ability to participate in it. That love is recorded as a breathing, a breeze, a shining, a warmth, a refreshment, a scent which all together 'in one rich flood/ O'er-ran my heart, and spirited my blood': an overwhelmingly pleasurable tide of sensations to which the conscious will surrenders. The experience was one of kinesis, for the tides of energy which softly swept into and through his soul quickened his 'powers' into new activity; catalysed the blood-begotten 'vital spirits'. Bathed in sensuous joy, he recognised the outside world as a cosmetic mockery of true beauty. The imagery is taken from the Song of Songs, a favourite Book of Vaughan's, with its garden of myrrh and spices, its well of living waters, and the inspirational wind that brings the lover to the beloved: 'Awake, O north wind; and come, thou south; blow upon my garden, that the spices thereof may flow out' (4:16). The landscape of the poem is all internal. The 'parched bank' represents Vaughan's old state of pathological drought. Sacred dew and rain could not touch him: he had been a closed person. He had wandered directionless, at the mercy of that meteorology of affliction so familiar in Christian iconography, the tempests of circumstance that drive the rootless scudding before them. Then comes the Herbert echo, or rather, direct quotation: 'And was blown through by every storm and wind' (14). Herbert had written in 'Affliction' [I]: 'Thus thinne and lean without a fence or friend,/ I was blown through with ev'ry storm and wind' (35-6). But the two lines succeeding the conscious or unconscious plagiarism are releasings of emotion touched into expression by the remembered quotation, the purest Vaughan, for whom the divine 'ray' is experienced with an all-but-physical intimacy, like sun on skin, but also as a human look of love and reassurance rests on us and gives us rest:

> I am so warmed now by this glance on me,
> That, midst all storms, I feel a ray of thee.

The quotation is a tribute to his predecessor's vital role in releasing Vaughan from his mind-set of agitation. God is the 'wind' or 'breath' or 'spirit' who is the source of inspiration, and hence, of course, is the 'thou' addressed here; but Herbert was the agency through which Vaughan achieved his release, and insofar as 'Mount of Olives [II]' concerns Vaughan's writing life, it is a testament to George Herbert as a channel of that inspiration. Vaughan marries Herbert's 'Affliction' [I] with 'The Flower' in this lyric. For the lingering inner warmth of his conversion transcends all ensuing storms: he compares its enduring comfort with the imagination's capacity to conjure up a fertile springtime scene in winter — in other words, the mind's power to live in its own reality. 'My withered leaves again look green and flourish' (22) recalls Herbert's 'And now in age I bud again,/ ... /And relish versing' (36, 39) of 'The Flower', for these 'leaves' are also the leaves of manuscript paper on which Vaughan composes his love-songs: 'I shine and shelter underneath thy wing/ Where sick with love I strive thy name to sing' (23-4). Henry Vaughan put on George Herbert, not like a suit of clothes as once he had assumed the hose of Habington, the doublet of Donne, but as that spiritual renewal of which St Paul speaks when he tells Christians to 'put on the new man, which after God is created in righteousness and true holiness' (Ephesians 4:24).

Four: Meditation, Reading and Night-Thoughts

Opening *Paradise Lost,* we encounter facing blocks of text, massive and weighty, like twin pillars. Marvell's lyrics are classically elegant; Herbert's pages intricately patterned. But as we leaf through Vaughan's pages, the poems swirl between long and short lines, playing tricks on the eyes to produce a visual effect of fluctuating motion and emotion on the page. Lyrics that open in one form may vary into another. Optical complexities draw our eyes to roam around these variable shapes, expressionist in their figuring of the irregular rhythms and cross-currents of inner experience. This variability makes the regular poems seem themselves a variation. Form seems dynamic rather than the result of a predestining order. The images that come to mind to describe these effects are of liquidity (Vaughan's poems flow, swirl or stream) or of energy (they pulse or radiate). Of course it is the writer's virtuoso art to conjure this illusion of impromptu exponential growth; yet his restless measures, in conjunction with perpetual fluctuations in poetic quality, are also germane to a temperament which experienced itself as unstable process:

> O knit me, that am crumbled dust! the heap
> Is all dispersed, and cheap ....
>
> I find my self the less, the more I grow;
> The world
> Is full of voices; Man is called, and hurled
> By each, he answers all,

Knows every note, and call,
Hence still
Fresh dotage tempts, or old usurps his will.
('Distraction', 1-2, 10-16)

'The world / Is full of voices' (11–12). The outside threatens invasion through the ear: the speaker dreads disintegration in the face of this polyphonic distraction. The verse-form, with its oscillation between the minimal line of two syllables and the maximal line of ten (11-12), huddles in and races out, toing and froing like the manic Man 'hurled' by commandeering voices making raids on his inner space. Vaughan has been compared with Rembrandt in his 'Protestant Baroque' dark illuminations, subjectivism and self-scrutiny (*Martz* [1991], pp.218-24); but the comparison breaks down when one recalls Rembrandt's deep commitment to portraiture. His paint reverences the private inner light of others in all their otherness. We go away looking at our fellow human beings with altered insight. Vaughan is nothing like this. He may take on the being of trees and birds; but not other people. The inner stillness of the 'new man' was always under threat from the 'many voices' of 'the noise, and throng' (32). His sensitive ear winced away from loud noise. Silence was his preferred medium. In the versified compendium of pious advice, 'Rules and Lessons', Vaughan advises the devout to keep their distance from the 'swarm' (31) and, after noon 'away with friends and mirth' (104). The impression is strong of a man in retreat from the social and sociable world, moving into himself and irked by all that interferes with this detachment.

How then did Vaughan spend his time in the period of the composition of *Silex Scintillans* (c.1647-55) when, by his own account, he was often in a state of emotional and spiritual delirium, striving for integration? Despite the scattered medical metaphors in *Silex* and his translation of Nollius' *Hermetical Physick* (published in 1655), my impression is that during the period of Vaughan's poetic flowering he was not yet following his profession. The quiet he sought was reclusive, and he manifests little of that feeling of fellowship which is such a vivid part of the religious experience of converts such as the Quaker, George Fox, and the gathered churches. These sects splintered from the core established religion, to found their own centres at the margin. But for Vaughan and the expropriated Anglicans, the centre was empty. He withdrew for replenishment into inwardness and solitude, which states he commends to his fellow Anglicans in the prose tract, *The Mount of Olives, or Solitary Devotions* (1652). This document is meant as a help or devotional manual for believers excluded from the given rituals provided by the church year and the Book of Common Prayer. Vaughan, from the resource of his personal routines of prayer and meditation, offers the reader 'Morning *and* Evening *sacrifices, with holy and apposite* Ejaculations *for most times and occasions*' (*HV*, p.140). The volume's title derives from the time when Jesus 'took up his *nights-lodging* in the cold *Mount of Olives*', emphasizing the affliction of the Anglican church in exile under the Commonwealth. Vaughan's account of the Christian's day, read in conjunction with the poems, yields a convincing account of the nature of the life he led, structured with a view to intensifying his opportunities for developing that state of stillness and withdrawal most receptive to the experience of Divine Presence. However, in various ways the prose contradicts the poetry. Vaughan's prose tends to be buttoned-up and stiff-collared: it preaches a conventionally Augustinian view of sin and the fall of nature at variance with the poetry.

On the face of it, his way of life seems dull and routine to excess, and it is hard to keep one's mind alert to the fact that Vaughan in this period was still in his late twenties and early thirties. His brother was in 1650 advertising himself as still hardly more than a lad. Henry's prose always sounds elderly; his pose too, in *The Mount of Olives*, mimes the stance of a senior church worthy. Yet one glimpses, under cover of the most conventional piety, an obsessive's alternative life-style, formulated to foster and sustain abnormal psychic states. The primary desideratum seems to have been to skimp on sleep. Vaughan's 'mystical' poems are the testaments of a person in a state of self-induced sleep-starvation. The light-headedness of this condition may well have furnished a valuable resource when seeking that state of reverie in which vision and poetry are most accessible; it may also have intensified the emotionalism and mood-swings to which he was constitutionally subject. In *The Mount of Olives*, Vaughan's first injunction to his reader is to keep awake at night, which 'was not therefore made, that either we should sleep it out, or passe it away idly .... *Christ* himself in the day-time taught and preach'd, but continued all night in prayer, sometimes in a Mountain apart, sometimes amongst the wild beasts, and sometimes in solitary places' (p.143). The aged and infirm, exempted from the extremer rigours of these nocturnal press-ups, are however exhorted to rise before sunrise. Immediately after waking, 'shut thy door against all prophane and worldly thoughts'. Vaughan goes on to elaborate a system through which the devout Christian can parcel out the day in the most prayerful manner possible. You wake and pray; then you get up and pray; after this you dress and do not neglect the chance to slip in another fortifying prayer 'before thou comest forth from thy Chamber' (p.144). The day is by these means timed according to a liturgical clock, the liturgy being supplied for those who do not have an adequate stock of extempore prayers of their own, from Vaughan's copious store.

The Mount of Olives, allowing due account for the conventional excesses prescribed by the devotional guidebook from Ignatius to de Sales and Richard Baxter (*Martz* [1962]), unconsciously displays symptoms of neurosis, which it is concerned to manage, and which undoubtedly he did manage in a positive way. For instance, it manifests Vaughan's fear of leaving home in prayers for journeys away from one's own hearth, which are given special weight as though the 'Ambushes and dangers' of the world beyond Llansantffraed parish posed a special threat (p.146). I am inclined to think that he had an anxiety about the loss of control that comes with sleep; an inability to trust his dreams as Thomas did, and to obtain spiritual release in them. In the poetry he rarely alludes to dreams: 'They Are All Gone Into The World Of Light' being the only significant exception I have found. The symbolism of light and darkness for which he is so justly famous and which is rightly associated with Vaughan's neo-Platonism, may have had its roots in night-fears of unconsciousness. His imaginative and susceptible temperament at once registered apprehension of darkness and found ways of healing and transcending the fear through preserving consciousness in Christian vigil: keeping the light on, so to speak. In young children, unwillingness to sleep is often an expression of separation-anxiety. A child refuses to sleep because to surrender consciousness is to lose contact with the presence of mother or father. Night-time in Vaughan's poetry is the time of mystery and sublime excitement: it also requires to be prayed through indefatigably. In 'Rules and Lessons', the speaker is already beginning to worry about night's incipience at mid-day: 'High noon thus past, thy time decays; provide/ Thee other thoughts; away with friends and mirth' (103-4). He advises sobriety, an act of contrition, an hour of meditation upon one's own death, and in bed that one should keep from nodding off as long as possible for 'one beam i' the dark outvies/ Two in the day' (134-5). We are to maintain vigilance against those lewd notions which arise at nights, for to God's eyes bedclothes are no barrier. In *The Mount of Olives*, this psychopathology issues in a rather beautiful meditation to ward off the evil of the night, making it clear that this evil resides in the fear of abandonment by the Beloved:

> When thou art present, all is brightnesse, all is sweetnesse, I am in my Gods bosome, I discourse with him, watch with him, walk with him, live with him, and lie down with him. All these most dear and unmeasurable blessings I have with thee, and want them without thee. Abide then with me, O thou whom my soul loveth! Thou Sun of righteousnesse with healing under thy wings arise in my heart; refine, quicken, and cherish it; make thy light there to shine in darknesse, and a perfect day in the dead of night.
>
> (p.151)

The mesh of texts from the Song of Songs ('O thou whom my soul loveth'), Malachi ('the Sun/ Son of righteousness' intimating the resurrection of Christ and hence man) and the Book of Common Prayer are levied as a spell to insulate the person about to enter the dark from the threatening loss of bearings.

Orthodox as the manual is, Vaughan manifests a chronic case of the separation-anxiety which can accompany belief: in this he is comparable with Saint Augustine in his memorably passionate prayers and meditations in the *Confessions*. Vaughan however reveals an unusual obsession with control. Sleep is the only state in which the ascetic cannot practise his techniques of control: therefore it is a perilous mental condition. He advises fellow-Christians, whenever they briefly surface into consciousness in the night, to give forth a pious ejaculation such as the following: '*Holy, holy, holy, Lord God of Sabbath! heaven and earth are full of the majesty of thy glory*'. This policy (which, if undertaken aloud, would drastically interfere with the sleep-patterns of the partner of the nuptial couch) is advised as likely to improve the quality of the believer's spiritual life. He even includes a medley of ejaculations suited to the particular state of mind and circumstances of the sufferer in these brief snatches of wakefulness, which he quaintly names as 'this handful of savoury herbs'. For instance, when the clock strikes, we are to cry out '*Blessed be the houre in which my Lord Jesus was borne, and the houre in which he died!'* and if we are weary of the cares and vanities of this world, we should call, *'Like as the Hart brayeth for the water-brooks, so thirsteth my soul after thee O God'* (pp.153, 155). None of the suggestions is intended to be ingenious or original: they lead the disorientated Anglican back into a verbal equivalent of the sheepfold of the church.

Vaughan's sole objective was to prepare himself for the coming of 'the Bridegroom'. The heart is the believer's marriage-bed, which must be fit for occupation by the husband-to-be. In the exercises recommended for the three days preparatory to receiving Holy Communion, he treats the Eucharist (with its mingling of the mystical expression of Christ's body and blood with the believer's) as a visit by the Bridegroom to the bride. The Church of England occupied a flexibly vague middle-ground between the Calvinist belief that Christ in the Communion was only present in the act of faith and the Roman Catholic commitment to the Real Presence. Vaughan seems to me to incline rather right than left. He admonishes us to examine our bosoms before the Meal:

> and if thou findest any sons of darknesse lurking under those fig-leaves, conceal them not but turne them out of doors, and wash thy Couch with thy teares; have a care that in the Bridegroom's bed, instead of myrrhe and flowers, thou strowest not thornes and thistles.
>
> (p.157)

Here marital imagery takes on a too solid literality and the believer's manual threatens to become a housewife's handbook, in which the soul is urged to diligent inspection of its bed-linen, lest the Spouse be offended by the presence of foul odours or spiked by a surprising thistle. The deficiency in humour which Vaughan betrays here is a corollary of the grave significance which he attaches to the Communion. The Sacrament ritually closes the gap of separation between man below and God above; the wafer of bread and the sip of wine are tokens of life-guaranteeing love that enters intimately into the whole person of the believer, and becomes, if not literally flesh of his flesh, spirit of his spirit. The Communion meal is a form of love-making; its consumption a sacred consummation. In this situation, all relevant preparation having been made, Vaughan could 'let go'. It is noticeable that he prescribes for the eve of this ceremony an even shorter sleep than usual (p.157); supplements the Prayer Book order with private devotions during the service; and forbids spitting, eating and drinking, until the Sacred Elements are fully digested (p.164).

There is a highly-charged dimension to Vaughan's inner life which, apparently contradicted by his life-style of austere, round-the-clock self-discipline, was probably intensified by the repressions he practised. Suppressed dreams customarily liberate themselves as day-dreams. Hence, the intense prayer-times which he practised in the early mornings (celebrated in the joyous 'The Morning-Watch' [p.134 below]) seem to have channelled dream-material into the substance of waking response. However, the pathological control he asserted probably explains the fact that he never achieved the 'ecstasy' or 'rapture' reported by mystics as the final stage of contemplation (*U*, pp.358-79). The conflict evident in some of his finest poems may be associated with these contrary drives of his psyche: the compulsion to respond in full to his Beloved's presence and the recoil from such yielding; his equivocal sense of God's 'almost-here' as simultaneously a 'beyond-there'. These are the positive and negative aspects of one search: their conflict generates the longing for transcendence of self. He wishes to be elsewhere and elsewhen, resituated at some prior or ultimate stage when the subconscious mind's intuitive responses are neither feared nor censored (the 'childhood' poems and those which desire the oblivion of death). Or these prior stages are located in Biblical history, whether when the species was still 'young' and theophany still a real possibility, or at the apocalyptic Day of Judgment when Time ends and the Bridegroom comes to claim the bride of Christendom.

The meditation-exercises he practised would have moved through a threefold sequence of imaginative stages. From 'composition of place' in which the meditator inserts himself as eye-witness into an intensely realised sacred event, subject or text, he passes to 'analysis' of its meanings and implications and finally to 'colloquy', a call to or dialogue with God, inspired by these thoughts. Several of Vaughan's lyrics are structured on this principle, the fruits surely of his daily rounds of meditative walking. When he speaks in 'I walked the other day (to spend my hour)', that hour is probably the period set aside for formal meditation. Entering a field, he finds and unearths the corm or bulb of a beautiful flower, now withered in winter: 'I saw the warm recluse to lie/ Where fresh and green/ He lived of us unseen' (19-21). In the fourth stanza he interrogates the flower which replies consolingly to the effect that his retirement is recuperative and a prelude to regeneration. So far the meditation seems to be going well: the meditator's steps have led him to unearth the mystery of the resurrection. But the centre of the poem breaks into an extraordinary emotional outburst:

> This passed, I threw the clothes quite o'er his head,
>   And stung with fear
> Of my own frailty dropped down many a tear
>   Upon his bed,
> Then sighing whispered, *Happy are the dead!*
>   *What peace doth now*
>   *Rock him asleep below?*
>   (29-35)

The traumatised feeling of this verse comes of the instability of its symbolism: there is the sense that Henry has been engaged in digging up the grave of his brother William, to get him back; at the same time we are at a bedside, recapitulating William's death-scene perhaps, in which 'I threw the clothes quite o'er his head'. But the buried flower, awaiting resurrection in its sanctuary, the cradling earth, is also a divine reason to hope: a hope he is able in the course of the remainder of the meditation to clarify. He prays to transcend the delusions of this life and to see again his brother's life 'hid in thee' (61). This lyric bears every sign of being the testimony of experience; Vaughan's life, like his poetry, was structured with a view to extracting the fullest insight and psychological benefit from the mundane. Through the exercise called 'meditation upon the creatures' he was able not only to explore that empathy with nature for which he is so famous but also to visit the depths of his own psyche, with their buried mental contents, as here in 'I walked the other day'. The poems are often self-ironising informal meditations upon his formal meditations, doubling back to retread the private pilgrimage of thought with the narrative wisdom of hindsight. Because they are going over the same path for a second time, such poems are doubly introspective. But when the poet surfaces, it is into the same unbrothered world where 'all the year I mourn' (63). It is typical of Vaughan to refuse to shrug off the pain. For such pain is the burden love must carry.

Vaughan's activities in these creative years, then, seem to have been solitary and ascetic. He prayed round the clock; sat and thought; walked out into the countryside and meditated. His advocacy of an abstemious attitude to sex (*Hermetical Physick, HV*, p.558) may have made his love-poetry to Christ all the more passionate through the expression of sublimated sexuality. He was also an omnivorous reader who must have spent literally years of his life with his head in a book. How he came by such a wealth of recondite reading matter, living impecuniously far from the centres of learning, is unknown: perhaps the small company of Breconshire intellectuals amongst whom Vaughan belonged operated an informal lending-network from their private libraries or Thomas sent books from London. He was also drawn to the translator's art, a kind of textual twinning which was congenial to his temperament. In *Flores Solitudinis* (1654), the fruits of a period of illness, he translated Jesuit works by Nierembergius, Eucherius and Rosweydus. He celebrated his love of reading in 'To His Books', a rhapsody of similitudes, each one concerned with light and vision: 'Bright books! the *perspectives* to our weak sights:/ The clear *projections* of discerning lights./ Burning and shining *thoughts*...' (1-3). To open a book is to gain optical entry into the past and to live in a book is to be companionate with the choicest spirits of history. Reading to him was realisation; the work of lifting words from the abstractness of their printed state into vitality and colour. This was especially true in relation to the Scriptures. The English Bible, for Vaughan as for his generation, was the Book of Books. It was the source and ground of all knowledge, a manual of all the arts and sciences, including alchemy and occultism (*Hill* [1991], pp.7-20, 23). From the Reformation until 1640, over a million Bibles were sold. In the 1640s and '50s, many owned pocket Bibles, which could be carried round and consulted wherever one happened to be. Yet the Bible was also explosive and incendiary. It was the alleged source of the opposite political philosophies that had split the nation from end to end. Milton's grandfather, as Vaughan's cousin, John Aubrey noted, disinherited his son 'because he kept not the Catholique Religion', an apostasy he detected when he 'found a Bible in English in his chamber' (*Darbishire* [1962] p.1). The Protestant duty of private meditation and interpretation of the vernacular Bible was at the centre of spiritual life. For the Puritan, this was paramount. For the Anglican after the eviction of the ministers, it could be the only resort. Henry Vaughan's Bible was therefore a kind of tabernacle into which he could withdraw from the world to look for Jesus. His country was the Bible; and the hillscape of Brycheiniog ascended into Biblical vistas which dropped back again to the Beacons. His pilgrim eyes travelled the tracks of print through the sacred pages, and Christ the Word was counsellor to his own words.

Vaughan's intensely imaginative temperament brought the events attested in the Bible to life in his mind so that they lived there as vividly as sense-impressions — or more so, challenging with a more vigorous reality. Here he could relate his own individual history to the epic history of the tribe, a three-part odyssey which began in Genesis with the Creation, fall and punishment; centred on the Nativity and Atonement; and would find journey's end in the Second Coming, Last Judgment and regeneration. His understanding of Scripture was typological: all events in the Old Testament foretold and were reinterpreted by those in the New. He loved the Old Testament with an especial attachment, for its people were not only elder brothers and very old friends but patriarchs who lived in the youth of the world, and were therefore in a sense 'younger' than we are. Their stories were familiar and immediate, and the subjects of frequent meditation. The ancient names got up from the page and became vivid people as Vaughan brooded over single verses. He walked and talked with Moses and Abraham; milked them of information and either had reluctantly to let them lie down again when their story was told, or carried them out into his own poems. In 'Isaac's Marriage', a spree of humorous inventiveness, he brings alive from a single commonplace verse of Genesis (24: 63) the vivid scene of Isaac, piously praying before his wife Rebecca is brought to him: 'Praying! and to be married? It was rare,/ But now 'tis monstrous ...' (1-2). But those were the unfashionable olden days when the wedding-guests were not gangs of foul-mouthed dissolutes but 'nobler guests: Angels did wind/ And rove about thee' (25-6), and simpering manners and the baroque inanity of bridal hairstyles 'In *rolls* and *curls*' were not known (34). Vaughan evokes a double image of yesterday's Biblical and primitive simplicity; today's loud, lewd profanity. For in those days they were closer to home by several thousand years.

Bible-reading transports the sophisticated spirit from a degenerate epoch to the time when the race was young and fresh from Eden; often Vaughan's Bible-readings carry a Blakean visionary freshness and conscious naivete, combined with such sensuous immediacy of imaginative response that they seem to spring not from the perusal of a book held at arm's length but from a personal outing newly enjoyed:

> My God, when I walk in those groves,
> And leaves thy spirit doth still fan,
> I see in each shade that there grows
> An angel talking with a man.
>
> Under a *juniper*, some house,
> Or the cool *myrtle*'s canopy,
> Others beneath an oak's green boughs,
> Or at some *fountain*'s bubbling eye;
>
> Here *Jacob* dreams, and wrestles; there
> *Elias* by a raven is fed,
> Another time by the Angel, where
> He brings him water with his bread;
>
> In *Abraham*'s tent the winged guests
> (O how familiar then was heaven!)
> Eat, drink, discourse, sit down, and rest
> Until the cool, and shady *even* ...
>
> (1-16)

It takes most readers — rightly — some time to recognise the 'groves' through which the speaker rambles as Books of the Old Testament rather than some imagined outdoor region; that the 'leaves' are pages rather than foliage. Textual trees can ripple and shimmer in a cooling breeze because their 'leaves' are breathed upon by the Spirit; this inspiration is then breathed in by the reader who walks in 'groves' of print equivalent to those where, once, angels might have been encountered chatting to men in the cool shade of some arbour. The book recapitulates this arbour which itself recapitulates the garden-groves of Paradise where God walked and talked with Adam in the cool of the evening. Perhaps we should see the columns of Scriptural print as signifying the trunks of trees in the oases and copses of the ancient desert landscape, those green spaces of juniper, myrtle, oak and fountain where Presences from the other world arrested the pious in their hour of need, bearing messages of hope and succour, to their undoubted surprise. You might even find yourself wrestling, like Jacob, with an angel — and throw him. You might dream of a ladder reaching to heaven, with angels ascending and descending. Vaughan's tone is plainly delighted, and delights. He bathes us in pools of reminiscence. We are struck by the economy of his gift as we move from 'grove' to 'grove', leafing back and forth through the Old Testament from Genesis to Zechariah. One after another the wonderful stories pop up, as though simultaneously. Narrated in the present tense, they are all going on now. This focuses us on the peculiar pleasures of the reading experience. Even as I look up the story of Elijah under the juniper in the First Book of Kings, I know that Zechariah is simultaneously in conference with an angel in a myrtle grove in the penultimate Book of the Old Testament; that meanwhile under an oak-tree in Judges, Gideon is being reassured, 'The LORD is with thee, thou mighty man of valour' (6:12), and I can turn at will to listen in to pregnant Hagar's conversation with an angel by a fountain in Genesis (16:7). The childlike simplicity of Vaughan's lilting octosyllabic quatrains relays the immanence of these stories and their instant accessibility in the record. Reading delivers a literary version of that 'commerce' through which messages were delivered more-or-less to the door in the Holy Land. Hence, reading is a place of vision and a version of theophany: 'I see...' (3).

But, however buried in a book we are, and however compelling and true the story, to read is to experience at second hand. Vaughan was an impatient and hungry man: his urge being always toward experience — to touch, taste, smell, hold, hear, and especially to see. The 'groves' even of Scripture are paper substitutes for tactile leaves. Face-to-face conversation is no longer possible in the modern world. Textual trees do not actually shelter anyone from the military on the Abergavenny road. The God whose angels visited Abraham's tent will not sit down as guests in the great hall of the house at Newton to break bread, nor after 1650 will Vaughan receive the bread and wine of the host in the locked church at Llansantffraed. And this is the real subject of the poem: lock-out, corruption and decline. 'Religion', for all its enchanting opening, was born from clueless darkness. The parenthesis ('O how familiar then was heaven!' (14)) invades the delighted telling, with characteristic Vaughan wistfulness. This corresponds to those moments at which we surface from a book and the world crowds in. God came to Moses and Job in personal theophany, 'in *fire,/ Whirl-winds*, and *clouds*, and the *soft voice*' (17-18) — but not now. Vaughan's voice takes on an ingenuous perplexity, wondering why this should be so. Grim symbolism of war creeps in, of broken 'truce' and cancelled 'treaties' between God and man. The poem ends in a powerful lament for the polluting of the church, run underground in the Interregnum, culminating in an expansion of metre and a great cry for renewal.

Henry Vaughan kept his Bible by his bed. He referred to it last thing at night and first thing on waking. One day, he knew, he would have to relinquish it; an uncomfortable thought, for, even though he would then be in the Eternity of which it spoke and there would theoretically be no need for the book, he could hardly imagine existence without it. The Bible bound his history together, linking it to his origins in childhood. As he nears the close of *Silex Scintillans II*, he pre-imagines the close both of his own life and that of his reading-life, in a sequence of three valedictory poems, 'The Book', 'To the Holy Bible' and 'L'Envoy'. The second lyric expresses the way in which a book can be loved as friend and companion. Addressed as 'thou' and spoken to intimately, it takes on a quietly active life which is understood to have intervened in his wayward career and been, in the most literal terms, a life-saver:

> O book! life's guide! how shall we part,
> And thou so long seized of my heart!
> Take this last kiss, and let me weep
> True thanks to thee, before I sleep.
>   Thou wert the first put in my hand,
> When yet I could not understand,
> And daily didst my young eyes lead
> To letters, till I learned to read.
>
> (1–8)

As a 'sacred parody' in the manner of Herbert, this poem redirects the familiar clichés of love-convention (here, the 'kissing and parting' trope) to a sacred subject. The first four lines have a threshold quality characteristic of Vaughan, between excess tending to absurdity and an almost painfully sincere intensity. There is a touch of Crashaw in the sexualisation of spirituality in the Dove's 'secret favours',' quickening kindness, smiles and kisses/ ... blisses,/ Fruition' (28-31). We cannot doubt that Vaughan's love of the Bible was so fervent that he would often be moved to kiss it — a species of behaviour repugnant to Puritans as savouring of the osculations of Catholic idolatry, worship of the representation rather than the represented. Vaughan was not ashamed of loving the paper, binding and the printer's ink on the page — the weight of the book in his hand, its particular smell and the very blemishes and mottlings that made it not just a copy but his copy. He loved the creatures that had been used to make it. Like most children of his period, he had been taught to read by spelling out the simpler passages of the Bible which stood *in loco matris* in the literary sphere. As the book of his childhood, the Bible therefore carries a deep emotional charge. Later, he recalls, he gave Scripture the slip, bolting from his 'nurse' (10) into the company of trashy reading matter, with fancy covers and novel ideas (10-15). This anathematised bibliography presumably includes the whole of world literature minus the Bible, a strict diet commended by Milton's Christ in *Paradise Regained* (IV. 334-64). Presumably Vaughan is thinking of his university period. Meanwhile, 'My first cheap book' (16) (held cheap by his callow self and a cheap way of owning a private library since it was viewed as an encyclopaedia) awaited its reader's return:

> And oft left open wouldst convey
> A sudden and most searching ray
> Into my soul, with whose quick touch
> Refining still, I struggled much.
> (19–22)

The Bible is viewed as angling a 'ray' of lucidity into the reader's soul, to 'refine' his impurities as he 'struggles' for meaning. The Bible is active; the reader passive until catalysed. This book 'searches' him; he does not research it. For the work of literature is in love with the reader and its *ars amatoria* undertakes the work not of *eros* but of *agape*, Charity, which extends as Grace from the Author to the reader. Ultimately the reader's defences being overcome, he is led home — that is, deeper into its text.

In Vaughan's day, Quakers and other Christians, including Milton, were placing the Bible in a secondary status, according priority to the inner light of the Spirit which, if it seemed to contradict Scripture, must be preferred. But Vaughan leaned absolutely on his life-guaranteeing Bible, with its assurance of peace in a fratricidal world. In its absence he would be bereft and even the prospect of Heaven might seem for an apprehensive moment less than Heavenly: 'Thy next *effects* no tongue can tell;/ Farewell O book of God! farewell!' (35-6). Part of Henry Vaughan's famous 'other-worldliness' consisted in the reclusive transcendence of life which is achieved with one's head in a book. The whole purpose of this life of prayer, meditation and reading was to move closer towards union with God. Vaughan never seems to have experienced the fulfilment of the mystic's quest in full union with the Deity. He reports neither the levitations, ecstasies nor hallucinations of St Teresa or Meister Eckhart.' It seemed to me,' wrote St Teresa, 'when I tried to make some resistance, as if a great force beneath my feet lifted me up. I know of nothing with which to compare it'(*U*, pp.376-7). Vaughan 'stuck' at the penultimate phase. The initial and often turbulent 'awakening' leads to 'purification' and 'illumination', that 'unitive' state of the psyche which is understood to be the soul's foretaste of union with her Beloved. The experience of 'illumination' in which Vaughan participated is painfully ambivalent, for the 'nearness' of the proximate God is also the remoteness of the absent God. On that threshold, incipient presence is also a withholding of presence. Christ is almost known — but not quite. And that 'not quite' means he might as well be a universe away. Near and far collapse their distinction; poles of desperate love and near-despair cross, and hope is betrayed in the moment of arousal. As in the Song of Songs, the Beloved always seems to have gone missing: 'my beloved had withdrawn himself, and was gone ... I sought him but I could not find him; I called him, but he gave me no answer' (Song of Songs 5:6). Vaughan's was the religion of Tantalus. He never knew the ecstasy of union which Crashaw celebrated in St Teresa ravished by the fiery arrows of the Seraphic archers: 'a sweet and subtle *paine*/ ... intollerable *joyes*/ ... a *death* in which who *dyes*/ Loves his *death*, and *dyes* againe' ('A Hymn to ... Saint Teresa', 98-101). Such orgasmic bliss of union was beyond the scope of Vaughan's experience; but he could record with melancholy integrity the search for the evasive God.

In the poem 'Love-Sick', Vaughan expresses with unparalleled urgency the frantic quality of his search to become one with his God — and the inexorable failure of the attempt. Surging rhythms and a violent heartbeat of stampeding alliterations, internal rhymes, assonances and repetitions in coupled words and phrases recall the Welsh *cynghanedd* tradition, especially the device of *dyfalu* (the running-on of appositional phrases which riddlingly elaborate an object or action in a sequence of vivid comparisons or analogues). Coupled and bonded words articulate the stress with which the poet's spirit rebels against his chain-linked condition of limitation. That urge towards transcendence which is the deepest passion Vaughan knows impels the desire to love more fully. But he recognises himself as poorly placed to perfect his love and yearns for the sublime license of a rising star, unfleshed, exalted:

> Jesus, my life! how shall I truly love thee?
> O that thy Spirit would so strongly move me,
> That thou wert pleased to shed thy grace so far
> As to make man all pure love, flesh a star!
> A star that would ne'er set, but ever rise,
> So rise and run, as to out-run these skies,
> These narrow skies (narrow to me) that bar,
> So bar me in, that I am still at war,
> At constant war with them. O come and rend,
> Or bow the heavens! Lord bow them and descend,
> And at thy presence make these mountains flow,
> These mountains of cold ice in me! Thou art
> Refining fire, O then refine my heart,
> My foul, foul heart! Thou art immortal heat,
> Heat motion gives; then warm it, till it beat,
> So beat for thee, till thou in mercy hear,
> So hear that thou must open: open to
> A sinful wretch, a wretch that caused thy woe,
> Thy woe, who caused his weal; so far his weal
> That thou forgott'st thine own, for thou didst seal
> Mine with thy blood, thy blood which makes thee mine,
> Mine ever, ever; and me ever thine.

The two-way impulse, at once pounding forward and retracting in internal rhyme, para-rhyme and assonance, is compounded in a verbal music which is at once a virtuoso technical exercise and a heart-felt expression of the double-bound condition of the human lover of a divine Beloved. 'Love-Sick' explores the possibilities and limitations of language as a reaching-out toward the transcendent in a closed system. Just as the universe is a sealed system, with God out there somewhere 'beyond', so language at its fullest extension strikes against and rebounds from its limits. The bounding soul cannot leap out of bounds.

In 'Love-Sick', the coupling of repeated and rhyming words within single lines grammatically retards the onward momentum of the sentences, setting up a dynamic struggle within the lines between the urge to go on and 'out-run these skies' and the constraints consequent upon detention within the word-order which always doubles back on itself. Hence the poet gathers energy for a grand leap in his wish to be 'A star that would ne'er set, but ever rise' and tries to take off in 'So rise and run', but seems to be running on the spot because he has repeated himself. Launching on the phrase 'as to out-run these skies', he bounds off in imagination towards 'These narrow skies', a noun in apposition which takes us nowhere except into the realm of irony. It should be an easy leap for a star. But the star is mere wish. The skies close on the speaker's fantasy of transcendence with the repetition of 'narrow', and the confines of his nature and its laws press against him. From 'narrow' he derives 'bar', and 'bar' begets 'war' against the boundaries of containment in the universe and separation from God. His high-flying space-odyssey boomerangs back to earth. Hence he calls out for Christ's intervention in an apocalyptic invocation: 'O come and rend,/ Or bow the heavens!' A new chain of coupled and repeated words assaults the gap: 'heart,/ My foul, foul heart', 'heat, heat', 'beat,/ So beat', 'hear,/ So hear'. The closed system must be made to 'open: open', to which end he reminds Christ of the passageway opened by the Atonement in which Christ's blood closes the gap between 'me' and 'Thee'. But the gap cannot in this life be closed.

Desire was a way of life. Indeed it was the principle on which the dynamics of Creation depended. The exquisite 'Cock-Crowing' compares the 'firm ... longing' of the rooster for the sun (14) with the magnetic attraction felt by man for God and expressed as 'A love-sick soul's exalted flight' (34). The universe of *Silex Scintillans* is charged with desire, down to the grass and stones beneath the poet's feet. Living in this Hermetic cosmos of mutual attractions which call from end to end of Creation, Vaughan is sensitively attuned to two-way influences of passionate attraction operating all around him. And in this force-field of vital sympathy, he experiences two oscillating moods, of estrangement and of inclusion. His own love ardently beckons and beacons to the remote Ardour which generated it in his own image. Night is his special time. In 'The Star', he looks up at the scintillations of light in the awareness that it is signalling to some affinity on earth. Further, he believes that the star is literally being moved by this fragment of perfection:

> What ever 'tis, whose beauty here below
> Attracts thee thus & makes thee stream & flow,

And wind, and curl, and wink and smile,
Shifting thy gate and guile ....
(1-4)

These typical Vaughan verbs 'stream ... flow ... wind ... curl ... wink ... smile' are all subject to the auxiliary 'makes': he admires the mystery whereby the lesser exercises power over the greater in a vitalistic universe not far removed from animism. Hermetism was the last hiding-place from the impersonal mechanist cosmos of modernity. Situated in this midnight recess, Vaughan could interpret his own sense of yearning by 'scientific' analogy as an incentive to the Creator to include him in the force-field of correspondences — in that 'commerce' which was such a precious word to Vaughan, since it represented a two-way conversation essential to his security and yet often in doubt. The lesson he can draw from the love-affair between the star and the lowly herb is:

For where desire, celestial, pure desire
Hath taken root, and grows, and doth not tire,
There God a commerce states, and sheds
His secret on their heads.
(25-8)

One-way conversations he dreaded; but here persuades himself that the greater the desire, and the more exhaustive its expression ('and doth not tire'), the more God is persuaded to enter into the same secret transaction with the lover as engages the plants and stars. Such dialogue was hard-won. For days or weeks on end all contact with God seemed lost. God seemed to turn his face away in an aversion which the lover must acknowledge as just (for he is sinful) but must try to coax or bargain away (for he is dependent). In 'Begging [II]', he presents his half of a dialogue with a silent other, opening with the blackmailing 'Aye, do not go! thou know'st, I'll die!'; in 'The Seed Growing Secretly', he cries out 'thy absence kills!' (6); in 'Anguish', he ends with a panic-attack: 'O my God, hear my cry;/ Or let me die! —' (19-20). The poem seems to react to a waning of the creative power, a doubt in the authenticity of the poetry he was labouring to compose — suggesting the profound importance of the act of writing to Vaughan in centring his spiritual experience. The exclamation of his love in words was a way 'To act as well as to conceive' (18). Bereft of its power to express the burning inner world, he was threatened with a frustration intimating total collapse.

In the night he either lay awake in bed in the house at Newton where his most passionate spiritual experiences were born, or walked out over the moonlit landscape. The skies above the Beacons are an immense dome, the Usk reflecting a trail of moonlight as do rain or dew on plants and grass; the dark bowl of the mountains would have harboured a stillness unknown to the city-dweller. It was a time of reverie in which he could contemplate without distraction and be open to the sense of Christ's immanent Being in the hills, trees and stars encircling him. Here too he was following in Jesus' footsteps, for, as he observed in *The Mount of Olives*, '*Christ* himself in the day-time taught and preach'd, but continued all night in prayer, sometimes in a Mountain apart, sometimes amongst the wild beasts, and sometimes in solitary places' (*HV*, p.143). Out of some such experience his most perfect poem, 'The Night', must have come. The poem is suffused with wonder and reverence; immaculately made in three groups of three stanzas whose six lines open on the page like pairs of wings — the wings of those nine orders of angels described by Dionysius the Areopagite, whose concept of 'the Divine Darkness' concludes the lyric. Nicodemus, the Pharisee whose eyes were opened by Jesus (John 3), appears in no other Gospel than John's. But there he appears three times, each time distinguished as 'he that came to Jesus by night' (7:50). He is one of the heart-shaking minor characters of the Gospel story, a shadowy figure like those witnesses who peer from the dark-brown obscurity of the sidelines of a sacred scene by Rembrandt or Honthorst, or move into a brief flare of light for a few significant actions. At his first visit rebirth is explained to him (3:5). He reappears to intervene on Jesus' behalf against his fellow Pharisees, who suspect him as a traitor to their caste (7:51-2). Finally and most movingly, he brings 'a mixture of myrrh and aloes' to anoint the body of Jesus after the crucifixion (19:39). These were the wise and loving actions of an undercover Christian, with complex and secret loyalties, who had the chance to witness in person the living temple of Christ's indwelling. Vaughan would have given his eyes for such vision. He conjures it in his poem:

John iii 2
Through that pure *Virgin-shrine,*
That sacred veil drawn o'er thy glorious noon

That men might look and live as glow-worms shine,
 And face the moon:
 Wise *Nicodemus* saw such light
 As made him know his God by night.

 Most blest believer he!
Who in that land of darkness and blind eyes
Thy long expected healing wings could see,
 When thou didst rise,
 And what can never more be done,
 Did at mid-night speak with the Sun!

 O who will tell me, where
He found thee at that dead and silent hour!
What hallowed solitary ground did bear
 So rare a flower,
 Within whose sacred leaves did lie
 The fullness of the Deity.
(1-18)

The tone is infinitely tender; the beauty of the sacred breathes from every line. Images of hiddenness and revelation, enclosure and disclosure haunt the poem, or rather hiddenness-which-is-revelation, enclosure-which-is-disclosure. In the matrix of the *'Virgin-shrine'*, Jesus' light appears to glow through the temple of his body as if filtered through the tabernacle of the Virgin's womb. A mysterious cosmology informs this imagery of incarnation. Sun appears as moon; son as mother, with possible Hermetic resonances (*Hermetica*, Lib. XIII, p.239). Nicodemus had uncomprehendingly asked Christ in his interview, 'How can a man be born when he is old? can he enter the second time into his mother's womb, and be born?' (3:4). Vaughan with tender irony seems to show Christ within the maternal body: birth imagery is re-echoed in the third stanza in which the speaker seeks the holy ground that 'did bear/ So rare a flower' (15-16) and repeats the sense of maternal enfolding of the beloved Lord 'Within ... sacred leaves' (17). The preposition 'within' centres the poem, which is a search for indwelling, spirit born into matter, so that we can be born from matter into spirit. An intense privacy covers the whole. For Nicodemus spoke with Jesus alone, hiddenly; and the speaker does not know how to find the birthplace of his Saviour. He too lives in a Pharisaical and garrisoned 'land of darkness and blind eyes', in a night as dead. He too must profess his faith in hiding. There exists no living tabernacle or temple to which he can go and be illumined with revelation. 'O who will tell me, where/ He found thee at that dead and silent hour!' (13-14). *Where*, out on a limb at the end of a line, searches into nothing for its point of attachment. Or rather, it searches into everywhere for a cosmic Christ:

> No mercy-seat of gold,
> No dead and dusty *Cherub*, nor carved stone,
> But his own living works did my Lord hold
> And lodge alone;
> Where *trees* and *herbs* did watch and peep
> And wonder, while the *Jews* did sleep.
>
> Dear night! this world's defeat;
> The stop to busy fools; care's check and curb;
> The day of Spirits; my soul's calm retreat
> Which none disturb!
> *Christ*'s progress, and his prayer time;
> The hours to which high Heaven doth chime.
>
> God's silent, searching flight;
> When my Lord's head is filled with dew, and all
> His locks are wet with the clear drops of night;
> His still, soft call;
> His knocking time; the soul's dumb watch,
> When Spirits their fair kindred catch.
>
> (19-36)

The abdication of the dead matter of synagogue or church is a Reformation rejection of the temple made with hands. Vaughan extends the temple to the whole creation. Christ gives birth to himself in nature and in the spirit of the believer, in a world-enfolding, self-unfolding process. Double grammar mimes the mutual inherence of Christ in nature, nature in Christ: when we read 'his own living works did my Lord hold/ And lodge alone', we at first suppose Christ held the works and lodged there alone; on a second reading, we decide that the works held and were sole lodging-place for Christ. Both would be right: they held him, he them. And if then, so now. Both Henry and Thomas Vaughan in their different ways were searching for the 'house of Light'. Each felt it could be found here and now, in nature, for in Thomas' words, 'Matter ... is the *House* of *Light*, here hee *dwells* and *builds* for himself ... hee takes up his *lodging* in *sight* of all the *World*' (*Aula Lucis, TV*, p.468). But where is it exactly, and how do we get at it?:

> of itself it is so *thin* and *spirituall*, wee can not lay *hands* upon it, and make it our *Possession*. We cannot *confine* it to any *one* place, that it may no more *rise*, and *set* with the *Sunne*; wee cannot *shut* it up in a *Cabinet*, that wee may *use* it when we *please*, and in the darkest *Night* see a glorious *Illustration*.
>
> (*TV*, pp.471-2)

This parallel elucidates the extent to which Henry and Thomas Vaughan were engaged on different versions of a physical search for the immanent Divine Light, Thomas through mystical science, Henry through contemplation. But Henry's search is passive rather than penetrative. An attitude of listening stillness develops through the poem, leading to the threshold state of the incomparably beautiful sixth verse with its intimation of beloved presence and nearness. If Christ inheres in nature, then the world has become his countenance, the great dew-starred, star-beaded nightscape his flowing locks, the night breeze his living breath. There is no main verb: the *dyfalu* form cedes all control to God-in-nature, whose 'still, soft call;/ His knocking time' seems to speak into the suspenses of the poem from the timeless world.

It cannot last. Time awakens, and the 'dark Tent', the tabernacle of indwelling, is swept away. Noise shouts it down as society resumes its loud pursuits. Norms that are really aberrations return with daylight that is really darkness, and the speaker pitches about with the rest. He ends by a desire for abdication into the Dionysian 'Divine Dark', a kind of re-encapsulation into the maternal body of God (*U*, p.347; *TV*, p.328):

> There is in God (some say)
> A deep, but dazzling darkness; as men here
> Say it is late and dusky, because they
> See not all clear;
> O for that night! where I in him
> Might live invisible and dim.
>
> (49-54)

From Christ's hiddenness he moves to his own disappearance.

Reversing the opening paradox of Christ's inherence within the Creation, he tentatively withdraws his imagination from the Creation and directs it into the core of Christ's light, so bright that it is experienced as its own opposite. For Vaughan the route to this Light could lead only through Llansantffraed Churchyard.

Five:
'Who Taught The Spider His Mathematicks?'

Will there be spiders in Heaven? Can we expect to see perfected blackbirds and thrushes nesting in the branches of the Tree of Life and to hear incorruptible frogs croaking their Redeemer's praises in the brooks of the next world? Will all cloven worms, both the genus *Lumbricus* and the human kind, be restored to their original unity and made to shine like glow-worms in the final light which renders all translucent? To these questions, laughable to those who trust to the anthropocentric prejudice known as 'common-sense' by *homo sapiens*, both Henry and Thomas Vaughan would have answered a heartfelt 'yes'. Thomas wanted to know from those who disparaged nature as low and corrupt '*who taught* the *spider* his *Mathematicks*?' and who had imbued the hare with an instinct that was in no sense hare-brained, to double-track and increase stride so as to elude predators? (*Anima Magica Abscondita, TV*, p.112). God is architect, 'chymist' and mathematician of nature. Having clothed the lilies of the field so that 'Solomon in all his glory was not arrayed like one of these', he is aware of every sparrow's fall (p.113: Matthew 6:28-30; 10:29). For Thomas, the creatures all display sparks of intelligence planted in them by their Creator and the labyrinthine elegance of the spider's purposeful web is in itself a demonstration of God's extension of his own wisdom into nature:

> Certainly this is a *well order'd policy*, enough to prove that *God* is not *absent* from his *Creatures* but that *Wisdom reacheth mightily from one end to another*, and that *his Incorruptible spirit filleth all things*. (p.112)

Thomas advised those readers who were serious in their desire to discover the secret magic instilled into nature to study indoors during the winter with the benefit of 'Fumigations and *spicie Lamps*', a kind of joss-stick study-aid believed to arouse the 'animal spirits' in the brain. But the return of clement weather should take the student out-of-doors:

> In the *Summer*, translate thy self to the Fields, where all are green with the Breath of God, and fresh with the Powers of Heaven. Learn to refer all Naturals to their Spirituals ... Sometimes Thou may'st walk in *Groves*, which being full of *Majestie* will much *advance* the *Soul*. Sometimes by *clear, Active Rivers* .... So Have I spent on the Banks of *Ysca* many a serious Hour. (p. 135)

Then he prints his lovely contemplation-poem beginning ''Tis Day, my Chrystal *Usk*' in which the reader is taught how to read the spiritual meanings of the book of Nature: 'I'm amaz'd to see/ What a *Clear Type* thou art of *Pietie*' (p.136). When we follow in the footsteps of Henry and Thomas Vaughan beside the River Usk as it curves through the wide plain between the mountains, we find it still 'Chrystal' in some lights — a 'Chrystal' which for Thomas did not merely mirror Heaven at one remove but was a flowing-out of God, just as flowers were his efflorescence and the sunlight his radiation. The green of the fields into which Thomas encourages us to come, throwing off our indoor stupor and staleness, was an exhalation of the Creator. God's works everywhere manifested his indwelling and the microscopic was an essential and valued part of his great temple of light, colour, sound, scent, motion and texture. Ponder a simple stone and its magnetic attraction draws you home to God. But taking this spiritual compass-direction does not entail leaving the stone behind. The stone is valuable in itself; the spider; the fern; dust and ashes. Clay ourselves, we are in a unique condition to admire God's chemistry in the laboratory crucible of the Creation.

The sense of wonder in the ordinary which both Thomas and Henry express is akin to Blake's reverence for the universe. The world is:

> a World of Imagination & Vision ... The tree which moves some to tears of joy is in the Eyes of others only a Green thing which stands in the way. Some see Nature all Ridicule & Deformity, &

> by these I shall not regulate my proportions; & some scarce see Nature at all. But to the Eyes of a Man of Imagination, Nature is Imagination itself. As a man is, so he sees. As the Eye is formed, such are its Powers.
>
> (Letter to Revd. Dr. Tusler, 23 August 1799)

Blake, deriving inspiration from Jacob Boehme, was close to seventeenth century mysticism's sacramental sense of Nature. That tree 'which moves some to tears of joy' is made of the same wood as that of Henry Vaughan's requiem 'The Timber'. During the Interregnum, few people were interested in trees, beyond their use as firewood and for carpentry, except for a minority of extreme radicals who believed, like Lawrence Clarkson in his Ranter period, that God was in all living things and all matter. Such doctrines lay on a perilous edge with blasphemies punishable under the Blasphemy Act of 1650 (*Hill* [1975], p.208). Pantheism, materialism and the denial of the transcendence of God informed radical heresies such as those described by John Holland in *Smoke of the Bottomlesse Pit* (1651): 'They maintain that God is essentially in every creature ... the essence of God was as much in the Ivie leaf, as in the most glorious Angel'. Jacob Bauthumley was punished by being burned through the tongue for writing:

> Nay, I see that God is in all Creatures, Man and Beast, Fish and Fowle, and every green thing, from the highest Cedar to the Ivey on the wall; and that God is the life and being of them all, and that God doth really dwell, and if you will personally ... and hath his Being no where else but in the Creatures ....
>
> (*The Light and Dark sides of God* (1650), *Cohn* [1957], pp.322,336)

The belief that God does not exist outside the creatures is next door to the ideology embraced by Gerrard Winstanley that if Christ is in us, we are Christ. The extreme of this view was denial of the reality of sin, Heaven and Hell and the afterlife. Thomas Vaughan's knowledge that he appeared to be on an ambiguous path no doubt contributed to the noisy apologetics of the 1650 tracts. His belief in the refining of nature so that the dross of corruption was purged off looked suspiciously like the Family of Love and the Grindletonians' belief that prelapsarian perfection could be attained in this life. The recondite magical works on which he relied were deeply associated with the revolutionary meliorism of his enemies, the works of

Hermes Trismegistus and other mystical writers having been translated by the heretical John Everard (*KT*, pp.270-1, 375). Thomas Vaughan was orthodox on sin, the established church, the afterlife, Heaven and Hell. On nature he was wildly controversial. In *Magia Adamica* (1650) he defined magic as 'nothing else but the *Wisdom* of the *Creator* revealed and planted in the *Creature*' (*TV*, p.150) and went on to a wily demonstration that its '*Signes*' were parallel to Church of England ritual symbolism (p.153).

Henry's Hermetic experimentalism was inner and spiritual rather than forensic and chemical, and he seems to have doubted the credibility of technical research in the light of the inscrutability of the Creator. His daily exercise of 'meditation upon the creatures' was performed in the spirit of Thomas's insistence that 'man stands in *Nature*, not above it' (*Euphrates*, *TV*, p.519). Thomas believed that the desire for knowledge of nature is innate and God-given: we are born greedy for understanding. He had observed the behaviour of very young children, who do not simply finger new objects but will introduce them into their mouths, in order to answer the question, 'What is it?' He accurately diagnosed these actions not as, in the first instance, play, but as curiosity (*Magia Adamica*, *TV*, p.144). Thomas labelled children's desire for knowledge 'the *Best* and most *mysterious part* of their *Nature*' (p.144). He was clear that God would never have planted in man 'a *Desire* to *know*, and yet *deny* him *Knowledge* it self' (p.145). Henry was not so sure. The poem 'Vanity of Spirit' ironises his own quest for knowledge as an obsession leading to the extinction of what little light we have. The search through nature involves a penetration of 'her' secrets which shatters what it measures:

> I summoned nature: pierced through all her store,
> Broke up some seals, which none had touched before,
> Her womb, her bosom, and her head
> Where all her secrets lay a bed
> I rifled quite, and having passed
> Through all the creatures, came at last
> To search my self, where I did find
> Traces, and sounds of a strange kind.
> (9–16)

A passage from Thomas's *Anima Magica Abscondita* is invariably but mistakenly cited to gloss this: 'But me thinks Nature complaines of a Prostitution, that I goe about to diminish her Majesty, having allmost broken her Seale, and exposed her naked to the World' (*TV*, p.111). For whereas Henry radically questions the ethic of scientific enquiry as a rape on a God-made sanctum, Thomas merely draws back from casting his pearls (the arcana of his trade) before swine (us): 'I must confesse I have gone very far, and now I must recall my selfe: For there is a necessity of reserving, as well as publishing some things ....' (p.111). Occult philosophy was the prerogative of an intellectual and spiritual élite: for this reason its language is intentionally cryptic. Its power to mystify guarantees the secrecy which is the basis of its fascination and the adept's authority. But Henry's qualm is with the provenance of scientific enquiry itself. In his own case, it rebounded into the Socratic obligation of self-scrutiny ('To search my self'[15]), on the basis that the self bears the image of God. He distrusted the pride latent in the *Hermetica*'s view that 'man is a being of divine nature ... a mortal god' (*Lib* X, p. 205). The image was too flawed. In 'Vanity of Spirit', he records that his conscious attempt to reconstruct unity from 'dismembered' hieroglyphs, though initially successful, has been counter-productive in obliterating the original intuition. Yet there are aspects of Hermetism which must have spoken to his temperament at a deep level. The *Hermetica* insists on God's universal immanence and accessibility:

> Everywhere God will come to meet you, everywhere he will appear to you, at places and times at which you look not for it, in your waking hours and in your sleep, when you are journeying by water and by land ... for there is nothing which is not God. And do you say 'God is invisible'? Speak not so. Who is more manifest than God?
>
> (*Lib.* XI, p.223)

The spirit only has to be receptive to receive God's presence. Rebirth delivers one into that diffusive presence by dissolving the boundaries of the self:

> I see myself to be the All. I am in heaven and in earth, in water and air; I am in beasts and plants; I am a babe in the womb, and one that is not yet conceived, and one that has been born; I am present everywhere ...
>
> (*Lib.* XIII, p.247)

says the initiate. We recognise here Henry's moving capacity to open himself to the being of other creatures in 'negative capability'. Though Henry knew enough practical alchemy to distil potions for his patients, his Hermetism did not take the form of science-mania but in the charting of the ups and downs of his soul's mercury, and witnessing the biochemical and astronomical wonders performed by the Creator between the Beacons and the Black Mountains.

St Francis of Assisi referred to the birds and animals as 'brother' and 'sister'. Meister Eckhart felt that, if one could understand just one flower 'as it has its Being in God', such knowledge would outweigh all other. Jacob Boehme sat out in the fields amazed to divine the transcendent beauty of mere grass (*U*, pp.255-6). Acute sensuous perception of natural beauty can be fed by sensual deprivation and the austere routines of a devout life. Henry Vaughan's sensitivity to the beauty of nature was in this tradition. Its theoretical foundation lay in the principles Thomas formulates rather beautifully in *Euphrates*:

> We must not therefore *confine* this *Restitution* to our own *Species* .... If it be true that *man* hath a Saviour, it is also as true, that the whole Creation hath the same .... And if it be true that we look for the *Redemption* of our *Bodies*, and a *New man*: It is equally true, that we look for a *New Heaven*, and a *New Earth*, wherein dwelleth Righteousness: for it is not Man alone, that is to be *Renued* at the general *Restauration*, but even the *world*, as well as *Man*, as it is written, *Behold! I make all things New* .... I speak this to shew, that God minds the *Restitution* of *Nature* in general, and not of *Man alone*, who though he be the noblest part, yet certainly is but a small part of Nature.
>
> (*TV*, p.518)

This belief in a mesh of being in which seeds, dogs, snails, trees and stars belong intrinsically together and from which man cannot be analysed out, to inhabit an estate of spiritual privilege, is a threat to the humanist eminence of 'man the measure of all things'. But it also offers a comforting vision of the world as an unbroken continuum of creaturely life. It allowed Henry Vaughan to love nature with uninhibited tenderness and released him into that characteristic empathy in which he could identify with birds, stones and trees. Hermetism placed a high spiritual value on imagination, for if the creation was the projection of God's imagination, then it followed that the God-given human imagination was the way through to reality. Vaughan's nature poetry suggests a new beatitude: 'Blessed are the imaginative for they already see God'.

Certainly, he thought so, lying awake on his bed in Newton as dawn rose outside his window and the morning chorus reached symphonic proportions. Anyone who has listened in knows how it issues out of the dark silence as the occasional exploratory cadence of a waking bird attesting to the hint of new light, to which more voices join, until the whole air reverberates with birdsong. The clamour can be tremendous, especially in a wooded country area, where the listener is aware of sounds of water and wind providing a continuo to the crescendo of sound. In Vaughan's 'The Morning-Watch' the sensual climax of sound is felt as almost unbearably pleasurable:

> O joys! Infinite sweetness! with what flowers
> And shoots of glory, my soul breaks, and buds!
> All the long hours
> Of night, and rest
> Through the still shrouds
> Of sleep, and clouds,
> This dew fell on my breast;
> O how it *bloods*,
> And *spirits* all my earth! hark! in what rings,
> And *hymning circulations* the quick world
> Awakes, and sings;
> The rising winds,
> And falling springs,
> Birds, beasts, all things
> Adore him in their kinds.
> Thus all is hurled
> In sacred *hymns*, and *order*, the great *chime*
> And *symphony* of nature.
>
> (1-18)

The poem, which is shaped in regular alternations of two long and six short lines, varied in the fifth short line by a foot, is not divided into stanzas. It can be analysed into nine sections (counting each unit of long and short lines as a section), to improvise a system of angelic hierarchies, crosses, or a ladder, upon which the poet can paradoxically 'climb/ When I lie down' (23-4). But the lyric protests against this anatomising tendency by every metrical device the lyricist can invoke. The natural 'order' which the poem praises and enacts is composed of a swirling pattern of perpetual flow in which rhyme and assonantal rhyme ('flower/ hours/ shrouds/ clouds/ blood'; 'rings/ sings/ winds/ springs/ things') keep the sounds circulating in our inner ear in a system of rhythmic echoes. Vaughan is well-known for his imperfect rhymes, which are variously attributed to Welsh pronunciation or slapdash disregard of the rules. For me, these imperfect rhymes are exactly right to express the '*symphony* of nature', the imperfect creatures' perfect impromptu. Vaughan's own rhapsodic tone, abandoned to the ecstasy of those far-flung voices in fugue to their Creator, breaks out in exclamation: 'O joys! ... O how it *bloods* ... In what rings ... O let me climb'. Yet the tumult of energy which opens the poem subsides in the second half. This is why most people who quote from the poem cut it off at the point I have done. This anti-climax, a common effect in a variable poet like Vaughan, is also a measure of the built-in limitation of the mystic life. I hope it is not irreverent to call the poem's energy orgasmic. This is implied in the powerfully transitive use of the verbs '*bloods*' and '*spirits*': the passive poet is aroused to a passion generated by the vital spirits released from the circulating blood, as the music vibrates in the inner chamber of the ear and through the body. This passion at second hand is then relayed to the reader. The whirling motion of planets, cycles of day, 'rings' of sound and reeving-on of lines all work to '*blood*' and '*spirit*' us with a version of the same patterned delirium of praise. Yet the poet always lies apart and sequestered. He eavesdrops on what is going on out there under his own eaves perhaps, and his nocturnal meditations take place in 'my bed/ That curtained grave' of the last couplet (31-2). The joy exhaled in the opening line is not faked, yet it is highly rhetorical, and has erupted from a sombre enclosure in which the speaker must nightly (in sleep) and ultimately (in death) give up the ghost. 'The Morning-Watch' is immediately followed in *Silex Scintillans* by the companion-piece, 'The Evening-Watch', a dialogue between soul and body instinct with sleep-resisting unease.

The first line of 'The Morning-Watch' varies upon the first line of Herbert's 'The Holy Scriptures [I]': 'O book! infinite sweetness!' For the Book of God it substitutes the Book of Nature. Thomas Vaughan's life's-work had been devoted to the attempt to prove the essential '*Harmonie* between *Nature* and the *Gospel*' (*Magia Adamica*, TV, p.185). Nature's hieroglyphic inscriptions must be read as typifying spiritual truths, like a living emblem-book. The reader of Nature saw both likeness and unlikeness to ourselves in this vital book, whose facing pages might spell out opposite perspectives. In that Nature was better than man (more holy and innocent) it could teach us a pattern of ideal behaviour; in that it was in the same boat (an Ark of corruption in need of regeneration), it spoke poignantly to the human condition. Thomas tended to the idealist perception; Henry to a tense conflict of idealism and pessimism. Hence, Thomas in ''Tis *Day*, my Chrystal Usk' derives lessons in metaphysics, purity, simplicity of life, plainness of dress, generosity to the poor, from the river. 'All This from *Thee* my *Ysca*?' he burbles, and of course replies 'yes, and *more*:/ I am for many *Vertues* on thy score' (*Anima Magica Abscondita, TV*, pp.136-7). In Henry's nature-poetry the picture is more complex and stressful. A double attitude to Nature parallels a double attitude to himself. In 'The Shower', whose 'drowsy lake' may refer to Llangorse Lake, four miles from Newton, Vaughan observes the cycle of evaporation and condensation in the exhalation of 'sick waters' (3) which aspire to a heaven too pure for them, and drop confounded back to earth: 'Thou fall'st in tears, and weep'st for thy mistake./ Ah! it is so with me ...' (5-7). Here the meteorology of a corrupted nature is sadly equivalent to that of the half-hearted prayers of a degenerate heart. Nature is all too like man. But that profound act of self-understanding, 'The Storm', places man (as so often with Vaughan) outside the logic of cause and effect which determines the natural order. Vaughan here confesses his pathological inability to keep calm, even when no external provocation exists, and from study of a river in torrent gives us a vivid picture of a mind uncontrollably at odds within itself. He is like nature in turbulence; unlike it in the arbitrariness of his tidal moods:

> I see the use: and know my blood
> Is not a sea,
> But a shallow, bounded flood
> Though red as he;
> Yet have I flows, as strong as his,
> And boiling streams that rave
> With the same curling force, and hiss,
> As doth the mountained wave.
>
> But when his waters billow thus,
> Dark storms, and wind

> Incite them to that fierce discuss,
> Else not inclined,
> Thus the enlarged, enraged air
> Uncalms these to a flood,
> But still the weather that's most fair
> Breeds tempests in my blood.
> (1-16)

In the third and final stanza, the speaker solicits a spiritual storm to allay the incontinence which fair weather only seems to exacerbate (17-23). The expressive power of Vaughan's participial adjectives ('boiling streams ... curling force ... mountained wave ... enlarged, enraged air') unites verb with epithet to generate the impact of a river in full flood, tempest at sea and a mind at odds with itself. Sound-effects ('rave ... hiss') unite with personification (the flood is 'he') and highly-wrought sound-patterning: 'enlarged' and 'enraged' are near-anagrams, which imply and deny one another in the 'fierce discuss' of the words on the page. 'Mountained' is an example of a grammatical sleight so familiar in Shakespeare and Milton, known as zero-morpheme derivation (*Davies* [1991], pp.42ff., 128), whereby, in this case, a noun is used as a verb (but by further shift, the verb is cited as a participial adjective). The stable and immovable object (a mountain) is thus fetched from its foundations and surges into flux ('to mountain', thence, 'to be mountained') in a grammar of disturbance at once concise and sublime. But if nature's turmoils resemble a disquietened mind, the speaker's throes are essentially mindless and delinquent — unmotivated, purposeless. They issue from a man who experienced himself and reproduced himself on the page as constitutionally driven and disorderly, and hence outside the order of nature. He tempers his frantic inner world through poetic form and by metaphor which allows a realignment with nature through typology: 'I see the use'.

It is ironically fitting that 'The Storm' has whipped up a minor critical storm of its own. Louise Guiney felt that 'use' must be a printer's error for 'Usk', and Gwenllian Morgan agreed. She kept her eye on the Usk for signs of redness, writing to her colleague in 1907 that 'There have been the reddest of red floods in the Usk: I never saw him redder .... In Welsh rivers are masculine' (*HV*, pp.733-4n.). In 1947, Sir Edward Marsh also proposed this emendation. As late as 1980 Geoffrey Grigson, anthologising it in *The Faber Book of Poems and Places*, printed:

I see the Usk, and know my blood
  Is not a Sea ....

on the grounds that 'use' makes poor sense. 'Usk' makes good sense and clarifies the fourth line. Vaughan compares his blood with the Usk which flows down through a red sandstone soil, and turns red in spate' (p.377n.). On such grounds as this, we might all prefer Vaughan to have written in 'The Shower': ''Tis so, I saw thy birth: Llangorse Lake ...'. But such picturesque local specificity is foreign to *Silex Scintillans*. The Silurist was not silurising as he had done in *Olor Iscanus* where classicisation of the Usk in 'To the River Isca' has perversely little to tell us about Vaughan's father-river. The poems of *Silex*, though they breathe the fresh air of mountain and river, refrain from direct reference to particular Welsh places. Miss Morgan kept vigil on the banks of the incarnadine Usk because she and Miss Guiney related their poet so deeply to the scenes of his experience, and because they wished to make sense of a rather refractory poem. Martin, in his edition, dismissed the 'red Usk' theory because ' "use" ... makes good sense with the obsolete meaning of a moral or application' (ibid).

At a first, second and even third reading, 'The Storm' may not actually make perfect sense to a reader, who (having decided between 'Usk' and 'use' — and surely 'use' is definitive) goes on to stagger at '*not* a sea' and fall flat at 'he'. As in so many of Vaughan's poems, the field of reference confounds before it enlightens the reader. Does 'he' refer to the sea or a river? If the poet is 'not a sea', why is the sea so powerfully evoked in place of the river? This indeterminacy is intrinsic to the meaning of the poems. When Vaughan says, ''Twas so, I saw thy birth: that drowsy lake ...', we are meant to ask, 'What was "so"? Who is "thy"? and in what sense "birth"? which lake is "that", and how can a lake be "drowsy"?' The problematic openness of these questions creates an instability proper to the shifting and soliloquistic ground upon which the speaker is standing — no ground at all in 'The Storm', but a waste of waters. The disorientated poet of *Silex Scintillans* passes on his vertigo by disorientating the reader. This instability of footing is an important aspect of our journey back to the landscape and mindscape of Henry Vaughan in the 1640s and '50s. He mourned it in 'Man', where he contrasted the instinctual life-cycle of bird, bee and flower. If a bird is a natural 'clock' which knows the time to mate, sleep, migrate, man's rootless search, 'restless and irregular', came down in an unusual industrial metaphor to no more than the 'winding quest' of a shuttle in a loom, to no end (17, 26-8).

But it is typical of Vaughan that he could transform his nightmare to a dream of endless motion. Thomas perhaps supplied the wherewithal. He shared the temperament and knew, not the cure, but how to glorify the symptoms. His Hermetism saw nature as eternal process, constantly reaching beyond herself to infinite variability of invention (*Magia Adamica, TV*, p.203). The prime matter existed in a 'restlesse' state of '*subtil perpetual Motion*', creating endless individualities rather than cloning replications in a set catalogue. Thomas quotes Hermes Trismegistus' pronouncement '*That Action was the Life of God*' (p.203) to authorise his embrace of a dynamic and kinetic model of nature. Under this lens, instability could be seen as literally magical; it was the very stuff of creativity. Henry seized on this dynamism both as an ethic and an aesthetic in 'Affliction [I]':

Beauty consists in colours; and that's best
  Which is not fixed, but flies, and flows;
The settled *red* is dull, and *whites* that rest
  Something of sickness would disclose.
      Vicissitude plays all the game,
        Nothing that stirs,
        Or hath a name,
      But waits upon this wheel ....
(25-32)

Henry has been trying to persuade his reader (and perhaps himself) that affliction is 'the great *elixir*' of a restorative cordial (4). For twenty-four lines the poem is sententiously parsonical: then it shakes free into the delighted vagrancy of these irregularly-measured lines. Here a word which would normally induce anxiety — 'Vicissitude' — is liberated from negative implications; conversely, comfort-words like 'fixed', 'settled' and 'rest' denounce themselves as restrictive and comatose; words signifying free motion stream out in a fast ripple of alliteration and assonance ('not fixed, but flies, and flows'). The verse corkscrews from long lines to a whirl of short lines (30-1), the hub of this wheel of exhilaration. Readers are invited to experience the release which comes when we stop resisting the current and, going with it, find ourselves buoyant after all. So also Vaughan's imagination could 'fly' and 'flow' from the graveyard of suppressions into the elements of nature.

He did not propose to waste time wondering 'why the first *believer*/ Did love to be a country liver' ('Retirement [II]', 3-4). It was obvious. In contrast to the polluted city (18-20), with its insanitary conditions, civil strife and over-population, as well as its spiritual dereliction, the countryside remembered Eden in every detail. The spirit of God was at home there and, refreshingly, 'the *Dove*/ Duly as *dew*' brought down her peace with every morning (25-6). 'Duly' and '*dew*' pun on '*duw*', the Welsh word for 'God'. Milton was to show Eden driven out to sea, in the wake of man's fall:

> With all his verdure spoiled, and trees adrift
> Down the great river to the opening gulf,
> And there take root an island salt and bare,
> The haunt of seals and orcs, and sea-mews' clang.
> (*Paradise Lost* XI. 832-5).

But Vaughan in a situation nearly as blighted felt that Paradise had not been entirely withdrawn, so that 'If *Eden* be on earth at all,/ 'Tis that, which we the *country* call' (27-8). In such poems it is easy to imagine that he had just come indoors, taken off his boots and picked up his pen to write: such an outdoor freshness seems transmitted to the page and the brisk couplets speak with an assured and artfully spontaneous naïveté of 'Fresh *fields* and *woods*', rains, mists, fields, flowers, hills, sky and planets. Believing comes naturally in these surroundings and the way of Abraham is more than good enough for a latterday believer.

Henry Vaughan observed his fellow-creatures with moving empathy. He not only felt for them but imagined what it must be like to be them. 'The Bird' and 'The Timber' are printed successively in *Silex II*. In tender cadences, protective and concerned, Vaughan addresses the bird, after a night of savage weather which the vulnerable creature seems scarcely equipped to survive; but Vaughan has heard it tuning up in the morning, presumably just outside his bedroom window. We are aware in 'The Bird' primarily of a certain tone, which is pure Vaughan and cannot be emulated, a quiet dwelling-upon the creature in an extension of imaginative fellowship toward the life of the other. If tenderness is sanctity, then this is a sacred poem. Jesus told us to love our neighbour as ourselves. But who is my neighbour? Is a bird my neighbour? a tree? Henry

Vaughan apparently found it easier to fulfil Christ's commandment in relation to the supposedly 'lower' species than with his fellow men; sequestering himself from society, he backs away into the green world to find there fitter company. This bird is not singing for worms, mate, territory, but, in accordance with the Vaughans' theory of natural philosophy, it sings hymns of praise to the Creator who has preserved it through the night:

Hither thou com'st: the busy wind all night
Blew through thy lodging, where thy own warm wing
Thy pillow was. Many a sullen storm
(For which course man seems much the fitter born,)
    Rained on thy bed
    And harmless head.

And now as fresh and cheerful as the light
Thy little heart in early hymns doth sing
Unto that *Providence*, whose unseen arm
Curbed them, and clothed thee well and warm.
    All things that be, praise him; and had
    Their lesson taught them, when first made.

So hills and valleys into singing break,
And though poor stones have neither speech nor tongue,
While active winds and streams both run and speak,
Yet stones are deep in admiration.
    Thus praise and prayer here beneath the sun
    Make lesser mornings, when the great are done.

For each enclosèd spirit is a star,
    Enlightening his own little sphere,
Whose light, though fetched and borrowed from far,
    Both mornings makes, and evenings there.
(1-22)

The bird is an immemorial emblem of the human spirit, from Plato's 'winged soul' of the *Phaedrus* to Marvell's soul-bird singing on the bough of his 'green thought in a green Shade', that 'Waves in its plumes the various Light' ('The Garden', 48, 56). To make this comparison is to show how far Vaughan's creature is from the bird of culture, which, like some origami fabrication, has been constructed from paper and flies only between books. For Vaughan intuits a real bird, not a metaphor. It could die. Apprehended through the senses, it is welcomed with a tender surprise into proximity with human territory: 'Hither thou com'st'. This bird is exposed to the elements in a rough pastoral where wind can blow right 'through thy lodging', its home-made shelter of woven twigs. But in the morning it chirps up, proving the God-given adequacy of its fledged wings to withstand the violence of the storm. Vaughan moves from his initial sense of the creature's frailty (an implicit criticism of the Creator) to a comprehension of the environmental balance between 'Curbed' storm and 'clothed' bird. But the hymning bird has always instinctively known these things better than the poet: even stones know better than poets and are not 'poor stones' at all, for their unconscious life is nothing but abstract meditation (14-16). In the fourth verse, the principle by which the universe emanates praise is explained: all creatures are instinct with spirit, the star-fire which sparks the soul of each, and all. But by this point, Vaughan is leaving the bird behind: only the repeated 'little' reminds us of the 'little heart' of the second stanza. With the introduction of ugly and allegorical 'dark fowls' in the fifth stanza, our bird is flown: the poem is over for us.

This sense of lyrical breakdown can be the cost of the formal structure of 'meditation upon the creatures' which moves from the realisation of the creature's qualities and dimensions to a contemplation of their divine meaning and application. An analogous difficulty is sometimes felt with Hopkins's nature-poetry, shaped by the same Ignatian meditation exercise: the secular reader cannot help but remember the thrush that 'Through the echoing timber does so rinse and wring/ The ear, it strikes like lightnings to hear him sing' ('Spring', 4-5), but willingly forgets 'Innocent mind and Mayday in girl and boy' (13). A more painful example occurs in 'The Timber', which opens with five stanzas of poetry so perfect that to have written only these twenty lines would have earned a place in literary history; and moves to an analysis of extraordinary bathos:

> Sure thou didst flourish once! and many springs,
> Many bright mornings, much dew, many showers
> Passed o'er thy head: many light *hearts* and *wings*
> Which now are dead, lodged in thy living bowers.
>
> And still a new succession sings and flies;
> Fresh groves grow up, and their green branches shoot

Towards the old and still enduring skies,
While the low *violet* thrives at their root.

But thou beneath the sad and heavy *line*
Of death, dost waste all senseless, cold and dark;
Where not so much as dreams of light may shine,
Nor any thought of greenness, leaf or bark.

And yet (as if some deep hate and dissent,
Bred in thy growth betwixt high winds and thee,
Were still alive) thou dost great storms resent
Before they come, and know'st how near they be.

Else all at rest thou liest, and the fierce breath
Of tempests can no more disturb thy ease;
But this thy strange resentment after death
Means only those who broke (in life) thy peace.

So murdered man ....

(1-21)

At the point of the allegorising 'turn' at 'So murdered man...', Vaughan loses his tree, and indeed in due course his entire drift, moralising sententiously and apparently unable to bring himself to terminate the poem, which runs to fifty-six lines. As the dead tree is sensitive to impending storm, so a dead victim is said to detect his murderer and the sinner to detest his sin. At the fifty-first line, the speaker vaguely plants 'trees of life' in his meanderings as if to compensate for the sap the lyric has lost. Probably many readers elect to read the first five stanzas as a requiem in its own right. They are capable of standing alone and make perfect sense in themselves, breathing an inspiration which is primary in Vaughan and inseparable from his childhood — a green inspiration which is full of love for rooted things.

Such love, bonding human beings to trees, is archetypally rooted in the mythology and poetry in all cultures. It is especially significant that 'The Timber' is an elegy: it stands with the requiems for William and with the 'Childhood' poems, recording the loss of an ancient home and shelter for generations of winged creatures. In this sense, the irreplaceable tree, like the Vaughan oak at Newton, is ancestral. The first verse records the cycles of season and procreation which the tree sustained — a fivefold 'many' in a mere three lines (1-3), which mimes the mortal brevity of the life-cycle both of habitat and tenants. Vaughan has chosen a gravely regular iambic quatrain for his requiem, with no virtuoso effects or variations. He tunes and turns it with eloquent restraint, so that first we view the 'light *hearts* and *wings*' ('light' meaning 'wellnigh weightless' to the great tree; 'not dark'; 'light-hearted' too) before the eye backtracks and moves down to the beginning of the next line, to encounter the sombre 'Which now are dead'. The second stanza emphasises the continuity of nature in 'a new succession' of nestlings and saplings, linking the ancient skies above with the exquisite detail of the 'low violet' (itself an emblem of beauty's evanescence) in the shelter of their roots. These lines are no comfort: a rueful knowledge is rooted in the poem that all growth is terminal, whether long-lived or short-lived. The dark corpse of the down tree rots at their base, where 'dreams of light' and 'thought of greenness' cannot penetrate, only the apparent premonitory quiver of the trunk before storms (its old antagonists) hit the forest. The tender dignity in the voice of the eyewitness who tells these things haunts us with the dignity of the great tree it laments.

Thomas Vaughan possessed a theory of recycling on which Henry may have drawn for 'The Timber'. In *Magia Adamica,* Thomas demands rhetorically,

> Is there any thing lost since the Creation? .... All things return to that *place* from which they *came,* and that very *place* is *Earth*.... What becomes of her *Grasse,* her *Corne,* her *Herbs,* her *Flowers*? True it is, both *Man* and *beast* doe use them, but this onely by the way, for they rest not till they come to *Earth* again.
>
> (*TV*, p.201).

Death, says the *Hermetica,* is just a word (*Lib* VIII, p.175); the cosmos 'renews the things that have been decomposed' (*Lib* IX, p.183). In a forest, this principle of recycling is at its most obvious, as the old fibre and leaves mulct down into a rich humus of decomposition, creating the conditions for new growth. In 'The Timber', Henry is aware of the cyclical regeneration of forests, as saplings spring amongst the ruins of the old trees and compete for the light (5-8). William Linnard, the expert on Welsh forest history, has told me that smallish woodlands would certainly have been a feature of Llansantffraed parish, consisting mainly of oak and likely to have been situated on the steeper rocky and north-facing slopes which were unsuitable for agriculture. In the Usk valley, the occurrence of 'gwern' place-names locally indicates the presence of alders (personal communications, 15 & 25 June 1994). Allt-yr-esgair, the name of the ridge behind Newton, means 'steep wooded slope of the ridge'. 'The Timber' shows a countryman's awareness of the organic community of a forest as a place of incessant decomposition and recomposition but a poet's attachment to the individual tree. Thomas's world-view also makes room for the mourning of the particular (and hence irreplaceable) individual, for, while the 'star-fire' which animates all creatures reunites with the 'General fire from whence it came', 'the *Astral* Mother doth *mourn*, and not *rejoyce* at the *Death* of her *Children*' (*Magia Adamica*, *TV*, p.163). In this mourning Henry shared, and sought the comfort of a holistic vision of nature which was not merely a palliative denial of the reality of loss and pain.

'The Water-fall' is a perfect image of life as fluidity and process, in which dissolution is the means of ultimate integration. The poem begins in a visual mnemonic of a water-fall, cascading down the steeps of the page and streaming out into broader pools, only to fall again. Onomatopoeia plays here like a god of water. Then the stream of verse broadens into the calm regularity of the mainstream river of meditation as it glides towards the sea:

With what deep murmurs through time's silent stealth
Doth thy transparent, cool and watery wealth
    Here flowing fall,
    And chide, and call,
As if his liquid, loose retinue stayed
Ling'ring, and were of this steep place afraid,
    The common pass
    Where, clear as glass,
    All must descend
    Not to an end:
But quickened by this deep and rocky grave,
Rise to a longer course more bright and brave.
Dear stream! dear bank, where often I
Have sat, and pleased my pensive eye,
Why, since each drop of thy quick store
Runs thither, whence it flowed before,
Should poor souls fear a shade or night,
Who came (sure) from a sea of light?
(1-18)

The long and short lines are antiphonal in their music. The long lines hold back, naturally reluctant, suspended at the precipice-edge; the short lines represent the rapid water channeled into the gulf, surrendered. The waters that fall call back to the waters that delay, arguing against their anxiety. Their liquid voices are heard as a series of purling modulations in the verbal music — mesmerising 'deep murmurs' of alliteration. As they cascade over the edge they slide into a play of 'f' and 'l's' ('flowing fall') with near-instant rhyme ('call'). Now they ripple out into a wider plateau of delay where the undercurrent of anxiety swirls in a melisma of 'l' sounds ('his liquid, loose retinue .../ Ling'ring'). 'Ling'ring' recoils as if loth to leave kin in the previous line but there is no lingering: the reader's eye travels with the precipitate stream of words down the final declivity where 'All must descend'.

As a poem of meditation, 'The Water-fall' is a free-flowing whole, where 'The Timber' chopped itself in two: the 'composition of place' and the 'analysis'. But Vaughan's river is from the first line not only emblematic of humanity's movement through death to resurrection but the image of a mind in process of interior dialogue. The object of thought therefore mirrors the processes of contemplation which lead the listening, witnessing poet to his reflections in the mainstream of the lyric. At the same time, the poem remains unerringly true to nature, an eye-witness report by a most noticing man: he notes the 'streaming rings' that fan out at the base of the waterfall and gradually ripple into stillness (34); the hydrodynamic energy generated by the fall, which gives new impetus to the water-course (11); the music of moving water. Listening attentively to a river, we may become aware that the polyphony of notes which are heard simultaneously as a generalised blur of bubbling sound are each generated sequentially in trills or syncopations from different points in the stream, by rocks or narrowings. The water seems to pass sound back and forth in discourse with itself. This sense of inner dialogue is intensified by the waterfall, the murmurous interval between two silences, calling back with one-and-many voices as it rushes on. Vaughan moves into dialogue with a mind in dialogue with itself: 'Dear stream! dear bank, where often I/ Have sat, and pleased my pensive eye'. The 'pensive eye', under the hypnotic spell of an eternal motion which repeats a single mesmerising message, appears with hindsight close to the Lake-poet's 'inward eye' or 'eye made quiet'. The verse glides in regular octosyllabic couplets away from the tonic force of the waterfall to a unanimous destination which is the source of all life, the sea. Vaughan in dialogue with himself calms his fears as he considers this reunion. The river is read as a natural hieroglyph, represented for us as a visual hieroglyph, shaped on the page so that the reader's 'pensive eye' may be awakened to the same reassurance against the fear that 'what God takes, he'll not restore' (22). Henry Vaughan phrases this negatively because his poem does not refuse the burden of anxiety that haunts everyone at the thought of personal annihilation. Thomas's ''Tis *Day*, my Chrystal Usk', sometimes printed as a companion-poem, is a fraternal not an identical twin. Blithe and ebullient, Thomas saunters along the bank picking up armfuls of salutory lessons in an exceptionally jolly way: 'I'le haste to *God* as Thou dost to the *Sea*' (*TV*, p.136). But Henry has taken with him the residue of his doubts as a believing Christian; and indeed they must go everywhere with him, for human nature is 'frail flesh' (21) in whom every kind of negative emotion is inherent. He brings those doubts — which are not just in him, but are himself, insofar as he is flesh — to be washed and blessed by water. This is part of the healing quality of the lyric; and its authority depends upon its human authenticity. The classic structure of a meditation exercise was intended not only to arouse the meditator to a state of devotion but also to calm and compose. In 'The Water-fall', motion is not commotion but release of energies:

O useful element and clear!
My sacred wash and cleanser here,
My first consigner unto those
Fountains of life, where the Lamb goes?
What sublime truths, and wholesome themes,
Lodge in thy mystical, deep streams!
Such as dull man can never find
Unless that Spirit lead his mind,
Which first upon thy face did move,
And hatched all with his quickening love.
As this loud brook's incessant fall
In streaming rings restagnates all,
Which reach by course the bank, and then
Are no more seen, just so pass men.
O my invisible estate,
My glorious liberty, still late!
Thou art the channel my soul seeks,
Not this, with cataracts and creeks.
(23-40)

Thomas genially enquired of the Usk its vintage and pedigree: 'Didst run with *ancient Kishon?* canst thou tell?/ So many yeers as *holy Hiddekel?*' (p.135): scenes of holy slaughters and visions. But Henry's river is a living memory of that *Aqua Vitae* upon which the Dove-Spirit 'moved [brooded] upon the face of the waters' (Genesis 1:2) and a pledge of the 'pure river of water of life' to which the Lamb will lead the just at the end of time (Revelation 22:1). In linking First Things with Last Things, it relates Genesis to regeneration; and leads the church, in indissoluble union, toward final invisible union with God. In the end, Vaughan abandons the natural for the divine: the 'dear' river is returned to the realm of analogy, the sign rather than the thing signified.

But this was not Vaughan's invariable practice. Nature was too dear to relinquish for the lonely triumphs of an immaterial transcendentalism. To evacuate his spirit from nature would have been to privilege himself above the fellowship of the creatures man had already betrayed to the curse. Vaughan tended to open for debate what most of us rest on as assumptions. When he opened a book, it occurred to him that it had been fabricated from the deaths and dismemberment of creatures. His anterior and recidivist vision, which looked to pre-birth experience for bliss, looked to pre-book experience for design. Unwishing development, he brooded on the predicament of animals and plants, undone so that human beings could be cultivated. Turning over in his hands an old book, it came to him with a vivid pang that lives had been sacrificed to supply him with reading-matter. Nature's innocents — the flax, the tree, the calf — had suffered death so that man could have the paper (made in those days of linen) and covers (made of wood bound in leather) of his books of knowledge. Vaughan revised the cultural perspective from the point of view of the natural creatures taken apart to construct it. He was unable to believe that a God of love would have allowed the creatures to suffer exploitation and rejection. In accordance with the promise in Romans (8:21) that 'the creature itself also shall be delivered from the bondage of corruption, into the glorious liberty of the children of God', he foresaw that at the end of time, the book of culture would be disbound so that the Book of Nature could be restored:

Eternal God! maker of all
That have lived here, since the man's fall;

The Rock of ages! in whose shade
They live unseen, when here they fade.
(1-4)

God is hailed as Creator and sustainer of his creation. 'The Book' develops an implied contrast between the creation of life and our manufacture of artefacts, which requires the destruction of the God-created originals. The holistic Vaughan gives a larger and more generous meaning to the word 'all' than Christianity can generally concede, with a quiet reminder to the reader that only man fell (2), dragging innocent nature in his wake. Collecting into his own imagination this 'all', Vaughan imitates the sanctuary offered by the 'Rock of ages' to every generation of creaturely life. He remembers that God's Omniscience has cared to mark the birth, growth, death and decomposition of every life-form since the beginning of time. Nothing has been too small or mean:

Thou knew'st this *paper*, when it was
Mere *seed*, and after that but *grass;*
Before 'twas *dressed* or *spun*, and when
Made *linen*, who did *wear* it then:
What were their lives, their thoughts & deeds
Whether good *corn*,or fruitless *weeds.*

Thou knew'st this *tree*, when a green *shade*
Covered it, since a *cover* made,
And where it flourished, grew and spread,
As if it never should be dead.

Thou knew'st this harmless *beast*, when he
Did live and feed by thy decree
On each green thing; then slept (well fed)
Clothed with this *skin*, which now lies spread
A covering o'er this aged book,
Which makes me wisely weep, and look
On my own dust; mere dust it is,
But not so dry and clean as this.
Thou knew'st and saw'st them all and though
Scattered thus, dost know them so.
(5-24)

This is a picture of Providence. Its beauty and pathos are felt in an entire gentleness of manner that enfolds each of the three creatures

— grass, tree, calf — and imaginatively remakes the lives that were over long ago. His tender concern echoes the Creator's watchful eye: 'Thou knew'st ... Thou knew'st ... Thou knew'st'. Each act of the imagination is at once poignantly retrospective and a foreshadowing of the final day in which the paper will be returned to the field as grass, the cover will recrudesce to the tree, the leather binding to the skin of the mild animal that browsed and slept in the eye of God. There is restrained irony throughout: the tree that had given the impression of rootfast permanence was telling the truth, for nothing can die that is fashioned and loved by God. All is process, and the book whose texture his fingertips admire ('dry and clean') is only one stage on the journey of all being back to source. The wisdom the book conveys is not through its writing but through its physical constitution, reminding the speaker-reader of his own less innocent 'dust'. The fear of 'scattering' had haunted Vaughan all his life. So too had a nervousness of exposure: in 'The Book', each creature needs and affords 'cover' — the linen dress, the tree a canopy of leaves, the calf its skin. The speaker 'wisely weeps' in the hope that the God who made all will gather and secure all:

> O knowing, glorious spirit! when
> Thou shalt restore trees, beasts and men,
> When thou shalt make all new again,
> Destroying only death and pain,
> Give him amongst thy works a place,
> Who in them loved and sought thy face!
> (25-31)

Vaughan's new Heaven and new Earth will be stocked full of trees soughing, the lowing of cattle and the come and go of human nature-lovers. The hospitality of his God contrasts with the sparsely-populated Heavens greedily awaited by some Calvinist sects, who had calculated that a hundred thousand males and ten thousand females were to be admitted as the elect. By contrast, Vaughan's ample Heaven extends the sense of community and fellowship into the green world: a house of many, and rooted, mansions. In the final prayer, Vaughan gently reminds the Creator of his love for the creatures, in whom he made out the face of God. This is of course Hermetic: God recreates an image of himself in Nature and in Man. Vaughan as an initiate knows the existence of this green track to Heaven which he has walked in reverie, reading as he goes. In 'The

Six:
Christ Coming In Triumph To Brecon

Under the 'Act for better Propagation and Preaching the Gospel in Wales' of 1650, Thomas Vaughan had been evicted as Rector of St Bride's Church:

> Thos: Vaughan out of Llansantfread for being a common drunkard, a common swearer, no preacher, a whoremastr, & in armes personally against the Parliament.
>
> (*H*, p.93)

In *Aqua Vitae* Thomas admits to having been a drinker; the prose works show him as such a rowdy element that it is not difficult to believe that he might have been 'a common swearer' when the fit took him; he did indeed fight for the King. The 'whoremastr' allegation might have been thrown in for good measure. Fighting against Parliament would have been enough to expel him from his incumbency. All the Vaughans' clerical friends were evicted from their livings during the period: Matthew Herbert from Llangattock, Thomas Powell from Cantref, Thomas Lewes from Llanfigan. The churches were closed and the ministers not replaced. To Henry Vaughan this was an unmitigated spiritual disaster. In *The Mount of Olives* he includes a '*Prayer in time of persecution and Heresie*':

> The wayes of *Zion* do mourne, our beautiful gates are shut up, and the Comforter that should relieve our souls is gone far from us. Thy Service and thy Sabbaths, thy own sacred Institutions and the pledges of thy love are denied unto us; Thy Ministers are trodden down,and the basest of the people are set up in thy holy place .... return and restore us, that joy and

> gladnesse may be heard in our dwellings, and the voyce of the Turtle in all our land.... *Behold, the robbers are come into thy Sanctuary, and the persecuters are within thy walls, We drink our own waters for money, and our wood is sold unto us.... Yea, thine own Inheritance is given to strangers, and thine own portion unto aliens.*
>
> (*HV*, p.166)

He adds a reminder to God of 'how furious and Implacable mine Enemies are' who have 'not only rob'd me of that portion and provision which thou hadst graciously given me, but ... also washed their hands in the blood of my friends, my dearest and nearest relatives' (p.167). The last statement is sometimes taken to refer to Henry's brother William but, as the prayer is intended to have general application to a war-scarred population, this inference seems rash.

Throughout South Wales, the churches had been cleared of their incumbents. The Book of Common Prayer had been banned, church assets siphoned off and the property of 'malignant' families seized. Vaughan's friends, Thomas Powell and Thomas Lewes, with Griffith Hatley of Abereskir, protested bitterly in 1654 at the persecution, gagging and imprisoning of politically incorrect ministers, who were forcibly prevented from giving the Gospel to the people of Wales who 'do as earnestly call for it, as the parched Earth after the dew and Raine of Heaven' (*H*, p.118). The group said it could 'name above 20 Parish churches in this County, in many whereof there have not been above two Sermons this 12 moneth, and in most of them none at all' (*H*, pp.119-20). Under Cromwell, known for his belief in liberty of conscience, the evicted ministers thought they might obtain some redress against Fifth Monarchist radicals like Vavasour Powell, a thorn in the Lord Protector's side as he tried to establish a settled state. This was not the case. Vaughan thought he was witnessing the death of true religion under the jackboot of inquisition. Evicted ministers and High Church Royalist gentry lived under the equivalent of voluntary house arrest. Where ministers were replaced, the new men were Puritans whom Vaughan viewed with contempt as 'the basest of the people ... set up in thy holy place'. The traditional èlite had been elbowed out of positions of authority and respect by elect members of the rabble. The Vaughan brothers, as descendants of an ancient local dynasty, smarted under the insult to God, King and lineage. Vaughan's neighbour, Rowland Watkyns, put this shock to caste more crudely and colourfully in his poem 'The new illiterate Lay-Teachers' when he complained that 'in the Temple every saucy Jack/ Opens his shop':

> Mad men by vertue of this propagation,
> Have Bedlum left, and preach't for Reformation ....
> The Tinkar being one of excellent mettle,
> Begins to sound his doctrine with his Kettle.
> And the laborious ploughman I bewail,
> Who now doth thresh the Pulpit with his flail.
> (7-8, 17-18, 21-4)

Being of a medical cast of mind, Watkyns concluded by prophesying that the 'itch of disputation' would inevitably break out into a scab of error whose suppurations would infect the entire flock (39-42).

Henry Vaughan could not know that the Commonwealth would ever come to an end. Nobody in 1650 could have realistically predicted the Restoration of Charles II; the execution of the remnant of the regicides; the suppression of the sects and the exhumation of the Lord Protector, whose corpse was to be gibbeted at Tyburn and his head stuck on a pole at Westminster Hall. From where Vaughan was positioned, the new regime looked invincible. He could not be a religious poet without being also a political poet. *Silex Scintillans* is an act of political resistance, written at an epoch at which history yielded no hope to people of his persuasion. He protested against a government established by force, against divine, natural and civil law. No poetic subject was unrelated to politics in a universe understood to operate on hierarchical macrocosmic laws. The Creation itself denounced the present turmoil. In 'The Constellation', he considers the quiet of the stars: 'Fair, ordered lights ... motion without noise' (1). The word 'order', with its antagonist, 'noise', becomes the focus of the poem. Humankind is deafened to the silent harmony of the spheres. In the nether world, loud-mouthed depravity has become a norm:

> But here commissioned by a black self-will
> The sons the father kill,
> The children chase the mother, and would heal
> The wounds they give, by crying zeal.

Then cast her blood, and tears upon thy book
Where they for fashion look,
And like that lamb which had the dragon's voice
Seem mild, but are known by their noise.

Thus by our lusts disordered into wars
Our guides prove wandering stars ....

Settle, and fix our hearts, that we may move
In order, peace, and love,
And taught obedience by thy whole Creation,
Become an humble, holy nation.
(37-46, 53-6)

Whereas the stars, commissioned by the Creator, assent to the laws of God and nature, man has reversed these laws. The English parricides have executed their king ('father of the nation' in the coronation-service, in the image of the Father-God); matricidal Puritans assault Mother Church in the name of Reformation 'zeal'. From their blood-stained Bibles, the Puritans cull texts to justify their malignity, and are apocalyptically identified by Vaughan with the hypocritical Beast of Revelation 13:11 whose mild lamb-horns were belied by its dragonish bellowing.

In *Silex II* (1655), the strain of anti-Puritan and anti-Commonwealth satire intensifies. Vaughan seems to have been offered a position in local government administration, which he has turned down. With hectic jubilation he lambasts the 'black parasites', 'poisonous, subtle fowls!/ ... flies of hell' ('The Proffer', 13-14) who have attempted to co-opt him, driving them off with much heroical credit to himself:

No, no; I am not he,
Go seek elsewhere.
I skill not your fine tinsel, and false hair,
Your sorcery
And smooth seducements: I'll not stuff my story
With your Commonwealth and glory.
(31-6)

The writer gloats over the impeccable way he has behaved. He relishes the opportunity to retort the Puritans' criticism of the Royalists back upon themselves. Having clambered into office, the Commonwealthsmen have shed their austerity: plush-clothed and bewigged, they offer sleazy incentives to the Royalist gentry to turn their coats in the same way. Vaughan presents himself as a member of the old ('primitive') church, keeping 'the ancient way' (43) and demonstrating the spurious novelty of the 'Good Old Cause'. Vaughan's attack was not entirely without point. Cromwell had Whitehall refurbished as his Court in 1654 with sumptuous items from velvet hangings, plumes of feathers and silk curtains to a chamber pot of red velvet for The Lord Protector's personal use (*Fraser* [1973], pp.458-9). No doubt minor provincial officials also displayed prosperity. Vaughan, whose spartan tastes and disdain for conspicuous consumption had often been offended by the decadence of fellow-Royalists, relished and no doubt exaggerated his enemies' corruptibility.

Vaughan interpreted this period of oppression as signalling the Latter Days predicted by the Book of Revelation. The millennarian impulse was not confined to the sectaries; fratricidal war and the execution of the King seemed to many to imply that they were living through the predicted cataclysms of the reign of Antichrist that would usher in the Day of Judgment and the final reign of the King of Kings. Vaughan's poems derive apocalyptic hope from the turmoil of the times. Again, Vaughan holds up a kind of reverse mirror to the Puritans: he longs for the Second Coming of Christ and sees every reason to believe that his return may be imminent. It was not only ill-educated Puritan prophets like Arise Evans who thought that Revelation 8 and 11 gave a blow-by-blow account of the Civil War, with special reference to the Battle of Edge Hill; traumatised Royalists thought so too, but located the marks of the Beast in the quarter where sectaries saw the triumph of the Saints. Reading the Bible and meditating its meanings hence became a subversive political activity in the safe house at Newton. Even the most spiritual and inward poems in *Silex Scintillans* are charged with counter-revolutionary energy.

The 'roving ecstasy' of 'The Search' with its hypnotic, filmic pilgrimage across the Holy Land in Jesus' footsteps, is a meditation-piece of great beauty. But secret political meanings are cryptically encoded in its lyrical narrative. The time-travelling tourist speeds across panoramic vistas by the magical power of the imagination, from Bethlehem to Calvary, only to find he has walked in the wake of an absence. The lines reeve over, fast-flowing, inconclusive as the search itself whose hurry reaches a point of turbulence: Christ cannot be found and the quest is vain (48). The Bible story leads to a dead end. The speaker, preparing to withdraw into the 'wilderness', is dissuaded by a new lyric voice which questions all such meditation exercises as fruitless, ironically deconstructing the whole poem. For the past cannot be a destination, though 'the calm, golden evenings' of Jacob and his sons at the well of Sychar (22-7) tempt us to dwell there, and the agony of Jesus requires our requiem. At the heart of the poem, the visitor had been shown the ruins of the Temple in Jerusalem, but found only:

> A little dust, and for the Town
> A heap of ashes, where some said
> A small bright sparkle was a bed,
> Which would one day (beneath the pole,)
> Awake, and then refine the whole.
> (16-20)

These five lines are revolutionary in kindling, under cover of austere restraint, the promise of ultimate conflagration; reminding the reader of the New Jerusalem in the Book of Revelation. This image of latent power camouflaged and in hiding links with many other symbols of buried resistance in *Silex Scintillans*: the underground survival and potency of the 'unseen and dumb' seed in 'The Seed Growing Secretly', awaiting its time to spring into vigour and fruit, 'Till the white winged Reapers come!' (46, 48). The Reapers refer to the promise to bring in 'the harvest of the earth' (the saints) in the Apocalypse (14:14-20). The persecuted remnant of God's people is seen by Vaughan as lying low but not defeated as long as it holds in its hand the book of God's promises and predictions. The desperate importance of the Bible to Vaughan in his tribulation is declared in the poem in *Silex Scintillans II* entitled 'The Agreement': 'my midday/ Exterminating fears and night!' (13-14); beside this, 'Most modern books' are dismissed as contemptible. Scripture becomes a radical instrument of political resistance, a millennarian survivor's manual. This illumines his personal fascination with the figures and stories of the Old Testament. They too often lived in eclipse, under punishment. But the throes of disaster were their birth-pangs of deliverance. Their world was similar but simpler. Noah's rainbow was a coded message for the 1650s. 'The youthful world's grey fathers' clung together in the waste of waters, looking out anxiously for the sign of God's peace with them ('The Rain-bow', 6). It came. But these aged men were paradoxically younger and hence more innocent than Vaughan's generation because they lived in the dawn of the world. Since then, humankind has gratuitously blasphemed the Covenant and trampled down Christ's sacrifice. The rainbow therefore appears to Vaughan's troubled eye as a comet, portent of disasters, 'thy light as luctual and stained with woes/ I'll judge, where penal flames sit mixed and close' (37-8). Vaughan's apocalyptic rainbow arches threateningly above a world of depravity which cannot be purged except through violence and fire.

This is a real but terrible hope, born of defeat and humiliation. In the highly-charged 1640s when Puritans (including Milton) had been in rough consensus that the fall of Antichrist, the Second Coming and the millennium of the reign of the saints were at hand, the tone had been active, optimist and utopian. 'We reck'n more than five months yet to harvest,' wrote Milton in *Areopagitica* in 1644; 'there need not be five weeks, had we but eyes to lift up, the fields are ripe already' (*CPW*, II, p. 554). The Reapers of Revelation were at hand. For Quakers and Levellers, the Second Coming had already occurred, and Jesus was present on this earth reigning in every new-eyed man, woman and child. The Digger Gerrard Winstanley wrote of the Apostles' prediction that Christ's spirit 'in the latter dayes be poured out upon sonnes and daughters, and shall spread in the earth like the shining of the Sun from East to West' (*Truth Lifting Up Its Head Above Scandals*, *W*, p.123). By the 1650s, this wave of energy had toppled and spent its force, and, despite the persistence of the Fifth Monarchist sect, radicals began to push the expected date of the End of the World further into the future. There was something of a consensus about the year 1666, with its beguiling coincidence of numerals, suggestive of the Sign of the Beast. For Royalists, millennarianism lay somewhat against the grain and had its roots in the black soil of despair. Millennarianism offered a compensatory fantasy for the defeated, in which persecution itself could be read as a sign of the Latter Days and triumph at hand. But that fantasy for Vaughan did not deny personal and corporate impotence. Only God could redeem history. Vaughan's position in the early 1650s was as passive as that of the republicans in the 1660s after the defeat of their 'Good Old Cause' (*Hill* [1985], p. 73). Standing and waiting — or sitting and writing — seemed the sole remaining way to serve. Between *Silex I* and *II*, Vaughan seems to have moved towards a position of quietism and even pacificism, comparable with that of the Quakers after the Restoration. He turned from the filth of bloodshed with revulsion, linking it with the fratricidal crime of Cain in two notable poems of *Silex II*, 'The Men of War' and 'Abel's Blood'. This second volume is more sombre and apocalyptic, as the seismic forces that had generated the Commonwealth settled into the Protectorate establishment.

The most memorable example of apocalyptic writing in *Silex I* is surely 'Corruption', a poem which exemplifies the appalled perception that his generation lived in a trough of history, not simply fallen, but fallen from fallenness. Through thirty-eight lines the speaker looks back in an agony of reminiscence to the epochs of Bible history in which men were only fallen and only just fallen:

> Sure, it was so. Man in those early days
> Was not all stone, and earth,
> He shined a little, and by those weak rays
> Had some glimpse of his birth.
> He saw Heaven o'er his head, and knew from whence
> He came (condemned,) hither,
> And, as first love draws strongest, so from hence
> His mind sure progressed thither.
> Things here were strange unto him: sweat, and till
> All was a thorn, or weed,
> Nor did those last, but (like himself,) died still
> As soon as they did *seed*,
> They seemed to quarrel with him; for that act
> That fell him, foiled them all,
> He drew the curse upon the world, and cracked
> The whole frame with his fall.
>
> This made him long for *home*, as loath to stay
> With murmurers, and foes;
> He sighed for *Eden*, and would often say
> *Ah! what bright days were those?*
> (1-20)

'Sure, it was so.' This beguiling opening sets the tone for a gentle turning-over of fancies evocative of the experience of Adam and his family, just evicted from Eden. The mode is human and intimate: it suggests that there remains plenty of time for such reminiscence —

a blind, as it turns out. Vaughan muses on how it must have felt and even supplies a chatty line of dialogue (*'Ah! what bright days were those!'*), amiably parodying his own typical posture of nostalgic head-shaking. The tone is tender, with delicate humour derived from the darker facts of Adam's experience: his disrelish for the thorns and weeds of his curse is answered by the vegetation's implacable and justified animosity to him. Contagion spreads through the verbal system: from *fell* derives *foil*; *foil* implicates *all* and *all* rhymes conclusively with the *fall* of the *whole* frame. Never were Vaughan's musical devices of pararhyme and assonance (the 'Welsh' inheritance) as skilfully deployed as here, in witnessing the propagation of the curse throughout the system of nature. Exquisite feminine rhymes together with lyrically irregular cadencing capture the childlike nearness to source enjoyed by these long-ago refugees. But at line 29, the tone changes dramatically to the prophetic. We are back in the deranging present, amongst contemporaries. Impotent and oppressed, their life-force seems blocked by fatalistic inertia and a darkness that travesties the sacred infusion of warmth by the Holy Spirit 'In the beginning', when 'the spirit of God moved upon the face of the waters' (Genesis 1:1-2):

Nor was Heaven cold unto him; for each day
    The valley, or the mountain
Afforded visits, and still *Paradise* lay
    In some green shade, or fountain.
Angels lay *leiger* here; each bush, and cell,
    Each oak, and high-way knew them,
Walk but the fields, or sit down at some *well*,
    And he was sure to view them.
Almighty *Love*! where art thou now? mad man
    Sits down, and freezeth on,
He raves, and swears to stir nor fire, nor fan,
    But bids the thread be spun.
I see, thy curtains are close-drawn; thy bow
    Looks dim too in the cloud,
Sin triumphs still, and man is sunk below
    The centre, and his shroud;
All's in deep sleep, and night; thick darkness lies
    And hatcheth o'er thy people;
But hark! what trumpet's that? what Angel cries
    Arise! Thrust in thy sickle.

(21-40)

There are forty lines in the poem: the number of the wilderness. The Children of Israel crossed it safely in forty years, through all vicissitudes; Christ's forty-day sojourn ended with the fall of Satan. Vaughan's poem breaks at the half-way point to recall the indwelling presence of God for early man in the landscape of the wilderness: 'still *Paradise* lay / In some green shade, or fountain'. Vaughan makes it appear as if a person with a butterfly-net might have snared hundreds of angels on that still enchanted ground. Man, graced with the vestige of his first shining, could still play host to heavenly guests. We are reminded of *Paradise Lost* as the full horror of eviction dawns upon Adam and Eve. The woman's desolate crie de coeur takes the form of a lament which has all the poignancy of a Mozart aria: 'Must I thus leave thee, Paradise? Thus leave / Thee native soil?' (XI. 269-70). But Adam's is pure Beethoven:

> This most afflicts me, that departing hence,
> As from his face I shall be hid, deprived
> His blessed countenance; here I could frequent,
> With worship, place by place where he vouchsafed
> Presence divine, and to my sons relate;
> On this mount he appeared; under this tree
> Stood visible, among these pines his voice
> I heard, here with him at this fountain talked.'
> (XI. 315-322)

His angel visitor, Michael, reassures him that 'in valley and in plain / God is as here ... / Present' (349-51) and later that humanity will enjoy 'A paradise within thee, happier far' (XII. 587). For Vaughan as for Milton's Adam, place is sacred because of its deep associations with Presence. The Puritan confidence in internals would help Milton to relocate his centre in 'the paradise within': 'One's native land is wherever it is well with one,' he wrote in a letter of 1666 (*CPW*, VIII, p.4). For Vaughan as a child of the Established Church and a lover of the green world, the question has a peculiar and stressful complexity. The final quarter of 'Corruption' moves suddenly into the tumult of the present day. Its visionary manner ('I see thy curtains are close-drawn ...') calls attention from the earth to the louring skies, in which God or God's withdrawal is manifest in doubtful or harrowing signs. What monster will 'hatch' from such 'thick darkness'? Vaughan catches the atmosphere of foreboding in his times as powerfully as Yeats was to do nearly three centuries later in 'The

Second Coming': 'And what rough beast, its hour come round at last,/ Slouches towards Bethlehem to be born?' (21-2). Vaughan, unlike Yeats, can answer directly. In the last two lines a fanfare strikes through the pregnant gloom like a reveille: 'But hark! what trumpet's that? what Angel cries/ *Arise! Thrust in thy sickle.*' The modern reader may raise an eyebrow not only at the loose and bathetic feminine rhyme ('people'/'sickle') but at the handiness of the angel. To contemporaries the idea that a squadroned militia was massing beyond the clouds could not have been dismissed as fantastic. This clarion-call of supernatural powers identified the black time of the English church as the phase of blight, blood and plague predicted in Revelation 8, in which 'the seven angels' with 'seven trumpets' herald a manifold woe to the tune of thunder, slaughter, stridor and universal devastation. The command to 'Arise! Thrust in thy sickle', quoting the reapers of Revelation 14, is less a revolutionary call to arms than a reminder that Christian history has a predetermined impetus, which should alert and re-energise the 'remnant'. Two lines of prophecy blast away thirty-eight of nostalgia.

When would Christ come, and what would it be like? Many bruised persons living through those times of holocaust dwelt on the Day of Judgment with lurid and retributive excitement, as bringing not only their deliverance but the annihilation of their enemies. This was not Vaughan's way. He seems to have found little consolation in the idea of vengeance but looked forward to the Judgment Day in a positive and generous light as the ending of human cruelty and a salutory reminder to look to the state of his own soul. There are two 'Day of Judgment' poems. The first, in *Silex I*, imagines the final conflagration as it devours all in its path:

> When through the north a fire shall rush
> And roll into the east,
> And like a fiery torrent brush
> And sweep up *south* and *west* ...
>
> When like a scroll the heavens shall pass
> And vanish clean away,
> And nought must stand of that vast space
> Which held up night, and day, ...
>
> O then it will be all too late ....
> (1-4, 13-16, 25)

The ruthless conciseness of the telling of each successive wave of destruction; the streaming verbs; the fanfare of six *whens*, leading to the inexorable *then*, intend to stagger the reader's mind with the knowledge that this *will happen*. In no time at all, Time will come to an end. So immediate is his sublime picture of this inferno that it is hard to resist the thought that Vaughan must have gone out onto the Beacons and literally imagined the fire 'rush' down from North Wales, 'roll' towards the Marches, 'sweep up *south*' (to Glamorgan) 'and *west*' (to the Irish sea). Vaughan's eschatological poetry is an attempt to realise the Bible prophecies in vivid actuality, for the purposes of personal chastening. For when he insists on 'Killing the man of sin' (32), he does not mean his enemies. There has been more than enough of that. He attacks the unregenerate Adam in himself.

In the *Silex II* poem 'The Day of Judgement', the emphasis is on resurrection and regeneration. 'O come, arise, shine, do not stay/ Dearly loved day!' (11-12), for the dead will bud like flowers from their graves. Evil seethes around him, all the more fiercely for knowing its time is almost up (30); he revolts against the falsification of the Gospel (35-8) but there is no touch of personal vendetta or desire to see others suffer. It simply does not seem to occur to Vaughan to take the opportunity offered by the two 'Judgement' poems to purge his bale by the legitimate means of imagining the enemy tortured and vanquished. In 'Abel's Blood', he struggles for a difficult forgiveness of those who have massacred the innocent in the war, bathing 'in a deep, wide sea of blood' (14). 'The Men of War' takes courage from John's prophecies in Revelation (13:9—10, which he paraphrases) that 'he that killeth with the sword must be killed with the sword'. He argues that it is a sign of Grace to leave vengeance to God. To be martyred, disarmed, led captive, is the paradoxical sign of future triumph, and the victors of the war are stigmatised by their very success. Hence he prays for 'A sweet, revengeless, quiet mind,/ And to my greatest haters kind' (43-4). By these psychological stratagems the defeated at all epochs have turned their mortifications to crowns purchased in advance.

What time of day would Jesus choose for his arrival? Reading his deliberations, again a reader has the feeling that Vaughan must have looked out of his window every morning wondering 'Will it be today?' This possible imminence may account for the tensely expectant quality of his passion in poems like 'The Night' which are not obviously apocalyptic. Intuitions brought the quivering intimation that final breakthrough might come very soon. The oak tree in front of the house at Newton would go up in flames and be replaced by the Tree of Life. His house would be burnt to ashes by the incendiary God and in its place would arise the new Temple. The very sheep would be resurrected from their condition as mutton or woollen jerkins and be put back together again by miraculous fiat, whiter now that they were grazing the pastures of The Lamb. His marriages, first to one sister, Catherine, then to the other, Elizabeth, would be dissolved, and he and the restored Catherine and the perfected Elizabeth would be married to their one love. We cannot overestimate the literality of the mind with which this naive sophisticate read and understood the mystic meanings of Scripture; and indeed it is the naïveté and literalism which so endear him to us and make his vision so radical-seeming. So he pondered the arrival of Jesus to make all new, nervous at his own inadequacy but thrilled at the extraordinary prospect before him:

Ah! what time wilt thou come? when shall that cry
The Bridegroom's coming! fill the sky?
Shall it in the evening run
When our words and works are done?
Or will thy all-surprising light
Break at midnight?
When either sleep, or some dark pleasure
Possesseth mad man without measure;
Or shall these early, fragrant hours
Unlock thy bowers?
And with their blush of light descry
Thy locks crowned with eternity;
Indeed it is the only time
That with thy glory doth best chime,
All now are stirring, every field
Full hymns doth yield,
The whole Creation shakes off night,
And for thy shadow looks the light ....
('The Dawning' 1-18)

The long opening line seems to stream out like the unfurling vision of Christ descending from the heavens of some Baroque ceiling; but this ceiling is the sky above Llansantffraed. Speedy octosyllabics now make the lines 'run' (3) to mime the commotion in the brief interim between the warning and the impact of 'all-surprising light', to climax in the shorter-still 'Break at midnight?' (6). Beneath the surface of this bravura poem stirs a nervous anxiety as to what time will find the believer best prepared. To put it plainly, he is troubled about being caught with his spiritual trousers down; and it is for this reason that he discards the second possibility of Christ's coming at midnight. To scramble blearily out of sleep when the King of Glory arrives would be unseemly enough but what if one were engaged at the moment of Jesus's arrival in 'some dark pleasure' (such as, presumably, having sexual intercourse with one's wife — legitimate but, for Vaughan as for St Paul, a regrettable expression of life in the flesh)? Vaughan shakily discards this possibility and hurries on to the desired solution: Christ, identified in the Apocalypse with the 'morning-star' (Revelation 22:16), must surely come in the freshness of morning, when sunrise and dewfall reciprocate the Lord's qualities and the birds are gospelling their sacred *aubade*. The second verse, abandoning his lyric wooing of the Bridegroom, is a prayer for the power to resist his distractibility so that, whatever the time appointed for Christ's Second Coming, 'Thou'lt find me dressed and on my way,/ Watching the break of thy great day' (47-8). This naïve anxiety about being caught out must have been a common enough millennarian neurosis.

The burden of guilt perplexed and oppressed him. In poem after poem he struggles with it, dumping it whenever possible at the base of the Cross. His Easter and Ascension poems are amongst his most emotional. From the jaunty balladic rhythms of 'Easter-Hymn' ('Death, and darkness get you packing,/ Nothing now to man is lacking' [1-2]) to the twin poems 'Ascension-Day' and 'Ascension-Hymn' which open the second volume of *Silex*, he looks to the New Testament promises, substantiated by Christ's atoning actions, as assurances of his own release from innate depravity, together with the loneliness that afflicts him in a world split off from direct eye-contact with the Saviour. I am writing this account on Ascension Day, which falls this year on 12 May 1994, some 340 years after Vaughan composed the lyric, very possibly on 4 May 1654: this planned coincidence is a reminder of the circularity of the church year, whose way-stages at once recapitulate the cycle of the seasons and bear witness to the cyclical character of Christian history. The date defined by 'Ascension-Day' is *now* — an eternally recurrent *now* in which all can share (8). I can experience the past Ascension '(though removed/ So many ages from me)' (5-6) in the present because of the eternal recurrence of this arousal and arising, spring by spring. The tears of the Magdalene are:

> Fresh as the dew, which but this dawning wears!
> I smell her spices, and her ointment yields
> As rich a scent as the now primrosed fields ....
> (20-22)

The spices and ointments were brought by Mary Magdalene and Mary the mother of James to the sepulchre to anoint the corpse, in sign of the preciousness of the man they mourned. But they were to find him risen. Mary Magdalene is important to Vaughan as the type of the sinner loved and purified by Christ. In comparing her gift of scent with that of 'the now primrosed fields', Vaughan draws us out of the Holy Land and into the England in which the primrose is the evanescent token of spring's return. The reader participates in a compound present tense, in which narrative time (the brink of Anno Domini); the narrator's time (spring 1654) and the reader's time (for me, May 1994) coincide as manifestations of one *now* — a *now* which, however, will not be over until the final cycle of Ascension is completed in eschatological time. The last lines of the poem are apocalyptic:

> Come then thou faithful witness! come dear Lord
> Upon the clouds again to judge this world!
> (61-2)

'Ascension-Day' coasts back to the beginning of Creation in the sabbath of Genesis (39) and forward to its ending. In that moment of an eternal *now*, Vaughan fantasises a communion with angels which haunts his imagination throughout his poetry:

> What stirs, what posting intercourse and mirth
> Of Saints and Angels glorify the earth!
> What sighs, what whispers, busy stops and stays;
> Private and holy talk fill all the ways!
> They pass as at the last great day, and run
> In their white robes to seek the risen Sun;
> I see them, hear them, mark their haste, and move
> Amongst them, with them, winged with faith and love.
> (25-32)

Trompe l'oeil tricks us into the illusion of an eavesdropping Vaughan literally encompassed by misty, fast-moving presences, in a soft tumult of joyful interchange. Between heaven and earth, earth and heaven, their gossiping congregations gad and speed; and, like some delighted wayfarer on fairy ground, the poet listens in as the air breathes and stirs around in him vivid animation. The passage climaxes in the development from 'Amongst them' (the poet apart) to 'with them' (part of their company). Fellowship with touchingly human angels was evidently easier for Vaughan than insufficiently angelic human company.

The second volume of *Silex Scintillans* contains a curious and topical poem entitled 'The Jews', which demonstrates the apocalyptic cast of Vaughan's mind at this period. Pro-Jewish sentiment in the early 1650s was not only the fruit of intense scrutiny of the Bible and Judaic custom but an aspect of millennarianism, for Fifth Monarchists believed that the programme leading to the establishment of the Kingdom of Heaven required the conversion of the Jews, and, if there were no Jews in England to convert (having been expelled in 1290), it was difficult to see how this could be accomplished without reintroducing them. Cromwell welcomed Menasseh ben Israel as spokesman for the Jews to London in 1655, and Jewish traders were informally admitted (*Fraser* [1973], pp.554-68). Vaughan's poem 'The Jews' belongs to this historical and religious matrix. The lyric begins with the prophecy of the Jews' ultimate recognition of Christ as their Messiah. To Vaughan this mass-conversion is a matter of *when* not *if*: three '*when*'s in the first stanza, drive home (or work up) the certainty of their acquiescence: 'When the fair year/ Of your deliverer comes ...' (1-2):

O then that I
Might live, and see the olive bear
Her proper branches! which now lie
Scattered each where,
And without root and sap decay
Cast by the husband-man away.
And sure it is not far! ....
So by all signs
Our fullness too is now come in,
And the same sun which here declines
And sets, will few hours hence begin

To rise on you again, and look
Towards old *Mamre* and *Eschol*'s brook.
(14-20, 26-31)

Vaughan's habitual concern with unity is here redirected onto the unification of the *diaspora,* the ten lost tribes scattered throughout the world. His reference to the reading of the 'signs' of history invokes a procedure familiar to every Puritan: it involved deciphering the meaning of political events according to their correspondence with the Bible's symbolic predictions. Joseph Mede's much reprinted *Clavis Apocalyptica* (1627; translated into English in 1650) argued that God would empty seven politically specific vials upon the earth, synchronised with the seven trumpet-blasts (the Reformation, the reign of Elizabeth I, etc). The sixth would be the conversion of the Jews and the destruction of the Turkish Infidel, which would finally weaken the hold of evil on human history (*Fixler* [1964], pp.37–45). For Vaughan, England's sunset will be the Jews' sunrise on the other side of the world. The Jews' sunrise will reciprocally usher in the morning of the English Church.

At the heart of 'The Jews', however, is an obliquely personal testament which displays a complex of feelings peculiar to Vaughan. As an address by an eldest son to God's eldest sons, the poem pleads for the primacy of the firstborn. First things for Vaughan are always most authentic:

Faith sojourned first on earth in you,
You were the dear and chosen stock:
The Arm of God, glorious and true,
Was first revealed to be your rock.

You were the *eldest* child, and when
Your stony hearts despised love,
The *youngest*, even the Gentiles then
Were cheered, your jealousy to move.

Thus, Righteous Father! dost thou deal
With brutish men; Thy gifts go round
By turns, and timely, and so heal
The lost son by the newly found.
(38-49)

Vaughan is preoccupied in this poem with fraternity, and the unifying of separated brothers. *'Mamre'* and *'Eschol'* who are to receive the sunrise on behalf of Jewry were a pair of brothers first mentioned in Genesis as in league with Abraham when he raided his enemies to release his brother's son, Lot, from captivity (14:12-24). Hence their story concerns the reinforcement of fraternal bondings and the restoration of the younger generation by the elder. There are strongly emotional reverberations for an 'unbrothered' man in a time of fratricidal civil war. Vaughan as 'younger' New Testament son is divided from the Jews, his elder brothers; God's only Son is the third principle which can unite the cloven pairing. But as an 'elder' son himself, he empathises with the Jews and interprets God's aversion from them and transference of attention to the Gentiles as a ploy to arouse their jealousy. He is anxious to heal the rift of sibling-rivalry by showing, in the final stanza, God's impartial but alternating dispensations, by which 'The lost son' will be healed by 'the newly found' (49). Twins of the one father, they will be restored under the wing of the arising Son.

Henry's twin believed that Adam had been a magician, handing down his occult knowledge to Abraham, Noah, Enoch and the other patriarchs. Thence it had travelled down through history by various routes to arrive in the mid-seventeenth century at the doorstep of Thomas Vaughan of Llansantffraed (*Magia Adamica, TV*, p.156). In 1655, the year of the augmented *Silex*, Thomas published *Euphrates*. Here he claims to be following in the footsteps of 'the ancient *Priests* and *Prophets*', not looking 'altogether in Bookes' for the *prima materia* but rather 'begging it at the hands of God, for it is properly his Gift' (*TV*, p.514). *Euphrates* acknowledges that the inspirational quality of Thomas's discoveries makes him superficially indistinguishable from an extreme Puritan, since to receive revelatory 'Visits' from God (one of Henry's core-words) is nowadays to be accounted 'amongst *Ranters* and *Anabaptists*' (p.515). Henry More had seen him as the very type of the zealot and fanatic, a force of unreason indistinguishable from a religious 'enthusiast' ([*Patrides*], pp.9-10). Thomas dismisses such misapprehension with contumely. He goes on to quote the *'Angel of the Waters'* of Revelation to demonstrate God as acting in or directly upon matter. He then cites Avicenna's opinion that John, the author of Revelation, was himself an alchemist: 'And certainly, if some *Passages* in the *Revelation* were urged, and that no farther than their own sense would carry them, it would be somwhat difficult to refell his opinion' (p.515). The Apocalypse hence becomes a recipe-book for the elixir. The various stages of the process, involving 'putrefaction' and disintegration into chaos as well as the conjunction of opposites, would correspond to the various pourings from vials and blasting of trumpets, the manifestations of the Beast and the wars predicted by John, culminating in the New Jerusalem. At times the whole thing was bound to appear a downright mess, but the millennarian 'Chymist' must convince himself that this chaos is intrinsic to ultimate success. Alchemy and millennarianism were both ways of maintaining an optimist vision without denying reality to the instability and despair of the age. The New Jerusalem becomes the philosopher's stone.

Seven:
'Such Low & Forgotten Things, As My Brother And My Selfe'

The creative period of Henry Vaughan's poetic life was now over. He survived his gift posthumously for nearly forty years, presumably maintaining his regular routine of meditation and practising medicine in Llansantffraed and neighbouring parishes. Louise Guiney liked to 'picture him on his hardy Welsh pony, drenched in the mountain mists, close-hatted, big-cloaked, riding alone, and looking abroad with those mild eyes which were a naturalist's for earth and sky, and a mystic's for the spiritual world' (*H*, p.194). One can understand the attraction of that picture, for it brings into the semblance of blurred telescopic focus a figure that has in point of fact all but vanished into the world of the hypothetical. Miss Guiney has dressed Vaughan for the part in Welsh gear and saddled up a native pony for her ghostly poet. She has situated him midway between the real and ideal worlds by sousing him in high-altitude cloud which at once reminds us of the discomforts of the life of a seventeenth century country doctor and sets him romantically within a misty dreamscape. Presumably he is on his way to or from some hill-farm patient but his mind is not on the practicalities of his trade: rather he is gazing with faraway eyes at and through hills and heavens, oblivious to the fact that he is wet to the skin. Miss Guiney is particular about his eyes: they are 'mild' eyes. In my illustrated childhood Bible, 'gentle Jesus' is portrayed thus, riding upon an ass, with an expression of humility. Complex, churning, emotional, ascetic, inchoate, my imagined Vaughan is a more turbulent ghost than Louise Guiney's nature-mystic. Both the humble ass and its self-willed rider, he had sought the difficult integrity of a life at the crossroads of duality: 'in this busy street / Of flesh and blood, where two ways meet' ('The Ass', 1–2). All the stress of the riven mid-century seems crowded into his poetry. There he had been busily creating an identity in the wake of William's death, Thomas's remoteness, the king's end and the church's closure; or rather, a sequence of identities, each volatile and stressful as the fluid, innumerable verse-forms he chose. Having merged with Herbert to find a voice, how did he emerge when the dual voice had had its say? Was he freed from his traumas into new identity; did he break through as some like to think into that full mystic union with his Maker which is beyond words; or did he just dry up?

Perhaps his life as a medical practitioner took over, absorbing his creative energies into the concocting of potions and powders, and the management of diseases. He may have become assimilated into the community as an authority-figure on whom people came to rely. In 1673 he told Aubrey that his practice was flourishing: 'My profession allso is physic, wch I have practised now for many years with good successe (I thank god!) & a repute big enough for a person of greater parts than my selfe' (*M*, p.488). He is often congratulated on his modesty. For me, his modesty in these letters is excessively self-conscious. He effusively thanks his cousin 'that you would be pleased to remember, & reflect upon such low & forgotten things, as my brother and my selfe'; it is an 'honour' hardly to be repaid (p.689). In part, this reflects the wave of regret that must pass through the heart of any provincial who once thought of making a name and career but who settled (for complex reasons) for a life out of the public eye. Vaughan sites himself on the margins and knows that he and Thomas must always count as marginalia, if remembered at all, at the 'centre'. He also points out, with humble pride, that he has made quite a name for himself as a doctor in these regions. So he is not no one. A public role may have come to substitute for a private persona, and the intense inwardness of his tumultuous inner life may have dwindled to a wraith as he became incorporated into the community as a respected professional.

The immediate causes of his silence after *Silex Scintillans* may have been prosaic. When his wife died, he married her younger sister, Elizabeth, perhaps in 1655, the year of the publication of the second edition of *Silex*. This marriage is a curiosity which extends roots into the depths of Henry's psychology. It was nominally against canon law to marry one's deceased wife's sister: but, handily, the Table of Kindred which asserted such marriages to be voidable had been suspended with the Book of Common Prayer. For a twin to marry his wife's sibling represents an inward-looking tendency toward replication in keeping with Henry's psychology of mirror-identification. Safety is found near to source. This marriage was soon fertile. By Elizabeth, Vaughan had four children, Grisell, Lucy, Rachel and Henry, the last being born in 1661. This means that Vaughan, whose house was already stocked with the children of his first marriage to Catherine Wise (Lucy, Frances, Catherine and Thomas), all aged under ten by the time of his second marriage, was packed in the second half of the 1650s with a second family of half-brothers and sisters who were also cousins because their stepmother was their aunt. There was also a difficult and senescent father living at home: the elder Thomas Vaughan did not die until the early summer of 1658. Still lurching from debt to debt in a chain of those dismal litigations that had played such a rude bass note to his entire life, Thomas was twice arrested during this period and, in Henry Vaughan's words in a deposition to the Radnor Commissioners in 1656, 'Thomas Williams ... with some foote-souldiers tooke my father prisoner & carryed him to Brechon goale, where he remayned till the rent was payed' (*H*, p.200). The first arrest was for debts to Brecon tradesmen; the second for alleged abuse of the tithes during the Interregnum. Henry's letter explains that an essential receipt has gone missing which 'I cannot find ... amongst all his papyrs, wch are still in my Custodie'.

This mislaying of a crucial document is typical of the disorderly state of affairs that seems to have prevailed at Newton. A threadbare family is hanging on by its fingernails to the rank of landed gentry. Hutchinson feels, in his tranquil way, that Henry 'would not readily forget the indignity that had befallen his old father' when hassled off by the Parliamentary soldiers to Brecon Gaol (p.200). This may indeed have been so: but Thomas must have been as easy to live with as a bed of thistles, and the indignity which his uncontrollable affairs brought upon a son dedicated to exemplary piety must have been hard to bear with filial fortitude. Meanwhile a medley of babies made itself known. Remembering that the house at Newton had only eight main living-rooms, there can have been little peace for poetry and the solitude without which Vaughan's inner life and Muse could not function. Children tend to disappear into the background of the biographies of famous males: in the cramped space of domestic reality, they cannot always be made to do so. John Donne in his cash-strapped 'Mitcham' years lamented his confinement: 'I stand like a tree which once a year beares, though no fruit, this mast of children' (*Gosse* [1899], I, p.154). In Vaughan's case there was also the poet's ageing mother whose date of death we do not know: if history is silent about her, it does not follow that she was in the life as inconspicuous. Thomas noted the death of his father but expressed no direct emotion about it, being more preoccupied by the fact that it had been foretold him in a dream by his dead wife (*Aqua Vitae*, p.589); though later he recorded the powerful guilt-dream in which his father and William appear beneath the oak tree (see p.41 above), suggesting complex upheaval in the depths of his subconscious.

Kinship ties were crucial to the gentry-families of Wales in the seventeenth century: but such bondings can also be bonds within which individuals struggle and quarrel. Hutchinson, who smooths out the conflicts of his subject's story where possible, feels that the Vaughan step-siblings probably got on well enough together at first. He infers this from the fact that Vaughan's daughter Frances made a bequest in a noncupative (oral, deathbed) will of 1670 in favour of 'her sister Lucy Vaughan the younger', with her stepmother as a witness. 'If the beneficiary is the half-sister, it is a welcome sign that the friction between the children of the two marriages was not yet acute' (*H*, pp.205-6). It is, however, just as possible that the stepmother had put pressure on Frances to make a will favourable to her own child. I am not accusing her of this: there is no indication either way. But the violent acrimony which exploded in public between the two Vaughan families in a later decade is of the sort that commonly has deep roots in childhood. The more likely picture of life at Newton in the late 1650s seems to me to be one of stress and friction: and, certainly, of noise and overcrowding. The death of Henry's father in 1658 would have meant a freeing of the son from Oedipal bondings, to become patriarch as well as paterfamilias. This event may well have brought a resolution of a portion of Henry's own inner conflict. It was closely followed, in 1660, by the Restoration of Charles II, the Good Father, *pater patriae* of his realm, and the restitution of the Church of England. Each of these events signals an inevitable slackening of tension within Vaughan and his fellow Royalist and Anglican gentry. Notwithstanding that the Restoration coincided with the deaths of his friends Matthew Herbert and Thomas Powell (cutting the bonds to his childhood), this easing of psychic pressure would have made the generation of poetry less likely for one of Vaughan's temperament.

He would never again need to live as intensely within himself, for from a clandestine and persecuted minority, he had come out vindicated as a staunch part of the visible majority. Vaughan could take communion again at Llansantffraed Church, at the hands of the new incumbent Dr Edward Games, then from Philip Roberts and finally from Thomas Powell's son Hugh; or ride over to Llanfigan to receive it from his old friend Thomas Lewes. There was no longer motivation to listen out morning by morning for the blast of the trumpet heralding Christ's Second Coming or to watch for the Final Conflagration across the Beacons. With victory came settledness, mundanity. Eschatological fervour is always a fantasy-product wrung from crushing misery and oppression. For all his eccentric interest in occultism, Henry Vaughan was not a natural fanatic. He was happiest in a pew participating in the approved Order for the Day. The guaranteed structure of liturgy replaced the improvisation of self-generated verse-forms. He had been driven inwards upon himself — the 'flinty heart' battered in *Silex Scintillans* — and the poetry had been sparked and squeezed out of this heart's ordeal, as the emblem to the book eloquently shows. But the continuity of the status quo was the natural home of his class and personality.

The extent to which Vaughan's short period of poetry was the product of personal identity-crisis in the throes of revolutionary national crisis is attested by his most famous poem, 'The World [I]', written before 1650:

1

I saw Eternity the other night
Like a great *Ring* of pure and endless light,
All calm, as it was bright,
And round beneath it, Time in hours, days, years
Driven by the spheres
Like a vast shadow moved, in which the world
And all her train were hurled;
The doting lover in his quaintest strain
Did there complain,
Near him, his lute, his fancy, and his flights,

Wit's sour delights,
With gloves, and knots the silly snares of pleasure
Yet his dear treasure
All scattered lay, while he his eyes did pour
Upon a flower.

2

The darksome states-man hung with weights and woe
Like a thick midnight-fog moved there so slow
He did nor stay, nor go;
Condemning thoughts, (like sad eclipses) scowl
Upon his soul,
And clouds of crying witnesses without
Pursued him in one shout.
Yet digged the mole, and lest his ways be found
Worked under ground,
Where he did clutch his prey, but one did see
That policy,
Churches and altars fed him, perjuries
Were gnats and flies,
It rained about him blood and tears, but he
Drank them as free.
(1-30)

The visionary opening of this poem is invariably quoted in wonderment for its beauty and magnificence as an image of the transcendental. The ring of endless light seems to have been fetched from the darkness of the imagination with dreaming ease and committed to paper with the plainest assurance. At the same time, there is a suave and Metaphysical *élan* about the irony with which 'Eternity' is brought into the focus of the elegantly casual 'the other night'. The remainder of the poem is usually regretted or suppressed. The ring of light floats complete in our memories like an imagist fragment, whole in itself, while the impressive image of whirling cosmic Time 'Like a vast shadow' may also be recalled. The sublimity which Vaughan seems to reach in this poem permits us to think of him as a pocket Dante of the Black Mountains; and we feel let down when the allegorical 'lover' appears, followed by a 'statesman' and a 'miser'. Grotesquely out of scale with the vision of the ring, they have seemed to generations of readers not only obvious but digressive and dated (Spenserian rather than Metaphysical). But this distortion of scale is proper to Baroque, whose unhinged perspectives are a true measure of the schismatic world Vaughan inhabited. The satire which takes over from visionary lyricism issued from a world governed by statesmen literally 'fed' on 'Churches and altars' and Mammon's *nouveaux riches* fattened by the profits of sequestration. The ring of light is explained by the voice of the final lines as God's provision for the Bride (of the true Church) (59-60), of whom only a faithful remnant could be seen as they 'soared up into the *Ring*' (47). Vaughan's visionary poetry had grown out of and existed in relation to his experience of alienation from the Commonwealth.

In February 1666, Henry's twin brother Thomas died. How great a disturbance this caused to Henry we have no way of measuring, though it may be felt that in real terms he had lost him years before and mourned the cutting of the bond before his passing. With the Restoration in 1660, Thomas could have been reinstalled as Rector of Llansantffraed Church and come home to kin and native land. He did not choose to do so. Under the patronage of Sir Robert Moray, the first President of the Royal Society, who lived in the vicinity of the King's laboratory in Whitehall, the widowed Thomas was living a life of practical experiment that suited him, near to the centre of scientific activity and on the skirts of power. The parochial life of a rural minister amongst a scattered congregation of inbred gentry and poor illiterates had nothing to offer him. Rosicrucian, controversialist, bosom friend of occultists and intellectuals of all sorts, the contrifugal twin had become metropolitan in his tastes and affinities. In September 1665, the Plague Year, the court retired to Oxford to escape the contagion; and Moray and Thomas Vaughan accompanied them. Thomas died at the village of Albury, near Oxford, the *alma mater* whose legitimate child he had proclaimed himself to be: 'a *notable wag* and a *saucy Boy*, whom she hath sometimes *dandl'd* on her *Knees*', as he had bragged to that 'illiterate *Chops*', Henry More (*The Man-Mouse, TV*, p.279). The *saucy Boy* was now forty-five or forty-six years old and died (if Wood is to be believed) *in flagrante delicto* with his adored calling, of mercury poisoning whilst attempting to distil the *elixir vitae*: 'Eugenius Philalethes died as twere suddenly wn he was operating strong mercurie, some of wch by chance getting up into his nose marched him off. So Harris of Jesus Coll.' (*TV*, 24). Thus the glorious endeavours of science descend into the farcical matter of Senior Common Room anecdote and the philosopher dies of an accidental sniff amongst his clutter of retorts and test-tubes: but if the story is apocryphal, it is true both to the spirit and to the common perception of Thomas, fanatically devoted to the life-and-death operation of 'the Work'. Thomas's writings would be translated into German during the next century. He would have the honour of being mocked first by Samuel Butler in *Hudibras* and then by Swift in *A Tale of a Tub* (1704) as a gibberish Welshman whose *Anthroposophia* 'is a piece of the most unintelligible fustian, that, perhaps, was ever published in any language' (*Swift* [1960], p.308). There is something truly lovable about Thomas. He is Jonson's Subtle minus the subtlety. He is the Emperor in his new clothes, nude as the day he was born, strutting amongst the gorgeous-suited vanities of Oxford and London with a certain impressive naïiveté. Thomas's inner life, jotted in the 1658-9 notebook, *Aqua Vitae*, was anything but ridiculous. Deeply in touch with the sources of his emotional life, he tried to be scrupulously honest with himself. Thomas trusted the intuitive, inspirational area of the psyche. His religious faith, his alchemical work and his love and grief for his newly-dead wife all belonged to this part of the mind; and he understood how they cohered there. It had been during his marriage (1551-8) that his mystical-chemical creativity had flourished, 'and though I brought them not to perfection in those deare Dayes, yet were the Gates open to mee then' (*TV*, p.588, and see pp.591-2). He used his dreams as means of healing and reintegration, reading them symbolically as God's and his dead wife's ministrations to his spirit. His faith comes through as passionate:

> 1859. April 8th ...
> In the Evening I was surprised with a suddaine Heavines of spirit, but without any manifest Cause whatsoever: but, I thank god, a great Tendernes of Heart came along with it: soe that I prayed most earnestly with abundance of teares, and sorow for Sinn. I fervently sollicited my gratious god for his pardon to my self, and my most deare Wife: and besought him to bring us together againe in his Heavenly kingdom ....
> (p. 92)

There is nothing sanctimonious about Thomas: he knows he is the same person as 'revelled away many yeares in drinking' and who was capable of petty meannesses to his wife, which now he will never be able to redeem (p.593). He is aware of mood-swings and unashamed of tears and 'Tendernes of Heart'. Whereas Henry disciplined himself to keep awake in order to sanctify the hours of darkness, Thomas abandoned himself to the release of sleep and dream according to the rhythms of nature. From his dreams he extracts an elixir which comes in answer to the spontaneous outpourings of his prayers:

> I went that night to bed after earnest prayers, and teares, and towards the Day-Breake, or just upon it, I had this following dreame. I thought, that I was againe newly maried to my deare Wife .... I thought, wee were both left alone, and calling her to mee, I tooke her into my Armes, and shee presently embraced mee, and kissed mee: nor had I in all this vision any Sinnful desyre, but such a Love to her as I had to her very soule in my prayers, to which this Dreame was an Answer. Hereupon I awaked presently, with exceeding great inward Joy. Blessed be my God, Amen.
>
> (pp. 592-3)

The wish-fulfilment aspect of Thomas's dreams carries an aura of effectual blessedness; his unconscious mind recovers night by night what it has lost and, when he awakens, he does not suffer the shock of realisation that this has only been a dream, but genuinely feels that Rebecca has visited him in God-given token of the beatitude to come, when he is laid to rest with her. A little later he confides, 'I am ready for Death, and withall my heart shall I wellcome it' (p.595). I shall leave him there, in the embrace of Rebecca, and return to Henry, that uneasy sleeper, who was to survive his twin by nearly thirty years.

In 1673, Vaughan's correspondence with John Aubrey and Antony à Wood began: this is the only source by which Henry Vaughan makes direct personal account of himself, a handful of letters ending in 1694 in which Vaughan responds to the biographers' attempts to grill him for information about Thomas's and his life and works, the natural history of Brecon, and Welsh culture. His letters exude gratification at being an object of interest to the intellectual milieu as one of the 'Oxford men' to be commemorated in Wood's *Athenae Oxoniensis*. At the same time, Aubrey found him infuriatingly slow to answer his letters, and lets fall tart remarks about his cousin's character which suggest he did not feel particularly endeared to him. In 1689, Aubrey wrote to Wood:

> I sent a letter to my cosen *Henry Vaughan* (Olor Iscanus) that very day the Prince of Orange came to London: but never received an answer. He was wont to be free enough of his pen. I will write againe....
>
> (*Powell* [1988], p.209)

In April 1690, he again expressed annoyance with Vaughan's tardiness: 'I have sent 2 if not 3 letters to *Olor Iscanus* and he has not been so civil as to answer me: he is ingeniose but prowd and humorous' (p.213). Vaughan's replies to Aubrey's letters do not answer this description. They tend to be stilted and fulsome, as though Vaughan felt uneasy in the relationship. He assured Aubrey that no papers:

> (wch I have the honour somtymes to receive from very worthie persons,) refresh me soe much, nor have soe dear an entertainment as yours.
>
> That my dear brothers name (& mine) are revived, & shine in the Historie of the Universitie; is an honour we owe unto your Care & kindnes: & realie (dear Cousin!) I am verie sensible of it, & have gratefull reflections upon an Act of so much love, and a descendinge from yor great acquaintance & Converse to pick us up, that lay so much below you.
>
> (*HV*, pp.691-2)

Henry apologises for the belatedness of his first reply by explaining that he has been detained at Brecon 'where I am still attendinge our Bishops Lady in a tertian feaver'(p.687). Twenty years later he apologises to the Brecon Sessions for non-attendance because of his 'present engagement with Mr.Serjeant Le Hunts Lady, who is most dangerously sick in a putrid feaver with most malignant symptoms' (p.699). In each case he makes it clear that his patients are persons of standing, who rely on his expertise and retain him on a long-term basis. It evidently mattered to Vaughan to be well-connected. He was related to 'his ever honoured & obliginge Kinsman' Aubrey through marriages of both families into the Walbeoffe family, and twice sends him the best regards of 'My Cousin Walbeoffe' — that is, Elizabeth, daughter of Thomas Aubrey, who had married Henry Vaughan's first cousin, Charles Walbeoffe of Llanhamlach.

A curious fact which emerges from the Aubrey correspondence is Henry's haziness about the resting-place of his twin brother: 'The name of the place, where my brother lyes buried, I doe not know;

butt tis a village upon the Thames side within 5 or 6 miles of Oxford, and without doubt well knowne to the University' (p.691). This ignorance is not presented as a transient lapse of memory but as a matter about which he is not in a position to furnish information. The twin who intimately shared his 'praeexistence' had been left to lie after death elsewhere, unvisited. It seems clear that Henry had not attended Thomas's funeral, though he knew its date (1 March [p.690]). Given contemporary obstacles to rapid communication, this might not have been within his power. However, it seems odd, in the light of Welsh custom and personal feeling, that Henry was not concerned with the whereabouts of his brother's grave. He also tells Aubrey in June 1673, that he has beside him ready for the press a volume called *Thalia Rediviva*, containing Thomas's surviving Latin poems, which he believes will be well received (p.688). But five years went by before the publication of *Thalia Rediviva: The Pastimes and Diversions of a Country-Muse in Choice Poems on Several Occasions*, twelve years after Thomas's death, when the surviving twin was in his late fifties. The subtitle is self-consciously old-fashioned. Henry himself had ducked out of the enterprise, by having it published under the editorship of an anonymous 'I.W.' or 'J.W' (probably John Williams, an ecclesiastic), who commends the volume to a contemporary audience prejudged as likely to have jaded palates for this sort of 'diversion'. He points out that '*the matchless* Orinda' (the poet, Katherine Phillips, one of Vaughan's few Parliamentarian friends) thought well of the poems and ends by making the editorial equivalent of a rude noise at anyone who dislikes them: '*who so thinks them not worth the publishing, will put himself in the opposite scale, where his own arrogance will blow him up*' ('To The Reader', p.319). The dedication to the Earl of Worcester is an instance of grovelling so witlessly hyperbolical as to make Vaughan's biographer Hutchinson sweat with embarrassed relief that Henry himself cannot be proved to have had a hand in composing it. 'I.W.' commends 'these twin poets' into the hands of a modern Caesar Augustus, imperial patron of the arts (pp.317-18). I cannot help reflecting that, though Henry may not be held responsible for the composition of this effusion, which is directed to a distant relative, he must have had a right of veto, which he forebore to exercise.

The joint volume, containing previously uncollected work by both twins, opens with a motto from Virgil's Sixth Eclogue: '*Nec erubuit silvas habitare Thalia*', the second of two lines which run, 'My earliest

Muse, Thalia, saw fit to play with light Sicilian verse. She dwelt among the woods, and did not blush for that' (1-2). Here Virgil disclaimed epic intention and insisted that he would devote himself to pastoral music. In quoting it, Henry apologises for the rusticities of a volume that must look archaic to a Restoration readership, by clinging to the skirts of the Augustan poet's pastoral and Georgic toga. The eclogue begins with the word *'Prima'* — 'first' or 'earliest' — agreeing with *'Thalia'*, the Muse of pastoral and sylvan lyric verse. For Vaughan, first things were always dear. But there is a melancholy sense in which first things are also antiques if one is reduced to scratching round in the past for mouldered inspirations. *Thalia* is a jumble of such antiques, dating mainly from the late 1640s and early 1650s, and including secular poems which Henry would have thought proper to suppress during the 'sacred' period of *Silex Scintillans*. The title is no doubt a compliment to Thomas. In the allegory opening *Lumen de Lumine*, Thomas had been led by a green-clad nature goddess through green walks and arbours toward a mountain of salt. She had told him, *'I have many Names, but my best and dearest is* Thalia: *for I am alwaies* green, *and I shall never* wither' (*TV*, p.306). She will lead him into the alchemical secrets topographically symbolised by Thomas as the Mountains of the Moon and the Origins of the Nile, areas so abstruse that no one has since been able to trace what Thomas meant by them. The word 'Thalia' is connected with a Greek verb implying growth or burgeoning. In entitling the volume *Thalia Rediviva*, Henry announces a return to his and Thomas's first private emerald world, a nostalgic haunting of the rural retreats of their childhood and the classicism of the twins' earliest inheritance.

But the green goddess is not very evident. Complimentary verse to persons mainly dead (a judge, an author, a female poet, a king, a librarian, a fiancé, a man-about-town) is succeeded by sapless love-poetry to Fida and Etesia, which finds its consummation in the daring description of the bosom of 'Fida: or the Country Beauty':

> Here like two *balls* of newly fallen snow,
> Her *breasts*, Love's native *pillows* grow;
> And out of each a *rose-bud* peeps
> Which *infant* beauty sucking, sleeps.
>
> (63-6)

This vision of mammary snowballs tipped with rosebud nipples, whose nursling, Beauty, has nodded off (perishing, presumably, in the general freeze) reminds us vividly of what a flop the Silurist had been as an amatory poet. The pious author of *Silex* must have averted his eyes from his own hands when he passed such titillating puerilities across to the editor. The volume as a whole is a bag of the twins' odds and ends, concluding with Henry's 'Daphnis: An Elegiac Eclogue' which echoes Virgil's Fifth, and laments the death of Thomas, though, as Hutchinson astutely saw (*H*, pp.220-1), it seems to be a cobbling-together of two elegies, one for a much younger man, perhaps William. The middle-aged Thomas cannot conspicuously have resembled a violet or a primrose (25-6), though he is clearly alluded to in the slur on Thomas's enemy, Henry More, as a 'true black Moor' (38), a racist crack which both twins seem to have thought the height of hilarity; and the account of Amphion's tales of Merlin beneath the oak, evoking their education under Matthew Herbert. Henry becomes muddled about the river which flows beside Thomas's remains, and throws in two for good measure (both wrong: Albury is beside the Thame, not the Thames or Isis):

> For though the *Isis* and the prouder *Thames*
> Can show his relics lodged hard by their streams,
> And must for ever to the honoured name
> Of noble *Moray* chiefly owe that fame:
> Yet, here his stars first saw him, and when fate
> Beckoned him hence, it knew no other date.
> Nor will these vocal woods and valleys fail,
> Nor *Isca's* louder streams this to bewail,
> But while swains hope and seasons change, will glide
> With moving murmurs, because *Daphnis* died.
> (113-22)

Here the national rivers of England and of Wales contend for the honour of having Henry's brother as their spirit-of-place: and though Oxford and London prefer a weighty claim on Eugenius Philalethes (ballasted by Moray, who gets a brief bow and scrape), the Usk valley's claim to Thomas Vaughan is upheld because of its priority in time. Here 'his stars first saw him': that is, his nativity astrologically determined him. The tussle for Thomas which in life Henry could not win, he can posthumously accomplish.

If Thalia cannot truly be resurrected in this volume because the well has dried up, a handful of jewels has been reserved here under the subsection, 'Pious Thoughts and Ejaculations', a series of nineteen sacred lyrics recalling the subtitle of *Silex Scintillans,* a very few dating from after the second edition, the remainder having perhaps been withheld from *Silex* for reasons of political prudence or because Vaughan doubted their quality. The impression given by this final gathering of sacred poetry is overwhelmingly of that 'east-meets-west' paradox which so often made this staunch Royalist and Anglican sound like a Puritan. On the one hand there is the militant Anglicanism of 'The Nativity. Written in the Year 1656' which compares the extortionate taxes levied on Royalists by the Protectorate (presumably the Decimation Tax of 1655 and '56) with the census in Galilee: 'A *tax*? 'tis so still! we can see/ The Church thrive in her misery' (9-10). But the attack on pagan Christmas festivities in 'The True Christmas', with its contemptuous dismissal of '*music, masque* and *show*', finery and parties, could be mistaken for a Puritan's (12). 'The Request' expresses a more-than-Puritan disdain for externals, 'rust, and rags and dregs' (34) and embraces the condition of the poor. The injustices of the world are vehemently disclaimed in 'The Bee', which turns to the solitudes of the wasteland: 'To the wild woods I will be gone,/ And the coarse meals of great *St. John*' (5-6). This withdrawal is from impious priests and rulers, factions and the lawless rule of force, but also from social injustice: a world where 'pity is not cold, but dead,/ And the rich eat the poor like bread' (9-10). This strikes an unusual note for Vaughan. At this moment there is a hair's-breadth between his perception and the Digger Winstanley's:

> The rich doth lock up the treasures of the earth; and hardens their hearts against the poor. The poor are those in whom the blessing lies, for they first *receive the Gospel,* and their gifts of love and tendernesse one to preserve another, shall be the condemnation of the rich.
>
> (*The New Law of Righteousnes,* 1648, *W,* pp.181-2)

But Winstanley went on to outline a social programme whereby 'the inheritances of the rich shall be given to those poor, and there shall be no beggar in *Israel*': Vaughan could only turn his back and refuse the burden of the vision. He was able to ascribe the cannibalistic consumption of the poor by the rich to the Puritan powers-that-be by an adroit manoeuvre whereby, in *Hermetical Physick,* he mistranslated the Latin for 'our men of *Europe*' as 'our Saints of *Europe*' (*HV*, p.554), adding that the poor 'are swallowed without much chewing, and there is none to deliver them'. From the conflict of the social world, he moves into the quietist unanimity of the natural world, where all creatures observe their due and meet times (35-46), a place of worship without pretension:

And are not *streams* at the *spring-head*
More sweet than in carved *stone,* or *lead?*
But *fancy* and some *artist's* tools
Frame a religion for fools.
(59-62)

At this point, the iconoclastic impulse of the verse becomes indistinguishable from the Puritan disgust with the statuary of Laudian church-architecture — all those artefacts which had been the targets of the wreckers' axes from Lollard times. However, in substituting the temple of nature for that of architecture, Vaughan shows that he craves some place to call a sanctuary, and finds his 'primitive church' in the wilds of the Welsh hills. The complex pleating of cross-currents in Vaughan's asceticism and nature-mysticism is clear as he runs for sanctuary as an Anglican whose church has been razed by Puritans, to a refuge which looks superficially so Puritan.

'The World [II]' picks up the familiar recidivist strain of *Silex* as he varies on Raleigh's 'The passionate man's pilgrimage': 'Give me my scallop-shell of quiet,/ My staff of faith to walk upon' (1-2). Vaughan joins the pilgrims on the narrow road. They are a shabby, ostracised bunch of undesirables, much like the itinerant beggars so plentiful in the seventeenth century. Identifying with the poverty-stricken, free of the 'silks, perfumes and glittering coaches' (71), Vaughan expresses an outsiderly consciousness of the consumerist society gaily processing along the broad high way that leads to destruction:

I observe only poverty,
And despised things: and all along
The ragged, mean and humble throng
Are still on foot, and as they go,
They sigh and say: *their Lord went so!*
Give me my *staff* then, as it stood
When green and growing in the wood.

(Those *stones*, which for the *altar* served,
Might not be smoothed, nor finely carved:)
With this *poor stick* I'll pass the *ford*
As *Jacob* did; and thy dear *Word*,
As thou hast dressed it (not as *Wit*
And *depraved tastes* have poisoned it),
Shall in the passage be my meat,
And none else will thy servant eat.
Thus, thus and in no other sort
Will I set forth, though laughed at for't;
And leaving the wise *World* their way,
Go through; though judged to go astray.
(73-91)

Possibly the hardest thing to bear for a person of Vaughan's earnestly eccentric disposition would be public derision. The very thought made Thomas paranoid. Henry, who generally camouflaged his oddity beneath a respectable persona, seems aware here that his beliefs would appear preposterous to the majority, settled in their conviction that, for instance, a tree is only there to be cut down, carved up and exploited for man's convenience. Vaughan refers Raleigh's 'staff of faith' back to source 'When green and growing in the wood' and would probably be happier not to mutilate the tree by stripping it away. Manufacture is consistently viewed as a product of the fall; a regrettable necessity, even when the artefact is plain and for holy use. In both literary and spiritual senses, this represents a wishing-away of symbol in favour of direct access to the literal and real: a complex attitude for one who lived so deeply in symbol and ritual. These are the poems of 'a country liver' ('Retirement [II]', 4), who felt that the primitive way of life of Jacob and Abraham could be emulated in the Welsh hills. In 'Looking Back', he reaches, for a few glorious lines, the lyric beauty of the elegies for lost childhood of *Silex*, walking in imagination the mountains 'of my first, happy age;/ An age without distaste and wars' — mountains flowered with stars seen alone when the curtains of every other house were drawn and human eyelids closed. It is our last haunting vision of the Vaughan retrospect; marred by one false note in the final stanza which reminds us of the vigil the sacred poet must keep against the common usage of the vulgar multitude: 'How brave a prospect is a bright *back-side*!'(15). Unfortunately, the anatomical usage was even then current.

Henry Vaughan, M.D., continued his career as a doctor well into old age, which argues that (despite the severe illnesses he records) he remained fit and mobile until near the end of his life. It is also possible that he needed the money. A physician's average fee was one pound per day for medical attendance, although he would expect to ask considerably less from poorer patients. Many people could not afford professional medical care at all. There is little doubt that Henry Vaughan as a committed Christian would have included a charitable element in his practice. As a 'Hermetic' doctor, his methods were significantly different from those of the academic establishment and claimed a measure of empiricism spectacularly lacking in the traditions of the Royal Society of Physicians. Established practice was based on the humoral principles of Hippocrates, Aristotle and Galen, whereby disease was understood as an imbalance of the four humours. Violent remedies were the rule, involving vomiting and excreting your way back to health through purges and emetics or losing quantities of blood by the application of leeches or wounding: plasters, ointments and potions backed up these basic treatments. Aubrey quotes an eminent physician of his time as confiding the opinion that if people knew how culpably ignorant the doctors were, 'they would throw stones at 'em as they walked in the streets'. The greatest physician of the seventeenth century, Thomas Sydenham, maintained that physicians were themselves health-hazards (*KT*, p.14). Little was known about the inside of the human body. Physicians' obsessive interest in the urine of patients inflamed Thomas Vaughan with disgust: he called them '*Quacks* and *Piss-pot Doctors*' who knew nothing of 'the *Philosophicall medicine*' because of their contumacious disregard of the study of nature (*Anthroposophia, TV*, p.71).

Henry set out his medical principles in his translation of Henry Nollius' *Hermetical Physick: or, The right way to preserve, and to restore Health* (1655), and, if we assume that these formed the basis for his practice, the book gives clues as to the system of healing he sought to operate. Typically, Henry embellished his translation with unmarked additions or altered inflections of his own, where he thought the sense incomplete or a felicitous thought popped into his mind. These elaborations are openings in the text through which we can detect his personal priorities. It is part of Henry's reclusiveness that he should have chosen to hide in the skirts of other people's texts; but his shape shows through the contoured way he 'Englishes' their

Latin, and occasionally there is a direct glimpse of an eye peeping out. For instance, he reinforces Nollius' claim to the empiricism of alchemy by adding in:

> Now all the knowledge of the *Hermetists*, proceeds from a laborious manual disquisition and search into Nature, but the *Galenists* insist wholly upon a bare received *Theorie* and prescribed Receits, giving all at adventure, and will not be persuaded to inquire further than the mouth of their leader.
>
> (p.550)

He and Thomas saw themselves as the natural descendants of Baconian empiricism, and however weird we might find it to have an alchemist turn up on our doorstep to treat us with mystical salts distilled under Capricorn, the Vaughan brothers were right to see themselves as a serious alternative, empirical at least in intention, to the credulous Galenists. Nollius insists that all prescriptions must be adapted to the specific needs of the patient; that medical interference should be minimal, allowing nature to cure herself; that preventative medicine was vital. He was aware of the importance of nutrition and life-style, advocating a temperate, consistent diet and good air (pp.555-7). Chew your food. Do not bolt. He was sensitive to the reality of psychosomatic illness (p.574) and to the crucial importance of the patient's confidence in the doctor in effecting cure (p.590). The transaction between doctor and patient was therefore holistic, involving the spiritual and emotional in the work of healing. Vaughan would have prayed with and for the patient and spent time with him or her, rather than just dispensing drugs. The policy of minimal interference would have limited the side-effects of the Hermetist's mineral medicines to the afflicted person. Vaughan saw himself as a radical alternative to the establishment physician:

> ...after all the coyl of Academical licentiated Doctors, he onely is the true Physician, created so by the light of Nature, to whom Nature her selfe hath taught and manifested her proper and genuine operations by Experience.
>
> (p.581)

The phrase, 'after all the coyl of Academical licentiated Doctors', is Vaughan's addition to the original text: it suggests that his 'M.D.' was self-generated, and that, having trained himself strenuously in his art, he considered himself qualified in a sense impossible to those with an official degree.

Rowland Watkyns, minor poet, Royalist and ejected Rector of Llanfrynach near Brecon, probably practised medicine in the area between 1650 and 1660. His principles would have been anathema to Vaughan. Watkyns, who practised traditional humoral medicine, versified his pharmacological wisdom in *A Looking-Glasse for the Sick: or, The Causes and Symptoms, or signs of several Diseases, With their Cures and Remedies*. Two thousand years of medical endeavour have led to an array of therapies as smelly as they were nauseous and unhealthy. Powdered goat's dung features in many prescriptions; vinegar poured on the head for headache; powdered snails for bladder-stones; burnt hare's skin; pig's fat; mercury mixed with spit; bull's blood for anointing the face; crow's dung packed into a tooth-cavity; a dog's turd for the alleviation of diarrhoea. If you have ear-ache, the expert recommends the following:

> *Stamp Emmets eggs, Earth-worms, and leaves of Rue*
> *In oil: which strain'd, the Hearing will renue:*
> *The juyce of Onion will afford relief,*
> *With Womans milk, and much assuage the grief.*
> (*Flamma Sine Fumo*, p.135)

He appends to this stomach-turning collection of home remedies a condensed account of how to diagnose your own imbalance of humours by study of urine. Simply by looking at a specimen, it is possible to tell whether the patient has a headache, chest pain or gastric complaint. Such divination of urine, which must be collected fresh in the morning, will decide between the ants' eggs and the goat-dung. Vaughan's Hermetic medicine at least offered remedies guaranteed palatable (*HV*, pp.550-1); and it is not difficult to account for the popularity of Vaughan's practice in the region, in view of the quality of the competition.

He chose therefore a life that was simultaneously active and contemplative, which took him away from home for considerable periods and turned his house into a chemical laboratory: for Nollius had said that the medical man should always be searching out the 'supreme, universall medicine' (p.578) to which the Almighty Physician might (or might not) guide the pious investigator. Though Henry explicitly disclaimed in a letter to Aubrey any flair for scientific research (p.693), he would have been involved in the preparation of the medicines he would dispense, comparable with that 'great glass full of eye-water, made att the pinner of Wakefield, by my deare wife, and my sister vaughan', which Thomas catalogued in 1658 (*TV*, p.587). If 'my sister vaughan' (Catherine, Henry's first wife) was involved in production of eye-lotion when on a visit to London, it is likely that she and Henry pursued their more modest version of the art at home in Wales. Such work, both creative and secret, may after 1655 have taken the place of his poetry. It would be pleasant indeed to think of Henry's long life moving to its close in the calm dignity of such employment. But his journey ended in acrimonious family dispute which spoils the saintly picture of Vaughan and leaves us staring at our poet stranded knee-high in the mire of human complexity. Outbursts of graceless public rage trouble our last view of the Swan of Usk as he encounters seismic disturbances to his domestic peace which had their origins in the conflict generated in the 1650s when Henry had married his first wife's sister and had by her a second family. Lawsuits mark this final phase of commotion, including unrelated litigations for theft and debt, and climaxing in the violent dispute between Vaughan and his elder son Thomas. This ended in Vaughan's covenanting to vacate and convey the estate of Newton to Thomas and his heirs, in return for an allowance of £30 per annum for life, use of grazing, stabling and timber, and payments of £100 to be made by Thomas to the children of the second family.

In 1689 Thomas took possession and Henry moved out of the house where he had been born, to a cottage at Scethrog, 'Holly Bush', which he rebuilt. He was sixty-eight years old; Thomas would have been in his late thirties. This cottage, which was demolished at the beginning of this century, was situated on the left hand side of the present road from Crickhowell to Brecon, overlooking the Usk, and seems to have been a spartan dwelling. Luxury had always made him feel uncomfortable so the cramped and austere character of his new house would rather have gratified than dismayed him; but to be dislodged from his childhood home may have been unsettling. He must at least have hoped for peace from the violent quarrels, slammed doors and general mayhem at Newton. He was to be disappointed. Thomas was not happy with his bargain. In a suit brought four years later, Thomas complains that he was swindled in the transaction, which he attributes to his stepmother's 'insinuation and persuasions ... under pretence of keeping peace & quietness in the family', with the ulterior aim of squeezing out capital sums for her own children (*H*, p.229). His hatred for his father's wife seems to have been intense. He refused to pay up the sums required and was taken to court. Protesting that his stepbrother Henry and his brother-in-law were threatening him with prison, Thomas began a Chancery suit against his father, and *sub poena*ed his father, stepmother, step-siblings and brothers-in-law. He accused his father and stepmother of breaking and entering Newton and making off with essential legal documents from a trunk. Ultimately an amicable and binding legal concordat was concluded between the feuding parties.

This affair is embarrassing to the Vaughan biographer. Just as you are preparing to lay the poet in the quiet earth with a few choice valedictory words expressive of his long, virtuous and poetical life, the mortifying fact of his human clay rudely intrudes. He is shown at the centre of an undignified family palaver which he, at the very least, could not control, and at the worst fuelled or aggravated. There is an inclination to save his face. Hutchinson makes much of Henry's sacrifice in renouncing the Newton house and helps Henry's cause by shifting the burden of responsibility for the resentment felt by Catherine's children toward Elizabeth's children across to the stepmother: 'Elizabeth Vaughan may have been more to blame than her husband' (p.228). But should we be looking for someone to 'blame'? The dynamics of a double family cloven by step-sibling jealousies and resentment of a new 'mother' by the old family, are the real subject of consideration. In this case the raw feelings may have been compounded by resurgence of original sibling-jealousy in Elizabeth for her predecessor, her dead elder sister Catherine. The ghost of a dead sister may be hard to live with but impossible to chase away. In this situation, ten people are fighting over love and precedence, in two groups: the four first children in one camp and the stepmother and her children in the other, with the father a floating quantity who as the centre of the whole group has a complex or ambivalent allegiance. This personal fight over love and precedence is betokened by dispute over money and property, in a situation where money is relatively tight. Such conflict was the stuff of life in seventeenth century Wales, where second families and under-aged heirs proliferated because of high mortality rates amongst spouses, and there was a tradition of rancorous litigation. The dispute in this first phase presents itself as a struggle over patrimony, throwing into relief the ancient tension between elder and younger sons which is as old as patriarchy and primogeniture. Thomas sees himself as a latter-day Esau, the patriarch Isaac's elder son, swindled by sly Jacob, egged on by his mother, out of his rightful inheritance: 'he took away my birthright; and behold, now he hath taken away my blessing' (Genesis 27:36). Louise Guiney was furious with Thomas. She used to call him 'horrid Thomas' (*H*, p.249), evidently feeling that he needed spanking for spoiling the poet's declining years with his public tantrum. But why was Thomas 'horrid'? Perhaps Aubrey's view of the Silurist as 'prowd and humorous' was not unjustified.

The next family ruction may be read as endorsing such a judgment. It concerned a suit for maintenance against her father by his disabled daughter, Catherine. Henry Vaughan's rejection of her claims is violent and harrowing to read. Hutchinson squirmed when he tried to defend the poet against the contemptible light in which he showed himself; and we are shaken by the contradiction between the absolute mercy of the poetry and the vicious retaliatoriness of the elderly poet's actions. The first impulse is to cover them up or distribute faults elsewhere, for we have grown to love 'our' poet and perhaps to believe that a true poet ought, as Milton said and Vaughan maintained, to be himself a true poem (*CPW*, I, pp.891-2; *Silex* Preface, p.142). But Vaughan's rejecting behaviour makes him (excruciatingly) human. It brings him into alignment with the reality we all inhabit in which gentle characters disclose razor edges and bountiful hands bunch spasmodically into fists. In April 1693 Catherine petitioned the authorities for maintenance when her father denied it, in the following terms:

> To the right honourable his Majesties Justices of the great Sessions for the severall Counties of Brecon Glamorgan and Radnor.
> The humble petition of Catherine Vaughan
> Sheweth unto your Lordshippes
> That your petitioner is a poore impotent person having one hand burnt in the fire when shee was uppon the breasts, and of late lame in one foot soe that shee cannot gett any thinge to relieve herselfe; may it please your Lordshippes to be advertized that her ffather is a gentleman of estate, and a Doctor of physicke and refuseth both uppon the request and order of ye Justices of the peace to relieve his daughter, the Parish also refuseth because her

> ffather is able, and fitter to relieve her, soe that she is on all hands remediles, and sure to perish for want ....
>
> (*H*, p.232)

An Order was issued whereby Vaughan was required to deposit thirty shillings per quarter with Hugh Powell, the Rector of Llansantffraed, who would disburse it to Catherine at the rate of half a crown each week. However, Vaughan defaulted on this undertaking, apparently insisting on putting the money in her hands himself week by week, a measure which suggests a desire to mortify her. When she complained to the local JPs, some of them turned on her threateningly, she alleged (p.233), so she reapplied to the Great Sessions for redress. Hutchinson points out that the local authorities probably knew her better and made a more just assessment of her troublesome character: it seems to me at least as likely that this was an instance of the old boys' network consolidating itself against the outspokenness of the kind of woman who was known as a 'shrew' or 'scold' and regarded as a public nuisance. Henry submitted to the court, though he did not turn up, and hit back hard:

> Honoured Syr!
>
> That I am accused by adversaries of all sorts & renderd to your Lordship as a person guiltie of all they can devise & declare against me: I doe not at all doubt; but I hope that you will give ear to what I allso have to say & shall make good...
>
> .... your Lordship will give me leave to tell you that among heathens noe parents were ever compelled to maintain or relieve disobedient & rebellious children, that both despise & vilifie their parents, & publickly give out most scandalous & reproachfull lyes concerning them: which this pious petitioner hath done, & still doth. How far this may enter into your Lordships breast, or whither it willbe of any weight, or value with your Lordship, I am uncertain: butt I am sure that among Christians & in all civil governments it is, or should be looked upon as a practise directly against his precepts & commands, who is the great Judge of all our actions.
>
> (*H*, pp.698-9)

The Justices were not impressed by this display of paternal indignation, nor presumably by the bad logic and worse theology that regarded the customs of the heathen as a model for Christian behaviour and implicitly denied that Love is the sole 'precept & command' of 'the great Judge of all our actions'. The letter bristles with hostility, expressed as sarcasm ('this pious petitioner') and a haughty manner toward the Court. The fact that this is the same man as the poet of *Silex* who prayed that he might be granted 'A sweet, revengeless, quiet mind,/ And to my greatest haters kind' ('The Men of War', 43-4) reminds us of the ferocity of the emotions engendered by family conflict, exposing the most sensitive nerves of the adversaries. Just as the row with Thomas exemplified a pathology endemic to patriarchy in its wrangle over patrimony, so the clash with Catherine plays out a variation on the *Lear* theme in which the daughters refuse the burden of the father's will. In the end, the magistrates consolidated the confederacy of dominant class and gender by reducing Catherine's maintenance to twenty shillings, and, in April 1694, to fifteen. But still Catherine would not be quiet or go away. After Vaughan's death the following year, she was filing a Bill of Complaint in which she claimed the right to the use of the Scethrog Cottage or its rent: she lost. She seems to have married and survived into her eighties. Miss Guiney fumed, 'I hope she caught a Tartar of a husband' (*H*, p.248). Hutchinson is evidently upset about the damage caused to the reputation of the Swan of Usk by an episode placed so awkwardly near to the conclusion of the story; he decides to close his account by forgiving the 'difficult and implacable' daughter on the allegedly charitable grounds that cripples are liable to be sour and vengeful to compensate for their infirmities (pp.236-7). The question of why fathers may be 'difficult and implacable' he does not tackle.

We are left with a ringing after-echo to the poet's life, jarring and discordant. But the life is not complete without it.

Conclusion: 'Into The World Of Light':

They are all gone into the world of light!
And I alone sit ling'ring here;
Their very memory is fair and bright,
And my sad thoughts doth clear.

It glows and glitters in my cloudy breast
Like stars upon some gloomy grove,
Or those faint beams in which this hill is dressed,
After the sun's remove.

I see them walking in an air of glory,
Whose light doth trample on my days:
My days, which are at best but dull and hoary,
Mere glimmering and decays.
(1-12)

Henry Vaughan died on 23 April 1695. We who succeed him and make a detour in our own journey to breathe briefly at his graveside now occupy the position of the speaker of 'They are all gone into the world of light', left behind in cloudiness at dusk. Vaughan beneath the green darkness of the yew has made the transcendent leap into the absenteeism of light. Our inheritance from him is a language in which to contemplate the paradox of optical limitation, and the imperative desirability of vision. This great elegy concerns failure of eyesight. When those we love die we keep looking for them. They are all gone — yes, but where? The eye restlessly travels the compass of the natural world as if it could disclose them through, behind or within the structure of physical reality. The mind resists unbeing and substitutes disappearance. It ought to be easier for a person of faith. He knows where they have all gone: the answer is simple, 'into the world of light'. But Vaughan was too human to accept that goodbye as a comfort. It left him in the dark.

He records the immobility of grief, its retrospective obsession. Strange and complex inner events are transacted. The firmament of the inner world 'glows and glitters' with the memory of these out-of-sight people, through the cloudy medium of mourning. Thrown up to heaven as stars, they filter down as points of light, or are shed from the set sun as weak beams 'in which this hill is dressed'. '*This* hill' locates us in a private here-and-now, lived through by Vaughan, transferred to us. In the third verse, a moment of astounding lucidity is announced with simple matter-of-factness. The other world arises on the horizon in a blaze of Baroque light: 'I see them walking in an air of glory,/ Whose light doth trample on my days'. Why 'trample'? They walk above; he sits below. Inevitably he must be bruised. The speaker is sensitive to his exclusion from the company of the departed. The clear light they inhabit collects and reflects them together; dissociates them from him. In their transcendent state, they no doubt see through and through one another and are all one. They don't seem able to look down from this towering advantage of radiance. The lyric enacts the complex fantasy of innocent betrayal that may accompany mourning: a wistful left-outness, envy pure of malice. Yet with what gentle art and composure this is expressed. Meditative stanzas each close upon the diminuendo cadence of a short line, circling to the solace of recurrent closure like a Mozart sonata that touches home whenever it wanders.

If only he could place the lost. But the harder he stares to 'outlook that mark' (20), the more the lens registers its own myopia:

> He that hath found some fledged bird's nest, may know
> At first sight, if the bird be flown;
> But what fair well, or grove he sings in now,
> That is to him unknown.
>
> And yet, as Angels in some brighter dreams
> Call to the soul, when man doth sleep:
> So some strange thoughts transcend our wonted themes,
> And into glory peep.
>
> If a star were confined into a tomb
> Her captive flames must needs burn there;

But when the hand that locked her up, gives room,
She'll shine through all the sphere.
(21-32)

The bird is an emblem of the soul's migration to its Maker: gone into the world of light. The Angel is an agent of mediation through divinatory dreams: from the world of light. The coffined star figures the forthcoming release of the soul from the body: translation to the world of light. Vaughan supplies a sequence of three persuasive pictures of and incentives to hope. Yet he also supplies a candid account of why these very incentives make us recoil in dismay. When the empty nest is discovered, all we know is emptiness; to us, the creature that has found its proper life is beyond tracing. Whereas we are condemned to live in locality, it has no known location. So the bird is not lost but we are. Vaughan seldom recounts lustrous dreams such as this of the Angel messenger; and here the 'strange thoughts' of transcendence which resemble them are tantalising 'peeps' only — hints and clues. The dark encasement of the star promises much — but not now. From the human perspective, hope is vestigial or fugitive, and what we are left with is the fact that our friends 'have all gone'. He ends:

Either disperse these mists, which blot and fill
My perspective (still) as they pass,
Or else remove me hence unto that hill,
Where I shall need no glass.
(37-40)

Meditation was supposed to fine the inner eyes so that, equipped with the equivalent of a spiritual telescope, they could divine what lay beyond human scope. Vaughan records the mistiness of the medium through which he strains, blurred perhaps through tears for those he can never have or see again; he prays for a clarity of perception, a focus, which may turn out to be accessible only on 'that hill', not 'this hill'.

Through the elegy the countryside appears, swathed in mists, haunted by generations of birds, mountainous and lit by stars and waning sunlight. Decade by decade lovers of Vaughan's poetry have come to Llansantffraed trying for glimpses of 'this hill': not as we visit Haworth and Grasmere, in coach loads, but quietly and privately in ones and twos, at intervals of months or years. Theophilus

Jones came in the early nineteenth century: the grave was neglected and overgrown and he found the inscription only just legible. A century later the stone was restored. Poets came, among them Siegfried Sassoon, survivor of another apocalyptic war, in search of healing. His visit shaped a sonnet, 'At the Grave of Henry Vaughan':

Above the voiceful windings of a river
An old green slab of simply graven stone
Shuns notice, overshadowed by a yew.
Here Vaughan lies dead, whose name flows on for ever
Through pastures of the spirit washed with dew
And starlit with eternities unknown.
Here sleeps the Silurist; the loved physician;
The face that left no portraiture behind;
The skull that housed white angels and had visions
Of daybreak through the gateways of the mind.
    Here faith and mercy, wisdom and humility
    (Whose influence shall prevail for evermore)
    Shine. And this lowly grave tells Heaven's tranquillity.
    And here stand I a suppliant at the door.

Select Bibliography

All references to Vaughan's poetry are to the following edition, unless otherwise stated:

Vaughan, Henry. *The Complete Poems.* Ed. Alan Rudrum. Harmondsworth, revised edn., 1983.

HV *The Works of Henry Vaughan*. Ed. L.C. Martin. Oxford, 1957 edn.
TV Vaughan, Thomas. *The Works of Thomas Vaughan.* Ed. Alan Rudrum with Jennifer Drake-Brockman. Oxford, 1984.
A Aubrey, John. *Brief Lives*. Ed. Oliver Lawson Dick. London, 1949.
H Hutchinson, F.E. *Henry Vaughan. A Life and Interpretation*. Oxford, 1947.
J Jones, Theophilus. *The History of Brecknock*, 1805. Brecon, 1898 edn.
L & O Lamont, William, and Oldfield, Sybil. *Politics, Religion and Literature in the Seventeenth Century*. London, 1975.
CPW Milton, John. *Complete Prose Works*. Ed. Don M. Wolfe. 8 vols. New Haven, 1953–82.
KT Thomas, Keith. *Religion and the Decline of Magic. Studies in Popular Beliefs in Sixteenth and Seventeenth Century England.* London, 1971.
U Underhill, Evelyn. *Mysticism. The Nature and Development of Spiritual Consciousness*, 1911. Oxford, 1993 edn.
W Winstanley, Gerrard. *The Works of Gerrard Winstanley, with an Appendix of Documents Relating to the Digger Movement*. Ed. G.H. Sabine. New York, 1965.

Abeleen, J.H.F. *The Genetics of Behaviour*. New York, 1974.
Blake, William. *Poetry and Prose*. Ed. Geoffrey Keynes. London, 1961.
Blunden, Edmund. *On The Poems of Henry Vaughan. Characteristics and Intimations*. London, 1927.
Boehme, Jacob. *The Signature of All Things*. Ed. Clifford Bax. New York, 1912.
--------*The Way to Christ*. Tr. Peter C. Erb. New York, 1978.
Bruno, Giordano. *The Expulsion of the Triumphant Beast* (1584).Tr. D.

Imerti. New Brunswick, 1964.
Calhoun, T.O. *Henry Vaughan*. Newark, 1980.
Cleveland, John. *Poems*. London, 1653.
Cohn, Norman. *The Pursuit of the Millennium*. London, 1957.
Cook, John. *King Charles His Case*. See Scott, Walter.
Cowley, Abraham. *Poems*. Ed. A.R. Waller. Cambridge, 1905.
Crashaw, Richard. *Steps To The Temple. Sacred Poems, With other Delights of the Muses*. London, 1646.
Darbishire, Helen. *Early Lives of Milton*. London, 1962.
Davies, Stevie. *John Milton*. New York, London, etc., 1991.
Dionysius the Areopagite. *The Mystical Theology and The Celestial Hierarchies*. Editor unnamed. Godalming, 1965.
Dryden, John. *The Works*. Ed. E.N. Hooker and H.T. Swedenborg. 18 vols. Berkeley and Los Angeles, 1965–76.
Donne, John. *Poetical Works*. Ed. H.J.C. Grierson. Oxford, 1971 edn.
Durr, R.A. *On The Mystical Poetry of Henry Vaughan*. Cambridge, Mass., 1962.
Eliot, T.S. 'The Silurist'. *The Dial* , 83 (1927).
Evans, J. Daryll. *The Churchyard Yews of Gwent*. Pontypool, 1988.
Figgis, J.N. *The Divine Right of Kings*. Cambridge, 1992.
Fixler, Michael. *Milton and the Kingdoms of God*. London, 1964.
Fraser, Antonia. *Cromwell. Our Chief of Men* . London, 1973.
---------*The Weaker Vessel. Women's Lot in the Seventeenth Century*. London, 1984.
Garner, Ross. *Henry Vaughan. Experience and the Tradition*. Chicago and London, 1959.
Gaunt, Peter. *A Nation Under Siege. The Civil War in Wales 1642–48*. London, 1991.
Gilman, Ernest B. *Iconoclasm and Poetry in the English Reformation. Down Went Dagon*. Chicago and London, 1986.
Gordon, D.J. *The Renaissance Imagination. Essays and Lectures Collected by Stephen Orgel*. Berkeley, Los Angeles and London, 1975.
Gosse, Edmund (ed.). *The Life and Letters of John Donne*. London, 1899.
Grant, Patrick. *The Transformation of Sin. Studies in Donne, Herbert, Vaughan, and Traherne*. Montreal, London and Amherst, 1974.
Grigson, Geoffrey (ed.). *The Faber Book of Poems and Places*. London, 1980.
Habington, William. *The Poems*. Ed. Kenneth Allott. Liverpool and London, 1948.
Herbert, Edward (of Cherbury), Lord. *Poems*. Ed. G.C. Moore Smith. London, 1923.

Herbert, George. *The English Poems*. Ed. C.A. Patrides. London, 1974.

Hermes Trismegistus (attrib.). *Hermetica*. Tr. and ed. Walter Scott. 2 vols. Oxford, 1924.

Hill Christopher. *The English Bible and the Seventeenth Century*. London, 1993.

------- *The Experience of Defeat. Milton and Some Contemporaries*. Harmondsworth, 1984.

------- 'Henry Vaughan', in *Collected Essays*,Vol. I. Brighton, 1985.

------- *Society and Puritanism in Pre-Revolutionary England*. London, 1964.

------- *The World Turned Upside Down. Radical Ideas During The English Revolution*. Harmondsworth, 1975 edn.

Holmes, Elizabeth. *Henry Vaughan and the Hermetic Philosophy*. Oxford, 1932.

Hopkins, Gerard Manley. *Poems and Prose*. Ed. W.H. Gardner. Harmondsworth, 1953.

Kermode, Frank. 'The Private Imagery of Henry Vaughan', *Review of English Studies*, NS I (1950), p. 225.

Linnard, William. *Welsh Woods and Forests. History and Utilization* Wales, 1982.

Mackenzie, Donald. *The Metaphysical Poets*. Basingstoke and London, 1990.

Manning, Brian. *The English People and the English Revolution*. London, 1976.

Martz, Louis L. *The Paradise Within. Studies in Vaughan, Traherne, and Milton*. New Haven and London, 1962 edn.

------- *The Poetry of Meditation. A Study in English Religious Literature of the Seventeenth Century*. Revised edition. New Haven and London, 1962.

------- *From Renaissance To Baroque. Essays on Literature and Art*. Columbia and London, 1991.

Milton, John. *The Poems*. Edited by John Carey and Alastair Fowler. London, 1968.

Mollenkott, Virginia Ramey. *The Divine Feminine.The Biblical Imagery of God as Female*. New York, 1983.

Marvell, Andrew. *The Complete Poems*. Ed. E.S. Donno. Harmondsworth, 1972.

Montaigne, Michel de (Sieur). *Essays*. Ed. J.M. Cohen. Harmondsworth, 1958.

Parfitt, George. *English Poetry of the Seventeenth Century*. London and New York, 1992 edn.

Patrides, C.A. (ed.). *The Cambridge Platonists* . Cambridge, London etc., 1980 edn.

Pettet, E.C. *Of Paradise and Light. A Study of Vaughan's 'Silex Scintillans'*. Cambridge, 1960.

Plato. *Phaedrus and Letters VII and VIII*. Tr. Walter Hamilton. Harmondsworth, 1973.

------ *Symposium*. Tr. Walter Hamilton. Harmondsworth, 1951.

Post, J.F.S. *Henry Vaughan*. Princeton, 1982.

Powell, Anthony. *John Aubrey and his Friends*. Revised edn. London, 1963.

Ralegh, Sir Walter. *The Poems*. Ed. A.M.C. Latham. London, 1929.

Rudrum, Alan. *Essential Articles. Henry Vaughan*. Connecticut , 1987.

------- *Henry Vaughan*. Wales, 1981.

Sassoon, Siegfried. *Collected Poems*. London, 1947.

Scott, Sir Walter (Ed.). *A Collection of Scarce and Valuable Tracts*. Collected by Lord Somers. Vols. 4,5,6. London, 1811.

Shumaker, Wayne. *The Occult Sciences in the Renaissance. A Study in Intellectual Patterns*. Berkeley, Los Angeles, and London, 1972.

Simmons, James D. *Masques of God, Form and Theme in the Poetry of Henry Vaughan*. Pittsburgh, 1972.

Smith, A.J. *Metaphysical Wit*. Cambridge, New York, etc., 1991.

Swift, Jonathan. *'Gulliver's Travels' and Other Writings*. Oxford, London, etc., 1960.

Traherne, Thomas. *Poems, Centuries and Three Thanksgivings*. Ed. Anne Ridler. London, New York and Toronto, 1966.

Virgil. *The Pastoral Poems* . Tr. E.V. Rieu. Harmondsworth, 1954 edn.

Watkyns, Rowland. *Flamma Sine Fumo*, 1662. Ed. Paul C. Davies. Cardiff, 1968.

Wedgwood, C.V. *The King's Peace, 1637–1641. The Great Rebellion*. London, 1955.

-------*The King's War., 1641–1647. The Great Rebellion*. London, 1958.

Wordsworth, William. *Poems*. Ed. J.O. Hayden. 2 vols. Harmondsworth, 1977.

Yates, Frances. *The Rosicrucian Enlightenment*. London and Boston, 1972.

Yeats, W.B. *The Collected Poems*. London, 1963.

Index

Abraham, 114, 116, 140, 169, 186
Adam, 37, 55
agriculture, 11, 22
Agrippa, Cornelius, 75
alchemy, 40, 75-6, 169-70, 177
Allt-yr-esgair, 22, 31, 145
Anglicanism, 18ff., 106, 110, 113, 153, 161, 174, 184
ap Llewellen, Dafydd, 13
ap Llewellen, Gwladys, 13
Apocalypse, 111, 114, 159ff., 169-70
Arminianism, 16
astrology, 34, 183
Aubrey, John, 12, 30, 32, 35, 38, 39, 57, 58, 70, 113, 172, 179ff., 187, 189, 192

Baroque, 13, 46, 60, 98, 164, 177, 196
Bautumley, Jacob, 130
Bible, 21-3, 40, 41, 42, 51, 53, 67, 74, 76, 79, 86, 90, 92, 96, 101, 102, 109, 113ff., 148ff., 156, 157, 159, 168, 171; *Apocalyse*, 157; *Corinthians*, 93; *Ephesians*, 104; *Exodus*, 92; *Ezekiel*, 67; *Genesis*, 92, 114, 116, 148, 60, 166, 169; *Hebrews*, 16; *Isaiah*, 42, 49, 67; *John*, 23; *Judges*, 116; *Kings I*, 116; *Malachi*, 109; *Mark*, 41, 53; *Matthew*, 51, 54, 86, 128; *Numbers*, 49; *Psalms*, 23, 49, 96; *Revelation*, 42, 92, 148, 155, 156ff., 169; *Romans*, 148; *Song of Songs*, 49, 103, 109, 119; *Timothy*, 16
Black Mountains, 2, 33, 133, 176
Blake, William, 114, 129-30
Blunden, Edmund, 101
Bodley, Sir Thomas, 57-8
Boehme, Jacob, 50, 130, 133
Boethius, 74
Book of Common Prayer, 19, 101, 107, 109, 111, 153, 173
Brecon, 9, 11, 23, 25, 26, 42, 58, 66, 67, 69, 71, 72, 79, 114, 152, 173, 180, 189, 190,
Brecon Beacons, 9, 20ff., 31ff., 46, 123, 133, 153, 163, 175
Brecon Priory, 24, 66, 67ff.
Bronte, Emily, 18, 99
Bruno, Giordano, 88
Bunyan, John, 17, 20, 21, 53
Butler, Samuel, 178

Calvinism, 16, 110, 150-51
Carew, Thomas, 74
Cartwright, William, 60, 74
Casimir, 74
Catholicism, 19, 21, 24, 110, 113, 117
Cavaliers, 25, 63ff., 71, 80
Charles I (King of England) 19, 24, 25, 48, 59, 60, 69, 71, 75, 78, 152, 155, 156, 172
Charles II (King of England), 26, 154, 174
Chester, 71
childhood, 29, 40-1, 43, 44-55, 82
Christ, 42, 47, 50, 53, 100, 107, 120ff., 123-27, 130, 141, 158, 163ff., 168
church, 9ff., 19-21, 23, 40, 48, 49, 74, 75, 92-3, 95, 98, 102, 107, 110, 124-25, 152, 155, 161, 174, 177, 185
Cicero, Tullius M., 57
Civil Wars (the English), 13, 18, 23ff., 44, 49, 59, 70, 74, 75, 81, 156
Clarkson. Lawrence, 130
Cleveland, John, 74
Commonwealth, 18, 75, 107, 154-56, 159, 177
Counter-Reformation, 19, 108
Crashaw, Richard, 19, 95, 117, 119
Cowley, Abraham, 26
Cromwell, Oliver, 58, 153, 154, 156, 167
cynghanedd, 47, 119-21, 160

Davenant, Sir William, 74
Davies, Stevie, 137
Dionysius the Areopagite ('pseudo-Dionysius'), 123, 126
Donne, John, 14, 16, 57, 59, 63, 64-5, 75, 76, 87, 89, 96, 104, 117, 174
Dryden, John, 26
dyfalu, 119, 126

Edgehill, Battle of, 156
Egerton, Sir Charles, 66
Eliot, George, 59
Eliot, T.S., 50-1
emblems, 78-9, 141-42, 143, 146, 197
Enoch, 169
Eucharist, 18-19, 96, 102, 110-11
Evans, Arise, 156
Evans, J. Daryll, 18
Everard, John, 131

Ficino, Marsilio, 43
Fletcher, John, 59
Fox, George, 20, 106
Francis of Assisi (Saint), 133
Fraser, Antonia, 48, 156

Games, Dr Edward, 175
Games family monument, 70
Geoffrey of Monmouth, 39
Gerard, Charles, 24
Grigson, Geoffrey, 137-38
Guiney, Louise, 9, 137-38,171, 182, 184

Habington, William, 65, 74, 104
Hatley, Griffith (of Abereskir), 153
Herbert, Edward (first Baron Herbert of Cherbury), 65
Herbert, George, 19, 25, 78, 93-104, 105, 172
Herbert, Matthew (of Llangattock), 20, 39, 42, 48, 49, 55, 152, 175, 183
Herbert, Sir William, 13
Hermeticism, 12, 32, 36, 40, 41, 43, 49, 75-6, 86-7, 89, 121ff., 124, 128ff., 132-33, 139, 144, 150, 187-88
Herrick, Robert, 80
Hill, Christopher, 113, 130, 158
Holford, J.P.W. Gwynne, 20
Holland, John, 130
Hopkins, Gerard Manley, 53, 142
Horace, 9
Hutchinson, F.E., *passim*

'indwelling presence' (*Shekhi-nah)*, 49, 123
Interregnum, 21, 07, 117, 130

Jacob, 186, 192
Jenkin, Thomas, 49
Job, 42
Jews, the return of, 167-69
Jones, Theophilus, 19-20, 197-98
Jonson, Ben, 63, 82, 178
Juvenal, 74

Laud, William (Archbishop of Canterbury), 16, 21, 60, 185
Levellers, 158
Lewes, Thomas (of Llanfigan), 20, 26, 152ff., 175
light (and dark), 27, 46, 76, 79-80, 91, 108, 123-7, 195
Linnard, William, 42-3, 144-45
Llangorse, Pool of, 22, 136-38
Llansantffraed Curch (st Bridget's), 9-26, 44, 116, 127, 152, 164, 175, 177, 193, 195-98
Lloyd, Marmaduke (Judge), 25, 66, 72
London, 31, 36, 44, 58ff., 113, 178, 183, 190
Lot, 12, 169
Lovelace, Richard, 63
Loyola, Saint Ignatius, 79, 108, 142

magic, 32, 129, 131, 169-70
magnetism (see 'sympathies')
Marsh, Sir Edward, 137

Martz, L.L., 106, 108
Marvell, Andrew, 105, 141
Mary Magdalene, 166-67
Mede, Joseph, 168
medicine, 11-13, 171, 187ff.
meditation, 105, 107-13, 145, 147, 151, 156
Merlin, 39
Metaphysical poetry, 86, 176
militarism, 23ff., 30, 70ff.
millenarianism, 15, 111, 156-70, 175
Milton, John, 13, 20, 23, 26, 27, 49, 52, 56, 62-63, 67, 93, 105, 113, 118, 137, 140, 158, 161, 192
Montaigne, Michel de (Sieur), 75
Moray, Sir Robert, 177, 183
More, Henry, 37, 80-81, 169, 177, 183
Morgan, Gwenllian, 9, 137-38
Moses, 22, 46-47, 56, 79, 114, 116
Mozart, Wolfgang Amadeus, 161
mysticism, 50, 107, 119ff., 171-72, 185

nature, 13ff., 16-18, 88, 89, 128-51; *as mother*, 49-50
Newton (home of the poet), 9, 22-23, 25, 30ff., 41, 42, 46, 48, 53, 95, 116, 123, 136, 143, 145, 156, 164, 173-74, 190, 191
Nicodemus, 123, 124
Nieremergius, I.E., 113
Noah, 2, 37, 157-8, 169
Nollius, Henry, 106, 187-8, 189

Oxford, 11, 24, 26, 31, 36, 55, 56ff., 177, 178, 179, 181, 183
Ovid, 74

Parfitt, George, 82-83, 89
patriarchy, 48-49, 50-51, 194
Petrarch, 74
Phillips, Katherine, 181
Plato (and Platonism), 34, 37, 40, 43, 56, 76, 80, 85, 108, 141
Powell, Hugh (son of Thomas), 26, 175, 193
Powell, Thomas (of Cantref), 20, 26, 34, 35, 48, 75, 152ff., 175
Powell, Vavasour, 153
Price, Goditha (wife of Herbert), 69-70
Price, Herbert (Colonel), 24, 25, 67ff.
promised land, 26, 46-47
'Propagation Act' of 1650, 20-21, 152, 172
Puritanism, 17, 19, 20, 21, 63, 70, 72, 117, 153-54, 155, 156, 158, 161, 168, 169, 184, 185

Quakers, 20, 106, 118, 158, 159
Quintilian, Spaniard, 58

Raleigh, Sir Walter, 185-86
Randolph,Thomas, 74
Reformation, 19, 21-22, 102, 113, 125, 155, 168,
regicide, 69, 75, 78, 154-55, 172
Rembrandt van Ryn, 106, 123
Rhees, John David ('Rhesus), 57-58
Rowton Heath, Battle of, 69, 71, 76
Royal Society, 177
Royalism, 19, 20, 24, 63, 72, 74, 152-56, 158, 174, 184
Rudrum, Alan, 33, 76, 89

St. David's, 26
Sassoon, Siegfried, 198
Scethrog (home of the poet), 9, 31, 38, 190, 194
Seneca, Lucius Annaeus, 56, 57
Shakespeare, William, 28, 66, 87, 137
Sidney, Sir Philip, 74
Silures, 12, 28
Socrates (and Socratic), 132
Somerset dynasty, 13, 19
Spencer, Edmund, 63, 65, 176
Strafford (Sir Thomas Wentworth, first earl of), 60
Swift, Jonathan, 178

Sydenham, Thomas, 187
sympathies, doctrine of, 75-76, 86, 88, 121

Tacitus, 12
Teresa of Avila (Saint), 119
Thalia, 67, 182-83
Time (Christian view of), 46-47, 111, 126, 162ff., 176
trees, 42, 43, 69, 77, 115, 134, 141, 142-45, 148-50; *oak*, 41-43, 53, 68, 143, 164, 174; *yew*, 9, 18, 195
Tretower, 11, 13, 29-30, 32, 49
twinship (fraternal and identical), 29-55, 75, 77, 87, 99, 169, 177

Usk, River, 9, 10, 20, 22, 26, 29, 31, 46, 49, 74, 76, 123, 129, 136, 137-38, 144-48, 183, 190

Vaughan, Catherine (née Wise, HV's first wife), 48, 66, 68ff., 164,172, 173, 190-92
Vaughan, Catherine (HV daughter by CV), 48, 173, 192-94
Vaughan, Charles (HV's uncle), 30
Vaughan, Denise (née Morgan, HV's mother), 30, 48-49, 174
Vaughan, Edward (HV's nephew), 30
Vaughan, Elizabeth HV's second wife), 164, 172-73, 174, 190-92
Vaughan, Frances (HV's daughter by CV), 48, 173, 174
Vaughan, Grisell (HV's daughter by EV), 173
Vaughan, Henry
ancestry of, 13, 28-30; *asceticism of*, 13, 28-30; *attitude to creatures of*, 11, 14, 15-16, 32, 43, 97, 128-51, 186; *attitude to mother of*, 32, 53, 62-63, 80, 185; *attitude to science of*, 122, 126, 131-32, 189-90; *attitude to TV of*, 33-43, 58-59, 189-90; *bilingualism of* , 37-38, 45-46, 82; *character of, 33ff., 65-66, 171-72, 186; childhood of*, 32-55, 143; *coat of arms of*, 11-14; *conflict in*, 18ff., 54, 83, 101, 135ff., 171ff., 184, 194; *conversion of*, 25, 93-104; *and death*, 84-93, 112, 195-98; *as doctor*, 11, 12-13, 171, 172, 180, 187-90; *economic status of*, 31-32; *education of*, 38, 55, 56ff.; *as eldest son*, 36, 42; *as father*, 53ff., 190-94; *grave of*, 9-24, 195-98; *identity problems of*, 58, 96, 106; *influence of Herbert on*, 25, 93-104; *love of books of*, 14, 56-57, 113ff., 117-19, 135; *litigiousness of*, 190ff.; *politics of*, 71-71, 152ff.; *recidivism of*, 28, 44ff., 148-51, 182, 185; *religious attitudes of*, 14, 20ff., 40, 78-79, 107ff., 116, 183ff.; *sexuality of*, 63-66, 113, 182-83; *sleep problems of*, 107-11; *and war*, 24ff., 70ff., 116-17, 158-59, 163

Poetry
Olor Iscanus, 10, 25, 27, 31, 34, 36, 44-55, 71, 73, 74, 76, 138
Poems 1646, 60-62, 63-65, 68, 71, 73, 76
Silex Scintillans, 18, 25, 27, 31, 44, 48, 53, 78, 79, 80, 82-104, 106, 117, 121-27, 135, 138, 154, 156, 157, 158, 159, 162, 163, 165ff., 169, 172, 175-77, 182, 183-84, 185, 186, 192
Thalia Rediviva, 27, 39, 62, 75-76, 181-87
'Abel's Blood', 159, 163
'Affliction[I]', 96, 99, 139-40
'The Agreement', 157
'And do they so?', 14-15, 97
'Anguish', 21, 122
'Ascension-Day', 27, 165-67
'The Ass', 172
'The Author's Emblem (Of Himself)', 78
'The Bee', 184
'Begging [II]', 31, 122
'The Bird', 15, 32, 140-42
'The Book', 149-51
'The British Church', 23

'Child-hood', 44, 50-55, 143
'Cock-Crowing', 88-89, 121
'The Constellation', 154-55
'Content', 32
'Corruption', 159-62
'Daphnis: An Elegiac Eclogue', 39, 42, 183
'The Dawning', 164-65
'Day of Judgement', 162-63
'The Day of Judgement', 163
'Divine Dark', 126
'An Elegy on the Death of Mr R.W.', 71, 76-77
'Employment [II]', 9
'The Evening Watch', 135
'The Garden', 141
'To the Holy Bible', 117-19
'The Holy Communion', 102
'Holy Scriptures', 22
'I walked the other day', 111-12
'Isaac's Marriage', 114
'The Jews', 167-69
'Joy of my life!', 90-93, 94
'The King Disguised', 24-25, 59
'Law and the Gospel', 21
'L'Envoy', 117
'Looking Back', 33, 186
'Love-Sick', 119-21
'Man', 31, 138
'Man's Fall, and Recovery', 22
'The Match', 99-101
'The Men of War', 159, 163
'Midnight', 80
'Misery', 36
'The Morning-Watch', 111, 14-36
'Mount of Olives [II]', 102-04
'The Mutiny', 36
'The Nativity Written in the Year 1654', 184
'The Night', 123-27, 163
'On Sir Thomas Bodley's Library', 56-58
'The Passion', 102
'Peace', 21
'The Pilgrimage', 16-18, 21
'Praise', 21
'The Proffer', 155-56
'The Rain-bow', 157-58
'To the Reader', 181
'Regeneration', 9, 79
'Religion', 116-17
'The Request', 184
'Retirement [I]', 13, 15
'Retirement [II]', 140, 186
'The Retreat', 44-47, 143
'A Rhapsody', 60-62
'Rules and Lessons', 102, 106, 108
'The Search', 126-27, 156
'The Seed Growing Secretly', 82, 122, 157
'The Shower', 136, 138
'Silence, and the stealth of days', 84-86
'Son-days', 19, 20
'A Song to Amoret', 65
'Spring', 142
'The Star', 121-22
'The Stone', 15
'The Storm', 36, 136-37, 138
'Sure, there's a tie of bodies!', 86-90
'The Tempest', 18, 99
'The Timber', 130, 140, 142-45, 146
'The True Christmas', 154
'They are all gone into the world of light', 108, 195-98
'Thou that know'st for whom I mourn', 83-84
'To Amoret, of the Difference 'Twixt Him, and Other Lovers, and What True Love is', 64
'To Amoret Gone From Him', 63-64
'To Amoret, Walking in a Starry Evening', 65
'To Etesias Going Beyond the Seas', 63-64
'To His Books', 113
'To His Learned Friend and Loyal

Fellow Prisoner, Thomas Powell...', 75-76
'To Lysimachus, the Author Being With Him in London', 62
'To my Worthy Friend, Master T. Lewes', 76
'To His Retired Friend, an Invitation to Brecknock', 25, 72-73, 76, 79
'To the River Isca', 10, 74-75, 138
'Upon a Cloak Lent Him by Mr. J. Ridsley', 70
'Upon the Priory Grove, His Usual Retirement', 68-69
'Unprofitableness', 184
'Vanity of Spirit', 131-32
'The Water-fall', 93, 145-48
'The World [I]', 175-77
'The World [II]', 185-86

Prose
Flores Solitudinis, 113
Hermetical Physick, 106, 113, 185, 187-88
Mount of Olives, 81-82, 95, 107-11, 123, 152-52
Vaughan, Henry (HV's son by EV), 173
Vaughan, Lucy (HV's daughter by CV), 48, 173
Vaughan, Lucy (HV's daughter by EV), 173, 174
Vaughan, Rachel (HV's daughter by EV), 173
Vaughan, Rebecca (wife of Thomas), 41-42, 43, 44, 66-67, 174, 179
Vaughan, Roger, 13, 29
Vaughan, Thomas ('Eugenius Philalethes', HV's twin brother), 9, 25, 32, 39, 41, 54, 80, 125, 107, 130, 169, 172, 174, 177, 180ff., 190
attitude to HV of, 43-44
character of, 35-37, 66-67, 80-81, 178ff., 186
dreams of, 41-42, 43, 66, 108, 174, 178-79
hatred of Aristotle of, 73, 81
occultist writings of, 37, 40, 73, 80-81, 86, 125-26, 128, 131, 135-36, 139, 144-45, 169-70, 182, 187
profession of, 58, 169, 177, 178
as Rector of Llansantffraed, 20, 44, 152, 177
Vaughan, Thomas (HV's father), 22, 29, 30, 41, 49, 66, 80, 173, 174
Vaughan, Thomas (HV's son by CV), 31, 48, 53, 173, 190-92
Vaughan, William (HV's younger brother), 25, 41, 73, 78, 80-94, 102, 112, 143, 153, 172, 174, 183
Virgil (Publius Vergilius Maro), 56, 74, 77, 181-82, 183
vision, 45-46, 51-52, 176-77, 195-98

Walbeoffe, Charles and Elizabeth, 180
Watkyns, Rowland, 69-70, 154, 189
Welsh language and literature, 37-40, 45-46, 47, 57, 119, 137, 160
Williams, John, 181
Winstanley, Gerrard, 130, 158, 184
Wood, Anthony à, 177, 179
Wordsworth, William, 41, 46, 147

Y Gaer, 23
Yeats, W.B., 161-62

Series Afterword

The Border country is that region between England and Wales which is upland and lowland, both and neither. Centuries ago kings and barons fought over these Marches without their national allegiance ever being settled. In our own time, referring to his childhood, that eminent borderman Raymond Williams once said 'We talked of "The English" who were not us, and "The Welsh" who were not us.' It is beautiful, gentle, intriguing and often surprising. It displays majestic landscapes, which show a lot, and hide some more. People now walk it, poke into its cathedrals and bookshops, and fly over or hang-glide from its mountains, yet its mystery remains.

In cultural terms the region is as fertile as (in parts) its agriculture and soil. The continued success of the Three Choirs Festival and the growth of the border town of Hay as a centre of the second-hand book trade have both attracted international recognition. The present series of introductory books is offered in the light of such events. Writers as diverse as Mary Webb, Raymond Williams and Wilfred Owen are seen in the special light — perhaps that cloudy golden twilight so characteristic of the region — of their origin in this area or association with it. There are titles too, though fewer, on musicians and painters. The Gloucestershire composers such as Samuel Sebastian Wesley, and painters like David Jones, bear an imprint of border woods, rivers, villages and hills.

How wide is the border? Two, five or fifteen miles each side of the boundary; it depends on your perspective, on the placing of the nearest towns, on the terrain itself, and on history. In the time of Offa and after, Hereford itself was a frontier town, and Welsh was spoken there even in the nineteenth century. True border folk traditional did not recognize those from even a few miles away. Today, with greater mobility, the crossing of boundaries is easier, whether for education, marriage, art or leisure. For myself, who spent some childhood years in Herefordshire and a decade of middle age crossing between England and Wales once a week, I can only say that as you approach the border you feel it. Suddenly you are in that finally elusive terrain, looking from a bare height down onto the plain, or from lower land up to a gap in the hills, and you want to explore it, maybe not to return.

This elusiveness pertains to the writers and artists too. It is often difficult to decide who is border, to what extent and with what impact on their work. The urbane Elizabeth Barrett Browning, prominent figure of the salons of London and Italy in her time, spent virtually all her life until her late twenties outside Ledbury in Herefordshire, and this fact is being seen by current critics and scholars as of more and more significance. The twentieth century 'English pastoral' composers — with names like Parry, Howells and Vaughan Williams — were nearly all border people. One wonders whether border country is now suddenly found on the English side of the Severn Bridge, and how far even John Milton's *Comus,* famous for its first production in Ludlow Castle, is in any sense such a work. Then there is the fascinating Uxbridge-born Peggy Eileen Whistler, transposed in the 1930s into Margiad Evans to write her (epilepsis-based) visionary novels set near her adored Ross-on-Wye and which today still retain a magical charm. Further north: could Barbara Pym, born and raised in Oswestry, even remotely be called a border writer? Most people would say that the poet A.E. Housman was far more so, yet he hardly visited the county after which his chief book of poems, *A Shropshire Lad,* is named. Further north still: there is the village of Chirk on the boundary itself, where R.S. Thomas had his first curacy; there is Gladstone's Hawardan Library, just outside Chester and actually into Clwyd in Wales itself; there is intriguingly the Wirral town of Birkenhead, where Wilfred Owen spent his adolescence and where his fellow war poet Hedd Wyn was awarded his Chair — posthumously.

On the Welsh side the names are different. The mystic Ann Griffiths; the metaphysical poet Henry Vaughan; the astonishing nineteenth century symbolist novelist Arthur Machen (in Linda Dowling's phrase, 'Pater's prose as registered by Wilde'); and the remarkable Thomas Olivers of Gregynog, associated with the writing of the well-known hymn 'Lo He comes with clouds descending'.

Those descending clouds...; in border country the scene hangs overhead, and it is easy to indulge in unwarranted speculation. Most significant perhaps is the difference between the two peoples on either side. From England, the border meant the enticement of emptiness, a strange unpopulated land, going up and up into the hills. From Wales, the border meant the road to London, to the university, or to employment, whether by droving sheep, or later to the industries of Birmingham and Liverpool. It also meant the enemy, since borders and boundaries are necessarily political. Much is shared, yet different languages are spoken, in more than one sense.

With certain notable exceptions, the books in this series are short introductory studies of one person's work or some aspect of it. There are normally no indexes. The bibliography lists main sources referred to in the text and sometimes others, for anyone who would like to pursue the topic further. The authors reflect the diversity of their subjects. They are specialists or academics; critics or biographers; poets or musicians themselves; or ordinary people with, however, an established reputation of writing imaginatively and directly about what moves them. They are of various ages, both sexes, Welsh and English, border people themselves or from further afield.

To those who explore the matter, the subjects — the writers, painters and composers written about — seem increasingly united by a particular kind of vision. This holds good however diverse they are in other, main ways; and of course they are diverse indeed. One might scarcely associate, it would seem, Raymond Williams with Samuel Sebastian Wesley, or Dennis Potter with Thomas Traherne. But one has to be careful in such assumptions. The epigraph to Bruce Chatwin's twentieth century novel *On the Black Hill* is a passage from the seventeenth century mystic writer Jeremy Taylor. Thomas Traherne himself is the subject of a recent American study which puts Traherne's writings into dialogue with European philosopher-critics like Martin Heidegger, Jacques Derrida and Jacques Lacan. And a current best-selling writer of thrillers, Ellis Peters, sets her stories in a Shrewsbury of the late medieval Church with a cunning quiet monk as her ever-engaging sleuth.

The vision (name incidentally of the farmhouse in Chatwin's novel) is something to do with the curious border light already mentioned. To avoid getting sentimental and mystic here — though border writers have sometimes been both — one might suggest that this effect is meteorological. Perhaps the sun's rays are refracted through skeins of dew and mist that hit the stark mountains and low hills at curious ascertainable angles, with prismatic results. Not that rainbows are the point in our area: it is more the contrasts of gold, green and grey. Some writers never mention it. They don't have to. But all the artists of the region see it, are affected by it, and transpose their highly different emanations of reality through its transparencies. Meanwhile, on the ground, the tourist attractions draw squads from diverse cultural and ethnic origins; agriculture enters the genetic-engineering age; New Age travellers are welcome and unwelcome; and the motorway runs up parallel past all — 'Lord of the M5', as the poet Geoffrey Hill has dubbed the Saxon king Offa, he of the dyke which bisects the region where it can still be identified. The region has its uniqueness, then, and a statistically above-average number of writers and artists (we have identified over fifty clear candidates so far) have drawn something from it, which it is the business of the present series to elucidate.

Both in seventeenth century culture and life, and in the history of Border literature, there are few phenomena to compare with the twins Henry and Thomas Vaughan of Breconshire. They merit separate studies, and Henry's established position in the canon (to use a currently questioned term) of metaphysical poets of the time accounts for his inclusion here; not to forget his death on 23 April — of all days in our calendar — exactly three hundred years ago. As to this book's approach: the passion and commitment for which Stevie Davies has become renowned, in her novels and critical work alike, prevents it being 'academic' in the pejorative sense still insisted on in some places; at the same time it is a specialist book, entailing among other things the essential scholarly apparatus such a study requires. In simpler terms, the more we find out about Henry Vaughan, the better.

John Powell Ward

Acknowledgement

The publisher gratefully acknowledges George Simon for permission to quote from 'At the Grave of Henry Vaughan' by Siegfried Sassoon.